# THE

# SAGE

# LEARNING

## OF

# LIU ZHI

*Islamic Thought in Confucian Terms*

Harvard-Yenching Institute Monographs Series 65

同治癸亥年重刊

# 天方性理

金陵劉介廉纂述

天方性理序

滇南藏板

# THE
# SAGE
# LEARNING
# OF
# LIU ZHI

*Islamic Thought in Confucian Terms*

Sachiko Murata, William C. Chittick,
*and* Tu Weiming
*with a Foreword by*
Seyyed Hossein Nasr

Published by the Harvard University Asia Center
for the Harvard-Yenching Institute
Distributed by Harvard University Press
Cambridge (Massachusetts) and London 2009

Printed in the United States of America

The Harvard-Yenching Institute, founded in 1928 and headquartered at Harvard University, is a foundation dedicated to the advancement of higher education in the humanities and social sciences in East and Southeast Asia. The Institute supports advanced research at Harvard by faculty members of certain Asian universities and doctoral studies at Harvard and other universities by junior faculty at the same universities. It also supports East Asian studies at Harvard through contributions to the Harvard-Yenching Library and publication of the *Harvard Journal of Asiatic Studies* and books on premodern East Asian history and literature.

Library of Congress Cataloging-in-Publication Data

Murata, Sachiko, 1943–
    The sage learning of Liu Zhi : Islamic thought in Confucian terms / Sachiko Murata, William C. Chittick, and Tu Weiming ; with a foreword by Seyyed Hossein Nasr.
        p. cm. -- (Harvard-Yenching Institute monograph series ; 65)
    Includes bibliographical references and index.
    ISBN 978-0-674-03325-2 (alk. paper)
    1. Islam--Relations--Confucianism. 2. Confucianism--Relations--Islam. 3. Liu, Jielian, fl. 1670–1724. Tian fang xing li. I. Chittick, William C. II. Tu, Weiming, 1940- III. Liu, Jielian, fl. 1670–1724. Tian fang xing li. English. IV. Title. V. Title: Islamic thought in Confucian terms.
    BP173.C65M84 2009
    297.2'8--dc22

                                                                                    2008037045


Index by the authors


♾ Printed on acid-free paper


Last number below indicates year of this printing
18  17  16  15  14  13  12  11  10  09

# *Foreword*

# Seyyed Hossein Nasr

It is said that a butterfly fluttering its wings in China can cause a storm in the Atlantic Ocean. Indeed, sometimes it is difficult to surmise how some causes can lead to very unexpected effects. Such is the history of how this book came into being. In 1993 my old friend and colleague Tu Weiming and I were attending a conference together at the East-West Center at the University of Hawaii in Honolulu. During the evening of the first day he handed me a typed essay and said that this was the text of an article entitled "Clash of Civilizations" by Samuel Huntington that was to be published soon in the journal *Foreign Affairs*. He added that the essay was also a plan of action and that it would probably disturb me as it disturbed him. That night I read the text and, as Tu Weiming predicted, was upset and disturbed by it. The next day we decided to do something to create at least better understanding between Chinese and Islamic civilizations, whose closeness Huntington saw as such a danger for the West.

A few days later I went to Malaysia, and before a very large audience, including some of the leading political figures of the country, I mentioned the idea of the clash of civilizations—surely for the first time in the Islamic world—and expressed my opposition to it. Considering the presence of a large Chinese population in this predominantly

Islamic country, the Malaysian deputy prime minister at that time, Anwar Ibrahim, expressed keen interest in having a dialogue between Islam and Confucianism held in Kuala Lumpur, and he appointed the Malay scholar Osman Bakar to arrange it. Having been one of my former students, Bakar consulted with me, and I suggested that, among others, Sachiko Murata and William Chittick should be invited to participate in the conference, which eventually took place in March 1995. Unfortunately, I could not attend, but I know that this gathering made it possible for a number of Muslim as well as non-Muslim Malay, Chinese, Japanese, and Western scholars to join together for the first time in discussing the relation between Islamic and Chinese thought and civilization.

After the conference in Hawaii, Tu Weiming and I decided to hold a meeting at Harvard. In April 1994, we met to discuss various ways to promote dialogue between Confucian and Islamic civilization. Each of us invited four or five scholars to participate in the meeting, and I included Sachiko Murata and William Chittick in my list. In the wake of that meeting, Murata spoke with Tu Weiming about the possibility of reading Neo-Confucian texts with him during her forthcoming research leave, when she was to be a fellow at the Center for the Study of World Religions at Harvard. They met together several times in the Fall of 1994, and then, along with Chittick, attended the Kuala Lumpur conference on Islamic-Confucian Dialogue in March of the following year. At that conference, they were introduced to Islamic thought in the Chinese language through a paper on Wang Daiyu delivered by the Singapore scholar Lee Cheuk Yin. This was the first they knew that such material even existed. Murata spent the remainder of her time at Harvard looking into the Harvard-Yenching Library's considerable collection of Islamic texts in Chinese, all the while sharing her findings with Tu. It was this series of events that led to their discovery of a whole new intellectual continent as far as Western scholarship was concerned.

It is true that the groundbreaking work of Françoise Aubin and a few other scholars had already pointed to the importance of Islamic works in the language of Neo-Confucianism and the rise of an intellectual current in China called the Han Kitab. Yet it remained for the newly formed team of Tu, Murata, and Chittick to start to study and analyze philosophically and metaphysically in English the contents of some of these works, including translations from Persian into classical Chinese. In 1997–98, Murata received an NEH Fellowship to study the works of Wang Daiyu and at the same time became an associate at the Harvard-Yenching Institute. It was during this period that she began her close readings of Wang Daiyu and Liu Zhi under Tu's guidance, with a good deal of input from Chittick concerning the Islamic context of the ideas and appropriate English equivalents for technical terms. Beginning around the same time, they held the first of a series of annual meetings at the Chitticks' house on Long Island, which I also attended. Unfortunately, my knowledge of matters Chinese is limited, but I would participate in these sessions by helping to create an intellectual framework as well as further elucidating the meaning of the original Islamic texts involved.

The first product of this collaboration, the remarkable work *Chinese Gleams of Sufi Light*, contains the translation of two Chinese texts into English, their analysis, a new English translation of 'Abd al-Raḥmān Jāmī's *Lawā'iḥ* (one of the texts studied in its Chinese translation) from the Persian by Chittick, and in-depth comparisons. The work became a landmark study in comparative philosophy, mysticism, and religion as far as the Islamic and Chinese traditions are concerned.

During these efforts the group became aware that they were dealing only with the tip of the iceberg and that there were many other important texts of the Han Kitab that deserved to be studied in depth. And so they turned their attention to the more extensive and highly influential work of the seventeenth-century master of this school, Liu Zhi, *Tianfang xingli* (Nature and principle in Islam), which was completed in 1704. The present book is the result of several years of effort to study and translate this work and to provide detailed commentaries and references to the Islamic sources. Among the most interesting features of this treatise is the explanation of metaphysical and cosmological ideas through the use of numerous diagrams. Perhaps the author made such extensive use of diagrams to appeal to the "visual genius" of Chinese culture. These diagrams nevertheless remind us of diagrams in the philosophical and metaphysical works of such Islamic authors as the Ikhwān al-Ṣafā', Ibn 'Arabī, and Sayyid Ḥaydar Āmulī.

It is interesting to look upon this work in the framework of the interactions of Islamic thought and the intellectual traditions of other civilizations. The civilizations of the West, India, and China remain in fact the main civilizations with whose intellectual dimensions Islamic thought had contact before modern times. The interaction of Islamic thought with the West during the Middle Ages has been studied extensively, and it is well known that the movement of thought at that time was only in one direction. Arabic texts were translated into Hebrew and Latin and resulted in the rise of Latin Scholasticism. Muslims, however, showed practically no interest in Latin texts and were not influenced by them.

The interaction between Islamic and Hindu and Buddhist thought is also known, although not studied to the same extent as the relation between Islamic philosophy and theology and Christian Scholasticism. In India Muslims continued to use Persian and Arabic and not Sanskrit. There were therefore translations of Hindu mythology, yogic teachings, and religious philosophies in general into Arabic and Persian and also of Islamic thought into Sanskrit and certain Indian vernacular languages used by Hindus. Persian itself spread widely in India and was known even by many Hindu pundits, and some of the Indian languages such as Sindhi, Punjabi, Gujarati, and Bengali became also Islamic languages. Moreover, a major Islamic language, Urdu, was born and spread in India. It is interesting to note, however, that, in contrast to the case of China, Muslim scholars did not use Sanskrit—which in India corresponds in many ways to Chinese in China—for imparting their teachings to other Muslims or even for the explanation of Islamic thought to Hindus.

The case of China was completely different. In this least-known interaction between Islamic thought and the intellectual tradition of another civilization, after using Arabic and Persian almost exclusively within their own communities for centuries, Chinese Muslim scholars decided from the seventeenth century onward to expound Islamic teachings in classical Chinese and in the philosophical and ethical language of Neo-Confucianism. This effort, moreover, was not primarily for non-Muslim Chinese, but most of all for the Islamic community itself. Thus in the case of China we face a unique situation, different from what we observe in the case of either the West or India.

Therefore this book is, needless to say, of great interest from the general point of view of comparative philosophy and religion as well as of the Islamic intellectual tradition and even Chinese intellectual history, even if the rest of the Islamic world and non-Muslim Chinese were little aware of the development of the Han Kitab. But more than any historical interest, this and similar works of this genre are of great interest for their innate metaphysical and philosophical value and for understanding the manner in which the masters of the Han Kitab crossed religious and civilizational frontiers and created harmony between two different intellectual worlds through an appeal to the underlying unity that constitutes the basis of the perennial philosophy. It would be of great interest to compare one day in detail their efforts with those of scholars and thinkers in India and the West involved in the interaction with Islamic thought.

Each of the three scholars who has collaborated in writing and editing this work as well as *Chinese Gleams of Sufi Light* has brought special expertise to this task. Tu Weiming is one of the leading authorities, if not the leading authority, on Chinese thought and especially Neo-Confucianism in America. William Chittick has a mastery of classical Arabic and Persian Sufi texts, upon which most of the Chinese texts are based, that is unparalleled in this country. As for Sachiko Murata, she forms the perfect link between the two, being a Japanese scholar with knowledge of Chinese who studied for many years in Iran and knows well various schools of Islamic thought. Her *Tao of Islam*, which is unique and has become widely known, is witness to her being a bridge between the Far East and the Islamic world. She is deservedly the lead author of this remarkable book.

I have been closely associated with Murata and Chittick since their student days in Tehran University, where I was then teaching, and I have known Tu Weiming since the early 1970s, when we met in Madras, for the first time, at a conference on philosophy in East and West. It is remarkable that the hands of destiny have brought these three exceptional scholars with such different backgrounds together. They have developed a close intellectual and human bond that has made this very significant work, as well as *Chinese Gleams*, possible. Let us hope that their cooperation will continue in the future to explore this whole continent of philosophical, mystical, and religious thought where the Islamic and Chinese traditions have met and created works whose significance is now being ever more realized beyond the confines of the Chinese world.

# Contents

## *Nature and Principle in Islam*

## Volume 1

## Volume 2

## Volume 3

# Volume 4

# Volume 5

## Reference Matter

# *Abbreviations*

For complete bibliographic information on the works cited in the following list, see the Bibliography, pp. 647–44. In the notes, when two sets of page numbers are cited, the first refers to the original text and the second to the translation cited in the Bibliography. Thus, in a citation such as *Path*, pp. 50–51/77, "pp. 50–51" refers to the edition of Rāzī's *Mirṣād* cited in the Bibliography and "77" to the English translation of this work by Hamid Algar.

## Liu Zhi's Sources in the Root Classic

Commentary     *Tafsīr-i Qāḍī* (The Koran commentary of Qāḍī [al-Bayḍāwī]). *Zhenjing zhu* 眞經注 (Commentary on the real classic).

Gleams     Jāmī, *Lawā'iḥ* (The gleams). *Zhaowei jing* 昭微經 (The classic of showing the concealed). For a translation, see *Chinese Gleams* in the next section.

Goal     Nasafī, *Maqṣad-i aqṣā* (The furthest goal). *Yanzhen jing* 研眞經 (The classic of searching for the real). English translation by Lloyd Ridgeon in *Persian Metaphysics*.

| | |
|---|---|
| *Path* | Rāzī, *Mirṣād al-'ibād min al-mabda' ila'l-ma'ād* (The path of the servants from the origin to the return). *Daoxing tuiyuan jing* 道行推原經 (The classic of the ongoing way of pursuing the origin). English translation by Hamid Algar, *The Path of God's Bondsmen from Origin to Return*. |
| *Rays* | Jāmī, *Ashi''at al-lama'āt* (The rays of "The Flashes"). *Feiyin jing* 費隱經 (The classic of exhausting the hidden). |
| *Standpoints* | al-Ījī, *al-Mawāqif fī 'ilm al-kalām* (The standpoints in the science of theology). *Gezhi quan jing* 格致全經 (The complete classic of investigating [things] and extending [knowledge]). |
| *Stars* | *Aḥkām-i kawākib* (The ruling properties of the stars). *Tianjing qingxing* 天經情性 (The feelings and nature of the heavenly classic). |

## Additional Abbreviations Used in the Notes

| | |
|---|---|
| *Chinese Gleams* | Murata, *Chinese Gleams of Sufi Light* |
| *Concepts* | Zhang Dainian, *Key Concepts in Chinese Philosophy* |
| *Flashes* | 'Irāqī, *Lama'āt*. English translation by William C. Chittick and Peter Lamborn Wilson, *Fakhruddin 'Iraqi: Divine Flashes*. |
| *Self-Disclosure* | Chittick, *The Self-Disclosure of God* |
| *Source Book* | Chan, *A Source Book in Chinese Philosophy* |
| *Sufi Path* | Chittick, *The Sufi Path of Knowledge* |
| *Terms* | Ch'en Ch'un (Chen Chun), *Neo-Confucian Terms Explained* |

# *A Note on*

# *Transliteration*

We have followed the *pinyin* system for Chinese. In *Chinese Gleams of Sufi Light*, we followed the Wades-Giles system. This explains why Liu Chih has become Liu Zhi, Wang Tai-yü has become Wang Daiyu, and so on. For Arabic and Persian words, we use the standard, modified *Encyclopedia of Islam* system, recognizable to any scholar in the field.

# Preface

This book extends research I began with *The Tao of Islam* and continued, with the help of my two collaborators, in *Chinese Gleams of Sufi Light*. In *The Tao of Islam*, I investigated basic Muslim concepts about ultimate reality, the cosmos, and the human soul in light of the correlative thinking that is typical of the Chinese intellectual tradition and especially the *Book of Changes* (*Yijing* 易經). By "correlative thinking" (the term used by Joseph Needham in *Science and Civilization in China*),[1] I mean the tendency to see harmony and complementary relationships among all things, conceptualized in terms like yin and yang, heaven and earth, male and female, light and dark. Benjamin Schwartz calls this typical Chinese approach to reading the world "correlative cosmology," although, he says, "correlative anthropocosmology" might be more accurate.[2] Tu Weiming has often written about "anthropocosmism" to designate this holistic, correlative vision of Heaven, Earth, and Man.[3] Anthropologists have pointed to diverse examples of correlative thinking in primal societies, but few scholars have bothered to point out that much of Islamic thought takes the same approach. The general trend has been to interpret Islam as another version of Semitic monotheism and to conceptualize its thinking in terms of categories derived from the modern study of Judaism and Christianity. I wrote *The Tao of Islam* to suggest that there are other, perhaps more plausible, ways to look at Islamic thought, and that these can be especially helpful in finding bridges to non-Western civilizations.

In 1995 I discovered sophisticated Chinese-language expressions of Islamic thought that took full advantage of the traditions of correlative thinking on both the Islamic and the Chinese sides. That led to my collaboration with Tu Weiming in exploring some of these works. My husband, William C. Chittick, was happy to join with us in our discussions and research. The first fruit of that collaboration was *Chinese Gleams*, in which we translated two short Chinese treatises, one by Wang Daiyu 王岱輿 and the other by Liu Zhi 劉智. There I summarized what I had learned about the unique blend of Confucianism and Islam that made its appearance in China in the seventeenth century, most notably with Wang's major work, *Zhengjiao zhenquan* 正教眞詮 (The real commentary on the true teaching).

Given the paucity of secondary sources at our disposal when we were working on *Chinese Gleams*, we had no real idea of the extent of the influence of this school on Chinese Muslim society and the tight relationships that bound its authors together. The gaping hole in the secondary literature has begun to be filled by Zvi Ben-Dor Benite's groundbreaking study, *The Dao of Muhammad: A Cultural History of Muslims in Late Imperial China*, which provides a wealth of information on the scholarly network and social institutions that allowed this school to flourish.[4] Liu Zhi himself is the focus of a recent Ph.D. dissertation by James D. Frankel, who summarizes his relationship with the Muslim and Chinese contexts, looks closely at his second major work, *Tianfang dianli* 天方典禮, (Rules and proprieties of Islam), and provides a thoughtful analysis of its contents and its significance for Chinese Islam.[5] Studies of Liu have also appeared recently in Chinese and Japanese.[6]

Our own interest in the Han Kitab has less to do with historical context than with the intellectual content of the works. Anyone interested in the significance of religious and philosophical thought for the human condition has much to learn from these books. All three of us have been working for many years on the contemporary religious and philosophical relevance of our respective specialties (Islam on one side, Confucianism on the other). At the same time, we have often engaged with the teachings of other traditions, sometimes through undergraduate teaching or discussion with colleagues, sometimes through international conferences, and recently through seminars aimed at dialogue between Confucian and Islamic thought. What we have found in the book translated here, Liu Zhi's *Tianfang xingli* 天方性理 (Nature and principle in Islam), is a deep interpenetration of the Confucian and Islamic traditions, without any of the syncretism (with its negative connotations) mentioned by some of the secondary literature. For Liu and others of the perspective, the "dialogue of civilizations" or the "ecumenical vision" is part of their own persons and perspective. In reading him, we have learned a great deal about the invisible harmonies that bind together two major worlds of thought.

*****

A great many people have helped me over the years, and I will not repeat all the names I mentioned in *Chinese Gleams*. Here I want to thank in particular Françoise Aubin, Akiro Matsumoto, and Yasushi Kosugi, who generously sent us photocopies of Chinese, Arabic, and Japanese works related to our research. I also thank Alma Giese and Wolfhart Heinrichs, our kind and generous hosts whenever we were in Boston. In addition, Alma put in a good deal of time proofreading the manuscript, and over the years Wolfhart has asked many thoughtful questions that helped us conceptualize various aspects of our work. Thanks also to my nephew Satoru Murata, who prepared the diagrams and inserted the Chinese characters into the text, and to my niece Kazuyo Murata, who typed the Arabic text.

Finally, I am especially grateful to the National Endowment for the Humanities, which supported me with a fellowship for the year 2005 to finalize the project.

Sachiko Murata<br>Mt. Sinai, NY

# THE

# SAGE

# LEARNING

## OF

# LIU ZHI

*Islamic Thought in Confucian Terms*

# Introduction

# ONE

# *Liu Zhi and the*

# *Han Kitab*

In *The Dao of Muhammad*, Zvi Ben-Dor Benite shows that Liu Zhi's 劉智 integrative approach to Confucian and Islamic learning guided the Islamic curriculum in China from the seventeenth to the nineteenth century. Among Chinese Muslims, this approach has often been called Han Kitab (Han Qitabu 漢克塔補), an expression that combines the Chinese word Han and a transliteration of the Arabic *kitāb*, or "book," meaning "(Muslim) books written in Chinese." Those who took this approach were often called Huiru 回儒, that is, Muslim literati, or Muslim scholars of Confucian learning.[1] Benite describes the appearance of the Han Kitab as an "unprecedented outburst of Chinese Muslim scholarship" between the 1630s and the 1730s.[2] The first major book was Wang Daiyu's 王岱輿 *Zhengjiao zhenquan* 正教真詮 (The real commentary on the true teaching), published in 1642, followed quickly by several other influential works. These books, however, did not appear in a vacuum. There was already a "far-flung network of educational institutions, teachers, and disciples," and it was through these that Islam "developed its own—distinctively Chinese Muslim—institutions, values, and ideals."[3]

The key figure in establishing this network was Hu Dengzhou 胡登洲 (also known as Puzhao 普照 and Muḥammad Ibrāhīm Ilyās), who died around 1597 and came to be called Taishi 太師, the Great Teacher. After spending some years in Islamic countries, he established a rejuvenated educational system in his home county of Xianyang 咸陽 in Shaanxi. His new approach to Muslim education spread by means of his students to four other major centers of Islamic learning (Xian 西安, Jining 濟寧, Kaifeng 開封, and Nanjing 南京). Although Hu Dengzhou published no books or treatises, his reorganization of Islamic education with an emphasis on the transmission of learning in the Chinese language had far-reaching results.[4]

With the publication of Wang Daiyu's *Zhengjiao zhenquan*, Muslim authors began producing books that crystallized and formalized the Chinese Muslim self-perception. Another extremely influential author was Wu Zixian 伍子先 (ca. 1598–1678), especially through his translation of *Mirṣād al-'ibād min al-mabda' ila'l-ma'ād*, which appeared in 1670. The original Persian text was written by a great Sufi shaykh, Najm al-Dīn Rāzī (d. 1256), and became one of the most influential handbooks of Islamic teachings in the Persianate world, from the Ottoman Empire through Iran, India, and Central Asia. Wu's translation became "probably the most popular text in the Chinese Muslim educational network and among its constituency. Every subsequent author, translator, and editor made reference to it."[5]

A third major author of the period was Ma Zhu 馬注. He was educated in the Chinese classics and passed the first level of the civil-service examinations at the age of eighteen. In the year 1669, at around the age of thirty, he went to Beijing, where he undertook serious study of Islamic texts. His major book is *Qingzhen zhinan* 清眞指南 in eight volumes, published in 1683; he translates the title into Arabic as *al-Murshid ila'l-'ulūm al-islām* (The guide to the sciences of Islam). According to Benite, it was "probably the single most respected of the many works written by Chinese Muslim scholars."[6]

## *Liu Zhi*

Liu Zhi was born around 1670. He studied in Nanjing at a school founded by Yuan Shengzhi 袁盛之, whose son, Yuan Ruqi 袁汝琦, took over its direction when his father died. Among the teachers at the school was Yuan's relative Liu Sanjie 劉三傑 (also called Liu Hanying 劉漢英), Liu Zhi's father. Liu Zhi studied with Yuan Ruqi, and he mentioned his own father's formative influence on his scholarly aspirations at the beginning of *Tianfang xingli* and elsewhere.

Liu's importance in the Han Kitab can hardly be overestimated. We are inclined to think that he is the most profound and subtle author of the whole school, although we will have to reserve final judgment until the many books written by its authors have been studied and analyzed. Benite calls Liu "the most systematic and prolific author of the scholarly network":

His work symbolizes the culmination of Chinese Muslim literary productivity over the course of the previous century, and he himself represents the maturation of the educational network and stands as one of its finest products. . . . Liu can be considered the quintessential Chinese Muslim scholar in that he existed at the center—chronological, dynastic, and geographic—of the Chinese Muslim educational system. . . . As the son of a teacher and the disciple of a major teacher, Liu's network of filiations brought him into contact with all the major teachers and scholarly figures of his time. Finally, his location in Nanjing put him at the hub of scholarly activity in the late seventeenth and early eighteenth centuries.[7]

Liu's last major book, a biography of the prophet Muḥammad called *Tianfang zhisheng shilu* 天方至聖實錄 (The true record of the utmost sage of Islam), provides autobiographical remarks that help us imagine him as a dedicated scholar with little inclination to involve himself in society. His family and friends did not honor him, because he refused to earn a living. He traveled all over China to visit libraries and find books. In 1721, a visit to the birthplace of Confucius in Shandong province inspired him to begin his biography of the Prophet. Not satisfied with the initial results, he set off again to visit libraries. In Hunan he discovered a text on the Prophet's life better than any he had seen before. He returned to Nanjing and completed the book at the beginning of 1724. During the three years it took him to compose this biography, he traveled several thousand *li* 里 (a unit of measurement equal to about one-third of a mile), changed his dwelling place ten times, and even read while traveling in a cart or mounted on a beast.

Liu tells us that he entered the path of learning at the age of fifteen. He must already have had some education, and he no doubt had in mind the sort of learning that Confucius meant when he said, "From fifteen, I set my heart on learning, from thirty I stood firm" (*Analects* 2.4). Liu related that he had spent eight years on the Confucian classics, six on the Islamic classics, three on the Buddhist canon, and more than a year on Daoism.[8] He then went on to read "137 Western books," which Benite, among others, argues would have been products of the Jesuit influx into China; Matteo Ricci, after all, was centered in Nanjing.[9]

In his quest for knowledge, Liu read thousands of volumes; he claimed to have composed hundreds of volumes but published only a tenth of them. He considered his three major books to be a trilogy. He completed the text translated here, *Tianfang xingli* 天方性理 (Nature and principle in Islam), in 1704. It focuses on what is commonly called in Arabic *uṣūl al-dīn*, the "roots" or "principles" of the religion. These are the foundational articles of Islamic faith; typically there are said to be three: *tawḥīd*, or the assertion of God's unity; prophecy (*nubuwwa*); and the Return to God (*maʿād*), that is, eschatology or "the last things" in a broad sense. Liu's approach, like that of the Huiru in general, is distinguished from that of other Muslim scholars in that he addressed the basic articles of Islamic thought with Confucian terminology and categories.

Liu's second book, *Tianfang dianli* 天方典禮 (Rules and proprieties of Islam), appeared in 1710. If his first book focuses on roots and principles, this book addresses branches and applications (*furūʿ al-dīn*). In other words, *Tianfang xingli* deals with the Islamic worldview, and *Tianfang dianli* with the practices that make it possible for people to bring themselves into conformity with that worldview. Alone among the titles of the Han Kitab, this book was included in the Siku quanshu 四庫全書, the largest compilation of books in Chinese history, initiated by the emperor in 1772.[10] James Frankel argues that this specific book caught the attention of the Confucian elite precisely because it focused on propriety or ritual (*li* 禮), the basis of Confucian activity both public and private and the source of social harmony and stability.[11]

In Islam, ritual practices as well as individual social rules and regulations are typically explained in the science of *fiqh*, or "jurisprudence." Liu's book, however, does not read like a typical manual of jurisprudence—far from it, in fact—because his discussions of issues are much more general and theoretical than is usually the case. He described the major Islamic practices, but it would not be possible on the basis of his comments, for example, to perform the daily prayers. He left detailed explication of elementary Islamic learning to teachers in the mosques. He was much more concerned with arguing that the Islamic proprieties and rituals coincide with the teachings of the ancient Chinese sages, and he even claimed that the Islamic forms preserve the original purity of those teachings.[12] Thus he wrote in the introduction:

What is recorded in the books of Islam (*tianfang*) is no different from what is in the Confucian canon. Observing and practicing the proprieties of Islam is like observing and practicing the teachings of the ancient sages and kings.[13]

*Rules and Proprieties* is divided into twenty chapters. The first provides an overview of Islamic theoretical teachings on divine unity, the creation of human beings, the role of prophets, and the specific function of Muḥammad; then it reviews the practical teachings that are the main subject of the book, including the Five Pillars of Islam and the Five Relationships (much discussed in Confucianism). Chapters 2 and 3 explain the Islamic concept of "Real Ruler," that is, God, and its difference from foundational notions of Daoism, Buddhism, and Confucianism. Chapter 4 explains the meaning of the first Pillar, the Shahadah or "witnessing," which is the verbal attestation that there is no god but God and that Muḥammad is God's messenger. Chapter 5 speaks generally about the "Five Endeavors," that is, the five basic practices of Islam, the indispensable means for achieving union with heaven.

Chapters 6 through 8 explain the four endeavors after the Shahadah: the daily prayers, fasting during Ramadan, the alms tax, and the hajj or pilgrimage to Mecca. Chapter 9 addresses the ritual slaughter of animals; its prominence in the book suggests that it was one of the practices that non-Muslim Chinese found strange. Chapters 10–13 explain the Five Relationships: husband and wife are the root of giving birth, father and son the root of honor and humility, superior and subject the root of governing by the Dao, elder brother and younger brother the root of affection and love, and friends the root of perfecting virtue. Chapters 14 through 17 address the necessity of the "four constants"—dwelling place, property, clothes, and food—and the proper way to deal with them. Chapter 18 describes various sorts of congregational prayer and the benefits of joint rather than private worship. Chapter 19 is dedicated to marriage, and Chapter 20 to funerals.

Liu's third major book is his life of the Prophet, *Tianfang zhisheng shilu*, which was completed in 1724. Although modeled on Islamic sources, especially a Persian translation of a work by Muḥammad ibn Mas'ūd Kāzarūnī (d. 1357),[14] it is colored throughout by Liu's attempts to bring out the heavenly nature of the Utmost Sage. The book was partially translated by Isaac Mason in 1921 and published under the title *The Arabian Prophet*, and some historians have opined that it is Liu's most important book. The most accessible of his three major compositions, it provides a quasi-mythic account of Muḥammad's life designed to elicit the awe and respect due the foremost among the sages.

In the introduction to this third member of what Frankel calls the "Tianfang Trilogy," Liu explained that the three books together form a unity. *Tianfang xingli* clarifies the Way (*dao* 道), *Tianfang dianli* explains the teaching (*jiao* 教), and *Tianfang zhisheng shilu* exposes the profound origin of the teaching and the Way. By "teaching," he meant the practical instructions of the religion; the Way is the Way of Heaven that underlies the practical instructions; and "profound origin" refers to the wondrous embodiment of both teaching and Way in Muḥammad.

Frankel, in his study of *Tianfang dianli*, has a long chapter discussing the relationship between *jiao* and *Dao*, teaching and Way, both in the Chinese tradition and in the Han Kitab. He looks closely at Ding Peng 丁澎, who was trained as a Confucian literatus and spoke of "our Islam" and "our Confucianism" and who was cited by Liu in *Tianfang dianli*.[15] Frankel points out that in the Chinese tradition, "*Dao* is the abstract, absolute and theoretical underpinning of *Jiao*; and *Jiao* is the concrete, relative and practical vehicle whereby *Dao* is manifested in the world."[16] By means of the teaching, the Sage bridges the gap between the Way of Heaven and the Way of Man.

In speaking of the Tianfang Trilogy, Liu said: "These three books are three and at the same time one. They are like stepping up the stairs, going into the hall, and then entering into the inner chamber." He was alluding to a passage in which Confucius says, concerning his well-known disciple Zilu, that he "has ascended the hall but has not yet entered the inner chamber" (*Analects* 11.14). Although Liu did not develop this analogy, the manner in which the three texts cover the gamut of traditional Islamic learning is fairly clear. He had in view a tripartite depiction of the Islamic tradition commonly found in Arabic and Persian texts (and explained under Diagram 4.6; see pp. 450–51). Ascending the stairs corresponds to practice, going into the hall is the ongoing process of transformation achieved by understanding the teachings and deepening the practice, and entering the inner chamber designates the goal of practice and teaching, which is reunion with the Origin.

These three stages accord with the traditional triad of Shariah (the revealed law), Tariqah (the path to God), and Haqiqah (the Reality, God himself), which are explained in detail later. Whether Muslim authors use these three or other terms, they commonly view their tradition as having three ascending stages: practice, or engagement of the body; faith, or engagement of the heart and mind; and perfection, or transformation of the soul and reintegration into the One.[17] All three stages are seen as essential to the tradition; hence, as Liu put it, "the three are three and at the same time one."

The unified purpose of Liu's trilogy is indicated in the titles, since each begins with *tianfang*, "heavenly square" or "heavenly direction." The word originally seems to have been used to refer to the Kaaba, the cube-like sanctuary in Mecca, which marks for all Muslims the direction toward which they face in performing the daily prayers (the *qibla*). By extension, it came to be applied to Mecca itself, to Arabia, and to the whole tradition.[18] It is in the last sense that Liu uses *tianfang* in the titles of his trilogy. These might be translated as "Principles of Islam," "Practices of Islam," and "The Sage Embodiment of Islam." The first explains the Tariqah in a broad sense as the realm of faith, understanding, and the awakening of the heart. The second describes the Shariah as the practices that complement faith and apply it to everyday life and ritual. The third describes the Haqiqah as embodied in the virtues, character traits, worthy activities, and wondrous realizations of the Supreme Sage, the person whose Sunnah (habit, wont, virtuous model) is imitated by all Muslims. All three books address what Liu called at the beginning of the text translated here *tianfang xue* 天方學, "Islamic learning."

## The Persian and Arabic Sources

*Tianfang xingli* is divided into three parts. In the introduction, Liu explained why he wrote the book and how he structured it. The second part is the "Root Classic" (Benjing 本經), which is a short text (1,600 characters) divided into five chapters and illustrated by ten diagrams. The majority of the book is occupied by the third section, which is divided into five volumes, each of which analyzes the discussion in one of the Root Classic's five chapters with the help of twelve diagrams. Thus, there are a total of seventy diagrams, ten at the end of the Root Classic without individual explanation, and sixty more with additional text.

In the introduction, Liu tells that he began the book by composing the Root Classic, which is "a collection of various classics formed into one classic." More specifically, he drew from "six great classics." The word *jing*, "classic," is sometimes used by the Han Kitab without qualification to mean the Koran, but commonly, as here, it simply means an important book written by a Muslim scholar. Liu is saying that the Root Classic is a collection of quotations drawn from six major Muslim texts. He called it the "root" because he used it as the springboard for the diagrams and his own explanations.

In writing the five explanatory volumes, Liu no doubt had many books in view, whether in Persian, Arabic, or Chinese. In both *Tianfang xingli* and *Tianfang dianli*, he provided lists of his Arabic and Persian sources (in Chinese transliteration and translation). The first list has forty titles, and the second forty-five. Nineteen of these overlap, giving a total of sixty-six titles, some of which have been identified by Donald D. Leslie and Muhammad Wassel.[19] The really important sources for the book, however, seem to be the six classics whose names are mentioned in the Root Classic itself in eighty-six interlinear notes. In these Liu referred in fact to seven books, five of which have been identified with certainty. We have a likely identity for the sixth; the seventh remains unknown.

The four most often cited books were written by three well-known Sufi teachers. One is the already mentioned *Mirṣād al-ʿibād* by Najm al-Dīn Rāzī. The second is by ʿAzīz Nasafī (d. ca. 1300), and two are by ʿAbd al-Raḥmān Jāmī (d. 1492). In terms of Sufi affiliation, both Rāzī and Nasafī belonged to the Kubrawī line, and Jāmī to the Naqshbandī lineage. Leslie and Wassel, among others, suggest that this affiliation has some significance, but we find it doubtful that the lineage of the authors would have had any direct influence on Liu's choice of the books. All four are true classics of Sufi literature and have been read by Muslims of all persuasions throughout the Persianate world. They show practically no characteristics that would differentiate them because of affiliation to one Sufi order rather than another.

The most often cited of the four books (thirty times) is Rāzī's *Mirṣād al-ʿibād min al-mabdaʾ ilaʾl-maʿād* (The path of the servants from the Origin to the Return).[20] Rāzī was a disciple of the great Najm al-Dīn Kubrā (d. 1221), the eponymous founder of the Kubrawī Order. He in turn became a guide on the path to God and wrote several books, of which *Path* is by far the most famous. The fact that he mentions "the Origin and the Return" in the title is not without significance, for, as we shall see, Liu employs a parallel notion as the organizing principle of *Tianfang xingli*.

At 550 pages, *Path* is the longest of the four Sufi texts. It is a beautifully written, poetic, and mythic presentation of the whole range of Islamic teachings, composed of five parts. After the first, introductory section, the second part provides an overview of Koranic cosmology: the creation of the universe, the distinction between the major worlds, the nature of spirits and bodies, the special place of human beings in the overall economy of creation, and the reason for human existence. The third part explains the roots of human ignorance, the necessity for prophets, the need for cultivation of the soul, and various practices over and above the usual Islamic rituals that can help people polish their hearts and achieve true awareness. The next section describes the differing returns to God experienced by the four basic sorts of human being. The final part explains the paths of conduct for people in the various stations of society.

*Maqṣad-i aqṣā* (The furthest goal) is the name of Nasafī's much shorter book (eighty pages);[21] Liu cited it fourteen times. Like Rāzī, Nasafī was a member of the Kubrawī line, although he belonged to another branch, that directed by Saʿd al-Dīn Ḥammūya (d. 1252), a great scholar of Shafiʿi jurisprudence who was also a direct disciple of Kubrā. Ḥammūya authored some fifty books and treatises, mainly in Arabic but also in Persian, many of them on metaphysics, cosmology, and spiritual psychology. Although not a follower of Ibn al-ʿArabī (d. 1240), known in Sufism as "The Greatest Master" (*al-shaykh al-akbar*), he made full use of the sophisticated philosophical and theological terminology for which Ibn al-ʿArabī is famous. Ḥammūya was much interested in explaining the hidden dimensions of the macrocosm in terms of the occult sciences. Jāmī, in his famous biography of the Sufis, *Nafaḥāt al-uns* (Breaths of intimacy), expressed exasperation at the difficulty of his writings, which, he tells us, are full of mysterious circles and diagrams;[22] Liu's use of diagrams would not have seemed strange to those versed in this tradition.

Nasafī, in contrast to Ibn al-ʿArabī or his own teacher Ḥammūya, was a popularizer. He wrote several books along the lines of *Goal*, each in straightforward and systematic language. He often reviewed the basic teachings of both Sufis and philosophers on various topics while juxtaposing his own explanations. This distinction between Sufism and philosophy is an important one in Islamic studies, although the exact line of demarcation between the two approaches is much debated. Generally, Sufism designates the "mystical" dimension of the Islamic tradition; it is characterized by an emphasis on the necessity of spiritual practice and the quest for inner illumination. Its great representatives—such as Ibn al-ʿArabī or the Persian poet Jalāl al-Dīn Rūmī (d. 1273)—are considered to have achieved in themselves a degree of holiness. In contrast, the philosophical approach, whose most famous representative is Avicenna (Ibn Sīnā, d. 1037), is marked by an indebtedness to the Greek tradition and a stress on the necessity of logical thought.

Nasafī's use of both Sufi and philosophical sources has led scholars to attempt to pinpoint whom he had in mind when he spoke of groups such as "The Folk of Oneness," or "The Folk of Unveiling," or "The Folk of Wisdom [i.e., philosophy]."[23] The differences between the philosophical and Sufi schools of thought appear significant in the context of thirteenth-century Islam, but, at a distance of a few centuries, their diverse viewpoints can be seen as harmonious variations on the same themes—themes on which Liu meditated in Confucian terms.

Nasafī was far less poetic than Rāzī, but he was a master of simple and fluent Persian prose. He began *Goal* by explaining that the "Furthest Goal" for all travelers on the path is to achieve true understanding of God, which comes by way of divine illumination. The path has three basic components—Shariah, Tariqah, and Haqiqah—and the person who reaches the goal is called the perfect human being (*insān-i kāmil*). Nasafī then set down the basic elements of the Tariqah, including the need for guidance on the way, various practices that must be performed, and the virtues to be achieved. In the remaining seven chapters and a conclusion, he ran through Islamic teachings on God's attributes and acts, the structure of the cosmos and the human soul, and the nature of the soul's transformation. In contrast to Rāzī, he employed a good deal of terminology drawn from the Muslim philosophers, although it is nicely integrated with the Sufi teachings.

The author of the two remaining Sufi texts, 'Abd al-Raḥmān Jāmī, was a prolific writer of both prose and poetry. He is one of the best-known and most influential writers of the later Persianate world. In many ways he was a popularizer like Nasafī, especially through his poetry, which included long retellings of the romantic sagas of Persian literature interspersed with teachings drawn from Ibn al-'Arabī and his followers. Jāmī made no secret of the fact that he spoke for Ibn al-'Arabī's school of thought. Given the prominence of his famous lives of the saints, *Nafaḥāt al-uns*, Jāmī has probably been more responsible than anyone else for giving currency to the idea that Ibn al-'Arabī stood for the doctrine of *waḥdat al-wujūd*, "The Oneness of Existence," a term that has been controversial among

Muslims down to modern times.[24] Jāmī was the first to highlight the importance of the lineage of Ibn al-'Arabī's students, beginning with his disciple Ṣadr al-Dīn Qūnawī (d. 1274).[25]

Of the two books by Jāmī cited by Liu, *Ashi' 'at al-lama'āt* (The rays of "The Flashes") is mentioned more often (fifteen times). This is a commentary on a famous Persian prose classic on divine love, *Lama'āt* (Flashes) by Fakhr al-Dīn 'Irāqī (d. 1289), a student of Ṣadr al-Dīn Qūnawī.[26] Before entering into a line-by-line explanation of the text, Jāmī's 150-page commentary provides a twenty-page introduction on the metaphysical principles of Ibn al-'Arabī's thought, and it is mainly from this section that Liu drew.

Jāmī's second book, the shortest of the four Sufi texts, is *Lawā'iḥ* (Gleams), which Liu cited eleven times. He later translated this book into Chinese, and we published English translations of both the original Persian and Liu's Chinese translation in *Chinese Gleams*. There we also explain a good deal more about Jāmī's importance in the Islamic tradition and the significance of *Lawā'iḥ* for Islamic thought.

The fifth book that Liu cited (nine times) is the Arabic *al-Mawāqif fī 'ilm al-kalām* (The standpoints in the science of theology). This is a famous exposition of dogmatic theology by 'Aḍud al-Dīn al-Ījī (d. 1355), a well-known Shafi'i jurist, who was a judge in Shiraz. Liu's bibliographers have been unsure about the exact identity of the book he cited simply as *Standpoints*, since a number of other books have the same name. When we wrote *Chinese Gleams*, we doubted that it was al-Ījī's *Standpoints*, because the passages in question have much to do with cosmology and little connection with the standard discussions of dogmatic theology. *Standpoints* is a late work, however, and by this time in Islamic history, theologians had become interested in many issues raised by philosophers, for whom cosmology is central.

The sixth book from which Liu cited seems to be the famous commentary on the Koran by Bayḍāwī (d. ca. 1300). In his list of sources, Liu mentioned two commentaries by the same Chinese term, differentiating them by the names of their authors (transliterated into Chinese), but he did not indicate which commentary he was citing in the Root Classic. The author of the first is "Qāḍī," "the judge," that is, Bayḍāwī; and of the second apparently "Zāhidī," who has not been identified with certainty. Liu cited the *Commentary* five times, and we have been able to find one passage in Bayḍāwī that could easily have been part of the inspiration for one of the discussions.

The seventh and last book is the still unidentified *Aḥkām-i ka-wākib* (The ruling properties of the stars), which Liu referred to twice while discussing the heavens.

## The Arabic Translation of the Root Classic

In 1898 a Chinese scholar by the name of Ma Lianyuan 馬聯元 published an edition of the Root Classic in Yunnan in south China with an interlinear Arabic translation, calling the Arabic text by the name *al-Laṭā'if* (The subtleties). Four years later he published an Arabic commentary on *Subtleties* in Kanpur in India, calling it *Sharḥ al-laṭā'if* (Explanation of the subtleties). Although the commentary explains the meaning of the Root Classic, Ma made relatively little use of Liu's five volumes of Chinese explanation, relying instead on his own learning in the Islamic sciences. He employed thirty-two of Liu Zhi's seventy diagrams, but added eight diagrams of his own, at least two of which he took from Ibn al-'Arabī's *Futūḥāt*.[27] He died in India in 1904.

In *Explanation of the Subtleties*, Ma introduced himself as 'Abd al-Ḥakīm al-Ḥājj al-Sayyid Muḥammad Nūr al-Ḥaqq ibn al-Sayyid Luqmān al-Ṣīnī, a name that suggests a family history of involvement in Islamic sage learning.[28] Below we refer to him as Nūr al-Ḥaqq, the name he called himself in the course of the book.[29] When we first read his translation of the Root Classic and his commentary several years ago, we were disappointed at how little it reflects the thoroughly Chinese character of Liu's text. Since then, however, we have spent a good deal of time studying his text and comparing it both to Liu's book and to Liu's sources, and we have revised our opinion.

In many ways Nūr al-Ḥaqq faced the same problem overcome by Liu and other authors of the Han Kitab: how to express Islamic notions in a foreign idiom. Chinese Muslims did not share the advantage of writers in languages like Persian, Turkish, and Urdu, all of which use the Arabic script. An author writing in Persian who wanted to be faithful to the text of the Koran or other Arabic sources, or who encountered difficulty translating an Arabic word into his own language, would simply employ the Arabic expression. Modern-day Muslims and scholars of Islam writing in European languages resort to transliteration for the same purpose. Given the nature of the Chinese script, however, neither Arabic script nor transliteration was an option. The Huiru could not write intelligible books if they employed more than a smattering of transliterated words. They were forced to rethink Islamic ideas in the context of Chinese thought, and that demanded thorough knowledge of the Chinese classics and the living tradition of Neo-Confucian learning.

When Nūr al-Ḥaqq translated Liu's book, he faced an analogous problem: "How do you say this in Arabic?" He could not transliterate Chinese terms without turning the text into gibberish, nor could he simply "translate" word for word, given the thoroughly Confucian style of Liu's thinking. He had to express the ideas as best he could in the technical language of the Islamic sciences, and that meant Sufism and philosophy, which are precisely the branches of Islamic learning that deal with the issues raised in *Tianfang xingli*. Along the way, he could try to recover the original concepts Liu had adapted to the Chinese context.

Nūr al-Ḥaqq did an excellent job of translating and explaining the Root Classic. His occasional quotations from all four of the Sufi texts that Liu used make it clear that he did his homework. He was not a historian, however, but a teacher occupied with training disciples. He was not worried about tracking down the original terminology; rather, he was concerned to express the Chinese notions in a language that his students, and Muslims in general, could understand. In order to do so, he employed terminology current in books on theoretical Sufism in his own time, two hundred years after the composition of *Tianfang xingli*. In drawing from the contemporary world of Islamic scholarship, he quoted directly from the massively influential writings of Ibn al-'Arabī, whose teachings also left their imprint on Liu's books, although apparently indirectly, mainly through Jāmī. On the whole, Nūr provided a helpful guide for understanding the parallel Islamic terminology, although he did not always employ the terms that Liu himself originally had in view.

Why did Nūr al-Ḥaqq bother to go to the trouble of translating the text into Arabic and then explaining it? He says that he considered it the best of the many works of the Han Kitab. Having instructed his Chinese students to memorize it, he then translated it "because of their affection for Arabic." Such "affection" (*shafaqa*) is universal among Muslims, but the act of translation may also point to changes in the situation of Muslims in China over the nineteenth century. More and more Chinese scholars were going abroad, spending several years in cities like Cairo and Medina and returning with what they considered a "pure" form of Islamic learning. The period was one of political and social turmoil throughout the Muslim world, and many responded by attempting to return to their religious roots. Some were attracted to Wahhabism and other narrow interpretations of the tradition, and China itself was by no means immune from the ensuing debates and conflicts, as Jonathan Lipman has documented in *Familiar Strangers*.

Without trying to sort out the various currents of Islamic teaching vying for the allegiance of Chinese Muslims in the nineteenth century—often summarized as the "Old Teaching/New Teaching" controversy, or the *khafiyya/jahriyya* conflict[30]—we can say with some degree of confidence that during the nineteenth century there was an influx of "reformist" currents of Islam often intensely hostile to the Chinese versions of Islamic teachings established by the Huiru. These reformist scholars considered the works of the Han Kitab distortions or syncretism and emphasized Arabic as the way to return to the sources of the tradition. Persian, which had once been of major importance for Islamic learning in China—witness Liu's Root Classic—was devalued and gradually became the language of "women," both literally and figuratively. Those who were serious and "manly" about their studies undertook the study of Islam in Arabic, whereas women continued to study Islam in Persian, often in the context of a specifically Chinese phenomenon, women's mosques.[31]

The social and cultural contexts of Islam in late nineteenth-century China no doubt help explain why Nūr al-Ḥaqq wanted to translate Liu's book. His students and many other Muslims probably thought that any book not in Arabic was not authentically Islamic (a notion very much alive today among Muslims all over the world). By translating the Root Classic into Arabic, Nūr al-Ḥaqq was bringing the Han Kitab into the context of the contemporary stress on Arabic-language Islamic learning. The fact that Nūr eventually left China—his reasons are as obscure as the other details of his life—suggests that he did not find China a congenial environment for this task; the publication of his commentary in Kanpur further confirms this.

Nūr al-Ḥaqq's attempt to synthesize the Han Kitab and the Arabic tradition seems to have had few repercussions in China or in the larger Islamic world. Nonetheless, his *Explanation of the Subtleties* was published in a second lithograph edition twenty-two years after the first, an indication that it must have had some readership, at least in India. The Arabic text has also been reproduced in China, and in 1983, it was even translated into Chinese.[32]

For several reasons, we thought it would be useful to provide not only an English translation of Nūr al-Ḥaqq's *Subtleties* but also the Arabic text. First, we found both *Subtleties* and its commentary helpful in clarifying some of Liu's discussions and in testing our conjectures concerning the Arabic/Persian terms that Liu might have had in mind. Those acquainted with Islamic languages will find a wealth of terminology that will help bridge the gap between the Islamic and the Confucian conceptual universes. Moreover, Nūr's commentary on the *Subtleties* has been helpful in providing plausible interpretations for some of Liu's ideas, and we have quoted from it extensively in our annotations, especially in the last two volumes, where Liu seems to be at his most original (and obscure). We thought it appropriate that readers have access at least to Nūr's version of the text that he is explaining.

A second reason for providing the Arabic text of *Subtleties* is simply to illustrate that members of the Han Kitab kept up an ongoing acquaintance with the Arabic and Persian languages and were always concerned to show the congruencies and differences between the Islamic and the Confucian traditions. Most educated Muslims nowadays—not to speak of the uneducated—have little or no familiarity with the intellectual tradition in Arabic and Persian that both Liu and Nūr al-Ḥaqq represent and about which a good deal more will be said. Many contemporary Muslims, especially those under the influence of Islamist ideology, would be shocked by the notion that the Root Classic—given its thoroughly "Confucian" color— could represent Islamic thought. Nūr al-Ḥaqq offers one example of a scholar proficient in the Islamic sciences who thought that Liu did in fact speak for the mainstream Islamic tradition.

A third reason is to show that "ecumenical" issues connected with the theological and intellectual relations between the Confucian and the Islamic traditions were very much part of the ambience that allowed the Han Kitab to flourish, as Benite is at pains to show, and these issues continued to play a role in Nūr's reading of the Root Classic. Like many other Chinese Muslim authors, Liu argued for a deep, underlying harmony in the teachings of the sages, whether they be of East or West. Nūr did not explicitly highlight this point, but the very fact that he heaped praise on Liu, even saying that he would have been a prophet if Muḥammad had not been the last, shows that he wanted to convince his readers that the great authors of the Han Kitab represented authentic Islam. Given the care that he exercised in finding ways to express Liu's ideas in an Arabic that any traditional Muslim scholar could appreciate, one can see a subtext to his book: he is bearing witness to the Koranic notion that God sent prophets to all peoples, and that everywhere the wisdom of the sages guides to the same ultimate goal.

# TWO

# *The Islamic Background*

Many people, in reading *Tianfang xingli*, will ask why it should be considered an "Islamic" text. Where are the markers by which such texts are recognized, such as quotations from the Koran, Muḥammad, and the great authorities? Where are the ritual instructions, the rules and regulations, the dogmatic statements of Muslim belief?

The immediate response is that this is a book on "principles," not applications. The rules and regulations can be found in *Tianfang dian-li*. Our decision to translate this text has everything to do with the fact that it deals with theory and not practice. When we first began to read it, we did not expect to encounter the typical Islamic markers, not least because we knew that the Huiru avoided Arabic terminology. More-over, Liu's list of sources and his translation of Jāmī's *Gleams* are in-dications that his inspiration derived in part from the specific strands of Muslim thought least beholden to the formal elements of the tradi-tion, namely, theoretical Sufism (what in recent Persian history has typically been called *'irfān*, "gnosis") and philosophy.

Theoretical Sufism in its later forms is commonly associated with Ibn al-'Arabī, who has been regarded by his followers as "The Greatest Master" (*al-shaykh al-akbar*) because of the unparalleled detail and profundity with which he unpacked the teachings of the Koran and the Hadith (the corpus of prophetic sayings). One can

20

speak of the "school" of Ibn al-'Arabī, but the word suggests a structure that did not in fact exist. Rather, many Muslim scholars took inspiration from his formulations of Islamic teachings and elaborated on them, often in commentaries on his most famous book, the *Fuṣūṣ al-ḥikam* (Ringstones of wisdom).

Ibn al-'Arabī based his approach squarely on the Koran and the Hadith, much more so in fact than did either the experts in Kalam (dogmatic theology) or the philosophers. He drew from all the major schools of Islamic learning—jurisprudence, Kalam, philosophy, and Sufism. He did not, however, call his own approach by any of these names, nor did he provide a label for what he was doing. When he did hint at appropriate names, he often spoke of *taḥqīq*, "realization" or "verification," and Ṣadr al-Dīn Qūnawī, his foremost disciple, spoke of his own approach and that of likeminded scholars as "the school of realization" (*mashrab al-taḥqīq*). *Taḥqīq* in fact had been used earlier by other authors—usually Sufis or philosophers—to designate a certain approach to learning. One of the best ways to understand how *Tianfang xingli* fits into the Islamic tradition is to investigate the meaning of this term.[1]

## The Quest for Realization

The primary aim of those who focused on *taḥqīq* was not to teach dogma or doctrine; nor was it to pass on the received learning or to instruct in proper morality and practice. Such scholars considered the formal aspects of the tradition, with its dogma and doctrines, less important than the goal that was to be achieved, namely, the transformation of the soul and conformity with the Supreme Reality. *Taḥqīq*, or realization, is a word they employed to designate both the method of achieving the goal and the goal itself. To gain an adequate understanding of what they meant, however, we need to review the question of the search for knowledge in Islam, a search required of all Muslims ("even unto China," as the famous saying of Muḥammad tells us).

People acquire knowledge in two basic ways, and these are given a variety of names in diverse religious and philosophical traditions. Muslims have often distinguished between them by calling one "transmitted" (*naqlī*) and the other "intellectual" (*'aqlī*). Transmitted learning depends on what has been received from the past. Examples include language, grammar, history, law, Koran, and Hadith—everything that is grounded in memory. In contrast, intellectual knowledge cannot be transmitted. It has nothing to do with memorization and rote, or with conclusions drawn on the basis of principles or observation. Rather, it is a living awareness and consciousness of the way things are, and it can be found only within oneself, in the "intellect" (*'aql*), also called the "heart" (*qalb, dil*).

A commonly cited example of an intellectual science is arithmetic, because its principles and details are latent in the human mind, waiting to be understood. We know that two plus two equals four because it is self-evident to our intelligence. At first we may need to be reminded of this, but once it is brought to our attention, we "re-cognize" it, that is, we come to know that we already know it. The use of the word *'irfān* (or its equivalent from the same root, *ma 'rifa*) for this sort of knowledge has much to do with the fact that this word is used in Arabic to render the notion of recognition, in contrast to *'ilm*, or "knowledge," which means knowing, learning, or a specific discipline and hence a "science."

The distinction between intellectual and transmitted knowledge is implied in the two Shahadahs that are the foundation of Islamic faith: "(There is) no god but God" and "Muḥammad is God's messenger." The Koran presents the first of these statements, commonly called "the words declaring [God's] Unity" (*kalimat al-tawḥīd*), as a universal, ahistorical, self-evident truth. It was known to Adam and was taught by every prophet and sage. It is accessible to human intelligence without prophetic intervention, because God created human beings in his own form (*ṣūra*) and gave them a primordial nature (*fiṭra*) that recognizes things as they are. The function of the prophets is not to teach Unity but to "remind" (*dhikr, tadhkira*) people that they already know it. In this way of looking at things, every normal, healthy intelligence recognizes that the universe is governed by One Supreme Principle, just as it recognizes that two plus two equals four. Such knowledge is innate to the human substance.

The second Shahadah takes a different standpoint and declares the importance of historical and transmitted knowledge. To say "Muḥammad is God's messenger" means to acknowledge that Muḥammad was sent by God with a message, and that the message tells people what God wants from them. This knowledge is conveyed first of all in the Koran, and then in the Hadith, dogma, ritual, and rules. The only way to gain it is to receive it by transmission. You cannot discover it in your own heart.

These two sorts of learning demand two different methodologies. The method of gaining transmitted knowledge is commonly known as "imitation" (*taqlīd*), that is, learning from others. All information about the historical tradition of Islam, whether known by Muslims or non-Muslims, is acquired by way of imitation. In contrast, intellectual knowledge cannot be acquired by this route—by studying books and memorizing the words of others or by carrying out historical or sociological or scientific research. Rather, it must be discovered in the heart. The process of discovery is called *taḥqīq*, realization. In order to achieve it, one must begin by imitating others, but imitation cannot provide true understanding. The goal is to know for oneself, directly and without an intermediary.

In order to gain reliable transmitted knowledge, people need authoritative teachers. Islam asks Muslims to follow the Shariah (the revealed law) as taught to them by the ulama (*'ulamā'*, i.e., the scholars who have mastered the law and thereby gained the authority to speak on its behalf).[2] But the ulama in turn have received their knowledge from their teachers; eventually the chain of transmission leads to the Koran and the Prophet. It is true that most "Islamic" knowledge is by definition transmitted, since its specifically Islamic color comes by way of its conformity with the Koran and the Hadith. But for Muslims the road to intellectual knowledge does not necessarily have the same Islamic color, because it does not depend on transmission. Moreover, this road has always been open, and it lies at the crux of the perspectives that eventually came to be known as philosophy and Sufism.

One debate among historians of Islamic philosophy is the extent to which this philosophy can be called "Islamic." If something is philosophy, then adding Islamic (or Christian or Confucian) simply confuses matters, as if philosophy depended on religion. Some scholars prefer to call such philosophy "Muslim," suggesting that it is indeed philosophy, but its authors and practitioners were Muslims. It seems to us that this reaction to the use of the word "Islamic" in this context derives from the recognition that genuine philosophy is an intellectual science, not a transmitted one. If it is intellectual, it must be universal and in some sense ahistorical; in contrast, religion is necessarily rooted in transmitted teachings and, as such, cannot escape from its historical limitations. Nowadays, of course, historians and philosophers generally reject any possibility of universal, impersonal, ahistorical knowledge. Nonetheless, most philosophers still seem to maintain that philosophy does not depend on knowledge transmitted from religious sources (even if many of them seem to reach this position by replacing the dogmas of religion with those of science or ideology).

Within the Islamic tradition, there has always been a tension between authorities who speak for transmitted knowledge and seekers of intellectual knowledge. Most Muslims have taken the position that "learning" means the Koran and Hadith, theological dogma, and the rules and regulations of the Shariah. Followers of the intellectual path have held that all this is necessary and good, but it is only preliminary to the real task. To be sure, it needs to be studied, but its purpose is to prepare the way for the advanced learning that comes through the awakening of the heart. In Chinese terms, transmitted knowledge is "small learning" (*xiaoxue* 小學), and intellectual knowledge "great learning" (*daxue* 大學).

The arguments and debates over the course of Islamic history between the teachers of transmitted knowledge and the seekers of intellectual knowledge have a certain similarity with the debates between Confucians and Daoists. Confucians advocated acquiring the transmitted knowledge of the Classics, but Daoists felt that transmitted knowledge can become a barrier to true understanding. "The name that can be named" is, after all, "not the name" (Laozi), and by the same token, the learning that can be transmitted is not the same as awareness and understanding. Sufis and philosophers, like Daoists and most Neo-Confucians, said explicitly that the real purpose of learning is to achieve transformation and realization. True awakening occurs when the heart is purified of all knowledge that has come from the outside.

## *Fields of Understanding*

In order to appreciate the contrasting natures of intellectual and transmitted knowledge, we need to pay attention to what seekers of intellectual knowledge were trying to understand. Despite many differences in approach and expression, philosophers and Sufis agreed that three basic sorts of knowledge can and should be sought in the heart. These are metaphysics, or knowledge of the Ultimate Reality that theologians call "God"; cosmology, or knowledge of the world out there, typically defined as "everything other than God" (*mā siwa'llāh*); and psychology or autology, which is knowledge of the knowing self (*nafs*).

Of course, these three topics are also studied as transmitted learning. The Koran and the Hadith have a great deal to say about them, as do books written by theologians, philosophers, and Sufis, and all these books can be studied and memorized. Nonetheless, the masters of philosophy and Sufism—in contrast to the experts in jurisprudence and dogmatic theology—never forgot that the purpose of learning is not only to acquire and apply the teachings of the past but also to transcend hearsay and to come to know God, the world, and the self for oneself and in oneself. True knowledge cannot be found by imitating the words and opinions of others, only by awakening the heart.

Some will object that Muslims must imitate the Prophet. The reply has always been: of course, and that is why transmission is the basis for all learning. Nonetheless, the Prophet did not know what he knew by hearsay. Part of imitating the Prophet is to come to know directly, not on the basis of someone else's words—not even on the basis of the words of God, when those words have been transmitted to us by others and we have simply memorized them. The great seventeenth-century philosopher Mullā Ṣadrā made this point in reference to all of God's prophets:

You should not suppose that the prophets used to hear revelation from the angels by virtue of imitation. What an idea! For imitation is not knowledge, whether the one imitated be a mortal man or an angel. But the prophets are knowers of God, His signs, His Sovereignty, His books, His messengers, and the Last Day. This is only a witnessing by the heart and an inward conversation in respect of insight and certainty, not mere imitation and surmise.[3]

## Wisdom

One way to understand the role of the intellectual path is to say that it provided forms of learning and praxis that could lead to the achievement of "wisdom" (*ḥikma*). The Koran often calls the knowledge that God gave to the prophets by this name, and it refers to God himself as "the Wise" (*al-ḥakīm*). For example, "He gives wisdom to whomsoever He will, and whoso is given wisdom has been given much good; yet none remember save those with minds" (2:269). For philosophers and Sufis, the search for wisdom was the quest to open their own minds, to remember what they already know in the depths of their hearts, and to receive "much good" from the Wise One, who is the giver of wisdom.

In this verse, the expression "those with minds" (*ulu'l-albāb*) literally means "the possessors of the kernels." Ibn al-'Arabī alluded to the difference between transmitted and intellectual knowledge while explaining the meaning of this expression as it is used in another Koranic verse: "Say: 'Are they equal—those who know and those who know not?' Only the possessors of the kernels remember" (39:9). True knowledge, according to Ibn al-'Arabī, is to know the kernel (*lubb*), not the shell (*qishr*). The shell is transmitted knowledge, and the kernel is the heart's remembrance and re-cognition of the way things are:

This verse tells us that they knew, then some of them were overcome by forgetfulness. . . . Others are reminded and remember, and they are the "possessors of the kernels." The "kernel" of the intelligence (*'aql*) is that which becomes the food of the intelligent. The "possessors of the kernels" are those who employ intelligence as it should be employed, in contrast to rationalistic thinkers, who are the people of the shell.[4]

Muslims often defined philosophy, following the Greek etymology, as "the love of wisdom" (*ḥubb al-ḥikma*). In both the philosophical and the Sufi approaches to knowledge, wisdom was understood as awareness of things as they truly are, along with activity appropriate to such awareness. The goal of searching for wisdom was not to gain information or the ability to control things; rather, it was to understand God, the universe, and oneself and, on the basis of this understanding, to become a sage, a wise man. The seeker of wisdom was trying to live in perfect conformity with the Supreme Principle. The sage is the person who has awoken to the presence of God in his own heart and lives correctly in the world. The fact that Chinese Muslims felt at ease calling the prophets "sages" (*sheng* 聖) has a good deal to do with the central place of wisdom and sagehood in the Koran and the constant emphasis on becoming a sage that was part and parcel of the intellectual tradition.

One of the best-known ways of distinguishing among the various approaches to knowledge in Islam is to divide the religion itself into the three levels or dimensions to which we have already referred: Shariah (*sharī'a*), or revealed law; Tariqah (*ṭarīqa*), or the path to God; and Haqiqah (*ḥaqīqa*), or Reality. This scheme was well known to Chinese Muslims and is mentioned in the prologues of Liu's two most important sources, Rāzī's *Path* and Nasafī's *Goal*. Liu himself mentioned it in Root Classic 4: 82–86 and provided a detailed description under Diagram 4.6. He calls Shariah "Propriety" (*li*), Tariqah "the Way" (*dao*), and Haqiqah "the Real" (*zhen* 眞).

In the first chapter of *Tianfang dianli*, Liu paid more attention to these three dimensions of the tradition, calling them the three "vehicles" (*sheng* 乘), the same term that Chinese Buddhists employed to translate *yana* as in Mahayana, the "Great Vehicle." He further stipulated a fourth, transcendent vehicle, which transforms heaven and humans such that "names and traces" disappear. He addressed this fourth vehicle in much of Volume 5 of *Tianfang xingli*, although he did not use the name.

The word Shariah literally means "road leading to water," or "avenue." In the Islamic sciences, it has two basic senses. Broadly, it designates the Koran and the Hadith along with all that these imply for our human situation; it is the whole body of transmitted learning inasmuch as it sets down a broad and inclusive path that must be followed in order to achieve the purpose of human life. In this sense, the word is often used as a synonym for *dīn* or "religion," and its plural, *sharā'i'*, is used to mean all the revealed religions, not just Islam. More narrowly, Shariah designates the instructions for activity and practice laid down in the Koran and the Sunnah that have been fleshed out by the jurists over the centuries. It is this second meaning of the term that is meant in the depiction of three stages or dimensions of the tradition.

Tariqah is the assimilation of the Shariah by the soul and the process of the soul's transformation. It is the road that needs to be traversed, the path that needs to be followed, so as to conform with God's instructions not only in bodily activities (the Shariah) but also in mind and heart. The goal is to find the presence of God in oneself and the world. In Islamic languages "Tariqah" is used far more commonly than *taṣawwuf* (Sufism) to designate the spiritual path—the steep path followed by especially dedicated Muslims. The Shariah is the broad path incumbent on all Muslims; the Tariqah is the narrow path for those who do not want to wait until death to meet God.

The goal of the Tariqah is, in short, to reach the Haqiqah, "the Reality." This word derives from the same root as *Ḥaqq*, "Real," as does *taḥqīq*, or realization. Both Haqiqah and *Ḥaqq* designate God himself, and *taḥqīq* means precisely reaching the Haqiqah—attaining to the Supreme Reality and actualizing the truly Real. The exact nature of this attainment is much discussed in Islamic sources, and Liu addressed the issue in the fourth and fifth volumes of his book. No matter how one understands it, Haqiqah remains the point of orientation for the whole discussion. Neither Shariah nor Tariqah makes any sense without the completing notion of Haqiqah.

The orientation of Shariah and Tariqah toward Haqiqah is commonly clarified by drawing a circle: the circumference, upon which all Muslims must walk, is the Shariah. The radii, which are open to everyone at any point on the circumference but demand a great deal more concentration and discipline, are the various paths that people must follow in order to reach God in the world and themselves. The center of the circle is the Haqiqah, the Reality that is the origin of both circumference and radii and that designates the "Furthest Goal"—as Nasafī put it—of all travelers. Wherever one stands on the circle, one's situation is determined by one's relation with the Center.

In terms of realization, the Shariah is the transmitted knowledge that seekers must learn and put into practice, the Tariqah is internalization of that knowledge through transformation of the soul and actualization of the innate human nature (*fiṭra*), and the Haqiqah is perfect realization of the Real. Only at the final stage does knowledge become truly "intellectual," that is, direct and unmediated, flowing forth of its own accord from the "intellect," which is none other than the true heart (*dil-i ḥaqīqī*) or, as Liu called it, "the first heart" (*chuxin* 初心).

## The Real

Throughout the Islamic tradition, but especially in philosophy and Sufism, God is called by the Koranic name *al-Ḥaqq*—Truth, Reality, Right, Real, Appropriate, Worthy. Although Haqiqah is derived from the same root and has basically the same meaning, it is not employed in the Koran and is not listed among the "most beautiful names of God." In contrast, *Ḥaqq* is one of the most commonly mentioned divine names; in Persian, for example, it is used more often than Allah.

*Tawḥīd*, or the principle of Unity, which is expressed in the sentence "There is no god but God," means that "There is no *ḥaqq* but the *Ḥaqq*." Only God, the Supreme Principle, is truly real, right, and appropriate. As for "heaven, earth, and everything between the two" (a common Koranic phrase designating the whole of creation), they fall short of the absolute reality and rightness of the Real. Nonetheless, the Koran and many hadiths tell us that *ḥaqq* is an attribute of created things as well as of the Creator. Everything has a truth, a reality, a rightness, and an appropriateness. The Prophet said that various things have *ḥaqq*s "against you" (*'alayka*), meaning that people must respond to the rightness and appropriateness of things in the proper manner. Hence the word *ḥaqq* means both "right" (as in "human rights") and "duty" or "responsibility." The fact that created things have rights signifies that human beings have the responsibility to observe and respect these rights. As the Prophet commanded, "Give to everything that has a *ḥaqq* its *ḥaqq*."

Some authors have taken this prophetic commandment as a nutshell definition of *tahqīq*, the literal meaning of which is "to actualize *ḥaqq*." Thus, "realization" means understanding the reality, truth, and right of God, the cosmos, and the human self; and, simultaneously, embodying this understanding by right and appropriate activity in every situation. It demands giving God, the cosmos, and the soul what is due to them, their "rights," and by doing so to live up to one's "responsibilities" as a human being.

In short, the "intellectual" knowledge sought in philosophy and Sufism calls for realization, or the transformation of the soul and the actualization of wisdom. The goal is to achieve "perfection" (*kamāl*), which is defined in terms of the Supreme Reality (God), the cosmos (the macrocosmic manifestation of the Supreme Reality), and the awakened heart (the microcosmic manifestation of the Supreme Reality). Only an awakened heart can grasp the truth and reality of the Real, the cosmos, and itself.

In reading *Tianfang xingli*, one should keep in mind that Liu was not speaking on behalf of the transmitted tradition. He acknowledged the importance of following the instructions that have reached us from the sages, especially the Utmost Sage, and he stressed the fact that the received learning is the foundation of the Way. But his purpose was not to repeat the teachings of the Koran, Hadith, and Islamic law, nor was it to provide information about the Supreme Principle and the cosmos. Rather, he was setting down a map of reality in order to guide people on the path to realization, a path that leads from ignorance to wisdom and from forgetfulness to awakening. He was not telling people *what* to think; rather, he wanted to help them learn *how* to think for themselves and to see for themselves. He wanted to make perfectly clear that each of us needs to know reality firsthand, not by hearsay and imitation. We cannot understand God, the cosmos, and our own selves by quoting the Koran and the Prophet, or the Chinese classics, not to mention the opinions of scholars and scientists.

For Liu, the transmitted knowledge that Muslims hear from their ulama (the learned, the scholars of Islam) is a necessary foundation for the Great Learning, but the Great Learning does not depend on the small learning for its expression. Once the intellect—the heart— is awakened through the Great Learning, it no longer belongs to the realm of forms and images; rather, it inhabits the realm of reality and principle. Because the heart is the master of forms, not their slave, it can express itself in ways appropriate to the audience. This can be what the Prophet had in mind when he said, "Speak to people in the measure of their intellects."

## *The World Map*

In order to put the methodology of *taḥqīq* into practice, one must understand where one stands in the cosmos. Where have I come from? Why am I here? What is the goal of human life? In other words, the first thing needed in the quest for realization is a map of the cosmos, situating human beings in the total picture and explaining their proper role in the context of heaven, earth, and the ten thousand things. This is what Liu provided in the book. He did so as a systematic teacher, and he surely had in mind that students should begin by memorizing the Root Classic and then analyze it with the help of the diagrams and their explanations. Their goal should be to assimilate its teachings as an aid on the path of realization. As he put it in the Summary of Volume 2, "If you scrutinize the diagrams and text every day only perfunctorily, how can that benefit your nature and mandate?"

Despite the book's Chinese vocabulary, it is setting down the overall Islamic worldview, specifically as elaborated by Ibn al-'Arabī and several generations of scholars after him. Of the three major figures from whom Liu is drawing, only one, however—'Abd al-Raḥmān Jāmī—belongs to Ibn al-'Arabī's main line of followers. Nasafī made use not only of Ibn al-'Arabī's teachings but also of parallel schools of thought, including Islamic philosophy. As for Rāzī, he shows no evidence of being directly influenced by Ibn al-'Arabī's specific doctrines and terminology or by Islamic philosophy. Nonetheless, his overall approach is explicitly that of *taḥqīq*.

As in any Islamic perspective, Liu's world map is built on the axiom of *tawḥīd*, which means that there is nothing real but the Real, no being but true Being, no knowledge but God's Knowledge. In its every application, the formula "No god but God" negates our everyday perception of the world and informs us that what we recognize as reality, life, awareness, truth, justice, and so on are not as they seem. The truth and reality of good, beauty, and perfection are found exclusively with the One God.

Nonetheless, as noted above, the cosmos is not devoid of reality. It and everything within it have their own *ḥaqq*s—not by virtue of themselves, but by bestowal, which is to say that all lesser reality derives from the true Reality. In philosophical terms, the Existence of the Real is "necessary" (*wājib*), which means that it cannot not be; the existence of everything else is "possible" or "contingent" (*mumkin*), which means that things may or may not exist, depending on the activity of the Real. Only the Real has existence in and of itself, which is to say that the Real is identical with True Being. Anything else, by existing in the manner that it does, makes manifest a certain possibility of being; hence, its existence is contingent on the Necessary.

## *Sovereignty and Kingdom*

In speaking of the universe, the Koran typically talks of heaven (or the heavens) and earth. Heaven is associated with the sky and everything "up," and earth with everything beneath our feet. The world as we know it comes into existence between heaven and earth, that is, as a result of their interrelationship. All things that appear in heaven and earth, along with heaven and earth themselves, are signs (*āyāt*) of the Real, symbols of and pointers to higher realms of reality.

Muslims have generally held that the universe has levels or worlds, the most prominent of which are precisely heaven and earth. In the intellectual tradition, heaven and earth were called by a number of parallel terms, such as unseen (*ghayb*) and visible (*shahāda*), spiritual (*rūḥānī*) and bodily (*jismānī*). In each set, the first term designates what is accessible to our intelligence but not to our senses, and hence philosophers commonly called it the "intelligible" (*maʿqūl*) realm. The second term designates what is accessible to the senses, at least in principle, and hence they called it the "sensory" or "sensible" (*maḥsūs*) realm.

The Muslim view of the relationship between the two worlds is that of traditional realism, parallel to what is seen in Platonism and some forms of medieval Christian thought. The intelligible, unseen, spiritual realm is that of real things, not of notions or abstractions. The sensory, visible, bodily realm is that of relative unreality, if not illusion. To use Liu's Neo-Confucian terms, heaven is the realm of principle (*li* 理), and earth is the realm of images (*xiang* 象); or, heaven is the realm of meaning (*yi* 義), and earth is the realm of forms (*xing* 形). These two pairs, *li*/*xiang* and *yi*/*xing*, coincide almost exactly with one of the more common Arabic/Persian pairs:

"meaning" (*ma'nā*) and "form" (*ṣūra*). Meaning or principle is the inner, spiritual reality of a thing, and form or image is the sensory appearance of the thing, an appearance that makes manifest the properties of the principle.

Both Nasafī and Rāzī commonly referred to the two basic worlds as *malakūt* (Sovereignty) and *mulk* (Kingdom). These two Koranic terms derive from the root MLK and have more or less the same meaning, designating what is possessed by a king or an owner. *Malakūt*, however, is typically used of a quality rather than a thing; it is the attribute of kingship, whereas *mulk* is the kingdom or empire that a king possesses. The Koran spells out clearly that both Sovereignty and Kingdom belong to God, whom it calls "the King" (*al-malik*) and "the Owner of the kingdom" (*mālik al-mulk*). A typical verse about God's kingdom says, "Do you not know that the kingdom of the heavens and the earth belongs to God?" (2:107). God's kingdom is mentioned dozens of times, but his sovereignty in only four verses, two of which say that the "sovereignty of each thing" is in the hand of God (23:88, 36:83). Another verse talks of God's showing "the sovereignty of the heavens and the earth" to Abraham (6:75), and the context suggests that this had everything to do with God's teaching him prophetic wisdom, in particular the significance of *tawḥīd*.

Long before Rāzī and Nasafī, Sovereignty and Kingdom had become common currency in discussions of the cosmos. Often they were cited as synonyms of the pair "command" (*amr*) and "creation" (*khalq*) mentioned in the verse, "His are the creation and the command" (Koran 7:54). The World of the Sovereignty (or the Command) is the realm in which the divine creativity is first expressed—in the invisible realm of spirit, intelligence, and meaning. The Creator then exercises his control, by way of the Command, over the World of the Creation (even though, in a broader sense, the word "creation" refers to the entire cosmos, both Sovereignty and Kingdom). Nasafī summed up the terminology like this:

The acts of God in the first classification are of two kinds: Kingdom and Sovereignty. The Kingdom is the world of sensory things, and the Sovereignty is the world of intelligible things. The world of sensory things is called the World of the Kingdom, the world of bodies, the world of the visible, the world of creation, and the low world. . . . The world of intelligible things is called the World of the Sovereignty, the world of spirits, the world of the unseen, the world of command, and the high world.[5]

## *Origin and Return*

Discussion of the two worlds addresses heaven and earth, or Sovereignty and Kingdom, or principle and image. From this standpoint, the world map is static, because it depicts the structure of the cosmos at the present moment. A second, equally important standpoint takes into account the dynamics of time and change. In this case, the discussion is likely to proceed in terms of the Koranic pair "this world" (*dunyā*) and "the afterworld" (*ākhira*). Philosophers generally prefer the less mythic terms, Origin (*mabda'*) and Return (*ma'ād*), although these are also derived from the Koran.

Even the most elementary Islamic catechism explains three implications of *tawḥīd*: everything originates from the One, everything returns to the One, and everything is sustained by the One—not just at the moment of its creation but at every moment of its continuance and subsistence in the world. The Koran makes this explicit in numerous verses; it is so obvious a theme that the mainstream Ash'arite theologians rejected any sort of causality other than direct divine activity at every moment. For their part, the philosophers preferred to deal with the issue in terms of the necessity of the Real Being and the contingency of everything else.

The parallel processes of coming from God and going back to God were central to both the philosophical and the Sufi depictions of the cosmos. Thus, there is nothing unusual about Rāzī's title *The Path of the Servants from the Origin to the Return*. The Koran refers to the two processes in dozens of verses. These are typical:

As We originated the first creation, so We shall bring it back again. (21:104)

To Him is your going back, all together—God's promise in truth. He originates creation, then He makes it return, so that He may justly compensate those who have faith and do worthy deeds. (10:4)

To God belongs everything in the heavens and the earth, and all things are taken back to Him. (3:109)

In theology and dogmatics, the word Return (*ma'ād*) is used to designate the third of the three basic articles of belief, after *tawhīd* and prophecy (*nubuwwa*). The Return is then viewed from two standpoints. In one respect, everything returns to the Origin because there is no other place to go; God is the only permanent reality, and everything remains in his hands, whether or not the thing happens to be present in the manifest realm. When something disappears from this world, it goes back where it came from. This is commonly called the "compulsory return."

In the second respect, certain things have a say in how they return to God, most notably human beings. This is called the "voluntary return." The point is that freedom of choice plays a role in the unfolding of a human soul, and to the degree that people are free, they participate in the creative process that shapes their souls and the world. They themselves must accept responsibility for their activities and their ultimate resting places. Yes, everyone goes back to God, but God has many faces, as indicated by his many names. He is merciful, loving, compassionate, tender, gentle; but he is also wrathful, vengeful, quick in retribution, severe. Returning to God under the care of the former sorts of names is called "paradise," and returning under the care of the latter is called "hell."

When Sufi authors talk of the Return, they stress the voluntary route, that of choosing "to die before you die," as a saying ascribed to the Prophet puts it. Dying to the ego and the world is to come to life in God. One can do so only by choosing to return to God before the compulsory return called death. The supreme model for this return is the Prophet's ascent to God, his *mi'rāj* (ladder) or *isrā'* (night journey).

In the traditional accounts of the Prophet's journey to God, the angel Gabriel awoke him from sleep, carried him on a miraculous beast to Jerusalem, and from there guided him up through the seven heavens, hell, and paradise. Eventually he sent him on alone for a solitary meeting with God; then the Prophet came back down to Gabriel, who took him back by the same route to his bed in Mecca. This journey, which the tradition has taken as the complement of the descent of the Koran to Muhammad—also on the hands of Gabriel—has provided the mythic model for the spiritual quest throughout Islamic history. The cosmological dimensions of the account were never neglected, and even philosophers like Avicenna analyzed the symbolism in cosmological terms.[6]

In the Koran, one of the passages said to refer to the Prophet's ascent includes this verse: "He [the Prophet] was two-bow's length away, or closer" (53:9). Significantly, this is the only Koranic verse that Liu quoted in *Tianfang xingli*. Many scholars, including Ibn al-'Arabī and his followers, read this as a reference to the special nearness to God achieved by the Prophet during his ascent. But they hardly stop there, given their recognition that God packs much meaning into brief words. To begin with, the word "bow" (*qaws*), like Latin *arcus*, also means "arc" of a circle; hence, the two bows can refer to two arcs making up a circle.

What, then, is this circle whose two arcs designated the Prophet's relationship with God at the moment of their encounter? In various Sufi readings, the germs of which long predate Ibn al-'Arabī, the two arcs are the Origin and the Return. By ascending to God, the Prophet completed the circle of creation. By going back to God voluntarily, he "died before he died," rejoined the Origin, and realized the furthest goal of the creative process. After this encounter with God, he returned to his community to guide them on the path, like a seasoned mountain climber. Thus, according to Nasafī's teacher Hammūya, "The ends of the prophets are the beginnings of the saints,"[7] which is to say that, by achieving perfection, the prophets establish the path that can then be followed by others to achieve the same goal.

In depicting the totality of the cosmos—everything other than God—as two arcs of one circle, Sufis and philosophers want to explain the directionality of all that exists (including the unfolding of time). God creates the universe in a descending, hierarchical series of worlds and beings, and things come into existence in successive degrees, from spiritual down to corporeal, from invisible and subtle down to visible and dense. The most common analogy for the descent is the shining light of the sun, which becomes dimmer as it moves away from its source. The brighter a being, the more unified, spiritual, and aware it is; the darker a being, the more dispersed, corporeal, and unaware.

Just as things originate from God on the circle's descending arc, so also they return to him on its ascending arc. Having reached the lowest point of the circle, the flow of existence reverses itself and heads back toward its Root. Like the descent, the ascent takes place in a series of hierarchical steps, called in the premodern West "the Great Chain of Being." Lowest on the scale are inanimate objects, which are the most dispersed, corporeal, and dense. Then come plants, then animals, and finally humans; each represents an upward movement toward unity, integration, spirituality, subtlety, and invisibility.

As Liu tells us repeatedly, the descending movement is from the inside to the outside, or from the nonmanifest to the manifest. It results in the proliferation of beings known as the ten thousand things. The ascending movement is from the outside to the inside, from the manifest to the nonmanifest, and it results in the unification of things through human consciousness and awakening.

In the early stages of the returning arc, the route is determined by compulsion, not free choice. Freedom enters the picture only at the human level or, rather, at the onset of human adulthood. As people grow and mature, free will and responsibility play an ever greater role in the unfolding of their lives and in the repercussions of their activities on the cosmic process. Given the peculiar human situation in the universe, people have the ability to distinguish between right and wrong and to make appropriate or inappropriate choices. In other words, their situations give them the ability to discern between *ḥaqq* (truth, rightness, realness, and appropriateness) and *bāṭil* (falsehood, wrongness, illusion, and inappropriateness). They do so by means of the *ḥaqq*, or revealed truth, that comes from God: "The *ḥaqq* has come, and the *bāṭil* vanishes; surely the *bāṭil* is always bound to vanish" (Koran 17:81).

At the human stage on the returning arc, a whole realm of ontological possibility opens up that is not available to minerals, plants, and animals. Since these new possibilities depend on human freedom, they are typically discussed in terms of responsibility, morality, ethics, spiritual transformation, and self-realization—not to mention culture, literature, religion, art, science, technology, and so on down the list of human activities and achievements. Ibn al-ʿArabī commonly situated these uniquely human possibilities within their cosmic context by referring them back to divine attributes, which are the qualities inherent in the Real Being simply because it is so. As Reality per se, Being is infinitely full of every ontological perfection, and these must manifest themselves, just as the sun must shine.

## Microcosm and Macrocosm

Both philosophers and Sufis discussed the cosmos—everything other than God—as having two basic realms, the unseen and the visible, and two basic orientations, originating and returning. They also spoke about the cosmos in terms of the "large world" (al-'ālam al-kabīr) and the "small world" (al-'ālam al-ṣaghīr). The large world is the cosmos as a whole, with its spiritual and corporeal realms and its originating and returning movements. The small world is the human individual, who also has invisible and visible realms and who also comes and goes.

Ibn al-'Arabī, as usual, went into more detail than most in explaining how this works. Basically, just as God created the microcosm in his own form, so also he created the macrocosm in his own form. In the universe as a whole, the traces, manifestations, and disclosures of Real Being are infinitely dispersed on both the horizontal continuum (the unfolding of time and space in this world and the next) and the vertical continuum (from spiritual to corporeal, from heaven to earth). The upshot is a never-ending succession of worlds and beings, all of which represent specific configurations of ontological possibility. Some are more spiritual, some more corporeal, some more conscious, some effectively unconscious.

The same ranking in degrees occurs in the manifestations of all divine attributes and qualities, which designate the diverse potentialities of being and becoming that are present in the Real. The list of the "ninety-nine names" of God contains a representative sampling of the qualities that come to be manifest and disclosed in the infinite beings of the beginningless and endless manifestation of Real Being that we call the universe or samsara.[8] Beings are ranked in intensity of light, life, awareness, desire, power, speech, hearing, seeing, mercy, love, vengeance, and so on down the list. But things are not fixed in their situations. Endless change and flux are characteristic of both macrocosm and microcosm.

If the macrocosm is infinitely dispersed, the microcosm is un-imaginably compressed. Infinity is found in a dewdrop. All reality is focused in this one human individual. Ibn al-'Arabī called the per-fected human being, who realizes the full potential of the divine form, "the all-comprehensive (engendered, or created) being" (*al-kawn al-jāmi'*). Just as the name Allah is the "all-comprehensive name" (*al-ism al-jāmi'*), designating God as the Reality that embraces all reality, so also the perfect human being (*al-insān al-kāmil*) embraces all mani-festations of the names and attributes of God to the extent possible in the created realm.

The first and most obvious difference between microcosm and macrocosm, after size, is that of focused awareness as opposed to infi-nitely dispersed consciousness. The perfected human being is a con-scious subject that takes as his or her object the whole macrocosm. This is the "knowledge of all the names" that God, according to Koran 2:30, taught to Adam, and it allows human beings to be God's vice-gerent (*khalīfa*), ruling over the cosmos in his stead. The human being can then be called the "spirit" of the cosmos, and the cosmos his "body," a point often discussed by Ibn al-'Arabī. For example:

Distinguish yourself from the cosmos and distinguish the cosmos from yourself. Distinguish the manifest from the nonmanifest and the nonmani-fest from the manifest. For within the cosmos, you are the spirit of the cos-mos, and the cosmos is your manifest form. The form has no meaning with-out a spirit. Hence the cosmos has no meaning without you.[9]

## Names and Attributes

Nothing determines the manner in which Islamic sources discuss Ul-timate Reality more than the notion that God has many names (*asmā'*), which theologians typically call his "attributes" (*ṣifāt*). The Koran is full of mentions of what it calls God's "most beautiful names," and it has a good deal to say on the general topic of names and naming.

The Sufi tradition talks about God's names and attributes con-stantly, and Liu devoted many pages to the interpretation of these teachings in Chinese terms. Especially important is the standard tri-fold way of depicting God—as Essence (*dhāt*), attributes, and acts (*af'āl*). The Essence is God in himself; the attributes are his revealed names, or the qualities and characteristics that can properly be attributed to him; and the acts are what he does, sometimes understood as the created things—heaven, earth, and everything between the two—and sometimes as designations for his activities, such as making, shaping, and forming.

The Koran is a book primarily about God and his doings, specifically the creation of the universe, the appointment of human beings as his chosen vicegerents, and the sending of prophets to guide people on the path of performing their duties and achieving ultimate happiness. The book mentions God by a variety of names, but it also insists that God is only one God; hence the primacy of *tawḥīd* in Islamic belief. Any reflective person faced with the text of the Koran will want to know how One God can be named by so many names without his oneness being compromised. This is the primary issue of Islamic discussions of God in general, and the answer is, in brief, that all names designate the same ultimate Reality, but from different standpoints.

Ibn al-'Arabī devoted much of his enormous corpus of writings to explaining how the One God gives rise to multiple things, and how the multiple things are reintegrated into the One—that is, Origin and Return. Each divine name has different implications for God and his relationship with the world—and indeed, Ibn al-'Arabī said that he preferred the word "relation" (*nisba*) to the theological term "attribute" as a designation for the divine names.

Almost none of the Koranic names of God has a mythic ring to it. It is true that "Allah" can be taken as God's personal name, but it is no more God's personal name than "God" is in English. The Koran frequently calls God *al-ilāh*, "the God," the word from which linguists say the word *Allah* derives. It uses *ilāh* to designate false gods, especially in its plural form, *āliha*, "gods." These include not only idols worshipped by misguided peoples, but also anything worshipped along with or in place of the Real, such as caprice or whim (*hawā*), as in the verse: "Have you seen him who has taken his own caprice to be his god?" (25:43). As for the God worshipped by the followers of all the prophets from the time of Adam, that is precisely Allah, God per se, "the God."

The names by which the Koran calls God designate cosmic and human qualities: merciful, compassionate, alive, knowing, desiring, powerful, speaking, generous, just, and so on. In every case, thoughtful Muslims have understood the names in terms of *tawḥīd*. In other words, to say that God is "merciful" means "None is merciful but God." There is no true mercy but God's mercy, and human mercy can at best be a pale reflection of his mercy. Nonetheless, people are called upon to be merciful, and they do so by following God's guidance. All the other names of God fit in analogous ways into the formula of *tawḥīd*, and each has been the object of elaborate discussion and explanation over long centuries of theological discourse.

From a certain point of view, the names can be divided into two categories. The first category consists of qualities we associate with existence and the cosmos; the second, with ethics and morality. On one hand, God is alive, knowing, desiring, powerful, hearing, seeing. On the other, he is merciful, loving, forgiving, generous, and just.

Muslim texts, however, do not usually draw a distinction between what we might call "ontological" and "moral," any more than Chinese texts do. Rather, all the divine attributes are essential to the reality of Real Being, and as such, they reverberate throughout the cosmos. Just as the trigrams and hexagrams of the Book of Changes can be applied to the Dao itself, to the cosmos and its operations, to society and human interrelationships, and to the inner workings of the human self, so also the divine names and attributes of Islamic texts—especially as discussed and explained by Ibn al-'Arabī and his followers—have applications to all realms of being, whether metaphysical, cosmological, social and ethical, or psychical and spiritual.

### Spiritual Anthropology

When Muslim thinkers focused on the implications of the Divine Essence, attributes, and acts for the human situation, they summarized their conclusions in terms of the three principles of faith. First, *tawḥīd*—everything comes from God, returns to him, and is sustained by him moment by moment. Second, prophecy—God sends messengers and sages to remind people of their own nature and the consequent responsibilities. Third, the Return—after death, people go back to the presence of God, and their final dwelling places conform to their own specific personhoods, which will have been shaped and determined by their activities, thoughts, intentions, and character traits in the present world.

The Koran teaches that human beings typically live in forgetfulness (*nisyān, ghafla*). God is the knowing and the aware, and everything else is by definition ignorant and unaware. Even though an understanding of Unity is innate to human nature, people forget Unity; hence, they neglect the duties and responsibilities that follow upon it. Although they were created for a special task, nonetheless, "Man was created weak" (Koran 4:28). As a result, Adam "forgot" (20:115) and, consequently, "he disobeyed" (20:121); that is, he ignored God's commandment to stay away from the tree. When God asked him why he approached the tree, he quickly remembered (*dhikr*), asked forgiveness, and was pardoned. It was only then that God placed him in the earth as his vicegerent, which was his *raison d'être* from the beginning.

Adam was worthy to be God's vicegerent because he fulfilled the duties of remembrance. These can be summed up in one word: servant (*'abd*). To be a servant is to live in conformity with the Supreme Reality. Not to be a servant is to rebel against the nature of things, to disrupt the harmony of heaven and earth, and to attempt to go against the flow of the Self-so.

In speaking of those who fulfill their human responsibilities, the Koran provides the examples of Adam, the prophets, and the sincere followers of the prophets. They lived in remembrance of God, acted as servants obedient to his instructions, and represented him on earth as his vicegerents. In the Koranic view, this human responsibility was embodied and taught by all the prophets, who are traditionally said to number 124,000.

What makes Adam (and his descendants) uniquely able to achieve the station of vicegerency is the fact that God "taught him the names, all of them" (2:30). This verse was often understood in terms of the prophetic saying, "God created Adam in His form [*ṣūra*]." One could translate *ṣūra* here as "image" in keeping with the English Bible, but that would obscure the rich associations of the word *ṣūra* in the Koran and the tradition (and it would also hide the fact that other Arabic terms do a better job of rendering the notion of image). The Koran lists among God's names "Form-giver" (*muṣawwir*, 59:24). Moreover, God is the subject of the verb "to form" in several telling verses, including these, which are addressed to the whole human race:

It is God who made the earth a fixed place for you, and heaven a building; and He formed you, He made your forms beautiful, and He provided you with the pleasant things.   (40:64)

He created the heavens and the earth with the *ḥaqq*, He formed you, and He made your forms beautiful; and to Him is the homecoming.   (64:3)

Because, as the Prophet said, "God is beautiful, and He loves beauty," the beautiful form that God gave to Adam and his descendents is precisely the form of God's own beauty, and his own beauty is described in terms of the "ninety-nine" most beautiful names.

### Actualization of the Divine Form

When God created Adam in his own form, he placed all his own attributes within him. It is this that makes human beings human—the presence of the form of God as such—that is, God inasmuch as he is the source of every beautiful and good attribute in heaven, earth, and the ten thousand things. At the beginning of human development in the womb, however, the divine attributes are potentialities, not actualities. They become manifest only gradually. First, the ontological potencies reveal their presence, though only dimly: life, awareness, desire, power. Gradually hearing, seeing, and speech become evident. Only around puberty do the implications of articulate awareness and rational thought come to be present to the degree that we can talk about "moral responsibility."

From this point on in human development, the issue of actualizing God's moral and ethical perfections comes into play. Attributes such as generosity, justice, compassion, and love are not present in any conscious way below the human level (that is, in minerals, plants, and animals). The obligation to submit (*islām*) to God's prophetic guidance, which is directed toward the full actualization of the divine form along with its moral and spiritual concomitants, thus appears as the fulfillment of human nature. It is to become what we already are in the depths of our own being. It is to "return" to God by way of free choice rather than compulsion. It is to acknowledge the moral and spiritual requirements of human nature and to strive for what the Chinese tradition knows as *ren* 仁—humanity, humaneness, benevolence, goodness, authentic human nature. The ultimate goal is to become God's "vicegerent" or representative, which is the actualization and realization of all the divine attributes naturally present in the human form. Or, in Confucian terms, the ultimate goal is "to become a sage."

In later Sufi texts, one of the most common ways of representing the human situation was to cite the hadith of the Hidden Treasure. The Prophet reported that David asked God why he created the universe. God replied, "I was a Hidden Treasure, and I loved to be recognized (*aḥbabtu an uʿraf*); so I created the creatures that I might be recognized." Usually "recognized" is translated as "known," but that obscures the common thread that runs through all discussions of knowledge in "theoretical Sufism." As noted, this branch of Islamic learning is often called *ʿirfān* or *maʿrifa*, that is, "re-cognition," usually translated as "gnosis."

In short, knowledge of the "intellectual" sort, the knowledge sought in the quest for realization, is recognition and remembrance of what we already know in our own true nature. Hence, a purported saying of the Prophet, which is perhaps the most often cited hadith in the later Sufi tradition, tells us, "He who recognizes (*ʿarafa*) his own soul/self (*nafs*) recognizes his Lord." The recognition that is achieved through self-knowledge and self-realization is precisely God's goal in creating the cosmos: "I loved to be recognized."

The real nature of the cosmos, then, circles around love and recognition. God's love of being recognized points to his being recognized by others, because he already knows himself in himself. In order for there to be others, he must bring the universe into existence, and for there to be true recognizers, he must create beings in the complete and all-comprehensive form of himself. Anyone who knows or recognizes anything at all knows something of God, because God reveals the Hidden Treasure to all things, and there is nothing else to be known. But human beings alone are able to recognize and know the Hidden Treasure in its totality and unity—they alone can recognize God in his Godhood—because they alone were taught "all the names."

The hadith of the Hidden Treasure also throws light on the traditional understanding of the Prophet's *mi'rāj*, whereby he ascended to God and reunited the two arcs of existence. God displayed the Hidden Treasure in all its diversity by creating the universe, which becomes manifest by means of the descending arc. But the goal is for the Treasure to be recognized and known as a unity and a totality, and this cannot happen until human beings follow the upward route of ever-increasing wakefulness and awareness. The final realization occurs when seekers rejoin the Knower and Creator of all and come to know the Hidden Treasure in the depth of its hiddenness as well as in the breadth of its manifestation.

In short, the quest for realization—knowing things through recognizing them within one's own microcosmic reality, without the intermediary of transmitted knowledge, and then acting in accordance with the rights and proprieties of things—lies behind the development of both the Sufi and the philosophical traditions in Islam. It is precisely this approach that Liu adopted as his own and presented to his readers as the fundamental teaching of Islam, the rationale for Islamic practice, and the path to the actualization of the knowledge and virtue fully embodied in the Prophet Muḥammad.

### The Divine Presences

Theoretical expressions of the intellectual tradition typically analyze the human situation in terms of the nature of things, that is, Existence or Being (*wujūd*)[10] and its concomitants. It was taken for granted that we cannot understand our own selves or fulfill our destinies without understanding Ultimate Reality and its goal in disclosing itself in the human form. We cannot understand our human form without grasping the reality of Real Being and its manifestations by means of the cosmos with the goal of "being recognized." Those who actualize the Real's goal in disclosing the Hidden Treasure are known as perfect human beings. Given that the Real *Wujūd* is none other than God in his Essence, attributes, and acts, the actualization of human perfection must in some way involve the realization of what Ibn al-'Arabī calls the "Divine Presence" (*al-ḥaḍrat al-ilāhiyya*), that is, God's Essence, attributes, and acts.

In the technical terminology of Ibn al-'Arabī and his followers, "Presence" designates the sphere of manifestation and influence of a reality or a name. In his lengthy chapter on the divine names in his magnum opus, *al-Futūḥāt al-makkiyya* (The Meccan openings), Ibn al-'Arabī discussed each name in terms of its "Presence," that is, the realm in which it discloses its properties. The "Divine Presence" is the sphere of influence of the Divinity, or the name Allah, which embraces the Essence and all the names; hence, nothing is outside its scope. All that is, for all eternity, is simply the Divine Presence, that is, the Presence of Real Being and its concomitants.

Beginning with Qūnawī, Ibn al-'Arabī's followers elaborated on the notion of "divine presence" by pointing out that the totality of all that exists—that is, the Divine Presence per se—embraces several distinct levels, each representing a plenary manifestation of the name Allah in an appropriate modality of existence. Since the typical number of levels enumerated was five, the discussion commonly proceeded under the rubric "the Five Divine Presences" (*al-ḥaḍarāt al-ilāhiyyat al-khams*).[11] These are the five realms in which the Real Being discloses itself in its fullness.

According to one common scheme, the first of the Five Presences is God's self-knowledge, in which God discloses himself to himself in himself. In other words, at the level of the first Presence, God is conscious of every potential of being and becoming that is latent in the infinity of his own Reality.

The second Presence is the realm in which God discloses himself as conscious light, that is, the spiritual realm, the World of the Sovereignty. This embraces the First Intellect and all other possibilities of spiritual existence, including the angels and the spiritual principles of everything that appears in lesser realms of existence.

The third Presence is the intermediate World of Imagination, which embraces and combines the attributes of spirit and body.

The fourth Presence is the realm in which God discloses the signs and traces of his names and attributes as the infinite multiplicity of bodily, divisible things, that is, the World of the Kingdom.

We have already discussed the second and fourth Presences—the Sovereignty and the Kingdom, or the realm of spirits and the realm of bodies—in some detail. For Ibn al-'Arabī and many of his followers, however, the third, intermediary Presence plays an equally important role. Jāmī suggests why:

It is impossible for spirits and bodies to be interrelated, because there is an essential difference between the simple [spirit] and the compound [body]. . . . Hence God created the World of Imagination as an isthmus (*barzakh*) bringing together the World of Spirits and the World of Bodies so that they can interrelate. . . . By means of the World of Imagination and its characteristics, spirits become embodied in imaginal loci of manifestation. . . . And spiritual men climb up to the World of Imagination in their spiritual ascents (*mi'rāj*)—they shuck off these natural, elemental forms, and their spirits put on spiritual loci of manifestation.[12]

In sum, the first Divine Presence—the first "locus of manifestation" (*maẓhar*)—is God's disclosure of himself to himself in his own knowledge. The next three are the three worlds of the cosmos: "heaven, earth, and everything between the two." The fifth is the Perfect Human Being, the full manifestation of the human reality, which brings together, actualizes, integrates, and synthesizes all realms of being. Jāmī explained that the Hidden Treasure created human beings precisely with this goal in view:

The One Ipseity desired to manifest Its Essence in a perfect locus of manifestation that would include all the luminous loci of manifestation and all the dark loci of disclosure . . . , for, that Ipseity, which is the Necessary by Its very Essence, perceives Its Essence in Its Essence for Its Essence with a perception that is in no way added to or distinct from Its Essence. . . .

Then, when It became manifest . . . in the loci of manifestation that are the [three] worlds, It did not perceive Its Essence in the respect that It brings together all actual perfections and all divine attributes and names, for Its manifestation in any locus of disclosure must accord with that locus. Do you not see that the manifestation of the Real in the spiritual world is not like His manifestation in the bodily world? In the first, it is simple, active, and luminous, and in the second, it is dark, passive, and compound.

That is why a desire arose in the Essence for the universal locus of manifestation, the all-comprehensive engendered being who embraces the Divine

Reality, that is, the Perfect Human Being. For his all-comprehensiveness acts as a locus of manifestation both for the Nondelimited Essence and for the [divine] names, attributes, and acts. This is because of the all-comprehensiveness and equilibrium of the Perfect Human Being's universal configuration and the breadth and perfection that he has in acting as a locus of manifestation. He also brings together the realities of Necessity and the relations of the divine names with contingent realities and creaturely attributes. So, he brings together the two levels of all-comprehensiveness and differentiation and he encompasses everything in the Chain of Existence such that all of it may become manifest within him in keeping with him.[13]

This may seem like an overly complicated way of interpreting the hadith of the Hidden Treasure, but it is by no means unusual in the intellectual tradition that extends from Ibn al-'Arabī down to modern times. Nor does it sound so complicated if one looks at it from the perspective of the great masters of Neo-Confucian thought. One can easily see why Liu, rooted in an Islamic tradition that is at ease with such formulations, found himself at home in the Neo-Confucian universe.

# THREE

# *Liu Zhi's Adaptations of*

# *Islamic Thought*

A look at some of the specific Chinese terms that Liu Zhi used and how he structured his argument will clarify the manner in which he assimilated the Islamic worldview into the Chinese context. Detailed explanations are left to the notes on the translation.

The title of Liu Zhi's book, *Tianfang xingli*, has usually been translated by historians and bibliographers as "The Philosophy of Arabia." Benite suggests "Metaphysics and Principle of Islam."[1] As already noted, *tianfang* was used by Muslims to refer to the Kaaba and Mecca specifically, Arabia generally, and to the Islamic tradition. In the context of Liu's Tianfang Trilogy, "Islam" seems an appropriate translation. As for *xingli*, it can certainly mean "philosophy" or "metaphysics" as these words are applied to the sophisticated theoretical discussions of the Neo-Confucian tradition. But, for scholars of Islam, the word "philosophy" typically translates the Greek loanword *falsafa*, which designates the tradition of thought among Muslims that takes inspiration from the Greeks, especially Aristotle and Plotinus. It would be misleading to suggest that Liu's book represents "philosophy" in this specific meaning.

The best known of the several schools of Muslim philosophy is the Peripatetic, whose most famous representative is Avicenna (Ibn Sīnā, d. 1037). Later schools did not become known to the West during the medieval period and for that reason were not studied by Western scholars until the twentieth century. These include the Illuminationist School, founded by Suhrawardī (d. 1191), and Transcendent Wisdom, founded by Mullā Ṣadrā (d. 1640). So far as we know, Liu was not directly familiar with any of these schools. This is not to say, however, that *falsafa* leaves no trace in his writings, because much philosophical terminology had been integrated into the theoretical Sufism that is the main source of his inspiration. In short, to say that *Tianfang xingli* is about the "philosophy" of Islam is true in certain senses of the word "philosophy" but not in the sense typically meant in Islamic studies.

The literal meaning of *xingli* is not "philosophy" or "metaphysics" but "nature and principle." Scholars sometimes translate it as "philosophy" because Neo-Confucianism itself is often called *xingli xue* 性理學, "the learning about nature and principle."[2] If this expression can be translated as "the philosophy of Neo-Confucianism," then it is equally plausible to translate Liu's title as "the philosophy of Islam." What is most significant, however, is the fact that Liu can only have chosen the title *Tianfang xingli* to indicate that he is presenting Islamic teachings with the Confucian tradition in view. In no sense can this be a reference to "Islamic philosophy" as *falsafa*.

There are many other telling instances in which Liu used Neo-Confucian terminology to suggest the congruence of the basic teachings of Islam and Confucianism. For example, in the Root Classic and elsewhere, he referred to Ījī's *al-Mawāqif fī 'ilm al-kalām* by the Chinese title *Gezhi quanjing* 格致全經 (The complete classic of investigating and extending). This famous handbook of Kalam, or dogmatic theology, seems to have been the most important text on the subject in the Chinese cultural sphere, which is hardly surprising, given its prominence elsewhere. Liu indicated the importance of the book by calling it the "complete" classic. He specified its subject matter by referring to the first two of the eight steps of Neo-Confucian learning: the "investigation" of things and the "extension" of knowledge. No educated Chinese reader would miss this reference to the eight steps.[3]

## Nature and Principle

Liu frequently used both *xing* and *li* in the text. Historians of Chinese philosophy typically translate *xing* as "nature," but there are problems with the English word *nature* that need to be highlighted if we want to appreciate how Liu understood the word. "Nature" is a good translation if we keep in mind this definition from Webster's: "a creative and controlling agent, force, or principle operating in something and determining wholly or chiefly its constitution, development, and well-being. . . . [S]uch a force or agency in the universe acting as a creative guiding intelligence." This specific definition, however, is one of several, and it is probably not the one that most people think of when they hear "nature" mentioned in discussions of Chinese philosophy.[4]

*Li* is the pattern, principle, or underlying order that determines the reality of things, and, in Neo-Confucian thought, it is the key concept in discussions of the ultimately Real, the Dao, the Great Ultimate (*taiji* 太極).[5] According to Zhu Xi 朱熹 (1130–1200), perhaps the foremost of the Neo-Confucians, "The Great Ultimate is simply the principle of the highest good."[6] "The Great Ultimate . . . is the ultimate of principle."[7] Or again,

There is no other event in the universe except yin and yang succeeding each other in an unceasing cycle. This is called Change. However, for this movement and stillness, there must be the Principle that makes them possible. This is the Great Ultimate.[8]

Zhu Xi explained the relationship between nature and principle in these terms: "Nature is the principle of Heaven that man received, and the Way of Heaven is the original substance of the Principle of Heaven. In reality, they are just one principle."[9] Or again, "Nature is principle. It is called nature in relation to the heart, and called principle in relation to things."[10]

According to Chen Chun 陳淳, a student of Zhu Xi and author of *Neo-Confucian Terms Explained*, nature and principle are synonyms, and their meaning is tightly bound up with the notion of "mandate" (*ming* 命), a term we will discuss shortly:

Nature is principle. . . . Principle is a general term referring to the principles common to all humans (*ren* 人) and things (*wu* 物) between heaven and earth, while nature is principle in the I's (*wo* 我). . . . It is called nature because from birth humans possess principle complete in their hearts. . . . Nature and mandate are basically not two different things. What lies in Heaven is called mandate and what lies in human beings is called nature. . . . Nature and mandate are only one principle.[11]

In other words, nature is a specific term referring to the principle inasmuch as it appears in an I, a self.

Liu Zhi distinguished between nature and principle in the same way, although he was more likely to refer to the side of the I as "spiritual awareness" (*lingjue* 靈覺). Under Diagram 1.6, for example, he used "things and humans" as a shorthand to refer to everything in the universe:

Why things are so is called "principle." Why humans are so is uniquely called "nature." This is because nature is their spiritual awareness, and the fact that they are designated by spiritual awareness makes them distinct from things.

In short, by speaking of *xing* and *li*, Liu was acknowledging his affiliation with Neo-Confucian thought. To see how he was simultaneously aligning himself with Islamic thought, it would be helpful to know which Arabic terms *xing* and *li* are meant to translate, and how these terms fit into the Islamic worldview.

The notion of "nature" deserves careful scrutiny. Those with a background in Islamic studies may be forgiven for jumping to the conclusion that nature means *ṭabīʿa*, the Arabic word that is typically translated as "nature" and that was used in early Arabic translations of Greek philosophy to render the Greek *physis*. In both Islamic and Western philosophy, "nature" can designate what we now call the "physical" world or the "natural" realm. In the early usage of nature in the Christian West, there was no clear distinction between natural and supernatural. There was an implicit if not explicit acknowledgment not only that God was the creator of nature but also that he himself was somehow identical with nature. Scholastic philosophers highlighted the divine side of nature by pointing to the sense of its Latin root, that is, "to give birth" (thus English "natal"). They distinguished between "Naturing Nature" (*natura naturans*), or God as the creative principle that gives birth to the universe, and "natured nature" (*natura naturata*), or the universe that is born from God's creative activity.[12] Nonetheless, in Western thought generally, especially since the Enlightenment, the natural realm has been sharply distinguished from the supernatural. When Rousseau spoke of "natural man," he had in mind a being totally cut off from Heaven.

Scholars of the Chinese tradition, in talking of nature, have often interpreted *xing* in Enlightenment terms; this accords with a general trend in the secondary literature to see Confucianism as a philosophy rather than a religion. One well-known authority tells us that "Chinese wisdom has no need for the idea of God."[13] Indeed, according to the outstanding historian of Chinese science, Joseph Needham, "The great tradition of Chinese philosophy had no room for souls." He goes on to explain: "The distinctive importance of Li [principle] is precisely that it was not intrinsically soul-like or animate."[14] Presumably, "nature," which according to Chen Chun is none other than "principle in the I," must also be unlike the soul, or the spirit, or life.

In short, many historians of the Chinese tradition have viewed nature as physical and material, or they have acquiesced to the modern understanding of nature as opposed to or utterly excluding the supernatural. They may do this explicitly, but more often they do it implicitly by employing the word "nature" without further elaboration. They also do so by adopting the common translation of *xing* as "human nature." This choice is justified by the fact that the word is often used to designate what distinguishes human beings from other things, as we just saw. But, in the modern understanding, "human nature" is typically understood in a purely humanistic way. This is one reason that scholars like Tu Weiming insist that Confucianism is not humanistic but rather "anthropocosmic"—it always has in view the situation of human beings in relation to the entire cosmos.

When we as Islamicists first began reading Liu's text, we found ourselves assuming that he was using *xing* as the equivalent of Arabic *ṭabīʿa*, but the more we read, the more it became obvious that, in contrast to *ṭabīʿa*, *xing* could not designate simply the "natural" side of things. It did not become clear which Arabic word Liu had in mind until we began studying his sources, although it took a while to find corresponding passages. Liu indicated his sources in the Root Classic "so that they can wait to be examined," that is, so that his readers could consult the originals. The 1,600-character text, however, contains eighty-six such references. The four known Persian books Liu cited total seven hundred pages, and the Arabic sources (assuming that one of them is Bayḍāwī's *Commentary*) add another fifteen hundred pages. Moreover, from what we have been able to discover, Liu did not "translate" any of the passages he cited. Rather, he recreated their gist in Confucian terms.

Liu's sources for "nature" are not difficult to find. He consistently used *xing* to translate the Arabic word *rūḥ*, which is normally rendered into English as "spirit." *Rūḥ* is an extremely important term in the Koran and the Islamic sciences. Cognate with Hebrew *ruwach*, it comes from the same Arabic root as *rīḥ*, "wind," which is precisely the meaning of Latin *spiritus*. *Rūḥ* is an invisible something that bestows life, animation, and awareness on visible things. It is "nature" in the sense of Webster's "creative guiding intelligence."

## Spirit

The Koran associates spirit with the unseen realm of the angels, and it calls Gabriel, the angel of revelation, "the spirit of holiness" (*rūḥ al-qudus*). Perhaps the most important Koranic use of the word for contextualizing Liu's interpretation of *xing* is the verses in which God says concerning Adam, "I blew into him of My spirit" (15:29, 38:72), or "He blew into him of His spirit" (32:9). Generally, Islamic thought maintains that God is the creator of spirit along with everything else. In contrast to Christianity, one cannot say that God himself is spirit. When Muslim texts talk about the "Holy Spirit" (*al-rūḥ al-qudsī*), they mean a created being, not the third person of the Triune God. But God's exact relationship with "His spirit" has been much discussed. Ibn al-ʿArabī and his followers often referred to this spirit as "ascribed" (*muḍāf, iḍāfī*), meaning that God ascribes it to himself in the verses about the creation of Adam. They also highlighted the fact that the Koran connects this Spirit to the divine "inblowing" (*nafkha*). Ibn al-ʿArabī called this inblowing, or the Spirit itself, "the Breath of the All-merciful" (*nafas al-Raḥmān*), and upon this notion he built an elaborate Koranic cosmology.

The general Koranic myth maintains that God blew of his own spirit into Adam after having created Adam's body from clay. Although other creatures also have spirits, the inblowing of the Ascribed Spirit somehow differentiates Adam from everything else. This spirit is the source of life, awareness, speech, and all other divine qualities that human beings actualize in themselves. In short, the human reality has two basic components, clay (or body) and spirit, just as the universe has two basic dimensions: earth and heaven, or visible and unseen, or Kingdom and Sovereignty. In later discussions, spirit is typically contrasted with body (*jism*), the visible, unconscious, passive, and dead dimension of the human reality. That the body in itself has none of the attributes of the spirit becomes obvious at death, when the spirit rejoins the subtle realm and the body goes back to the clay from which it had been shaped.

Three other terms play especially important roles in Islamic discussions of the invisible, aware, and subtle dimension of the human being: soul or self (*nafs*), heart (*qalb*), and intellect (*'aql*). Al-Ghazālī (d. 1111), one of the foremost Muslim theologians and thinkers, points out that all four terms designate the same invisible reality, often called "the human subtlety" (*al-laṭīfat al-insāniyya*), but from different standpoints.[15] "Spirit" designates the human subtlety in its linkage with the divine inblowing. More generally, it is the invisible, heavenly dimension of reality that ties all things to the divine. The philosophical tradition divides spirit into several kinds according to the bodily composition of that in which its influence appears. Thus we have mineral, vegetal, animal, human, and angelic spirits.

*Nafs*—self or soul—is the most ambiguous of the four terms. It derives from the same root and is written exactly the same (in the normal, unvocalized Arabic script) as *nafas*, "breath," and many authors take it as a synonym for *rūḥ*. It is both a standard reflexive pronoun and a Koranic designation for the human subtlety. The Koran speaks of "heaven, earth, and what is between the two," and many authors consider the human *nafs* to be the microcosmic analogue of the in-between realm (that is, the Presence of Imagination in the Five Divine Presence scheme). In this understanding, the *nafs* is neither spirit nor body, neither unseen nor visible, neither one nor many, but the intermingling of the two sides or, to use the Koranic image, "the meeting place of the two seas" (*majma' al-baḥrayn*). It is the locus of our individual awareness, our selfhood. Each of us represents a unique combination of spirit and body, light and darkness, intelligence and ignorance, remembrance and forgetfulness.

The Sufi tradition stresses the forgetful side of the soul and gives the word *nafs* a strong negative connotation. The philosophical tradition looks at the soul as the neutral field in which the qualities of our selfhoods become established. The budding philosopher searches for wisdom in order to transform the soul into a pure and luminous intelligence, often called an "actualized intellect" (*'aql bi'l-fi'l*). The sage is someone whose soul has been transmuted into spiritual light and who makes this transmutation manifest through wise and virtuous activity.

The third word that plays an important role in analyses of the human substance—*'aql*—means intellect, intelligence, reason, rational faculty. All human beings are born with this faculty, but intelligence can be actualized fully only by self-realization. Although the Koran does not use the nominal form of this word, it uses the verbal form fifty times and repeatedly stresses the importance of the understanding for which the intellect should be striving. For example:

Surely the worst of beasts in God's eyes are those who are deaf and dumb and do not intellect.   (8:22)

Have they not traveled in the earth that they might have hearts with which to intellect and ears with which to hear? Surely the eyes are not blind, but blind are the hearts within the breasts.   (22:46)

Heart—*qalb*—the seat of intelligence, is the fourth important term used in discussing human nature. It is practically synonymous with Chinese *xin* 心, a word that is usually translated as "mind" or "heart-and-mind."[16] Like *xin*, *qalb* designates not only the physical heart but also the locus of human awareness and consciousness. The Koran and the Hadith place it at the center of the human reality—embracing the physical, psychical, and spiritual dimensions. It is associated primarily with awareness and intelligence, and only secondarily with emotions and feelings. The heart is where people grow intellectually and spiritually, and, the Koran tells us, the human predicament arises because of the heart's illness (*maraḍ*) and rust (*rayn*).

To say that the heart is rusty recalls an image that is universal in the Sufi tradition (and well known in China). Mirrors used to be made of iron. The original substance of the human heart is like a shiny mirror, reflecting the light and wisdom of God. In the ordinary human state, however, it is rusty with ignorance and forgetfulness, and it needs to be polished. In Islamic terms, polishing the heart is accomplished by remembering (*dhikr*) God. As 'Alī, the son-in-law of the Prophet, said, "God made remembrance the polish of hearts."[17] Concerning the fully polished heart, Zhuangzi says, "The heart of the Utmost Human functions like a mirror, going after nothing, responding to nothing."[18]

Given the importance of the heart in the Koran and its connotations of spiritual transformation, the Sufis prefer "heart" to the philosophers' "intellect" when talking about realization. They like to quote sayings attributed to the Prophet that the heart is God's Throne in the microcosm, or that the heart alone, of all created things, is able to embrace God.[19] Some of them criticize intellect as a limited human faculty, cut off from the divine spirit. Most philosophers, however, do not acknowledge that intellect has such limitations. They claim that the goal of human existence is to actualize the true intellect, which transcends rational processes, and that this can happen only when the human soul awakens to its innate linkage with the divine spirit, which is nothing but the First Intellect or the Ascribed Spirit, the means whereby God creates the universe.

It is important to keep in mind that the heart/intellect has cosmic functions. It is none other than the very spirit ("nature"—"guiding intelligence") that gave rise to the universe in the first place. Scholars of Chinese thought generally give short shrift to *xin* as "heart" and stress its meaning as "mind," but they do this because of the relatively late Western association of the heart with sentiments and its complete disseverance from the realm of rationality. Since this split never occurred in the Islamic world, the word *qalb* has retained its Koranic meaning as the seat of intelligence and personhood, and the notion that the fully actualized heart "embraces God" has remained a constant theme of Islamic spirituality. To translate *qalb* as "mind" in the context of Islamic thought, where it designates a range of meanings from the physical organ to the highest realization of selfhood, would introduce a dichotomy that is simply not present in the texts.

In sum, the word *rūḥ*, or "spirit," designates the invisible, intelligent, active, living dimension of the human reality, and it cannot be properly understood apart from its quasi-synonyms: soul, intelligence, and heart.

## Xing, Li, *and* Rūḥ

Liu consistently spoke of *xing*, or "nature," when his sources discuss *rūḥ*, or "spirit." He was less consistent when employing the word *li*, or "principle," but he did use it for both *'aql* (intellect) and *nafs* (soul). An example will both illustrate the correspondence between *xing* and *rūḥ* and help pinpoint the Arabic for *li*. Diagram 1.6 is labeled "The Beginning of the Differentiation of the Natures and the Principles." The diagram is meant to illustrate that the creative flow from the Origin transforms the Mandate (the topic of Diagram 1.5) into the principles and natures of the ten thousand things. The discussion represents a detailed explanation of two lines (eight characters) from the first chapter of the Root Classic: "This one reality [the Mandate] has ten thousand differentiations / and equips both humans and heaven with principles" (1:14–15).

Liu noted that these two lines are based on Rāzī's *Path*. Rāzī does have a corresponding discussion, but much of both the diagram and its explanation is also derived from Nasafī's *Goal*, specifically the enumeration of nine levels of nature pertaining to human beings and nine corresponding levels of principle pertaining to the cosmos.[20] Nasafī, however, did not use any words in this specific discussion that would correspond to "nature" and "principle." The Arabic words that Liu had in mind are found in *Path*.

Rāzī explained that God brought the universe into being by creating first the spiritual, invisible world, and then the corporeal, visible world, that is, first the Sovereignty and then the Kingdom. God began the process by creating the Muhammadan Spirit (*rūḥ-i Muḥammadī*). In Diagram 1.6 and elsewhere, Liu translated this expression as "the nature of the utmost sage." He made it the top circle in the diagram and identifies it with Aershi—that is, Arabic *'arsh*, the "throne" of God. This is none other than the Mandate of Diagram 1.5, which we have also met as the Ascribed Spirit blown into Adam.

Then, Rāzī wrote: "When the Real created that [Muhammadan] Spirit and looked upon it with the gaze of love, shame overcame it, and the Spirit split into two because of the shame. Half of it became Intellect."[21] Because of this split, the invisible, spiritual realm has two poles, Spirit and Intellect, which are related to each other in the same way as Adam and Eve. Spirit is the male, active pole, and Intellect the female, receptive pole; Spirit is yang and Intellect yin. The yang Spirit gives rise to a multiplicity of other spirits, and the yin Intellect gives rise to a multiplicity of souls (*nafs*). As a result, everything in the visible universe has an invisible root, either a spirit or a soul. These spiritual, intellectual, or "soulish" realities exist independently of the visible universe, but they determine its manifestation.

According to Rāzī, the creatures of the visible world are divided into two sorts: those that have active, yang spirits and those that have receptive, yin souls. Those with spirits include angels, humans, jinn, satans, and animals; these are beings that, according to Liu's diagram, have *xing*, "natures" or, in Chen Chun's terms, "I's." Entities with souls include stars, planets, heaven, earth, elements, inanimate things, and plants; these, in Chen Chun's terms, are "things" rather than "I's" and are associated with principles rather than with natures.

Although this passage from *Path* makes clear that the Arabic term corresponding to *xing* is *rūḥ*, it does not allow us to conclude that Liu had a single equivalent in mind for "principle." He may have meant *nafs* (soul) or *'aql* (intellect), or he may have used *li* as an equivalent for both. Most likely, however, he had *'aql* in mind. Rāzī told us that souls derive from the Intellect, and hence their "intellectual" side presumably dominates over their "soulish" side. Moreover, the usage and connotations of the Chinese *li* (which is sometimes translated as "reason") are closer to *'aql* than to *nafs*. Nūr al-Ḥaqq seemed to agree, because in translating this diagram into Arabic, he rendered *li* as *'aql*, not *nafs*.[22]

## Xing *and* Ṭabī'a

It is important for those who have some familiarity with Islamic thought—or Western thought, for that matter—to remember that, as far as Liu was concerned, "nature" does not mean *ṭabī'a*; it is not the "physical" or "natural" realm in any sense of the word that would set up a dichotomy with the "supernatural." Understanding *xing* in a humanistic sort of way as "human nature" ignores the cosmological and metaphysical context central to both Islamic and Neo-Confucian thought. Moreover, as Liu made eminently clear, nature is shared by all ten thousand things. By no means is it an exclusively human possession, although it does have degrees, and hence we can say that the nature of the human is higher than the nature of animals, and the nature of animals is higher than that of plants.

There is, in short, nothing "natural" about *xing*—if we mean something that is opposed to the "supernatural." Rather, nature is the spiritual, intelligible realm. What we nowadays call the "physical" and "natural" realm is the images and traces of Liu's nature and principle. Liu wrote of the nature embedded in the Mandate: "This nature is the chief of all the spiritual awarenesses of the thousand antiquities" (under Diagram 1.5). It is, in other words, the supreme awareness in the universe, which is precisely what is meant by Arabic expressions such as "the Greatest Spirit" (*al-rūḥ al-a'ẓam*) and "the First Intellect" (*al-'aql al-awwal*).

In classical Arabic, *ṭabī'a*, or "nature," is often contrasted sharply with *rūḥ*, or "spirit," although not in a dualistic, dichotomous sense. Literally, *ṭabī'a* means "that which receives an impression." This is why the word *ṭab'*—which comes from the same root and has more or less the same meaning—is used in modern Islamic languages to mean "printing." According to Ibn al-'Arabī, *ṭabī'a* is the domain of earthly receptivity; it is the lower, material, visible realm that receives all its properties as "imprints" or "impressions" from the spiritual realm, which is the heavenly, conscious, invisible world. Thus, *ṭabī'a* is the receptacle for the traces of spirit; spirit and nature work together in harmony, exactly as do heaven and earth, or Sovereignty and Kingdom. The union of spirit and nature brings about manifestation, just as, in Neo-Confucian thought (and in Liu Zhi's text) principle makes itself manifest in the vessel of vital-energy (*qi* 氣).[23]

In short, if Liu called his book *Tianfang xingli*, "nature and principle in Islam," he did so at least partly because he found *xingli xue*, "Neo-Confucian learning"—"the learning of Nature and principle"—congruent with *tianfang xue*, "Islamic learning." He saw Neo-

Confucianism as focusing on the realm of the spirit, soul, intellect, and heart, which pertain to the invisible, heavenly realm, the unseen dimension of reality that governs the human relationship with God, who is the Great Ultimate or Real Substance. On the Descending Arc of the Origin, God employed "nature and principle" to create human beings. On the Ascending Arc of the Return, humans rediscover their own true natures—that is, their spiritual and intellectual roots—on the path of achieving perfection.

## Mandate

As we saw in Chen Chun's discussion of nature and principle, the concept of nature is closely tied to that of mandate (*ming*)—a word often translated as "destiny." In its earliest uses in Chinese, it seems to have referred to the command of God. By the time of Mencius, it was being used in the sense of everything outside human ability to change.[24] Its centrality to Chinese thought has everything to do with the debate over the extent of human freedom and the role of ethics and morality. Is our destiny determined by Heaven—God, karma— or are we free to shape our own becoming? Does nurture make us the way we are, or does nature, or do the two work together?

As in Muslim discussions of free will and predestination, the Chinese debate gives prominence to the heavenly mandate, the divine power over human affairs that establishes our nature, but human freedom is also seen to play a significant role. The crux of the discussion is precisely, "How significant a role does freedom play?"

*The Doctrine of the Mean*, one of the four classics that were the center of attention in Neo-Confucian scholarship, illustrates the intimate relationship between mandate and nature in its first lines: "Heaven's mandate is called 'nature'; following nature is called 'the Way'; cultivating the Way is called 'the teaching.'" Thus, by issuing the Mandate, Heaven (the Real Principle, God) bestows nature. If people follow nature, they are following the Way (Dao). To follow nature is to follow the Mandate. The problem arises because people have somehow lost touch with nature. As Benjamin Schwartz put it:

Yet the fact remains that Heaven has not guaranteed the immanent presence of its patterns within the human sphere. In the human being, Heaven has mysteriously engendered a creature that has the ominous capacity to obstruct Heaven's immanent presence and to create disorder. He or she is a creature who manages to create a fatal breach within the organismic whole. The gap that has thus been created makes possible the existence of moral evil.[25]

The human dilemma has to do with the apparent conflict between the Mandate of Heaven as the way things are—the nature that is bestowed by God—and the Mandate of Heaven as the moral order to which we should conform. A. C. Graham expresses the problem nicely:

If Heaven has established an order within which each thing has its own nature, is it not self-evidently good that man like other things should pass through his life-cycle in accordance with his nature? Since Heaven is the highest authority, on what grounds are we to prefer morality to the nature with which Heaven has endowed us?[26]

The grounds for preferring an ideal over an actual situation are provided precisely by the "teaching" (jiao), which was embodied and instituted by the sages. They alone have been able to heal the breach between Mandate as nature and Mandate as moral order, and they alone provide guidance for others. Only by following the sages can people practice the Way, cultivate their hearts, and achieve healing and wholeness.

Confucius, in his famous description of the stages of his life, described the main steps of the Way. At fifteen he set his heart on learning, at thirty he was firmly established, and by forty he had no lingering doubts. Then, at the age of fifty, "I knew the Mandate of Heaven." At sixty, his ear was obedient to the truth, and at seventy he could follow his heart's desire without overstepping the right.[27]

What exactly did Confucius come to know when he knew the Mandate? Did he know things as they are, did he know things as they should be, or did he know both? In other words, does the word "Mandate" here mean destiny and fate, which firmly fix the flow of becoming, or does it mean the instructions of Heaven, the clear path designating what is required of us so that we can become fully human and achieve ren? Is the issue ontological or moral, or, as seems much more likely, does it transcend this dichotomy? A. C. Graham puts it this way: "Within the concept of Heaven there is consequently a tension between factual and normative requirements; the Way of

Heaven must somehow be both how things do happen and how they ought to happen."[28]

Another key passage on the Mandate is found in the commentary on the Trigrams in the ancient Book of Changes: "Investigate principle to the utmost and fully realize nature until you reach the Mandate."[29] Here we can see the program of Confucian learning. One must study the teachings of the sages and undergo transformation of the soul to the point of achieving the full realization of nature, which is none other than the goal of the path, union with the Mandate.

In the Root Classic, Liu seamlessly integrated these typical Chinese discussions of Heaven, Mandate, nature, and Way into the threefold description of Islam as Shariah, Tariqah, and Haqiqah—Propriety, Way, and Real:

> Only by emulating the Sage's endeavors,
> cultivating the body with Propriety,
> clarifying the heart with the Way,
> and fully realizing nature and going back to the Mandate,
> does the complete substance [of the human reality] come
>     home to the Real. (4:82–86)

In this passage, Liu brought together the two sides of the Mandate, the ontological and the moral. The Mandate is the means whereby Heaven bestows nature, and nature gives us our humanity. But, the human condition involves free choice, and that allows us to go against the moral, ethical, and spiritual demands that the Mandate makes on us. In order to reintegrate ourselves into the Mandate that brought us into existence, we need to cultivate our souls, polish our hearts, and clarify our root substance. The only way to do so is to follow the teaching of the sages.

Liu and other Chinese Muslims use the word *ming* or Mandate to translate Arabic *amr*, "command," a word with precisely the same ambiguity as *ming*: the divine command is at once the destiny that God sets down for the world and the commandments and instructions that God issues for human guidance. The ontological sense of the word, however, predominates in Liu's understanding, as it often does in the Islamic context. Ibn al-'Arabī and others refer to this sense of the term as "the engendering command" (*al-amr al-takwīnī*). It is the creative act by which God "engenders" things, that is, brings them into existence. It consists of the single word *kun*, "Be!," and is mentioned in several Koranic verses, such as "His only command, when He desires a thing, is to say to it 'Be!' and it comes to be" (36:82).[30]

Theologians distinguish the engendering command from the "prescriptive command" (*al-amr al-taklīfī*), which is God's commandments in the form "Do this!" or "Don't do that!" The prescriptive command, embodied in God's revelations to the prophets, establishes the moral order. On its basis the prophets came to know the Way of achieving union with Heaven, and they established Shariahs, or religions. In other words, the prescriptive command gave rise to the "teaching" (*jiao*) transmitted from the sages. By following this teaching, one can bring oneself back into harmony with the engendering command.

### Former Heaven and Latter Heaven

Heaven is a central concept in Liu's book. It is, after all, Heaven that "mandates nature." And, for those who follow the Path, the goal is to realize one's original nature and thereby rejoin the Mandate of Heaven. But, when we look at the human situation in these terms, it is clear that Heaven, Mandate, and nature need to be understood from two different standpoints. On one hand, Heaven issues the Mandate (the engendering command), and that gives rise to our nature. On the other hand, nature needs to be realized by following the Teaching (the Mandate, the prescriptive command), and that brings about reunion with Heaven.

From the first standpoint, nature exercises its influence on the ten thousand things by way of what Liu called "the Former Heaven" (*xiantian* 先天). From the second standpoint, those who follow the Way strive to realize true human nature in "the Latter Heaven" (*houtian* 後天). The contrasting standpoints of two Mandates or two natures allow us to speak of two heavens, and the contrast between the two heavens provides the overall structure of Liu's book.

In both Islamic and Chinese thought, heaven (*samā'*, *tian* 天) is paired with earth (*arḍ*, *di* 地). The Chinese word, like the English, has a range of meanings from the blue sky to God. In contrast, the Arabic word never refers to God, who, in Koranic terms, is "the

Creator of heaven and earth." The word may refer to the sky, but in theological and especially in Sufi writings, it is more likely to denote the invisible, spiritual dimension of the created realm. Also, in contrast to English usage, Arabic "heaven" can never mean "paradise," the generic word for which is "Garden" (*janna*).[31]

In both Chinese and Islamic thinking, when heaven and earth are contrasted, the two work together as yang and yin. Heaven is active, earth receptive. Rūmī summed up the traditional Islamic position with the verse,

> In the view of intelligence, heaven is man and
>   earth woman—
> whatever the one throws down, the other nurtures.[32]

From early times, Chinese thinking associated Heaven with nature, especially perfected human nature; for the Neo-Confucian authors, the goal of the Way is to actualize the identity of Heaven, principle, and the human heart. Mencius, for example, wrote: "He who fully realizes his heart knows his nature. He who knows his nature knows Heaven" (7.A.1.1). To the Huiru, this must have seemed a Chinese version of the hadith "He who recognizes himself recognizes his Lord."

The centrality of the concept of Heaven to Liu's book and indeed to the Tianfang Trilogy is suggested by the literal meaning of Tianfang. Certainly, Liu used it to designate the Islamic tradition, but he was also pointing to the fact that Islamic teachings are orientated toward Heaven. Heaven, in turn, can be viewed from two perspectives, which are simply standard implications of *tawḥīd*: everything comes from Heaven, and everything also returns to Heaven. But, from the human standpoint, the Heaven from which we have come is behind us, and the Heaven to which we are returning is ahead of us. The first of these is the Former Heaven, and the second the Latter Heaven.

To a large degree, Liu conflated the two basic ways of looking at the cosmos discussed in the previous chapter, that is, the static (Sovereignty and Kingdom) and the dynamic (Origin and Return). The preceding discussion focuses on these two viewpoints as complementary and overlapping, but Liu seemed not to make a clear distinction between them (as is sometimes seen in Arabic and Persian texts as well). In his depiction, the World of Principles (the Sovereignty) is the Former Heaven, and the World of Images (the Kingdom) is the Latter Heaven. That is, the visible realm of images and traces, having made manifest the natures and principles latent in the Former Heaven, unfolds in the direction of the Latter Heaven.

Liu clarified the relationship between the Former and the Latter Heavens in the Summary at the beginning of Volume 1. This is the only instance in the summaries of the five volumes in which he defined his terms, and this again points to the importance of the notion of the two Heavens for the book as a whole.

The World of Principles is where images and numbers are not yet formed, although the principles are already embedded; this is the so-called Former Heaven. The World of Images is where heaven and earth are already established and the ten thousand things are already begotten; this is the so-called Latter Heaven.

When human beings enter the World of Images, they make manifest the World of Principles, whose differentiation is discussed in Diagram 1.6. They can then reintegrate themselves into the Mandate by engaging in self-cultivation and returning to the World of the Principles. In the Latter Heaven, however, the natures and principles are given different names, not least because their full realization depends on passing beyond the images and entering into the realm of the heart.

The Chinese discussion of the Former and Latter Heavens goes back to ancient cosmological charts that exist in many versions. One set of charts was associated with the mythic ruler Fu Xi 伏羲, another with King Wen 文王 of the Zhou 周 dynasty. The first set was called "Former Heaven Charts" (*xiantian tu* 先天圖), and the second "Latter Heaven Charts" (*houtian tu* 後天圖).[33] Perhaps the best-known example of the two contrasting charts is found in two different arrangements of the trigrams of the Book of Changes.[34]

The Former Heaven arrangement of the trigrams is commonly understood to pertain to a nonmanifest realm in which everything works together in perfect harmony and balance. The Latter Heaven arrangement then refers to the phenomenal world, in which things can come into conflict and disturb the flow of the creative transformation. The two arrangements were well known, and their significance often discussed. But, if we want to find an earlier Chinese scholar whose understanding of the Former and Latter Heavens was similar to that of Liu, perhaps the best person to investigate is Shao Yong 邵雍 (d. 1077). Although he was a contemporary and friend of the great Neo-Confucians Zhou Dunyi 周敦頤, Zhang Zai 張載, and the Cheng 程 brothers, he had Daoist leanings and was not included in Zhu Xi's list of correct Neo-Confucian transmission.[35] We do not know if Liu read the works of Shao Yong, but this seems likely, given the breadth of his learning.

Anne Birdwhistell, in her study of Shao Yong, explains that Former Heaven and Latter Heaven refer to two sorts of reality, the first that of "theory" and the second that of "experience." Shao Yong focused on the first realm, in contrast to mainstream Neo-Confucians, who focused on the second, and his thought came to be known as "Former Heaven Learning" (*xiantian xue* 先天學).[36] According to Birdwhistell, the Former Heaven is an "abstract structure whose pattern the phenomenal world, called *hou-tian*, follows." Moreover, it is "a level of conceptualization abstracted from the level of particular human experience." She supports this by quoting Shao Yong to the effect that the Former Heaven pertains to the mind (i.e., the heart, *xin*), and the Latter Heaven to the traces (*ji* 跡).[37]

Whether or not Birdwhistell is correct in her interpretation of Shao Yong's position, Muslim thinkers have rarely if ever understood the realm of the heart to be that of ideas abstracted from the phenomenal world. Rather, the true heart dwells in the domain of spirit and intelligence, the domain from which the phenomenal world draws its reality. The visible realm comprises the "traces" (*āthār*) of the spiritual realm, thereby making manifest the influence of heaven on earth. These traces are precisely what the Koran calls the "signs" of God.

For Liu, the Former Heaven is the nonmanifest realm, the World of Principles, whose existence precedes the appearance of the ten thousand things. This does not mean that the Former Heaven came first in time; rather, it has an ontological priority over the World of Images, which is oriented toward the Latter Heaven. Thus, when we observe the unfolding of life, awareness, and consciousness in the world and see them culminate in the qualities of our own humanity, we see the flow of existence in an upward direction toward the Latter Heaven and reunion with the Mandate.

From the standpoint of the Former Heaven, the creative flow moves from up to down, from inside to outside, from nonmanifest to manifest, from principle to image. It begins in pure and undifferentiated life, consciousness, and awareness and becomes dissipated in the unawareness, multiplicity, and dispersion that characterize the visible world. From the standpoint of the Latter Heaven, existence flows from down to up, from outside to inside, from dense to subtle, from manifest to nonmanifest, from unawareness to consciousness. It begins in plurality and difference in the World of Images, and it culminates in unification and unity in the realm of nature and the Mandate. It begins in sleep and ends in wakefulness.

We observe the ascent toward unity most clearly in our own self-awareness. The further we progress on the path of learning and understanding, the more we become integrated and unified and the closer we get to enlightenment. Full awakening is the point at which the Return rejoins the Origin, that is, where the Latter Heaven becomes one with the Former Heaven. It is through this return that the prophets and saints—known in Chinese as the sages and worthies—achieve the realization of the ultimate meaning of *tawḥīd*: the unity of the Real and the integration of all that there is.

Briefly then, the Former Heaven designates the realm from which we and all things have descended into the world, and the Latter Heaven the direction in which we are headed. The Former Heaven is the realm where things come down from invisibility, awareness, consciousness, and life. The Latter Heaven, although it appears outwardly as dispersion, visibility, ignorance, and death, is the realm where things ascend inwardly toward invisibility, light, and consciousness. The Former Heaven is the Descending Arc, the Latter Heaven the Ascending Arc (a point made completely explicit in Diagram 4.3).

In this way of looking at things, the goal of human life is to ascend in harmony with the flow of heaven and earth and to achieve contiguity and continuity with the invisible principles that gave rise to the visible universe. It is to reach the point where the Latter Heaven rejoins the Former Heaven and to complete the circle of existence by uniting the end of the Ascending Arc with the beginning of the Descending Arc. It is to achieve the heart's awakening, which is none other than its original oneness with Heaven. Only then does a person become a sage.

## Complete Substance and Great Function

Liu discussed the Real Principle in terms of the standard theological scheme of Essence/attributes/acts, but with certain modifications taken from Ibn al-'Arabī's followers, probably by way of Jāmī. He devoted Diagrams 1.2–1.4 to these three topics. He called the Essence "substance" (*ti* 體) and the names and attributes "function" (*yong* 用), a pairing that is prominent in both Buddhist and Confucian thought. Generally, substance is the thing in itself, function its movement or activity; substance is a thing's fundamental reality, function its expression; the two are typically discussed together and designate a relationship.[38] Julia Ching has explained the importance of the *ti/yong* pairing in Zhu Xi's thought:

Underlying such usage is a metaphysics that distinguishes between the inner and the outer. The inner is assumed to be good and perfect. Being hidden and latent, it cannot always make itself manifest. This depends on the outer. Frequently, the inner, or latent, is called *t'i* [*ti*], and the outer, or manifest, is called *yung* [*yong*]. Often *t'i* refers to a deeper reality in a still mode, whereas *yung* refers to its active manifestation.[39]

Several Arabic/Persian pairs are used in more or less the same way.[40] These include meaning (*ma'nā*) and form (*ṣūra*), nonmanifest (*bāṭin*) and manifest (*ẓāhir*), and essence (*dhāt*) and attributes (*ṣifāt*), the last being the typical way of talking about God. In Islamic philosophy, the same sort of relational discussion can proceed in terms of the ten Aristotelian categories: substance (*jawhar*) and the nine accidents (*'araḍ*), which are general designations for what can be said about the substance's appearance and manifestation. Rarely, however, is the Arabic term for substance, *jawhar*, used to designate God or the Divine Essence.

Diagram 1.3 talks about the divine attributes as "the Great Function of the Complete Substance" (*quanti dayong* 全體大用), an expression apparently used for the first time by Zhu Xi in his commentary on the

*Great Learning.*[41] Diagram 1.12 explains the peculiar nature of human beings compared to everything else by saying that they are "that in which 'the Complete Substance and the Great Function' of the Real Ruler are collected together."

In Islamic terms, Liu was saying that God created human beings in his own form. In so doing, he placed within them the signs and marks of both his Essence (complete substance) and his names and attributes (great function). Ibn al-'Arabī calls Adam "the all-comprehensive (engendered) being" precisely because, alone among all things engendered by the word "Be!"(*kun*), this "being" (*kawn*) makes manifest both the Divine Essence and all the divine attributes. Thus, "Adam emerged in the form of the name God, because it is this name that comprises all the divine names."[42] The difference between God and humans lies not in all-comprehensiveness but in the Necessity of the Real Existence (*al-wujūd al-ḥaqq*) and the contingency of the existence that humans receive from the engendering command.

In the Root Classic, Liu mentioned Zhu Xi's expression once, in explaining that the heart has seven levels, the highest of which is called "the first heart" (*chuxin* 初心). When "the first heart reveals the functions,/the subtle responses have no limits,/for the Complete Substance and Great Function/do not exclude or hide anything" (4:14–17). So, the perfect heart is all-inclusive, which is to say, it embraces all knowledge and awareness. Liu's words here can certainly be taken as a gloss on Zhu Xi's use of the term in his commentary on the *Great Learning* in explaining the first two of the eight steps of learning, that is, the investigation of things and the extension of knowledge:

If we wish to carry our knowledge to the utmost, we must investigate the principles of things, for there is nothing unknown to the spirituality of the heart. Among the things under heaven, there is nothing that does not have principle, but as long as all principles are not investigated, knowledge is not fully realized. . . . After exerting himself in this for a long time, [the seeker of knowledge] will one day suddenly achieve an all-pervading penetration. Then he will attain the outward and the inward, the coarse and the fine, and the Complete Substance and Great Function of the heart will reach full clarity. This is called the investigation of things. This is called the utmost knowledge.[43]

· Although Liu's words in the Root Classic echo this passage, he added a typical Islamic qualification in explaining Diagram 4.2, which illustrates the Root Classic's lines. "Based in clear discernment," he says, "[seekers] reach authentic realness to the extent that the hidden issues forth. Then the Complete Substance and Great Function of the Real Ruler appear." In other words, Liu confirmed Zhu Xi's remarks concerning the heart's realization of the Complete Substance and Great Function, but he pointed out that this substance and function belong not to the heart per se but to the Real Lord.

Liu emphasized this point under Diagram 4.6, where he used Zhu Xi's expression in a way that connects it with the tripartite division of Islam into Shariah, Tariqah, and Haqiqah. Having explained that Propriety (Shariah) is the perfection of practice and that the Way (Tariqah) is the perfection of the heart, he then said that the Real (Haqiqah) is none other than "the Complete Substance and Great Function" realized by "those in whose natures the Root Suchness flows."

Generally in Islamic metaphysics, as in Liu, the full realization of the heart—which, according to the purported hadith, "embraces God"—coincides with the full realization of the Real, or the return to the Origin. This is because, in realizing the true substance of the heart, human limitations are effaced before the Essence and attributes of God. To use the standard Sufi terminology, the heart undergoes the "annihilation" (*fanā'*) of its own illusory reality and reaches true life and awareness through the "subsistence" (*baqā'*) of the reality of the Lord, the only reality that truly is. Then it dwells in the station described by the Neo-Confucian scholar Lu Xiangshan 陸象山 (d. 1192), who is explaining the meaning of Mencius's statement, "He who fully realizes his heart knows his nature. He who knows his nature knows Heaven":

There is only one heart. My heart, my friends' heart, the heart of the sages thousands of years ago, and the heart of the sages thousands of years to come are all the same. The substance of the heart is infinite. If one can completely develop his heart, he will become identified with Heaven. To acquire learning is to appreciate this fact.[44]

In sum, we can say that Liu's "Complete Substance and Great Function" stresses the presence of God that sages and worthies find when they return to the Real. Zhu Xi, in contrast, spoke only of the heart. Nonetheless, we can and should argue that for Zhu Xi, Lu Xiangshan, and other Neo-Confucians, the true heart is identical with the Supreme Principle; so what he is saying is hardly different from what Liu is saying. But, by first discussing the Complete Substance and Great Function as the origin of the natures and principles that give rise to the manifest universe, Liu added an important clarification to the heart's cosmological situation: full enlightenment is reached, as he later explained in some detail, at the summit of the Ascending Arc, that is, through contiguity with the Latter Heaven. The heart achieves its entelechy by closing the Circle of Existence and returning to what it already was at the outset. Julia Ching sums up the Neo-Confucian discussion of substance/function (*tiyong*) in parallel terms: "Truth is therefore discovered after a process of un-veiling. Self-perfection is seen as an effort at interior liberation for the sake of exterior manifestation—of making known what one already possesses: the seeds of perfection."[45]

## *Prophethood and Sagehood*

The goal of human life, then, is to achieve perfection, but perfection cannot be defined simply in humanistic terms or on the basis of so-cial and cultural norms. It is rooted in the nature of things, in the Self-so. Far from being cosmic accidents, human beings are central to the overall economy of reality. They are the means whereby the cosmos achieves its ultimate purpose. Only through them does the Hidden Treasure come to be recognized for what it is; only the heart can awaken to the Complete Substance and Great Function.

Those who achieve the goal of creation are, as Ibn al-'Arabī put it, "perfect human beings," but all perfect human beings are not the same. One of the major discussions and debates among Muslim thinkers was how to distinguish among different sorts of "prophets" (*nabī*) and how to differentiate the prophets from those whom the Koran calls the "friends" (*walī*) of God (this term is commonly translated as "saints" outside the Koranic context).

Generally it was held that prophethood is predicated on moral and spiritual perfection, but it is bestowed by divine designation and cannot be achieved by human effort. There have been 124,000 prophets, beginning with Adam himself, and these can be classified in different categories in keeping with Koranic designations, such as "messenger" or "possessor of constancy." As for Muḥammad, he was the "seal" of the chain of prophets; with him the doorway to prophethood was closed. That leaves "friendship" with God, or "sanctity," as a station of human perfection achievable by those who follow in the footsteps of the prophets. Ibn al-'Arabī was not being too controversial when he said that the friends of God can attain the level of human perfection reached by the prophets themselves—but only by following in their footsteps and with divine help, not simply by their own efforts.

In the sources that Liu employed, the friends or saints are clearly distinguished from the prophets, but they are described as having achieved the moral and spiritual perfections of the prophets by virtue of adhering to their guidance. Liu translated prophet as "sage" (*sheng* 聖) and saint as "worthy" (*xian* 賢), and there was much discussion in the Confucian tradition concerning how to distinguish these two ranks of human beings.

Benite devotes a long chapter of *The Dao of Muhammad* to showing how the key concepts of Dao and sage were adopted by the Huiru. As he points out, Chinese Muslims were well aware that Confucians considered sagehood a universal human phenomenon, not limited to China, and they liked to quote this passage from Lu Xiangshan: "Sages appeared tens of thousands of generations ago. They shared this heart; they shared this principle. Sages will appear tens of thousands of generations to come. They will share this heart; they will share this principle. Over the four seas sages appear. They share this heart; they share this principle."[46]

One can see an echo of this passage in Liu's wish in his introduction that his readers will open up their hearts and minds to the real teachings of the Islamic classics: "May they not become stagnant in the opinions of one corner, but rather awaken to the sameness of heart and principle." He was even more explicit when he related that he spent ten years in the forest in isolation, and then, "I suddenly came to understand that the Islamic classics have by and large the same purport as Confucius and Mencius." He wrote in a similar vein in the introduction to the second book of his trilogy, *Tianfang dianli*, when he remarked that Islamic instructions about practice and conduct are not much different from the rites and proprieties laid down in Confucian teachings. As a result, to observe the Muslim practices is simply to observe the practices and teachings of the former sages and righteous kings, for the teachings of the sages in East and West have always been the same.

In speaking of the universality of truth and virtue, the Huiru use language and imagery that are thoroughly Chinese, but the notion is also Islamic and strongly rooted in the Koran, especially when we understand "sage" as they did: as the designation for those who stand in the highest stations of human perfection, those who see things as they truly are. These sages are precisely those who are called "prophets" in Islamic terms, and all of them share "this heart," which is the heart that "embraces God," and "this principle," which can be the First Intellect, another name for the Ascribed Spirit, or the vision of *tawḥīd*, which the Koran affirms as being common to all prophets (21:25).

In explaining the degree to which the Han Kitab adopted Chinese teachings on sagehood, Benite goes a bit too far when he tells us that they diverged markedly from the Koranic position. His one-paragraph summary of the Koran's teachings is inadequate, and he is oblivious to the complex ways in which the relevant issues were discussed in the interpretive tradition, not least in the Persian and Arabic texts that the Chinese Muslims were reading. He concludes: "In the Chinese context, Muhammad remains central but not as a prophet. Rather, he is a sage, one in a chain marked by the gradual completion of the Dao."[47] He does not explain, however, how or why one should distinguish between "sage" and "prophet."

Our own understanding of what Liu is saying puts his interpretations of the meaning of sagehood fully in line with the traditional Muslim expositions of the meaning of prophethood. It is true that some Muslims might take exception to Liu's position because of his use of the word "sage" in both a strict sense as a reference to the prophets and a loose sense as a reference to wise men or saints. But the same is true of the Arabic word *ḥakīm*, which can be applied to prophets, saints, and perfect human beings. In this loose sense, Liu sometimes used the expression "sages and common people" to designate the human race, and clearly he wanted to include the worthies with the sages, not the common people. In referring to the Root Classic, he mentioned "the sages who authored the classics," meaning the six books on which it is based. He was not declaring that Nasafī, Rāzī, Jāmī, Ījī, and Bayḍāwī were prophets; rather, they were *ḥakīm*s. No one on the Islamic side would object to his use of this term.

Generally Liu held sagehood up as the supreme human station, one that everyone should strive to achieve. Islamic texts do practically the same with prophecy, especially in their great stress on following the Sunnah of Muḥammad. In his summary of Volume 4, Liu referred to a saying of Mencius and declared: "When people settle down in the ordinary without hoping to become sages, then, whether in heavenly or human affairs, they are simply 'throwing themselves away.' If they know shame, they will be courageous, and if they are constant, they can become sages."

In the Islamic context, authors are generally careful to assert that the way to achieve human perfection lies in emulating the prophets, but there always remains the caveat that no one can "become a prophet" in the strict sense of the word, because Muḥammad was the last one; hence, people can become at best saints. Generally, scholars differentiated between prophets and saints by declaring that every prophet is a perfect human being, but each also has a cosmic and social function given by the Lord Ruler on high. It is this bestowal of a specific function that came to an end with the prophecy of Muḥammad. No one can aspire to such a function, but anyone can aspire to follow Muḥammad in body, soul, and heart with the aim of achieving realization, which is precisely the station of the most perfect of the saints. The whole discussion of Shariah, Tariqah, and Haqiqah is modeled on Muḥammad's human substance. A saying that is attributed to him makes the point: "The Shariah is my words, the Tariqah is my acts, and the Haqiqah is my [inner] states."

The Muslim debate over the exact relationship between prophets and saints has been going on for centuries. Liu was aware of the subtlety of the issues involved, and he was careful to avoid saying explicitly that people can actually hope to become sages (in the sense of prophet), although he insisted that everyone should strive for the perfection embodied in sagehood. What remains completely clear is that, in keeping with both the Confucian and the Islamic traditions, he held up the station of human perfection as both the model that needs to be followed in daily life and the ultimate goal that needs to be pursued and actualized. This perfection, moreover, is not to be understood simply in moral, ethical, and social terms. Rather, it is human conformity with the Real Principle, and it is achieved by the union of heaven and earth—understood as designations for the actual forces that determine the entire universe.

## One Body with Heaven and Earth

In Diagram 1.3, Liu depicted the function (divine attributes) of the Root Substance (Divine Essence) as "knowledge and power" (*zhi-neng* 知能), using the latter expression here (and elsewhere) to designate the whole range of divine attributes. Diagram 2.2 explains that each of the fourteen levels of nature manifests "knowledge and power" in its own way. The first and highest level of nature is that of the Utmost Sage (i.e., Muḥammad), whose knowledge and power is "undifferentiatedly the same with the knowledge and power of the Real Ruler in one body." According to Diagram 4.7, "The true action and real knowledge [of the sages] are undifferentiatedly the same with the Root Suchness in one body." These are the only places in the text where this phrase "in one body" (*yiti* 一體) occurs. We can understand some of what the expression implies by looking at Diagram 5.3, which depicts three sorts of body and three levels of embodiment (*ti* 體) achieved by the sages in their return to the highest level of human perfection.

The word *ti*, translated under 5.3 as both "body" and "embodiment," is the same as *ti*, or "substance," which is paired with *yong*, or "function." From earliest times the basic meaning of the word was "body" in both its corporeal or physical and its living or spiritual dimensions. As Chung-ying Cheng explains, "On its most elementary level *ti* is the concrete, corporeal human body in terms of which human life is maintained and developed. But *ti* is not simply a matter of organization of physical components. It is a structure and system of organic functions and vital spirit in the vehicle of the physical body."[48] Cheng goes on to explain that as a verb, *ti* means to embody something and to form an organic system with it:

In terms of this embodiment the *Yizhuan* (Ten Commentaries) in the *Yijing* [Book of Changes] speaks of a superior man forming one body with heaven, earth, and the "ten thousand things." . . . In the "*Wenyan* Commentary" of the *Yizhuan* it is said, "When a superior man embodies *ren* (*tiren*), he will lead others." . . . In the "Great Appendix" it is said that a sage must understand and embody the creativity of heaven and earth (*ti tiandi zhi zhuan*). This must be the basis for the human participation in the creative transformation of things as described in the *Zhongyong* (*Doctrine of the Mean*).[49]

The first person to bring out explicitly the full symbolic resonance of the term *ti* seems to have been Wang Bi 王弼 (226–49), who used it in a commentary on the *Daodejing* to describe the ultimate reality, *wu* 無, "Nonbeing."[50] There also he used the term in conjunction with *ben* 本, "root," "origin," "source." After him the term *benti*, or Root Substance, "becomes the unique general term for ultimate reality in all branches and all schools of Chinese philosophy."[51]

Throughout Chinese thought, then, *ti*—body or substance—has played a major role in discussions of both Ultimate Reality and human perfection. Generally, historians have translated *ti* in one of two ways, depending on context, and we have followed this practice, with some hesitation. The problem for translators is fairly clear: the English language does not have a single term that could designate both the human body and the Ultimate Reality and, at the same time, preserve all the connotations of *ti*. One might argue for "substance," since it is common to speak of "the human substance," but, to speak of "forming one substance with Heaven" implies a substantial continuity that is belied by the transcendence of the Root Substance, the Divine Essence. Moreover, "substance" is a philosophical term typically used in contexts that limit its semantic field; in contrast, "body" serves as a symbol in various traditions for levels of being that lie beyond the strictly physical level.

But to return to the issue at hand, in the Book of Changes, one can find the cosmological notion that human beings, by achieving *ren* or true humanity, come to form one body with heaven, earth, and the ten thousand things. So basic is this to the Confucian worldview that, as Tu Weiming puts it,

The highest Confucian ideal is the "unity of Man and Heaven," which defines humanity not only in anthropological terms but also in cosmological terms. . . . Humanity in its all-embracing fullness "forms one body with Heaven, Earth, and the myriad things."[52]

The cosmological implications of forming one body with all things was developed in detail by the Neo-Confucian thinkers, beginning especially with the Cheng brothers.[53] For example, Cheng Hao 程顥 wrote, "The man of *ren* forms one body with all things without any differentiation."[54] Zhang Zai remarked, "Therefore that which fills the universe I regard as my body and that which directs the universe I regard as my nature."[55] The greatest champion of this way of explaining *ren* was Wang Yangming 王陽明, who stated at the beginning of his *Inquiry on the "Great Learning,"*

The great man regards Heaven and Earth and the myriad things as one body. He regards the world as one family and the country as one person. As for those who make a cleavage between objects and distinguish between the self and others, they are small men. That the great man can regard Heaven, Earth, and the myriad things as one body is not because he deliberately wants to do so, but because it is natural to the nature of his heart that he does so.[56]

As we have seen, Liu declared that the knowledge and power of the Utmost Sage specifically and that of the sages generally are no different from the knowledge and power of the Real Lord, and that this sameness means that the two have "one body." This one "body" (*ti*) is of course none other than Zhu Xi's Complete "Substance" (*ti*), and this "knowledge and power" is none other than Zhu Xi's Great Function. But how can this issue be addressed in terms that preserve the basic notion of human beings as creatures of God expounded in Islamic texts?

Liu devoted much of Volume 4 to explaining the interrelationships among three basic levels of the human reality: body (*shen* 身 rather than *ti*), heart (*xin*), and nature (*xing*). The highest level of nature is then the Nature of Continuity (*jixing* 繼性). As becomes clear in both the texts and the diagrams, the Nature of Continuity is none other than the Nature of the Utmost Sage, which is the first level of cosmic manifestation, as explained under Diagram 1.6. It is this

Nature that gave birth to the diverse natures and principles in the Former Heaven, but now, in the Latter Heaven, this same Nature is the goal that is to be reached through awakening and self-realization. To rejoin the Nature of Continuity is precisely to actualize the Complete Substance and Great Function (Diagrams 4.2, 4.6).

The expression "Nature of Continuity" provides a good example of how Liu mined the Chinese classics to find appropriate terms. One of the earliest uses of the word *ji*, or "continuity," is found in a famous passage of the Book of Changes: "One yin, one yang, this is called 'Dao.' That which *continues* it is the good, that which perfects it is nature."[57] Clearly "that which continues it" is "in continuity with" the Dao. Liu consistently used "Nature of Continuity" to translate "Ascribed Spirit." It is this spirit that God ascribes to himself when he says in the Koran, "I blew into [Adam] of My own spirit." By ascribing this Spirit to himself, God is surely affirming its "continuity" with himself.

As noted, however, the exact nature of this Spirit and its continuity with God was much debated by Muslim scholars. Generally, among Ibn al-'Arabī's followers, the Ascribed Spirit is considered to be the point of contact between the Uncreated and the created, the intermediary between the divine and the cosmic. It is called by many other names, one of the most famous of which is First Intellect (*al-'aql al-awwal*), in keeping with the prophetic saying, "The first thing God created was the intellect." We will meet other names in the course of the annotations on the text.

The three levels of body, heart, and nature that Liu describes in Volume 4 are respectively the realms to which the three levels of cultivation have been addressed "from ancient times until now" (Diagram 5.3). The body is brought into harmony with the Real One through the Shariah (Propriety), the heart through the Tariqah (the Way), and nature through the Haqiqah (the Real). Pursuing these three is "the true practice of sage endeavor" (Diagram 4.6).

In Diagram 5.3, Liu discussed the fullness of sage nature, that is, the station of the Perfect Human Being, who is the fifth Divine Presence embracing the other four. Liu, however, spoke of these presences as *ti*—body, or substance, or embodiment. Human beings have three bodies—bodily body, heart body, and nature body—and these are given to them by the productive activity of the creative transformation. The goal of sage endeavor is to follow the Shariah, Tariqah, and Haqiqah in order to embody the Real One "by means of these three bodies."

If we read Liu's explanation of the three bodies in terms of the Five Divine Presences, we can say that the Real One that comes to be embodied in the three bodies is none other than the first Divine Presence, that is, the Complete Substance whose function is knowledge and power. The perfected body of the sage then corresponds to the fourth Presence (the World of the Kingdom). His perfected heart is the third Presence (the World of Imagination), and his realized nature is the second Presence (the World of the Sovereignty). In the totality of his integral unity, the sage himself is the fifth Presence, the Human Ultimate (renji 人極). He alone achieves the fullness of the creative transformation and deserves to be described as forming one body with heaven, earth, and the ten thousand things.

FOUR

# *The Structure and Argument of* Tianfang xingli

Liu developed the argument in *Tianfang xingli* in three stages. Chapter 1 of the Root Classic summarizes the whole book. Chapters 2–5 of the Root Classic expand on the first chapter. The third part consists of five volumes, each with twelve diagrams and text explaining the first and second stages.[1]

The structure of the book suggests that Liu expected students to begin by memorizing the Root Classic, as they would any "classic" text.[2] The next step would be to investigate the meaning of the memorized text with the help of the diagrams and commentary, under the guidance of a teacher. Eventually they would become familiar with a broad range of Islamic and Confucian teachings on the Real Substance, nature and principle, heaven and earth, the Mandate, the ten thousand things, and the human situation. They would then be able to recall most of the details simply by reviewing the Root Classic or by reciting its first chapter.

Certainly the popularity of the book over a period of two centuries had much to do with its pedagogical usefulness. Nūr al-Ḥaqq said as much in his brief explanation of why he chose to translate the Root

81

Classic into Arabic. According to Nūr, the eloquence of Liu's Chinese is unmatched by any other Muslim scholar. Letting hyperbole get the best of him, he then exclaimed: "By God, were Muḥammad not the Seal [of prophethood], Liu Zhi would have been a prophet in China." Moreover, *Tianfang xingli* is the best of all Muslim books on the "realities" (*ḥaqā'iq*, plural of *ḥaqīqa*), that is, the truths understood by those who achieve realization and attain to the Haqiqah:

I saw that among the books about the realities, this is the clearest in meaning, the most concise in words, and the most beautiful in arrangement. Despite its explanations, there is nothing extraneous or tiresome, and despite its concision, it explains perfectly everything in the two worlds. I commanded my followers to memorize it. However, some of its meanings were obscure for them. Because of their affection for Arabic, I elucidated it. Then, in order to increase its benefits, I explained it. I named it The Five Subtleties, because it is arranged in five chapters.[3]

## *Chapter 1*

The gist of the first chapter, and hence of the whole book, can be seen in Diagram 0.6, "The Macrocosm's Following in the Circle of Creation and Transformation." This is a version of what Ibn al-'Arabī and others call "the circle of existence" (*dā'irat al-wujūd*), made up of the descending and ascending arcs. Although the two arcs are not clearly differentiated in Liu's circle, Nūr al-Ḥaqq knew perfectly well that this was the issue, and his version of the diagram (see Fig. 1) makes it obvious. He gives the diagram the title "The Circle of Creation," makes a slight change in the orientation of the individual circles, adds a vertical, bisecting line, and names the two sides "the Descending Arc" and "the Ascending Arc."

The Circle of Existence illustrated in Diagram 0.6 with its two arcs is the organizing scheme of the book. The Descending Arc is what Liu called "the Former Heaven," and the Ascending Arc "the Latter Heaven" (as he makes explicit in Diagram 4.3, a much more complete version of the whole picture). That the two Heavens are at issue is clear from Diagrams 0.2 and 0.3, which together provide a more detailed statement of the stages of creation.

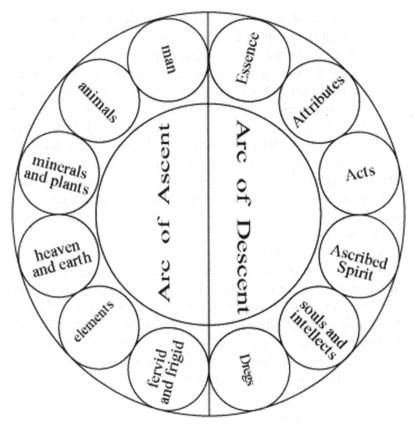

Fig. 1     Nūr al-Ḥaqq, The Circle of Creation

Diagram 0.2 depicts "the sequence of the transformation of principles in the Former Heaven" by showing the Descending Arc in six levels, from the Real Substance down to its lowest point, the Vast Sediment. The first three levels represent the Divine Reality or "the Divine Presence," that is, God's Essence, attributes, and acts. Substance is the Real in itself without regard to anything else, Function the Real inasmuch as it can be understood in relation to others, and Act the divine activity that brings others into existence.

The second set of three levels in Diagram 0.2 represents the World of Sovereignty. First is the level of the Mandate, second the level of the Mandate's differentiation into natures and principles, and finally the furthest descent of the circle of existence into a realm that makes possible the appearance of visible things. Muslim philosophers often call this third level "universal hyle" or "prime matter."

Diagram 0.3 illustrates "the sequence of the transformation of forms in the Latter Heaven" and depicts the Ascending Arc, again in six stages. The original vital-energy at the top of the diagram is none other than the Vast Sediment mentioned in Diagram 0.2 (as is made explicit in Diagram 0.6). The next three levels—image, form, and stuff—represent stages of increasing complexity that give rise to the World of Images. Only at the stage of the images themselves, called "wood/metal" in Diagram 0.6, do minerals and plants appear as bodily things. Then come the living kinds, that is, animals, including human beings.

If Diagram 0.6 differentiates human beings from other living things, this is because it takes into account their cosmic function, the fact that only they can complete the Circle of Existence by returning to the Origin. This final return to Unity is indicated schematically by the empty circle of Diagram 0.10, "The Undifferentiated Transformation of Heaven and Humans." This is the culmination of the circle of creative transformation, or the achievement of the station of Complete Substance and Great Function.

## Chapter 2

The second chapter of the Root Classic discusses the qualities and characteristics that become manifest in humans and things, that is, the ten thousand beings of the World of Images. The basic point is that the World of Images makes manifest the natures and principles concealed in the World of Principles; in a mysterious way, the images are none other than the principles. As Liu puts it at the very end of the chapter, "Observe the forms and discriminate the meanings,/ look at the images and awaken to the principles—/The Former Heaven and the Latter Heaven/are on one thread, nothing more" (RC 2:87–90).

The expression "one thread" derives from the *Analects*. It was typically interpreted to mean an underlying unity that ties together all of reality. Liu wanted to say that all things disclose their invisible natures and principles, which are in the last analysis nothing but the functions and acts of the Real Substance.

In Chapter 2 Liu delineated the general characteristics of the principles as understood in terms of their images. None of the ten diagrams of the Root Classic illustrate this chapter, but its structure can be seen when we look at the topics discussed under the twelve diagrams pertaining to Volume 2. Diagrams 2.1 and 2.2 review the fourteen levels of nature depicted in Diagram 1.6, from the nature of the Utmost Sage (the Muhammadan Spirit) down to that of the Vast Sediment. Following Rāzī, Liu explained that the Ascribed Spirit overflows to produce, level by level, all the spirits of humans and things. The fourteen levels are ranked on the basis of the intensity with which they manifest the functions of the Real Substance, that is, the attributes of God.

Diagram 2.3 explains the fourteen levels of principle in terms of their "forms and vessels," which are the images that make them manifest in the Latter Heaven. Diagram 2.4 reveals the hidden characteristics and qualities of these same levels. Diagram 2.5 stresses the unity of principle and image. Diagrams 2.6 to 2.11 provide detailed descriptions of the qualities and characteristics that appear in the major phenomena of the macrocosm—the heavens and their revolutions, the four agents (elements) and four seasons, the climes of the earth, and atmospheric events. Diagram 2.12 reminds us that all these natures, principles, images, forms, and vessels are strung on One Thread or, as Ibn al-'Arabī's followers often put it, are unified by the Oneness of Existence (*waḥdat al-wujūd*).

## Chapter 3

Chapters 1 and 2 describe the macrocosm in terms of its overall structure from Origin to Return along with the sorts of humans and things that appear within it. Chapters 3 and 4 turn to the bodily and spiritual makeup of the human microcosm and the necessity of learning, cultivation, and practice for the achievement of awakening.

The relationship between microcosm and macrocosm can be seen by comparing Diagram 0.6, "The Macrocosm's Following in the Circle of Creation and Transformation," with Diagram 0.7, "The Microcosm's Original Beginning and Final Return." Diagrams 0.4 and 0.5 break up Diagram 0.7 into two stages, just as Diagrams 0.2 and 0.3 divide Diagram 0.6 into two.

Diagram 0.7 provides the overall scheme of Chapter 3 and depicts the microcosm as a circle from Origin to Return. Diagrams 0.4 and 0.5 comprise eleven of the twelve levels of Diagram 0.7, the first showing six stages of the development of the embryo in the womb, and the second six stages from infancy to perfection. The final stage of Diagram 0.4, "the spiritually living," is identical with the first stage of Diagram 0.5, "hardness and firmness" (as can be seen in Diagram 0.7).

Diagram 0.4 corresponds to the Former Heaven in the macrocosm (Diagram 0.2). The movement is from the invisible and unified toward the visible and differentiated, that is, from the "seed" in the womb to the developed child. Diagram 0.5, which is the microcosmic analogue of the Latter Heaven (Diagram 0.3), maps out the developmental stages of the invisible powers inside the human being—growth, awareness, self-consciousness, and full awakening, the last of which is identity with the Nature of Continuity, that is, the level of Complete Substance and Great Function.

## Chapter 4

Having discussed the unfolding of the stages of nature, Liu turned to the specific characteristics of the microcosm that make it possible for people to engage in self-cultivation. He provided an overview of the path to perfection, discussed the trials that people face in their quest, and finally described the return to the Real. Since none of the Root Classic's diagrams pertain to this chapter, we summarize it in terms of Volume 4.

Diagrams 4.1 and 4.2 address the nature of the heart and the virtues that it needs to actualize. Diagram 4.3 reviews the relationship between the Former and the Latter Heavens and explains that human perfection means reaching the pinnacle of the Arc of Ascent, which is none other than the return to the origin of the Arc of Descent. Diagram 4.4 describes the Human Ultimate, the person who has achieved the reunion of the two Heavens, in terms of the symbolism of the famous Light Verse of the Koran. Diagram 4.5 describes the cosmic function of human beings and the manner in which they can re-establish the harmony of the creative flow.

Diagram 4.6 turns to a description of the sage practice that can lead to the goal, and 4.7 describes the four basic sorts of human being in terms of the degree to which they follow or ignore this practice. Diagrams 4.8–4.10 detail various sorts of obstacles that block the path to perfection. Diagram 4.11 describes the three transformations—of body, heart, and nature—that need to be achieved, and 4.12 depicts the return to the Real that is the goal of cultivation.

## Chapter 5

The final chapter of the Root Classic looks again at the whole picture, but with a view toward the union of heaven, earth, and the ten thousand things that is achieved through human perfection. It is summarized by Diagrams 0.8, 0.9, and 0.10.

Diagram 0.8 illustrates the basic structure of the universe. The divine unity appears as three Ones that give rise to the entire cosmos: the Real One in itself; the Numerical One, which becomes manifest as the myriad ones that are the multiple things; and the Embodied One, which is the sage through whom the universe becomes aware of its origin and return. Diagram 0.9 shows that the Three Ones and the cosmos are in fact the differentiation of a single reality. Diagram 0.10 depicts the levels once they are reintegrated into the One from which they arose, an integration that is achieved when the sage forms one body with heaven, earth, and the ten thousand things.

# FIVE

## *The Translation*

We had already decided before the publication of *Chinese Gleams* to
work on *Tianfang xingli* because it appeared to us as philosophically
and religiously the most significant of the several Han Kitab books
with which we had some familiarity. We began meeting on a semi-
regular basis at the Harvard-Yenching Institute. Before our meetings,
Murata would prepare a rough translation of a passage. Chittick, who
does not know Chinese, would then polish the English while consult-
ing with her about the original Chinese terms and the various possible ways of understanding them. Then the three of us would meet.
Chittick would read the translation aloud as Tu compared it with the
Chinese text and offered advice on corrections and modifications.
This process was accompanied by long discussions of the significance of the ideas in both Islamic and Confucian terms. Having
blackened several pages with corrections and notes, Murata and
Chittick would then return home to prepare the next draft and move
on to the next chapters.

It took us about three years to complete the first draft of the whole
book, but it was obvious to us that we were still not catching a good
deal of Liu's purport. We then started the process over from the beginning and spent another two years revising and correcting the first

draft. Once we were satisfied with the translation, we began tracking down Liu's sources, annotating the text, and writing the introduction.

We have arranged the text exactly as it is found in our editions of Liu's book. First, the two introductory statements, then the Root Classic followed by ten diagrams, then the five volumes, each beginning with a summary and containing twelve diagrams with explanation. We have provided our own annotations throughout. We omitted only Liu's list of forty sources, which is located between the two introductory statements, because most of the books have still not been identified, despite the pioneering efforts of Kuwata Rokurō and the more recent work of Donald Leslie and Muhammad Wassel. We also left out the laudatory prefaces written by other authors, the number of which varies according to the edition.

Given the fact that the book is basically the Root Classic plus explanation, we have provided the Root Classic's Chinese text. On the pages facing it, we have also provided Nūr al-Ḥaqq's Arabic version with English translation. The book titles enclosed in parentheses at the ends of some lines of the English translation of the Root Classic indicate Liu's sources as he noted them. For their full names, see the List of Abbreviations at the beginning of the book.[1]

The numbers along the righthand margin of the translation of the Root Classic specify the diagrams that explain the meaning of the text. These are our additions to the text (they do not occur in the original), and, in placing them, we have followed our own understanding of the text (with occasional help from Nūr al-Ḥaqq).

Our translation has undergone many revisions. In the early stages we were concerned simply with decipherment. We made numerous changes as we gradually came to understand where Liu was coming from and what he was trying to say. We again revised the text thoroughly as we read it through for the second time. Still further revision has been undertaken with the goal of consistency—choosing appropriate English terms for the technical terminology and making sure the same term is used wherever that character occurs in the text or the diagrams.

Given the multivalent meanings of many Chinese characters, consistency has been extremely difficult and sometimes impossible, but we have felt it more important to illustrate the manner in which basic concepts are used in different contexts than to try to come up with different translations appropriate to the various contexts. We are, after all, dealing here with a conceptual universe far from our modern ways of looking at the world. Making the English too familiar and too idiomatic has the drawback of suggesting that the concepts behind the language are the same old concepts with which we deal in everyday discourse. This would be unfair both to the author of the text and to the reader.

Responsibility for the final version of the translation, introduction, and notes rests with Murata and Chittick. Tu Weiming provided explanation, clarification, and advice at every stage, but he did not participate actively in the final details. His thoughts on the significance of the book are provided in the Epilogue.

In the annotations we have tried to clarify the meaning of the text by referring back to the Islamic sources that Liu used and by highlighting some of the references to the Chinese classics and some of the important technical terms as explained by Neo-Confucian scholars. Although we provide references to English translations of the Persian and Arabic works that we cite, all translations are our own. We also take responsibility for the translations of the Chinese texts used in the annotations, unless we state specifically that we are quoting from an existing translation.

# Nature and Principle
# in Islam

———•———

# *Personal Narrative*

Although I am indeed a scholar of Islamic Learning, I privately venture to say that unless there is an exhaustive prying into the [Chinese] Classics and Histories and a wide inquiry into the hundred families of books, Islamic Learning will stay in a corner and not become public learning under heaven.

When I was young, I followed my deceased father, Master Hanying, receiving teachings from him on how to investigate and learn, and I liked to read widely in various books. My deceased father went deep into the purport of the nature and mandate of Heaven and humans. He used to exhibit to his colleagues what he had silently become acquainted with. He would often beat his breast in lamentation and say, "The Islamic classics elucidate the principles in their furthest essence, but unfortunately I am unable to translate them into Chinese so that they might be shown widely in this land."

That is why I was inspired by my deceased father to engage in this affair. I searched deeply and inquired energetically in seeking to penetrate the Islamic classics, but I did not dare to consider myself right. After a while my father passed away, and I searched out and looked at the classics he had left behind, scouring the relics of his work. I wept and lamented, and my own efforts became even stronger. I shut out people and affairs and did not grudge to use up my savings. I purchased the books of a hundred scholars and read them. I also extended this attitude to the books of Daoism and Buddhism. Having dwelt in seclusion in a mountain forest for ten years, I suddenly came to understand that the Islamic classics have by and large the same purport as Confucius and Mencius. However, I still did not dare to consider myself right. I asked about questions concerning which I had doubts and difficulties from the scholars of Islam. Indeed, I sought to go through thoroughly, from beginning to end, outwardly and inwardly, both the fine and the coarse, to reach the ultimate in each.

Then I sighed deeply and said, "The classics are the Islamic classics, but the principle is the principle under heaven. If the people under heaven do not come to have a share in hearing and clarifying the principle under heaven, that is by no means the intention of the sages who authored the classics. If I make them public under heaven, then the intentions of those who authored the classics will be satisfied and the will of my deceased father will also be satisfied."

This is why I chose, from the midst of several voluminous classics, those whose principles are the same and whose meanings are united, and I compiled them as one book: *The Chinese Translation of the Nature and Principle of the Root Classics*. Altogether it is five chapters. First I talk about the order of the manifestation and display of the principles and images of the macrocosm. Then I extend this talk to the endeavor and power embedded in each of heaven and earth, humans and things, and to the reasons for alteration and transformation, begetting and more begetting. Next I talk about the order of the manifestation and display of the body and the nature of the microcosm. Then I extend this talk to the functions stored in body and heart, nature and mandate, and to the causes of sagehood and ordinariness, good and evil. The final chapter comprehensively unifies the subtle principles of the differentiation and union of the macrocosm and microcosm and the fine meanings of the undifferentiated transformation and the coming home in the end to the One Real. The text is concise and its purpose comprehensive. Displayed here will be the beginnings of the mysterious depth and rich content of Nature and Principle in Islam.

I was still afraid, however, that those who are beginners in learning may have some doubts, and so, on the basis of the classics, I established diagrams that display the principles of the classics, and, on the basis of the diagrams, I established explanations to transmit the meaning of the diagrams. Altogether the explanations are sixty, arranged in five volumes.

Humbly I hope that students of Islamic Learning will understand the meaning by looking at the diagrams and that they will be opened up to the classics by looking at the text. May they not become stagnant in the opinions of one corner, but rather awaken to the sameness of heart and principle. May they not wade in the flow of heresy, but rather rely on the teaching of the great public.

I hope I have not betrayed the intention of the former sages who authored these classics and have brought to fruition the persistent will of my deceased father. That is all.

> Respectfully recorded by the student of Islam,
> Liu Zhi of Jinling [Nanjing]

# The Plan of the Book

This book consists of the Root Classic, the diagrams, and the commentaries.

The Root Classic has five chapters arranged in the head volume. Following it are the diagrams and commentaries, which have sixty sections differentiated into five volumes.

You should know that I established the diagrams on the basis of the Classic, and I established the commentaries on the basis of the diagrams. With the diagrams I display the principles of the Classic, and with the commentaries I detail the meaning of the diagrams, so that most of the deep meanings of Nature and Principle can be obtained.

The Root Classic is a collection of various classics formed into one classic. Its text can be seen in the midst of six great classics. I note below that certain passages are seen in certain sections so that they can wait to be examined. The text of the commentaries has the meaning of a commentary on the Root Classic, which I edited and completed to form a text. It is not that I dared to obtain stealthily from various scholars, nor that I composed according to my own private opinion. The pattern of the text and each word and phrase can be clearly examined.

The titles of the classics from which I selected and compiled are attached to the beginning of the book without making separate notations in the midst of the commentary.[1]

I composed the diagrams by assembling the meanings with the aim of transmitting the meaning that has not been exhaustively transmitted. "What is signified by words has a limit, but what is signified by meaning has no limit."[2] By examining the diagrams, you may be able to understand the meaning beyond the words.

There are comprehensive diagrams and specific diagrams. The comprehensive diagrams are for clarifying the sequence of principles in the classics. The specific diagrams are separated out from the comprehensive diagrams and given their own places. I was afraid that the meanings of some of the commentaries on the classics would not be transparent, and so I added several more diagrams to clarify them.

The words and meanings of this book are totally rooted in the Islamic classics. Now and then since some texts of the classics are difficult to translate into Chinese, I could not escape from using different texts to comment on them. Although the texts do not match, their meanings are never incompatible.

This is a book that talks about principles, not about images and numbers.[3] Hence it talks about principles in detail, but it talks about numbers briefly. Although it talks briefly about images and numbers, it is impossible not to talk about images and numbers, for images and numbers are images and numbers rooted and existing in the midst of the principles. Thus, it is impossible not to mention them when talking about principles. I hope that those who read this book will not say that the book is excellent on principles but only summarizes the numbers.

Everything throughout is translated into Chinese to give form to the text, except the two uppermost heavens, for which I used Islamic names and designations. This is because each of the seven heavens below them rules over one governance; so the name of the heaven is the name and designation of the governance ruled by that heaven. The two uppermost heavens rule everywhere; so their names do not have specific designations. Since they have no specific designation,

it would be impossible to translate them into Chinese and fully realize the meaning of the two heavens. Therefore the ninth heaven is
designated and called Aershi, and the eighth heaven is designated
and called Kuerxi.[4]

I authored this book hoping only that I do not betray the intention
of the Creator of things in giving me life. When the Creator of things
gives life to humans, each of them has his own function for which he
is granted a spirit. If I had used my spirit in the world, then it surely
would have appeared there. But I did not enjoy using it there and instead I have enjoyed using it here, perhaps because the Creator of
things has decreed that I follow this affair.

## Notes

1. For a list of the books that Liu cites—some still unidentified—see Leslie and
Wassel, "Arabic and Persian Sources Used by Liu Chih."

2. The quotation is from the Great Treatise of the *Yijing* 1.12.2 (translated by
Wilhelm as, "Words cannot express thoughts completely" [*I Ching*, p. 322]). The
passage is explaining why the *Yijing* uses images and hexagrams: "The sages set up
the images in order to realize their intentions fully; they established the hexagrams
in order to express true and false completely."

3. Numbers (*shu* 數)—as is evident from its pairing here and elsewhere with images (*xiang* 象)—refers to the multiplicity represented by the images. Liu Zhi is saying, in other words, that the book focuses not on the phenomena of the world or the
ten thousand things but on the principles—the spiritual roots—of the manifest
world.

4. Aershi is a transliteration of Arabic *'arsh*, "throne" (of God), and Kuerxi of
Arabic *kursī*, "footstool." Their cosmological significance is explained under Diagram 2.3.

# THE
# COMPILED
# INTERPRETATION OF
# NATURE AND PRINCIPLE
# IN ISLAM

纂譯天方性理

# *Head Volume*

# 首卷

[Note: Numbers to the right of the text of the Root Classic refer to the relevant diagrams. Book names in parentheses are Liu's own designations of his sources as indicated in the Chinese text (for the complete titles, see the List of Abbreviations). The Arabic text is *al-Laṭā'if* by Nūr al-Ḥaqq, paired with its translation as *The Subtleties*.]

本經
第一章
總述大世界造化流行之次第

　　清哉本然
　　最初無稱
　　眞體無着
　　惟茲實有
5　　執一含萬
　　惟一含萬
　　妙用斯渾
　　惟體運用
　　作爲始出 (昭微經)
10　　眞理流行
　　命昭元化
　　本厥知能

## The Root Classic
### Chapter One
*Comprehensive Statement on the Sequence of the Ongoing
Flow of the Creative Transformation in the Macrocosm*

How pure is the Root Suchness![1]                                   0.1, 1.1
　The Earliest Beginning has no designation,
　the Real Substance has no attachment.                              1.2
　Only this is True Being,
5　holding the One and containing the ten thousand.
　The Only One contains the ten thousand,
　but the subtle functions are not differentiated.                  1.3
　When the Only Substance turns and functions,
　activity begins to emerge. (*Gleams*)[2]                          1.4
10 The Real Principle flows and goes,                               0.2
　and the Mandate shows the original transformation.[3]
　At root it is knowledge and power

اللطائف

بسم الله الرحمن الرحيم

الفصل الاوّل

فى بيان تنزّلات العالم الكبير

سبحان من كان كنزاً مخفياً

و هو مبدأ بلا ابتداء غير متصف

ذات بحت غير ملا بسة

و انما هذا وجود حقيقى

و أحدية اندرجت فيها الشؤونات 5

و لاندراج الشؤونات فيها

كانت صفاته غير متمايزة عنها

فبتجلّى ذاته بالصفات

صدرت افعاله ابتداءً

فيُجرى الحقيقة المحمّدية 10

فبالامر يكون الكون الاوّل

فبتضمّنها بالعلم والقدرة

## The Subtleties
### *In the Name of God, the All-merciful, the Ever-merciful*

### The First Chapter
### Clarifying the Descents of the Macrocosm[4]

Glory be to Him who was a Hidden Treasure!
    He is an Origin without beginning, unqualified,
        an utter Essence, unclothed.
This alone is a True Existence
5     and an Exclusive Unity within which are enfolded the tasks.
    Since the tasks are enfolded within [the Exclusive Unity],
    His attributes are not distinct from It.
    When His Essence discloses Itself through the attributes,
    His acts emerge at the beginning.
10    He brings to pass the Muhammadan Reality,
    so, the First Engendered Being comes to be by the Command.
    Since [the Muhammadan Reality] comprises knowledge
        and power,

爰分性智
一實萬分
15　人天理備
中含妙質
是謂元氣
先天之末
後天之根
20　承元妙化
首判陽陰
陽舒陰斂
變爲火水
火水相搏
25　爰生氣土
氣火外發
爲天爲星
土水内積
爲地爲海
30　高卑既定

   and then differentiated into nature and wisdom.　1.5
   This one reality has ten thousand differentiations
15　and equips both humans and heaven with principles.
   In their midst is contained the subtle stuff,
   which is called the "original vital-energy."　1.6
   It is the end of the Former Heaven
   and the taproot of the Latter Heaven.　1.7
20　Following the origin, the subtle transforms,　0.3
   dividing first into yin and yang.
   Yang expands and yin contracts,
   altering into fire and water.　1.8
   Water and fire wrestle together,
25　thereby begetting air and soil.　1.9
   Air and fire issue outside,
   making heaven and making the stars.
   Soil and water accumulate inside,
   making the earth and making the ocean.　1.10
30　When high and low are made firm,

قسّمه الله الى نفس وعقل
فيانشعابهما
تمّت ملكوت الانسان والسماء    15
ثمّ بقيت فى ضمنهما درادى لطيفة
و سمّيت الهباء الاولى
و هى آخر الملكوت
و اساس الملك
فيتقسّم اصلها    20
فرّقها الله اوّلاً الى حَرّانية وقَرّانية
فانبسطت الحرّانية وانقبضت القرّانية
فجعلهما الله ناراً وماءً
فبامتزاجهما وتضادّهما
أحدث الله الهواء والتراب    25
امّا الهواء والنار فيتوجّهان الى الخارج
فجعل الله الهواء السماوات والنار كواكبها
و امّا التراب والماء فباقيان فى الداخل
فجعل الله التراب الارض والماء بحاراً
فلمّا أسكن الفوقانية والتحتانية    30

God divided [the First Being] into a soul and an intellect.
When these two branch out,

15    the Sovereignty of humans and heaven is complete.
Then within the two remained subtle dregs,
which were named "the First Dust."
It is the last of the Sovereignty
and the foundation of the Kingdom.

20  By the division of the root [of the Dust],
God separated it first into a fervid and a frigid.
The fervid expanded, and the frigid contracted;
so God made the two fire and water.
Through their commingling and mutual opposition,

25    God brought forth air and soil.
As for the air and the fire, they face outside;
so God made the air the heavens, and the fire their stars.
As for the soil and the water, they remain inside;
so God made the soil the earth, and the water oceans.

30    When He stilled the aboveness and the belowness,

庶類中生 (道行推原經)
造化流行
至土而止
流盡則返
35　返與水合
而生金石
金與火合
而生草木
木與氣合
40　而生活類 (格致全經)
活與理合
而人生焉 (道行推原經)
氣火水土
謂之四元
45　金木活類
謂之三子
四元三子
謂之七行

every kind is begotten in the midst. (*Path*)[5]
When the creative transformation flows and goes,
it stops upon reaching soil.
When the flow fully realizes itself, it returns.
35    When it returns, [soil] unites with water,
and metal and stone are begotten.
When metal and fire unite,
grass and wood are begotten.
When wood and air unite,
40    the living kinds are begotten. (*Standpoints*)[6]
When the living and the principles unite,
humans are begotten. (*Path*)[7]
Air, fire, water, and soil
are called "the four origins."
45    Metal, wood, and the living kinds
are called "the three children."
The four origins and the three children
are called "the seven agents."

أحدث بينهما الاجناس
بأنّ نزول التخليق
الى التراب انتهى
ثمّ بعد انتهائه انقلب الى العروج
فبتركيب التراب مع الماء     35
أحدث اللّه المعادن والاحجار
ثم بتركيب المعدنى مع النار
أحدث النباتات
ثم بتركيب النباتى مع الهواء
أحدث الحيوانات     40
ثم بتركيب الحيوان مع الروح الانسانية
أحدث الانسان
اما الهواء والنار والماء والتراب
فمسمّاة بالوالدات الاربع
والمعادن والنباتات والحيوانات     45
بالمواليد الثلاثة
و الوالدات والمواليد
بالاركان السبعة

He brought forth between them the kinds,
  because the descent of creation
  comes to an end at the soil.
Then, after coming to an end, it turns back toward the ascent.
35   By compounding the soil with the water,
  God brought forth the minerals and the stones.
  Then, by compounding the mineral with the fire,
  He brought forth the plants.
  Then, by compounding the vegetal with the air,
40   He brought forth the animals.
  Then, by compounding the animals with the human spirit,
  He brought forth humans.
As for the air, fire, water, and soil,
  they are named "the four progenitors";
45   the minerals, plants, and animals,
  "the three progeny";
  and the progenitors and the progeny,
  "the seven pillars."

七行分布
50      萬彙生成 (格致全經又研真經)
殊形別類
異質分宗 (格致全經)
理隨氣化
各賦所生 (費隱經)
55      大化循環
盡終返始
故惟人也
獨秉元精
妙合元真
60      理象既全
造化成矣 (道行推原經)

When the seven agents spread out,
50      ten thousand classes are begotten and come to be.
    *(Standpoints, Goal)*[8]                                    1.11
The forms come to be particularized, the kinds distinct,
    the stuffs different, and the families differentiated.
        *(Standpoints)*
    The principles accompany the transformation of
        vital-energy,
    and both are bestowed on what is begotten. *(Rays)*
55  The great transformation follows a circle;                 0.6
    when the end is fully realized, it returns to the beginning.
    Since only humans
    grasp uniquely the original essence,
    they are subtly united with the original Real.
60      When principles and images are completed,
    the creative transformation is perfected. *(Path)*       1.12

فبانبساط هذه السبعة

حصّل الله الاجناس نتيجةً    50

و بتباين صورها جعلها انواعاً متغائرة

و بتفاوت موادّها جعل خواصّها متفاوتة

و ملكوت كلّ شىء انما تظهر بمتابعة ملكه

و هو بها يُنتج

و تخليق العالم الكبير كدائرة    55

عاد مُنتهاها الى مَبدئها

و لكون الانسان منتهى المخلوقات

عليهم انطبع ما فيها من الخلاصة

و اتّصلت لطافتهم الى الحقّ

فلمّا اتمّ الملكوت والملك بهم    60

حصّل التخليق

 

By deploying these seven,

50     God actualized the kinds as the result.

Through the dissimilarity of their forms, He made them
       different species,

     and through the disparity of their matters, He made their
       characteristics disparate.

     Each thing's Sovereignty becomes manifest only by following
       its Kingdom,

     and [the thing] gives results by means of [the Sovereignty].

55  The creation of the macrocosm is like a circle

     whose endpoint returns to its origin.

     Since human beings are the endpoint of the created things,

     the quintessence of these is imprinted within them

     and their subtleness conjoins with the Real.

60     When He completed the Sovereignty and the Kingdom with them,

     He actualized the creation.

第二章
分述天地人物各具之功能

一眞衍化
理象章陳
理具於知
象見於能 (費隱經)
5    知預先天
能衍後天
先以象著
後以理形 (道行推原經)
理象相屬
10    性命以位 (研眞經)
理象附形
妙用以呈 (道行推原經)
人曰知能
物曰功用 (同上)

## Chapter Two
### *Specific Statement on the Endeavor and Power Embedded in Each of Heaven and Earth, Humans and Things*

The One Real expands and transforms,
    ornamenting and arranging the principles and images.
    The principles are embedded in knowledge,
    the images are seen in power. (*Rays*)[9]
5    Knowledge is beforehand in the Former Heaven,
    and power expands in the Latter Heaven.
    The Former is displayed by the images
    and the Latter is formed by the principles. (*Path*)[10]
Principles and images belong to each other,
10    so the natures and mandates take up their positions. (*Goal*)[11]
    When principles and images adhere to the forms,
    the subtle functions are disclosed. (*Path*)
    In humans one speaks of knowledge and power,
    in things one speaks of endeavors and functions. (Ibid.)

الفصل الثانى
فى بيان خواصّ المخلوقات

لمّا تجلّى وجود الحقّ
ظهرت حقائق الاشياء وصورها
فالحقائق مودعة فى علمه تعالى
والصور مرئية بقدرته تعالى
فعلمه تعالى قبل الملكوت                    5
و قدرته منها الى الملك
و الملكوت انما ظهرت باجسام
و صور الملك انما تصوّرت بارواح
فلمّا توافقت طبقاتهما
استقرّت كلّ درجة من الارواح فى طبقة        10
فلمّا اجتمعتا وتصوّرتا
ظهرت صفات الحقّ تعالى فيها
الّا انّها فى حقّ الانسان مسمّاة بالعلم والقدرة
و فى الاشياء بالخاصّة

## The Second Chapter
### *Clarifying the Characteristics of the Created Things*

When the Existence of the Real disclosed Itself,
    the realities of the things and their forms became manifest.
The realities are deposited in His knowledge,[12]
    and the forms are visible through His power.
5    His knowledge is before the Sovereignty,
    and His power is from it to the Kingdom.
The Sovereignty becomes manifest only through bodies,
    and the forms of the Kingdom take form only
        through spirits.
Since the layers of the two correspond,
10    each degree of the spirits settles down in a layer.
When the two combine and take form,
    within them become manifest the attributes of the Real.
In humans, however, these are named "knowledge and power,"
    and in things, "characteristics."

15    理同氣異
      以辨愚智
      體圓用虧
      以適時宜 (費隱經)
      渾同知能
20    是至聖性
      任用知能
      是大聖性
      順應知能
      是欽聖性
25    顯揚知能
      是列聖性
      希望知能
      是大賢性
      體認知能
30    是智者性
      堅守知能
      是廉介性

15  The principle is the same, but the vital-energy different;
        so the ignorant are distinguished from the wise.
        The substance is full, but the function deficient,
        thereby suiting what is right at the time. (*Rays*)              2.1
      Making knowledge and power an undifferentiated sameness
20      is the nature of the Utmost Sage.
        Efficaciously using knowledge and power
        is the nature of the great sages.
        Obediently responding to knowledge and power
        is the nature of the ambassador sages.
25      Manifesting and elevating knowledge and power
        is the nature of the average sages.
        Hoping for and looking toward knowledge and power
        is the nature of the great worthies.
        Embodying recognition of knowledge and power
30      is the nature of the wise.
        Firmly guarding knowledge and power
        is the nature of the pure and upright.

و الروح الانسانية سواء والنفسانية متفاوتة 15
و لذا صار بعضهم جاهلاً و بعضهم عالماً
و لانّ ذات الحقّ احدية وصفاته متفاوتة
فمظاهرها توافق حالها
و اتحاد العلم والقدرة مع الحقّ تعالى
لنفس خاتم الانبياء 20
و بالخيار استعمالهما منه تعالى
لنفوس اولى العزم
و بهما الانقياد والاجابة
لنفوس المرسلين
و بهما اظهار الدعوة والتبليغ 25
لنفوس الانبياء
و بهما الطمع والتمنّى
لنفوس الاولياء
و بهما تحصيل معرفة الحقّ
لنفوس العارفين 30
و بهما اتقان المحافظة
لنفوس الزاهدين

15 The human spirit is the same, but the psychical [spirit] is disparate.
   That is why some of them become ignorant and some knowing,
   and because the Real's Essence is unitary and His attributes
      disparate,
   so the loci of manifestation [of the attributes] conform with
      their state.
   Unification of knowledge and power with the Real
20 belongs to the soul of the Seal of the Prophets.
   Employing them by choice on His behalf
   belongs to the souls of the Possessors of Constancy.
   Acquiescing and responding to them
   belongs to the souls of the messengers.
25 Making manifest the call and conveying [the message] with them
   belong to the souls of the prophets.
   Craving and wishing by them
   belongs to the souls of the saints.
   Actualizing recognition of the Real by them
30 belongs to the souls of the gnostics.
   Making observance firm with them
   belongs to the souls of the ascetics.

循習知能
是善人性
35    自用知能
是庸常性
禽獸知覺
草木生發
金石堅定
40    同是知能
弗稱知能 (研眞經又道行推原經)
惟阿而實
代行化育
惟庫而西
45    錯合變化
創無爲有
厥惟土天
發隱成著
厥惟木天

Following and practicing knowledge and power
is the nature of good people.
35    Selfish use of knowledge and power
is the nature of the common people.
Birds and beasts have knowledge and awareness,
grass and trees begetting and issuing,
metal and stone hardness and firmness;
40    these are the same as knowledge and power,
but they are not designated as knowledge and power.
(*Goal, Path*)                                    2.2
Only Aershi                                       2.3
acts on behalf [of the Real] to transform and nurture.
Only Kuerxi
45    mixes and unites, alters and transforms.
Creating being from nonbeing is
only the soil-heaven (Saturn).
Issuing the hidden and bringing forth the displayed is
only the wood-heaven (Jupiter).

و بهما طلب العبودية
لنفوس العابدين
و بهوى النفس استعمالهما     35
لنفوس العاصين
و اما احساس الطيور والبهائم
و حياة النباتات ونموّها
و شدّة الصلابة فى المعادن والاحجار
فكلّها من علمه تعالى و قدرته     40
و لم توصف بهما
و امّا خاصّة العرش
فمُفيضة التكوين والتربية عن الحقّ
و اما خاصّة الكرسي
فموقّقة بين الخواصّ و متصرّفة فيها     45
و اخراج المعدوم الى الوجود
بخاصّة فلك زحل
و انبات الخبايا واظهارها
بخاصّة فلك المشترى

Seeking servanthood with them
    belongs to the souls of the worshipers.
35    Employing them in the soul's caprice
    belongs to the souls of the disobedient.
As for the sense-perception of birds and beasts,
    the life and growth of plants,
    and intense hardness in minerals and stones,
40    all of those are from His knowledge and power
    but are not described by them.
As for the characteristic of the Throne,
    it is to effuse engendering and nurturing from
        the Real.
The characteristic of the Footstool
45    is to reconcile and control the characteristics.
Sending forth the nonexistent into existence
    is by the characteristic of the sphere of Saturn.
Making concealed things sprout and become
        manifest
    is by the characteristic of the sphere of Jupiter.

50    化小爲大
      厥惟火天
      章明貴顯
      厥惟日天
      結交離合
55    厥惟金天
      化蠢爲靈
      厥爲水天
      改移流動
      厥惟月天
60    風以動之
      火以發之
      水以滋之
      土以奠之
      金以定固
65    木以建立
      活類運行
      凡是功用

50    Transforming the small into the great is
      only the fire-heaven (Mars).
      Ornamenting clarity and ennobling manifestation is
      only the sun-heaven.
      Connecting and exchanging separations and unions is
55    only the metal-heaven (Venus).
      Transforming the doltish into the spiritual is
      only the water-heaven (Mercury).
      Altering and shifting, flowing and moving is
      only the moon-heaven.
60  Wind moves,
      fire issues forth,
      water soaks,
      soil settles down,
      metal firms and fixes,
65    wood erects and establishes,
      the living kinds turn and travel.                    2.4
    On all these endeavors and functions

و جعل الصغير كبيراً 50
بخاصّة فلك المرّيخ
و اظهار الخواصّ والخلاصة
بخاصّة فلك الشمس
و تلصيق الاجزاء و توفيق الاضداد
بخاصّة فلك الزهرة 55
و جعل الكثائف لطائف
بخاصّة فلك عطارد
والتغيير والازالة والتبديل
بخاصّة فلك القمر
و خاصّة الريح التحريك 60
والنار تقوية النماء
والماء الترطيب
والتراب التسكين
والمعادن التثبيت والتوثيق
والنباتات الاقامة 65
والحيوانات الحركة والمشى
و كلّ خاصّة

50    Making the small large
    is by the characteristic of the sphere of Mars.
    Manifesting the characteristics and quintessence
    is by the characteristic of the sphere of the sun.
    Sticking parts together and reconciling opposites
55    is by the characteristic of the sphere of Venus.
    Making dense things into subtle things
    is by the characteristic of the sphere of Mercury.
    Altering, removing, and exchanging
    is by the characteristic of the sphere of the moon.
60  The characteristic of wind is to cause movement,
    of fire to strengthen growth,
    of water to moisten,
    of soil to induce stillness,
    of minerals to fix and firm,
65    of plants to raise up,
    and of animals to move and walk.
    Every characteristic

萬化仰藉
一粟之生
70    九天之力 (格致全經又天經情性)
日星景麗
元象以見
東西運旋
變化以出 (同上)
75    四行專注
方位以定
四氣流通
歲時以成 (格致全經)
七洲分地
80    物產以異
四際分空
化育以從
雲雨雪雹
霧露沙塵
85    皆所由資

the ten thousand transformations depend and rely.                    2.5
The begetting of one grain
70    is the strength of the nine heavens. (*Standpoints, Stars*)[13]    2.6
In the brightness and beauty of sun and stars
the original images are seen.
East and west turn and rotate
and alteration and transformation emerge. (*Standpoints, Stars*)  2.7
75    When the four agents are specifically focused,
the directions and positions are made firm.                            2.8
When the four vital-energies flow and pervade,
the times and seasons come into being. (*Standpoints*)[14]           2.9
The seven climes differentiate the earth,
80    so things and products are different.                                  2.10
The four boundaries differentiate the emptiness,
and transformation and nurture follow.
Cloud, rain, snow, and hail,
fog, dew, sand, and dust—
85    all are caused by the assistance

ممّا يحتاج اليه جميع المخلوقات
لانّ انبات حبّة
70    بتقوية الافلاك التسعة
و بظهور الشمس والنجوم
أبصرت الافلاك
و بحركتها من المشرق والمغرب
يصدر التحويل والتصوير
75    و يتمكين أربعة عناصر
تعيّنت الجهات
و بتعاقب تأثيراتها
تحصُل الاوقات الاربعة فى كلّ سنة
و بتقسيم الارض الى سبعة اقاليم
80    تتفاوت الاشياء والنتائج
وبتقسيم آثار الاربعة فى الهواء
يخلق منها اشياء التربية
لانّ السحاب والمطر والثلج و البرد
والبخار والندى والرمل والغبار
85    انما خلقها الله بتأثيرها

is needed by all created things;
the spheres are seen.
for making a grain sprout
70    is by the strengthening of the nine spheres.
When sun and stars become manifest,
the spheres are seen.
When they move from east and west,
transmuting and form-giving emerge.
75    When the four elements are firmly established,
the directions are designated.
When they leave successive traces,
the four seasons happen every year.
By the division of the earth into seven climes,
80    things and results become disparate.
By dividing the traces of the four [elements] in the air,
He creates from them the things of nurturing,
for clouds, rain, snow, and hail,
vapor, dew, sand, and dust,
85    these God creates only by [the elements'] leaving traces

以妙元功 (同上)
察形辨義
觀象悟理
先天後天
90　　一貫而已 (昭微經)

    of the subtlety of the original endeavor. (Ibid.)[15]　　　　2.11
Observe the forms and discriminate the meanings,
    look at the images and awaken to the principles—
    the Former Heaven and the Latter Heaven
90　  are on one thread, nothing more. (*Gleams*)　　　　　　2.12

و بلطافة خواصّ اصولها
فاذا تتبّعتَ فى الاجسام و ميّزت بين معانيها
و أبصرت صورها و تأمّلت فى حقائقها
فالملكوت والملك
تجلّى الذات الاحدية　　90

and by the subtlety of the characteristics of their roots.
So, when you investigate the bodies, distinguish among
　　their meanings,
　gaze upon their forms, and ponder their realities,
　the Sovereignty and the Kingdom
90　are the self-disclosure of the Unitary Essence.

第三章
總述小世界身性顯著之由

溟漠運精
元祖誕降
髭乳感孕
支裔衍生 (道行推原經)
5  初惟一點
是爲種子
藏於父脊
授於母宮
承繼先天
10  妙演後天
胚胎兆化
分清分濁
本其二氣
化爲四液


## Chapter Three

*Comprehensive Statement on the Cause of the Manifestation
and Display of the Body and Nature of the Microcosm*


Vastly and boundlessly the essence turned,
    and the original ancestor was begotten and descended.
    The influence of moustache and breasts led to pregnancy,
    and branches and descendents were begotten and spread. (*Path*)
5  In the beginning was only the One Spot,                0.4
    and this was the seed
    stored in the father's spine
    and then conferred on the mother's womb.
    It followed by continuity from the Former Heaven,
10    it extended by subtlety into the Latter Heaven.       3.1
The embryo gave signs of transformation
    and was differentiated into pure and turbid.          3.2
    Rooted in these two vital-energies
    it transformed to become four liquids—

الفصل الثالث
فى بيان خلق البشر

جمع اللطيف الجليل سبحانه الصفوة
فخلق منها ابا البشر
ثمّ عند ظهور الشارب والثدى بالازدواج والحمل
تتوالد الشعوب والقبائل
و ابتداؤه انما كان بنطفة                                    5
و هى بذرة
كانت مختفيةً فى صلب الاب
فأُمنيت فى رحم الامّ
و عينها متّصلة بنزول الملكوت
و لطافتها سائرة الى عروج الملك              10
والحمل كالهباء الاولى
حيث انقسم الى لطيفة وكثيفة
فبنضج هاتين
صارتا أربع طبقات

### The Third Chapter
*Clarifying the Creation of Mankind*

The Subtle, the Majestic—glory be to Him!—gathered the
    most limpid
    and from it created the father of mankind.
When moustache and breasts became manifest, by pairing
    and pregnancy
    branches and tribes were born.
5  His beginning was only a sperm-drop,
    and it is a seed
    that was hidden in the father's loins,
    then emitted into the mother's womb.
    Its entity was conjoined with the descent of the Sovereignty,
10    its subtleness traveling to the ascent of the Kingdom.
Pregnancy was like the First Dust
    inasmuch as it divided into subtle and dense.
    By the ripening of these two
    they became four layers—

15      黑紅黃白
        層包次第
        四本升降
        表裏形焉
        紅者爲心
20      黃者其包
        黑者爲身
        白者其脉
        身心既定
        諸竅生焉
25      肝脾肺腎
        眼耳口鼻
        體竅既全
        靈活生焉 (研眞經又道行推原經又格致全經)
        靈活爲物
30      包備萬性
        與種俱存
        與胎俱生

15      black, red, yellow, and white,
            whose layers were wrapped in sequence.                   3.3
    The four roots ascended and descended,
            forming outward and inward.
            The red became the heart,
20          the yellow its wrap,
            the black the body,
            the white its veins.                                      3.4
    When body and heart became firm,
            the diverse apertures were begotten—
25          liver, spleen, lungs, and kidney,
            eyes, ears, mouth, and nose.                              3.5
            When the bodily apertures were completed,
            the spiritually living was begotten. (*Goal, Path, Standpoints*)[16]
    As a thing, the spiritually living
30          completely enwraps the ten thousand natures.
            It was preserved along with the seed,
            and was begotten along with the embryo.

سوداء وحمراء وصفراء وبيضاء　15

و أحاطت طبقة منها بأخرى على الترتيب

فاذا ارتفعت هذه الاربع و تنزّلت

تصوّرت الظاهرية والباطنية

فصارت الحمراء قلباً

والصفراء محيطة به　20

والسوداء جسداً

والبيضاء عروقاً

فلمّا تمكّن الجسد والقلب

أحدث الله الاعضاء

و هى الكبد والطحال والرية والكلية　25

والعين والاذن والفم والانف

فلمّا أتمّ الله القالب والاعضاء

نتجت الروح الملكوتية

و هي حقيقة

متضمّنة بجميع النفوس　30

كانت مودعة فى النطفة

فوقعت معها فى الرحم

15　black, red, yellow, and white,
　　one layer encompassing another in order.
When the four went up and came down,
　　outwardness and inwardness took form.
　　The red became a heart,
20　while the yellow encompassed it,
　　the black a body,
　　and the white veins.
When body and heart were firmly established,
　　God brought forth the organs,
25　which are liver, spleen, lungs, and kidneys;
　　eyes, ears, mouth, and nose.
　　When God completed the frame and the organs,
　　the Sovereigntarial spirit was the result.
It is a reality
30　that comprises all the souls.
　　It was deposited in the sperm-drop,
　　so it fell along with it into the womb.

隨厥形化
而運其機
35    俟其體全
而著其跡 (道行推原經)
子吸氣血
由臍入胃
而堅定啓
40    是爲金性
百體資之
由胃入肝
而長養生
是爲木性
45    吸化資之
由肝入心
而活性成
是爲生性
運動資之
50    自心升腦

It accompanies the transformation of the forms
and it turns with its own mechanism.
35    It waits for the body to be completed,
and then displays its traces. (*Path*)[17]
When the child sucks in vital-energy and blood,
which enter the stomach by way of the navel,
hardness and firmness begin;
40    this is "the nature of metal,"
which assists the one hundred bodily members.
When it enters the liver by way of the stomach,
growth and nourishment are begotten;
this is "the nature of wood,"
45    which assists sucking and transforming.
When it enters the heart by way of the liver,
the nature of the living comes to be;
this is "the nature of begetting,"
which assists turning and movement.
50    When it ascends to the brain from the heart,

فباتّباع تحوّل صورتها
تتحرّك قرينتها
حتّى اذا أتمّ الله القالب    35
أظهر آثارها
فجذب الجنين البخار والدم
فدخلا من سرّته الى معدته
فيبتدئ الوثاقة والتثبيت
وهى الروح المعدنية    40
فيتغذّى بهما جميع قالبه
فاذا دخلت خلاصة ذلك من معدته فى كبده
حدث النشو والنماء
و هي الروح النباتية
فيتقوّى بها الجذب والهضم    45
فاذا دخلت من كبده الى قلبه
فيها حصلت الحياة
و هى الروح الحيوانية
فيحدث بها الحركة
فاذا دخلت من قلبه الى دماغه    50

By following the transmutation of [the sperm-drop's] form
the form's comrade [i.e., the spirit] moves.
35    When God completed the frame,
He made manifest the [spirit's] traces.
The embryo attracted vapor and blood,
which entered its stomach from its navel,
so firmness and fixity begin,
40    and this is the mineral spirit,
and its whole frame is nourished by the two [vapor and blood].
When the quintessence of that [nourishment] entered its liver from
its stomach,
configuration and growth came forth,
and this is the vegetal spirit,
45    through which attraction and digestion are strengthened.
When [the quintessence] entered its heart from its liver,
thereby life was obtained,
and this is the animal spirit,
through which movement comes forth.
50  When it entered its brain from its heart

而知覺具
是爲覺性
外之五官
內之五司
55  一切能力
皆所資之
是諸所有
四月而成
五月筋骨
60  爲堅定顯
六月毛髮
爲長性顯
七月豁達
爲活性顯 (研眞經又格致全經)
65  生四十日
愛惡言笑
爲氣性顯
長遵禮節

knowledge and awareness come to be embedded;
this is "the nature of awareness."
The five external senses,
the five internal managers,
55  and every power and strength
are all assisted by it.
Whatever these diverse things may be,
all are perfected in four months.                          3.9
In the fifth month muscles and bones
60  manifest hardness and firmness.
In the sixth month locks and hair
manifest "the nature of growth."
In the seventh month volition
manifests "the nature of the living." (*Goal, Standpoints*)[18]
65  Forty days after birth,
love, hate, speech, and laughter
manifest "the nature of vital-energy."                      3.10
Growing to respect propriety and ritual

فبها حدث الادراك والاحساس
وهى الروح النفسانية
والحواسّ الخمس الظاهرية
والخمس الباطنية
و سائر القوى 55
كلّها منها حادثة
و هذه المذكورة
فى الشهر الرابع حاصلة
و فى الشهر الخامس صلبت أعصابه وعظامه
بظهور الروح المعدنية 60
و فى السادس نشأت شعراته
بظهور النباتية
و فى السابع تحرّك بالارادة
بظهور الحيوانية
و بعد اكمال ولادته اربعين يوماً 65
حدثت الشهوة والغضب حتى يبكى ويضحك
بظهور النفسانية
حتّى اذا بلغ و عمل بالآداب والعبادات

thereby perception and sensation came forth,
and this is the psychical spirit.
The five outward senses,
the five inward,
55 and the rest of the faculties
all come forth from it.
All these mentioned things
are obtained in the fourth month.
In the fifth month [the embryo's] sinews and bones become hard
60 by means of the manifestation of the mineral spirit.
In the sixth its hair is configured
by means of the manifestation of the vegetal [spirit].
In the seventh it moves by volition
by means of the manifestation of the animal [spirit].
65 Forty days after it completes its birth,
appetite and wrath come forth, so that it may weep and laugh,
by means of the manifestation of the psychical [spirit].
Finally, when he matures and performs acts of courtesy and worship

善用明悟
70   爲本性顯
功修既至
窮究既通
理明物化
神應周徧
75   爲德性顯
德性既顯
本然乃全
是謂返本
是謂還原
80   生人能事
至此而全 (道行推原經又研眞經)

and good use of clarity and awakening
70   manifest "the root nature."                              3.11
When he reaches the utmost in endeavor and cultivation
and achieves penetration in exhaustive examination,
then the principles will be clarified, things transformed,
and the spirit will respond wholly and impartially,
75   making manifest "the nature of virtue."
When the nature of virtue becomes manifest,               0.7
the Root Suchness is complete.
This is called "return to the Root"
and is called "circling back to the Origin."
80   The powerful affair of begetting humans
reaches its completion here. (*Path, Goal*)[19]            3.12

و حسّن صفاته والتمييز والفكر
ظهرت الروح الانسانية    70
و اذا استكمل العبادات والرياضات
و استوفى معرفة الله
و انكشف عنده الحقائق و فنى عن الاشياء
حتّى تؤثّر صفات الحقّ على قواه
ظهرت الروح الاضافية    75
و اذا ظهرت فيه
فهو مظهر ذات الحقّ وصفاته
و تسمّى وصال الله
و فناء فى الله
و غاية ايجاد الخلق    80
كاملة بوصوله الى هذا

and beautifies his attributes, discernment, and thought,

70    the human spirit becomes manifest.

When he perfects the acts of worship and ascetic disciplines
and he achieves full recognition of God,
and when the realities are unveiled for him and he is
annihilated from the things
such that the Real's attributes leave traces in his faculties,

75    then the Ascribed Spirit becomes manifest.

When it becomes manifest within him
he is the locus of manifestation for the Real's Essence
and attributes.
This is named "arrival at God"
and "annihilation in God."

80    The final goal of giving existence to the creatures
is perfected when he arrives at this.

第四章
分述小世界身心性命所藏之用

非性無心
非心無性
心性會合
全德昭焉 (道行推原經)
5    心含七德
作是靈明
順於心包
信於其表
惠於其裏
10   明識在靈
篤眞在仁
發隱其妙
眞現初心
初心著用

## Chapter Four

### *Specific Statement on the Functions Stored in the Body, Heart, Nature, and Mandate of the Microcosm*

There is no heart without nature,
    and no nature without heart.
    When nature and heart meet and unite,
    complete virtue is shown. (*Path*)        4.1
5   The heart contains seven virtues
    which bring about spiritual clarity.
    Obedience is in the heart's wrap,
    faithfulness in its outward,
    kindness in its inward;
10    clear discernment is in the spiritual,
    authentic realness in the kernel,
    issuing forth the hidden is the subtlety,
    and the appearance of the Real is the first heart.    4.2
When the first heart displays the functions,

الفصل الرابع
فى بيان خواصّ الانسان

لا يوجد القلب بدون النفس
ولا تظهر النفس بدون القلب
فمتى اتّفقا
ظهر كلّ الجمال
اما القلب فمتضمّن بسبعة كنوز          ٥
بها صارت الروح متنوّرة
امّا الاسلام ففى الصدر
و الايمان فى القلب
و الرقّة فى الشغاف
و حقّ المعرفة فى الفؤاد          ١٠
و خلوص التوجّه الى الحقّ فى حبّة القلب
و كشف الاسرار المختفية فى السويداء
و تجلّى الحقّ فى مهجة القلب
و اذا انكشف هذا القلب

### The Fourth Chapter
*Clarifying the Characteristics of*
*the Human Being*

The heart does not come into existence without the soul,
    and the soul does not become manifest without the heart.
    When the two coincide,
    every beauty becomes manifest.
5   As for the heart, it comprises seven treasures[20]
    through which the spirit becomes illuminated.
    Submission is in the breast,
    faith in the heart,
    gentleness in the heart's cover,
10   true recognition in the inner heart,
    purity of facing the Real in the heart's seed,
    unveiling of the hidden mysteries in the core,
    and the self-disclosure of the Real in the heart's lifeblood.
When this heart is unveiled,

15    妙應無方
      全體大用
      莫或遺藏 (道行推原經)
      先天來降
      後天復升
20    來自此心
      復於此心 (道行推原經又研眞經)
      兩弧界合
      復滿圓形 (眞經注又費隱經)
      人若燈具
25    眞光其火
      不獲眞光
      徒爲人具 (眞經注又研眞經又道行推原經)
      人極大全
      無美不備
30    既美其形
      復美其妙 (道行推原經又研眞經)


15    the subtle responses have no limits,
         for the Complete Substance and Great Function
         do not exclude or hide anything. (*Path*)[21]
      The Former Heaven comes in descent,
         and the Latter Heaven goes back in ascent.
20    The coming is from this heart
         and the going back is to this heart. (*Path*, *Goal*)
      "When the worlds of the two arcs are united,"[22]
         they go back to the fullness of the round form. (*Commentary*,
            *Rays*)                                                          4.3
      Humans are like a lamp's apparatus,
25    and the Real Light is its fire.
      If it does not catch the Real Light,
         then the human apparatus acts in vain. (*Commentary*, *Goal*,
            *Path*)[23]
      The Human Ultimate is the great completion
         equipped with every beauty.
30    When the form is beautified,
         the subtlety's beauty goes back. (*Path*, *Goal*)                   4.4

15 فليس لظهور كراماته نهاية
لانّ أسماء الحقّ وصفاته
لا تشذّ ولا تخفى
و ظهور الملكوت بالمجيئ والنزول
والملك بالاعادة والعروج
20 والمجيئ منذ هذا القلب
و اليه الاعادة
فاذا انطبق القوسان
فبانتهاء الاعادة صارا دائرةً
والانسان كآلات المصباح
25 و نور الحقّ ناره
فمن لم يصل اليه
فهو مجرّد الآلات الانسانية
و انسان كامل واصل
فما من جمال الا و هو فيه منتظم
30 فانّه اذا جمّل آلاته
عاد جمال نور الحقّ

15 the manifestation of its miracles has no end,
    because the names and attributes of the Real
    are neither lacking nor hidden.
The Sovereignty becomes manifest in coming
        and descent,
    and the Kingdom in return and ascent.
20 The coming is from this heart,
    and to it is the return.
    When the two arcs coincide,
    by reaching the end of the return, they become
        a circle.
Humans are like the apparatus of a lamp,
25 and the light of the Real is its fire.
    Anyone who does not arrive at it
    is merely the human apparatus.
As for a Perfect Human Being who arrives,
    every beauty is arranged within him.
30 For, when he beautifies his apparatus,
    the beauty of the light of the Real returns.

本然流行
貫合粗精
自眞來我
35　造化爲之
自我復眞
人爲爲之 (費隱經)
本其各具
尋其公共
40　渾融沕合
卷其跡相 (同上)
惟是聖人
實踐其境
眾則難之
45　自取暗昧
陷於疑逆
徒致瀆累 (道行推原經)
聖賢智愚
由是而分

The ongoing flow of the Root Suchness
　　threads through and unites the coarse and the fine.
　　Coming from the Real to the I
35　　is the work of the creative transformation.
　　Going back from the I to the Real
　　is the work of human acts. (*Rays*)
The root embedded in all
　　searches for what is shared in common.
40　　When there is undifferentiated melting and deep uniting
　　the traces and guises are rolled up. (Ibid.)
Only the sages
　　truly practice this realm.
　　As for the multitudes, it is difficult,
45　　for they bring darkness and obscurity upon themselves.
　　They are trapped in doubt and rebellion,
　　resulting in vain dispersion and burdens. (*Path*)
Sages, worthies, wise, and ignorant
　　are thereby differentiated.

و سريان وجود الحقّ
ممتلئ فى الغلائظ واللطائف
و المجيء من الحقّ الينا
بمجرّد تخليقه     35
والاعادة منّا اليه
بأعمالنا البشرية
فنكون بوجودنا المقيّد
طالبين للمطلق
حتّى اذا تواصلا وامتزجا     40
اندرجت الآثار البشرية
و انما الانبياء
واصلون بالحقيقة الى هذا المقام
و هو على سائر البشر متعذّر
فانّهم بما كسبوا من الظلمة     45
غمسوا فى الشكّ والشرك
و ذهبوا الى التفرّق والتعب
والانبياء والمخلصون والعلماء والجهلاء
من هذا المقام منقسمون

The flow of the Existence of the Real
   fills all things coarse and subtle.
The coming from the Real to us
35   is simply by His creating,
The returning from us to Him
   is by our human acts.
With our delimited existence we are
   seeking the Nondelimited.
40   When the two arrive together and commingle,
   the human traces are enfolded.
Only the prophets
   truly arrive at this station.
It is not feasible for the rest of the people,
45   for they, because of the darkness they have acquired,
   are plunged in doubt and association [of others with God]
   and have gone into dispersion and drudgery.
The prophets, the sincere, the knowers, and the ignorant
   become divided from this station.

50　　迷異奸邪
　　　從此以判 (同上)
　　　聖人全體
　　　本無明暗
　　　賢則有虧
55　　暗於本然
　　　智暗於性
　　　愚暗於心
　　　暗此蔽彼
　　　本然弗見 (同上)
60　　賢障於己
　　　智障於知
　　　愚障於欲
　　　障淺礙深
　　　本然弗通 (同上)
65　　信理疑事
　　　則爲異端
　　　信事疑理

50　　Deluded, heretic, wicked, and depraved
　　　are thusly divided. (Ibid.)[24]
　　The complete substance of the sages
　　　at root has no clarity or darkness.
　　　Worthies have some defects,
55　　for they are dark in·the root suchness.
　　　The wise are dark in nature,
　　　and the ignorant are dark in the heart.
　　　The darkness of this shades that,
　　　and the Root Suchness is not seen. (Ibid.)　　　4.7
60　Worthies are blocked by self,
　　　the wise are blocked by knowledge,
　　　and the ignorant are blocked by desire.
　　　Though the blockage is shallow, the obstacle is deep,
　　　and the Root Suchness does not pervade. (Ibid.)　　　4.8
65　Being faithful to the principle and doubting affairs
　　　is to become a heretic.
　　　Being faithful in affairs and doubting the principle

والضالّون والمبتدعون والمنافقون والكافرون    50
من هؤلاء متفرّقون
امّا الانبياء بكلّيتهم
فليس لهم حجاب نورانى وظلمانى
والمخلصون لهم نقص
اذ حقائقهم مظلمة    55
والعلماء نفوسهم مظلمة
والجهلاء قلوبهم مظلمة
فان ظلمة هذا تحجب ما وراءه
و به كان الحقّ غير منكشف
فحجاب المخلصين الانانية    60
والعلماء علومهم
والجهلاء شهواتهم
والحجاب بارز والمانع عميق
فيه كان الحقّ غير متّصل
فمنهم من صدّق بالحقّ وفى امور الدين مال    65
فهو من المبتدعين
و من استقام فى الامور ومال عن الحقّ

50   The misguided, the innovators, the hypocrites, and the unbelievers
     split off from these.
   As for all of the prophets,
     none has any luminous or dark veil.
   The sincere have a deficiency
55   because their realities are dark.
   The knowers have dark souls,
     and the ignorant dark hearts.
   The darkness of this veils what is beyond it,
     and because of it the Real is not unveiled.
60  The veil of the sincere is the I-ness,
     of the knowers their sciences,
     and of the ignorant their appetites.
   The veil is prominent and the obstruction deep,
     so because of it the Real is not conjoined [with them].
65  Among them those who acknowledge the Real but deviate in the
       affairs of the religion
     are among the innovators.
   Those who go straight in the affairs but deviate from the Real

則爲疑貳
疑信交衷
70  悵悵無知
則爲迷惑 (眞經注)
心順身逆
是爲疎忽
身順心逆
75  是爲奸佞
心身皆逆
是爲邪逆 (同上)
疑離之漸
逆悖之深 (同上)
80  沉淪物我
本然隔絶 (道行推原經又費隱經)
惟法聖功
修身以禮
明心以道
85  盡性復命

is to be double-minded.
Interweaving faithfulness and doubt in the heart
70  and aimlessly wandering without knowledge[25]
is to be deluded and perplexed. (*Commentary*)                4.9
Those whose hearts obey and whose bodies rebel
   are careless and indifferent.
Those whose bodies obey and whose hearts rebel
75  are wicked and hypocritical.
Those whose bodies and hearts both rebel
   are deprived and rebellious. (Ibid.)                       4.10
Doubt is to depart gradually
   and rebellion is to become deeply perverse. (Ibid.)
80  The things and the I become drowned, ruined,
   and cut off from the Root Suchness. (*Rays, Path*)
Only by emulating[26] the Sage's endeavors,
   cultivating the body with Propriety,
   clarifying the heart with the Way,
85  fully realizing nature, and going back to the Mandate,

فهو من المشركين
و من اجتمع الباطل والحقّ فى قلبه
و لم يعلم ايّهما أصوب 70
فهو من الضالّين
و من اطاع قلبه وعصى جسده
فهو من المقصّرين
و من اطاع جسده وكذّب قلبه
فهو من المنافقين 75
و من أعرض جسده وكذّب قلبه
فاولئك هم الكافرون
والشكّ هو البعد عن الحقّ تدريجةً
والشرك هو الاعراض عنه دفعةً
ويهما غمسوا فى الاشياء والانانية 80
حتى ينقطع عنهم الحق
الا الذين اتّبعوا النبى عليه السلام فى العبادات
فانّهم اذا روّضوا أبدانهم بالشريعة
وجلّوا قلوبهم بالطريقة
و وصلوا نفوسهم الى الروح الاضافية 85

are among the associators.
Those in whose hearts the unreal and the Real come together
70    and who do not know which is more proper
are among the misguided.
Those whose hearts obey but whose bodies disobey
are among the negligent.
Those whose bodies obey but whose hearts deny
75    are among the hypocrites.
Those whose bodies turn away and whose hearts deny—
"those are the unbelievers" [Koran 4:151].
Doubt is to become distant from the Real gradually,
and association is to turn away from Him all at once.
80    Through the two they immerse themselves in things and in I-ness
until the Real is cut off from them;
except those who follow the Prophet—upon whom be peace—in
acts of worship,
for, when they discipline their bodies with the Shariah,
polish their hearts with the Tariqah,
85    and make their souls arrive at the Ascribed Spirit,

全體歸真
本然獨湛
大用全明
是謂人極
90    乃復初心 (道行推原經)

does the Complete Substance come home to the Real.    4.11
The Root Suchness becomes uniquely transparent,
the Great Function completely clear.
This is called the Human Ultimate
90    and going back to the first heart. (*Path*)    4.12

فقد رجعوا بالكلّية الى الحقّ
و فى شهودهم بقيت ذاته تعالى وحدها
و ظهرت صفاته تعالى كلّها فيهم
و سمّوا انساناً كاملاً
لانّهم معادون الى القلب الابتدائى    90

they go back entirely to the Real.
His Essence alone remains in their witnessing,
and all His attributes become manifest within them.
They are named Perfect Humans Beings,

90    because they have returned to the beginning heart.

第五章
總述大小兩世界分合之妙義與天人渾化之極致

惟一非數
是數皆一 (費隱經)
厥初實有
統一統數
5    一者其體
數者其用 (昭微經)
體用渾然
是名眞一
由體起用
10   是名數一
返用歸體
是名體一
三一非三

## Chapter Five
### *Comprehensive Statement on the Subtle Meaning of the Differentiation and Union of Macrocosm and Microcosm and the Ultimate Extension of the Undifferentiated Transformation of Heaven and Human*

Only the One is not a number,
  but all numbers are the One. (*Rays*)[27]
  At the beginning, the True Being
  governs the One and governs the numbers.
5    Oneness is its Substance,
  and the numbers are its functions. (*Gleams*)[28]
The undifferentiated suchness of Substance and function     0.8
  is named "the Real One."
  The Substance's giving rise to the functions
10   is named "the Numerical One."
  The functions' returning and coming home to the Substance
  is named "the Embodied One."
The three ones are not three:

الفصل الخامس
جامع ما تقدّم فى الفصول السابقة

انما الواحد ليس بعدد
و جميع الاعداد عين الواحد
امّا الوجود الحقّ المَبدئى
فجامع للاحدية والتعدّديات
والاحدية ذاته تعالى　　5
والتعدّديات شؤوناته
و عدم تمايزهما
مسـمّىً بالاحدية
و من الذات ابتداء الشؤونات
مسـمّىً بالواحدية　　10
ثم عادتها فى الذات
مسـمّىً بالمتّحدية
والآحاد الثلاثة ليست بثلاث

## The Fifth Chapter
### Comprehensive of What Went Before in the Previous Chapters

Surely the One is not a number,
　　but all numbers are the same as the One.
　　As for the original, Real Existence,
　　It comprehends Exclusive Unity and the
　　　　numerous things.
5　　Exclusive Unity is Its Essence,
　　and the numerous things are Its tasks.
The lack of distinction between the two
　　is named "Exclusive Unity."
　　The beginning of tasks from the Essence
10　　is named "Inclusive Unity."
　　Then their return into the Essence
　　is named "Unifiedness."
The three ones are not three,

一而三義 (同上)

15 眞一起化
數一成化
體一化化 (道行推原經)
起化以爲
從體著用

20 成化以命
先理後聖
化化以順
進以知見
盡於無間 (道行推原經)

25 化如循環
盡終返始 (同上)
化出自然
終歸自然
少不自然

30 即非本然 (研眞經又昭微經)

They are one with three meanings. (Ibid.)[29]

15 The Real One gives rise to transformation,
the Numerical One perfects transformation,
the Embodied One transforms transformation. (*Path*)        5.1
The acts give rise to transformation,
displaying the functions that follow the Substance.

20 The Mandate perfects transformation
as principle in the Former Heaven and sagehood in the Latter.  5.2
Obedience transforms transformation,
advancing from knowledge to seeing
and full realization without distance. (*Path*)        5.3

25 Transformation is like following a circle—
when the end is fully realized, it returns to the beginning.
(Ibid.)        5.4
Transformation emerges from the Self-so
and comes home to the Self-so in the end.
It cannot be without the Self-so,

30 or else it would not be the Root Suchness. (*Goal,*
*Gleams*)        0.9, 5.5

بل حقيقة لها ثلاثة معانٍ

فالاحدية مُبدئة التخليق     15

والواحدية محصّلته

والمتّحدية مُفنيته

اما ابتداء التخليق فبأفعاله

و هى اظهار الصفات من الذات

و تحصيله بالامر     20

و له فى الملكوت ولاية وفى الملك نبوّة

و افناؤه بالطاعات

والشروع فيها بالعلم ثمّ الشهود

و غايتها عدم انقطاع عن الحقّ

والتخليق كدائرة     25

عاد مُنتهاها الى مبدئها

و صدور التخليق باقتضاء الذات الاحدية

و فى العاقبة اعادته باقتضاء ذلك

فالذى لم يكن بالاقتضاء

فليس من الذات الاحدية     30

rather, a reality with three meanings:

15     Exclusive unity originates creation,

Inclusive Unity actualizes it,

and Unifiedness annihilates it.

As for the beginning of creation, that is through His acts,

which make manifest the attributes from the Essence.

20     It is actualized by the Command,

which has sanctity in the Sovereignty and prophecy

in the Kingdom.     5.2

It is annihilated by acts of obedience,

which begin in knowledge, then witnessing,

and whose final goal is not to be cut off from the Real.

25 Creation is like a circle

whose end point returns to its origin.

Creation emerges by the requirement of the Unitary Essence,

and, at the end, its return is by Its requirement.

Whatever is not by this requirement

30     is not from the Unitary Essence.

本然無着
着於名相
名相無附
附於意識
35    意識無恒
故曰皆朽 (昭微經又費隱經)
是故萬物
只朽其相
弗朽其理
40    夫理即眞 (費隱經)
凝目視一
散目視二
着疑陷礙
見物皆幻 (昭微經又費隱經又道行推原經)
45    物何非眞
事何非實 (昭微經)
物物純全
孰云偏駁 (昭微經又費隱經)

The Root Suchness has no attachment—
    the attachment is in the names and guises.
    The names and guises have no adherence—
    the adherence is in intentional discernment.
35    Intentional discernment has no constancy,
    so it is said that all decays. (*Gleams, Rays*)[30]
Hence the ten thousand things
    decay only in their guises.
    There is no decay in their principle,
40    for the principle is the Real. (*Rays*)
The concentrated eye sees one,
    the scattered eye sees two.
    Attached to doubt, they are trapped by obstacles
    and see all things as illusory. (*Gleams, Rays, Path*)[31]
45    How can things not be the Real?
    How can affairs not be the True? (*Gleams*)[32]
    Everything is pure and complete.
    Who says it is partial and mingled? (*Gleams, Rays*)

و اما هى فغير ملابسة
انما الملابسة باسمائها وصورها
والاسماء والصور لا تحقّق لهما
و انما تحقّقهما على معرفة الذهن
والمعرفة لا تدوم    35
و لذا قيل وجب فناؤهما
و لذلك كلّ شىء
انما فنت صورته
لا حقيقته
لانّها هى الحقّ    40
و عين الجمع انما رأت الواحد
و عين الفرق رأت وجودين
و بالشكّ غمسوا فى الموانع
و رأوا كلّ شىء وجوداً باطلاً
و أىّ شىء ليس بوجود الحقّ    45
و أىّ شأن ليس بشأن الحقّ
فكلّ شىء خالص كامل
و من ذا الذى قال ناقص مختلط

As for It, It is not clothed—
    being clothed is only in Its names and Its forms.
    The names and forms have no realization—
    their only realization is in the recognition of the mind.[33]
35    The recognition does not continue;
    so it is said that both must undergo annihilation.
That is why everything's
    form alone is annihilated,
    not its reality,
40    for that is the Real.
The eye of gathering sees only the One,
    and the eye of dispersion sees two existences.
    Because of doubt they immerse themselves in obstructions
    and see everything as an unreal existence.
45    But which thing is not the Real's Existence?
    And which task is not the Real's task?
    So, each thing is pure and perfect—
    who would say "deficient and mixed"?

一塵一粟
50    全體本然 (研真經)
一呼一吸
終古限量 (費隱經又道行推原經)
小中見大
天納粟中
55    大中見小
天在塵外 (研真經又道行推原經)
舒其光陰
一息千古
卷其時刻
60    千古一息 (道行推原經又費隱經)
一歸本然
天人渾化
物我歸真
真一還真 (費隱經又昭微經)
65    物無相礙
人無欲累

One dust-speck, one grain,
50    is the Root Suchness of the Complete Substance. (*Goal*)        5.7
In one inhalation and one exhalation
is the full measure of the final antiquity. (*Rays, Path*)
The great is seen in the small,
and heaven is received in the midst of a grain.        5.8
55    The small is seen in the great,
and heaven exists outside a speck. (*Goal, Path*)        5.9
When time stretches out,
one breath is a thousand antiquities.        5.10
When the present moment is rolled up,
60    a thousand antiquities are one breath. (*Path, Rays*)        5.11
The Ones come home to the Root Suchness,        0.10
and heaven and humans are undifferentiated transformed.
The things and the I's come home to the Real,
and the Real One circles back to the Real. (*Rays, Gleams*)        5.12
65    The things are not obstructed by the guises,
and humans are not burdened by desire.

لانّ كلّ غبارة وحبّة
حقيقتهما من شؤون الحقّ 50
و فى نفس خرج ودخل من الفانى
انكشف عنده ما من اوّل العالم الى آخره
فقد يبصر فى صغير اكبر
حتّى يرى السماوات موسوعة فى حبّة
و قد يبصر فى جلال الحقّ صغر الاشياء 55
حتّى يرى السماوات وراء غبارة
و اذا انبسط زمانه
ففى كل نفس اوّلى وآخرى
و اذا اندرجت الاحيان
فالاوّلى والآخرى كنفس 60
و اذا رجعت الآحاد الى الذات
اضمحلّت السماوات والانسان
فحينئذ انردّت الاشياء وانا الى الحقّ
بل الاحدية الى الوجود المطلق
فما من صورة شىء تحجبه 65
و لا من شهوة بشرية تمنعه

For, of each speck and each grain,
50　　the reality is one of the tasks of the Real.
　　In a breath that leaves and enters the one who is annihilated,
　　　everything from the first to the last of the cosmos is
　　　　unveiled to him.
　　He may see inside the small something larger,
　　and even view the heavens embraced by a grain.
55　　He may see in the majesty of the Real the things' smallness,
　　and even view the heavens beyond a speck.
　　When his time undergoes expansion,
　　in each breath are a first and a last.
　　When the moments are folded up,
60　　the first and the last are like a breath.
　　When the Ones go back to the Essence,
　　the heavens and the human fade away.
　　Now the things and the I withdraw to the Real,
　　or rather, Exclusive Unity to Nondelimited Existence.
65　　So no form of anything veils him,
　　and no human appetite holds him back.

妙義各呈
本然見焉 (道行推原經又研眞經)
初爲實理
70　今爲實相
實有相見
種果全焉 (研眞經又昭微經)

The subtle meaning of each is disclosed
and thereby the Root Suchness is seen. (*Path, Goal*)
In the beginning was the True Principle
70      and now is the True Guise.
When the True Being is seen as Guise,
the seed and fruit are complete. (*Goal, Gleams*)

فباظهار كلّ شىء معانيه اللطيفة
شاهد الحقّ
ففى الابتداء تجلّى الحقّ بالحقائق
والآن بصورها     70
و اذا شاهد الحقّ فى الصور
فقد تمّ البذر والثمر

والحمد لله ربّ العالمين

When everything makes manifest its subtle meanings
he witnesses the Real.
At the beginning the Real disclosed Himself through the realities
70     and now through their forms.
When he witnesses the Real in the forms,
the seed and the fruit are complete.
And praise belongs to God, Lord of the worlds.

## Notes

1. The first line is found in the text provided and translated by Nūr al-Ḥaqq but not in the editions of *Tianfang xingli* we used.

2. Derived from Gleam 13 (*Chinese Gleams*, pp. 152–53).

3. These two lines may be a translation of this sentence: "When the Real wanted to create the existent things, He first made the Muhammadan spirit appear from the radiance of the light of the Unity" (*Path*, pp. 37/60–61).

4. The title of the first chapter is not found in *Subtleties* but is given in *Explanation of the Subtleties*.

5. Derived at least partly from *Path*, pp. 50–51/77, 57/86–87.

6. This is probably based on Ījī's discussions of the elements, specifically *Standpoints*, pp. 222–23.

7. Rāzī says in Chapter 2.4 (*Path*, pp. 65–66/94–95) that humans are created from the highest of the high (i.e., the First Intellect, or Muhammadan Light) and the lowest of the low (i.e., the elemental body).

8. Compare *Goal*, p. 267/108: "From the self-disclosure of the Ascribed Spirit, the fathers and the mothers appeared. The fathers and the mothers are perpetually in self-disclosure. From the self-disclosure of the fathers and the mothers, the three progeny appeared and are appearing." Ījī refers to the appearance of plants and animals from the four elements in *Standpoints*, pp. 223–24.

9. In contrast to his practice in most of the Root Classic, Liu began Chapter 2 with ten lines that are not elaborated upon in the diagrams. He reviewed what we learned in Chapter 1 in order to prepare for the detailed discussion of the macrocosmic levels that pertain to the Latter Heaven. Although the principles and natures are present in the Former Heaven, and the images and numbers appear in the Latter Heaven, this is not to say that the images derive simply from the principles; rather, both are prefigured in the Real Being, specifically in its two primary functions, knowledge and power. In citing *Rays* here, Liu Zhi may have had in view this passage: "The Real Being leaves traces in the fixed entities in respect of manifestation. In other words, the entities and their states become manifest in the external realm (*'ayn*) as they were in knowledge" (*Rays*, p. 13).

10. Here Liu is explaining that the dual functions of the Substance—knowledge and power—manifest themselves macrocosmically as the Former and Latter Heavens. In his translation, Nūr al-Ḥaqq rightly took principles and images as quasi-synonyms of Former Heaven and Latter Heaven. One of the passages in *Path* that Liu may have had in mind here is:

The outwardness of the cosmos is called "the Kingdom," and its inwardness is called "the Sovereignty." In reality, each thing's Sovereignty is the thing's spirit through which it abides; and each thing's spirit abides through the Real's attribute of Self-Abiding, as He said: "In His hand is the Sovereignty of everything" [Koran 36:82]. (*Path*, p. 46/71)

11. In *Goal* (p. 257/96), Nasafī made the point like this: "The outward of the Ascribed Spirit is the bodies of the spheres, the stars, and the elements, so that the World of the Kingdom may appear. The inward of the Ascribed Spirit is the life of the spheres, the stars, and the elements, so that the World of the Sovereignty may appear."

12. This is the first of several instances in which the Arabic text has the invocatory formula "exalted is He!" (*ta'ālā*), showing that the pronoun (in this case, "His") refers to God; in English, a capital letter performs the same function, so translating the formula is superfluous. If the author were demonstrating his piety, he would have included invocatory formulas after the most holy name of God (Allah), which has already been mentioned several times in the text.

13. In *Standpoints* (p. 200), Ījī named the nine spheres in the midst of explaining the opinions of the philosophers concerning the heavens, but he said nothing about their qualities and characteristics; nor did Jurjānī in his commentary on *Standpoints*.

14. *Standpoints*, pp. 200–224. These few lines indicate the general topics that Ījī discussed in the first three parts of the fourth *mawqif*, on substances, specifically the parts dealing with spheres, stars, and elements. Little of what Liu Zhi said in his commentary, however, reflects the explanations offered by Ījī or his commentator Jurjānī.

15. These few lines are drawn from sections of *Standpoints* (pp. 215–24, 224–28) that deal with compound things that have constitutions (minerals, plants, and animals) and those that do not (atmospheric phenomena).

16. Cf. *Path*, pp. 176–78/192–94.

17. This passage may have been inspired by a discussion in which Rāzī compared the spirit to an infant placed in a cradle (the body); its traces do not become manifest until the appearance of intellect after puberty. In the womb, the spirit is connected to the body through the attribute of life, which appears in movement. When the body emerges from the womb, the spirit attaches itself to the senses, and at each stage of bodily growth, its qualities become more manifest (*Path*, p. 215/224).

18. As pointed out in the notes on the Diagrams, this discussion is drawn largely from *Goal*. Ījī did not talk about the months in the womb, but he did

analyze in some detail the characteristics of minerals and the faculties of plants and animals (*Standpoints*, pp. 228–42).

19. *Path*, pp. 178ff/194ff. For more on the sources, see the notes under Diagrams 3.10 and 3.11.

20. "Treasures" (*kunūz*) follows the text in *Explanation of the Subtleties*. *Subtleties* itself has *karāmāt* (miracles), but the commentary repeats the word "treasure" for each of the seven levels, so there can be no doubt that Nūr al-Ḥaqq considered it the correct reading. Moreover, in line 4.16, Nūr al-Ḥaqq used the word *karāmāt* to render "subtle response." *Karāmāt* has the technical sense of a miracle performed by a saint, similar to but contrasted with a miracle (*mu'jiza*) performed by a prophet. Nūr remarked in the commentary that these miracles are achieved through reaching the furthest stage of the heart and that "their wonders have no end" (*Sharḥ*, p. 108/84).

21. *Path*, pp. 195–97/208. See Diagram 4.2 and the notes there.

22. The quotation is a paraphrase of Koran 53:9, as becomes clear under Diagram 4.3.

23. *Commentary*, p. 470; *Goal*, pp. 274–75; *Path*, pp. 121–24/143–47. See the notes under Diagram 4.4.

24. For the division into four human types, see *Path*, p. 345/336. Rāzī devoted each of the four chapters of Part 4 to one type of soul.

25. Reading *zhi* (knowledge) instead of *zhi* 之 (this), which is found in our editions of the original text. "Knowledge" is given as an alternative in the text's margin and followed in Nūr al-Ḥaqq's version.

26. This is the only time Liu uses this word *fa* in the book. Since he highlighted it in *Tianfang dianli*, Frankel ("Liu Zhi's Journey," pp. 171–86) discusses it in detail. Frankel suggests that as a noun it should be translated as "law," although he acknowledges the verbal meaning of "imitating." The word has a long history of use in Chinese thought and, from earliest times, was closely associated with *li*, Propriety, as here. Daoists see it as a cosmic principle; Chapter 25 of Laozi's *Daodejing*, for example, has this passage centering on *fa* or emulation: "Humans emulate the earth, the earth emulates heaven, heaven emulates the Way, and the Way emulates the Self-so." Buddhists commonly used *fa* to translate the notion of *dharma*. As Frankel points out, the word does not correspond to Shariah, which is often translated as "law," but he seems to be unaware that Shariah is also used as a synonym for *dīn* or "religion" in a broad sense. Nor does he point out that the Sunnah—which means precisely the "exemplary model" (= *fa*) of the Prophet—is often said to have three dimensions, corresponding to the Prophet's bodily activity (Shariah), his moral and spiritual qualities

(Tariqah), and his inner reality (Haqiqah). So, here in this passage, "emulation" of the Prophet is exactly what Liu meant, that is, emulation on all three levels of Propriety, Way, and Real.

27. That "one" is not a number, but rather the origin of the numbers, is a common statement in Islamic mathematics, and Ibn al-'Arabī often refers to its metaphysical significance (e.g., *Self-Disclosure*, pp. 167ff; *Sufi Path*, p. 411, note 3). The passage here is probably derived from Jāmī's explanation of Flash 14, where 'Irāqī wrote:

The One (*aḥad*) flows in the things like "one" *wāḥid* in the numbers. If "one" were not, the entities of the numbers would not become manifest and the numbers would have no names. If one were to become manifest in its own name, no number would become manifest in its entity. (*Rays*, p. 99/99)

28. Gleam 25 (*Chinese Gleams*, pp. 184–85).

29. Gleam 17 (*Chinese Gleams*, pp. 160–63).

30. Gleam 18 (*Chinese Gleams*, pp. 164–65); *Rays*, p. 9.

31. Gleam 2 (*Chinese Gleams*, p. 136).

32. Gleam 25 (*Chinese Gleams*, p. 184).

33. The word *taḥaqquq* (realization) follows the text in *Explanation of the Subtleties* (*Sharḥ*, p. 150/109). *Subtleties* has instead *i'timād* (reliance).

## 0.1

## 最初無稱圖

## 0.1
## Diagram of the Nondesignation
## of the Earliest Beginning

## 0.2
## 先天理化次第圖

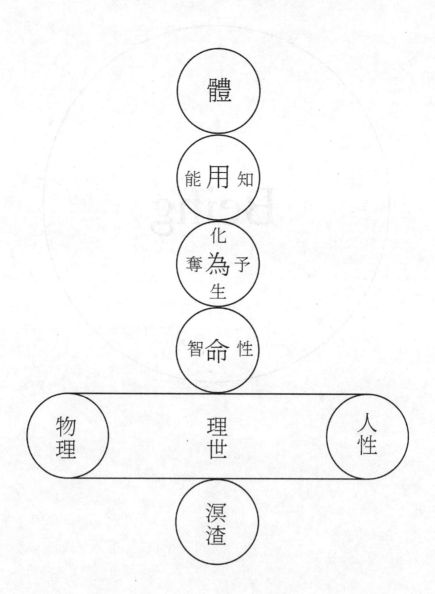

## 0.2
## Diagram of the Sequence
## of the Transformation of Principles
## in the Former Heaven

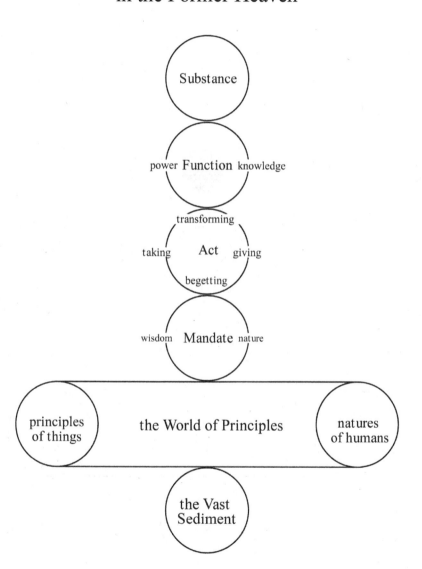

0.3
後天形化次第圖

## 0.3
# Diagram of the Sequence
# of the Transformation of Forms
# in the Latter Heaven

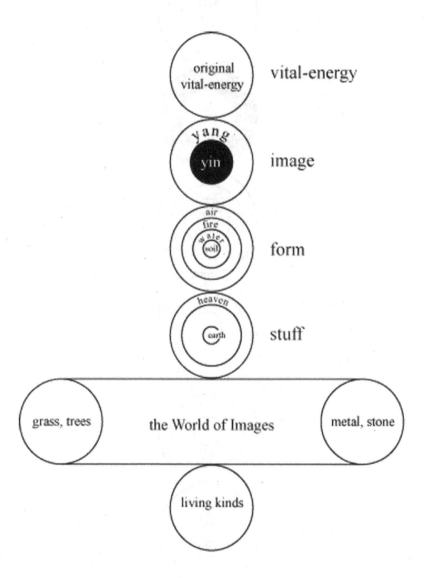

## 0.4
## 胎形變化次第圖

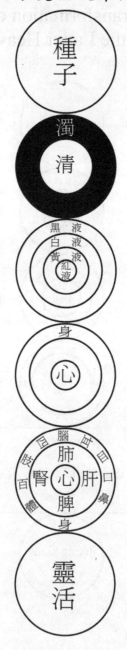

## 0.4
## Diagram of the Sequence of the Alteration and Transformation of Forms in the Womb

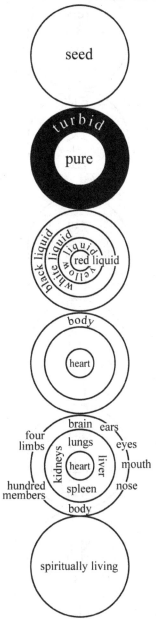

0.5

靈性顯著次第圖

## 0.5
# Diagram of the Sequence of the Manifestation and Display of the Nature of the Spiritual

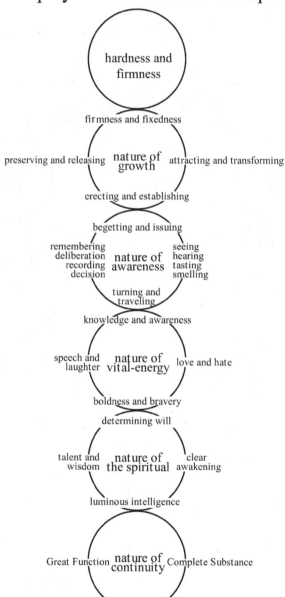

## 0.6
## 大世界造化循環圖

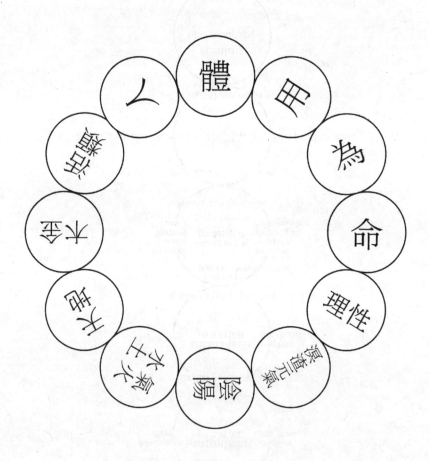

## 0.6
# Diagram of the Macrocosm's
# Following in the Circle of Creation
# and Transformation

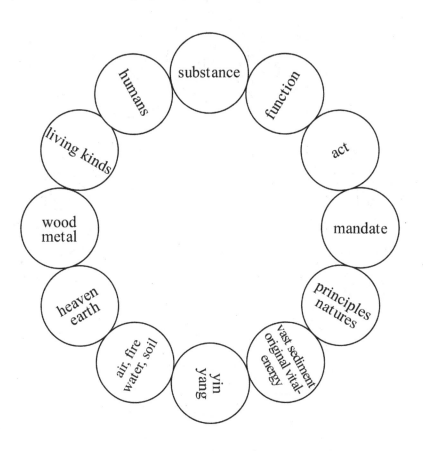

## 0.7
## 小世界原始返終圖

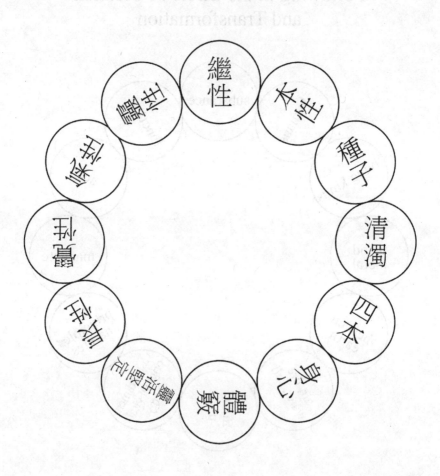

## 0.7
## Diagram of the Microcosm's
## Original Beginning and Final Return

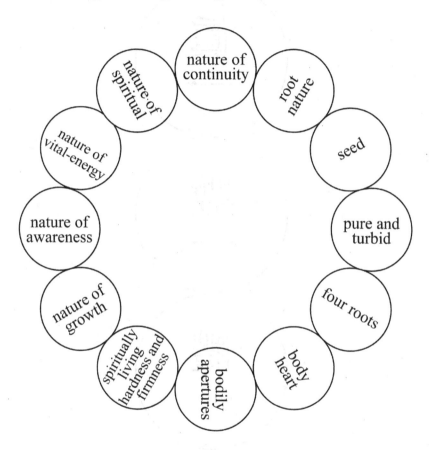

## 0.8
### 天人分品圖

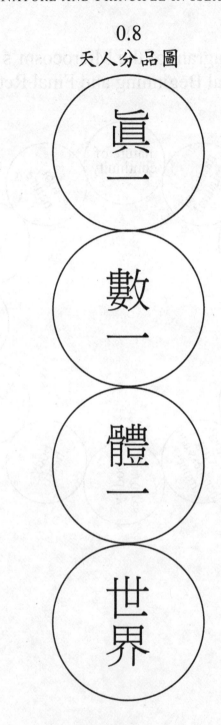

## 0.8
## Diagram of the Differentiated Levels
## of Heaven and Humans

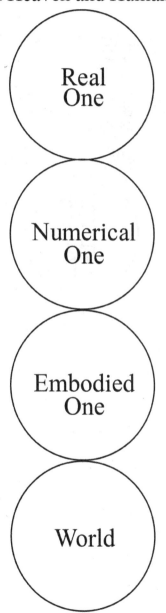

0.9

天人合一圖

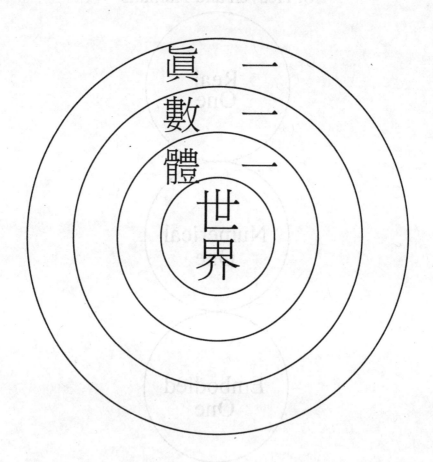

## 0.9
## Diagram of Heaven and Humans
## United as One

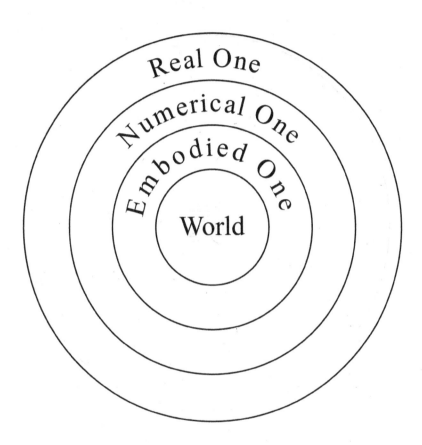

## 0.10
### 天人渾化圖

## 0.10
## Diagram of the
## Undifferentiated Transformation
## of Heaven and Humans

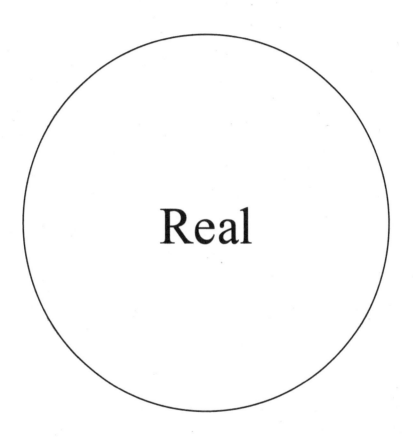

# *Volume 1*

## *Summary*

Volume 1 is a sequential description of the causes by which the macrocosm becomes manifest and displayed.

There are the World of Principles and the World of Images. The World of Principles is where images and numbers are not yet formed, although the principles are already embedded; this is the so-called Former Heaven. The World of Images is where heaven and earth are already established, and the ten thousand things are already begotten; this is the so-called Latter Heaven.

The One Real causes all the manifestation and display of both worlds, such that there seems to be distinction in sequence and moments. Each of the diagrams explains how to discern the rough outline. Looking at the text and understanding its meaning can awaken you both to the details of the subtlety of the ongoing flow of the creative transformation and to the principles of perfection bestowed on humans and things. If these are put aside, there is no way for Realness to be seen with certainty.

## 1.1
## 最初無稱圖

## 1.1
## Diagram of the Nondesignation of
## the Earliest Beginning

The creative transformation[1] has a beginning; so it must have an earliest beginning. Before the images and numbers are formed, all principles are already embedded within, and this is the beginning of the creative transformation.[2] When no principles can be named, that is the earliest beginning.

The Root Suchness[3] of the creative transformation cannot be designated by name.[4] Because it cannot be designated, various scholars have called it "nonbeing."[5] How can this be possible? Someone said that calling it nonbeing does not mean the nonbeing of the void. Rather, it means that there is the Real without illusion,[6] there is Substance without function.

However, there is already the Real,[7] and the Real is Being. How can it be called nonbeing? There is already Substance, and Substance is Being. How can it be called nonbeing?

Here the sages[8] do not say "nonbeing" but rather "nondesignation." The scholars of Nature and Principle[9] refer to it not only as "Being" but also as "True Being." True Being has no peer and stands by itself. Real and illusory are not differentiated, substance and function are not distinguished. There is nothing that has being, yet in reality everything has being.[10]

Someone said: When you already call it "Being," then Being is the designation. How can you say there is no designation?

I say: Being is a meaning, and designation is a name. Embedded in the realm of the earliest beginning are all the meanings of real and illusory, substance and function; so it is called "Being." But real and illusory, substance and function, are names without any specific belonging;[11] so it is called "Nondesignation." It is wrong to say that "Being" is a designation without scrutinizing the distinction between name and meaning.[12]

Someone said: In the realm of the earliest beginning, there is no void or illusion whatsoever; so it is permissible to designate it as "Real." There is no working or functioning whatsoever; so it is permissible to designate it as "Substance." How can you say there is no designation?

As for this: As soon as you say "Real," this is confined to the level of the Real; so it is differentiated from the illusory. As soon as you say "Substance," this falls into the position of Substance; so it is divided from function. That is not the meaning of this diagram. The meaning of this diagram is that the Real is the illusory, the Substance is the function, and the One Root is the ten thousand variations. Outward and inward, fine and coarse, beginning and end, principle and vital-energy[13]—the One threads through without its designation and name falling to one side.[14] Therefore it is called "Nondesignation."

Once it moves, then it becomes manifest and differentiated into numerous levels:[15]

First is the level of nonmovement, which is Substance [Diagram 1.2].

Second is the level of the first movement, which is function [1.3].

Third is the level of the Lord-Ruler, which is the differentiation of Substance and function [1.4].

Fourth is the level of the First Mandate, which is the appearance of the Real Principle [1.5].

Fifth is the level of nature and mandate, which is the differentiation of the ten thousand principles [1.6].

Sixth is the level of form and vital-energy, which is the display of vital-energy and images [1.7].

Once all six levels have been provided, the creative transformation is completed.

## Notes

1. "Creative transformation" (*zaohua* 造化) is Liu's designation for the process of ongoing change and transformation, which is a central topic for Muslim philosophers and Sufis. In the Chinese tradition, talk of creation and the Creator is associated with Zhuangzi. One of his characters remarks, "So now I think of heaven and earth as a great furnace, and the creative transformation as a skilled smith" (6.12). The discussion of change, alteration (*bian* 變), and transformation is of course central to the *Yijing*. According to its commentary on the first hexagram, "The way of Heaven is to change and transform so that everything will obtain its correct nature and Mandate" (Wilhelm, *I Ching*, p. 371). Or again, "In heaven images are perfected, in earth forms are perfected. Thus are seen alteration and transformation" (*Dazhuan* 1.1; Wilhelm, *I Ching*, p. 280; see also *Concepts*, pp. 197–207).

2. As Zhu Xi put it, "When considered from the standpoint of principle, before things existed, their principles of being had already existed" (*Source Book*, p. 637). Or again: "Fundamentally, principle cannot be interpreted in the senses of existence or nonexistence. Before Heaven and Earth came into being, it already was as it is" (ibid.).

3. The Root Suchness (*benran* 本然) is the Real Being, or the Root Substance. The character *ran* is an emphatic particle, meaning "yes," "certainly," "verily" (similar to Arabic *inna*). As a noun, it can be used as here to designate that which can ultimately be affirmed as Real. In this sense, it parallels the Arabic word *inniyya* ("that-it-is-ness," derived from the emphatic particle *inna*, "verily," "truly"). In Islamic philosophy, *inniyya* is used as a synonym for existence (*wujūd*), and is often contrasted with *māhiyya* (what-ness), i.e., quiddity or essence. Speaking of the Real Being, Muslim philosophers often say that "Its whatness is its that-it-is-ness" (*māhiyyatuhu inniyatuhu*). In other words, the Real per se has no whatness other than the fact of being so; so it has no name. All other things, whatever they may be, have specific essences and specific names, and their existence is an open question.

4. As befitting its depiction of "nondesignation," Diagram 1.1 does not fit into the Former Heaven / Latter Heaven scheme that organizes the rest of Volume 1. As indicated under Diagrams 1.1 and 1.7, eleven of the twelve diagrams in this volume are divided into two groups of six: 1.2–1.7 and 1.7–1.12, with 1.7 pertaining to both. This is almost the same scheme that is seen in Diagram 0.6, beginning with Substance (1.2) and ending with humans (1.12)—although in 0.6, wood/metal and living kinds are represented as two circles, and here they are treated together under Diagram 1.11.

In typical Islamic theology, God is understood in terms of Essence, attributes (or names), and acts, as explained in the Introduction. Especially in the school of Ibn al-ʿArabī, however, authors found it useful to further refine this scheme, envisaging the Essence in itself as beyond conceptualization, whether negative or positive, apophatic or kataphatic. This is what Liu called "Nondesignation," an apt translation of Ibn al-ʿArabī's "Nondelimitation" (*iṭlāq*) and Ṣadr al-Dīn Qūnawī's "Nonentification" (*lā taʿayyun*).

Once the Nondesignation of the Real in itself is acknowledged, then we can conceptualize it, first in terms of negating attributes from it and second in terms of affirming its attributes; God is described negatively in one respect and positively in another. These two respects are commonly known as Exclusive Unity (*aḥadiyya*), meaning that the One Real excludes all otherness and multiplicity, and Inclusive Unity (*wāḥidiyya*)—or, as we translated it in *Chinese Gleams*, One-and-Allness—meaning that the One embraces the principles and roots of all multiplicity and all otherness.

Here Liu devoted one diagram each to these four ways of envisaging the Real (in contrast to 0.6, where he left out Nondesignation). He called God as Exclusively One "Substance" and God as Inclusively One "function." He called the fourth level "act," a direct translation of a standard Arabic term for this level. He then depicted the World of Principles (the World of the Sovereignty) in terms of three levels in Diagrams 1.5–1.7. Together, Diagrams 1.2–1.7 represent the Former Heaven or the Descending Arc, the movement from absolute unity and invisibility toward differentiation and manifestation. Diagrams 1.7–1.12 show the Latter Heaven or the World of Images (the World of the Kingdom) in terms of the ascent from the original vital-energy to the human level, where the circle of existence can rejoin its origin, the Real Substance.

Ibn al-'Arabī commonly referred to the nondesignation of the Real Being as *iṭlāq*, which means "nondelimitation," "unboundedness," "absoluteness." For example, he wrote, "God possesses Nondelimited Being, but no delimitation prevents Him from delimitation. On the contrary, He possesses all delimitations. Hence He is Nondelimited Delimitation; no single delimitation rather than another exercises its property over Him" (Ibn al-'Arabī, *Futūḥāt*, 3: 162; *Sufi Path*, p. 109). Ibn al-'Arabī's disciple Qūnawī used the same term but also gave prominence to the word *lā ta'ayyun*, "nonentification," "nondesignation," "nondetermination":

Know that it is not correct, in respect of the Real's Essential Nondelimitation . . . for Him to be recognized by any description, or to have any relation whatsoever ascribed to Him—whether oneness, the necessity of Existence, originatingness, the demand of existence-giving . . . , for all this demands entification and delimitation, but there is no doubt that the intellection of an entification demands the precedence of nonentification. Everything that we mentioned precludes nondelimitation. (*al-Nuṣūṣ*, first *naṣṣ*)

Use of *ta'ayyun*, or "entification," as a specific technical term apparently began with Qūnawī. It is often translated as "determination" and sometimes as "designation," but these terms obscure the word's connection with *'ayn*, "entity," one of the most important technical terms in this school of thought. *Ta'ayyun* means basically "to become an *'ayn*" or "to take on the characteristics of an *'ayn*." *'Ayn* means "entity," that is, "thing" (*shay'*) as distinct from other things. The "First Entification" is Real *Wujūd* inasmuch as it discloses itself in characteristics and attributes that allow us to understand and conceptualize it as an entity distinct from that which is absolutely nondelimited and nondistinct, i.e., the level of Nonentification or Nondesignation.

5. Zhu Xi remarked, "Whereas the Buddhists talk about non-being, the Confucianists talk about being" (*Source Book*, p. 648). This is one of several points on which Liu and the Han Kitab aligned themselves with the Neo-Confucians and criticized Buddhists and Daoists (cf. Wang Daiyu's remarks in his *Great Learning*; *Chinese Gleams*, pp. 109–11). On the long debate over the relationship between being and nonbeing (or "beingless"), see *Concepts*, pp. 150–61; and *Source Book, passim*.

6. To describe the cosmos as illusion (*huan* 幻) is typical of a Buddhist (or Hindu) approach, but notice that Liu was careful to make the pair Real-illusory synonymous with Substance-function. Maya—the realm of illusion—is always two-sided, because it simultaneously veils and reveals. Ignorance is to be deceived by the veils, and enlightenment is to recognize the veils as *nama-rupa*, the names and forms of Brahman.

The pair of terms that most closely coincides with Real-illusion in Koranic Arabic is *ḥaqq* and *bāṭil* (e.g., Koran 17:81). The word *ḥaqq* we have met as "real," "true," "right," "worthy," and the corresponding substantives. *Bāṭil* designates the opposite or negation of *ḥaqq* and can be translated as "false," "unreal," "illusory," "vain," "wrong," "unworthy." But, as the rest of this discussion shows, Liu knew that the illusory is the function of the Real Substance, which is to say that it is the self-disclosure of the Real (he returned to this issue under Diagram 5.4). Ibn al-'Arabī summed up this discussion in these terms:

The illusory (*bāṭil*) becomes manifest in the form (*ṣūra*) of the Real, but the illusory is nonexistence. It has no existence, but the form does exist; so it is Real. So where is the entity of the unreal that became manifest, when the form is only Real? (*Futūḥāt*, 3: 97; for a slightly different translation, see *Sufi Path*, p. 133)

Ibn al-'Arabī and his followers often carried out this discussion in terms of the word *khayāl*, which means both "imagination" and "image" and, in some contexts, "illusion." All manifestation, they explained, is an image of the Real, just as our imaginings are images of our own selfhoods. Hence everything is both a face and a veil of the Real. Each thing is Real/not Real, He/not He. Ibn al-'Arabī captured the discussion in two lines of poetry:

The realm of being is only images,
   but in reality it is the Real.
Whoever understands this fact
   has grasped the mysteries of the Path.   (*Fuṣūṣ al-ḥikam*, p. 159)

7. Compare Lu Xiangshan: "Principle exists in the universe from the very beginning. How can it be said to be non-being?" (*Source Book*, p. 578).

8. Here Liu is using the term loosely to refer to Ibn al-'Arabī and his followers.

9. Scholars of Nature and Principle (*xingli jia* 性理家) would normally mean Neo-Confucians, but here the reference seems to be to Muslim thinkers. Certainly Existence (*wujūd*) has been a central term in Islamic theological discussions at least from the time of Avicenna (d. 1037), and it gained even greater importance with the writings of Ibn al-'Arabī and his followers, for whom "the Real Existence" (*al-wujūd al-ḥaqq*) is a typical designation for God in his all-comprehensive reality. It is no accident that Ibn al-'Arabī came to be known as the founder of the doctrine of "the Oneness of Existence" (*waḥdat al-wujūd*), even if he did not use this specific expression. For the importance of *wujūd* in Jāmī (whom Liu seems to be calling a "sage" in 5.2), see *Chinese Gleams*, pp. 116–21.

Nūr al-Ḥaqq labeled his version of this diagram "Existence" (*wujūd*) and explained that it is the level called "the Hidden Treasure" in the famous hadith. Then he said, quite rightly, that it is also what 'Irāqī, in *Flashes*, calls "love" (*'ishq*). In support of this, he quoted from the beginning of the first chapter of *Flashes*: "Love, in the resting place of Its exaltation, is free of any entification" (*Rays*, p. 39; *Flashes*, p. 73).

10. In Ibn al-'Arabī's terms, this is to say that the Real Being alone has being, and everything else is strictly nonexistence (*'adam*); nonetheless, given that the Real Being knows all things as possible entities, they "exist" as concomitants of its awareness. It then brings them into being but does not give them being of their own, because It alone is being. In other terms, the universe is It / not It, that is, simultaneously identical with and different from Real Being. In terms of delimitation or entification, the thing is what it is, but, in terms of the Nondelimitation and Infinity of the Real Being, it can be nothing other than the self-disclosure (*tajallī*) of that Being. All things, in other words, are God / not God—God, inasmuch as the actual existence of the things is none other than the Real Being; and not God, inasmuch as things are specifically themselves and thus nonexistent, that is, other than True Being, which is nonspecified and nondesignated (see *Sufi Path*, pp. 113ff).

Parallel passages in Chinese writings are not uncommon. In discussing the Ultimate One as *shen* 神 or spirit, Shao Yong wrote, "There is no place *shen* is and no place *shen* is not" (Birdwhistell, *Transition*, p. 58).

11. In Ibn al-'Arabī's terms, all the divine names designate exactly the same reality, which in itself transcends naming; only when we take the

cosmos into account do the names designate the diverse relations that are established between the Unnameable and the things. Ibn al-'Arabī also says that the names of God that we do know are in fact the "names of the names," the latter being the meanings that transcend specification and entification (see *Sufi Path*, chap. 2).

12. This paragraph is important to show that Liu often used "meaning" (*yi* 義) and "principle" (*li* 理) as synonyms. Root Classic 2:87–88 also illustrates this: "Observe the forms and discriminate the meanings, / look at the images and awaken to the principles." In both cases, "meanings" and "principles" designate the realities of things in the divine knowledge or in the Former Heaven, whereas "forms" and "images" designate the things as they appear in the Latter Heaven. The corresponding Arabic terminology, as noted in the Introduction, is *ma'nā* (meaning) and *ṣūra* (form), a pair used to differentiate between the fixed entities and the existent entities, or between intelligible things and sensory things, or between things as they are with God or the First Intellect and things as they appear in the world. Both Chinese *yi* and Arabic *ma'nā* can also designate "meaning" in the usual sense of the purport of a word.

13. In a broad sense, vital-energy (*qi* 氣) is the underlying "matter" of which the universe is composed but not dead and passive matter; hence Wing-tsit Chan's translation as "material force" (*Source Book*, *passim*). For this broad meaning of *qi*, Liu used the phrase "the original vital-energy." In narrower senses, *qi* designates the sum of a thing's subtle qualities and characteristics; thus earth, water, air, and fire are themselves vital-energies, and all things have vital-energies specific to them, whether they be metal, wood, and the living, or body and heart. The basic meaning of the word *qi* is "breath," "air," and "vapor" (see *Concepts*, pp. 45–63); scholars have pointed out a similar role given to parallel terms in other traditions, such as Greek *pneuma* and Sanskrit *prana* (Ching, *Religious Thought*, p. 29). The most striking parallel in the Islamic context is found in Ibn al-'Arabī's "Breath of the All-merciful," within which all creatures are articulated as divine words. The Neo-Confucian Zhang Zai gave *qi* special prominence as the undifferentiated primal substance from which the myriad things take shape and to which they return. The passage here reflects the mainstream Neo-Confucian position, voiced clearly by Zhu Xi, that principle dwells in the realm above form, and vital-energy is the vessel that receives its influence and gives rise to the things: "Before heaven and earth existed, there was after all only principle. . . . As there is principle, there is therefore vital-energy to operate everywhere and nourish and develop all things" (*Source Book*, p. 635).

14. "The One that threads through," or "the One Thread" (*yiguan* 一貫), is the topic of Diagram 2.12. The expression goes back to *Analects* 4.15 and 15.2. Legge rendered it there as "all-pervading unity." In his notes, he remarked, "To myself it occurs to translate, 'my doctrines have one thing which goes through them,' but such an exposition has not been approved by any Chinese writer" (*Chinese Classics*, 1: 169). This suggests that Nūr al-Ḥaqq's translation of the term in *Subtleties* 2:90, "the self-disclosure of the unitary Essence" (*tajallī al-dhāt al-aḥadiyya*), is not far from the way it was understood in the Chinese tradition. According to Chen Chun:

"One" is simply principle, which is undifferentiated in its totality, the one great foundation. "Thread" is this one principle spreading out in its operation and penetrating the ten thousand things. The heart of the sage, undifferentiated in its totality, is simply one principle, which is the great foundation. . . . When spoken of as one undifferentiated principle, all principles are luxuriantly present. When spoken of as the ten thousand manifested and evident principles, they are all but this one principle. The one penetrates the ten thousand and the ten thousand are all based on the one. (*Terms*, pp. 94–95)

15. The six levels are derived from Jāmī, Gleam 24. The names of the first three are practically the same as in Liu's translation of this Gleam, but not the second three (*Chinese Gleams*, pp. 180–83). Jāmī discussed the levels in similar terms in *Rays*, p. 6.

1.2

真體無著圖

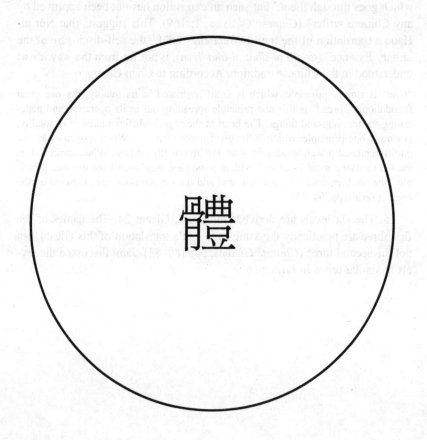

## 1.2
## Diagram of the Nonattachment
## of the Real Substance

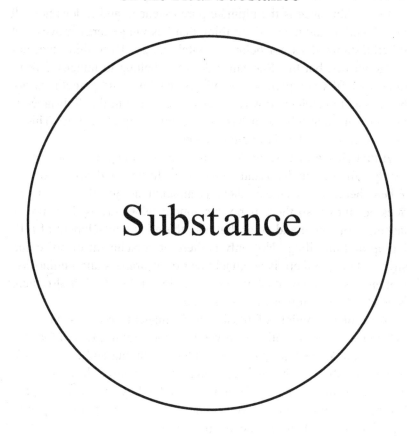

This is the first differentiated level of the first diagram.[1] It is Substance, the level of nonmovement.

Someone said: When there is Substance, there is movement.[2] Why do you say "nonmovement"?

I say: Substance is the ultimate pure essence,[3] and it does not fall into direction and place. Everything that has vital-energy moves, but this Substance does not belong to vital-energy. Everything that has image moves, but this Substance does not belong to images. Everything that fills completely, sometimes reaching and sometimes not being able to reach everywhere, has movement, but this Substance is neither void nor full; so it has no use for complete filling. This is why we call it the level of nonmovement.

Although we discuss its level in terms of nonmovement, yet, in reality, all the ten thousand movements follow and arise from it. When there is movement, there is attachment, yet this Substance does not move; so there is no attachment. Not only is there no attachment of sound and color, but also there is no attachment of rolling up and unrolling.[4] Not only is there no attachment of noise and silence, but also there is no attachment of awareness and luminosity. Not only is there no attachment of direction and place, but also there is no attachment of being and nonbeing.

None of the realms of illusion is permanent,[5] but this one Real Substance is permanently preserved and does not decay. All that belongs to the formed and the formless has beginning and end, but this one Real Substance has no beginning or end. Since it has no beginning, you cannot obtain a differentiated boundary by tracing what is before. Since it has no end, you cannot obtain an end point by pursuing what is after. How can people ponder it?

Someone said: As things, meanings and principles have neither movement nor attachment. Perhaps this Substance belongs only to meaning and principle, which subtly pervade without any obstacle. Is that why it does not move and has no attachment?

I say: This Substance is the origin; meanings and principles have followed it and emerged from it from ancient times until now.[6] At this moment [of Substance], it is by no means possible to seek the meanings and principles. Whoever thoroughly investigates this diagram cannot seek them where there is movement, nor can he seek them where there is attachment.

## Notes

1. In the title, attachment (*zhuo* 着) is the same word used in Buddhism to mean clinging to things or ideas. Liu means that here Substance is to be considered apart from its normal correlative, function. From this standpoint, Substance has no relationship with anything, and nothing has any relationship with it; so it cannot be known. "None knows God but God," as Ibn al-'Arabī liked to say. In the two instances in which "nonattachment" occurs in the Root Classic (1:3 and 5:31), Nūr al-Ḥaqq translated it as "unclothed" (*ghayr mulābis*), which is to say that the Substance is being considered without regard to its "clothing," that is, its functions, or its names and attributes; or, as he remarked, it is seen as "disengaged" (*mujarrad*) from any relationships or standpoints. The second edition of his commentary has a marginal note, quoting from *Rays* (p. 5), that employs the word *ta'alluq*—also commonly translated as "attachment"—to explain the meaning: "This level is too high for the attachment to it of knowledge, unveiling, and witnessing" (*Sharḥ*, p. 4). In other words, it is inaccessible to any sort of cognition whatsoever, whether it be discursive or mystical, conventional or visionary, indirect or unmediated.

2. This is because substance is normally understood as the correlative of function. Together they express "the relation between an object and its inherent movement or activity, between the fundamental metaphysical nature of a thing and its expression, between moral principles and their being carried out by individuals" (*Concepts*, p. 240). As for "movement" (*dong* 動) and its correlative, "stillness" (*jing* 靜)—or, as they are often translated, "activity and tranquility"—these are present in all things, but the Real Being, while possessing them, is not affected by them. Zhou Dunyi wrote in his commentary on the *Yijing*, "Things cannot be still while moving or moving while still. Spirit [*shen*], however, can be moving without movement and still without stillness" (*Source Book*, pp. 471–72).

3. This and the following paragraph may be based on Jāmī, *Gleams*, Gleams 13 and 14 (*Chinese Gleams*, pp. 152–55).

4. Judging from the other passages in the book where the word "rolling up" is used (e.g., Root Classic 4:41, 5:59), the appearance of the World of Images is being compared to the unrolling of a scroll, and its return to non-manifestation to its being rolled up. The Koran uses similar imagery in the verse, "On the day when We shall roll up heaven as a scroll is rolled for the writings" (21:104). For Liu, the issue is not simply that phenomena like noise and silence are not connected to the Real Substance; rather, nothing whatsoever is connected to it, because, to use Ibn al-'Arabī's term, it is

"nondelimited," whether by manifestation or nonmanifestation, being or nonbeing, delimitation or nondelimitation.

5. Impermanence is stressed in Buddhism, but it is no less basic to the Islamic worldview. As the Koran puts it, "Everything is perishing but His face" (28:88); "Everything on the earth is undergoing annihilation" (55:26). In Ibn al-'Arabī's terms,

Everything other than the Essence of the Real is in the station of transmutation, speedy and slow. Everything other than the Essence of the Real is intervening image and vanishing shadow. . . , undergoing continual change from form to form constantly and forever.   (*Futūḥāt*, 2: 313; *Sufi Path*, p. 118)

6. Here Liu seems to be objecting to the Neo-Confucian use of "principle" to designate the Ultimate Reality. As he explained under Diagram 1.6, principle (as well as meaning, as noted under Diagram 1.1) should instead be considered on the same level as nature, and as such it is inherent and undifferentiated in the Mandate, which is the means by which the Real Substance makes the Hidden Treasure manifest.

## 1.3
### 大用渾然圖

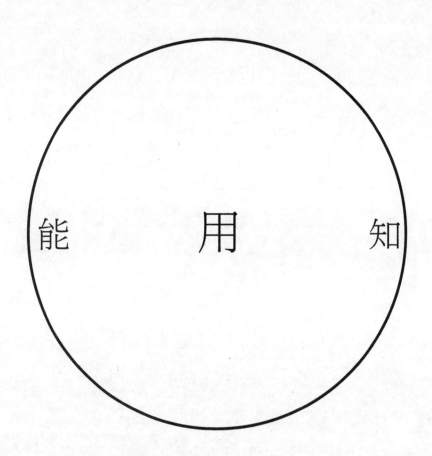

## 1.3
## Diagram of the Undivided Suchness
## of the Great Function

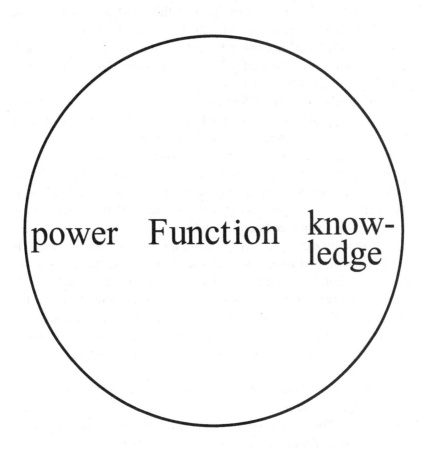

This is the second differentiated level of the first diagram.

At this moment, the Root Substance,[1] which is utterly empty and void,[2] has no movement whatsoever, but the mechanism[3] of movement is already lodged therein. You cannot help naming and calling it the "First Movement."[4] The level of this First Movement is the Great Function of the Complete Substance.[5] The Great Function has not yet issued forth,[6] nor has it been disclosed in any way; it is only that the subtlety[7] of the Self-so[8] contained in the Root Substance is expediently named "function."

How can the subtlety of the Self-so be function? When there is the subtlety of the Self-so, there must be the harmonious mechanism of desiring to move.[9] Hence it is named "function."

The great functions are only two: knowledge and power.[10] The subtlety of the Self-so does not yet have knowledge, yet the subtlety of knowing everything is already embedded within. The subtlety of the Self-so does not yet have power, yet the subtlety of power over everything is already embedded within.

To say knowledge is to say luminous awareness.[11] To say power is to say settling and arranging. Luminous awareness has not yet become manifest, yet luminous awareness of all ten thousand seeds[12] begins abundantly here. Settling and arranging have no trace, yet the meaning of the settling and arranging of all ten thousand seeds is stored here. There is knowledge without knowing, and power without being powerful,[13] for the functions have not yet departed from the Substance.

Master Chami[14] said that the meaning of knowledge is the meaning of lordly sustaining, but at this time the level of Lordship is not yet separate. The meaning of power is the meaning of bringing to be, but at this time the mechanism of bringing to be is not yet seen. The level of the Great Function wholly enwraps all the movements of the necessity of Lordship and all the movements of the powerful acts of thingness in the midst of the abundance of undifferentiated suchness.

It can be said that the explanation of Master Chami grasps the essentials of this diagram.

## Notes

1. As noted in the Introduction, Root Substance (*benti*) is used by various schools of Chinese thought to designate Ultimate Reality. In summarizing its significance, Chung-ying Cheng says that it designates the boundless source of creativity and transformation, embraces the notion of human identity, and "integrates and fuses heaven, *dao*, *daiji* [the Great Ultimate], and *wuji* [the Non-Ultimate]" (Cua, *Encyclopedia*, pp. 719–20).

2. Utterly empty (*kongkong dongdong* 空空洞洞) and void (*xu* 虛) are standard terms in Daoism and Buddhism. Although Liu was critical of using them to designate the Real Being per se, he clearly had no hesitation in employing them to conceptualize the Real Substance. The words are in fact good translations of the Arabic terms that we render as "nondelimited" and "nonentified." The point is that there is nothing to be said about the Real Substance in itself, because it is beyond all and nothing can "attach" to it.

3. Mechanism (*ji* 機) refers to the natural way something comes to be. The classical reference to a "mechanism of movement" is Zhuangzi's story of a one-legged beast who asked a millipede how he could manage with all those legs. The millipede replied, "All I do is put into movement the heavenly mechanism within me, but I don't know why it is so" (17.10). In another passage, Zhuangzi writes, "Men return and enter into the mechanism. The ten thousand things all emerge from the mechanism, and all enter into it again" (18.7). In the second of these passages, Watson translates *ji* as "mysterious workings," and Chan renders it as "the originative process of Nature" (*Source Book*, p. 204).

4. This is what Jāmī and others called the First Self-Disclosure, the First Entification, or the First Descent. It is the eternal self-knowledge of the Real and is discussed from several points of view, each of which demands a different name, including Muhammadan Reality, Exclusive Unity, Inclusive Unity, Oneness, and First Isthmus. As has been pointed out by various observers, it corresponds in many respects to the Logos discussed in the Gospel of John and some forms of Christian theology. In the present context, Liu probably has in mind Jāmī's explanation in Gleam 16, which begins:

The Essence as such is denuded of all names and attributes and rid of every relation and attribution. It is qualified by these affairs in respect of Its attentiveness toward the world of manifestation in the "First Self-Disclosure," which is that It discloses Itself by Itself to Itself. Then the relations of knowledge, light, existence, and witnessing are realized. (*Chinese Gleams*, p. 158)

5. As noted in the Introduction, the expression "Great Function of the Complete Substance" (*quanti dayong*) can be traced to Zhu Xi. Given that Liu used Substance and function as equivalents for the theological terms Essence and attributes (or names), he was saying here that the Great Function is the sum total of the names and attributes of the Essence. In other words, it is the divine self-expression in divinis, or the Logos that is with God and that is none other than God himself, the single reality through which all things are made. It is, to use the Aristotelian expression commonly cited in Muslim texts, "the first in thought" that latterly becomes "the last in action." It is the Muhammadan Reality addressed by the divine words, "But for thee, I would not have created the spheres." Jāmī provided another designation for the Great Function when he called it "the universal task" (*sha'n-i kullī*):

The first level of descent in His knowledge is His descent in a universal task that comprehends all the divine and creaturely tasks, without beginning and without end. This is by way of His knowing Himself in this universal, all-comprehensive task, such that He knows the form of the Essence clothed in that [universal task] in a universal, undifferentiated manner, without the distinction of the tasks from each other. (*Rays*, p. 6)

The word "task" (*sha'n*) goes back to the Koranic verse, "Each day He is upon some task" (55:29). Ibn al-'Arabī interpreted this day as "the Day of the Essence," which is none other than the everlasting present moment. His followers commonly use "task" to denote all the divine acts, both as known to God within himself and as made manifest in the cosmos.

6. It has not yet issued forth because it is simply the Real Being's awareness of itself in itself, not in its manifestations.

7. "Subtlety" (*miao* 妙), or "mystery," designates nature or principle as invisible and impalpable and is associated with the realm of the spirit or the numinous (*shen*). Thus the *Yijing*: "The spirit is subtle in the ten thousand things and gives expression to them" (*Shuogua* 1.2.6; Wilhelm, *I Ching*, p. 272). Liu often used the word "subtlety" in contrast to "trace" (*ji* 跡), another designation for the appearances that make up the World of Images.

8. The Self-so (*ziran* 自然) or Self-suchness is often translated as "nature" or "spontaneity" (see *Concepts*, pp. 162–66) and is much discussed in Daoism. Chapter 65 of the *Daodejing*, for example, speaks of the sage in these terms: "He learns by not learning and goes back to what the multitude has passed over. Thus he supports the ten thousand things in their self-suchness without venturing to do anything." Zhuangzi tells us that the distinct attribute of human beings is their ability to interfere with the self-

so. They need to follow the Way precisely because their self-centeredness disturbs the spontaneous flow of things.

9. In Islamic thought, this "desire to move" is expressed in terms of the divine attribute *irāda*, "desire," as in the Koranic verse, "His only command, when He desires a thing, is to say to it 'Be!' and it comes to be" (36:82). One version of the hadith of the Hidden Treasure uses the same verb: "I desired to be known; so I created the creatures." Jāmī discussed the relationship of desire with other divine attributes in Gleams 15 and 17.

10. Perhaps Liu limited the great functions to knowledge and power instead of describing them as four or seven—as is commonly done in Islamic texts—to establish an ontological root for the yin-yang style complementarity that he perceived in the cosmos. He may also have wanted to provide a divine source for the Former Heaven / Latter Heaven dichotomy since he wrote: "Knowledge is beforehand in the Former Heaven, / and power expands in the Latter Heaven" (Root Classic 2:5–8). We need not attribute such motives to him, however, because there is plenty of precedent in Islamic texts for discussing the cosmos in terms of two primary and complementary attributes, typically beauty (*jamāl*) and majesty (*jalāl*), or gentleness (*luṭf*) and severity (*qahr*), or mercy (*raḥma*) and wrath (*ghaḍab*). Often the discussion proceeds in terms of the "two hands" of God, which, according to the Koran (38:75), God employed in creating Adam (see Murata, *Tao*, chaps. 2 and 3; Murata and Chittick, *The Vision of Islam*, pp. 67–77).

In his depiction of Diagram 1.3, Nūr al-Ḥaqq translated function as "attributes" and eliminated the problem of explaining why only two divine attributes are mentioned by listing seven attributes around the circle. Beginning at the top and moving clockwise, these are desire, hearing, knowledge, life, speech, power, and seeing (*Sharḥ*, p. 8/7).

11. Luminous awareness (*juezhao* 覺照), or illuminated consciousness, is a good clarification of what is meant by God's knowledge (*'ilm*). It is self-evident in Islamic texts that this knowledge is the act of knowing and understanding, which is to say that is inseparable from awareness and consciousness. When applied to human beings, however, *'ilm* can mean "the sum total of what someone knows" (*ma'lūmāt*). The Chinese language can have the same sort of ambiguity, which may be why Liu added this clarification. Certainly in English "knowledge" is often understood to mean "information," which obscures its association with life, consciousness, and awareness. Talk of "artificial intelligence" further muddies the waters.

12. The ten thousand seeds are what Ibn al-'Arabī and his followers commonly called the "fixed entities" (*al-a'yān al-thābita*). According to Liu, at the level of the First Entification, these entities are not yet differentiated; they become distinct only at the level of the Second Entification, which is the topic of the next diagram. In Ibn al-'Arabī's perspective, the Real Being has knowledge and awareness of the infinite things because these things are simply the possibilities of manifestation latent in itself. Moreover, Being is eternal and unchanging, which is to say that it knows everything eternally. Nothing can be "new" to the Real. The things or entities are "fixed" in Being's eternal awareness but have no existence of their own. "Creation" is the process whereby the Real brings them from the state of nonexistence in knowledge to the state of existence for themselves in the world. In other words, creation is God's word "Be!" uttered to things, through which they come to be, but without having any true being of their own. The ten thousand things are words articulated in the Breath of the All-merciful, which is nothing but the deployment of infinite existence.

In the language preferred by the Muslim philosophers, the fixed entities are called quiddities (*māhiyyāt*). Arabic *māhiyya*, like Latin *quidditas*, derives from the phrase "What is it?" A thing's quiddity (often called its "essence" in medieval philosophy) is the thing in its own specific whatness or suchness, which is precisely what differentiates it from other things. When we answer the question "What is it?," we have in mind the thing's name or definition or reality, but we have not yet discussed whether or not it exists. Hence the discussion of quiddity, like the discussion of fixed entity, typically goes on in tandem with the discussion of existence or being.

13. Ibn al-'Arabī often reminded us that the divine names require the existence of the world. Creator (*khāliq*) demands the created (*makhlūq*), Merciful (*rāḥim*) demands objects of mercy (*marḥūm*), Lord (*rabb*) demands vassals (*marbūb*), and the God (*al-ilāh*) demands the "godded over" (*al-ma'lūh*). But, the divine names that we know are in fact "the names of the [real] names," and those real names, of which the known names are simply labels, are real "before" there can be any talk of differentiation and multiplicity, which is to say that they are always and forever latent in the divine Essence, which is nondelimited and nonentified. See *Sufi Path*, chaps. 2–4.

14. This is a reference to Gleam 24, where Jāmī discussed the two sorts of entifications within the First Entification, that is, active/necessary/divine and passive/possible/created. As Liu translated this passage, "This

movement embraces all the necessary movements of Lordship and all the powerful movements of thingness." Only at the next level does Lordship become differentiated from thingness, Creator from creature (*Chinese Gleams*, pp. 180–81).

# 1.4
# 體用始分圖

## 1.4
## Diagram of the Beginning of the
## Differentiation of Substance and Function

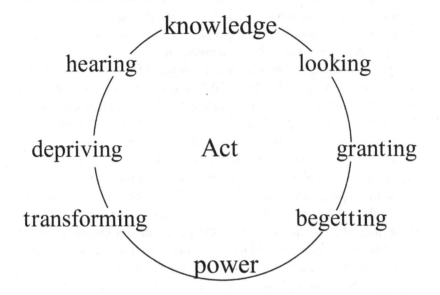

This is the third differentiated level of the first diagram.[1]

Function is contained in Substance. At this moment, there is the slightest mechanism of issuing and disclosing. This is the level of the second movement. There is no action whatsoever, yet the power to act is already abundantly embedded. If we talk about this as a whole, it is knowledge and power. If we talk about it separately, it is begetting[2] and transforming, granting and depriving, and all the kinds of settling, arranging, spreading, and laying out.[3]

When function and substance are not yet differentiated [1.3], this is called "the Chief Manifestation."[4] When function and substance begin to be differentiated, this is called "the Second Manifestation."

The Chief Manifestation is like the root clarity of fire when clarity and fire are one and have not reached further. The Second Manifestation is like the outside light of fire. Even though the light does not depart from the fire, it still has the power to illuminate everything.

At this moment the level of the Lord-Ruler becomes manifest. The act is the act of the Lord-Ruler, so, because of the act, one knows lord-rulerness. When the level of the Lord-Ruler is manifest, all the powerful acts embedded within arise like steam and reach the outward from the inward. When we probe the Great Function of knowledge and power as a whole, then, whenever there is the act of beauty, there is also the act of exaltation.[5]

"Beauty" means harmony and obedience. The settling and arranging of all of the ten thousand seeds,[6] the designations and names of the ten thousand seeds, and the meanings and principles of the ten thousand seeds all belong to harmony and obedience.

"Exaltation" means authority and gravity. All self-strength, all constant superiority, and all eternal perseverance belong to authority and gravity. The function of the self-strength of the Lord-Ruler is preserved only in Himself, but He does not use it. Were He to use it, heaven and earth would be ruined and the world destroyed.[7] This function of self-strength does not allow the preservation of a single thing. The man of discernment gets the taste of this realm and calls it "predetermination."[8]

When the Lord-Ruler desires to create things, there is an abundance of the Great Function beforehand, and this is also called the "inkwell."[9] This means that the essences of the ornamented patterns of heaven and earth and the meanings and principles of the ten thousand things are all collected beforehand in the midst of the inkwell.

Master Chami[10] says that this level means that the Real One enwraps and contains all the movements of the conferred traces of the Root Act, and that this is the outward of the Real Being.

The reason it is called "the conferred traces of the Root Act" is that the Real Ruler bestows upon things what He possesses in the Root Substance just like the trace of a seal.

## Notes

1. The discussion here concerns the internal divine relationships that must be grasped if we are to understand how the cosmos can come into being from the "empty" and "void," that is, from the nondesignation of the Essence. Ibn al-'Arabī and his followers commonly addressed this issue by differentiating between two sorts of divine oneness, to which we have already referred: *aḥadiyya*, or "Exclusive Unity," and *wāḥidiyya*, or "Inclusive Unity." The words are derived from two Koranic names of God, both of which mean "One," *aḥad* and *wāḥid*. The first sort of oneness is that of absolute transcendence and exclusiveness, belonging only to the Unknown Essence. The second sort designates the fact that God's unity encompasses all of reality. This way of envisaging the divine oneness gives rise to three levels of conceptualizing the Real Being in itself: first its utter nondesignation, then its Exclusive Unity, and then its Inclusive Unity. These are also known as Nonentification, the First Entification, and the Second Entification. All three names designate the same Being, but from three different standpoints (*i'tibār*). As Liu remarked in Root Classic 5:13, "The three ones are not three."

The same basic discussion commonly goes on in terms of the words "Essence" (*dhāt*), "attributes" (*ṣifāt*), and "acts" (*af'āl*). These are the three labels that Nūr al-Ḥaqq gave to his translations of Diagrams 1.2–1.4. He provided a good explanation of the interrelationships among these three standpoints in his commentary:

It is necessary that you recognize that these three levels (*martaba*), in relation to the Unitary Essence, are one. In regard to the rational faculty, however, there are three states (*ḥāl*): Nonentification, First Entification, and Second Entification.

Nonentification is the Unitary Essence, which, in regard to Its disengagement from all relations and respects, is called "the Level of the Essence."

The First Entification is also the Unitary Essence, but, in regard to the attributes present within It, It is named "the Level of the Attributes."

The Second Entification is also the Unitary Essence, but, in regard to the emergence of acts from It, It is called "the Level of the Acts."

All three states are beginningless concomitants of one another, but they leave no trace in the external realm. The priority of the Level of the Essence over the Level of the Attributes, and of the Attributes over the Acts, is only in regard to our rational faculties, not in reality, or in time, for God's knowledge is attached to its objects from eternity without beginning to eternity without end, without any taint of new arrival or renewal. So also, the rest of His attributes and acts subsist in His Essence without beginning and end, even if their attachments are made present only with the new arrival of the objects to which they attach.   (*Sharḥ*, pp. 10–11/10)

2. The character for "begetting," *sheng* 生, represents a shoot sprouting from the ground. In some contexts translators render it as "life" or "production," but we have chosen "begetting" not only for reasons of consistency but also because "life" does not suggest dynamism and motion, and "production" can be impersonal and dead. The *Yijing* identifies *sheng* with the principle of change itself: "Begetting and more begetting are what is meant by change" (*Dazhuan* 1.5.6; Wilhelm, *I Ching*, p. 299). In explaining the meaning of this sentence the Neo-Confucian Cheng Hao wrote, "This is what heaven takes as the Way—heaven simply takes begetting as the Way" (cf. *Concepts*, p. 116).

3. These are good examples of "names of acts," because each designates one of God's activities in bringing the world into existence. Liu, however, did not seem to have specific Arabic terms in mind; rather, he employed standard Chinese terms. Altogether he mentioned ten acts—six in the diagram, of which four are repeated in the text, plus four more. In his version of the diagram, Nūr al-Ḥaqq (*Sharḥ*, p. 9/8) mentioned five acts: engendering (*takwīn*, that is, bringing into being by saying "Be!"), life-giving (*iḥyāʾ*), death-giving (*imāta*), providing (*tarzīq*), and form-giving (*taṣwīr*).

According to Jāmī, this second level of entification is called by several names, including the Level of Divinity, the World of Meanings, the Presence of Designation (*ḥaḍrat al-irtisām*), the Presence of Beginningless Knowledge, and the Presence of Possibility (*Naqd*, pp. 39–40). He described it in these terms:

After [the first level of descent] is His descent in the differentiations of this universal task. This is called "the Second Entification." It is that He knows Himself differentiatedly through all the divine and creaturely, beginningless and endless tasks that were included in that universal task.   (*Rays*, p. 6)

4. That is, the First Entification as contrasted with the Second Entification.

5. The complementarity of beautiful and majestic divine attributes, as mentioned under the previous diagram, is much discussed in Islamic texts. This passage may be inspired by Gleam 27, in which Jāmī spoke of the contrary names of the Real in terms of gentleness (*lutf*) and subjugation or severity (*qahr*).

6. As already noted, these are the fixed entities or quiddities. In several passages Jāmī explained that the Second Entification is the level at which the fixed entities become differentiated (e.g., *Chinese Gleams*, p. 166). His clearest explanation is probably this:

The realities of the things are the entifications and distinctions of the Real Existence at the level of knowledge. The source of these entifications and distinctions is the specific characteristics of the tasks and standpoints that are concealed in the Unseen Essence. Existence discloses Itself in one of the attributes, and thereby It becomes entified and distinct from Existence disclosed in another attribute. This then becomes one of the realities derived from the names. The form of this reality in the knowledge of the Real is called the "quiddity" and the "fixed entity." Or, if you want to say that the reality itself is the quiddity, that also is correct. Thus the "fixed entities" are the forms derived from the divine names and entified in the Presence of Knowledge. (*Naqd*, p. 42)

7. That God's majesty and wrath, if untempered by his beauty and mercy, would destroy the world is a common theme, often discussed in connection with the hadith "God's mercy takes precedence over His wrath."

8. Wang Daiyu spoke of the differentiation of things in God's awareness as the root of predetermination (*qianding* 前定) in these terms: "The Classic says that the Real Lord is the Original Being, the Unique One, and at root nothing was with Him. Afterward, He mentioned and recorded the ten thousand things according to His own will. This is predetermination by the Real Lord's movement and quietude" (*Chinese Gleams*, p. 91). Ibn al-'Arabī explained the connection between God's eternal knowledge of the entities and the destinies of people and things in many passages, often in terms of God's "conclusive argument" (*al-ḥujjat al-bāligha*, Koran 6:149) against his creatures (see *Self-Disclosure*, pp. 26, 187). In no way should it be imagined, however, that this "predetermination" negates human freedom, a point to which all our authors often return (for Wang on this, see *Chinese Gleams*, p. 49).

9. Wang Daiyu also used the word inkwell (*mochi* 墨池) while talking about the level of the Acts (*Chinese Gleams*, pp. 91, 95). The Koranic basis for it is the verse "*Nūn*! By the Pen and what they inscribe!" (68:1). Although

*nūn* here is taken as the Arabic letter N, the word when spelled out means inkwell, and no one could miss its association with the Pen. Its cosmological interpretation goes back at least to Ja'far al-Ṣādiq (d. 764; see Murata, *Tao*, pp. 153 ff). Chinese Muslims may have taken it from Nasafī, who gave a long explanation in *Insān-i kāmil* (ibid., pp. 163–64). What he said there he summarized in *Goal* in these terms:

*Nūn* consists of the world of strength (*quwwa*), and the world of strength is the inkwell (*dawāt*) of God. The Pen consists of the First Substance, and the First Substance is the Pen of God. "What they inscribe" consists of the simple things, and the simple things are the writers of God. They are constantly writing, and their work is always to write the compound things.   (*Goal*, p. 241/78)

10. Liu apparently misread Gleam 24, which says that the third and the fourth levels together are the "Manifest of Existence" (*ẓāhir-i wujūd*). As he translated this passage, "These two levels pertain to 'the outward of the Real Being'" (*Chinese Gleams*, p. 183).

## 1.5
### 真理流行圖

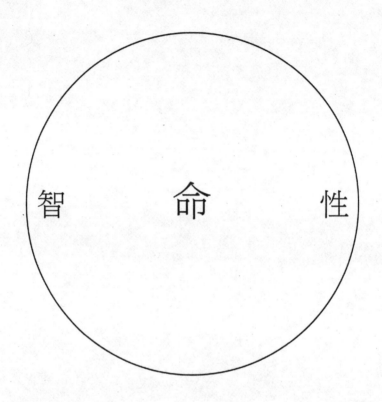

## 1.5
## Diagram of the Ongoing Flow
## of the Real Principle

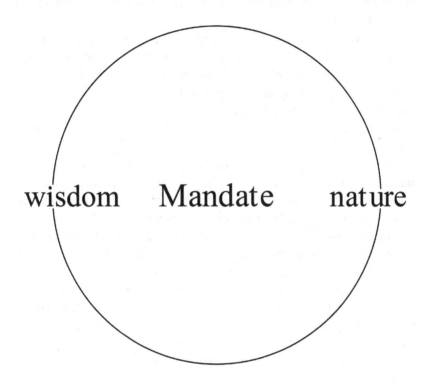

This is the fourth differentiated level of the first diagram.

The Mandate is the meaning[1] of the majestic ongoing flow.[2] It is the chief level of the issuing appearance of the Real Ruler. It is neither the Substance, nor the Function, nor the Act.[3] But, the issuing appearance that becomes the Mandate is the issuing appearance of the Real Ruler.

When there is already issuing appearance, then, if you desire to designate it as Lord-Rulerness, that is not permissible, and if you desire to designate it as thingness,[4] that also is not permissible. At the very moment of the majestic ongoing flow, the Real Ruler has in the midst of His Root Substance the all-possessing subtlety,[5] the issuing appearance of which is fully realized in the midst of this chief level.

The chief level is the one, whole mandate of the groups of the mandates[6] of the thousand antiquities.[7] Hence, the creative transformation is all that issues and appears from the Real Ruler within this chief level; it is an issuing appearance one by one.

The chief level is the chief level of Real-Rulerness. However, it is not permissible to designate this as the Real Ruler. What is possessed by the chief level is the one totality of what is possessed by the Real Ruler.[8] The principles and images contained in the chief level are the one totality of the principles and images contained in the Real Ruler. Hence, the affairs of the creative transformation are all affairs of the chief level, yet it is as if the Real Ruler has no share in these affairs. Therefore it is called "the representative."[9]

What is possessed in the midst of the ongoing flow is differentiated into two: one is nature, the other wisdom. What is called "nature" is the transformation of knowledge in the midst of the Great Function, and what is called "wisdom" is the transformation of power in the midst of the Great Function. Nature and wisdom are the knowledge and power of the Real Ruler.[10]

This nature is the chief of all the spiritual awarenesses[11] of the thousand antiquities. This wisdom opens up all the beginnings of the works and functions of the thousand antiquities. Both nature and wisdom act on behalf of the capability of the creative transformation.

Hence, all things having spirit are deeply rooted in this nature in order to begin; these are the kinds of humans, spirits, birds, and beasts. All things having action are deeply rooted in this wisdom in order to begin; these are the kinds of heaven, earth, and the ten thousand things.[12] Thus, this chief level is also named and called "the Great Brush."[13] This is to say that all the principles and images of the thousand antiquities emerge from the writing of this Great Brush.

It is also named and called "the Way," for it is the path of the coming and returning of the principles and images from ancient times until now. All giving rise and transforming by the Real Ruler must follow this realm to arise. All coming home to the Real by the ten thousand transformations must also follow this realm to come home. A person of discernment said that the ten thousand transformations follow this realm to come home to the Real. This realm is not together with the ten thousand transformations, but then they come home together to the Real. When ultimately this realm comes home to the Real, why then should we distinguish the chief level [from the Real]?

## Notes

1. Mandate (*ming*), as noted in the Introduction, corresponds to Arabic *amr*, "command." "Meaning" (*yi*) designates principle or spiritual reality. In this chapter Liu is concerned with the Mandate as destiny, or what in Arabic is called the "engendering command" or the "being-bestowing command" (*al-amr al-takwīnī*). The issue here is not moral commandments or ethics, because these are established by the prescriptive command (*al-amr al-taklīfī*).

2. The "ongoing flow" (*liuxing* 流行) is the constant unfolding of the cosmos. Mencius used *liu*, or flow, to illustrate that the nature of human beings is to do good:

Gaozi said, "Nature is like whirling water. Give it an outlet in the east and it will flow east; give it an outlet in the west and it will flow west. . . ."

Mencius said, "Water is indeed indifferent to east and west, but is it indifferent to up and down? The nature of the human is good, just as water goes down." (VI.A.2.1–2)

Ibn al-'Arabī and his followers commonly talked about the creative process as the "flow" (*sarayān*) or the "effusion" (*fayḍ*) of the Real Being. They called the All-merciful Breath "deployed existence" (*al-wujūd al-munbasiṭ*) and said that it flows in all things. This Breath is nothing but the Real Being, but it is simultaneously other than the Real Being inasmuch as it undergoes articulation, and that articulation (or entification) is nothing but the entire cosmos in all its infinity; hence the flow of the Real makes manifest (*ẓāhir*) all that is nonmanifest (*bāṭin*) in the Hidden Treasure.

3. That is, it is other than God, the Real Principle, conceived of in terms of Essence, attributes, or acts. Rather, it is what appears from God and makes his creative power manifest.

4. In other words, the Mandate is neither God nor creation. It is, to use one of Ibn al-'Arabī's well-known designations, "the third thing" (*al-shay' al-thālith*), the other two "things" being the Real and creation. It is "the Supreme Isthmus" (*al-barzakh al-a'lā*), because it stands between Real Being and absolute nothingness; or, it is the Breath of the All-merciful, within which all the divine words—that is, the infinite entities—become articulated (*Sufi Path*, chap. 8).

5. The all-possessing subtlety (*wusuo buyou zhi miao* 無所不有之妙) can be the Muhammadan Reality (*al-ḥaqīqat al-Muḥammadiyya*), as contrasted with the Muhammadan Spirit (*al-rūḥ al-Muḥammadī*), which is the Mandate. In Ibn al-'Arabī's terms, the Muhammadan Reality is the Logos as uncreated root of all things, embracing and comprising all the divine names and attributes in an undifferentiated, unitary manner; it is the prototype of the whole cosmos in divinis, and it is no different from God himself. This one, all-comprehensive Word "issues forth and is fully realized in the midst of this chief level," which is the Muhammadan Spirit, the First Intellect. As Nūr al-Ḥaqq explained,

Before manifestation, the First Engendered Being (*al-kawn al-awwal*) is identical with the Muhammadan Reality. It is this which, after manifestation, is the First Engendered Being. So, it is the locus of manifestation for the Real by means of this all-comprehensive reality. How great and noble [the First Being] is, for nothing is able to receive the Real's effusions but it!    (*Sharḥ*, p. 12/11)

6. In the Koran God says, "Our command is but one, like the glance of the eyesight" (54:50), and this is "the Chief Mandate." The command also entails manyness, however, because the single word "Be!" addresses all things. In this context, Ibn al-'Arabī liked to talk about the "specific face" (*al-wajh al-khāṣṣ*), that is, the face of God turned specifically to each individual entity to bring it into existence (*Self-Disclosure*, pp. 135ff). Liu

frequently spoke of the mandates of individual things, often in the expression "nature and mandate."

7. I.e., time immemorial. We use the term antiquity (*gu* 古) because of the important role the word plays in Diagrams 5.10–5.11.

8. Liu here explained why he used the term "all-possessing subtlety." By "one totality" he can mean what Ibn al-'Arabī called "the Word of the Presence," that is, "Be!" or the creating Logos. Ibn al-'Arabī and his followers called this chief level, as we have already noted, by a number of other names, including First Intellect, Supreme Pen, Greatest Spirit, Ascribed Spirit, and Muhammadan Light. When it issues forth from the One, it is "the Original Transformation," as Liu called it Root Classic 1:11. In other words, it is the first created thing, or "the first engendered being" as Nūr al-Ḥaqq translated it.

9. This term is discussed in some detail in 5.2. The original Arabic is not clear; probably it is *khalīfa* or vicegerent, one of the titles of the Perfect Human Being (*al-insān al-kāmil*), whose complete manifestation is Muhammad. In any case the point is that this first creation becomes the means for the creation of the rest of the cosmos. Nasafī, for example, cited the following prophetic saying, and he often reminded us that the First Intellect is identical with the Muhammadan Spirit:

The first thing God created was the Intellect. God said to it, "Come forward," so it came forward. Then He said, "Turn away," so it turned away. Then He said, "By My exaltation and majesty, I have created no creature more honored in My eyes than you. With you I shall give, with you I shall take, with you I shall reward, and with you I shall punish." (*Goal*, p. 239/76; cf. pp. 240–41/77–78)

10. Nature manifests knowledge, which Liu described as "luminous awareness" (Diagram 1.3), and wisdom manifests power, which is "settling and arranging." Calling nature "luminous awareness" suggests precisely the general meaning of the Arabic term *rūḥ*, "spirit." As for wisdom (*zhi* 智), Liu often used it to translate "intellect" (*'aql*), which is associated with both discernment and the ordering and arranging of things. Wisdom's connection with power (a yang attribute) rather than knowledge (a yin attribute) plays a role in what follows (e.g., Diagram 1.8).

In Confucian teachings, wisdom is one of the five constant virtues or the five natures, along with humanity or benevolence (*ren* 仁), righteousness (*yi* 義), propriety (*li* 禮), and faithfulness (*xin* 信); so it is much discussed as a human ideal. According to Chen Chun:

Wisdom is consciousness in the mind. To know the right is right and the wrong is wrong and to be absolutely sure is wisdom. Mencius said, "To know these two things, *ren* and righteousness, and not to depart from them is real wisdom' [4A.27].'' (*Terms*, p. 73)

As noted in the Introduction, Liu's division of the mandate into wisdom and nature is based on Rāzī's discussion of the creation of the spirits in *Path* (Chapters 2.2 and 2.3). There he wrote that the Muhammadan Spirit split into two, giving rise to spirit and intellect. Thus "nature" here translates spirit, and "wisdom" intellect. In Diagram 1.6, however, Liu seemed to translate intellect as "principle," which is entirely appropriate to its Arabic meaning, given that *'aql* is not only the subject that knows but also the intelligible reality that is known. The identity of "intellect, intellecter, and intellected" is an important philosophical principle discussed by Mullā Ṣadrā and others.

In *Subtleties* 1:13, Nūr al-Ḥaqq translated wisdom as "intellect," but he translated nature as "soul" rather than "spirit." In his version of Diagram 1.5 (*Sharḥ*, p. 17/13), he called the Mandate the Greatest Spirit (*al-rūḥ al-a'ẓam*), wisdom Universal Intellect (*'aql-i kullī*), and nature Universal Soul (*nafs-i kulliyya*). All three are much discussed in Islamic texts. Nūr al-Ḥaqq explained that the two are called "universal" because they embrace all the "particular" (*juz'ī*) souls and spirits detailed in Diagram 1.6.

11. We have met "awareness" (*jue*) in Liu's explanation of knowledge as "luminous awareness." "Spiritual" (*ling* 靈) refers to the living reality of awareness and consciousness in the heart. *Mathews' Chinese-English Dictionary* defines *ling* as "the spirit of a being, which acts upon others. Spirit; spiritual; divine. Supernatural. Efficacious." Zhuangzi puts the word *ling* into the mouth of Confucius, whom he quotes as saying, "Life, death, preservation, loss. . . . these are the alternations of the world. . . . They should not be enough to destroy your harmony; they should not be allowed to enter the Spirit Storehouse" (5.7, Watson).

12. "Spirit" translates *shen*, which is different from *ling* or "spiritual" in not having the same close association with the heart. Mathews says it means "A spirit; a god. Spiritual, inscrutable, divine, supernatural. The soul." Liu's discussion here, as noted under Diagram 1.5, is derived from Rāzī and corresponds with Chen Chun's correlation of nature with I's and principle with things (*Terms*, pp. 46–47). As possessors of spirit, Rāzī listed humans, angels, jinn, satans, and animals; as possessors of intellect, he listed stars, planets, heaven, earth, elements, inanimate things, and plants. Liu's mention here of "spirits" along with humans, birds, and beasts seems to be the only allusion in the text to angels, jinn, and satans (all three of which can be called "spirits" in Arabic). From this point on in the text, Liu often differen-

tiated between possessors of spirits and possessors of action with the shorthand "humans and things."

13. This is of course the "Supreme Pen," a synonym for the First Intellect, which takes its ink from the "Inkwell" mentioned under the previous diagram. The Arabic *qalam*, like English calamus (Gk. *kalamos*), is a reed pen. Chinese Muslims, however, use a brush for both Chinese and Arabic calligraphy.

## 1.6
## 性理始分圖

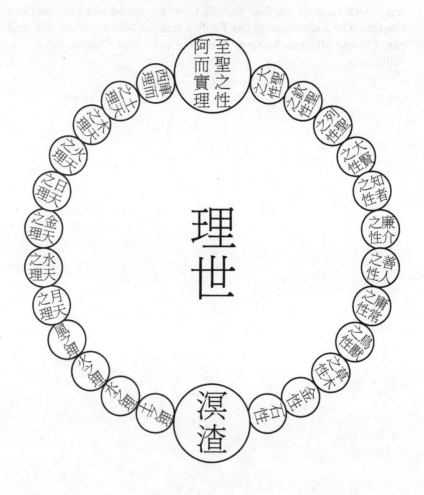

# 1.6
# Diagram of the Beginning
# of the Differentiation of the
# Natures and Principles

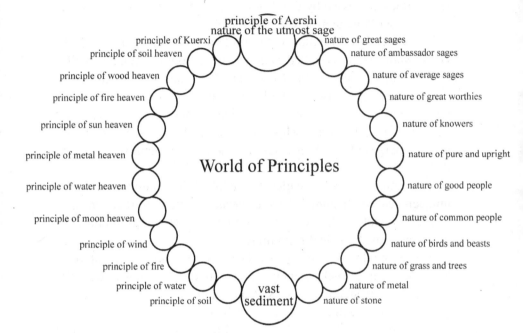

This is the fifth differentiated level of the first diagram.[1]

The signs of differentiation and separation come gleamingly to be from the Chief Manifestation in the midst of the Great Mandate.[2] Although colors and images[3] are not yet formed, the principles are already lushly embedded. All humans and things, sages and common people, upper things and lower things, and all the principles and vital-energies possessed by the World of Images[4] are seen in this realm as the trace of one undifferentiated suchness.[5]

The Chief Manifestation is the root suchness in the midst of the Great Mandate. It is called "nature and wisdom."[6] What is called "nature" here is deeply rooted in nature in the midst of the Great Mandate and gives rise to why humans are so. What is called "principle" here is deeply rooted in wisdom in the midst of the Great Mandate and gives rise to why things are so. Why humans and things are so emerges all together from the One Origin within which are no distinctions.[7]

Why things are so is called "principle." Why humans are so is uniquely called "nature." This is because nature is their spiritual awareness, and the fact that they are designated by spiritual awareness makes them distinct from things.

Nature is why humans are so. Generally speaking, the nature of humans has nine levels. Principle is why things are so, and generally speaking, the principle of things also has nine levels.

The earliest beginning of nature, which is near to the Real Ruler, is the nature of the Utmost Sage. It is followed by the nature of great sages, then the nature of ambassador sages, after that the nature of average sages, then followed by great worthies, knowers, pure and upright, good people, and then common people, all of whom together are nine levels.

At the earliest beginning of the principle of things and united with the Real Principle is the principle of Aershi. Aershi enwraps and contains eight heavens and supports their functions as a whole. It is the greatest level of heaven. It is followed by the principle of Kuerxi. Kuerxi enwraps and contains seven heavens and acts on behalf of their functions. It also exists inside of what is contained in Aershi. Next is the principle of the soil heaven [Saturn], then the principle of the wood heaven [Jupiter], then the principle of the fire heaven [Mars], then the principle of the Great Yang [sun], then the principle of the metal heaven [Venus], then the principle of the water heaven [Mercury], then the principle of the Great Yin [moon], all of which together are nine levels.

Once the nature and principle of humans and the heavens have been provided, then the surplus of the nature of humans is transformed into the root suchness of all birds and beasts. The surplus of the root suchness of birds and beasts is transformed into the root suchness of all grass and trees. The surplus of the root suchness of grass and trees is transformed into the root suchness of all metal and stone. These numbers and grades also flow and go in order to emerge from the nine levels in the midst of the nature of humans.[8]

The nature of humans has begetting and growth, knowledge and awareness, and spiritual intelligence, and may obtain the completeness of nature.[9] The nature of birds and beasts has begetting and growth, and knowledge and awareness, without spiritual intelligence. The nature of grasses and trees has only begetting and growth. The nature of metal and stone has only hardness and firmness.[10]

The surplus of the principles of the nine heavens is transformed into the principles of the four agents—wind, fire, water, and soil. The principles of the heavens turn and go ceaselessly; so the principles of wind, fire, water, and soil all turn and go ceaselessly. Only in the principle of soil are we slightly aware of hardness and congealedness. All are differentiated and separated in the sequence of flowing and going so as to emerge.

Then the surplus of the differentiation and separation of all of the ongoing flow becomes the Vast Sediment.[11] This is what is called "vital-energy." Vital-energy is the root of the forms and images of the ten thousand beings.

Someone said:[12] When nature and principle begin to be differentiated, there are different levels like this, and before and after are not the same. Does the creative transformation act like this, or is it that it does not act and instead complies with the Self-so?

I said: When the ongoing flow of the Real Principle reaches this ultimate point, it complies with the Self-so. There is a sequence of high and low in the midst, but this does not result in the slightest deficiency or going beyond, for there is one, firm, lordly sustaining, which settles and arranges. Therefore this cannot be called "acting," nor can it be called "not acting."

## Notes

1. This diagram depicts the differentiated details of the World of Principles mentioned in Diagram 0.2 (i.e., the World of Sovereignty), which itself is the manifestation of the Mandate. This world is differentiated into two sorts of realities—principle and nature—which correspond to Rāzī's intellect and spirit and make manifest the wisdom and nature of the previous diagram. These natures and principles are in turn ranked hierarchically as determined by their nearness to or distance from the unity of the Mandate, which is called here the principle of the Throne / the nature of the Utmost Sage. The higher a thing on the scale, the more intense are its life, light, consciousness, and so on (that is, the attributes or functions inherent to the Real Being).

Although Liu did not make the point explicit here, the left side represents the successive principles whose manifestations appear as the levels of the Descending Arc, and the right side represents the levels of spirit that become manifest on the Ascending Arc (as can be seen in Diagram 0.6). The diagram draws from discussions of the World of Sovereignty by both Rāzī and Nasafī. At the very top we have the Muhammadan Spirit—the nature of the Utmost Sage—whose station (maqām), according to Nasafī, is the Throne. This is none other than the seat of the All-merciful, within whose Breath the cosmos is articulated. The names of the nine human levels are fairly standard, but Liu is obviously basing himself on Nasafī's list, because Nasafī provides the same cosmic correlations, which are not nearly as common. Nasafī's original terms are as follows:

> Utmost Sage: khātam, "Seal" of prophecy, namely Muhammad
> Great sage: ulu'l-'azm, possessor of constancy (a Koranic term applied to some prophets)
> Ambassador sage: rasūl, messenger
> Average sage: nabī, prophet
> Great worthy: walī, friend (of God), or saint
> Knower: 'ārif, knower or gnostic
> Pure and upright: zāhid, renouncer or ascetic

Good person: *'ābid*, worshiper
Common person: *mu'min*, believer (*Goal*, pp. 269–70/109–10)

In his biography of the Prophet, Liu repeated the fourfold classification of prophets. Remarking on this and basing himself on a large number of Chinese discussions of the significance of Muḥammad as a sage, Benite argues that, although Liu mentioned only Muḥammad as the Utmost Sage (and provides no examples of the other sorts), he did not necessarily mean that no other sage could have the same status. "In stating that Muhammad's status as sage is 'supreme,' he was not implying that there might not be other sages in the same category" (*Dao*, p. 180). Benite's argument is plausible in the Chinese context, but anyone familiar with the teachings of Liu's Islamic sources would naturally interpret this mention of the supreme or utmost sage to mean that Muḥammad's status was unique.

Nasafī has a parallel explanation of the structure of creation in *Insān-i kāmil* (pp. 55–58), which Liu may have seen. There he said that God created fourteen levels of spirits in the World of Sovereignty and fourteen levels of simple (i.e., noncompound) bodies in the World of the Kingdom, the levels corresponding to what we have in this diagram. His discussion begins like this:

When God wanted to create the cosmos, which is substances and accidents, the first thing He created was a substance, and that is called "the First Substance" (*jawhar-i awwal*). When God wanted to create the world of the spirits and the bodies, He gazed upon that First Substance, and it melted and began to boil. That which was the cream and quintessence of that Substance came to the top, like the cream of sugar, and that which was the dregs and opaqueness of the Substance sat on the bottom, like the dregs of sugar. God created the levels of the world of the spirits from the luminous cream, and He made the levels of the world of the body appear from the dark dregs. (*Insān*, p. 55)

Nūr al-Ḥaqq interpreted this diagram as an elaboration of Rāzī's statement that spirit (nature) and intellect (principle) give rise to two sorts of creatures, possessors of spirits and possessors of intellects, and he revised the diagram to follow Rāzī, whereas in fact Liu is closer to Nasafī. Instead of what we have here—twelve levels each of spirit and intellect between Throne and Vast Sediment—Nūr depicted fourteen, for a total of sixteen. On the right, instead of the four levels beginning with birds and beasts, he has hypocrites, unbelievers, angels, jinn, satans, and animals. On the left, he adds plants and minerals after soil.

2. In other words, the roots and principles implicit in the First Entification (and differentiated in the Second Entification as things and entities) be-

gin to come into manifestation by means of the Engendering Command, the word "Be!"

3. By "colors" (*se* 色) and "images" (*xiang* 象), Liu meant the realm of appearances and phenomena, that is, the visible (Arabic *shahāda*) as opposed to the unseen (*ghayb*); or the Latter Heaven as opposed to the Former Heaven. The Great Commentary on the *Yijing* says, "What is visible is called 'image' " (*Dazhuan* 1.11.4; Wilhelm, *I Ching*, p. 318). On images, see *Concepts*, pp. 210–15.

4. As already noted, Liu's World of Images is the World of the Kingdom, which manifests the signs and traces of the Sovereignty on the level of elements, minerals, and plants. In other words, it represents the corporeal images of the principles and natures. It should not be confused with the World of Images (*'ālam al-mithāl*) or World of Imagination (*'ālam al-khayāl*) central to Ibn al-'Arabī's teachings.

5. Here the undifferentiated suchness is the Mandate, the Ascribed Spirit. In Islamic texts, the process of differentiation is commonly discussed in terms of the Supreme Pen (the First Intellect), which takes the undifferentiated ink from the Inkwell and then differentiates it by writing on the Guarded Tablet (the Universal Soul); Pen and Tablet are the yang and yin of the World of Sovereignty (see Murata, *Tao*, pp. 153ff).

6. As we saw under the previous diagram, the differentiation into nature and wisdom—nature being the principle of humans and wisdom that of things—derives at least partly from Rāzī's discussion of the split of the Muhammadan Spirit into spirits and souls. Here Liu was talking in shorthand when he wrote that possessors of natures are "humans"—in the diagram he put animals, plants, and minerals into the same category.

7. Compare Chen Chun:

Heaven is nothing but the vital-energy of the One Origin, operating like this without cease. This is the great foundation, this is the Great Ultimate. All things come out of it, whether small or large, . . . each fulfilling its own mandate. . . . It is not that heaven manipulates in each case but each naturally flows from the great foundation. This is how Heaven penetrates all with the One. (*Terms*, p. 96)

8. For more explanation of how this "surplus" of light determines the levels, a discussion drawn largely from Rāzī, see under Diagram 2.1.

9. By "completeness of nature," Liu has in mind the perfection and completion of the human being achieved by returning to the Origin and reaching the "nature of continuity," as made clear by Diagram 1.12 (and Root Classic 3:76–81).

10. In this paragraph, which is unpacked in Volume 3 (Diagrams 3.7–3.12), "nature" clearly cannot mean "human nature," as it is often rendered in translations of Chinese texts. Wing-tsit Chan, for example, is not untypical when he translates the first line of *The Doctrine of the Mean*, which reads "What Heaven mandates is nature," this way: "What Heaven imparts to man is called human nature" (*Source Book*, p. 98). He may simply be following the usual Chinese commentaries, but Zhu Xi among others understood "nature" here to refer to animals as well as humans (Legge, *Chinese Classics*, 1: 383).

11. As Nūr al-Ḥaqq recognized in his translation of Root Classic 2:17, this corresponds to what Ibn al-ʻArabī called the Dust (*al-habāʼ*), a word that designates not dust on the ground but particles floating in the air. According to Ibn al-ʻArabī, it is the Koranic term corresponding to what the philosophers call *hylē* (*hayūlā*), or prime matter. Within the Dust all the bodily things in the World of the Kingdom take shape. As noted under the next diagram, however, there are other Islamic concepts that also correspond with vital-energy (*qi*).

The word "sediment" translates *darādī* (pl. of *durdī*, from Persian *durd*), the "dregs" at the bottom of the wine bottle—frequently lamented by the Persian poets, not least because of the *dard*, "pain," that accompanies the dregs. Liu had in mind Rāzī's detailed discussion of how God created the spirits in a series of levels, each successive level being configured from the leftover of the previous level (Nasafī used "dregs" in a similar context, as already noted). Rāzī held that when God brought forth the light of the Muhammadan Spirit from the light of his own Unity, he looked upon that Spirit with the gaze of love, and it was overcome by shame and began to sweat. From the drops of its sweat, God created the spirits of the prophets. From the spirits of the prophets, he created the spirits of the saints, from the spirits of the saints, the spirits of the believers, and so on down the line: the disobedient, the hypocrites, unbelievers, angels, jinn, demons. Having created all these spirits, God then took their dregs and created the other spiritual realities, including those that pertain to plants, minerals, and the elements (*Path*, pp. 37–38/60–61).

12. The questioner wants to know if everything is determined by the Mandate of Heaven, or if there is room for things to have their own self-nature; this is a version of the predestination / free will debate. Liu took the middle position, refusing to say that it is one or the other, in typical Islamic fashion. The most famous example is the response of Jaʻfar al-Ṣādiq to a similar question: "It is neither compulsion nor freedom—the actual situation is between the two."

## 1.7

## 氣著理隱圖

## 1.7
## Diagram of the Display of Vital-Energy and the Hiddenness of Principle

This is the sixth differentiated level of the first diagram.[1]

When the level of the ongoing flow of the pure essences of the Former Heaven reaches here, there begins the awareness of having the undifferentiated, whole image. This is the so-called original vital-energy. When the colorless and imageless subtleties of the Former Heaven reach here, they come to an end, and the traces[2] of the Latter Heaven, with color and image, begin here.

This realm is nearly the one great pillar of the mechanism of following the flow and proclaiming the transformation. Although the original vital-energy is the outward of the majestic ongoing flow, yet, as a thing, it does not exist outside nature and principle [1.6], or outside the Great Mandate of the Chief Manifestation [1.5], or outside the Great Function [1.3] of the Complete Substance [1.2].

At the time of the nondesignation of the Earliest Beginning [1.1], the root suchness of the original vital-energy is already lodged in the midst.[3] At the time of the Earliest Beginning, however, differentiation and separation have not yet been formed. When the ongoing flow reaches here, the Root Suchness issues and discloses. This is the meeting place where the inward reaches the outward.

As a thing, [the original vital-energy] resembles the turbid, but it is pure; it resembles the traces, but it is subtle. In terms of sequence, it is the surplus of the whole flow of the Former Heaven. In terms of issuance and disclosure, it is everything that is within the Former Heaven. Without exception humans and the nature of humans, things and the principles of things, are issued and disclosed according to the issuance and disclosure of this original vital-energy. Thus, in the midst of the Earliest Beginning, without exception the so-called Great Function of the Complete Substance[4] is also issued and disclosed according to the issuance and disclosure of this original vital-energy.

Its turbidity cannot be outside its purity, and its traces cannot be separated from its subtlety. Hence we cannot simply name it "vital-energy"; rather, we should name and call it "original vital-energy." The "origin" is that within which are collected all the pure essences; the "vital-energy" is the container within which are lodged all the pure essences.

This diagram is designated as "the Display of Vital-Energy and the Hiddenness of Principle." The principle is hidden but not because of the vital-energy. As a thing, the principle has little movement and much stillness; as a thing, vital-energy has much movement and little stillness. At this moment, vital-energy moves, but the principle is still, so it is called "hidden." Every hidden thing has to wait in order to become manifest; that is all.

The issuance and disclosure of the original vital-energy is also differentiated into six levels. First is the level of undifferentiated sameness, where the position is differentiated [1.7].

Second is the level of arising transformation, where yin and yang are differentiated [1.8].

Third is the level of broadening transformation, where the four images are displayed [1.9].

Fourth is the level of the true position, where heaven and earth are made firm [1.10].

Fifth is the level of flourishing multitudes, where the ten thousand things are begotten [1.11].

Sixth is the level of the completeness of perfection, where the human kinds emerge [1.12].

When the six levels are provided, the powerful affairs of the original vital-energy are concluded.

## Notes

1. This diagram represents the furthest limit of the manifestation of the Sovereignty, which is simultaneously the beginning of the World of the Kingdom. In other words, it is the point at which the Arc of Descent changes direction and turns back on the Arc of Ascent. Nūr al-Ḥaqq called it the Dust (*habā'*), which, as noted, is one of Ibn al-'Arabī's designations for Prime Matter. It is the pure potentiality to receive forms (*ṣūra*), a potentiality that underlies all appearance on the Arc of Ascent. Mullā Ṣadrā, having described the cosmos in terms of the levels of the Real Being's manifestation on the Arc of Descent, wrote concerning Prime Matter:

So [the descent] continues, until it comes to an end at a common matter in which there is no good save the potency and preparedness to receive things. You will come to know that, although this matter reaches the utmost meanness and evil in its essence, it is the means for the approach to all good things, and, because of it, existence goes back and returns to perfection after deficiency, nobility after meanness, and ascension after fall. (*al-Asfār al-arba'a*, 7: 72–73)

Other terms might also qualify to translate *qi* into Arabic. Given that the basic sense of the word is "breath," perhaps the closest Islamic concept is the Breath of the All-merciful. The notion is rooted in two Koranic themes—that God's mercy embraces all things and that God creates the universe by speaking (e.g., by saying "Be!" to it). It follows that each individual being is a word enunciated by God in the womb (*rahim*) of mercy (*rahma*). Just as the "matter" of our own speech is our breath, so also the matter of God's Speech is his "breath," which is none other than the creative flow of mercy, compassion, life, and awareness.

Another term that can have the same sort of significance as *qi* is *tabī'a* or "nature," which was discussed in the Introduction as a designation for the receptivity of things to the action of the spiritual realm, the earthly side that receives the influence of heaven. According to Ibn al-'Arabī, in the broadest sense of the term, "nature" designates precisely the Breath of the All-merciful, which is the matter underlying every articulated and entified thing, that is, everything that takes shape and form because of the creative activity of the Ascribed Spirit, the Engendering Command (see *Sufi Path*, chap. 8).

2. The subtleties (*miao*) are the formless natures and principles of the Former Heaven (the World of the Sovereignty), and the traces (*ji*) are the forms, colors, and images of the Latter Heaven (the World of the Kingdom).

3. The inseparability of vital-energy from principle is stressed by Zhu Xi (*Source Book*, p. 634). Chen Chun wrote: "Before heaven and earth existed, there was already principle. However, as soon as there was principle, there was vital-energy. The principle resides in the vital-energy and is never separate from it. As vital-energy is everywhere, principle penetrates everything" (*Terms*, p. 109).

4. Which is to say that the human perfection that is achieved on the Arc of Ascent is already present at the beginning of the Arc of Descent. On Liu's use of this term, borrowed from Zhu Xi, see Chapter 3 of the Introduction.

1.8

### 陰陽始分圖

### 陰陽終分圖

### 陰陽變化圖

# 1.8
## Diagram of the Beginning of
## the Differentiation of Yin and Yang

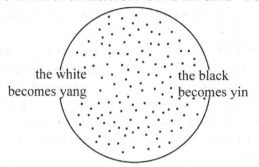

the white becomes yang

the black becomes yin

## Diagram of the End of the
## Differentiation of Yin and Yang

yang

yin contracts inside    yin    yang issues outside

## Diagram of the Alteration and
## Transformation of Yin and Yang

fire

yin alters to become water    water    yang alters to become fire

This is the level of the arising transformation of the original vital-energy.[1]

The original vital-energy is the vast sediment of the majestic on-going flow. All the abundant things contained in its midst are the surplus of nature and wisdom in the midst of the Great Mandate of the Former Heaven.

The root of differentiation into yin and yang[2] is that, when the surplus of nature and wisdom is obtained, the two become differentiated. Wisdom is the beginning of having action and the germ of taking pleasure in movement. Thus, in the midst of the original vital-energy, what is obtained from the surplus of wisdom surely has by itself the mechanism of taking pleasure in movement. It moves because it cannot not move.

Nature is settled without having any share in movement. Thus, in the midst of the original vital-energy, what is obtained from the surplus of nature also does not have any share in movement.

Of the surpluses of nature and wisdom, one moves and one does not move. Hence in their midst there is an image that is differentiated into two. The one that moves is called "yang" and the one that does not move is called "yin." This is why one vital-energy transforms and becomes differentiated into two.

When it is first differentiated, the two mix together and hardly depart from each other. After that, yang piles up in one place, and the mechanism of facing outward comes swiftly to be. Yin piles up in another place, and the tendency of facing inward comes hiddenly to be. The surplus of wisdom transforms to become yang, and the surplus of nature transforms to become yin; so the taproots of yin and yang arise from the surplus of nature and wisdom.

Someone said: When we speak about principle in the Former Heaven, nature is prior to wisdom.[3] When we speak about vital-energy in the Latter Heaven, wisdom is prior to nature.[4] In the ongoing flow of the original vital-energy, has the latter become former and the former latter?

I say: In the Former Heaven, principle is superior;[5] so wisdom is stored in nature, and, in reality, nature enwraps wisdom. In the Latter Heaven, vital-energy is superior;[6] so nature is stored in wisdom, and, in reality, wisdom enwraps nature.

Here there is the great beginning of yang, which arises from the surplus of wisdom and occupies the prior position, and the great beginning of yin, which arises from the surplus of nature and occupies the posterior position. The sequence of prior and posterior cannot but act like this.

## Notes

1. This diagram depicts the first level of the World of the Kingdom and the start of the return to God. In other words, it is the beginning of the Latter Heaven, as we see in Diagram 0.3, where it corresponds to the topmost circle. From this point on, the qualities and characteristics hidden in the Former Heaven—the World of the Sovereignty and the Arc of Descent— gradually come to be manifest by the interaction of principle and vital-energy.

Under Diagram 1.5, Liu explained that knowledge and power, the primary functions of the Real Substance, differentiate themselves into nature and wisdom (spirit and intellect). Nature is "luminous awareness," and wisdom is "settling and arranging." In other words, nature is a consciousness that illumines and observes, but it does not act (like Purusha in the Samkhya *darshan*). Hence, it is a yin attribute, though yin and yang per se are not yet manifest. Wisdom settles and arranges, thereby acting; so it is a yang attribute (like Prakriti). Nature and wisdom together give rise to the diversification of the natures and principles in the World of Principle. Once nature and wisdom have made their properties fully manifest in the Former Heaven, they reach their lowest point of descent as the Vast Sediment, which becomes the seedbed of the Latter Heaven.

With the appearance of yin and yang, nature and wisdom reassert their authority over the realm of manifestation. They leave no trace in the Vast Sediment per se, given that it is undifferentiated and inchoate by definition, but they begin the process of bringing the ten thousand things into existence in a hierarchy that leads to the various levels of human perfection, the highest of which is conjunction and continuity with the Original Being.

2. Islamic thought is full of complementary principles that are understood to interact in much the same way as yin and yang (cf. Murata, *Tao*), but no pair of terms corresponds exactly. This is presumably why Nūr al-Ḥaqq, in his translation of the Root Classic, resorted to the Arabic neologisms *qarrāniyya* (frigid) and *ḥarrāniyya* (fervid)—although these two words may well have had a previous history among Chinese Muslims. In

any case, *qarrāniyya* derives from the root QRR, whose basic meanings include rest, settling, stability, coolness, and cold. *Ḥarrāniyya* derives from the root ḤRR, which signifies heat, thirst, and achieving freedom. Nūr al-Ḥaqq explained that in the Dregs, the fervid is the trace of the intellect (wisdom), "because the root of the intellect is power, which requires movement, that is, creation and existence-giving, and the requisite of movement is heat." The frigid is the trace of the soul (nature), "because the root of the soul is knowledge, which requires stillness, that is, the fixity of the known things in knowledge, and the requisite of stillness is cold" (*Sharḥ*, p. 23/18).

3. In other words, the yin principles (spirit, knowledge) are prior to the yang principles (wisdom, action). This is because the various levels of descending manifestation are knowing and aware "before" they come into activity through differentiation. Ibn al-'Arabī made the same point by saying that God's knowledge precedes his activity. When God exercises power, he must first desire to do so ("His only command, when He *desires* a thing, is to say to it 'Be!' "; Koran 36:82); in order to desire something, God must already know it. Hence knowledge is prior to activity. The "thing" known by God, to which he says "Be!," is precisely the "fixed entity," forever present in his awareness. When God says "Be!" to the entity, its traces appear in the universe. Jāmī explained how this works by comparing the Engendering Command to light shining through pieces of colored glass, which thereby determine the way in which the light becomes manifest:

> The entities are all colored glass
>   upon which fall the rays of Being's sun.
> When the glass is red, blue, or yellow,
>   that is how the sun itself appears.    (*Rays*, p. 86)

4. Nature is luminous awareness, but on the Arc of Ascent, this is not achieved until after activity. First there must be the bodily receptacle, settled and arranged, and then the spirit can grow, mature, and achieve the fullness of awakening.

5. Principle—the invisible, spiritual, divine dimension of reality—is primary on the Descending Arc, moving from inside (nonmanifestation) to outside (manifestation), that is, from luminous awareness to wisdom, which settles and arranges things in their places.

6. Vital-energy, the manifestation of principle, is observed in the various forms and shapes assumed by the creatures on the Ascending Arc—minerals, plants, animals, humans. What has "settled and arranged" these levels is wisdom, and the spiritual dimension of things—their "nature"—

remains internal and hidden. Awareness and consciousness become more intense as we move up the ladder toward the human level, which then has nine degrees of ever greater awareness, awakening, illumination, and wisdom.

## 1.9

四象始形圖

清升濁降圖

上下分形圖

# 1.9
## Diagram of the Beginning of the Forms of the Four Images

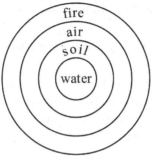

## Diagram of the Ascending Pure and the Descending Turbid

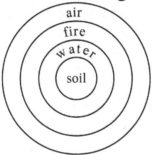

## Diagram of the Differentiating Forms of Above and Below

This is the level of the broadening transformation of the original vital-energy.[1]

At this very moment yin and yang transform and become water and fire. When water obtains fire, air is begotten. When fire dries water, soil is begotten. Therefore the four images of water, fire, soil, and air come to be.

Someone said: How do yin and yang transform to become water and fire?

I say: Yang is deeply rooted in wisdom in the midst of the First Mandate, and wisdom is deeply rooted in power in the midst of the Great Function. Wisdom and power are outward clarity. Here yang transforms and becomes fire, and fire is outward clarity.[2]

Yin is deeply rooted in nature in the midst of the First Mandate, and nature is deeply rooted in knowledge in the midst of the Great Function. Nature and knowledge are inward luminosity; so yin transforms and becomes water. Water is inward luminosity.

Water receives the blaze of fire, and air is begotten. Air is the subtle transformation of water and desires to ascend and leap. Although the body[3] of water goes down, it contains real yang; so, when water receives the blaze of fire, air just desires to ascend and leap.

Fire fights with water, and soil[4] is begotten. Soil is the preserved trace of fire and desires to fall and drop. Although the body of fire goes up, it contains real yin, so when fire fights with water, soil cannot but fall and drop.

All four—water, fire, soil, and air—have the meaning of clinging to the low in the midst of the high and the cause of adhering to the high in the midst of the low. They are designated by the names "four origins" because they are the foundational origins of the forms and colors of the ten thousand beings.

Their root meaning is four singles.[5] The "single" is the simple. What are called "the four images" are all simple, for each comes to act by itself without any companion. After this, metal and wood are begotten, and they act in pairs.

## Notes

1. Liu also called the four images "the four agents" and "the four vital-energies." In Chinese thought, there is much discussion of the "five" agents, i.e., soil, water, fire, metal, and wood; and various explanations are offered for different ways of arranging them (*Concepts*, pp. 95–103). Liu did not mention five-agents schemes per se, but he did explain the rationale for including air and excluding wood and metal (see the discussion under Diagram 2.8).

In Islamic sources, the elements are typically four, just as Liu listed. According to Rāzī, to whom the relevant lines of the Root Classic are referenced, the elements are themselves spiritual principles:

The four elements from which the human frame was made were also created from the dregs of the spirits. . . . Not a single mote remained without having within it the flavor of the attributes of the World of the Spirits. Even though the four elements are the furthest existent things from the World of the Spirits, something of the limpid attributes of the World of the Spirits is contained within them. (*Path*, pp. 67/95–96)

2. That is, the contrasting qualities of the four elements appear from yin and yang in terms of the correspondences mentioned earlier: the functions of knowledge and power (Diagram 1.3) give rise to nature and wisdom in the Mandate (Diagram 1.5). Thus yang (power, wisdom, settling and arranging) is contrasted with yin (knowledge, nature, luminous awareness).

Ibn al-'Arabī and his followers often correlated divine attributes with the four elements, but usually without an intervening binary relationship. Rāzī quoted an Arabic saying that mentions fire and water as an initial dyad:

When God desired to create this world, He created a substance and gazed upon it with the gaze of awesomeness and melted it. Then it became two halves because of awe of the All-merciful: half fire and half water. He made the fire flow upon the water, and from it rose smoke. From the smoke He created the heavens, and from the water's froth, the earth. (*Path*, pp. 57/86–87)

Ibn al-'Arabī correlated the four elements with the divine functions in more than one way. Usually the arrangement is like this (but see under Diagram 2.8, where another scheme is mentioned):

| Knowledge | Earth | (cold and dry) |
| Desire | Air | (hot and wet) |
| Power | Water | (cold and wet) |
| Speech | Fire | (hot and dry) |

In a typical passage concerning the elements, Ibn al-'Arabī explained the order of their appearance:

Water was the first of the elements. That of it which was dense became earth, and that which was insubstantial became air. Then the insubstantial part of air became fire, which is the globe of ether. So, in our view, the root of the elements is water. (*Futūḥāt*, 2: 677)

Nasafī had much to say about the qualitative relationships among the four elements. For example,

Know that soil is coarse, and water, in relation to soil, is subtle. Air is subtler than water, and fire is subtler than air. Whatever is subtler has a higher location in this world. . . . Know also that each of these four things, by reason of subtlety and density, has a separate location in this world, and also a location within each other. (*Goal*, p. 232/68)

3. The word for body (*ti*) here is the same as that for substance. Generally, "substance" is an appropriate translation of *ti* when the discussion is about *tiyong*, substance and function. But here there is no reference to function and, on the Islamic side, the discussion concerns what is commonly called the world of bodies (*'ālam al-ajsām*), as contrasted with the world of spirits.

4. The element is usually called "earth," but the word used, *tu* 土, is different from the word employed for the earth (*di* 地) paired with heaven. In Arabic, the word for "earth" in the heaven/earth pairing is *arḍ*; sometimes this word is used for the element, and sometimes *turāb*, "soil," is used. In Persian, however, soil (*khāk*) is always distinct from earth (*zamīn*).

5. Calling the elements "singles" (*ji* 奇) is parallel to Islamic texts, where the elements in their pure form are said to be simple (*basīṭ*, *mufrad*), that is, without parts. Everything perceived in the visible realm, however, is compounded (*murakkab*) of many parts, including what we call earth, water, air, and fire. In other words, the discussion is not about what we call by the names of the elements in the world, but about the energies and qualities that they make manifest. Thus Rāzī wrote:

You should know that when the human frame was going to be made from the four elements—water, fire, wind, and dust—these were not kept in the attribute of elementality and simplicity. Rather, they were carried down through further descending degrees. The first descending degree was that of compoundedness, for the element at the stage of simplicity is closer to the World of the Spirits. (*Path*, p. 65/94)

## 1.10
## 天地定位圖

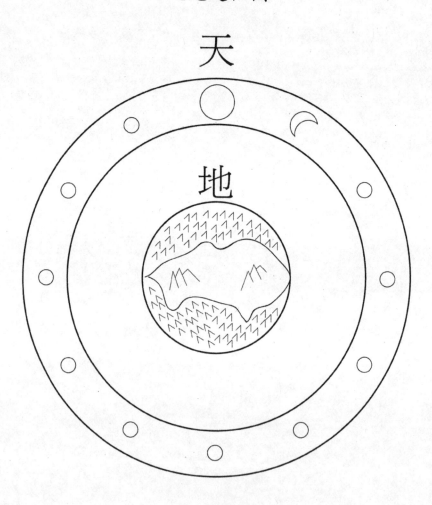

## 1.10
## Diagram of the Firm Position of
## Heaven and Earth

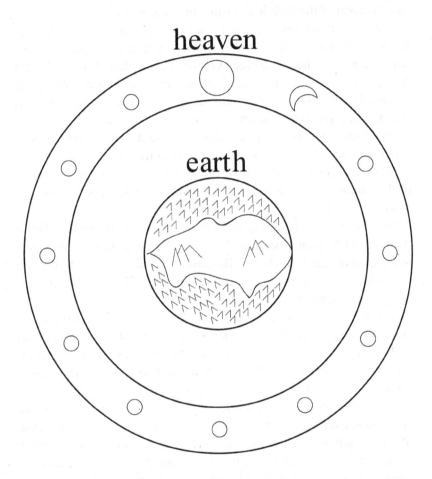

This is the true position of the level of the original vital-energy. The vital-energy of real yang issues outside and becomes heaven. The stuff[1] of real yin contracts inside and becomes earth. Because of this, heaven enwraps earth, and earth is housed in the midst of heaven, like the form of the yolk in the white of a hen's egg.[2]

When the positions of heaven and earth are made firm, water and fire are preserved in their midst. Know that heaven is air; air is that which leaps up when water receives the blaze of fire. This is why the firm position of heaven is up. Earth is soil; soil is that which falls down when fire fights with water and preserves the traces. This is why the firm position of earth is down.

The firm positions of up and down are the differentiated forms of inside and outside. When we look at heaven from earth, it seems that heaven is high and earth is low. But, if we look from the standpoint of the complete form of heaven and earth, in reality heaven is outside and earth inside.

Fire has no attachment to anything and adheres to heaven. When the body of heaven first came to be, air flew and became elevated, and sequence came into being. Because of the sequence of flying and becoming elevated, fire scattered and entered into its midst until the images of sun, moon, and planets came to be.

The nature of water tends to come down and adhere to the earth. When the body of earth first became firm, its tendency was sometimes high, sometimes low, sometimes hard, sometimes porous. Accordingly, water flowed over the high, low, hard, and porous and soaked into them, and the forms of lake, sea, river, and ditch came to be.

The preserved traces of fire fall down, but the pure of it goes up and adheres to heaven. The real yang of water ascends, but the turbid of it descends and adheres to earth. Thus neither the images existing in heaven nor the forms existing in earth have ever been without the cause of the interlacing of water and fire in order to come to be. The reason water and fire cannot but interlace is that yang contains real yin in the midst, and yin contains real yang in the midst.[3] It is not that yang is one in yang, and yin is one in yin.

*Notes*

1. Stuff (*zhi* 質) is a general designation for anything fixed in form and substance. It is commonly used as a near synonym for vital-energy, although it is usually considered to be more consolidated and solid (*Concepts*, pp. 63–65). In Diagram 0.3, Liu depicted stuff as the fourth stage in the consolidation of the Latter Heaven, when heaven and earth have taken up their positions, which is precisely what this diagram is showing.

2. The depiction of the earth as an egg yolk is found in the writings of the first-century astronomer Zhang Heng 張衡 (Needham, *Science and Civilisation*, 3: 217).

3. This is indicated in the usual yin-yang diagram by the black spot on the white side, and the white spot on the black side.

# 1.11
## 萬物始生圖

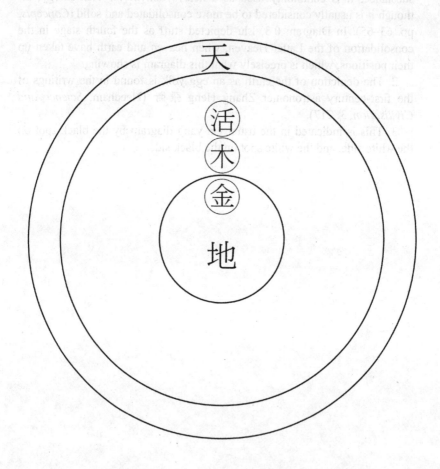

## 1.11
## Diagram of the Beginning of the
## Begetting of the Ten Thousand Things

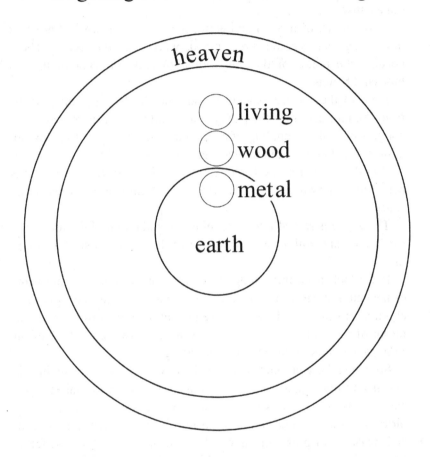

This is the level of the flourishing multitudes of the original vital-energy. Heaven and earth are firm in their positions, and water and fire are interlaced; so the affairs of transforming and nurturing arise, for the ten thousand things cannot be transformed and nurtured without a cause.

In the midst of heaven and earth, the water and fire that are first united together become three: metal, wood, and the living.[1] These become the bonds of the transformation and nurturing of the ten thousand beings.

Each of these three—metal, wood, and the living—comes to be from the unification of the [four] companions. Metal is rooted in the congealing and coagulating of earth and water; it comes to be by obtaining the alteration and transformation of air and fire.

Wood is rooted in the bestowal and conferral of air and fire; it is begotten by obtaining the nourishment and cultivation of earth and water.

The living is rooted in the combination and union of the four—air, fire, water, and soil. It overspreads and fills up the midst of the emptiness.[2]

If we look from the standpoint of the transforming and nurturing of heaven and earth, then metal, wood, and the living become three children of heaven and earth.[3] If we look at the transforming and nurturing of these three, then these three in turn are the mothers of the forms and colors of the ten thousand beings.

So, when the vital-energy of metal[4] flows and goes, mountains obtain it and make jade and stone, water obtains it and makes pearls and oysters, soil obtains it and makes the mines of the five metals, birds and beasts obtain it and bring into being the treasures of birds and beasts, and grass and trees obtain it and make the essence of grass and trees. All ten thousand things obtain it, and hardness, clarity, firmness, and solidity come to be in each.

When the vital-energy of wood flows and goes, mountains obtain it and beget excellent plants, water obtains it and begets duckweed and aquatic grasses, fertile soil obtains it and begets crops in general, and barren soil obtains it and begets grass and moss. Among four plants, that endowed with the superiority of soil is hard in its stuff, that endowed with the superiority of air is empty in the middle, that endowed with the superiority of water has a great many flowers, and that endowed with the superiority of fire has numerous fruits. In sum, all obtain this vital-energy of wood and by it are transformed and nurtured.

When the vital-energy of the living flows and goes, what is begotten in the mountains becomes running beasts, whose bodily forms are similar to hill and mound. What is begotten in the forest becomes flying birds, whose hair and feathers resemble branches and leaves. What is begotten in water becomes the scaled and finned, whose scales and armor resemble the waves of water. What is begotten in soil becomes crawling worms, whose form and stuff resemble soil and earth.

Among these four things begotten, that endowed with the superiority of air and fire is capable of flying, that endowed with the superiority of soil and water is capable of running, that endowed with the superiority of air and soil is mild in nature, that endowed with the superiority of fire and soil is ardent in nature, that endowed with the superiority of air and water is greedy in nature, and that endowed with the superiority of water and fire is violent in nature. In sum, all obtain the vital-energy of the living and by it are transformed and nurtured.

The three that are metal, wood, and the living exist in the midst of the transformation and nurturing of heaven and earth, and they are the three children. Afterward, they assist all the ten thousand things to begin. Thus in reality they are also the mothers of the forms and colors of the ten thousand beings.

### Notes

1. In other words, once heaven and earth have been established in their places, the elements interact and bring the ten thousand things into existence, beginning with minerals, plants, and animals.

2. "Emptiness" (*kong* 空) refers not to the utter emptiness of the Root Substance (Diagram 1.2), but to the space between heaven and earth, as can be seen in Diagrams 1.9c and 2.11.

3. Islamic texts call these three the "progeny" (*muwalladāt*), because they are born from the "parents" (*wālid*), that is, the "fathers" (*ābā'*), which are the heavenly spheres, and the "mothers" (*ummahāt*), which are the four

elements along with the four "natures" (*tabā'i'*, that is, the four qualities of the elements—hot, cold, wet, and dry). Nasafī wrote:

The spheres, stars, elements, and natures are called "the fathers and mothers." The fathers and mothers disclose themselves perpetually, and the three progeny have appeared and are now appearing from their self-disclosure.    (*Goal*, pp. 257/96–97)

4. The corresponding expression in Islamic texts is "mineral spirit" (*rūḥ-i ma'danī*) or "inanimate spirit" (*rūḥ-i jamādī*). Despite the fact that metals and minerals exhibit none of the usual signs of spirit, such as life and awareness, their qualities illustrate the active presence of the heavenly principles. As Nasafī remarked, "The fathers, the mothers, the minerals, the plants, the animals, and the humans—each partakes of the inward of the Ascribed Spirit in the measure of its own preparedness [*isti'dād*]" (*Goal*, p. 268/109).

## 1.12
## 大成全品圖

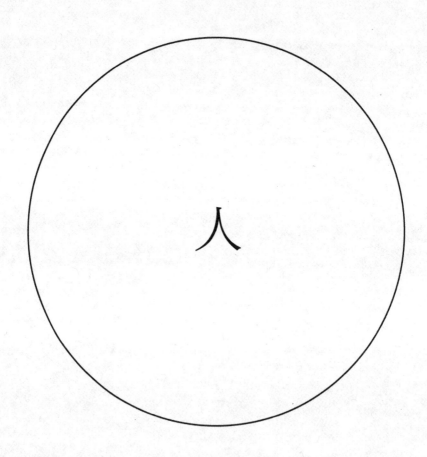

## 1.12
## Diagram of the Level of the
## Completeness of the Great Perfection

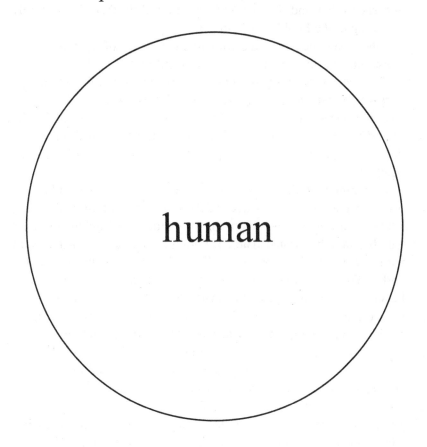

This is the perfect and complete level of the original vital-energy.[1]

Once heaven, earth, and the ten thousand things have all been provided, humans are begotten. The begetting of humans is not that they wait for the vital-energies of yin and yang to interact and ally with each other and then come to be. In reality, there is the lordly sustaining of the Real Ruler in the midst.

If there were heaven and earth without humans, of what use would be establishing the positions of heaven and earth?[2] If there were the ten thousand things without humans, to whom would the taking and using of the ten thousand things belong? From here we know that begetting heaven, earth, and the ten thousand things was all for the sake of humans. The human is that in the midst of which the Complete Substance and Great Function of the Real Ruler are collected together.[3]

In keeping with the suchness of the Self-so, knowledge and power turned around the pure essences of the four agents of air, soil, water, and fire and watched over them for forty mornings,[4] and the [human] body began to be formed. There is nothing in his outward and inward bodily apertures that does not tally with what is contained in the world.[5] The human body totally encloses all the bodies that exist, the human heart enwraps all the hearts that exist, and the nature of the human undifferentiatedly contains all the natures that exist. Because of this, human beings are the spiritual of the ten thousand things.[6]

When we speak from the standpoint of the principles of the Former Heaven, what makes humans human is the seed of all principles and vital-energies; this means that the original vital-energy also follows this seed in order to issue forth. When we speak from the standpoint of the principles of the Latter Heaven, what makes humans human is the fruit of all principles and vital-energies. The original vital-energy differentiates itself into yin and yang and threads directly through to the bottom for the sake of this fruit, and thus does the being of all things begin to be issued and disclosed. The fruit of the Latter Heaven is the seed of the Former Heaven.[7]

The bodily apertures are provided with all beauty, but the finest and subtlest of all are only two: heart and nature.[8]

Nature has ten virtues.[9] Five are outer luminosity and five inner luminosity. Seeing, hearing, speaking, smelling, and touching are called "the five awarenesses." These become differentiated from the heart and issue to the surface. Remembering, deliberating, recording, awakening, and comprehensive awareness are called "the five strengths."[10] These become differentiated from wisdom and are lodged in the brain.

The heart has seven layers,[11] and it has ten feelings[12]—pleasure, anger, love, hate, sorrow, joy, worry, desire, hope, and fear. When the heart's ten feelings are united together with the ten virtues of nature and issue forth, this is the upper level. It is this that makes humans human.

The one who received the creative transformation in the beginning and became the human body is named and called "Adam."[13] After this, the numerous human kinds are all begotten from Adam. This means that his companion also emerged from his left rib.[14] Adam is the original ancestor of the ten thousand generations.

## Notes

1. The perfection and completeness of the human level has everything to do with the fact that all qualities and vital-energies that appear in other things are present, at least potentially, in the human being. In Islamic texts, one of the several notions that is used to explain this capacity and preparedness is "constitution" (*mizāj*). The Arabic word means literally "blend," referring to the fact that everything is composed of a mixture of the four elements. Nasafī discussed its significance in a passage in which he was explaining the Koran's mention of the "proportioning" (*taswiya*) of the clay of Adam when God created him (e.g., 82:7: "Who created you, proportioned you, and balanced you"). He explained that in the human case, this means that the constitution has a unique "equilibrium" (*i'tidāl*), because all the elements are present in equal measure.

Every constitution in which the parts—the elements and natures—do not correspond and are not equal is a constitution without equilibrium and equality. "Proportioning" is in reality the constitution, that is, the reception of the spirit. . . . A constitution outside equilibrium has one of three states: it is near to equilibrium, far from equilibrium, or midway between near and far. Those that are far become the constitutions of the minerals, and then the mineral spirit appears. Those that are midway between near and far become the constitutions of plants, and the vegetal spirit appears. Those that are near become the constitutions of animals, and the animal spirit appears. (*Insān*, p. 265)

As for human beings, they are distinguished from other creatures by their balanced constitution. Thus Ijī wrote: "Everyone agrees that the most balanced among all species of compound things, that is, the nearest of them to true equilibrium, is the human species" (*Standpoints*, p. 227). His commentator, Jurjānī, explained that here is no stinginess on God's part. Rather, the creatures are differentiated by their preparedness and receptivity (*qābiliyya*)—their ability to receive the divine light and make it manifest.

Parallel discussions are not hard to find among the Neo-Confucians. Cheng Hao, for example, explained human exceptionalism in these terms: "Man is not the only perfectly intelligent creature in the universe. The human heart is the same as that of plants and trees, birds and animals. It is only that man receives at birth the Mean of Heaven and Earth [balanced vital-energy]" (*Source Book*, p. 527).

2. In Islamic terms, this discussion goes on in terms of the human role as God's vicegerents on earth. Ibn al-'Arabī offered numerous Koranic proofs and rational arguments to show that human beings are the "intended entity" (*al-'ayn al-maqṣūda*) in the creation of the universe, not least the fact that humans alone have the full capacity to return to God by way of the Ascending Arc and achieve what Liu called "the nature of continuity," that is, union with the Ascribed Spirit. Indeed, no concept is more central to Ibn al-'Arabī's worldview than *al-insān al-kāmil*, the Perfect Human Being. Many Sufis like to quote in this context the purported saying of God, "But for thee [O Muḥammad!], I would not have created the spheres." They also call to witness the hadith of the Hidden Treasure, which says that God desired to be known. Full knowledge of God can be achieved by his own image only when it reunites with its prototype.

Parallels in the Chinese tradition and especially Neo-Confucianism are numerous. Shao Yong wrote: "Man occupies the most honored position in the scheme of things because he combines in him the principles of all species. . . . The spirit of man is the same as the spirit of Heaven and Earth. . . . The perfect man can penetrate the hearts of others because he is based on the One" (*Source Book*, p. 492).

Commenting on *Analects* 15.28, "It is man that can make the Way great," Zhu Xi said, "Humans are the heart of Heaven and Earth. If there were no humans, no one would attend to Heaven and Earth" (Chan, *Zhu Xi*, p. 193).

3. Which is to say that God created Adam in his own form, embracing all of the divine names and attributes.

4. Wang Daiyu also referred to the forty days of Adam's creation (*Chinese Gleams*, p. 61). A well-known hadith, cited twice by Rāzī, quotes God as saying, "I fermented the clay of Adam for forty mornings with My own two hands" (*Path*, pp. 63/94, 211/221). God's "two hands" have generally been interpreted as complementary divine attributes, such as mercy and wrath (see Murata, *Tao*, chap. 3). Ibn al-'Arabī suggested the nature of the fermentation precisely in the context of explaining how God brings the three progeny into existence from the four elements with the final goal of creating human beings:

No form became manifest among the elements for the human being, who is the object sought from the existence of the cosmos. Hence God took sticky earth and mixed it with water, thus making it into a clay with His own two hands. . . . He left it for a period so that it might ferment through the hot air that permeated the parts of its clay. . . . Hence God says, "We created the human being from a dry clay of stinking mud" [Koran 15:26].   (*Futūḥāt*, 3: 296)

5. This brief reference to the correspondence between microcosm and macrocosm is probably at least partly inspired by Rāzī's long and poetical explanation in Chapter 2.4 of *Path*, "On the beginning of the creation of the human frame" (especially the detailed list of correlations on pp. 75–77/104–5). He summed up the discussion in this passage:

God created the heavens, the earth, and everything within them in six days . . . , even though that was the macrocosm. When He created Adam, who is the microcosm, He assigned forty days. . . . All these honors pertained to Adam's frame, which is the microcosm in relation to the macrocosm. But the [Divine] Presence singled out his spirit for Himself, for He said, "I blew into him of My own spirit" [15:29]. Given that this world, the next world, and everything within them are but a microcosm in relation to the infinitude of the World of the Spirit, see what an honor he was given! (*Path*, pp. 81–82/108–9)

6. As seen in a passage quoted in Chapter 2 of the Introduction, Ibn al-'Arabī held that the human being is the spirit of the macrocosm. He also wrote: "God created the cosmos as a well-proportioned body and made Adam its spirit" (*Naqsh al-Fuṣūṣ*, in Jāmī, *Naqd al-nuṣūṣ*, p. 3). Or again, "The level of the perfect human being in relation to the cosmos is the level of the rational soul in relation to the human being" (*Futūḥāt*, 3: 186).

Among Neo-Confucians, Wang Yangming often discussed the spiritual function of human beings vis-à-vis the cosmos. For example, in explaining a passage from the ancient Book of Rites that says, "Humans are the heart of Heaven and Earth," he remarked that this is true only when people attain to clarity of intelligence.

We know, then, in all that fills heaven and earth there is but this spiritual clarity [*lingming* 靈明]. It is only because of their forms and bodies that men are separated. My spiritual clarity is the lord-ruler of heaven and earth, of spirits and demons [*shengui* 神鬼]. . . . Separated from my spiritual clarity, there will be no heaven and earth, spirits and demons, or ten thousand things. (*Source Book*, p. 690)

7. In other words, from the viewpoint of the Descending Arc, the seed of all principles and vital energies—the Muhammadan Reality or Logos— gives rise to the Ascribed or Muhammadan Spirit (the Mandate), which em- braces all natures and principles. Everything present and potential in the Vast Sediment, also known as the Original Vital-Energy, is the result of the manifestation of that seed. The seed sprouts in the various stages of ascent—mineral, plant, animal—and comes to fruition at the human stage, when people close the circle by achieving the Nature of Continuity (Dia- gram 3.12), which is none other than reunion with the Ascribed Spirit from the standpoint of the Ascending Arc. It is at the point of reunion that the di- vine form in which Adam was created comes to be fully realized. This is the fruit of the seed. Wang Daiyu offered a parallel discussion:

The Non-Ultimate belongs to the Former Heaven and is the time of the first planting of the seed. Since this is from above to below, it is called "descending." This is the origi- nal seed, and it is the beginning of no-bearing-witness. The Human Ultimate belongs to the Latter Heaven and is the time of cultivation. Since this is from below to above, it is called "ascending." This is the root cause for producing fruit. The tree is hidden in the seed, and the fruit becomes manifest according to the tree. In the final analysis, the fruit is the seed and they are not two. (*Chinese Gleams*, pp. 100–101)

Both Wang Daiyu and Liu may have had this passage from Rāzī in mind:

The origin of the created and existent things is the human spirits, and the origin of the human spirits is the pure Muhammadan Spirit. Thus he [Muḥammad] said, "The first thing God created was my spirit," and, in another version, "my light." That Master was the cream and quintessence of the existent things and the fruit of the tree of the beings—for, "But for thee, I would not have created the spheres"—so he was also the origin of the existent things, and it cannot be otherwise. For creation is like a tree, and the Master is the fruit of that tree, and in reality the tree derives from the seed in the fruit. (*Path*, p. 37/60; cf. pp. 402–3/391)

8. Heart and nature are the topics of Volumes 3 and 4.

9. Discussed in some detail under Diagram 3.9.

10. These are clearly the internal faculties of the mind, for which the most typical Arabic word is *quwwa*, literally "strength" or "potency."

11. These are discussed under Diagram 4.2.

12. Feelings (*qing* 情), or "emotions," are much discussed in relation to heart and nature. The standard list of seven, which is taken from the Book

of Rites and is mentioned by Liu under Diagram 3.10, includes pleasure, anger, sorrow, fear, love, hate, and desire. Chen Chun called nature and feeling the substance and function (*tiyong*) of the heart: "The substance of the heart is nature, referring to its state of stillness, and the function of the heart is its feeling, referring to its state of movement" (*Terms*, p. 58). Thus, feelings are "nature when aroused" (ibid., p. 61). Liu Zhi, by saying here that the "upper level" is achieved when the ten feelings are "united together with the ten virtues of nature and issue forth," seems to mean that only human beings among the ten thousand things are able to bring together all the levels and capacities of nature and principle, that is, the spiritual realm.

13. The Chinese is *adan* 阿丹, a transliteration of Arabic Ādam.

14. Although not mentioned in the Koran, the creation of Eve from Adam's left rib is generally accepted by the tradition; Ibn al-'Arabī drew interesting conclusions from the symbolism (Murata, *Tao*, pp. 179, 181, 200).

# Volume 2

## Summary

The second volume clarifies the meaning that was not fully realized in the first volume. When it discusses principles, the earlier discussion of principles that was not fully realized will become sufficient; and when it discusses images, the earlier discussion of images that was not fully realized will become sufficient.

It is not, however, that principles are principles by themselves or images are images by themselves. Rather, the images are the principles.[1] To talk about images is precisely to explain clearly the principles that cannot be seen.

If those who have hearts can seek the principles and images through their bodies, they will obtain both. If they cannot seek the images and principles through their bodies, they will remain far away from them. If you scrutinize the diagrams and text every day only perfunctorily, how can that benefit your nature and mandate?

## Notes

1. Volume 2 describes how the natures and principles of the Former Heaven exercise their influence on the ten thousand things that appear in the

Latter Heaven. Liu's basic point is expressed succinctly in this sentence: "The images are the principles." Although the volume addresses the macrocosm in terms of the images that appear within it, it is in fact explaining the principles.

Liu pointed to the unity of principles and images in Chapter 2 of the Root Classic in a way that is worth remarking on here, because he does not expand on it in this volume. There he wrote, "Knowledge is beforehand in the Former Heaven, / and power expands in the Latter Heaven. / The Former is displayed by the images / and the Latter is formed by the principles" (2:5–8). In other words, knowledge, or "luminous awareness," is the essential attribute of the World of Sovereignty, the spiritual realm that is "before" (logically and causally, not temporally) the World of the Kingdom, the visible world. Power, or "settling and arranging," becomes manifest in the latter realm. The images are all things that appear in the visible realm; through them becomes manifest what is hidden in the Former Heaven, that is, the principles or spiritual realities that bestow form and shape on the Latter Heaven.

## 2.1
## 先天性品圖

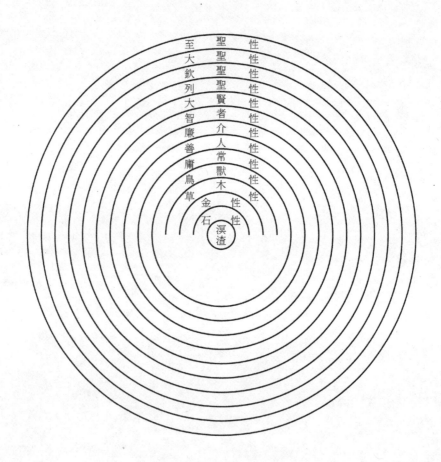

## 2.1
# Diagram of the Levels of the Natures
# of the Former Heaven

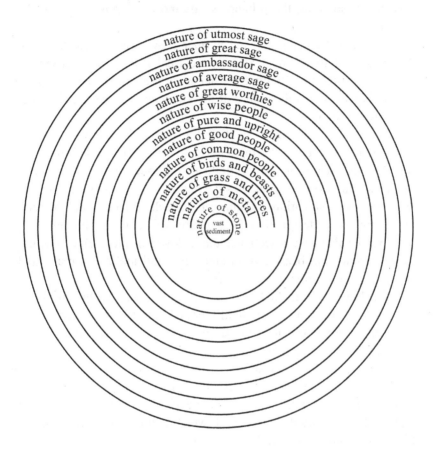

The explanation of the levels of the natures of the Former Heaven was already clarified in the Diagram of the Beginning of the Differentiation of the Natures and Principles [1.6]. Now diagrams will again be enumerated and explained in detail. The more detailed the text in investigating the principles, the more the principles will be revealed.

Altogether the natures of the Former Heaven are fourteen levels. The nature of the Utmost Sage is the Real Ruler's self-activity of chief manifestation. Although its name is "the nature of the Utmost Sage," in reality it is the nature of the knowledge, power, and virtue[1] of the Real Ruler.

What is below the nature of the Utmost Sage is differentiated and revealed in a sequence. All the levels and orders obtain their own natures by following the surplus light of this one nature.[2] Below this one level, three are designated as the natures of sages. The great worthies are one designation, the knowers[3] one designation, and the pure and upright one designation. The natures of good people and common people also have a sequence that is lower in succession. The natures of birds and beasts, grass and trees, and metal, minerals, and stones are even further below them.

As a thing the Vast Sediment comes to be when all the surpluses of nature and mandate are mutually united, altered, and transformed. In all there are fourteen levels from the nature of the Utmost Sage down to the Vast Sediment.

The nature of the Utmost Sage is neither the same as nor different from the Root Suchness of the Real Ruler.[4] The levels of its surplus nature are also not far apart from the Root Suchness of the Real Ruler. The most stubborn and dull, which is utterly dissimilar, is the border and limit of the levels and orders.

When the diverse levels of nature have been issued and disclosed in forms and colors, the numbers have been exhausted, the principles have reached their ultimate, and the ten thousand beings have come home to the taproot, then their return must be realized fully so as to enter into the nature of the Utmost Sage.[5] Only then will they be able to come home to the Root Suchness of the Real Ruler—because of the nature of the Utmost Sage. This may be why the nature of the Utmost Sage is the beginning and end of the ten thousand natures.

## *Notes*

1. "Virtue" translates *de* 德, a term that from ancient times was employed to mean goodness, strength of character, and worthy conduct; Daoism highlights its sense as power and strength (as in the common translation of *Daodejing* as "The Classic of the Way and the Power"). Chen Chun explained that virtue, in contrast to the Way of heaven and earth, "is concerned with human effort. . . . In general, the Way is what is common, while virtue is what is achieved in the self, thus becoming one's possession" (*Terms*, pp. 114–15).

2. Rāzī explained how the surplus of light delineates the levels with the analogy of candy-making, which could be observed in any local bazaar (*Path*, pp. 38–40/61–63). First the candy-maker extracts pure white sugar (the pure light of the Muhammadan Spirit), then he boils it for a time to produce white rock candy (the spirits of the prophets), then, by continuing to boil the syrup, he makes white sugar (saints), browned sugar (believers), caramel (sinners), black candy (unbelievers, angels, jinn), and the dregs. The dregs have both subtle and dense parts, the subtle being the animal and vegetal spirits, and the dense the four elements along with the bodies produced by their combination.

Rāzī expanded on this analogy in some detail, employing it, for example, to answer the perennial question of theodicy: Why does a good God create a world infected with evil? First, the darkness and blackness that appear in the sugar are inherent to the created state; pure light belongs to God alone. Second, God has the two basic attributes of gentleness and severity, or mercy and wrath; the purity of the spirits is the trace of gentleness and mercy, and their darkness is the trace of severity and wrath. Third, the darkness that increases level by level displays the activity of fire, and fire is love. It was God's love for creation that caused him to bring it into existence in the first place, which is to say that love causes the separation of things from their source. But God's love gives rise to human love: "He loves them, and they love Him" (Koran 5:54). When the fire of love is nurtured in the human breast through awareness of the pain of separation from the Source (a pain that parallels Buddhist *duhkha*), it intensifies the aspiration and need that drive human beings to engage in the quest for God. In other words, the very blackness of the human spirit demands the existence of the road to liberation, the Shariah and Tariqah through which people can return to the Haqiqah.

It is worth noting that Wang Daiyu employed Rāzī's image of candy-making in a similar context in his major work, *Zhengjiao zhenquan*, pt. 1, chap. 2.

3. Although this diagram, like Diagrams 2.2 and 2.5 (and in contrast to 1.6), has "wise people," the text has "knowers."

4. As explained in the notes to Diagram 1.5, the nature of the Utmost Sage, which is none other than the Muhammadan Spirit, is mentioned in the Koranic verses that refer to the creation of Adam, such as, "He blew into him of His spirit" (32:9). This spirit is neither the same as God nor other than God; rather, it is that which brings God and others together. Hence Ibn al-'Arabī calls it the Supreme Isthmus, or the Third Thing. Nasafī's favorite designation for it is "the Ascribed Spirit," an expression that Liu translated almost literally as "the nature of continuity" (Diagram 3.12). By ascribing it to himself, God declares its continuity with himself.

5. Having been created by means of the Ascribed Spirit, creatures can return to their ultimate source only by rejoining that same Spirit. The cosmos—whether we have in view the macrocosm, the microcosm, or both—returns to the Real Lord once it has exhausted its possibilities, but it returns by way of the intermediary that brought it into existence, which is precisely the nature of the Utmost Sage. On the Chinese side, Liu probably had Laozi in mind: "The things proliferate, and each goes back and comes home to its taproot. Coming home to the taproot is called stillness. This is said to be going back to the Mandate" (*Daodejing*, chap. 16). Liu quoted part of this passage in the first chapter of *Tianfang dianli*: " 'Coming home to the taproot' is returning to the beginning of the I. 'Going back to the Mandate' is completing the affairs of the I's governance."

## 2.2
## 性品知能圖

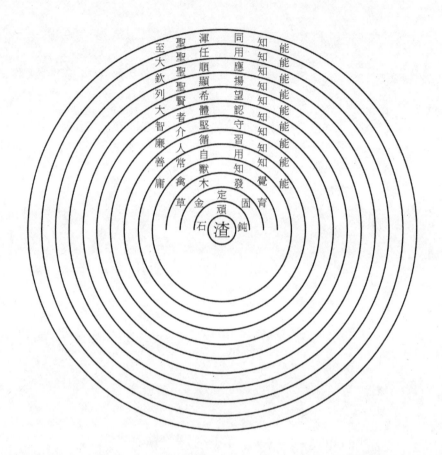

## 2.2
# Diagram of the Knowledge and Power
# of the Levels of the Natures

The natures of the Former Heaven are altogether fourteen levels. What differentiates and distinguishes them and makes each of them different is only the distinction of knowledge and power in their nature. The knowledge and power of one sage are not the same as the knowledge and power of another sage, and their levels and orders are decisively differentiated.[1] The knowledge and power of the ignorant and degenerate are not the same as the knowledge and power of the worthies and the knowers. The knowledge and power of things are not the same as the knowledge and power of humans. The disparity of their levels and orders is doubled and redoubled countless times.[2]

The knowledge and power of the Utmost Sage are undifferentiatedly the same. "Undifferentiated sameness" means that his knowledge and power are undifferentiatedly the same with the knowledge and power of the Real Ruler in one body,[3] without lack or surplus.

Great sages use[4] knowledge and power efficaciously. "Using efficaciously" means that their knowledge and power do not reach undifferentiated sameness, but they are allowed to use the knowledge and power of the Real Ruler efficaciously. For example, the bonds and ties of heaven and earth are the knowledge and power of the Real Ruler; but great sages can raise the dead and revive them, rotate and shift heaven and earth, and so on, and in all this they use [knowledge and power] efficaciously.

Ambassador sages respond obediently to knowledge and power. "Obedient response" cannot be to use efficaciously; rather they respond obediently to the Real Ruler's turning and function.

Average sages manifest and elevate knowledge and power. "Manifestation and elevation" means that, by obtaining all the issuing and disclosure of the Real Ruler's knowledge and power, they fully realize what was proclaimed for mankind.

Great worthies hope for and look toward knowledge and power, and knowers have embodied recognition[5] of knowledge and power. Those who hope for and look toward [knowledge and power] cannot be called "sages,"[6] yet they desire and seek to reach sagehood. Those who have embodied recognition are those who seek the clarity of the one root and embody its recognition.

The pure and upright firmly guard knowledge and power, and good people follow and practice knowledge and power. The common people use knowledge and power selfishly, and those who use knowledge and power selfishly are very near to being things.

Although knowledge and power are embedded in everything, these cannot [always] be designated as knowledge and power. Birds and beasts are said to have knowledge and awareness, grass and trees issuing and begetting, and metal and stone hardness and firmness. All are the same as knowledge and power.[7] The various kinds of things can obtain them only at the very last; so their levels are lower, and we are aware that they are further from the Real Ruler.

If the traces of the things' differentiation and distinction were to disappear and the forms of before and after were to be released, and if they returned again to the One Origin, then humans and things would not be seen as far apart.

## Notes

1. Since Liu took the nine human types and their cosmic correspondences from Nasafī (as explained under Diagram 1.6), he may also have been inspired by Nasafī's discussion of the differences among the nine types, although Nasafī explained them from bottom up instead of top down:

Know that when the human being acknowledges the prophets, he reaches the station of faith, and his name becomes "believer." When, along with acknowledging the prophets, he also performs many acts of obedience, divides the night and day [by periods of practice], and spends most of his time in worship, he reaches the station of worship, and his name becomes "worshiper." When, along with much worship, he turns his face away from this world altogether and expels love of this world from his heart, he reaches the station of asceticism, and his name becomes "ascetic." When along with asceticism, he recognizes God, and after recognizing God, he knows and sees all the substances of the things and all the wisdoms of the substances of the things as they truly are, he reaches the station of gnosis [*ma'rifa*], and his name becomes "gnostic." When in addition to that gnosis, he is singled out [*ikhtiṣāṣ*] by the Real for His love and inspiration, he reaches the station of sanctity, and his name becomes "saint."

When, along with that love and inspiration, the Real singles him out for His revelations and miracles and sends him with a message to the creatures so that he may call them to the Real, he reaches the station of prophethood, and his name becomes "prophet." When, along with revelations and miracles, the Real singles him out for His scripture, he reaches the station of messengerhood, and his name becomes "messenger." When along with scripture, God gives him power to abrogate a first Shariah and put another Shariah in its place, he reaches the station of the possessors of constancy, and his name becomes "possessor of constancy." When, along with abrogating the first Shariah and putting another in its place, the Real makes him the seal of prophecy, he reaches the station of sealing, and his name becomes "seal." (*Goal*, pp. 268–69/109–10)

2. The diversity of human levels is a general Koranic theme, expressed in many different ways, not least in terms of knowledge: "Are they equal— those who know and those who know not?" (39:9). "Not equal are the blind and the seeing man, the darknesses and the light, the shade and the torrid heat; not equal are the living and the dead" (35:19–22). Metaphysically, creatures must be infinitely diverse because each thing, as a face or self-disclosure of the One, has its own uniqueness. Ibn al-'Arabī expressed this notion in the axiom, "There is no repetition in the [divine] Self-disclosure."

3. See the discussion of this expression "one body" (*yiti*) in Chapter 3 of the Introduction.

4. "Use" translates *yong*, which, when paired with *ti*, or "substance," means "function." Given the reference to *ti* (body/substance) in the previous sentence, one might stretch the Chinese grammar a bit and translate this sentence like this: "Great sages function efficaciously according to knowledge and power." Liu could then be alluding to Zhu Xi's concept of Complete Substance and Great Function and be saying that the Utmost Sage is one body with the Complete Substance and Great Function, whereas the Great Sages are distinct from him inasmuch as they manifest the Great Function without having the same identity ("undifferentiated sameness") with the Complete Substance (under Diagram 4.7, however, he distinguished sages from worthies by saying that the sages reach this one body). This would be in line with the sort of distinction drawn in Islamic texts between the Muhammadan Reality and the realities of other prophets. Mythically, this distinction is represented, for example, by Muḥammad's saying, "I was a prophet when Adam was between water and clay" (*Sufi Path*, p. 239).

Qūnawī's student Farghānī expressed the distinction between Muḥammad and other prophets in terms of the Koranic verse of the Two Bows (the only verse Liu cited in this book): "[Muḥammad] was two-bow's length away, or closer" (53:9). According to Farghānī, all prophets reach the station of "Two-Bows' Length," technically known as *jam' al-jam'*, "the gathering of gathering"; in other words, all prophets complete the circle of existence and reach the Nature of Continuity. Among the prophets, however, Muḥammad alone achieved the station of "Or Closer," technically *aḥadiyyat al-jam'*, "the unity of gathering" (Farghānī, *Mashāriq al-darārī*, pp. 186, 395–96; idem, *Muntaha'l-madārik*, 1: 226, 2: 45). Jāmī employed this terminology in the introduction to *Rays* (p. 16) and explained it while commenting on Flash 14 (*Rays*, pp. 96–97; *Flashes*, pp. 98–99).

5. Wang Daiyu also used the expression "embodied recognition" (*tiren* 體認), or recognition with body, but he understood it as the station of "the Embodied One," which is the third of the Three Ones (*Chinese Gleams*, pp. 96–100).

6. In Arabic and Persian texts, this point would typically be made more forcefully: Muḥammad is by definition the Seal of the Prophets, that is, the one who brought the function of prophethood to a close, so that no one can become a prophet after him. Nonetheless, the saints can walk in the footsteps of the prophets and achieve much of what they achieved; what exactly they can achieve is the issue that stirs up debate. From the Sufi perspective (contra many philosophers), the final stages of ascent on the path cannot in fact be "achieved." This is why Nasafī was careful in the text just cited to refer to God's "singling out" or "specifying" (*ikhtiṣāṣ*) the saints and prophets for their stations. Such specification is discussed in contrast to "earning" (*iktisāb*), that is, what seekers can achieve on their own by following the prescriptive command.

7. By saying that all are the same as knowledge and power, Liu meant that the divine attributes become manifest in these levels in the appropriate modalities of existence. In Gleam 33, Jāmī used the specific example of knowledge to show that the Real Being is present in every existent thing, animate or inanimate. Liu entitled this Gleam "Knowledge and Power" and translated part of it as follows:

Truly, the Real Being's knowledge goes throughout the ten thousand beings. Therefore, without any doubt, all things large or small, manifest or concealed, have knowledge. However, there are two sorts of knowledge. One can be called "knowledge" according to the common people's opinion, and the other cannot be called "knowledge" according to their opinion. Both kinds are called "having knowledge" by those who possess real eyes. (*Chinese Gleams*, p. 203)

## 2.3
## 後天形器圖

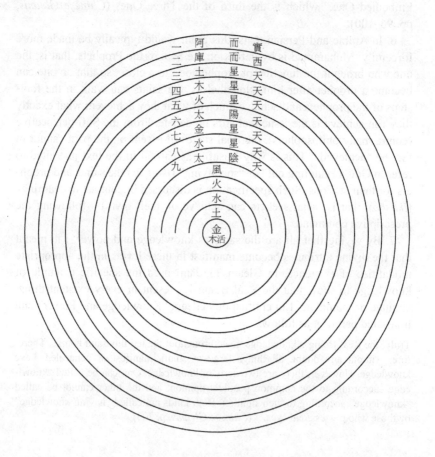

# 2.3
# Diagram of the Forms and Vessels
# of the Latter Heaven

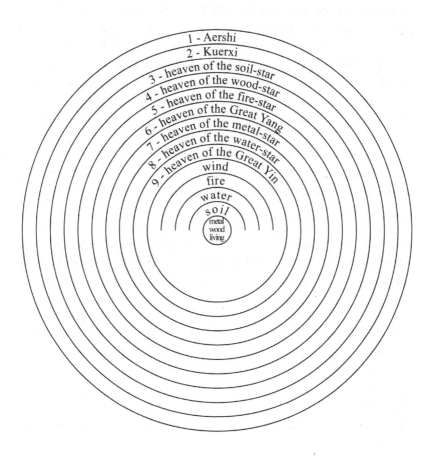

The forms and vessels of the Latter Heaven are altogether fourteen layers.[1] Their number corresponds to the number of the levels of the natures of the Former Heaven. The layers of the upper world are nine orders, which are the positions of the nine heavens. The layers of the lower world are five orders, which are the four vital-energies and the three children begotten from the four vital-energies.

Aershi[2] is the heaven of the ultimately pure with nothing beyond. The positions of the diverse heavens suspended in its midst are like pearls suspended in a shell. This is the body of the first heaven. In one respect it has form and faces downward, and in another respect it is formless and faces upward. It is formless and faces upward because it still belongs to the Former Heaven, and it has form and faces downward because it has begun to enter the Latter Heaven. At this moment the positions are differentiated, and Heaven is differentiated into Former and Latter, yet the two worlds are not separated and cut off from each other.

The second layer is called Kuerxi.[3] This is the heaven to which the twenty-eight mansions[4] and the constellations cling. Although it has forms, in reality these forms cannot be thought about or deliberated upon. When the original fire comes forth and enters the body of heaven, the images come to be; its [the original fire's] strength is able to reach only here, and then it stops. Above and beyond this is the ultimate purity to which nothing can cling, and below this are the seven heavens, to each of whose layers only one star clings.

The soil-star [Saturn] clings to the third layer, the wood-star [Jupiter] to the fourth layer, the fire-star [Mars] to the fifth layer, the Great Yang [sun] to the sixth layer, the metal-star [Venus] to the seventh layer, the water-star [Mercury] to the eighth layer, and the Great Yin [moon] to the ninth layer.

The heavens are nine. The uppermost is designated as the first layer, and the lowermost is designated as the ninth because the numbers run from the highest [heaven] to the lowest. This is counting according to the sequence. If the lowermost is designated as the first heaven, then the uppermost is designated as the ninth heaven. This is counting contrary to the sequence.[5]

In each heaven one star is settled in place. Each heaven has the endeavor and function[6] of that heaven. The one star that is placed in each works according to the mechanism and circumstances of the root heaven's endeavor and function.

Below the ninth heaven, the heavens are followed by wind.[7] Wind is followed by fire, fire is followed by water, and water is followed by soil.

When soil returns and faces water, it congeals and unites with water. Then metal is begotten. Metal is able to absorb fire and descends. Fire descends and air accompanies it and enters soil. Then wood is begotten. Wood is able to beget, and metal is able to make sounds. If the two come together and are suitably united with the effects of the four vital-energies, then the vital-energies of flying, rising, begetting, and living are begotten.

These three—wood, metal, and the living—are the three children begotten by the four vital-energies, which are wind, fire, water, and soil.[8] The unity of the three children makes up only one of the fourteen layers.

## Notes

1. Here Liu explained the fourteen levels of manifestation in the Latter Heaven (the World of the Kingdom), the principles of which were listed under Diagram 1.6. Forms (*xing* 形) and vessels (*qi* 器) are the things of the visible world, within which both the principles and the natures of the Former Heaven make their characteristics manifest. The terms go back to the Great Commentary on the *Yijing*, which makes clear that they are practically synonyms: "What is form is called 'vessel'" (*Dazhuan* 1.11.4; Wilhelm, *I Ching*, p. 318). The Great Commentary also says, "What is above form is called the 'Way'; what is below form is called the 'vessel'" (*Dazhuan* 1.12.4; Wilhelm, *I Ching*, p. 323). Wing-tsit Chan explains that the Dao is "what exists before physical form and is therefore without it" and the vessel is "what exists after physical form and is therefore with it" (*Source Book*, p. 786). In *Terms* (pp. 106–7), Chan translates *qi* as "concrete thing" rather than vessel. See *Concepts*, pp. 221–27.

The Arabic term for "form," *ṣūra*—which is contrasted with *ma'nā*, "meaning"—was discussed in Chapter 2 of the Introduction. A common equivalent for *qi* in Liu's sources is *qālab* (frame, mold), within which the spirit ("nature") is poured like molten metal. The typical Arabic word for "vessel," *inā'*, never became a technical term, although Junayd used it in a famous saying that explains how the Ascribed Spirit appears appropriately in all things: "Water takes on the color of its vessel."

2. According to the Koran, the *'arsh*, or Throne, is the place where the All-merciful "sits." Cosmologically, it is identified with the starless sphere, also called the "sphere of the spheres" (e.g., *Goal*, p. 241/79). In other words, the Throne is the furthest limit of the bodily realm and is contiguous with the spiritual realm, as shown by the fact that nothing indicates its presence but the blackness of the night sky beyond the stars, a blackness that signifies the invisibility of the World of the Sovereignty. Liu's explanation of the Throne as facing the formless on one side and the formed on the other may be derived from this passage, in which Rāzī clarified how the All-merciful "sits" upon it:

The Throne is singled out for the "sitting" of the attribute of All-mercifulness because the Throne is the furthest limit of the World of Bodies. It is a vast expanse, one of whose faces is toward the World of Sovereignty, and one of whose faces is toward the World of Bodies. The replenishment of the Real's effusion that reaches the World of Bodies derives from the attribute of All-mercifulness.   (*Path*, pp. 187–86/201)

3. The *kursī*, or Footstool, is where the All-merciful lets down his "two feet" and is identified with the sphere of the fixed stars. According to Ibn al-'Arabī, the fact that the All-merciful sits on the Throne means that beyond the cosmos there is nothing but the divine mercy. The two feet that he lets down are the foot of mercy and the foot of mercy mixed with wrath (Murata, *Tao*, pp. 86–88, 156). In Rāzī's terms, mercy mixes with wrath because the pure light of the Muhammadan Spirit finds the first trace of darkness at the level of the Footstool.

4. The twenty-eight mansions play a significant role in cosmological thinking in the Chinese, Arabic, and Sanskrit traditions (see Yampolsky, "The Origin of the Twenty-Eight Lunar Mansions"). For Ibn al-'Arabī, they mark the cosmic reverberations of twenty-eight divine names, each of which also becomes manifest as one of the twenty-eight letters of the Arabic alphabet. These twenty-eight letters articulate the creatures that are uttered by the Breath of the All-merciful. See Burckhardt, *Mystical Astrology*; and *Self-Disclosure*, pp. xxix–xxxii.

5. Ibn al-'Arabī numbered the spheres in either of these two sequences. When he described the overall structure of the cosmos in terms of the Descending Arc, he called the sphere of Saturn "the first heaven" and ended with the sphere of the moon, "the seventh heaven." When he discussed the Ascending Arc, he spoke of "the first heaven" as the sphere of the moon.

6. "Endeavor and function" (*gongyong* 功用) can be translated simply as "function," or "operation"; Nūr al-Ḥaqq translated it with the single word *khāṣṣa*, meaning "characteristic," or "specific quality." In the Root Classic, Liu made clear that he was using the expression to refer to the characteristics, qualities, and activities of things, and that these are the analogue of the knowledge and power of human beings: "In humans one speaks of 'knowledge and power,'/in things one speaks of 'endeavors and functions'" (2:13–14).

7. In Islamic texts fire is closest to heaven, then wind (e.g., *Goal*, p. 232).

8. In other words, the three kingdoms—plants, minerals, and animals—known in Arabic as the progeny (*muwalladāt*)—are compounded from the four elements, which are their mothers (as explained under Diagram 1.11).

## 2.4
# 形器功用圖

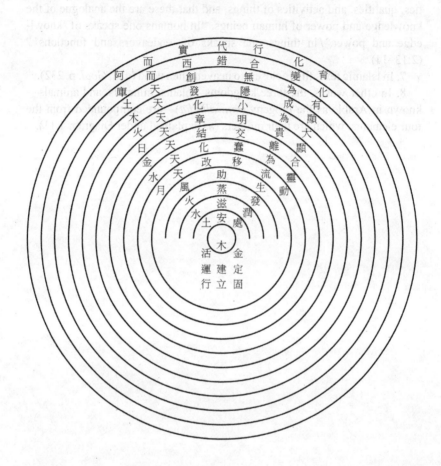

## 2.4
# Diagram of the Endeavors and Functions
# of the Forms and Vessels

The vital-energies of the forms are fourteen layers, each of which has its own endeavor and function.[1] The intermixings of the ten thousand things and the differences in human affairs are nothing but the endeavors and functions of these fourteen layers, which illuminate and brighten, connect and unite.

Aershi[2] acts on behalf of the endeavor and function of creating things. Thus it occupies the very beginning of form and vessel and obtains the omnipotence of the Real Ruler's transforming and nurturing. On one hand it faces the World of Principles, and on the other it faces the World of Images. If something in the World of Principles desires to come to the World of Images,[3] it must rely on this realm to come. Only then can humans and things come to be in the World of Images. All the endeavors and functions of the diverse heavens below this heaven are also obtained by relying on it. Therefore its endeavor-and-function is the general sustainer of all the endeavors and functions of the diverse heavens.

Kuerxi[4] has the endeavor and function of mixing and uniting, altering and transforming. Each of the endeavors and functions of the diverse heavens has its one firmness that cannot act on behalf of the others, yet this heaven is uniquely able to act on behalf of the endeavors and functions of the other heavens. It acts on behalf of Aershi above, which brings about the whole movement of the various heavens, and it acts on behalf of the diverse heavens below, which enact the functions of the root heaven. This is so because each of the diverse heavens carries one star, and so also its endeavors and functions come home only to one affair. But, the stars of this heaven are countless, and all the twenty-eight mansions and the constellations cling to what is above. So, their endeavors and functions are also countless.

The soil-star heaven[5] creates being from nonbeing. Humans and things assume form and gain stuff, and they hasten forth from nonbeing into being, all because of the endeavor and function of this heaven.

The wood-star heaven[6] issues the hidden and brings forth the manifest. Things are begotten, grow, mature, and culminate; humans display flourishing talent and perspicacity; and signs become auspicious and omens good, all because of the endeavor and function of this heaven.

The fire-star heaven[7] transforms the small into the great. Humans and things grow from small to great by being sheltered from others, and from suffering, poison, disease, and perversity, all because of the endeavor and function of this heaven.

The heaven of the Great Yang[8] ornaments clarity and ennobles manifestation. Its endeavors and functions do not reach specifically either of the two heavens of Aershi and Kuerxi, but, in comparison to the six heavens above and below it, it is the most prosperous. Each one of the six heavens above and below it must borrow the strength of this heaven's endeavors and functions—only then is it able to enact by itself the endeavor and function of the root heaven. This is so because its position occupies the midmost of the seven governances,[9] and in reality it is the lord-ruler of the seven governances. The six heavens above and below it are only its specific assistants. Therefore the begetting and livingness of humans and beasts, the growing and issuing of grass and trees, the altering and transforming of metal and stone, the flourishing and ripening of flowers and fruits, the nobility and eminence of humans and things, and the health and longevity of age and strength are all the acts of the endeavors and functions of this heaven. Clouds and rain, thunder and lightning, fog and dew, frost and snow, cold and heat, wetness and dryness, the coming and going of the four seasons, the waning and waxing of the ten thousand things, all alterations and transformations, and all activity come to be through the endeavors and functions of this heaven.

The metal-star heaven[10] performs the endeavor and function of connecting and exchanging separations and unions. The exchanging, joining, uniting, mutual influence, and partnership of humans and things; and sounds, voices, colors, appearances, fragrances, flavors, and tastes are all nothing but the acts of the endeavor and function of this heaven.

The water-star heaven[11] transforms the doltish into the spiritual. If humans and things are doltish, it gradually transforms them into the spiritual. If they are dark, it gradually transforms them into clarity. The removal of filth, the rejection of impurity, and all the causes of immersing, moistening, translucence, and shining are nothing but the acts of the endeavor and function of this heaven.

The heaven of the Great Yin[12] is good at altering and shifting so as to flow and move. All the sudden increases and sudden decreases, quick successes and quick failures, waning and waxing of morning tides and evening tides, and alteration and confusion of affairs and things are nothing but the acts of the endeavor and function of this heaven.

The endeavor and function of wind[13] is the ability to expand and burgeon so as to assist begetting and the living.

The endeavor and function of fire[14] is the ability to smoke and evaporate so as to assist tepidness and warmth.

The endeavor and function of water[15] is the ability to nourish and moisten so as to enhance tasting and begetting.

The endeavor and function of soil[16] is the ability to bear and carry so as to settle and place.

Metal is good at firming and fixing, wood at erecting and establishing, and the living at turning and traveling.

When the endeavors and functions of the upper world and lower world are complete, the powerful affairs of the forms and vessels are concluded.

Endeavors and functions are the traces of the subtle function of the Real Ruler. Subtle function is the lively ongoing flow of the Complete Substance, and it does not stick to one firmness.[17] We discern the endeavors and functions of the forms and vessels by the forms and vessels. Furthermore, we awaken to the Complete Substance and Great Function of the Real Ruler by the endeavors and functions of the fourteen layers.[18] Thus we can say that form and vessel are form and vessel, and we can also say that form and vessel are not form and vessel.[19]

## Notes

1. As is clear from the concluding paragraph, this whole discussion aims at showing that the divine attributes and functions appear in the qualities and characteristics of the cosmic phenomena, which are the "signs" (āyāt) of God. Ibn al-'Arabī, among others, devoted much space to explicating the correlations between the divine names and the signs, which he often called the "properties" (aḥkām) and "traces" (āthār) of the names. In the Root

Classic, Liu attributed this discussion to the unknown *Aḥkām-i kawākib* ("The ruling properties of the stars"). To illustrate the type of thinking that this book no doubt contains, we cite a few examples of Ibn al-'Arabī's parallel discussions, partly from a long passage in which he described, in the same descending order, the specific properties of the nine spheres, then of the four elements (although in his scheme fire precedes air), and then of the animals, plants, and minerals (*Futūḥāt*, 3: 444–46).

2. The Koran tells us that "The All-merciful sat upon the Throne" (20:5), and according to various commentators, God then let down his "two feet" on the Footstool, which in turn "embraces the heavens and the earth" (2:255). Ibn al-'Arabī explained that the Throne is the pure mercy of the engendering command; since the Footstool is the locus of the appearance of duality, at this level wrath begins to exercise its effects, even though "God's mercy takes precedence over His wrath" (Murata, *Tao*, pp. 86–88).

The Throne is the most tremendous bodily thing in respect of its all-encompassingness; so it is "the Tremendous Throne" [Koran 9:129] in size and measure. Through its movement it bestows everything in its power upon those within its compass and grasp; so it is "the Generous Throne" [23:116]. It is far above being encompassed by any other bodily thing; so it possesses eminence and is "the Splendorous Throne" [85:15]. . . .

In the Throne the Word coming from the All-merciful Breath is one. It is the divine command bringing the engendered things into existence [i.e., "Be!"]. The Breath flows to the utmost end of the Void [*khala'*]. Through it everything comes to life, for "The Throne is upon the water" [11:7]; so it receives life through its very essence, because "from water" God created "every living thing. Will they not have faith?" [21:30], that is, in what they see—the life of the earth through the rain and the life of the trees through watering. (*Futūḥāt*, 2: 436)

3. Nasafī explained how things descend from the World of Principles in these terms:

When God wants to create something in the world, first the form of that thing is in God's knowledge. It comes to the Throne, then it comes from the Throne to the Footstool, then it hangs in the light of the fixed stars, then it passes through the seven heavens. It becomes the fellow traveler of the planets' light and comes to the lower world. Nature (*ṭabī'at*), which is the king of the lower world, comes to welcome this unseen traveler that is coming from God, and it brings as a gift a horse made of the four elements and appropriate to the rider. Then the thing comes to exist in the World of the Visible. When it comes to exist in the World of the Visible, the thing that was known to God becomes the act of God. Thus, the spirit (*jān*) of everything that exists is from the World of Command, and its frame (*qālab*) is from the World of Creation. (*Insān*, p. 144)

4. Ibn al-'Arabī:

The Word [the engendering command "Be!"] became divided only below the Throne—from the Footstool to everything below it—for the Footstool is the position of the two feet, and this is nothing but the division of the Word. Hence there became manifest [the World of] the Command and [the World of] the Creation, prohibition and commandment, obedience and disobedience, and the Garden and the Fire. All these derive from one root—the mercy that is the attribute of the All-merciful. (*Futūhāt*, 4: 274)

5. Ibn al-'Arabī:

God deposited in [Saturn] everything black and murky, and He linked to it the narrowness of the roads, rocky paths, hard ground, distress, grief, regrets for what was missed, the agonies of death, the mysteries of the darknesses, the deserts of destruction, thorny trees, vipers, snakes, harmful animals, desolate wildernesses, ruined roads, trouble, and hardships. (*Futūhāt*, vol. 3, p. 445)

6. Ibn al-'Arabī:

He deposited in [Jupiter] the lofty palms, justice in litigations and governments, the causes of good and felicities, the pure and beautiful blessing-givers, equilibriums, and completions; and the mysteries of the acts of worship, the means of nearness, the charities that act as proof, and the light-giving prayers. (Ibid.)

7. Ibn al-'Arabī:

He deposited in [Mars] the defense of the religious schools through ill-natured cuts and spearing counterpoints, . . . acts of partisanship and zeal, the instigation of tribulations and wars among the people of the paths of guidance and misguidance, and the counter-positioning of misleading obfuscations and clear proofs between the people of sound rational faculties and those of imaginings. (Ibid.)

8. Ibn al-'Arabī:

He deposited in [the sun] the mysteries of the spiritualities, the shining lights, the sparkling brightnesses, the dazzling lightning flashes, the illuminating rays, the light-giving bodies, the perfected levels, the balanced equilibriums, the pearl-like knowledges, the high rubies, the bringing together of the lights and the permeating mysteries, . . . the climbing of the spiritual meanings to the ultimate heights, the repelling of defects through profitable consolations and beneficial words, fragrant perfumes, and the likes of these. (Ibid.)

9. The seven governances (*zheng* 政) are the seven sorts of ruling power represented by the seven planets. Ibn al-'Arabī has an elaborate explanation of the cosmos as an empire governed by ranks of angels, including twelve administrators (corresponding to the constellations of the zodiac), seven lieutenants (the planets), and thousands of helpers (*Futūhāt*, 1: 294–96; partly quoted by Mullā Ṣadrā, *Elixir*, pp. 70–73).

10. Ibn al-'Arabī: "He deposited in [Venus] complete form-giving, beauty of arrangement, pleasant audition, beautiful and splendid views, awe, beauty, intimacy, and majesty" (*Futūḥāt*, 3: 445).

11. Ibn al-'Arabī:

He deposited in [Mercury] imaginal faculties, illusions, revelation, inspiration, the perils of corrupt opinions and analogies, vile dreams, dream-visions, artifactual inventions, practical deductions, mistaken and correct thoughts, active faculties, imaginings, auguries and divinations, physiognomy, sorcery, incantations, and talismans. (Ibid.)

12. Ibn al-'Arabī: "God deposited in [the moon] increase and decrease, growth, transformations, and dwindlings" (ibid.).

13. Ibn al-'Arabī:

Air is the breath and life of the macrocosm and possesses strength and power. It brings about the existence of melodies through the movement of instruments, such as the movements of the spheres, the boughs of the trees, and the intersection of sounds. . . . When it moves, it is the strongest thing that leaves traces in nature. . . . If it were to be still, every breathing thing would perish—and everything in the cosmos breathes, for the root is the Breath of the All-merciful. (*Futūḥāt*, 2: 451)

14. Ibn al-'Arabī:

In actual fact, fire is a noble angel who has a specific glorification and a strong authority. But the lowest heaven is extremely cold. Were it not for that fact that between us and its coldness God placed this fire that is between the air and the heaven, there would be no animal, plant, or mineral in the earth, because of the intensity of the cold. (*Futūḥāt*, 2: 450)

15. Ibn al-'Arabī:

Among the elements, God chose water as the best, because "of water We made every living thing" [Koran 21:30], even the Throne, for when He created it, it was only "upon the water" [11:7]. Thus life permeated the Throne from the water, so it is the most tremendous element. (Ibid., p. 174)

16. Ibn al-'Arabī:

The earth is the lowly that does not accept transmutation. . . . Each element manifests its authority within it, while it is the patient, the receptive, the fixed, the stable. . . . It is the mother from whom we emerged and to whom we shall return, and from it we will emerge once again. To it are we submitted and entrusted. Earth is the subtlest of the elements in meaning. It accepts density, darkness, and hardness only because God in His jealousy has covered over the treasures He has deposited within it. (Ibid., p. 455)

17. This sentence could almost be a translation of Ibn al-'Arabī's axiom, "There is no repetition in the self-disclosure," which means that at every

moment, each thing is unique, and no two things or two moments are ever the same. As Jāmī put it in *Gleams*, "The Presence of the Real discloses Itself at each breath with another self-disclosure, and there is no repetition whatsoever in Its self-disclosure" (*Chinese Gleams*, p. 188).

18. Given that "the human is that in the midst of which the Complete Substance and the Great Function of the Real Ruler are collected together" (Diagram 1.12), in understanding the cosmos we understand ourselves. Zhu Xi, among others, based self-knowledge on "the investigation of things." Ibn al-'Arabī stated repeatedly that the Koranic doctrine of the "signs" of God means that everything we come to know is informing us not only of God's Essence and attributes, but also of ourselves. For example, he cited a Koranic verse commonly taken as referring to the macrocosm and microcosm and explained it in terms of self-knowledge:

God says, "We shall show them Our signs upon the horizons and in themselves until it is clear to them that He is the Real" [41:53]. Hence the Real turned us over to the "horizons," which is everything outside of us, and to our "selves," which is everything that we are upon and in. When we come to understand these two affairs together, we recognize Him and it becomes clear to us "that He is the Real." (*Futūḥāt*, 2: 298; *Self-Disclosure*, p. 8)

19. Cf. Ibn al-'Arabī's notion of He/not He (explained under Diagram 1.1).

2.5
理象相属圖

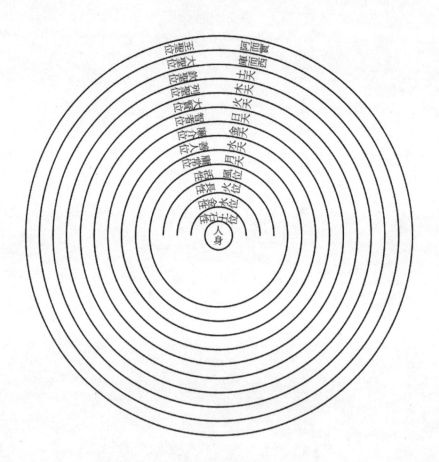

# 2.5
# Diagram of the Belonging Together
# of Principles and Images

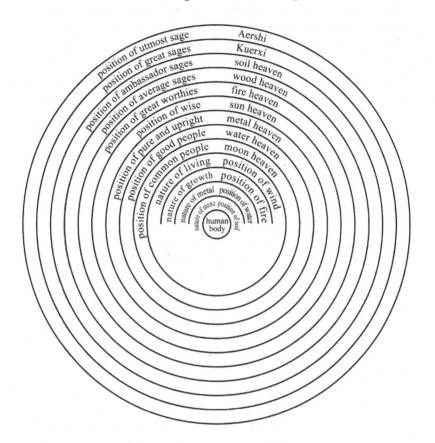

The natures and principles belong to the Former Heaven, and the forms and vessels belong to the Latter Heaven. The forms and vessels of the Latter Heaven emerge from the natures and principles of the Former Heaven. The natures and principles of the Former Heaven are stored and lodged in the forms and vessels of the Latter Heaven. At root, therefore, principle and image belong together.

Someone said: The forms and vessels are where the natures and principles are stored and lodged, but we do not know how they are stored and lodged.[1] Are the natures and principles stored and lodged in the midst of the forms and vessels? Or, do they not need to depend on and adhere to the forms and vessels? Is there rather something else in which they are subtly stored and lodged?

I said: The forms and vessels of the Latter Heaven are the position and allotment of the natures and principles of the Former Heaven. The position and allotment refer to the direction faced by nature and principle. This is not to say that a certain level of nature and principle is enclosed in the midst of that level.

Someone said: The images of each level are not confused with one another. But, do we not know that the natures of each level are undifferentiatedly the same as the One Principle that completely fills up the invisible and inaudible spaces? Does each have its own place that is not confused with the others?[2]

I said: The natures and principles of the Former Heaven are differentiated and distinct because the meanings and principles are differentiated and distinct. The meanings and principles have no traces. Although they are differentiated, the traces of the differentiation are not visible. In the midst of the One Principle of undifferentiated suchness, there is by itself a subtlety without any mutual confusion.[3]

If we look from the standpoint of the majestic flow, there is nothing up or down that is not completely filled with the One Principle. This can be called "union without differentiation."

If we look from the standpoint of the time of issuing appearance, there is not the slightest deficiency or going beyond for sage or commoner, human or thing. This can be called "union with differentiation."[4]

As for the belonging together of principles and images, this pertains only to the meanings and is not bound to the traces.[5]

Aershi is the position of the Utmost Sage, Kuerxi the position of the great sages, the soil heaven the position of ambassador sages, the wood heaven the position of average sages, the fire heaven the position of great worthies, the sun heaven the position of knowers, the metal heaven the position of the pure and upright, the water heaven the position of good people, and the moon heaven the position of common people. In short, all belong to their positions because of their levels and orders. Each takes up its position according to the proximity of its nature to the meaning and principle of its own heaven.

As for the natures of the things in the lower world, each takes up its position following the kind of its begetting. Those that come into being by obtaining the nature of the living follow wind. Those that come into being by obtaining the nature of wood follow fire. Those that come into being by obtaining the nature of metal follow water. Those that come into being by obtaining the nature of stone follow soil. All belong together based on the kind of begetting at root.

The belonging together of principles and images in the case of sages and common people, humans and things, is all the same.

## Notes

1. The questioner wants to know if spiritual realities are localizable. Liu tells him that they are not; rather, the images inform us of the orientation of the principles, that is, their hidden qualities that give rise to specific forms of manifestation.

2. The questioner is asking how natures can be differentiated within the One Principle itself. If the Principle is one, how can it be differentiated; and if it is differentiated, how can it be one? The basic answer goes back to Substance and function, or Essence and attributes. Ibn al-'Arabī and his followers often dealt with it by illustrating that the Real Being possesses all attributes in its own Oneness, which is to say that all possibilities are present in the very reality of "being," including life, knowledge, desire, power, and so on down the list of divine attributes. We know these attributes because we face them constantly in our everyday experience; they animate the universe and ourselves. From our standpoint they are many, but in God they are identical with the One Being.

Jāmī and others frequently addressed the issue of One and many by speaking of two "effusions" (*fayḍ*), a word that means "to flow," "overflow," "pour forth," "issue." The two effusions are called "the most holy" (*aqdas*) and "the holy" (*muqaddas*). The most holy effusion is God's disclosure of himself to himself in himself, which is to say that he is fully aware of his own reality. Along with his awareness of himself, he is aware of the infinite possibilities and modalities of existence that he encompasses. The holy effusion is God's disclosure of himself to others in the form of the others, or the manifestation of the infinite possibilities of existence within their own limitations. These limitations are precisely what God knows by knowing the things in their thingness (*shay'iyya*), that is, the specific attributes and qualities that distinguish them from Being as such. The specific thingness of the things determines their "preparedness" (*isti'dād*) or "receptivity" (*qābiliyya*), their capacity to receive and make manifest the Real Being, the Light of heaven and earth.

To put this slightly differently, the most holy effusion is God's knowledge of the fixed entities as possibilities latent in his own infinite Being. The holy effusion is his engendering command, "Be!," addressed at the entities; they come to be as heaven, earth, and the ten thousand things. In his translation of *Gleams*, Liu called the two effusions "the silent transformation" and "the creative transformation." Jāmī described them like this:

The Presence of the Real has two self-disclosures. One is the unseen self-disclosure in knowledge, which the Sufis have called "the most holy effusion." It is the Real's manifestation to Himself from eternity without beginning in the Presence of Knowledge within the entities' forms, receptivities, and preparednesses.

The second is the witnessed, existential self-disclosure, which is called the "holy effusion." It consists of the manifestation of the Existence of the Real colored by the properties and traces of the entities. This second self-disclosure is put in order by the first self-disclosure. It is the locus of manifestation for the perfections that came to be included through the first self-disclosure in the receptivities and preparednesses of the entities. (*Chinese Gleams*, pp. 206–8)

3. This "subtlety" can be the divine knowledge, within which the fixed entities are known without any confusion, much as our own ideas are distinct in the midst of the unitary awareness of our selfhood.

4. The holy effusion, also called the Breath of the All-merciful and the "deployment" (*inbisāt*) of Being, is present in all things, thereby bestowing upon them their existence. As the Koran puts it, "He is with you wherever you are" (57:4). Thus all things are "He" (*huwa*), that is, the One, Nondesignated Being, to which proper reference can be made only with pronouns, called in Arabic nouns of "allusion" or "pointing" (*ishāra*). If, however, we look at the unfolding of the holy effusion as successive self-disclosures and remember that "there is no repetition in self-disclosure," then each thing is uniquely

itself, each is "not He," because it is designated and delimited. Nonetheless, since each is still nothing but a self-disclosure of the Real, each remains identical with the One.

5. Principles and images, or meanings and traces, are united in their spiritual reality, which is ultimately the Muhammadan Spirit, the Logos, but not in the level of bodily manifestation.

2.6
# 九天遠近圖

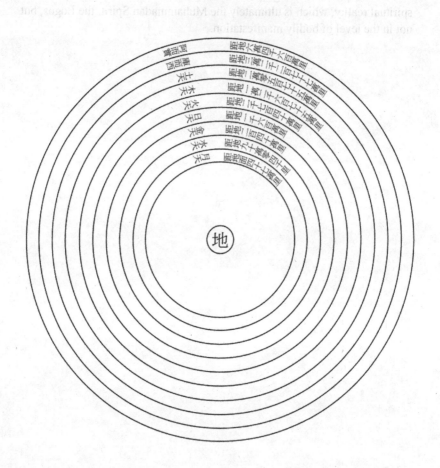

## 2.6
# Diagram of the Distance
# of the Nine Heavens

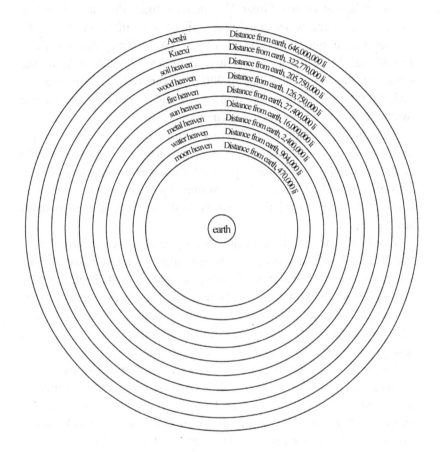

Aershi — Distance from earth, 646,000,000 li

Kuerxi — Distance from earth, 322,770,000 li

soil heaven — Distance from earth, 205,750,000 li

wood heaven — Distance from earth, 126,750,000 li

fire heaven — Distance from earth, 27,400,000 li

sun heaven — Distance from earth, 16,000,000 li

metal heaven — Distance from earth, 2,400,000 li

water heaven — Distance from earth, 904,000 li

moon heaven — Distance from earth, 470,000 li

earth

Heaven is differentiated into nine layers, but what brings about differentiation is formless. Even though it is formless, we can still know about the distance because, if we look at the distance of the star of the root heaven, we will know the distance of that heaven.[1]

The distance of the Great Yin heaven from the earth is about 470,000 *li*,[2] of the water-star heaven about 904,000 *li*, of the metal-star heaven about 2,400,000 *li*, of the Great Yang heaven about 16,000,000 *li*, of the fire-star heaven about 27,400,000 *li*, of the wood-star heaven about 126,750,000 *li*, of the soil-star heaven about 205,750,000 *li*, of Kuerxi about 322,770,000 *li*, and of Aershi about twice the distance from earth as Kuerxi.

Each heaven's numerical distance from the earth is fixed by the length of its radius. Knowing the length of the radius enables you to know the length of the diameter. If the diameter is one, then the circumference will be three. Thus you may know the length of the circumference and size of the complete body of each heaven without any deviation.

You know that the distance and size of each heaven is based on its star. The body of the star of each heaven also has a fixed size. All the mansions and constellations of Kuerxi are differentiated roughly into seven grades. The first grade is 110 times as large as the earth, the second ninety times as large, the third seventy times as large, the fourth fifty-three times as large, the fifth thirty-five times as large, the sixth seventeen times as large, and the smallest seven times as large.

The soil-star is ninety times as large as the earth, the wood-star seventy-four times as large, the fire-star one and one-half times as large, and the sun 165 times as large. The metal-star is thirty-six times smaller than the earth, the water-star about 20,000 times smaller, and the moon thirty-eight times smaller.

The distance of the heavens and the size of the stars are as clear as the arrangement of the eyebrows. Those who look at their forms and vessels cannot fail to know their greatness.

The position of the earth in the midst of the nine heavens is like a grain of sand in the midst of the Great Desert. The position of the nine heavens in the midst of the nature of the human, whether large or small, is like the position of earth in the midst of the nine heavens.[3]

## Notes

1. This diagram and the numbers mentioned in its commentary are derived from Matteo Ricci, who provides them in two works: *Kunyu wanguo quantu* 坤輿萬國全圖, pp. 222–23, 228; and *Qiankun tiyi* 乾坤體義, pp. 605–6, 610. The latter is a translation of Christopher Clavius's commentary on the Sphere of Sacrobosco, one of the most popular medieval treatises on astronomy. For a table of the exact distances of the planets given by Ricci, see Bernard, *Matteo Ricci's Scientific Contribution to China*, p. 64.

2. One *li* is about one-third of a mile. In his version of the diagram, Nūr al-Ḥaqq provided the distance in *farsakh*s (parasangs), taking ten *li* as equal to one *farsakh* (*Sharḥ*, p. 60/45). Typically a parasang is about four miles.

3. Given that the nature of humans contains all natures (Diagram 1.6) and is ultimately no different from the Nature of Continuity, the universe is in fact contained in the human essence. This led Ibn al-'Arabī and others to say that in the last analysis, what appears to us as the macrocosm is in fact the microcosm, and our own deepest selfhood is the macrocosm. Jāmī wrote:

Everything that is differentiated in the cosmos is included in an undifferentiated way in the configuration of the human being. Hence, in terms of form (*ṣūra*), the human is the undifferentiated microcosm (*'ālam-i ṣaghīr*), and the cosmos is the differentiated macro-anthropos (*insān-i kabīr*). But, in terms of [ontological] level (*martaba*), the human being is the macrocosm, and the cosmos is the micro-anthropos. (*Naqd*, p. 91)

## 2.7
## 九天旋轉圖

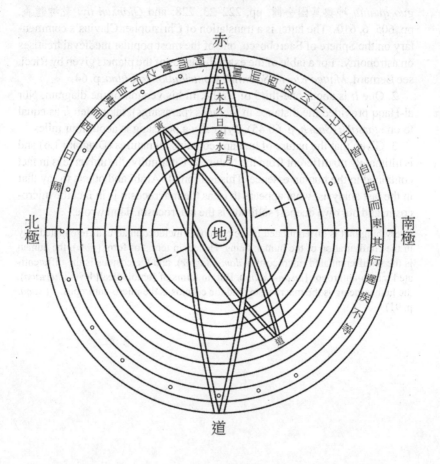

## 2.7
# Diagram of the Rotation and Revolution of the Nine Heavens

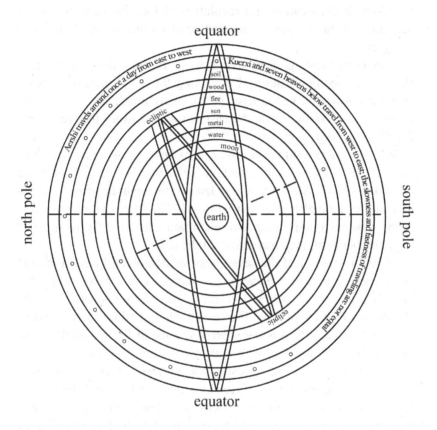

equator

north pole

south pole

equator

Aershi rotates and revolves from east to west, and this is its self-so movement.[1] The remaining heavens rotate and revolve from west to east, and this is the opposite and contrary movement. If the explanation of the two movements is clear, then you should know that the functions of the rotation and revolution of the nine heavens are all activities of the mutual connections and unions of the four vital-energies.

Why does Aershi go from east to west? Because the eastern direction is the specific position of collecting the air of begetting.[2] Air's specific position is in the east; so its rotation and revolution arise from the east. Arising from the east, it travels toward the west. This is called the "self-so movement."

Why do Kuerxi and the seven heavens below it move from west to east? Because the western direction is the true position of the fixed allotment of soil. All the root mandates of the eight heavens have the meaning of mutual connection with soil. The true position of soil is in the west; so their rotation and revolution arise from the west. Arising from the west, they travel toward the east.

Why do Kuerxi and the seven heavens below it all have a mutual connection with soil?[3] Because the images come to be when the original fire comes forth and enters the heavenly bodies. It is only Aershi to which the original fire cannot cling; it clings to the remaining eight heavens. Soil is the preserved trace of fire; so all the eight heavens have the meaning of mutual connection with soil.

Why do they have the opposite and contrary movement? Because the rotation and revolution of Aershi is from east to west. This is the leading movement; so the eight heavens below it have the tendency to move from east to west. In reality, however, the root traveling of the eight heavens is from west to east. So, although they have the tendency to be pulled by and to move with Aershi, their root traveling does not go along with this. Although they have an east-to-west tendency, in reality they travel from west to east. Therefore this is called the opposite and contrary movement.

In the rotation and revolution of the nine heavens, one movement is self-so, and eight are the opposite and contrary movement. Neither movement comes to rest. Thus, not only do the air of the east and the soil of the west melt and enter into each other, but also the fire of the south and the water of the north are caused by these rotations and revolutions of the leading movement, and so they turn, travel, and spread out. Then the four vital-energies blend together and originate the transforming and nurturing of the ten thousand things. All this is the act of the strength of the rotation and revolution of the nine heavens.

Those who talk about extending [the knowledge of] principles and investigating things cannot but know this.[4] Since the explanation of equator and ecliptic and the designation of the south pole and the north pole are constantly discussed by those who look at the images of heaven, I will not repeat it.

## Notes

1. As noted under Diagram 1.3, "self-so" (*ziran*) means that which is so of itself and can also be translated as "spontaneous" or "natural." The diagram is based on the image of the armillary sphere by Ricci in both *Qiankun tiyi*, p. 608, and *Kunyu wanguo quantu* 坤輿萬國全圖, p. 230 (see also Chen, "The Human Body as a Universe," p. 540). For the original from an edition of Clavius's Latin work, see http://www.hps.cam.ac.uk/starry/sacroarmill.html.

2. The relationship between the directions and the four vital-energies is explained under the next diagram.

3. Liu's answer may be inspired, at least partly, by Koran 41:8ff, according to which God created the earth, went up to heaven when it was "smoke" (*dukhān*), then transformed the smoke into seven layers, which he then adorned with lamps. In one of many discussions of the implications of these verses, Ibn al-ʿArabī wrote:

Once the elements—which are a prepared, feminine locus for the reception of reproduction and birth—came to be actualized, and once burning became manifest from the element fire in the wetness of both air and water, there rose up from them a smoke seeking the most tremendous, which was the highest, furthest sphere. But the smoke found that the sphere of the stars prevented its ascent to the highest sphere, so it returned in waves, piled up, and became a sewn-up mass (*ratq*). Then God unstitched it (*fatq* [cf. Koran 21:30]) as the seven heavens. (*Futūḥāt*, 2: 677)

4. This is a reference to two of the eight steps of learning as set down in the *Great Learning*: "The extension of knowledge consists in the investigation of things" (*Source Book*, p. 86). Liu may equally well have had in mind Muslim scholars, given the manner in which he translated the title of Ījī's *Standpoints in Theology*: "The Complete Classic of Investigating and Extending."

## 2.8
## 四行正位圖

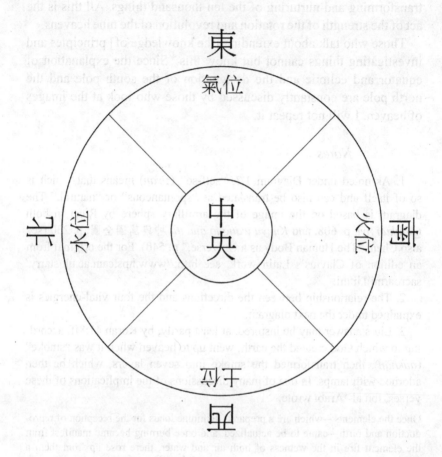

東

氣位

北    水位    中央    火位    南

干位

坎

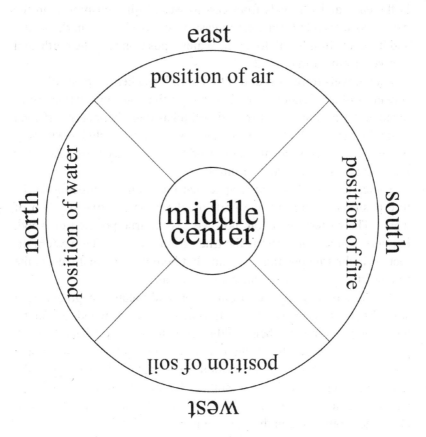

## 2.8
### Diagram of the True Position
### of the Four Agents

The four agents are four images. Air is begotten from water, and soil emerges because of fire. Air, soil, water, and fire are the four agents, and the four agents are the mothers of the ten thousand things.

Each agent has its own position of specific focus. Air's position is in the east, and it travels from east to west. Soil's position is in the west, and it travels from west to east. Fire's position is in the south, and it travels from south to north. Water's position is in the north, and it travels from north to south.

Each travels from its root position until it reaches the place of overflowing fullness without gap. This means that the four vital-energies blend, enter into one another, and boil up as one vital-energy. If each of the four traveled alone, the ten thousand things would have no way of being begotten. When the four blend together, then the ten thousand things are transformed and nurtured.[1]

Someone said:[2] It is not strange that the southern direction is the true position of fire and the northern direction the true position of water. The eastern direction, however, is the true position of wood, but here you say that east is the true position of air. The western direction is the true position of metal, but here you say that west is the true position of soil. What does all this mean?

I said: Wood is begotten from water, and metal is begotten from soil. When the four agents are first differentiated, wood and metal have not yet come into being. When sons have not yet been formed, in reality the mother dwells there. Air is real yang that ascends in the midst of water. Although air is not named "water," in reality it is the essence of water, which is the mother of wood. Therefore its position and allotment dwell specifically in the east. Until wood is begotten, child and mother live in the same palace.

Metal is the child of soil. When metal has not yet been begotten, the true position of its mother is arranged specifically in the west. Until metal is begotten, child and mother are together in the same palace.

When the true position of wood is east and the true position of metal is west, this is the Latter Heaven. When the true position of air is east and the true position of soil west, this is the Former Heaven. This is before that.

The meaning of mother and child, Former and Latter, has been clarified. The more we search for the subtle functions of their positions in the east and west, the more these become obvious.

## Notes

1. A parallel discussion arises in the Muslim philosophical tradition, well represented by Nasafī. In that perspective, the four elements are "simple" (*mufrad*), and everything made from the elements—e.g., minerals, plants, and animals—is "compound" (*murakkab*). Simple things are by definition invisible; they can be perceived only by the traces they leave in compound things.

2. Having assigned the four agents to the four directions, Liu needed to explain why he did not follow the standard Chinese arrangement, which puts metal in the west and wood in the east (e.g., Wilhelm, *I Ching*, p. 310; *Terms*, p. 69). His answer is that the four agents pertain to the Former Heaven, but metal and wood (minerals and plants) come into existence only after the four agents combine in the Latter Heaven.

Shao Yong, known for his "Former Heaven Learning," may be one inspiration for Liu's explanation here. In his major work, Shao spoke of four agents (water, fire, dust, and stone) rather than five. When asked why he had done so, his son and commentator responded,

The four images [sun, moon, stars, and zodiacal space] and the four forms [water, fire, dust, and stone] are the Former Heaven. The five agents are the Latter Heaven. The Former Heaven is that from which the Latter Heaven emerges.    (Birdwhistell, *Transition*, p. 82)

Nūr al-Ḥaqq's version of this diagram reverses the position of fire and water, placing fire in the north and water in the south. He also added four divine attributes, saying that east (air) is the locus of manifestation (*maẓhar*) for life (*ḥayāt*), south (water) for knowledge (*'ilm*), west (soil) for existence-giving (*ījād*), and north (fire) for power (*qudra*). He then provided a diagram from Ibn al-'Arabī's *Futūḥāt* that makes correlations between the elements and four divine attributes (but not the directions). The original diagram, however, has desire (*irāda*) in place of "existence-giving" (*Futūḥāt*, 1: 260; *Self-Disclosure*, p. 230). Nūr said nothing about his reversal of the positions given by Liu, but he did explain the rationale for the correlation with the divine attributes:

Water is specified for the south and fire for the north (*shimāl*) instead of the opposite because south is the right (*yamīn*), and that is more excellent than the left (*shimāl*); and water is one of the traces of knowledge, and these are prior to the traces of power. (*Sharḥ*, p. 70/52)

· The priority of the traces of knowledge (i.e., nature) over those of power (i.e., wisdom) is discussed under Diagram 1.8, and the correlation of attributes with elements under Diagram 1.9.

Nūr al-Ḥaqq had his own explanations for the correlations of the attributes and elements (*Sharḥ*, p. 68/51): Air manifests life because wind, as the Prophet said, is from "the breath of the All-merciful," and the life of living things is sustained through breathing. Fire manifests power because it is the trace of the Universal Intellect, and water manifests knowledge because it is the trace of the Universal Soul. Earth manifests existence-giving—which is to bring the nonexistent things (the fixed entities) into existence—because it causes seeds to sprout.

## 2.9
## 四時往復圖

## 2.9
## Diagram of the Going and Coming Back
## of the Four Seasons

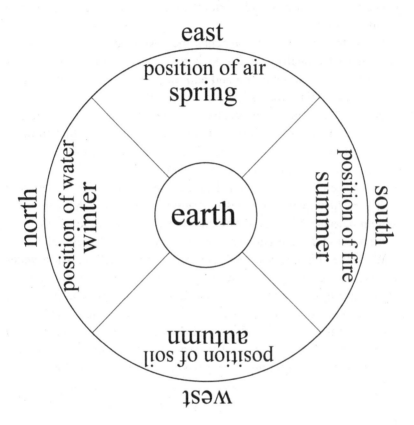

Before the existence of the four vital-energies, the four seasons were not in the midst of the emptiness.[1] The four seasons came to be when the four vital-energies turned around in the ongoing flow. In the midst of turning around and the ongoing flow, each vital-energy has a specific position in which it flourishes; so each is designated for a specific season.

When the ongoing flow reaches the eastern direction, where air flourishes specifically, the season is spring.[2] We know that spring is spring because it has melting and harmony; so we know that air is air because it contains what is in keeping with this.

When the ongoing flow reaches the southern direction, where fire flourishes specifically, the season is summer. We know that summer is summer because it has heat and flourishing; so we know that fire is fire because it contains what is in keeping with this.

When the ongoing flow reaches the western direction, where soil flourishes specifically, the season is autumn. We know that autumn is autumn because it has gathering and harvesting; so we know that soil is soil because it ejects and gives out what is in keeping with this.

When the ongoing flow reaches the northern direction, where water flourishes specifically, the time is winter. We know that winter is winter because it has hardness and congealing; so we know that water is water because adhering to soil and storing are in keeping with this.

Know that the ongoing flow of air and fire is the ongoing flow of issuing and going beyond; so their seasons, spring and summer, also have images of issuing and going beyond. The ongoing flow of soil and water is the ongoing flow of gathering and storing; so their seasons, autumn and winter, also have the meaning of gathering and storing.

When the strength of gathering and storing has been fully realized, the mechanism of issuing and going beyond rises again. When the mechanism of issuing and going beyond rises, the air that flourishes specifically in the eastern direction comes back to begin here. This is the going and coming back of the four seasons.

Someone said: The order of the four seasons follows the five agents in a circle.[3] But here you say that that is the acts of the four vital-energies and that wood and metal have no share in it. In which ground do you place these two agents, wood and metal? Moreover, without wood, fire is not begotten, and without metal, water is not begotten. When fire is not begotten, how can summer come abruptly in the midst of the four seasons? When water is not begotten, how can winter be there suddenly in the midst of the four seasons?

I said: Air, fire, water, and soil are in the Former Heaven, the mothers of wood and metal. The agents wood and metal are in the Latter Heaven, the children of the four single agents. If we grant that without wood, fire will not be begotten, from whence came the fire of the Former Heaven before wood was begotten? If we grant that without metal, water is not begotten, from whence emerged the water of the Former Heaven before metal was begotten?

Know that the fire and water of the Former Heaven are not begotten from wood and metal. The four agents gather together and in reality become the mothers of the wood and metal of the Latter Heaven. When wood has been begotten, the strength of wood is able to assist fire; this is the explanation of wood's ability to beget fire. When metal has been begotten, the strength of metal is able to assist water; this is the explanation of metal's ability to beget water. Because wood can assist fire, we say that wood can beget fire even before wood is added to help the fire. Because metal can assist water, we say that metal can beget water even before metal is added to help the water.

Know that the subtle function of the transforming and nurturing of the Real Ruler lies in the midst of the pairing of the four vital-energies; and it lies in the midst of all the rotation and interconnection of the two agents—metal and wood. Thus the Latter Heaven helps what was not fully realized in the Former Heaven.

## Notes

1. Liu attributed the relevant Root Classic lines (2:77–78) to Ījī's *Standpoints*, which discusses the four seasons in the *mawqif* on substances (pp. 220–21). Rāzī mentioned the four seasons as the macrocosmic analogues of the four natures and the four humors: spring is heat and yellow bile, autumn cold and black bile, summer wetness and phlegm, winter dryness and blood. Then he said that each season has its wind. "The spring [wind] impregnates the trees, brings out the leaves, and makes the green

things grow; the summer ripens the fruit, the autumn dries it, and the winter makes it fall" (*Path*, p. 76/104).

In his version of this diagram, Nūr al-Ḥaqq again reversed the position of water and fire, and made correlations with four Koranic divine attributes: east/air/spring—gentleness (*luṭf*); south/water/winter—severity (*qahr*); west/earth/autumn—contraction (*qabḍ*); and north/fire/summer—expansion (*basṭ*). He explained that in winter the sun is in the south, and in summer it is in the north. He continued:

The season of spring is influenced by the wind, and its nature refreshes and gives movement to bodies; so people are refreshed by it, and plants begin to be configured and grow—because of the manifestation of His attribute of gentleness. . . .

Summer is influenced by fire. Its nature is heat, expansion, and elevation. This is why heat is intense and growth is strengthened—because of the manifestation of the attribute of expansion.

Autumn is influenced by soil. Its nature is to induce stillness and contraction. That is why crops are harvested in it—because of the manifestation of the attribute of contraction.

Winter is influenced by water. Its nature is cold and concealing, which is to say that it inserts things into its inwardness. That is why cold is intense and growth hidden—because of the manifestation of the attribute of severity.    (*Sharḥ*, pp. 70–71/53–54)

2. The four seasons are often correlated with the four qualities of change described in the *Yijing* at the beginning of the commentary on the first hexagram: origination, flourishing, advantage, and perseverance (Wilhelm, *I Ching*, pp. 369–72). Zhu Xi stressed the importance of these four qualities so much that he identified them with "the heart of Heaven and Earth" (Chan, *Zhu Xi*, p. 191). Chen Chun wrote: "When spring has finished producing, summer grows, and when autumn has finished destroying, winter preserves. Origination, flourishing, advantage, and perseverance begin and end in rotation and have been this way forever" (*Terms*, pp. 97–98).

3. The questioner again brings up the fact that this way of looking at seasons is different from the traditional Chinese way, and again Liu has recourse to the distinction between the Former and Latter Heavens in his explanation.

## 2.10
## 七洲分地圖

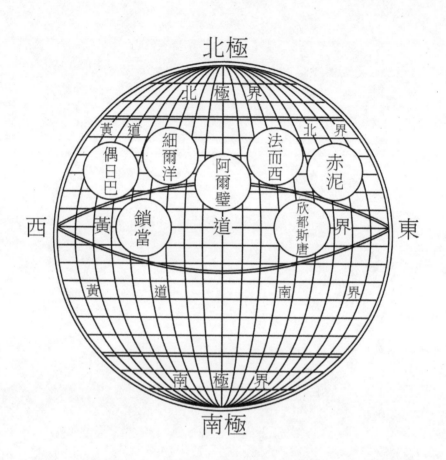

## 2.10
# Diagram of the Differentiated Earth
## of the Seven Climes

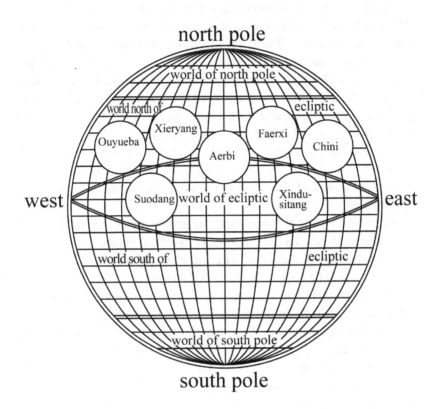

Earth is the form that has come to be from the mutual adherence of soil and water; its body is undifferentiated roundness, and its position is the center of the middle of the emptiness.[1] Its circumference is 90,000 *li*, and its depth and thickness are 28,600 *li*.

There are seven differentiated forms that make seven climes. These are called Aerbi, Faerxi, Ouyueba, Chini, Xieryang, Xindusitang, and Suodang.[2] These seven climes correspond to the seven governances.[3] Each clime belongs specifically to a governance. The nature and feelings of humans and things in that earth are mutually similar with the nature and feelings of the star that belongs to it.[4] The happiness, calamities, and good omens of this one clime are related to the brightness and luminosity of this one star.

Aerbi is the chief position of the seven climes. Mankind was first begotten here; its earth belongs to the sun. The nature and feelings of people are clear and true, with self-strength. Its things are products of much value.

Faerxi belongs to the wood-star. Its people are strong, mighty, and powerful in affairs. Its earth has many excellent plants.

Chini belongs to the moon. The will of its people shifts hastily and easily. Its earth has much moisture and dampness.

Ouyueba belongs to the fire-star. Its people like to argue and are happy to fight. Its things have many hidden poisons.

Xindusitang belongs to the water-star. Its people are clever, clear, honorable, and skillful. Its things have many unusual shapes.

Xieryang belongs to the metal-star. Its people are elegant, beautiful, upstanding, and honest. Its things are good and beautiful and its earth has many exotic products.

Suodang belongs to the soil-star. Its earth is very salty. Grass, trees, birds, and beasts are scarce and few. Its people are dull, withdrawn, black, small, and able to carry heavy burdens. The people of the Muslim lands (*tianfang*) say that this earth is a country of slaves.

There are seven earths, and in the midst are differences of cold, hot, warm, and cool, because each of them corresponds to different distances from the degrees of the ecliptic. If you unite the great earth and look at it as a whole, it is differentiated into five large worlds from south to north. One is the world of the ecliptic; its earth is very hot because the sun's disk truly illuminates it. One is the world of the south pole and one is the world of the north pole. These two worlds are very cold because they are far from the sun's disk. One is the world south of the ecliptic, and one the world north of the ecliptic. In these two worlds cold and heat are moderate, because they are neither far from nor near to the disk of the sun. The reason the vital-energy of the earth is cold and hot, warm and cool, is because the ecliptic is shiny and illuminates all these worlds.

## Notes

1. As made clear by Diagram 2.8. The numbers are based on Ricci, *Qiankun tiyi*, p. 606; and *Kunyu wanguo quantu*, p. 222.

2. These are loose geographical designations, all transliterated from the Persian: Arabia, Persia, Europe (which Nūr al-Ḥaqq translated as "the Western regions"), China, Syria, Hindustan (India), and Sudan. In his study of the text, Sha Zongping tries to suggest which regions Liu really had in mind, but Sha's opinion appears to depend on a modern knowledge of geography and nomenclature with which Liu would not have been familiar. In any case, some of Liu's personal opinions of peoples may well be reflected in the text, given that he put Arabia at the center of the world and saw Europe as full of "hidden poison," which many would consider an astute reading of the Jesuit presence in China.

In discussing the diagram, Nūr offered a rough translation of Liu's text, explaining that just as God made heaven into seven layers, he also made the earth into seven climes, and each of the climes has a spiritual or supra-formal correspondence (*al-tanāsub al-maʿnawī*) with one of the planets.

The Root Classic indicates that this discussion is drawn from *Standpoints*, and Ījī did refer to the influence of the climes on human character traits, but not in any detail. After having explained that human beings have the most balanced constitution of all creatures (see notes under Diagram 4.10), Ījī referred to Avicenna and Fakhr al-Dīn Rāzī on the question of which sort of human constitution is the most balanced. Avicenna held that it is the constitution of the inhabitants of the regions around the equator, because their states of heat and cold are equal, for their days and nights are equal. Rāzī said it is that of the inhabitants of the fourth clime, who have the best colors, the tallest statures, the most astute minds, and the noblest character traits—all of this being derived from their constitution. Those of regions closer to the equator, such as Abyssinia and Zanzibar, suffer from an excess of heat (*Standpoints*, p. 227).

This sort of discussion is also well-known in Neo-Confucianism. For example, Cheng Hao explained that only true human beings are able to achieve proper balance between yin and yang: "The principle of the Mean is perfect. Nothing can be begotten with yin or yang alone. Those who possess them partially are animals and barbarians, while those who possess them in balanced proportion are men" (*Source Book*, p. 540).

3. I.e., the seven governances of the planets, as seen under Diagram 2.4.

4. To speak of the "feelings" (*qing*) of the planets sounds odd in English, but no odder than speaking of the "spirits" of the planets, which is precisely what their "natures" designate. As noted in the discussion of *qing* under Diagram 1.12, Chen Chun defined feelings as "nature when aroused." Liu is saying that the natures and feelings of the seven planets are expressed in the natures and feelings of the humans and things that fall under their respective spheres of influence. Notice also how Liu translated the title of his seventh source, *Aḥkām-i kawākib*, which means literally "The ruling properties of the stars." The Persian phrase is synonymous with *aḥkām-i nujūm*, which historians of science typically translate as "astrology." Liu called this book *Tianjing qingxing*, "The feelings and natures of the heavenly classic." By speaking of the stars as the "heavenly classic," he seems to be comparing them to a book waiting to be read.

## 2.11
## 四際分空圖

## 2.11
### Diagram of the Differentiated Emptiness of the Four Boundaries

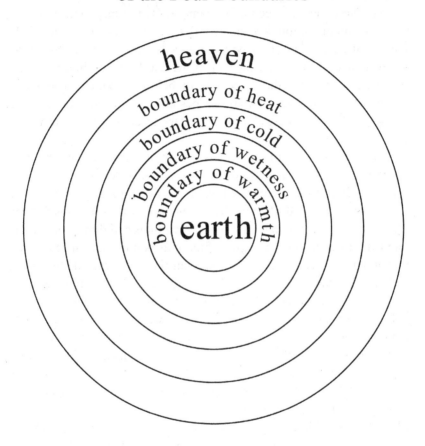

There are four boundaries in the midst of the emptiness between earth and heaven.[1] That near earth is the boundary of warmth. Above the warmth is the boundary of wetness. Above it is the boundary of cold. The one near heaven is the boundary of heat.

The four boundaries come into being rooted in the connection and composition of the four agents—wind, fire, water, and soil. The vital-energy of each of the four boundaries acts from above to below to cultivate and nurture the endeavor of the ten thousand things—it has never been the case that it acts from below to above.[2] The vital-energy of the boundary of warmth does not travel to the boundary of wetness. The vital-energy of the boundary of cold does not travel to the boundary of heat.

The boundary of warmth belongs to soil;[3] its vital-energy is harmonious and peaceful. The boundary of wetness belongs to water; its vital-energy is rather cool. The boundary of cold belongs to wind; its vital-energy is dreadfully cold. The boundary of heat belongs to fire; its vital-energy is blazingly hot. All the ten thousand things look up to and lean upon the vital-energies of the four boundaries, since the nature and mandate of each is adjusted according to the time it obtains.

It is also said that the four boundaries are soft membranes that support heaven and nourish earth. In the same way, if there were no soft membranes to connect and stretch between skin and flesh, flesh could not nourish skin and skin could not act as the guardian of flesh.

As for the vital-energy of yang that is accumulated in the midst of the earth, sometimes it ascends and goes up. Some of it reaches the boundary of warmth, some of it passes the boundary of warmth and reaches the boundary of wetness and the boundary of cold, and some of it reaches the boundary of heat. The height of its ascent is not the same, and thus it becomes dust, fog, cloud, rain, hail, sand, shooting stars, and comets.

There are diverse kinds of forms and shapes. The vital-energy of yang that is accumulated in the midst of the earth is that which was shot out by the sun and then entered into [the earth]. Some of it ascends and goes up, some of it floats and roams in going up, and some is shot out directly and goes up. Some of that which is shot out directly goes up calmly, and some goes up vigorously. That which goes up by floating and roaming barely reaches the boundary of warmth. Some of this vital-energy carries soil and becomes dust. The vital-energy that goes up alone becomes fog. Some of that which is shot out directly goes up and becomes clouds. If the clouds enter deeply into the boundary of wetness, it rains, and if the clouds only reach the boundary of warmth, it does not rain.

Of that which is shot out directly, what goes up calmly while carrying soil becomes sand; this vital-energy is unable to reach fully the boundary of wetness, because its body is heavy. What goes up vigorously enters directly into the boundary of cold; when it becomes cold, its vital-energy congeals, freezes, and becomes hail.

The strength of what goes up vigorously is so strong that it is like issuing an arrow or a volley that directly enters the boundary of heat, and the boundary of heat is the root position of fire. When the vital-energy of accumulated yang encounters fire, it burns and transforms into fireballs, and when it falls, it becomes shooting stars. This vital-energy exists only on the days when the sun dominates; so there are more shooting stars in summer than in winter.

If the vital-energy of accumulated yang is very fierce, the strength of directly going up is stronger. Then it is able to shoot out and enter the extreme boundary of heat and go near to heaven. When it is near to heaven, this vital-energy is sucked in by the vital-energy of heaven and cannot fall; so it travels along with heaven. It becomes comets and the like. It must wait very long and gradually dissipate and scatter into nothing.

## Notes

1. Islamic texts often call these four boundaries the "globes" (*kura*) of the elements, and they are ranked from dense to subtle as soil, water, air, and fire (or ether). Notice that Liu followed the standard Islamic order, whereas earlier (Diagrams 2.3–2.4), he had put wind above fire. Nūr al-Ḥaqq explained the diagram like this:

Between heaven and earth are four layers arranged in terms of the traces of the elements: First is the dusty, which is the trace of soil; second, the vapory, which is the trace of water; third, the bitterly cold, which is the trace of air; and fourth, the etheric, which is the trace of fire. (*Sharḥ*, pp. 77/57–58).

Ibn al-ʿArabī enumerated the elemental globes as four of the twenty-eight levels of the cosmos and explained that they manifest the traces of four divine attributes: contraction (fire), life (air), life-giving (water), and death-giving (soil; *Self-Disclosure*, p. xxxi).

2. This is because, as Nasafī put it, "Anything more subtle is also more penetrating, more inclusive, and more encompassing." As a result, "the subtle has a location inside the dense, but the subtle does not perforate the dense, nor does it constrict the place of the dense" (*Goal*, pp. 233/68, 69).

3. From here on Liu's discussion seems to be inspired mainly by Ijī, who often referred to the four elemental globes, although he held that they have seven levels: pure fire, fire mixed with air, pure air (also called *zamharīr*, "bitter cold"), air mixed with water (or vapor, *bukhār*), air mixed with earth, water mixed with earth (clay), and pure earth (*Standpoints*, p. 224). The following passage seems to have inspired Liu:

The heat of the sun rises as parts that are either airy and watery, and that is vapor, or fiery and earthy, and that is smoke. From these two all the higher traces come to be.

As for vapor, if the heat intensifies, the watery parts dissipate and pure air remains. If the vapor reaches the [layer of] bitter cold, it freezes because of the cold and becomes clouds, and the watery parts fall as drops, either without freezing, which is rain, or with freezing: if the cold was before the gathering together [of the drops], that is snow, and if after it, then hail, which becomes spherical by movement.

If the vapor does not reach the intense cold, it becomes mist. A small amount of it may be condensed by the cold of the night; so it falls, either without freezing, as dew, or with it, as frost.

As for smoke, it may become mixed with the clouds and then break out of them, either by its natural rising, or by falling as a result of condensation from the cold. Because of the breaking and banging together, there is sound, which is thunder. There may also be lighting up because of the strength of the warming that is begotten by the movement and the banging together. The subtle parts are quickly extinguished, and those are lightning flashes, and the dense parts are not extinguished until they reach the earth, and those are thunderbolts.

The smoke may reach the globe of fire, and then it begins to burn, like a candle that has been extinguished and is placed below a burning candle; its smoke flames up and connects to the lower candle so that it begins to burn.

The part that is subtle becomes flame, and the fire quickly penetrates it, as if it were a star dying out. This is a "flaming star" (*shihāb*). The part that is dense becomes completely connected to fire without flaming up, and it remains joined to it without becoming extinguished. Such are comets, meteors, and shooting stars. (*Standpoints*, p. 242)

Although Liu's source here is *Standpoints*, the discussion would not appear out of place for any number of Chinese thinkers. Shao Yong, for example, wrote: "When the vital-energy of water moistens and flows downward, it becomes rain. When the vital-energy of fire flares up and expands, it becomes wind. When the vital energy of earth rises and moistens, it becomes dew. When the vital-energy of stone strikes within and attacks, it becomes thunder" (Birdwhistell, *Transition*, p. 110; cf. *Source Book*, pp. 484–85).

2.12
一貫洋溢圖

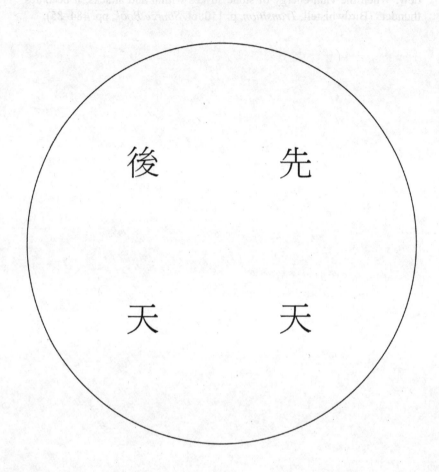

# 2.12
## Diagram of the Overspreading
## of the One Thread

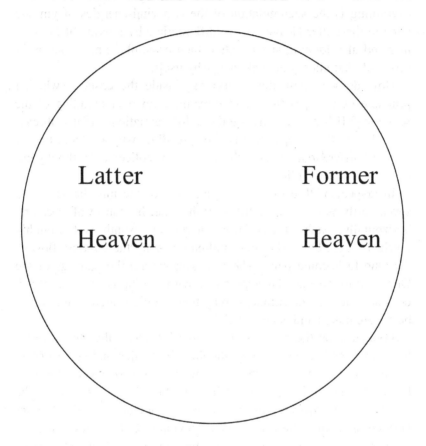

[The One Thread goes] from differentiated principles and differentiated forms to all beings.[1] When we look at the principles, we must look at them before forms and colors come to be. When we look at the forms, we must seek them from the images, which means that everything is the accumulation of the two vital-energies of yin and yang in the Latter Heaven. It we differentiate by looking at the Former and also looking at the Latter, then principle is principle by itself, and vital-energy is vital-energy by itself.

How do we know that everything inside the cosmos, whether principle or form, is the direct threading and overspreading of the Real One? If it is one, why are there differentiations? If it is threading, why are there gaps? If it is overspreading, why are there limits? Without differentiation, even the scattered is collected. Without gaps, even emptiness is fullness.

In respect of threading vertically, each of the nine heavens and seven earths is completely filled by the One. In respect of threading horizontally, each of east, west, north, and south is thoroughly reached by the One. The four vital-energies are the ongoing flow of the One to become pairs. The four seasons are the pairings of the One to flow and go. Overspreading with liveliness and activity, it does not stick to one firmness. Why then should principle and image be differentiated and become two?

Looked at on the basis of the Former [Heaven], the One is formless and threads directly. Why should it be hidden and concealed in the forms? Looked at on the basis of the Latter [Heaven], the One has form and threads directly. Why should it fly and rise up in the formless? The formless does not belong inevitably to the Former Heaven, and form does not belong inevitably to the Latter Heaven. So how is it possible to differentiate the Former Heaven and the Latter Heaven?

This may well be why the One Thread overspreads and fully embraces the limitless. That which fully embraces the limitless without effort and without exhaustion creates and re-creates ceaselessly in itself.[2] There is ceaseless creation and re-creation because the One pays attention to the ten thousand things. If it did not pay attention to the ten thousand things, there would not be the ten thousand things, and without them, there would be no assistance to nourish humans. The reason it pays attention to the ten thousand things is to pay attention to humans.[3]

## Notes

1. On the One Thread, see the explanation under Diagram 1.1. Most of the text here is explaining that the differentiation between Former Heaven and Latter Heaven, spiritual and bodily, principle and image, has to do with our situation in the world. All things, however, are self-disclosures of the same Real One, a notion that Jāmī and other late authors call *waḥdat al-wujūd*, "the Oneness of Existence."

In the four lines of the Root Classic illustrated by this diagram (2:87–90), Liu referred to *Gleams*. The lines can be taken as the gist of several passages, including Gleams 24, 25, and 27. In explaining the meaning, Nūr al-Ḥaqq cited Gleam 25: "It is one Reality, and manifestation and nonmanifestation, firstness and lastness, are its relations and respects. 'He is the First and the Last and the Manifest and the Nonmanifest' [Koran 57:3]" (*Chinese Gleams*, p. 184). He also cited a purported hadith: "Glory be to Him who made Himself subtle and named it 'Real' and who unveiled Himself and named it 'creation'" (*Sharḥ*, p. 80/60).

2. This recalls Zhu Xi's doctrine of ceaseless begetting by Heaven and Earth (Chan, *Zhu Xi*, pp. 188–91). Ibn al-ʿArabī called this "the renewal of creation at each instant" (*tajdīd al-khalq fī'l-ānāt*; *Sufi Path*, pp. 18, 96ff). At the beginning of Gleam 26, Jāmī explained Ibn al-ʿArabī's position:

[Ibn al-ʿArabī said that] the cosmos consists of accidents gathered together in the One Entity, which is the reality of Being. It undergoes change and renewal at every breath and every instant. At every instant a world goes to nonexistence and its likeness comes into existence, but most of the world's folk are heedless of this meaning. (*Chinese Gleams*, p. 186)

3. This is a restatement of the standard Islamic teaching that God created the universe for the sake of human beings (see the notes under Diagrams 1.12 and 3.1).

# Volume 3

## Summary

Volume 3 is a sequential description of the causes of the manifestation and display of the microcosm.[1] In the microcosm there are the manifestation and display of form and the manifestation and display of the formless. When we look at the manifestation and display of form, we can know the subtlety of the self-suchness of created things. When we look at the manifestation and display of the formless, we can know the essence of humans' becoming one with heaven.

The form of the microcosm is later than heaven and earth and smaller than heaven and earth. The principle of the microcosm is before the two and broader than the two. This is because the macrocosm has borders and boundaries, but the microcosm has no borders and boundaries. The principle of the macrocosm has rising and perishing, but the principle of the microcosm has rising but no perishing, even though there has never been anything without both rising and perishing.[2]

339

*Notes*

1. Volume 3 is dedicated to describing how the human microcosm comes into being on the analogy of the macrocosmic stages explained in Volume 2. Much of the discussion is derived from Nasafī's *Goal*.

2. Liu noted that the microcosm is greater than the macrocosm under Diagram 2.6. Here he added that one of the differences between the two lies in the fact that the universe has a beginning and an end, and the human self has a beginning but no end. This is one of the implications of Mullā Ṣadrā's famous dictum, "The soul is bodily in origination, spiritual in subsistence" (*al-nafs jismāniyyat al-ḥudūth rūḥāniyyat al-baqā'*). See, e.g., Mullā Ṣadrā, *The Elixir of the Gnostics*, p. xxviii, a passage in which he reviewed the ascending stages of the human substance in the Latter Heaven—from vegetal soul in the womb to holy soul in union with God.

3.1
人生元始圖

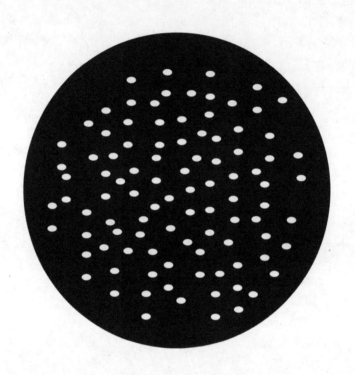

## 3.1
## Diagram of the Original Beginning
## of the Begetting of the Human

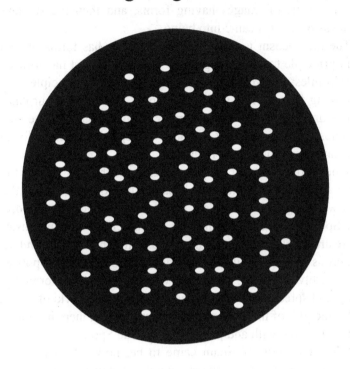

Heaven and earth are the macrocosm, and the human body is the microcosm.[1] Before there was the macrocosm, first there were the six levels of the formless principles, and then the six levels of the images having forms came into being. As for the microcosm, first there were the six levels of images having forms, and then the six levels of formless principles came into being.[2]

The macrocosm is first formless and later has forms; it advances from principle to vital-energy. The microcosm first has forms and is later formless; it circles back from vital-energy to principle.[3]

Having forms arises in the One Spot,[4] which is the surplus of the nature and principle of the Former Heaven that became the Vast Sediment. It is the taproot and seed of begetting humans for the ten thousand generations under heaven.

When Adam grasped the pure essence[5] of the four agents, they became connected together and became the body, in which the One Spot was lodged. When Adam begot children and grandchildren, the One Spot flowed and branched off into indefinitely numerous bodies. There are surely indefinitely numerous One Spots for the indefinitely numerous bodies, but these indefinitely numerous One Spots are not by themselves Adam's One Spot, which altered, transformed, multiplied, and spread out so as to emerge. As for the world of the natures and principles of the Former Heaven, everything there has one nature and is endowed with and possesses this One Spot.

When the body of Adam came to be, however, the indefinitely numerous One Spots all accompanied and entered into the body of Adam, where they were lodged and stored.[6] As a thing [the One Spot] is subtle and cannot be glimpsed; it leaps beyond the outwardness of color and image, voice and smell. That which is housed and stored in Adam's body is an undifferentiated single root. Although it enwraps and stores the bodies of the ten thousand generations, it is not aware of their manyness. It flows and branches off in children and grandchildren, each of which is from the one root, but it is not aware of its littleness. Almost in continuity with the Former Heaven, it becomes the ultimate subtle thing.[7]

Humans have heart and body. The body has outward and inward; it has bodily apertures, knowledge and awareness, nature and feeling, movement and doing, words and actions, failure and success, long life and short life. All these are abundant in its midst, making it subtle. The showing forth and display of its ongoing flow also becomes differentiated into six levels.[8] First is the level of the original beginning, which is the seed [3.1]. Second is the level of the proliferation of begetting, which is the beginning of the connection to the embryo [3.2]. Third is the level of alteration and transformation, when the four roots come to be [3.3]. Fourth is the level of perfecting the form, when the outward is differentiated from the inward [3.4]. Fifth is the level of the firmness of stuff, when the bodily apertures are completed [3.5]. Sixth is the level of display and disclosure, when the spiritually living appears [3.6].

The six levels of the microcosm's form are not less than the six levels of the macrocosm's form.

## Notes

1. Cf. Nasafī: "Know that the human being is the microcosm, and everything other than the human being is altogether the macrocosm" (*Goal*, p. 254/93). The discussion under this diagram and the next seems to be based on Nasafī's explanation of the correlation between the "four oceans" of macrocosm and microcosm (*Goal*, pp. 255–56/94–95). The four oceans of the macrocosm are the Divine Essence, which is the Hidden Treasure; the Ascribed Spirit (the First Intellect), the World of the Kingdom (the bodily realm), and the World of the Sovereignty (the spiritual realm); in other words, they are Substance, the Mandate, the Former Heaven, and the Latter Heaven. The four oceans of the microcosm are the sperm-drop in the father, the womb that receives the drop, the body of the child, and the child's spirit; in Liu's terms, these are the One Spot, the womb, the body, and the heart.

2. These are the twelve levels described in Volume 1 and depicted in Diagram 0.6. The formless principles pertain to the Former Heaven and extend from Substance down to the Vast Sediment, and the images having forms pertain to the Latter Heaven and extend from vital-energy to humans. The first six are necessary preconditions for the manifestation of the second six, but the order of the appearance of the second six is reversed: the first six represent stages of descent from subtlety to density, and the second six are stages of ascent from density to subtlety.

3. This is precisely the relationship between the Descending and the Ascending Arcs in Islamic texts: each successive level of the Origin is more

differentiated and dense, and each successive level of the Return is more unified and subtle; the descent is away from the light of Being and Awareness into the darkness of nonbeing and unconsciousness, and the ascent moves back into the realm of light and wakefulness.

In Nasafī's terms, the macrocosm begins with the undifferentiated and nondesignated Essence, the first ocean. Its attributes and qualities then become manifest in the three subsequent oceans, culminating in the visible world, the most outward of the levels. As for the microcosm, it begins as an undifferentiated sperm-drop, which is then deposited in the womb, and then appears in the world as the union of body and spirit. The microcosm's true possibilities, however, can be reached only when the divine attributes of life, knowledge, desire, and power are actualized on the formless level of spirit, although, of course, these attributes leave traces in the body. Thus the macrocosm develops from inward to outward, or from nonmanifest to manifest, in stages that follow the Descending Arc. In contrast, the microcosm develops from manifest to nonmanifest, from bodily to spiritual, as it realizes its invisible potentialities on the Ascending Arc.

Nasafī sometimes explained this process in terms of "simple things" (*mufradāt*) and "compound things" (*murakkabāt*), a standard philosophical pairing. The simple things are those that have no parts. They are "the fathers and mothers" and pertain to the Descending Arc, in both its heavenly and earthly aspects, and to the initial, invisible stages of the Ascending Arc, that is, the elements and their natures. The compound things are the children found on the Ascending Arc, which also have their heavenly (spiritual) and earthly (bodily) aspects. "The simple things of the cosmos are the intellects, souls, spheres, stars, elements, and natures. . . . The compound things of the cosmos are the minerals, plants, and animals" (*Goal*, p. 241/78).

Again in Nasafī's terms, the Descending Arc begins with the Ascribed Spirit, also called the Intellect, since, as the Prophet put it, "The first thing God created was the Intellect." As for the Ascending Arc, it ends with the Intellect. Nasafī summed up the parallelism between the two arcs in these passages:

Then the three progeny appeared and are appearing—the minerals, the plants, and the animals. . . . At the end of all, human beings appear, and when human beings reach the Intellect, they become complete. There is nothing after the Intellect. Thus it is known that the Intellect existed at first, because whatever appears at last was there at first. When human beings reach the Intellect, the circle is completed. The beginning was from the Intellect, and the sealing is through the Intellect. The descent was in the simple things, and the ascent is in the compound things. The descent is in the fathers and the mothers, and the ascent is in the progeny. (*Goal*, p. 242/79)

At the end of all, human beings appeared and are now appearing. When human beings reach perfection and become knowing, the First Ocean, which is the Hidden Treasure that wanted to become evident and recognized, becomes evident and recognized. What was intended from the spheres, stars, elements, natures, and progeny—that is, what was intended from both the simple things and the compound things—was for human beings to come from potentiality into actuality, and from outward to inward. If human beings could exist without these things, or if they could live without them, none of them would have come into being. What was intended from all of them was humans.   (*Goal*, p. 257/97)

4. This expression probably translates "first substance" (*jawhar-i awwal*), although it also refers to the sperm-drop (*nuṭfa*), which is mentioned in the Koran as the first stage of becoming in the womb. Nasafī (*Goal*, p. 255/94) explained that both macrocosm and microcosm have a first substance from which everything else appears. The first substance of the macrocosm is the Ascribed Spirit, and that of the microcosm is the sperm-drop. Arabic *jawhar*, or "substance," derives from Persian *gawhar*, "pearl," and was used by philosophers, in Persian as well as in Arabic, to designate the first of the Aristotelian categories, as opposed to "accident." In Ash'arite theological writings the same word *jawhar* was used to designate the indivisible "atom."

In his book *al-Insān al-kāmil* Nasafī went into detail about the sperm-drop as the first substance:

At first the human being was one substance, and everything that gradually comes to exist in him already existed in that one substance, but each came to be manifest in its own moment. That one substance is the sperm-drop. All was existent in the sperm-drop; it had everything useful for it to reach human perfection with itself and from itself. . . .

The sperm-drop of man is the first substance of the microcosm, the essence of the microcosm, and the seed of the microcosm. The world of love is the microcosm, and the sperm-drop loves itself. It wants to see its own beauty and witness its own attributes and names. It will disclose itself, become clothed in the attribute of activity, and come forth from the world of undifferentiation into the world of differentiation. It will become manifest in many forms and shapes, meanings and lights, so that its beauty may become manifest and its attributes, names, and acts may appear. (*Insān*, pp. 16–17)

5. "Essence" (*jing* 精) here might also be translated "spiritual essence." What is meant is the most subtle and invisible dimension of the human reality. Mathews lists these meanings among others for the character: essential, fine and delicate, spirit, ethereal, subtle, ghost.

6. Adam's body here should probably not be understood as his biological body, since, according to standard Islamic teachings, he dwelt in the Garden

before he was "sent down" to the earth. Liu more likely had in mind the Covenant of Alast, mentioned in Koran 7:172, according to which God brought forth Adam's "descendents," *dhurriyya*, from the loins of his children and had them testify against themselves. The word is derived from a root that means "to make numerous," "to scatter," "to sow," "to create"; from the same root we have *dharr*, which means "tiny particles" or "atoms." Some scholars talk about the "world of the particles" (*'ālam al-dharr*), meaning the realm in which the descendents of Adam agreed to the Covenant, and this is typically understood as a semi-spiritual (or imaginal) realm before physical embodiment.

7. The One Spot is "almost in continuity" because it manifests the Ascribed Spirit, which, from the standpoint of the Latter Heaven, is none other than the Nature of Continuity.

8. This outlines the program for the first half of Volume 3: explanations will be given for the six levels of increasing complexity and subtlety that appear when the seed is deposited in the womb and undergoes transformation, finally achieving the level of the spiritually living, which is "the nature that makes humans human" (Diagrams 3.1–3.6). These six levels correspond to the six levels of increasing complexity that bring the macrocosm into manifestation (Diagrams 1.7–1.12). The second half of Volume 3 then explains how human nature is defined by six increasingly formless levels that culminate in the Nature of Continuity.

### 3.2
### 胚胎初化圖

濁

清

## 3.2
## Diagram of the First Transformation
## of the Embryo

# turbid

This is the image of the One Spot when it enters the mother's belly, where it is transformed for the first time. It is the level of the proliferation of begetting. Before the One Spot enters the mother's belly, it is preserved as pure, subtle, and imageless in the father's spine.[1] When it departs from the root position and enters the womb, the imageless comes to have an image.[2] The image comes to be when it obtains the vital-energy of the interplay between father and mother.

The yang of the father moves and begets water. Water carries the vital-energy of yang and bestows it upon the mother. The yin of the mother moves and begets fire. Fire carries the vital-energy of yin and inserts the One Spot in the womb. The intercourse of yin and yang collect water and fire together; so the one is transformed and becomes two. The pure is stored on the inside, and the turbid guards the outside.[3]

The pure belongs to yang; it was rooted in the father's yang and became enwrapped in the mother's yin and was thereby transformed. The turbid belongs to yin; it was rooted in the father's water and became burned by the mother's fire and was thereby transformed.

Someone said: If the pure already belongs to yang, the principle should issue outside, yet here it gathers inside. If the turbid already belongs to yin, the principle should gather inside, yet here it issues outside. Why?

I said: The number of levels in transforming and begetting the microcosm is no more and no less than in transforming and begetting the macrocosm. Nonetheless, in reality, the differentiated forms of inside and outside are mutually opposed. The differentiated forms of the macrocosm issue and increase on the outside. Thereby they become great and go up, and so the yang issues outside [1.8]. When the yang issues outside, the yin gathers inside by itself.

The differentiated forms of the microcosm are stored and lodged on the inside. Thereby they become great and go up; hence the pure is stored inside. When the pure is stored on the inside, the turbid surrounds it on the outside by itself. The reason why the differentiated forms are mutually opposed is precisely so that the wonder of the creative transformation may be sufficiently seen. Compared to the macrocosm, the microcosm is finer and more concealed.[4]

The macrocosm is formless by itself and is transformed to reach form.[5] All its influences reach the outside from the inside. Reaching the outside from the inside means that its meanings are fully realized outside.

The microcosm has form by itself and is transformed to reach the formless. All its influences reach the inside from the outside. Reaching the inside from the outside means that what is connected and united inside is concealed.[6]

For example, in the body of the human, the heart occupies the inmost. The heart can pervade what the body cannot pervade. The heart pervades the position of the formless; this is like Aershi, which pervades the position of the World of Principles.[7] That is why what is hidden and lodged on the inside of the microcosm becomes great and goes up.

It is also said that the human heart is like heaven, and the human body is like earth.[8] What is like heaven is up, and what is like earth is down. Basing oneself in the body and reaching the heart is to ascend, and basing oneself in the heart and reaching the body is to descend.

This subtlety of the mutual opposition of the differentiated forms is sufficient for the wonders of the creative transformation to be seen, but bestowing and receiving between the boundaries of heaven and humans are kept concealed.[9]

## Notes

1. Nasafī wrote: "As long as the sperm-drop is in the man's back (*pusht*), it is the First Ocean of the microcosm" (*Goal*, p. 255/94). Persian *pusht*, like Liu's "spine," translates the Koranic term *ẓahr* (back, or loins), which is found in the verse of the Covenant, 7:172.

2. Nasafī:

When the sperm-drop comes to the woman's womb, it itself is the Hidden Treasure, but here it becomes evident. When it comes to the woman's womb, it becomes the First Substance of the microcosm. Here the attributes of the human being are distinguished, and here the [divine] names become manifest. (*Goal*, pp. 255/94–95)

3. This is the reverse of the second, macrocosmic circle in Diagram 1.8, where yang is on the outside, and yin on the inside. In Islamic terms, inside or nonmanifest (*bāṭin*) corresponds to the invisible (*ghayb*) and spiritual,

which is subtle (*laṭīf*). Outside or manifest (*ẓāhir*) corresponds to the visible (*shahāda*) and bodily, which is dense (*kathīf*) and coarse (*ghalīẓ*). According to Nasafī:

The sperm-drop has an outward and an inward, and some have said that the sperm-drop has a subtlety and a density. From the outward of the sperm-drop, the outward of the child appears, and that is the World of the Kingdom. From the inward of the sperm-drop, the inward of the child appears, and that is the World of the Sovereignty.  (*Goal*, p. 256/95)

4. As the macrocosm develops (Diagrams 1.7–1.12), it moves from simplicity and invisibility to complexity and visibility, from the undifferentiation of the Vast Sediment to the infinite diversity of the forms in the universe. Once the microcosm receives a differentiated form, it develops its inner powers and moves from ignorance to intelligence, from visibility to invisibility, from the darkness and dullness of the body to the awakening of the heart. Like Nasafī, the Muslim philosophers track this movement in terms of levels of soul or spirit—the mineral, vegetal, animal, human, and angelic spirits, culminating in the Ascribed Spirit.

5. This is one of the many implications of the hadith of the Hidden Treasure. The Treasure is formless in itself, but it becomes manifest as the forms of the cosmos, thus allowing human beings to know it and to follow it back to formlessness. All things are signs pointing at the formless Origin. All things are jewels that had been concealed in the undifferentiated Treasure and have now become manifest.

6. These inner connections and unifications occur through knowing, awareness, and consciousness, all of which lead in the direction of the Nature of Continuity, which is union with Heaven.

7. The correlation between heart and Throne is a common one, even mentioned in a purported prophetic saying. According to the Koran, the Throne is the seat of the All-merciful and embraces heaven and earth, which are the overarching forms of the macrocosm. Given the reversal that occurs because the microcosm develops from form to the formless, the most formless level of human existence is the most interior, which is the heart. A famous saying ascribed to the Prophet tells us that God says, "My heaven and earth do not embrace Me, but the heart of My believing servant does embrace Me." Inside the heart, then, the All-merciful is "sitting," and the goal of the spiritual path is to find God inwardly, sitting on his microcosmic Throne. Rāzī explained the correlation between heart and Throne in these terms:

Know that the heart in the human body is like the Throne in the cosmos. Just as the Throne is the locus of manifestation for the sitting of the attribute of all-mercifulness (*raḥmāniyyat*) in the macrocosm, so also the heart is the locus of manifestation for the sitting of the attribute of spirituality (*rūḥāniyyat*) in the microcosm.   (*Path*, p. 187/201)

8. This is probably a reference to Rāzī: "Know that the heart in the human is like heaven, and the body is like earth" (*Path*, p. 195/207).

9. In other words, the World of the Kingdom makes the Hidden Treasure manifest and allows us to see the wondrous signs of God, but since humans unite with Heaven in the luminous consciousness of the heart, the spiritual dimension of things remains concealed.

### 3.3
### 四本分著圖

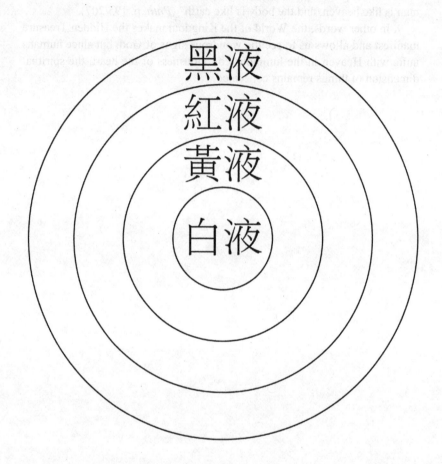

## 3.3
## Diagram of the Differentiation and
## Display of the Four Roots

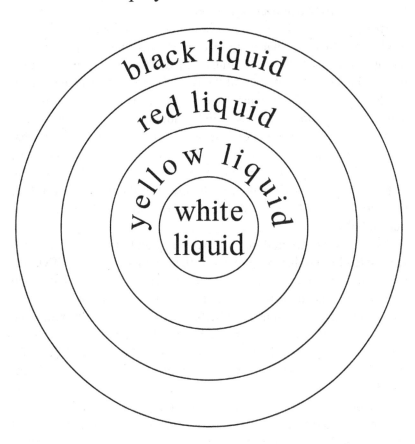

This is the image of the first month of the embryo.[1]

What enters the womb, having shifted from the father's spine, is the pure and the turbid. These two obtain the warmth and nourishment of the womb and are differentiated into four layers. This is the level of alteration and transformation.

The One Spot is differentiated into pure and turbid; this is like the original vital-energy that is divided into two wings [1.8]. Rooted in the pure and the turbid, it is transformed into four layers, and this, too, is like the differentiation of the two wings into four images [1.9].

The color of the outermost layer is black, belonging to soil. The color of what is near the black is red, belonging to wind. The color of what is near the red is yellow, belonging to fire. The color of what occupies the midmost is white, belonging to water. White is the most pure, yellow is slightly turbid in the midst of purity, black is the most turbid, and red is slightly pure in the midst of the turbid. These four become the root of the blood, flesh, and essential vital-energy of the human body.[2]

The four roots are nothing but two—pure and turbid. They are differentiated by the differentiations of their colors. Color is differentiated into four in the womb by the burning of the yin fire. That which occupies the outside is nearest the fire, so its color is black. The second layer interacts slightly with the fire, so its color is red. That which is slightly nearer the inside barely obtains the vital-energy of fire, so its color is yellow. That occupying the middlemost is far from the fire, so its color is white. Once the four colors are differentiated, then each of the four agents—wind, fire, water, and soil—has its own domain because of the color's coming to be.

Someone said that at root the color of the pure is white, and at root the color of the turbid is red. This is because at root the pure is transformed from the water of yang, and the water of yang is white in color; and at root the turbid is transformed from the fire of yin, and the fire of yin is red in color. Red and white are already divided, and they are again warmed and nourished by the yin fire of the womb. Therefore the outside of the red alters and becomes black, and the outside of the white alters and becomes yellow. This also is an explanation of how the four roots are differentiated and become four colors.

## *Notes*

1. Diagrams 3.3–3.6 detail the first four months in the womb. In the first month the four elements appear, in the second the microcosmic heaven and earth (heart and body), in the third the various bodily organs, and in the fourth the beginning of human nature. This follows Nasafī's organization, but not his details. Notably, Nasafī did not have a stage corresponding to Liu's second month, and Liu's third month combines the qualities of Nasafī's second and third months.

According to Nasafī, the four elements differentiated in the first month give rise in the three succeeding months to the qualities of minerals, then plants, then animals. In the second month, the organs take shape. In the third, the seven vegetal faculties appear—attraction, retention, digestion, excretion, nourishment, growth, and form-giving—and the vegetal spirit takes up its seat in the liver. In the fourth month, the next two levels of spirit become manifest—the animal (*ḥayawānī*) and the soulish or psychical (*nafsānī*). The primary quality of the animal spirit is life (*ḥayāt*) or animateness, which appears in the heart. The qualities of the psychical spirit are sensation and volitional movement, which appear in the brain.

2. Nasafī (*Goal*, pp. 259–60/99–100) also explained that the sperm-drop separates first into two and then four because of subtlety and coarseness. His treatment of the four elements, however, is completely different. He spoke of them in terms of a standard correlation with the four humors: soil is black bile, water is (white) phlegm, wind is (red) blood, and fire is yellow bile. The sperm-drop is layered exactly like the four elements in the macrocosm; so, beginning at the center, the elements take the order soil, water, wind, and fire; or black, white, red, and yellow. Liu, in contrast, ranked them in the order in which they appear through the cosmic flow: water/white, fire/yellow, wind/red, and soil/black.

## 3.4
## 表裏分形圖

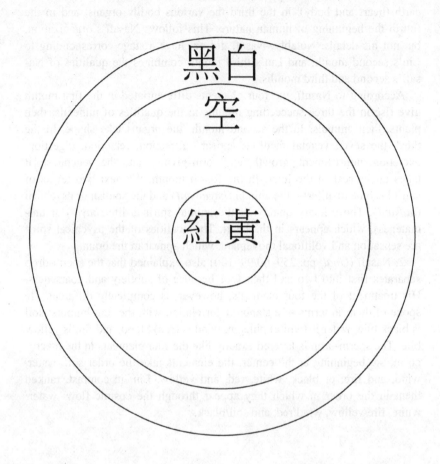

## 3.4
## Diagram of the Differentiated Forms
## of Outward and Inward

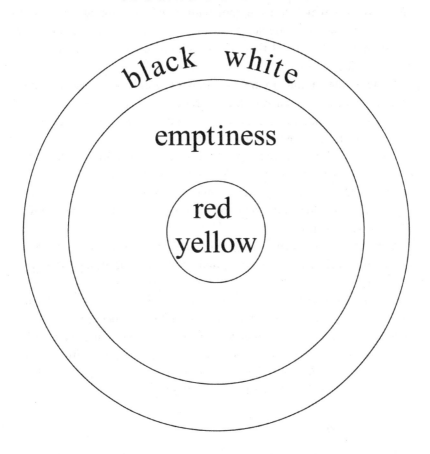

This is the image of the second month of the embryo.

At this moment, the four that are white, yellow, red, and black obtain the vital-energy of the warmth and nourishment in the womb longer than before. Since this lasts longer, flying, spreading, issuing, and moving—which are the root natures of the four agents, wind, fire, water, and soil—depart from the layered sequence of the four colors that came to be at first. Then each comes home to the root position of the four agents.[1]

Wind comes home to the position of wind; so it ascends and reaches inward. In regard to the microcosm, the inside is up; so the utmost inside is also the furthest up. Wind ascends and comes home to the inmost; so it comes home to the highest.

Fire comes home to fire's position; so it ascends and reaches next to wind. Its position is also inside. When wind and fire occupy the inside, water cannot be preserved inside; so it can only tend to descend and go down, adhering together with soil. What goes down goes to the outward.

Wind and fire ascend inside, and their form becomes the heart. Water and soil descend outside, and their form becomes the body. The heart is heaven, the body earth. Once the forms of outward and inward are differentiated, the heaven and earth of the microcosm are firmly positioned. Fire and wind unite together and become the heart; water and soil adhere together and become the body, and their midst is empty. This is similar to the meaning of heaven's position being up, earth's position being down, and the midst being empty [1.10].

This is the level of the perfection of the form.

### Notes

1. The "root positions" represent the arrangement of the elements in the fully differentiated cosmos, as in Diagrams 1.9 and 2.3: soil, water, air, and fire. In the macrocosm, soil/black and water/white are at the bottom, which is located in the center, given that it is surrounded on all sides by air, fire, and the heavens. In the microcosm, soil and water are also at the "bottom," but this means on the outer, bodily, dense side, as opposed to the inner, spiritual, subtle side. The body is outside, the heart inside.

3.5

内外體竅圖

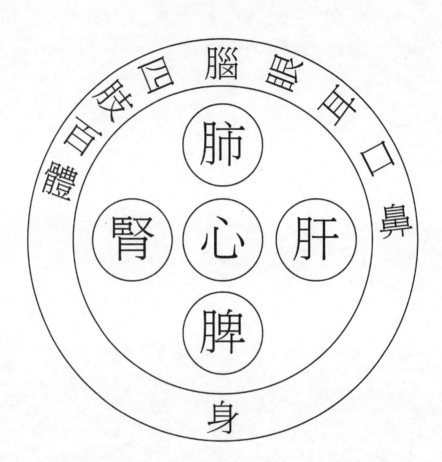

## 3.5
### Diagram of the Bodily Apertures
### of Inside and Outside

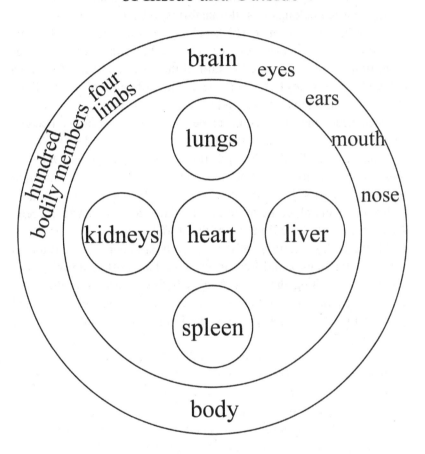

This is the image of the third month of the embryo.

In the second month, first the embryo is differentiated into the forms of outward and inward. When it reaches here, outward and inward each has its own alteration and transformation. That of the outward which belongs to soil transforms to become the flesh of the entire body, and that of it which belongs to water flows to become the paths of the veins and arteries. That of the inward which belongs to air transforms to become the stuff of the heart, and that of it which belongs to fire issues to become the opening of spiritual clarity; these stand opposed on the left and right sides of the heart.

Once heart and body come to be, the four storehouses[1] become connected to one another in the space between heart and body. These become the specific dwelling positions of the four agents. Once the four storehouses have come to be, all six treasuries[2] are embedded in sequence; so ears, eyes, mouth, nose, four limbs, and the hundred bodily members all come to be differentiated and displayed entirely. This is the level of the firmness of the stuff.

All the bodily apertures of the one body are connected and united with the storehouses and treasuries. What has most to do with connecting and uniting the entire body's bodily apertures is the brain alone. Each of the storehouses and treasuries connects with and unites only what it manages, but the brain manages all connecting and uniting.[3]

The brain joins and connects together the spiritual vital-energy of the heart and the essential vital-energy of the body in order to transform them. Its function is to receive forms in the formless and to make the formless pervade the forms, because it is the comprehensive origin of the hundred veins. The knowledge and awareness, the turning and moving, of the hundred bodily members all rely upon it.

What does it mean to receive forms in the formless? Everything seen by the eyes, heard by the ears, and known by the heart is received and gathered together by the brain and contained and stored within. This is what gives it the ability to receive.

What does it mean to make the formless pervade the forms? In the midst of the brain is lodged the virtue of comprehensive awareness.[4] Vessels and arteries from the brain pervade the eye; so the eyes obtain the strength of the comprehensive awareness and are able to see.

Vessels and arteries pervade the ears; so the ears obtain the strength of the comprehensive awareness and are able to hear. Vessels and arteries pervade the mouth and nose; so the mouth and nose obtain the strength of the comprehensive awareness, and the mouth knows taste and the nose knows smell.

Thus the liver opens apertures in the eyes, and what enables the eyes to see is the strength of the brain. The kidneys open apertures in the ears, and what enables the ears to hear is the strength of the brain. The spleen opens apertures in the mouth, the lungs open apertures in the nose, and what enables the mouth to know taste and the nose to know smell is the strength of the brain.[5]

Vessels and arteries from the brain pervade the entire body; so the strength of the comprehensive awareness is obtained throughout the body. Hands are able to hold, feet able to walk, and all the hundred bodily members know pain and itchiness.

Although the heart is the treasury of spiritual clarity, it cannot but seek assistance from the brain. If the brain obtains nourishment, the spiritual clarity of the heart will be doubled. If the brain loses nourishment, the will and vital-energy of the heart will darken. This is the meaning of making the formless pervade the forms.

It is also said that the heart is a chamber, and the brain a hall. Everything arranged in the chamber will always be manifested and disclosed in the hall. The brain accepts the giving of the heart, and then it gives to the hundred apertures. Once the bodily apertures have been completed, the human form is perfected.

From now on, what takes nutrition and nourishment has two taproots. The outside taproot is called the "navel," and the inside taproot is called the "gall bladder." The navel is able to pull the mother's blood and vital-energy into the stomach, thereby taking nutrition and nourishment. The gall bladder is able to differentiate and distinguish between the good and the bad that are pulled into it by vital-energy and blood. It uses the good and expels the poisonous. So, the inside and outside bodily apertures depend upon these two taproots to obtain their nutrition and nourishment.

## *Notes*

1. As is clear from the diagram and the text, the four storehouses are liver, lungs, kidneys, and spleen.

2. The six treasuries are ears, eyes, mouth, nose, four limbs, and the hundred bodily members.

3. Concerning the relation between heart and brain, Nasafī wrote:

Configuration and growth become manifest, the plant becomes complete, the vegetal spirit gains strength, and the stomach and liver become capable of digesting food. Then the heart attracts the cream and quintessence of the vegetal spirit, which is in the liver. When it enters the heart and is once again digested and ripened, all of it becomes life. The cream and quintessence of the life that is in the heart becomes the animal spirit. The animal spirit sends the leftover through the arteries to all the organs, and it becomes the life of the organs. The distributor of life in the body is the animal spirit, whose site is in the heart, which is on the left side.

Then the brain attracts the cream and quintessence of the animal spirit, which is in the heart. When the blood enters the brain and is once again digested and ripened, it becomes the psychical spirit. The psychical spirit sends the leftover by way of the nerves to all of the nerves; so sensation and volitional movement appear in all of the organs. This is the reality of the animal, and all of this is in another month. In four months, the elements, natures, minerals, plants, and animals are completed, each in one month.   (*Goal*, p. 261/101)

4. This is the *sensus communis*, the faculty that unites and coordinates all the faculties. See the explanation under Diagram 3.9.

5. Nūr al-Ḥaqq went into more detail in making correlations:

The liver is the storehouse of the microcosm's fire, and within it is the faculty of wrath (*ghaḍab*). The lungs are the storehouse of soil, and within it is the origin of stillness (*sukūn*). The spleen is the storehouse of air, and within it is the origin of movement (*ḥaraka*). The kidneys are the storehouse of water, and within it is the faculty of appetite (*shahwa*). Between heart and body these four are the traces of the four elements that are between heaven and earth. Rather, they are four of the heart's viziers for, by means of them, it exercises control over the body. As for the external organs, they are in the head, hands, and legs. The eyes are linked to the liver; so the eyes hurt when there is heat in the liver. The ears are linked to the kidneys; so the ears ring when the kidneys are weak. The mouth is linked to the lungs; so the mouth becomes hot and dry when there is heat in the lungs. The nose is linked to the spleen; so the nose becomes sore when there is heat in the spleen.   (*Sharḥ*, pp. 90–91/68–69)

## 3.6
### 靈活顯用圖

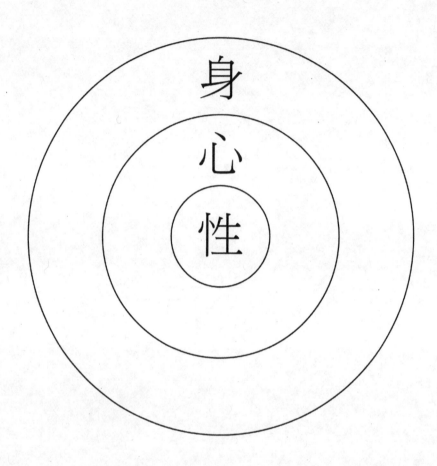

## 3.6
### Diagram of the Manifestation of the Function of the Spiritually Living

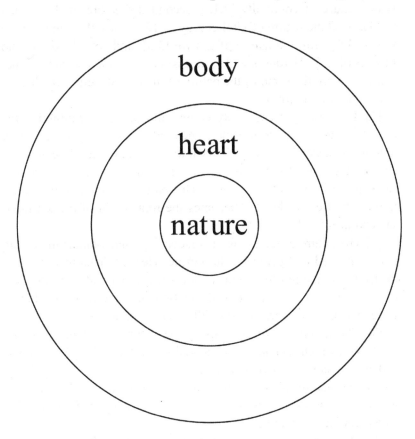

This is the image after the bodily apertures have been completed.

Once the bodily apertures have been completed, the spiritually living is begotten. The spiritually living is the nature that makes humans human. This nature has one root and comprises six levels. First is the nature of continuity [3.12], second the nature of the human [3.11], third the nature of vital-energy [3.10], fourth the nature of the living [3.9], fifth the nature of growth [3.8], and sixth hardness and firmness [3.7].[1] Hardness and firmness are not called a "nature" because they are the same as the nature of metal and stone, which does not beget or issue forth.[2]

[1] The nature of continuity comes into being by continuing the Root Suchness of the Real Ruler. The nature of the Real Ruler is that nothing precedes it, although after it there is continuity. Because this nature takes the Root Suchness of the Real Ruler as its own root suchness, it is called "continuity." This nature is the chief manifestation of the Real Ruler and becomes the root origin of the ten thousand natures.[3]

[2] The nature of the human is that each human obtains the nature that is allotted and given by the Former Heaven. This nature is not far from the nature of continuity, but, since it is allotted by the Former Heaven, there is a subtle distinction in name and meaning of which we are not aware. This is called the "root nature."

[3] The nature of vital-energy is the nature of vital-energy and stuff, with which humans are endowed in the Latter Heaven.[4] This is called "the nature of love and hate."

[4] The nature of the living is adherence to the bodily frame by which one knows, becomes aware, turns, and moves. This is called "the nature of food and color."[5]

[5] The nature of growth is that through which the bodily frame grows from small to large. This is called "the nature of issuing forth and nurturing."

[6] Hardness and firmness are what harden and adjust the bodily frame so that it does not become loose and scattered. Although this is not named a nature, it also is a nature.

One root comprises these six levels. This is the subtle meaning that surely cannot be differentiated when you want to differentiate it, but there is surely a difference of self-suchness when you want to unify it. This is what makes the spiritually living.

Beginning with the One Spot, the human body is differentiated into forms and gradually reaches the manifestation of the functions of the spiritually living. This is how the microcosm transforms from form into the formless. The spiritually living has form in the midst of the formless, and formlessness in the midst of form.[6]

This is the great mechanism whereby humans, having come from Heaven, unite with Heaven by way of being human. When there is adherence to the formless, what makes humans human is complete. When there is going back to the formless, what unites humans with Heaven reaches its ultimate.

This is the level of display and disclosure.[7]

## Notes

1. The six levels of human nature can be translated back into Nasafī's terms as (1) the Ascribed Spirit, (2) the human spirit, (3) the psychical spirit, (4) the animal spirit, (5) the vegetal spirit, and (6) minerals. In speaking of the Ascribed Spirit, Nasafī said that it is identical with the human spirit (*Goal*, pp. 263/104, 271/112, 275/116), but he also talked about the human spirit as the second level of spirit, as here. He explained that once the human spirit is purified, strengthened, and perfected, it recovers its true nature as Ascribed Spirit (*Goal*, p. 274/116).

2. Nasafī did not mention "mineral spirit" in *Goal*, but he did elsewhere (e.g., *Insān*, p. 265), and the term was often used by other authors. A few paragraphs down, Liu said that hardness and firmness are in fact a nature.

3. Liu used the term "chief manifestation" in at least two ways. Under Diagram 1.4, he identified it with the Undivided Suchness of the Great Function, discussed in Diagram 1.3; so it is the Divine Essence envisaged as embracing all names and attributes in unity. Under Diagram 1.6, he said it is the Root Suchness in the midst of the Great Mandate, and this is what he meant here. The Great Mandate is the Engendering Command, or the Ascribed Spirit, and the Root Suchness is the divine reality that animates it and is present within it; or, it is Breath of the All-merciful. Despite the terminological profusion (which is even greater in Liu's sources), it is clear that he meant to identify the Nature of Continuity with the Ascribed Spirit (and in-

deed, as already pointed out, it can be taken as a nearly literal translation of the term).

4. The nature of vital-energy and stuff (*qizhi zhi xing* 氣質之性) is an expression first used by Zhang Zai in order to distinguish between the nature of heaven and earth, which is common to all, and the nature of individual things, which is partial. According to Zhu Xi, "There are two kinds of nature: There is what is called the nature of principle, and there is what is called the nature of vital-energy and stuff" (*Concepts*, pp. 370, 372). Wing-tsit Chan and others (e.g., Kalton, *To Become a Sage*, p. 123) translate the term as "physical nature." Chan writes that, with this concept, "for the first time Confucianism has found an at least tentatively satisfactory answer to the question of evil. . . . In the physical nature is the occasion for evil, and how to use this occasion depends on man" (*Source Book*, p. 511; for Zhu Xi's use of the term, see pp. 623–26).

5. This expression is typically said to refer to appetite and sexual passion, qualities shared by all animals and hence innate to the animal spirit. In translating these two characters plus that for nature in Mencius 6.A.4.1—a passage that says literally, "Food [and] color [are] nature"—Legge has "*To enjoy* food and *delight in* colors is nature." Lau renders this as "Appetite for food and sex is nature."

6. This point is often made in Islamic texts by discussing the soul (*nafs*) as the interface between the formless spirit and the formed body. Jāmī explained that it is impossible for the luminous and subtle spirit to have a direct relationship with the dark and coarse body. As a result,

God created the animal soul as an isthmus between the transcendent spirit and the body. In respect of being an intelligible faculty, the soul is simple and corresponds with the transcendent spirit. In respect of comprising by essence diverse and multiple faculties scattered throughout the body and controlling it in many ways . . . it corresponds with the [bodily] constitution compounded of the elements. (*Naqd*, p. 55)

7. This sentence clarifies why Liu used the phrase "the manifestation and display of" in the titles of each of the next six diagrams. During each of the six levels of the spiritually living, the invisible qualities and characteristics of the macrocosmic levels come to be more and more manifest and displayed in the consciousness of the microcosm.

3.7
堅定顯著圖

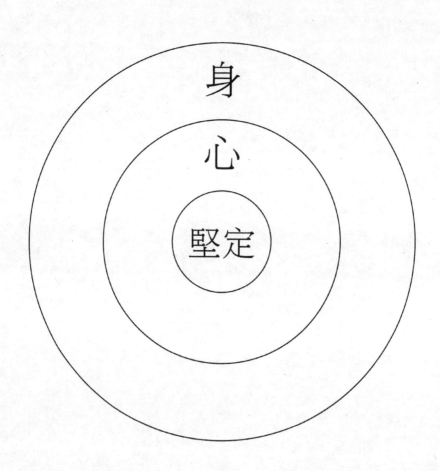

### 3.7
## Diagram of the Manifestation and Display of Hardness and Firmness

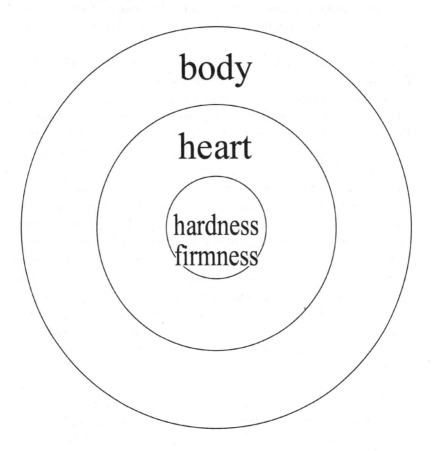

This is the first level of the manifestation of the function of the spiritually living.[1]

As a thing, the spiritually living has one root and comprises six levels. It goes from the fine to the coarse by going from the nature of continuity and the nature of the human to the nature of vital-energy, the nature of the living, the nature of growth, and hardness and firmness.

In manifestation, hardness and firmness come first, followed by the nature of growth, the nature of the living, and the nature of vital-energy, then followed by the nature of the human and the nature of continuity. This is reaching the fine from the coarse. Reaching the fine from the coarse is the meaning of still following form and then undergoing transformation to reach the formless. It is this sequence as such that makes the microcosm the microcosm.

The reason why hardness and firmness come into manifestation first is that hardness and firmness are the nature of metal and stone, whose occupation is not to beget and issue forth. Rather, hardness and firmness surely have the ability not to change at all. When hardness and firmness are manifest, each of the viscera and entrails is tied down to its root position without shaking and moving. The flowing and pervading of both vital-energy and blood come home through the meridians, without collapsing or transgressing. Each of the hundred bones, large and small, is at ease in its allotted inch without overstepping. Everything throughout the body is hardened and adjusted, connected and bound; so nothing can be loosened and scattered. All this is because of the strength of this hardness and firmness.

Just as the microcosm obtains strength from the nature of hardness and firmness, so also the macrocosm obtains strength from the nature of hardness and firmness. Since the macrocosm obtained the strength of hardness and firmness, the nine heavens and seven earths have not changed their positions from oldest antiquity. The sun, stars, rivers, and high mountains have not altered their constancy from oldest antiquity. The creation of things binds and ties together heaven and earth through this tying and binding.

Once the microcosm obtains the strength of this hardness and firmness, then everything throughout the body is adjusted and put at ease, and nothing changes its position, just as the macrocosm has not altered its constancy from oldest antiquity. Thus, the nature of hardness and firmness is the capability of the creation of things to tie and bind together the microcosm. The complete power of the creation of things is fully entrusted to the human body, and this is what is seen first in the manifestation of its functions.[2]

## Notes

1. This section is derived partly from Nasafī's description of what takes place in the second month in the womb:

When the elements and natures are completed, the three progeny appear from the four elements and natures: first minerals, second plants, third animals. In other words, the distributor distributes these four elements and natures and brings all the inward and outward organs of the human being into manifestation. In this state these organs are minerals. It sends to each organ a designated measure of all four; to some, equal measures of all four, and to others, disparate measures, as wisdom requires. It binds them all to each other, and brings forth the channels of life, sensation, and volitional movement. Then the minerals are completed. This all takes place in another month.   (*Goal*, p. 260/100)

2. Body here is *shen* 身, not *ti*, so the point is not a substance/function correlation. Liu is saying that when the body is fully formed (by means of the stages indicated in Diagrams 3.1–3.6), the first thing we observe about it is the "physical" characteristics and activities made possible by hardness and firmness. Diagrams 3.8–3.12 subsequently consider the nonphysical characteristics and functions that appear inwardly during the Arc of Ascent, that is, the return to the Nature of Continuity.

3.8
發育顯著圖

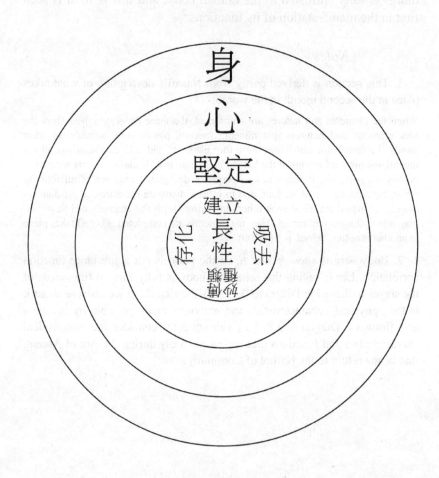

## 3.8
## Diagram of the Manifestation and
## Display of Issuing Forth and Nurturing

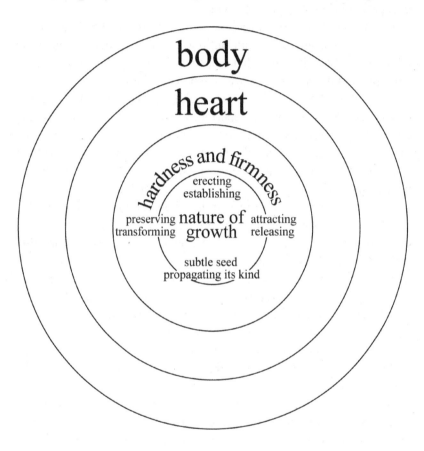

Once hardness and firmness become manifest, the nature of issuing forth and nurturing becomes manifest.[1] Issuing forth and nurturing are the nature of growth, which is the nature of grass and trees. The nature of grass and trees is embraced everywhere, and its specific occupation is begetting and growing.

Before the nature of growth becomes manifest, the fetus cannot rely on its own attracting and pulling to receive nourishment from the mother. It awaits only what reaches it from the mother's essential strength, and it obtains its nourishment accordingly.

When it reaches here, this is the time of manifestation. The strength of vital-energy is strong and superior. It can rely on its own attracting and pulling to take assistance from the mother. Regardless of whether or not the mother's essential strength reaches it, it knows—without knowing why it is so—to take essential strength from its mother to nourish itself. When it obtains nourishment, it grows.

As a thing, the nature of growth has the strength of attracting, the strength of transforming, the strength of preserving, and the strength of releasing.[2] When it can attract, it selects the cause of nourishing and nurturing. When it can transform, it ripens what has been attracted, and then emerge altering and transforming. When it can preserve, it completely gathers the subtle essence of what has been transformed and distributes it among the viscera and entrails and the bodily limbs. When it can release, it completely eliminates and releases the leftover and excess of the subtle essence without retaining it. These four strengths are the subtle root of what is contained in the nature of growth.[3]

When someone becomes an adult through issuing forth and nurturing, two [more] strengths of the root being become manifest and disclosed in the midst of the undifferentiated collectedness of the four strengths. One of these is the strength of the subtle seed, the other the strength of the propagation of images. These reach manifestation and disclosure at the time of the proliferation of begetting.[4]

The subtle seed comes before transformation of drinks and edibles into vital-energy and blood. This strength selects the utmost essence of the allotment, invigorates the nourishment of the original veins, and subtly makes the seed. As for the propagation of images, when there is desire for the seed to be implanted in the womb, this strength completely impresses and bestows therein the forms, shapes, natures, and feelings embedded in the root substance. This is the function of propagating its kind.

The position of the nature of growth is in the liver. This nature already has the power of growing and issuing forth, but it borrows the fire of the liver to assist its strength. Thus we become aware that growing and issuing forth will be twice as easy.

When the macrocosm obtains the strength of the nature of growth, the images come to be, and the images do not decay. The forms come to be, and the forms flourish daily. The nature of begetting and growth in the microcosm is virtually the same as the nature of begetting and growth in the macrocosm.

## Notes

1. This section is based on a passage in which Nasafī described how the vegetal spirit appears in the embryo:

When the organs are completed, the minerals are completed. Then faculties appear in each outward and inward organ: the faculties of attraction, retention, digestion, repulsion, nourishment, growth, and form-giving. Once the organs, limbs and faculties appear, the child begins to search for food. By way of the navel the child attracts to itself the blood that is gathered in the womb of the mother. . . . By way of the veins the vegetal spirit distributes the blood to all of the organs as their nourishment. The distributor of food in the body is the vegetal spirit, whose site is the liver, and the liver is on the right side. When nourishment reaches all of the organs, configuring and growing become manifest. This is the reality of the plant, and it is all in another month.   (*Goal*, pp. 260–61/100–101)

2. "Strength" (*li* 力) translates *quwwa*, "strength," "faculty," "potency." "Transforming" is digestion, "preserving" retention, and "releasing" repulsion. "Subtle essence" renders *zubda wa khulāṣa*, "cream and quintessence." The corresponding passage in *Goal* reads:

When the blood enters the child's stomach and is once again digested and ripened, the liver, by way of the mesentery, attracts to itself the chyle that is in the stomach. When it enters the liver and is digested and ripened once again, the cream and quintessence, which is the chyme in the liver, becomes the vegetal spirit. Some of what is left over becomes yellow bile, some blood, some phlegm, and some black bile. The gall bladder pulls the yellow bile to itself, the spleen pulls the black bile to itself, and then the vegetal spirit distributes the phlegm to the whole of the body for various wise reasons.   (*Goal*, p. 260/100)

3. The text of *Goal* lists seven vegetal faculties, the standard number, but elsewhere Nasafī began his discussion of the vegetal spirit by talking only about the four faculties that Liu mentioned here (Nasafī, *Bayān al-tanzīl*, p. 200; idem, *Kashf al-ḥaqā'iq*, p. 87).

4. In other words, the two faculties that make reproduction possible in adulthood also pertain to the nature of issuing forth and nurturing. These two faculties become manifest after the maturation of the plant or animal. They correspond to the faculty of reproduction (*muwallida*), not mentioned by Nasafī, and the faculty of form-giving (*muṣawwira*), which is mentioned but not explained; it bestows on the offspring a form and shape appropriate to the species.

## 3.9
## 知覺顯著圖

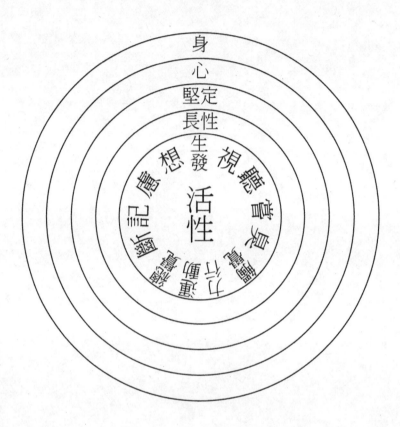

# 3.9
# Diagram of the Manifestation and Display of Knowledge and Awareness

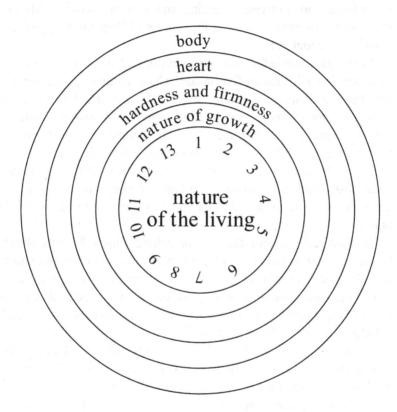

1. begetting and issuing
2. seeing
3. hearing
4. tasting
5. smelling
6. awareness of touch
7. acting with strength
8. turning and moving
9. comprehensive awareness
10. decision
11. recording
12. deliberation
13. thought

Once the nature of growth becomes manifest, the nature of the living is displayed.[1] There was no knowledge and awareness before this, but now there is knowledge and awareness. There was no turning and moving before this, but now there is turning and moving. Knowledge and awareness, turning and moving, arise at this moment, and their nature becomes the taproot of [appetite for] food and color[2] throughout life.

As things, knowledge and awareness have ten functions.[3] Five of these are lodged outside, five inside. Those lodged outside are seeing, hearing, tasting, smelling, and touch; they are housed in the eyes, ears, mouth, nose, and bodily limbs. Those lodged inside are called comprehensive awareness, thought, deliberation, decision, and recording; none of their positions is separable from the brain.

Comprehensive awareness manages as a whole all knowledge and awareness, inside and outside. The hundred bodily members are assisted by it to be aware. Its position is lodged in the front of the brain.[4]

Thought reflects upon the reasons behind what it has already obtained in order to respond to the function of comprehensive awareness. Its position follows behind that of comprehensive awareness.[5]

Deliberation scrutinizes and measures what has been thought in terms of right and wrong, permissible and impermissible. Its position is lodged in the middle of the brain.[6]

Decision is spiritual clarity that resolutely judges and straightforwardly decides the appropriateness of what has been deliberated. Its position follows behind that of deliberation.[7]

Recording contains and stores without loss everything seen, heard, known, and every object of awareness outside and inside. Its position lodges in the back of the brain.[8]

Turning and moving are that which, relying on what is reached by knowledge and awareness and, corresponding to it, turns and moves.[9] What turns in the viscera and entrails is the affair of vital-energy. What moves in the four limbs and the one hundred bodily members is the affair of the deeds of both vital-energy and blood.

There is the strength of directing, and there is the strength of serving. Directing is lodged in the heart and gives rise to turning and moving. Serving is lodged in the body and responds to the directing, and then turning and moving come to be.

The nature of the living is embedded in all ten thousand things. However, some have knowledge and awareness, and some do not have knowledge and awareness; some have turning and moving, and some do not have turning and moving. It is not that some are complete and some incomplete in their natures. If we look from the outside, it may seem that there is no knowledge and awareness, no turning and moving. But, in reality, there are always knowledge and awareness, turning and moving. It is only that, although there are knowledge and awareness, people cannot see the knowledge and awareness, and although there are turning and moving, people cannot glimpse the turning and moving.[10]

Take, for example, metal and stone as things. Humans regard them as having no knowledge and awareness, no turning and moving. But, when melted, they transform, and when struck, they give off sound. Is this not their knowledge and awareness? Begotten in the mountains, they flow in water; begotten in the bottom of the mines, they are seen at the surface of the mine. Is this not their turning and moving? If metal and stone are like this, how much more so are things more spiritual than metal and stone!

## *Notes*

1. This section is based generally on *Goal*, pp. 261–62/101–2, where Nasafī summarized the teachings of the Muslim philosophers on life (*ḥayāt*), the chief attribute of the "animal spirit" (*rūḥ-i ḥayawānī*). Life, it is worth remembering, was not considered an attribute of the vegetal spirit, a point taken for granted by Liu. In Arabic, this is indicated by the derivation of *ḥayawānī* from *ḥayāt*, and in English by the derivation of "animal" and "animate" from *anima*, and "vegetal" from *vegetare*, "to grow." The primary attribute of the vegetal spirit is configuration (*nashw*) and growth (*namā'*). Life, in contrast, is defined in terms of the ability to manifest the qualities of sensation (*ḥiss*) or perception (*idrāk*) and of volitional movement (*ḥarakat-i irādī*). In Liu's terms, the nature of the living appears first in knowledge and awareness and second in turning and moving.

2. As noted under Diagram 3.6, this expression refers to appetite for food and sex. In Arabic, *shahwa*, which is a basic characteristic of the animal soul, means precisely "appetite" in this sense.

3. Nasafī differentiated between the animal and the "psychical" (*nafsānī*) spirit, and he ascribed the five external and five internal senses to the latter. Not surprisingly, the five external senses are the same in Liu's account, but he diverged in his explanation of the five internal senses. The correspondence between the Arabic expressions and Liu's Chinese terms becomes clear not so much because of the meanings of the words as because of the order in which the two authors explained them and the manner in which they located them in the brain.

4. "Comprehensive awareness" (*zongjue* 總覺) translates *ḥiss-i mushtarik*, commonly rendered as *sensus communis*, given that English "common sense" is far indeed from the medieval notion, which was that of a single mode of internal perception that united all the faculties. The discussion of the three or five internal senses has a long history, going back at least to Aristotle. See Wolfson, "The Internal Senses."

5. "Thought" (*xiang* 想) is Nasafī's "imagination" (*khayāl*), a term similar to our notion of thinking, given that "concepts" (*taṣawwur*) are "forms" (*ṣūra*) of ideas and meanings. In Islamic psychology the ideas and meanings (*ma'nā*) themselves—that is, the transcendent realities, of which our thoughts are the forms and images—are generally held to dwell in the intelligible realm of pure spirits, a realm directly accessible only to the fully actualized intellect. The philosopher strives for this actualization in his quest for wisdom.

6. "Deliberation" (*lü* 慮) stands in place of *mutaṣarrifa*, which means "the controller," or "that which puts to use." Nasafī explained that this faculty, when under the sway of intellect, is also called "the thinking" or "reflective faculty" (*mufakkira*). If it is dominated by sense-intuition, it is also called "the imagining faculty" (*mutakhayyila*).

7. "Decision" (*duan* 斷) corresponds to *wahm*. Although commonly used as a synonym for "imagination," technically it designates one of the internal senses. The Latin medievals rendered *wahm* as *estimatio*, but there is no agreement among experts as to whether any modern English word adequately conveys its meaning. We normally opt for "sense-intuition." Nasafī defined it in standard fashion: "Sense-intuition is that which grasps the meaning of friendship in the friend and the meaning of enmity in the enemy" (*Goal*, p. 262/102).

8. "Recording" (*ji* 記) is *ḥāfiẓa*, "memory." Nasafī explained how the five internal faculties relate to each other in these two passages:

> Imagination is the storekeeper of the *sensus communis*, and memory is the store-keeper of sense-intuition. The *sensus communis* and imagination are in the front of the brain, and sense-intuition and memory are in the back of the brain. The controller is in the middle of the brain.
>
> The *sensus communis* perceives the forms of the sensibles, which is to say that the *sensus communis* perceives what is witnessed, and sense-intuition perceives what is absent [from perception]. The *sensus communis* perceives everything perceived by the external senses. All of it is gathered in the *sensus communis*, which is why it is called "*sensus communis*." This is to say that the objects of hearing, sight, smell, taste, and touch are all gathered in the *sensus communis*. In other words, it can perceive all of these. . . .
>
> The controller is that which uses perceptions that are stored in imagination for compounding and differentiating. (*Goal*, p. 262/102)
>
> The controller takes control of the perceptions stored in the imagination by way of compounding and differentiating them, as, for example, by compounding a man with two heads and conceiving of him as two-headed; or, by separating the head from a man and conceiving of him as headless. If intellect puts this faculty to work, it is called "the thinking faculty," and if sense-intuition puts it to work, it is called "the imagining faculty." (*Kashf al-ḥaqā'iq*, pp. 88–89)

9. "Turning and moving" (*yundong* 運動) translates *quwwat-i muḥar-rika*, "the motor" or "movement-inducing faculty." It is of two sorts, inciting (*bā'itha*) and activating (*fā'ila*), which Liu called "directing" and "serving." Nasafī explained the nature of the latter's service when he wrote: "The activating faculty is obedient to the inciting faculty and accepts its commands" (*Goal*, pp. 262/102–3). He placed the inciting faculty in the imagination (rather than in the heart, as Liu would have it), and the activating faculty in the organs and limbs.

10. Although Nasafī did not discuss the presence of life in all things, this is one of Ibn al-'Arabī's common themes. His metaphysical argument is simply that all things disclose the Real Being, which is never divorced from any of its essential attributes, including life, knowledge, desire, and power. Whether these become manifest in any given thing depends on its receptivity (cf. the discussion under Diagram 1.11). Jāmī offered a parallel argument for life's first corollary, knowledge (awareness, consciousness). Liu's translation of the passage sums up the discussion like this: "All the powerful affairs possessed by the Real Being pervade fully and go throughout the ten thousand beings" (*Chinese Gleams*, pp. 202–5).

## 3.10
## 氣性顯著圖

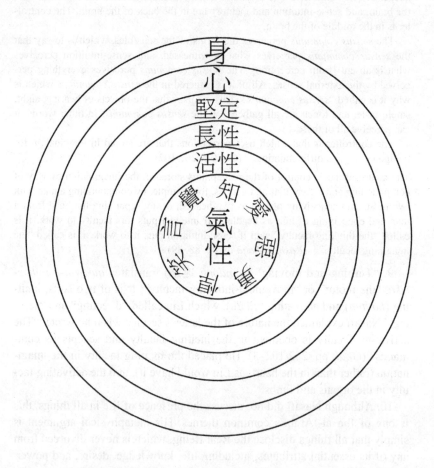

# 3.10
## Diagram of the Manifestation and
## Display of the Nature of Vital-Energy

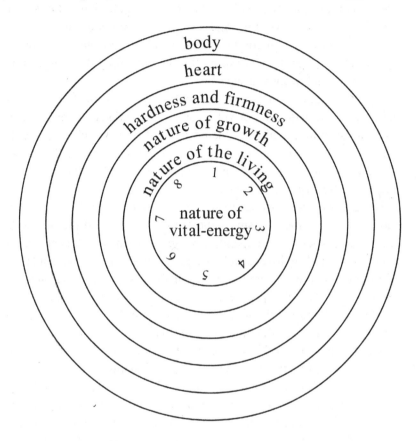

1. knowledge
2. love
3. hate
4. bravery

5. boldness
6. laughter
7. speech
8. awareness

The three levels of hardness and firmness, growth, and the living are manifest at the time when there is no departure from the mother's belly. Forty days after the emergence from the mother's belly, the nature of vital-energy becomes manifest.[1] When the nature of vital-energy is manifest, there is knowledge of love and hate.[2] Looked at superficially, these two, love and hate, are nothing more than a comprehensive designation for the seven feelings and the six desires.[3] When they expand, they are in reality the capability to emerge from the ordinary and become a sage.[4]

At the beginning of emergence and departure from the mother's belly, love and hate are not yet clearly differentiated. Their germ is probably seen in the midst of the crying and laughter of the heavenly suchness.[5] So, the crying and laughter of the heavenly suchness are the place where the germ of love and hate are seen and where the nature of vital-energy first becomes manifest.

Humans are the spiritual of the ten thousand things[6] and are embedded with the mechanism of the ability to love and the ability to hate. Later, when these expand,[7] love gives strength to enact the affairs that should be loved, and hate gives strength to leave aside the affairs that should be hated. All are for the sake of this strength and vital-energy. Thereby people advance daily toward sagehood and worthiness. Although the nature of vital-energy belongs to the Latter Heaven, it is connected to humans like this.[8]

The former worthy Yezide[9] said: The nature of vital-energy is to receive obediently the function of the root nature and to function accordingly. What the nature of vital-energy is capable of doing is everything that the root nature desires to do. The knowledge and power that are possessed by the root nature are fully entrusted to the nature of vital-energy so as to issue forth and appear. The nature of vital-energy is rooted in vital-energy and stuff,[10] and vital-energy and stuff are rooted in the four agents of wind, fire, water, and soil so as to come to be. When humans obtain equally the four agents, the nature of their vital-energy is harmonious and peaceful, and the root nature is also able to borrow from it and become completely manifest. When they obtain the four agents unequally, the nature of their vital-energy is not able to be harmonious and peaceful, and the root nature will also not become completely manifest.

He also said: The nature of vital-energy has four names that are differentiated by belonging to the four agents. The first is called "the nature of settled firmness," and it belongs to wind. The second is called "the nature of constant alertness," and it belongs to water. The third is called "the nature of awakening regret," and it belongs to fire. The fourth is called "the nature of self-indulgence," and it belongs to soil. Those in whom the four natures function generally are the middle humans. Those in whom the specific natures of wind and water function are above the middle humans. Those in whom fire and soil function are below the middle humans.

Someone said: Wind is not firm. Why does the nature of settled firmness belong to wind?

I said: As a thing, wind fills completely all that is up, all that is down, and the four directions, without overflowing and without falling short. It seems to be unsettled, but in reality it is settled. It seems to be infirm, but in reality it is firm. Therefore the nature of settled firmness belongs to the wind.[11]

Those who function specifically according to the nature of settled firmness are the same as those who function according to the root nature; they are the class of sages.[12] They are followed by those who function according to the nature of constant alertness, as if they function according to the root nature; they are the class of the worthies and the wise. They are followed by those who function according to the nature of awakening regret, still not failing to function according to the root nature. Below this are those who function according to the nature of self-indulgence, who are purely perverse and rebellious; this is not the same as the root nature.

This is how the nature of vital-energy is differentiated. It is worthwhile for those who function according to the nature of vital-energy to know how to inquire into it.

## Notes

1. This corresponds to Nasafī's psychical spirit (*rūḥ-i nafsānī*), which begins to manifest itself during the fourth month in the womb. On the meaning of vital-energy (*qi*), see the note under Diagram 1.1.

2. In Nasafī's terms, these are appetite (*shahwa*) and wrath (*ghaḍab*), two basic tendencies of the animal soul that are much discussed in both philosophy and Sufism; the medieval translators rendered them as "concupiscence" and "irascibility." As Nasafī explained, the function of appetite is "to attract benefit and to gain pleasure," and the function of wrath is "to repel harm and domination" (*Goal*, p. 262/103).

3. As noted under Diagram 1.12, the seven are pleasure, anger, sorrow, fear, love, hate, and desire. As for the six desires, they seem to be a subdivision of the last feeling.

4. Here and in much of what follows Liu was inspired by Rāzī, who developed a sophisticated psychology of love based on appetite and wrath, although he calls appetite by its near synonym, *hawā*, "caprice" or "whim." Generally, "appetite" is used in more philosophical approaches, and "caprice" in more theological or Koranic approaches. The Koran mentions appetite twice to mean sexual desire, but without negative connotations. In contrast, it condemns *hawā* in several verses and describes it as the tendency of the forgetful soul to fall away from God by following its own whims. Rāzī explained caprice and wrath as negative faculties of the soul, but then he said that they can be transformed into positive forces ("sublimated" we might say), in which case they will drive the soul in its quest to achieve perfection. In his chapter on "the cultivation of the soul" (*tazkiyat al-nafs*), he describes the soul as the child of the spirit (its father) and the four elements (its mother):

The soul has two essential attributes inherited from its mother; other blameworthy attributes are progeny of these two roots and the attributes of their activity. These two essential attributes are caprice and wrath, both of which are characteristics of the four elements, which are the soul's mother. Caprice is inclining and aiming toward the low, as God says, "By the star when it declines (*hawā*)" [Koran 53:1], that is, when it goes down. . . . This inclining and aiming toward the low is the characteristic of water and soil.

Wrath is seeking elevation, greatness, and domination, and this is the attribute of wind and fire. . . .

The soul must have these two attributes of caprice and wrath so that it can attract beneficial things to itself with caprice and repel harmful things from itself with wrath. Thus its existence will remain and be nurtured in the world of generation and corruption. But these two attributes must be kept in equilibrium. (*Path*, pp. 178–79/194)

5. By "heavenly suchness" (*tianran* 天然) Liu clearly meant the purity of the newborn infant. Nowadays this expression is understood to mean natural or innate or inborn nature, without anyone imagining that Heaven or the Divine is somehow involved. What Liu meant is the human substance as endowed by Heaven, which is so of itself without the intervention of human acts. In his later uses of the term, the heavenly implication of the term is more pronounced. The notion itself is not far from what Islamic sources call *fiṭra*, a Koranic word meaning "creation" in the specific sense of an original, God-given nature.

6. As was explained under Diagram 1.12.

7. The reference to "expansion" derives from the famous chapter in *Mencius* concerning the child who is on the verge of falling into a well. In discussing the innate human tendency to save the child, Mencius mentioned "the four beginnings" that give rise to virtue: commiseration gives rise to *ren*, shame to righteousness, modesty to propriety, recognizing right and wrong to wisdom. He then said, "All have the four beginnings in themselves, so they should know to expand them. When they are fully expanded, that will be enough to bestow protection on the four oceans" (*Mencius* 2.1.6).

8. Liu's text here parallels Rāzī's discussion of the purification of caprice and wrath. Rāzī said that when the soul follows the discipline of the Shariah and the alchemy of religion, it gradually undergoes transformation, like a horse that is tamed.

When the soul's attributes of caprice and wrath return to equilibrium, . . . then praiseworthy attributes will appear in the soul, such as shame, generosity, liberality, courage, forbearance, humility, manliness, contentment, patience, gratitude, and others. (*Path*, pp. 182–83/197–98)

In the rest of the chapter, Rāzī explained why the soul cannot follow the Way without caprice and wrath. As these two become purified and strengthened, their focus turns away from the distractions of the lower realm, and they motivate seekers in their quest for God.

When caprice aims for the high, all of it becomes intense affection and love. When wrath turns its face to the high, all of it becomes zeal and aspiration. Because of intense affection and love, the soul turns its face to the Divine Presence, and because of zeal and aspiration, it does not come to a halt in any station and does not pay attention to anything other than the Exalted Presence. These two instruments are the most complete means for the spirit to arrive at the [Divine] Presence. (*Path*, p. 184/199)

9. This is presumably the same person quoted under Diagram 5.9, that is, the famous Sufi Abū Yazīd Basṭāmī (d. ca. 261/874). These two paragraphs, however, have little in common with any of the numerous sayings ascribed to him (for a rather complete compilation of these, see Nurbakhsh, *Bā-yazīd*). There is one passage, however, in which he extolled the qualities of soil as the source of love (cited in Murata, *Tao*, p. 141). The discussion sounds more like Zhu Xi. For example:

> Although nature is the same in all men, it is inevitable that the various elements in their endowed vital-energy be unbalanced. In some men the vital-energy of wood predominates. In such cases, the feeling of commiseration is generally uppermost.... In others the vital-energy of metal predominates.... So also with the vital-energies of water and fire. It is only when yin and yang are harmonized and the five moral natures are all complete that a man has the qualities of the Mean and correctness and becomes a sage. (*Source Book*, p. 625)

10. On the importance of the nature of vital-energy and stuff in Confucian thought, see the note under Diagram 3.6.

11. Ibn al-'Arabī seems to make a similar point in arguing that, in contrast to what Sufis typically say, the path does not lead from variegation to stability, but from variegation to stability in variegation (*Sufi Path*, p. 108).

12. Rāzī also divided human beings into four basic types, but according to the original creation (*fiṭra*) of their spirits and without reference to the elements (see the notes under Diagram 4.7).

## 3.11
## 本性顯著圖

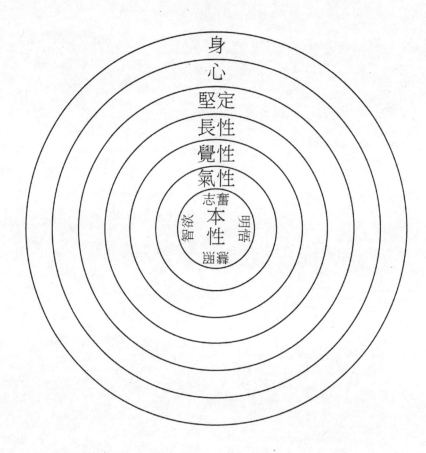

# 3.11
## Diagram of the Manifestation and Display of the Root Nature

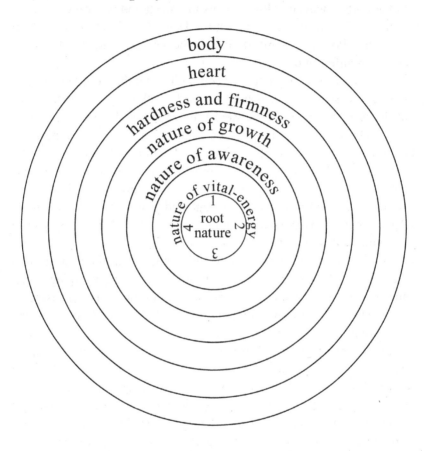

body
heart
hardness and firmness
nature of growth
nature of awareness
nature of vital-energy
1
root nature
2
3
4

1. determining will
2. clear awakening
3. luminous intelligence
4. desire and wisdom

The root nature is rooted in what is allotted and shared in the Former Heaven and equipped with every beauty. This nature is undifferentiated from and one with the nature of vital-energy, the nature of the living, the nature of growth, and the nature of hardness and firmness in the Latter Heaven.[1] However, its manifestation is differentiated in terms of the Former and the Latter. These four levels in the Latter Heaven follow the manifestation of the Former, and this level becomes manifest at the very last.

The root nature, the nature of continuity, and the Root Suchness of the Real Ruler have a sequence, but without this or that. On the basis of the Root Suchness of the Real Ruler, there is the nature of continuity. On the basis of the allotted share of the nature of continuity, there is the root nature. It is this that makes the sequence. In reality, however, the knowledge and power of the root nature are not different from the knowledge and power of the nature of continuity, nor are they different from the knowledge and power of the Real Ruler's Root Suchness. This is the meaning of saying that there is a sequence but without this or that.

Within the root nature are embedded all the ten thousand principles and all the ten thousand affairs without leaving anything aside, and it is equipped with all the ten thousand things.[2] The measure of its substance is vast and great, and its pervading light goes through everything.

In the midst of going through everything, it contains a kind of pure and subtle wisdom, which integrates all the knowledge and awareness possessed by the nature of the living; and it contains a kind of pure and subtle desire, which integrates all the love and hate possessed by the nature of vital-energy. These are called "the two strengths."[3] The two strengths pertain specifically to the Latter Heaven. They are the capability to issue and appear in the outer world.

So also, in the midst of going through everything, [the pervading light] manifests the reflected luminosity of its heavenly suchness and intentionally breaks off from the Latter Heaven. It sees directly that which the root nature follows in order to emerge. It manifests the tendency of its heavenly suchness and, because of the clarity of the luminosity, it hastens directly to the reality of the Real Ruler's

Root Suchness. These are called "the two virtues."[4] The two virtues pertain specifically to the Former Heaven. They are the capability of the root beginning to issue and appear. In order to become manifest, the two virtues must wait until someone arrives at the cultivation of clarity.

Everyone is embedded with this nature, which is to say that everyone is embedded with these virtues, these strengths, and the light that goes through everything.[5] Some manifestations, however, are complete and some are incomplete.

Master Chami said: Nothing is unknown and nothing is impossible for the nature of the human. If the function is not fully realized, it is only because people have not fully realized the function; it is not that knowledge and power are complete or incomplete.[6]

The explanation of Master Chami is based on a deep insight into the root nature of humans, which is the nature of the continuity of the Real Ruler's Chief Manifestation and also the Real Ruler's Root Suchness.

## Notes

1. As Liu mentioned under Diagram 3.6, this is the nature of the human, what Nasafī (and many others) called "the human spirit" (*rūḥ-i insānī*). It is one with the other natures because the human spirit embraces the qualities and characteristics of all the lower levels: psychical, animal, vegetal, and mineral. In the same way, each of these levels embraces the qualities lower than itself; even minerals manifest the attributes of the four elements.

2. There is a reference here to *Mencius* (7.1.4.1): "All things are already complete in us" (Legge); "All the ten thousand things are there in me" (Lau). In Islamic terms, this is simply to say that God created Adam in his form and taught him "all the names." The microcosm embraces the principles of everything that appears in the macrocosm.

3. These two may be the love and zeal that Rāzī discussed in the passage quoted under Diagram 3.10, that is, the means whereby the soul is able to arrive at the Divine Presence.

4. Given Liu's quote from Jāmī in what follows, the two virtues may simply be "knowledge and power," the primary functions of the Real Substance (Diagram 1.3).

5. Perhaps this sentence is illustrated by the four sets of qualities in the Diagram: "The light that goes through everything" would be luminous intelligence, "the two strengths" desire and wisdom, and "the two virtues" determining will and clear awakening.

6. This quote could be a conflation of Gleam 6, in which Jāmī said that the rational soul can take on the guise of all of existence, and Gleam 33, in which he explained that the degree of knowledge achieved by the soul depends on its receptivity (*Chinese Gleams*, pp. 142–43, 202–3).

## 3.12
## 繼性顯著圖

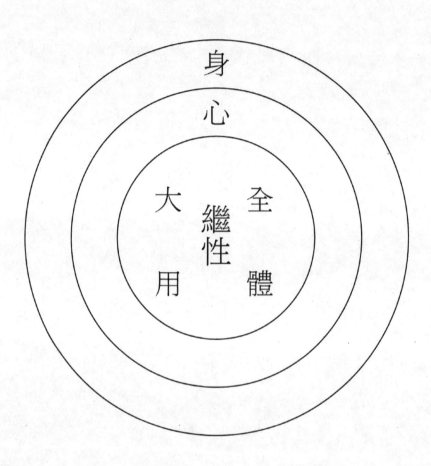

# 3.12
## Diagram of the Manifestation and Display of the Nature of Continuity

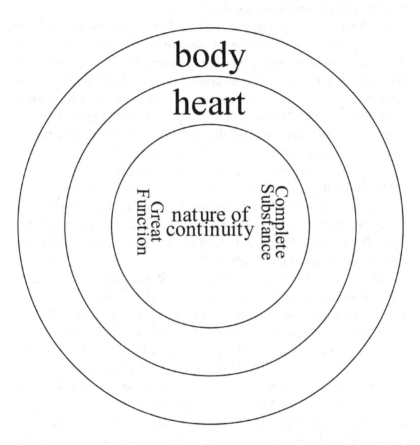

The nature of continuity is the original nature of the Real Ruler's Chief Manifestation.[1] All the natures and mandates of humans and things, ancient and modern, follow this and are imprinted and separated by it. It is called "the one comprehensive mandate of all the mandates of a thousand antiquities."

The Real Ruler's giving rise and transforming follow this realm to give rise. The coming home to the Real of the ten thousand transformations follows this realm in coming home. This one nature is the one, great meeting place of both arising from the beginning and coming home to the lodging.[2] This nature encompasses the whole world everywhere, without coming or leaving. It is shared in common by heaven and earth, humans and things.[3] The root nature is the nature embedded in each human. When what is embedded in each becomes manifest, the shared in common also becomes manifest.

Originally the root nature and the nature of continuity are not two. Before the root nature is differentiated, there is only this nature of continuity, without the root nature. After the nature of continuity has been allotted and shared, it is named the "root nature" and is not named "the nature of continuity."

Before the root nature becomes manifest, the nature of continuity that is shared in common never fails to manifest itself daily between heaven and earth, but its manifestation has nothing to do with the I. When the root nature becomes manifest, this manifestation is united with that manifestation, and the two manifestations become one manifestation. This is like light that is united with light such that it is impossible to differentiate between "this light" and "that light." It is like water that is united with water such that it is impossible to differentiate between "this water" and "that water." The two lights have become one light, the two waters have become one water. This is the meaning of "the two manifestations become one manifestation."

When the manifestation embedded in each comes home and enters into the manifestation shared in common, the manifestation shared in common becomes as if uniquely manifest in the I. Thereby the nature of continuity is able to become the I's nature of continuity. This is how the nature of continuity becomes manifest and displayed.

When the root substance of the nature of continuity becomes manifest, then it is the root substance of the I. How much more so in the case of knowledge and power, and how much more so in the case of work and function!

When the root substance of the I becomes manifest, then the root substance of the nature of continuity is forgotten. How much more so in the case of knowledge and power, and how much more so in the case of work and function!

Thus the I's mandate is the one comprehensive mandate of all the mandates of the ten thousand antiquities, and the I's circumstances are the great meeting place of arising from the beginning and coming home to the lodging. Is it not that the Real Ruler and the I have become the same substance with different names?

The human body is the microcosm, and what it makes manifest at the very last is what arose and was transformed at the very first.

The macrocosm is based in the formless and reaches manifestation in having forms. It takes the former [the formless] as former and the latter [having forms] as latter. Since the Real Ruler's act of lordly sustaining is in the midst, heaven, earth, and the ten thousand things cannot be self-relying.

The microcosm is based in having forms and reaches manifestation in the formless. It takes the latter [having forms] as former and the former [the formless] as latter. Since the Real Ruler's act of lordly sustaining is in the midst, humans also cannot be self-relying.

When the latter [having forms] is taken as the former [the formless] and becomes further manifest, what is reached is the former beyond which there is no former. Then the Real Ruler cannot have lordly sustaining in the midst. To the extent that He cannot have lordly sustaining in the midst, this is self-reliance, although there cannot be self-reliance without the Real Ruler.[4]

### Notes

1. In other words, the Nature of Continuity is the Muhammadan Spirit, the First Intellect, the Ascribed Spirit, etc., as described especially under Diagram 1.5. The difference is that we are now looking at it from the viewpoint of the Latter Heaven rather than the Former Heaven, as the goal of the creative transformation rather than its origin. Notice that the Nature of Continuity is identified in the Diagram, although not explicitly in the text,

with Zhu Xi's Complete Substance and Great Function (as under Diagram 1.12).

2. In other words, this One Nature, which is the Ascribed Spirit or First Intellect, is both the first and the last point on the Circle of Existence, the point where the Ascending Arc rejoins its origin. Nasafī wrote:

The First Intellect is also there from the beginning. Relative to the going back, however, it is at the end. Relative to the coming, it is the Origin (*mabda'*), but relative to the going back, it is the Return (*ma'ād*). (*Goal*, p. 242/80)

The folk of wisdom say that when a human being reaches the Intellect and becomes intelligent, he has completed the ascent, and the circle is complete, for the Intellect was first, and when he reaches the Intellect, the circle is complete. The folk of oneness say that when a human being reaches the Intellect and becomes intelligent and when he works according to the Intellect, he has reached God's Essence and the circle is complete, for God's Essence was first, and when he reaches God's Essence, the circle is complete. (*Goal*, p. 258/98)

3. Among Neo-Confucians, Zhang Zai stressed that nature is not something individual: "One's nature is the one source of all things and is not one's private possession. It is only the great man who is able to know and practice its principle to the utmost. Therefore when he establishes himself, he will help others to establish themselves. . . . He will love universally" (*Source Book*, p. 508). In Islamic terms, to say that nature is shared in common is to say that all things are the traces of the First Intellect, which is the Supreme Pen that writes out every detail of the universe; or, that all things are "existents" (*mawjūd*), that is, self-disclosures of Existence (*wujūd*).

4. The issue here is the relationship between the fully realized human selfhood and the Real. One of the common ways in which Islamic texts deal with it is in terms of annihilation (*fanā'*) and subsistence (*baqā'*), which are discussed under Diagram 4.5. The basic position of Ibn al-'Arabī is that the seeker who reaches the Real realizes that he is nothing but the face of the Real undergoing constant self-disclosure. He sees and experiences the nothingness of his own separative self and participates with full awareness in the Real's self-disclosure. He is the living embodiment of He / not He. His own individual selfhood is "not He," and what manifests itself through him is "He." So, are the sages "self-reliant"? No inasmuch as their individual selves have been utterly negated, but yes inasmuch as their selves have been replaced by the true Self, which is nothing but the Real, who alone can say in truth, "There is no I but I."

# Volume 4

## Summary

Volume 4 clarifies the meaning that was not fully realized in Volume 3. In reaching the surpassing subtlety of the Human Ultimate, there are suddenness and gradualness. In the differentiation of the classes of sage and ordinary, there are heavenly and human. Although the sudden may be known without knowing the gradual, the sudden cannot be considered the rule, for suddenly surpassing is the path of one or two people, and gradually entering is the path of hundreds of thousands of people.[1]

When people settle down in the ordinary without hoping to become sages, then, whether in heavenly or human affairs, they are simply throwing themselves away.[2] If they know shame, they will be courageous, and if they are constant, they can become sages.[3] If people are not courageous and not constant, they will find it difficult to desire to surpass the three worlds[4] so as to enter into that which has no beyond. Even worse are those who are not courageous and constant and who even foolishly criticize the courage and constancy of others. They throw themselves even further away than those who throw themselves away.

## Notes

1. The debate among Buddhists over whether enlightenment is to be reached suddenly (*dun* 頓) or gradually (*jian* 漸) is well known. In China the Northern School of Zen is commonly said to have advocated gradual enlightenment, and the Southern School sudden enlightenment; in any case, "from the ninth century onward, the story of Zen has been that of the Southern School" (*Source Book*, p. 427). Liu offered an Islamic solution to the conflict between sudden and gradual under Diagram 5.4.

2. There is a reference here to *Mencius* 4.A.10: "With those who throw themselves away, it is impossible to do anything. . . . *To say*, 'I am not able to dwell in benevolence or pursue the path of righteousness,' is what we mean by throwing one's self away" (Legge).

3. The first half of this sentence refers to *The Doctrine of the Mean* 20.10, and the second half to *Analects* 7.25.2.

4. In Chinese thought, the three worlds (*sanjie* 三界) can be Heaven, Earth, and Humans; or the higher, lower, and middle worlds. The latter division corresponds to what is usually meant by the expression in Islamic texts: the World of the Spirits, the World of the Bodies, and the Isthmus or World of Imagination. In Koranic terms, these are "heaven, earth, and what is between the two."

## 4.1
## 心性會合圖

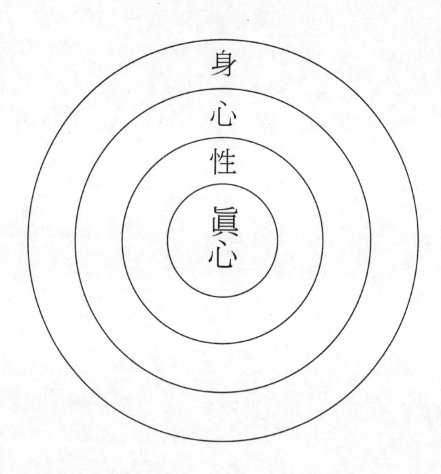

## 4.1
## Diagram of the Meeting and
## Uniting of Heart and Nature

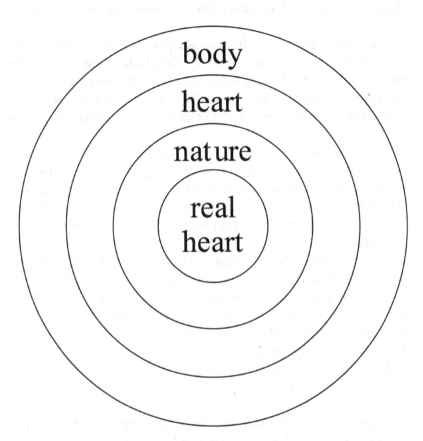

Before the differentiation of natures and principles, there is only this one heart,[1] and this heart has no direction or place. After the differentiation of natures and principles, it is no longer named heart but "nature." When nature hastens forth from the World of Principles to the World of Images, it has neither form nor substance, and it lodges in the heart.[2]

The subtle substance of the heart is empty and silent, having nothing outside.[3] The heart possessed by the inside of the body is the heart's position, the lodging-place of nature. The subtle substance of the heart is nature in the Former Heaven. The square inch of the heart is where nature lodges and belongs, and this square inch is in the Latter Heaven.[4]

The heart of the Former Heaven is the fountainhead of nature's differentiation and separation. The position of the square inch assists nature in manifestation and disclosure. Why? Although the square inch belongs to the Latter Heaven, the talent and wisdom[5] embedded within it are in reality enough to know nature and in reality enough to see nature.

The void and subtlety of nature exist everywhere.[6] Although [nature] is subtle, it is unable to manifest and issue forth by itself; so it must obtain the heart's talent and wisdom to be sufficient to issue forth. Nature borrows assistance to become manifest. Nature is like fire, and the heart is like charcoal. Without fire, how can charcoal burn? Without charcoal, to what does fire attach itself?

In sum, the principle of the Former Heaven must borrow from the heart of the Latter Heaven, and it also must borrow from the vital-energy of the Latter Heaven. After there is the heart of the Latter Heaven, the principle will shine forth, and after there is the vital-energy of the Latter Heaven, the principle will act.

How does the heart of the Latter Heaven have the power to make the principle shine forth? When the bodily apertures belonging to the embryo in the womb are first differentiated, there is already something that belongs to fire. It issues forth to become the openings of spiritual clarity that stand opposite each other in the left and right of the heart.[7] The openings of spiritual clarity are the taproot of talent and wisdom, and the power to make the principle shine forth is latent within them.

How does the vital-energy of the Latter Heaven have the power to realize nature fully? The nature of vital-energy receives obediently the function of the root nature as its own function. It rides on the horse of the root nature. The talent and wisdom of the heart are sufficient for it to know, and the root capacity of vital-energy is sufficient for it to act.[8]

Given that there are beginning and end along with the regulated principles of nature, there is the mechanism for everything to meet and come together. Hence, the Former Heaven must borrow from the Latter Heaven. It is not possible to say, however, that the nature of the Former Heaven never uses its strength by itself, for heart and nature function together, and the Former and Latter Heavens illuminate and brighten the midst, each by way of its own capability.

If the talent and wisdom possessed by the square inch meet and unite with the pure and subtle wisdom contained in the root nature, then knowledge will become stronger. If the talent and wisdom possessed by the square inch meet and unite with the reflected luminosity of the heavenly suchness that is manifest in the root nature, then the observation of the principles will become more real.[9]

Thus we know that it is not that the nature lodged in the square inch never uses its strength by itself. It borrows the position of the square inch as its lodging, and it takes the clarity of the square inch as its function; then the heart's talent and strength may reach full realization.[10] When the six levels of nature's substance meet and come together as one, the position of the square inch is no longer of any use,[11] yet the subtle substance of the heart can perfect its activity as before without falling into direction and place. So, we can say that the heart is nature, and we can also say that nature is the heart.

### Notes

1. In other words, the one, true heart is present in the Former Heaven at the stage of the Mandate (Diagram 1.5). It is the undifferentiated root of both nature and principle, spirits and souls; it is the First Intellect, or the Muhammadan Spirit. In Confucian thought, this cosmic dimension of the heart (typically translated as "mind") is implicit in the discussion of the

"heart of Heaven and Earth" and the association or identification of the human heart with the Great Ultimate, which is the Supreme Principle:

The heart is the Great Ultimate.   (Shao Yong, *Source Book*, p. 492)

The Principle and the heart are one.   (Cheng Hao, ibid., p. 536)

The heart is the Principle.   (Lu Xiangshan, ibid., p. 579)

There is only one heart. . . . The substance of the heart is infinite. If one can completely develop his heart, he will become identified with Heaven.   (Lu Jiuyuan, ibid., p. 585)

The principle of the heart is the Great Ultimate.   (Zhu Xi, ibid., p. 628)

2. The heart in which nature lodges is the bodily heart, the seat of the human spirit. Rāzī, who inspired much of this discussion of the heart, went to some length to clarify the difference between the bodily and spiritual hearts. The heart, for him, is both the physical organ and the most subtle level of our spiritual nature, deriving from the luminosity of God's love.

Know that the heart has a form, and it is what the Prophet called the "lump of flesh." All creatures and animals have that. It is a pinecone-shaped lump of flesh on the left side in the breast. This fleshly heart of man has a spiritual anima (*jān-i rūḥānī*) that the heart of animals does not have. In the state of limpidness (*ṣafā'*), however, the anima of the heart has another heart derived from the light of love, but not everyone has this heart. Thus God says, "Surely in that is a reminder for him who has a heart" [Koran 50:37]. In other words, the person with a heart has an intimacy with God. God did not affirm that everyone has a heart. One must have a true heart, which is what I call "the heart of the anima and the heart." . . . The heart has a soundness and a corruption. Its soundness lies in its limpidness, and its corruption in its opacity. (*Path*, pp. 191–92/205)

Rāzī explained that the limpidness and clarity of the heart are found in the health of its "five senses," which are the spiritual analogues of the five external senses. Liu translated this passage under Diagram 4.11.

Nasafī also said much about the purification of the heart as the means to re-establish contact with the Ascribed Spirit, that is, to realize the Nature of Continuity. In the following passage, for example, he referred to the "rust" of the heart (following Koran 83:14):

Know that the inward of the Ascribed Spirit, which is the life of the cosmos and its inhabitants, encompasses the cosmos. When someone makes his interior limpid and purifies his heart from the imprints of the cosmos, then the inward of the Ascribed Spirit will become manifest within him. It will brighten his insides and become his life.

The inward of the Ascribed Spirit does not come from anywhere, come to anywhere, or go anywhere. It is constantly present and encompasses the cosmos. When you polish and purify the mirror of your heart, the inward of the Ascribed Spirit will become manifest inside you and brighten your insides. So, the Ascribed Spirit does not come from anywhere, nor does it go anywhere. The Ascribed Spirit is present, but your heart has become rusty. Once you purify the heart of rust, your heart will be illuminated by the Ascribed Spirit and it will live through the Ascribed Spirit. (*Goal*, pp. 268/108–9)

3. In Rāzī's terms, the heart's subtle substance is "the true heart" (*dil-i ḥaqīqī*) or "the reality of the heart" (*ḥaqīqat-i dil*), and it is situated in the Unseen World (*'ālam-i ghayb*).

4. Cf. Chen Chun: "Although the heart is no larger than a square inch, all the ten thousand transformations issue from it; it is truly the source" (*Terms*, p. 59). "The heart is simply like a vessel; what it contains is the nature" (ibid., p. 57). Rāzī called "the square inch" by both the Arabic *muḍgha*, "lump of flesh," and its Persian translation, *gūsht-pāra*, "piece of flesh."

5. Talent (*cai* 才) and wisdom (*zhi* 智) are the human analogues of the two Great Functions, knowledge and power. If talent comes first, it is because we are dealing here with the reversal of order that occurs on the Ascending Arc of the Latter Heaven. "Talent" refers to all the human abilities and capacities that need to be utilized to follow the Way. For Mencius, talent is the innate moral worth that Heaven bestows on humans. For Zhu Xi, it refers more to ability (*Concepts*, pp. 388–91; *Terms*, p. 64). The broad applicability of the term is suggested already by its use in the *Yijing*:

The *Yijing* is vast and great, and within it everything is provided: the Way of Heaven, the Way of Humans, and the Way of Earth. It combines these three talents and doubles them; that is why there are six lines. The six lines are nothing other than the Ways of the three talents.    (*Dazhuan* 2.10.1; Wilhelm, *I Ching*, pp. 351–52)

6. The invisible omnipresence of the spiritual realm is a common notion in Confucianism. Liu Zhi expanded upon the implications of this under Diagram 4.11. According to *The Doctrine of the Mean* (16.1–2), "The Master [Confucius] said, 'How abundantly do spiritual beings display the virtues that belong to them! We look for them, but we do not see them. We listen to them, but we do not hear them. They are embodied in things, and nothing is without them.'"

7. The openings of spiritual clarity are discussed under Diagram 3.5.

8. As is clear under Diagram 3.10, the nature of vital-energy, which is Nasafī's psychical spirit, has the animal faculties of love and hate (appetite and wrath). These need to be transformed so that they can gaze on the Real Lord instead of being entranced by the forms and images of the manifest realm. In order for this to happen, vital-energy must obey the root nature (the human spirit). The psychical spirit, however, distorts the normal

aspiration toward self-realization—that is, the desire "to realize nature fully." In Islamic philosophy, this discussion commonly proceeds in terms of a tension between the intellect (*'aql*) or the rational soul (*nafs nāṭiqa*) and the animal soul. The lower soul must submit to the higher soul and follow its directives, not vice versa. Thus Avicenna argued that virtue and good character can be acquired by making the animal faculty subservient to the intellect; otherwise, the rational soul will follow the animal soul.

The intellect [must] gain the disposition to seek ascendancy. . . . When the animal faculty is strong and gains the acquired habit of seeking ascendancy, a disposition to yield is occasioned in the rational soul. Once the effect of receptivity becomes deeply rooted in the rational soul, this strengthens its attachment to the body. (Ibn Sīnā, *al-Najāt*, p. 296)

For many examples of how Muslim texts deal with achieving the proper balance between intellect and soul, see Murata, *Tao*, chaps. 8–10.

9. On the pure and subtle wisdom and the reflected luminosity, see under Diagram 3.11.

10. Liu frequently used the term "full realization" (*jin* 盡) in this volume, no doubt with an eye toward the saying of Mencius, "He who fully realizes his heart knows his nature. He who knows his nature knows Heaven" (7.A.1.1).

11. The six levels are those discussed in 3.6–3.12. They come together as one when the circle of creation has been completed at the sixth level, the Nature of Continuity, and the corporeal level of existence has fulfilled its function.

## 4.2
## 心品藏德圖

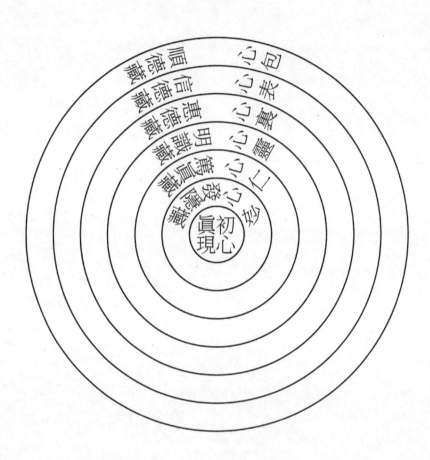

# 4.2
## Diagram of the Virtues Stored in the Levels of the Heart

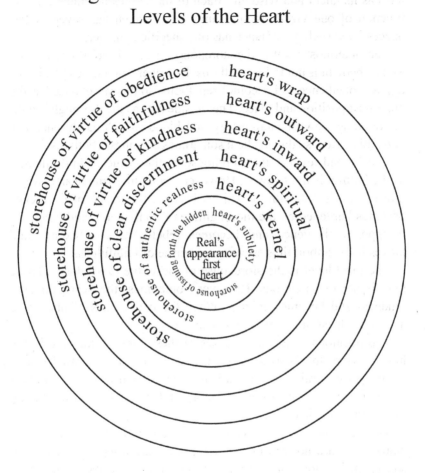

The heart's form and color are at root one thing having seven levels.[1] Each level has the virtue of one level. Virtue is what the heart obtains as its talent and wisdom.[2] Each of the virtues has the work and function of one virtue. In the same way, heaven has seven governances,[3] and each governance has one specific manager.

The outermost level is the storehouse of the virtue of obedience.[4] To be obedient is not to be rebellious. However, sometimes [the heart] opposes obedience and becomes rebellious; so this storehouse has the outermost position and place. The outside acts as the thoroughfare for the ongoing flow of vital-energy and blood, which easily encroach upon this virtue; so the obedient sometimes becomes rebellious.[5]

The second level is the storehouse of the virtue of faithfulness.[6] To be faithful is not to sway. However, sometimes [the heart] sways, moves, and is not faithful. This is because the virtue of obedience becomes burdened by the thoroughfare of vital-energy and blood; so it opposes obedience and becomes rebellious. This excites and moves its neighbor, thus swaying the virtue of faithfulness.

The third level is the storehouse of the virtue of kindness. To be kind is not to be callous. However, sometimes [the heart] opposes kindness and becomes callous. When the two virtues of obedience and faithfulness alter, this virtue also alters.

The positions of the storehouses of these three virtues are in the heart's wrap, the heart's outward, and the heart's inward [respectively]. In general, since all fall into the allotted moments of form and color, it is easy for vital-energy and blood to encroach upon them and make them alter.

The positions of the storehouses of the four virtues after this are neither outward nor inward. Although they are inseparable from the square inch of form and color, they do not fall into the allotted moments of form and color. Vital-energy and blood cannot encroach upon them and shade them to make them alter. When the four virtues after this issue forth in clarity, the three virtues before this are able to maintain their constancy.

The fourth level is the storehouse of clear discernment. When this virtue becomes manifest, it lights up the principles with clarity and transparency, and no other knowing and seeing can confuse it or make it perplexed. When the heart has this level, it is like heaven that has the sun. The light of the sun is able to efface the diverse lights, but the diverse lights are not able to efface it.

The fifth level is the storehouse of authentic realness. When this virtue becomes manifest, it hastens toward its root, without being pulled or blocked. This level of the heart is like fire. The nature of fire is to flare up and hasten directly inside. To hasten inside is for it to become distant from the outside.

The sixth level is the storehouse of issuing forth the hidden. The principles possessed by everything in the Former and Latter Heavens have the utmost depth and the utmost hiddenness, and all that is unthinkable and unimaginable is stored and compiled in the midst of this level. Principle in itself is without boundary and without moment. When it reaches here, this is called issuing forth. When the heart is able to be joyous and to investigate, it reaches the One, without separation. This also is called issuing forth. What issues forth appears gradually.

The seventh level is the storehouse of the appearance of the Real. The Substance and Function of the Real are both small and great, with nothing outside or inside. From the moment there is the heart, the Real is stored and lodged in the midst of this level. But, when endeavor and strength have not yet been added, and talent and wisdom have not yet been fully realized, what is stored is stored forever, and nothing causes it to appear. When talent and wisdom are fully realized, and endeavor and strength reach the utmost, then, from [the storehouse of] clear discernment, [the heart] has reached [the storehouse of] authentic realness and [the storehouse of] issuing forth the hidden. It is here that the Complete Substance and Great Function of the Real Ruler appear. Once they appear, the traces of the square inch disappear, and the subtlety of the directionless and placeless allows for no differentiation into this and that.

## Notes

1. The seven levels are derived from *Path*, pp. 195–97/208, although Liu's explanations seem to be largely his own. For "level," the original Arabic word is *ṭawr*, "stage" (not, as Algar renders it in his translation, "face"). The Arabic and Persian terms used in *Path* are as follows:

A. *Islām* (submission) in the *ṣadr* (breast), explained as the "skin" (*pūst*) of the heart (*dil*).

B. *Īmān* (faith) in the *qalb* (heart).

C. *Maḥabbat* (love), *'ishq* (intense love), *shafaqat* (affection), in the *shaghāf* (pericardium).

D. *Mushāhada* (witnessing, contemplation) and *ru'yat* (vision) in the *fu'ād*, which is another word for "heart," the reference here being to its use in Koran 53:13: "The heart [of the Prophet] did not lie about what it saw," that is, during his ascent to God, the *mi'rāj*.

E. *Maḥabbat* (love) for God in *ḥabbat al-qalb* (the seed of the heart).

F. *Mukāshafāt-i ghaybī* (unveilings of the Unseen) and *'ulūm-i ladunī* (sciences from God) in the *suwaydā* (core).

G. *Ẓuhūr-i anwār* (manifestation of the lights) of the self-disclosures of the divine attributes in the *muhjat* (lifeblood).

Nūr al-Ḥaqq's translation of the Root Classic has the same, fairly standard terms for the seven levels, but his rendering of the virtues after the first two suggest that he did not base his translation of this section on *Path*.

2. The importance of virtue (*de*) is discussed under Diagram 2.1. In defining "virtue" in terms of "obtaining" (*de* 得), Liu used a pun over two thousand years old. Zhu Xi also used it: "As a word 'Virtue' is 'obtaining.' This means to practice the Way and obtain its fruits in the heart" (*Concepts*, p. 342). As already noted, the basic virtues in Neo-Confucianism are five: humanity (*ren*), righteousness (*yi*), propriety (*li*), wisdom (*zhi*), and faithfulness (*xin*). In what follows, Liu included only one of these as a virtue of the heart.

3. Rāzī put it this way:

Just as each layer of heaven is the locus of a planet, such that the seven heavens are the loci of seven planets, so also every stage of the heart is the mine of a different jewel, for [as the Prophet said,] "People are mines, like mines of silver and gold." (*Path*, p. 195/208)

4. Liu discussed obedience as the opposite of rebellion under Diagram 4.10; on the Chinese terms, see the note there.

5. Like Muslim philosophers, Liu preferred relatively abstract and "scientific" terminology to the mythic and anthropomorphizing explanations offered by many Sufi texts, including *Path*. This passage provides a good example. Instead of relegating the heart's shortcomings to "vital-energy and blood," Rāzī wrote:

Whenever [the breast] is deprived of the light of submission, it becomes the mine of darkness and unbelief—"he whose breast has been expanded for unbelief" [Koran

16:106]—and the locus of Satan's whisperings and the ego's enticements: "He whispers in the breasts of men" [114:5]. Of the heart, only the breast is the locus of Satan's whispering and the ego's enticements, and that is the heart's skin. These things have no way into the heart's inside, for the heart is the storehouse of the Real and has the attributes of heaven, and they have no way to go there. "We guard it from every accursed Satan" [15:17].   (*Path*, p. 196/208).

6. Neo-Confucians consider faithfulness the fifth of the five constant virtues but exclude it from the four virtues of human nature (see *Terms*, pp. 69, 85–88). Here, as elsewhere in this discussion, Liu's explanation departs from that of Rāzī, who confined himself to showing how the Koran uses the relevant term:

The second stage of the heart (*dil*) is called "heart" (*qalb*), and it is the mine of faith, for "He wrote faith in their hearts" [58:22]. It is the locus of the light of the intellect, for "that they may have hearts with which to intellect" [22:46]. It is the locus of seeing, for "the eyes are not blind, but blind are the hearts within the breast" [22:46]. (*Path*, p. 196/208)

## 4.3
## 升降來復圖

## 4.3
# Diagram of the Ascent and the Descent, the Coming and the Going Back

In the cosmos the principles of the thousand beginnings and the ten thousand branches can never be exhausted. However, there is only the one act of the Real Ruler Himself, ascending and descending, coming and going back.[1] Descent is from the seed, and ascent is to the fruit, coming to the lowermost and going back to the uppermost.[2]

The descent and ascent of the macrocosm are the coming and going back of the microcosm. The coming and going back of the microcosm is more subtle than the descent and ascent of the macrocosm.[3] The macrocosm's ascent after descent is such that the ascent is fully realized in forms. The microcosm's going back after coming is such that the going back is fully realized in the formless. Compared to forms, the formless is of the utmost essence.

In the majestic beginning, before the descent and the coming, the name is "Lord Ruler." When human affairs have been fully realized and have ascended and gone back, the name is "heart."[4]

The Former Heaven undergoes transformation through the ongoing flow of the One Principle. This brings forth the nature of continuity, the nature of the spiritual,[5] the nature of the living, the nature of growth, the nature of minerals, and the nature of the four agents. They descend in succession and stop when they reach the original vital-energy. At root the Real Ruler is ascended, and He descends on His own.[6] The descent of the macrocosm is based upon this, and the coming of the microcosm is also based on this.

The Latter Heaven undergoes transformation through the differentiation and display of the original vital-energy. This brings forth soil, water, fire, and wind; metal and stone; grass and trees; and birds and beasts. Gradually they issue forth in clarity and stop at the human. This is how the macrocosm ascends from its descent, but in reality this is the Real Ruler's ascending from His descent on His own.[7]

This is the meaning of "Descent is from the seed, and ascent is to the fruit." The fruit of the Latter Heaven is the seed of the Former Heaven. The coming of the microcosm is that it comes at the same time that the macrocosm descends from its ascent. Its going back is that it goes back after the macrocosm has completed its ascent from descent. To go back as the very last is to go back as the utmost essence.

The coming [of the microcosm] in the Latter Heaven is that it comes from the One Spot. Based on the One Spot, there is bodily form. Based on bodily form there are hardness and firmness, begetting and growth, knowledge and awareness, and spiritual awakening. They advance in succession until they reach the Chief Manifestation's Nature of Continuity and then stop. This is the microcosm's going back from its coming.

The going back reaches the ground of the Root Suchness of the Real Ruler, in the midst of which stands the macrocosm, like one grain of sand in the midst of a great desert. Coming to the lowest and then going back to the highest is called the "going back of the formless"; it is of the utmost essence compared with the going back of having forms.

The sage Ersa[8] said, "Without being begotten again, humans are not able to catch the meaning of heaven and earth." To be begotten (*sheng* 生) means to ascend (*sheng* 升). "Again" means for the second time. The first time was in accompanying the ascent of the macrocosm to perfect the image, and the second was in following the ascent of the microcosm to realize fully its principle. This is the meaning of being begotten again. When the two ascents have been completed, then the foundational meaning of the great creation is fully realized here.

The Classic says, "When the worlds of the two arcs were united, he went back to the utmost nearness."[9] The two arcs are the coming and descent, which make one arc, and the going back and ascent, which make the other arc. When the descent and ascent have been completed, the worlds of the two arcs are united. He who goes back to the utmost nearness surpasses and goes beyond the world of names and guises[10] and stands in the Not-Even-Anything Village.[11] The Complete Substance is undifferentiatedly transformed and deeply united with the Root Suchness. This is the realm of the practice of the Utmost Sage alone.[12]

## Notes

1. This is the most complete diagram of Liu's overall scheme. Nūr al-Ḥaqq's version uses the standard Arabic terminology that we have been mentioning in the notes. "Nature" is *rūḥ*, "spirit," and its levels are depicted in terms of the typical mineral, plant, animal, human scheme, with the

Ascribed Spirit at the top. "Lord Ruler" is *haḍrat al-ḥaqq*, "the Presence of the Real." For "the nature of the four," Nūr's diagram has the not quite correct form *'anāṣiriyya*, "spirit of the elements." For "bodily form," it has *qālab*, "frame." "Former Heaven" becomes "Sovereignty," and "Latter Heaven" "Kingdom" (*Sharḥ*, p. 119/87).

2. The seed being discussed here is located at the top of the diagram; in other words, it is identical with the Real Ruler / nature of continuity, as becomes completely clear in Liu's subsequent explanation (for more on seed and fruit in this sense, see under Diagram 1.12). The seed mentioned at the bottom of the diagram refers rather to the One Spot, the microcosmic analogue of the Vast Sediment discussed under Diagram 3.1.

3. Nasafī made the same point:

In the Descent, the further things go from the Origin, the baser (*khasīs*) they become. In the Ascent, the further they go from the Origin [and the closer to the Return], the more eminent (*sharīf*) they become.    (*Goal*, p. 242/80)

In the Descent, whatever level is nearer to the Origin is more eminent and more subtle, and in the Ascent, whatever level is further from the Origin [and closer to the Return] is more eminent and more subtle. The reason for this is that in the Descent, opacity falls to the bottom, and in the Ascent, the limpid rises to the top. . . . Whatever is first in the Descent is last in the Ascent.    (*Insān*, p. 73)

4. Again, that the heart in its true nature should be indistinguishable from the Great Ultimate is the position of Confucianism (see the first note under Diagram 4.1).

5. The diagram here has "nature of the human." The text has "the nature of the spiritual," which is the same as "the spiritually living"; as Liu wrote under Diagram 3.6, "The spiritually living is the nature that makes humans human."

6. Here the text is affirming God's independence (*ghinā*) of all things and the world's dependence on his creative activity. In his Essence God is "ascended." He "descends" of his own volition inasmuch as he discloses himself (*tajallī*) through the traces and properties of his names.

7. In Islamic terms, both the Arc of Descent and the Arc of Ascent are the manifestations or self-disclosures of the Real Being. In other words, both are strung on the One Thread.

8. Ersa is "the prophet 'Īsā," that is, Jesus. The saying is a version of John 3:3, commonly quoted in Sufi texts (e.g., *Path*, pp. 240/246–47).

9. This is a reference to Koran 53:8–9, "Then he [Muḥammad] drew near and came close, two-bows' length away, or nearer." As noted in the introduction, this verse is commonly read as a description of the special nearness to God achieved by Muḥammad during his *mi'rāj*, that is, his ascent to the divine

presence. The two "bows" are the two "arcs" of the circle depicted in the diagram. As indicated by Liu's note on Root Classic 4:22–23, this discussion is based on *Rays* (specifically the commentary on Flash 14), where 'Irāqī wrote:

Suppose that the lover and Beloved are one circle, cut in half by a straight line, such that it appears as two arcs. If this line that appears to be there, but is not, falls out of the diagram at the moment of Meeting, the circle will appear to be one as it is. The secret of Two Bows' Length appears. . . . But, there is something more to say: you should know that, although the line falls away from the circle, the circle does not appear as it did at first. The property of the line does not disappear. Though the line disappears, its trace remains. (*Rays*, pp. 96–97; *Flashes*, p. 98)

In his explanation of this passage, Jāmī reverted to the distinction that philosophers make between the Necessary Being (the Beloved) and the possible or contingent beings (the lover). This duality arises from the Essence, the level of Nondesignation.

This comparison means that the Nondelimited, Unseen Ipseity is like a circle, and its descent to the levels of Necessity and contingency is like the division of the circle into two arcs. The entifications that distinguish the contingent from the Necessary, whether they be on the level of the [divine] knowledge or on the level of the external things, are a line dividing the two arcs. These entifications are illusory (*mutawahham*), which is to say that they do not have real existence. Rather, they are among the relations and aspects of the Nondelimited Reality. (*Rays*, p. 96)

10. The world of names and guises (*mingxiang* 名相) is clearly the World of Images, the Latter Heaven (see also Diagram 5.6).

11. The expression is Zhuangzi's (1.10; Watson, p. 35). It corresponds almost exactly to Persian *nā-kujā-ābād*, "Nowheres-ville," a term used by the twelfth-century philosopher Suhrawardī in *Āwāz-i par-i Jibra'īl* (The sound of Gabriel's wing). The Persian is probably a translation of the Arabic *lā makān*, "no-place" or "no-location," often used to designate the realm beyond the cosmos that is the goal of travelers on the path to God. Rūmī said of one of the saints: "His form is in soil, his spirit in No-place—a No-place beyond the imaginings of the travelers" (*Mathnawī*, Book 1, verse 1581).

12. Practice (*jian* 踐) is the means whereby transformation is achieved. According to Confucius, "By nature humans are nearly alike; by practice they get to be far apart" (*Analects* 17.2). In Islamic terms, this is to say that God blew of his spirit into everyone, and they become differentiated to the degree that they follow the prescriptive command. By saying that only the Utmost Sage reaches this realm, Liu accorded with the teachings of Ibn al-'Arabī and his followers, who hold that Muḥammad's supreme station among the prophets is asserted by the words "or nearer" (Liu's "utmost nearness") in this Koranic verse.

## 4.4

## 人極大全圖

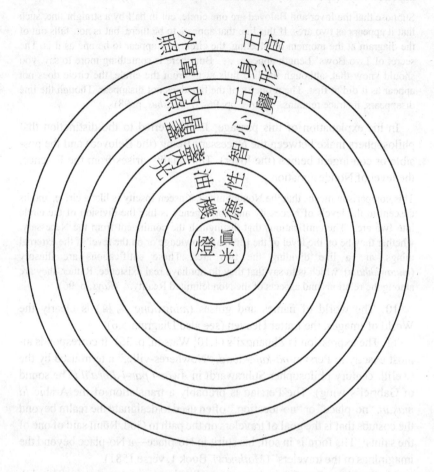

# 4.4
# Diagram of the Great Completion
# of the Human Ultimate

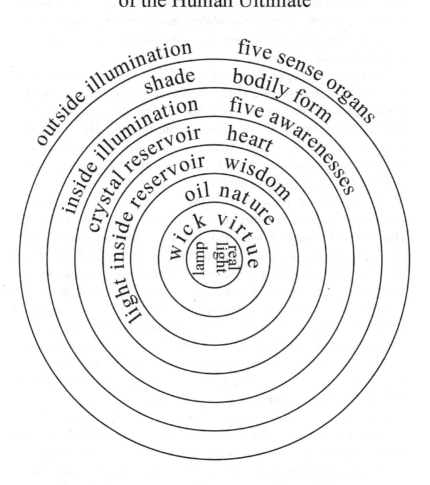

To speak of the "ultimate" is to speak of the utmost.[1] The subtlety that makes humans human[2] is the utmost ultimate to which nothing more can be added. If there were another subtlety more subtle than this, then humans could not be called subtle, nor could their subtlety be called ultimate. There is no subtlety more subtle than this; so only the human subtlety can be considered the utmost ultimate to which nothing more may be added.

The five sense organs,[3] the bodily body,[4] the five awarenesses, the heart, wisdom, nature, and virtue are the apparatus of this subtlety.[5] If the real light has not been reached, having the apparatus of the subtlety is not enough to reach the ultimate subtlety. The real light is the ultimate subtlety. If the ultimate subtlety has been reached, then the subtlety is subtle and the subtlety's apparatus fully perfects its activity, and so everywhere is subtle.

The real light is like a lamp.[6] If the lamp does not have wick, oil, reservoir, and shade, then the lamp has no place to adhere and attach. The wick, oil, reservoir, and shade are the lamp's necessary apparatus. If the wick, oil, reservoir, and shade are all complete but the lamp does not yet adhere and attach to them, then the wick, oil, reservoir, and shade perfect their acts only as the lamp's apparatus.

If there is the lamp's apparatus without the lamp, then the apparatus is a useless instrument. If there is the apparatus and the lamp adheres and attaches to it, but the lamp does not fully realize the reason for its subtlety, this is not because the lamp is not subtle. It is because the apparatus of the lamp has not fully realized the reason for its subtlety. This also is why the lamp cannot fully realize its subtlety.

The crystal reservoir is there, but it is not yet brightened and cleaned; the oil is there, but it is not yet limpid and purified; the wick is there, but it is not yet upright and correct; the shade is there, but it is not yet translucent and transparent. If the subtlety of the lamp's apparatus is not yet fully realized, then the subtlety of the lamp will also not be fully realized.

If the inside luminosity is not bright and the outside luminosity not pervading, then the light inside the reservoir will not fully realize its own flourishing. How can one hope that it will have the ability to illuminate things from afar? If the wick, oil, reservoir, and shade each fully realizes its subtlety, and the lamp adheres and attaches to them, how can the lamp not keep things bright from afar?

The subtlety of the crystal reservoir is its brightness and cleanliness. The subtlety of the oil is its limpidness and purity. The subtlety of the wick is its uprightness and correctness. The subtlety of the shade is its translucence and transparency. If the lamp's apparatus is all subtle, then the lamp's subtlety is a hundred times greater than before.

Humans have the five sense organs, the bodily body, the five awarenesses, the heart, wisdom, nature, and virtue, all of which are the apparatus of the subtlety. These are similar to the wick, oil, reservoir, and shade of a lamp. As long as the lamp's wick, oil, reservoir, and shade do not fully realize their subtlety, the lamp also will not fully realize its subtlety. As long as the subtlety of the wick, oil, reservoir, and shade of humans is not fully realized, the lamp of the real light will not be manifest in the apparatus of the subtlety.

The heart is like the lamp's crystal reservoir, and its subtlety is its ultimate brightness and cleanliness. The body is like the lampshade, and its subtlety is its ultimate untaintedness. Nature is like the lamp's oil, and its subtlety is its ultimate purity and limpidness. Virtue is like the lamp's wick, and its subtlety is its ultimate issuing appearance. When body, heart, nature, and virtue are all subtle, how can the subtlety of the real light not be subtle here? When the subtlety of the real light arrives, how can the inside and outside luminosity leave anything out?

Only when subtlety reaches here can one consider the ultimate, utmost subtlety to have been reached. This is the utmost ultimate to which nothing more can be added. It is the great completion of the Human Ultimate.

## Notes

1. The expression "Human Ultimate" (*renji* 人極) became established in Neo-Confucian thought by means of Zhou Dunyi's highly influential *Explanation of the Diagram of the Great Ultimate*, which also discusses the "Non-Ultimate" (*wuji* 無極). Concerning the sage, Zhou wrote, "The sage settles these affairs by the mean, truth, humanity, and righteousness, taking stillness as chief. Thus he establishes the Human Ultimate." Chan translates the term as "the ultimate standard for man" (*Source Book*, p. 463), which conveys one of the senses of the term but loses the obvious parallelism with the other two Ultimates. Wang Daiyu often discussed the three terms to-

gether in his Real Commentary, as in the passage from his *Great Learning* quoted in the notes to Diagram 1:12, where he says, "The Non-Ultimate is the seed, the Great Ultimate is the tree, and the Human Ultimate is the fruit" (*Chinese Gleams*, p. 64; cf. ibid., pp. 99–100). Wang's three Ultimates correspond to Liu's "three Ones," in Volume 5.

2. In the Sufi tradition, one of the common designations for what makes humans human is *al-laṭīfat al-insāniyya*, "the human subtlety." Liu used subtlety (*miao*), a word often translated as "mystery," to translate both *laṭīfa*, "subtlety," and *ghayb*, the "unseen" or "absent" realm, which is the counterpart of *shahāda*, the "visible" or "witnessed" realm. The "utmost subtlety" is yet another synonym for the Muhammadan Reality (Diagram 1.3), the principle *in divinis* that gives rise to the Ascribed Spirit.

3. The word translated as "sense organ," *guan* 官, means literally "office" or "official," and thus a thing's appointed function. Cf. Mencius 1.15.2: "It is not the *guan* of the ears and eyes to think. . . . The *guan* of the heart is to think." In this diagram it designates the organs themselves, not the senses for which the organs act; seeing, hearing, and so on are the "five awarenesses," as explained under Diagram 1.12.

4. The expression is *shenti* 身體, which might also be translated as "bodily substance." Liu commonly used *ti* for body, but he tended to use *shen* as a contrast for the heart. He used *shenti* again under Diagram 5.3 in talking about "the three bodies," the other two being the heart body and the nature body.

5. Liu seems to be employing the word "apparatus" (*ju* 具) because of the analogy of the lamp, which is developed in this section. The Arabic word *āla*—tool, instrument, apparatus—is used in a similar way in philosophical texts. Thus the five senses and all the faculties are "tools" of the human spiritual essence, the "subtlety." The knowledge realized by the true heart is then called "noninstrumental" (*ghayr ālī*), because it is the self-awareness of the spirit, without any intermediary (see Mullā Ṣadrā, *The Elixir of the Gnostics*, p. 115n29).

6. This sentence can be taken as a translation of part of the Koranic verse upon which this diagram is based, the famous "light verse" (24:35):

God is the light of the heavens and the earth. The likeness of His light is as a niche wherein is a lamp—the lamp in a glass, and the glass as it were a glittering star. [The lamp is] kindled from a blessed tree, an olive that is neither of the East nor of the West, whose oil would almost shine, even if fire did not touch it. Light upon light—God guides to His light whomsoever He will.

This verse was often interpreted as an image of the human microcosm, the most famous example being that by al-Ghazālī in his *Niche of Lights* (*Mishkāt al-anwār*), which is named after the imagery. Some of the Arabic/ Persian terms used by Rāzī in explaining the verse (*Path*, pp. 121–23/143–45) are similar to the Chinese, but the designations for the innermost levels diverge rather sharply. In the Root Classic, Liu referred the discussion to *Path*, *Goal*, and *Commentary*. All three provide microcosmic interpretations of the verse, but the explanation that is most similar to Liu's own is Rāzī's in *Path*, the terminology of which can be compared to what we have here as follows:

A. Outside luminosity: the rays (*partaw*) outside the windows of the niche. The five sense organs: the five senses (*ḥawāss-i panjgāna*).

B. Shade: niche (*mishkāt*). Bodily form: body (*jasad*).

C. Inside luminosity: the reflection of the luminosity (*'aks-i nūrāniyyat*) of the glass. Five awarenesses: human faculties (*quwā-yi basharī*).

D. Crystal reservoir: glass (*zujāja*). Heart: heart (*dil*).

E. Light inside reservoir: the reflection of the luminosity of the spirit. Wisdom: intellect (*'aql*).

F. Oil: oil (*rawghan*). Nature: spirit (*rūḥ*).

G. Wick: wick (*fatīla*). Virtue: the hidden (*khafī*).

In *Commentary* (p. 470), Bayḍāwī offered a number of explanations for the meaning of the Light Verse, but the longest by far meditates on the structure of human faculties. Briefly, it goes like this: the niche is the five senses, which are like windows to the outside. The glass is imagination, which receives the forms of perceived things from the senses, stores them within itself, and passes them on to the higher faculties. The lamp (*miṣbāḥ*) is intellect, which perceives universal realities and divine sciences, thereby casting light on the lower faculties. The blessed tree is reflection (*fikr*), which gives rise to numerous branches through its power of reasoning. The tree is "neither of the east nor the west" because it is situated between forms (*ṣūra*) and meanings (*ma'nā*) and is able to exercise control over and take benefit from both. The oil is the holy faculty (*al-quwwat al-qudsiyya*), "within which are disclosed the flashes of the Unseen and the mysteries of the Sovereignty that pertain specifically to the prophets and the saints." Because of the oil's purity and limpidness, it shines without having to employ reflection or learning (this, in other words, is the faculty that achieves "realization," knowing things in their realities).

In Goal (pp. 274–75/115–16), Nasafī's scheme is relatively simple and is based on his division of spirit into three basic levels—animal (*ḥaywānī*), psychical (*nafsānī*), and human (*insānī*). The glass is the human frame (*qālab*), i.e., the body. The wick is the animal spirit (in the heart). The oil is the psychical spirit (in the brain). The flame is the human spirit.

## 4.5
## 本然流行圖

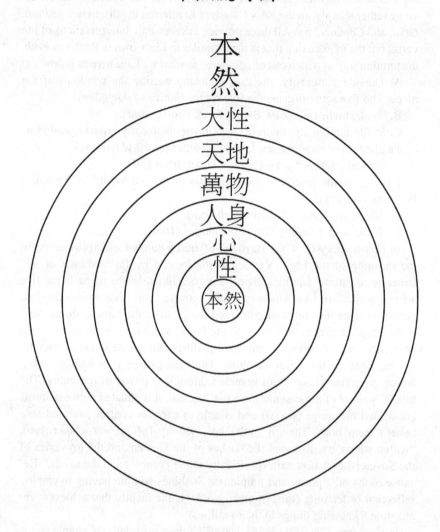

## 4.5
## Diagram of the Ongoing Flow of
## the Root Suchness

# Root Suchness

Ever since there have been heaven and earth, the things and the I's,[1] there have been many realms of illusion, but there has been nothing but the ongoing flow of the Root Suchness.[2] Sometimes it flows and goes from the outermost to the inmost; sometimes it flows and goes from the inmost to the outermost.

Flowing and going from the outermost to the inmost belongs specifically to the affairs of the creative transformation.[3] This is the ongoing flow of the suchness of the Self-so. It is the ongoing flow from the Root Suchness, outside which is nothing. It brings forth the great, commonly shared nature, heaven and earth, the ten thousand things, the human body, the heart, and nature.[4]

In the same way, the Root Suchness of the one, ongoing flow is embedded in each human being. This is the ongoing flow of the suchness of the Self-so. It is the ongoing flow from the inmost to the outermost that belongs equally to the affairs of human activities, although not everything emerges from the ongoing flow of the suchness of the Self-so.[5]

The issuing appearance from the inmost of the Root Suchness is such that when humans obtain it, they can realize fully the nature embedded in themselves.[6] When they fully realize nature, they rectify the heart of the ongoing flow of the Root Suchness. When they rectify the heart, they rectify the body of the ongoing flow of the Root Suchness. When they rectify the body, they rectify all things and nurture the ten thousand things. When they nurture the ten thousand things, they come to assist in the nurture and transformation of heaven and earth, and heaven and earth are put in position.[7]

When nothing is excluded from the position of nurture, then heaven and earth, the things and the I's, circle back as a whole to the great nature of the ongoing flow of the Root Suchness. The great nature goes back and enters undifferentiatedly into the Root Suchness, outside which there is nothing. This is called "the ongoing flow from the inmost to the outermost," and it belongs equally to the affairs of human activities. Although these are named "the affairs of human activities," in reality all are the ongoing flow of the self-activity of the Root Suchness.[8]

Humans are the human of the ongoing flow of the Root Suchness. Humans, in whom the Root Suchness flows and goes, are embedded in the one, ongoing flow of the Root Suchness; so the inside and outside of the body are nothing but the Root Suchness. Rooted in the Root Suchness embedded within each of them, they seek and inquire into the Root Suchness that is shared in common.[9] This is to seek and inquire into the Root Suchness with the Root Suchness.[10] The Root Suchness embedded within each enters undifferentiatedly into the Root Suchness that is shared in common. This is to enter undifferentiatedly into the Root Suchness with the Root Suchness. When the Root Suchness circles back to the Root Suchness, then originally there is no differentiation in the Root Suchness between this and that.

Yet, there is manyness in the sequence of this one, ongoing flow, although in reality, there is no manyness in the sequence of this one, ongoing flow. It is only that when people see it, they become aware that there is a sequence in the ongoing flow. If one talks about the Root Suchness based on the reality of the Root Suchness, then the Root Suchness neither leaves nor comes.

Why, then, is there manyness in the sequence of the ongoing flow? When people see it, they regard it as if there were nature, but there is no nature in the midst of the Root Suchness. When they see it, they regard it as if there were heaven and earth, things and I's, body and heart, but in reality there are no heaven and earth, things and I's, in the midst of the Root Suchness. In reality there are no body and heart. Why? Humans who come home to the Real are those who circle back to the Root Suchness with the Root Suchness. Following this, at that moment, heaven and earth are rolled up and the traces of time and place disappear. This is the very day of rebirth.[11]

How can heaven and earth be rolled up specifically for this one person? Because, in the midst of the Root Suchness, there is originally nothing of heaven and earth. When people see it, they regard it as if there were heaven and earth.

How can the traces of time and place disappear specifically for this one person? Because, in the midst of the Root Suchness, there is originally nothing of time and place. When people see it, they regard it as if there were time and place.

This realm is known only by those who come home to the Real. Those who do not reach the stage of coming home to the Real do not know it.

## Notes

1. "The things and the I's" (*wuwo*) designates the ten thousand beings that become manifest in the Latter Heaven. As noted in the Introduction, this expression takes into account the distinction between principles and natures, as reflected in Diagram 1.6. Things manifest principles, and I's manifest natures, even though, at root, natures and principles are the same reality.

2. Nūr al-Ḥaqq translated "the ongoing flow of the Root Suchness" as *sarayān wujūd al-ḥaqq*, "the flow of the Existence of the Real" (*Subtleties* 4:33). The word *sarayān* means "to flow," "pervade," and "permeate." Ibn al-ʿArabī and his followers frequently used it to express the manner in which the Real Being pervades all things. Jāmī, for example, wrote: "So, in reality, Being is not more than one. It flows in all these levels [of the cosmos] and in all the realities ordered within them. Within these levels and realities, It is the same as these levels and realities" (*Chinese Gleams*, p. 182).

3. As the diagram indicates, the "outermost" is the Root Suchness pictured as the all-encompassing reality whose flow gives rise to all things "inside" itself; in Arabic, this is the meaning of the Koranic divine name *al-muḥīṭ*, "the All-Encompassing" or "the Circumference" (see *Self-Disclosure*, pp. 223ff).

4. In Ibn al-ʿArabī's terms, this spontaneous unfolding of things is simply the nonrepeating self-disclosures of the Real that result from the engendering command, "Be!" The "great, commonly shared nature" is the Ascribed Spirit, that is, the Breath of the All-merciful within which all things become articulated, ending with the appearance of the heart and, within it, the Nature of Continuity.

5. Liu seems to be saying that the Root Suchness flows out from the deepest recesses of the human spirit into the realm of human embodiment and activity, at which point "not everything emerges from the Self-so," because the human ego interferes. As Chen Chun explained, "As soon as there is the slightest selfish human desire mixed in it, the Principle of Heaven is cut off" (*Terms*, pp. 70–71). In Islamic terms, selfish human desire can appear because of human freedom. Freedom is then addressed by the prescriptive command, which tells people to overcome selfishness and bring themselves back into conformity with the flow of the Real. Liu posed the discussion here in terms of the Daoist notion of *ziran*, the self-so or spontaneous. Angus Graham nicely explains the Daoist view:

While all things move spontaneously on the course proper to them [since everything follows the engendering command], man has stunted and maimed his spontaneous aptitude. . . . To recover and educate his knack he must learn to reflect his situation with the unclouded clarity of a mirror, and respond to it with the immediacy of an echo to a sound or shadow to a shape.   (Cited in *Concepts*, p. 162)

This sort of responsiveness can be achieved only when free will coincides exactly with the engendering command, such that the flow of being in the individual self is indistinguishable from the Self-so. As Confucius put it, "From seventy, I could follow my heart's desire without overstepping the right" (*Analects* 2.4). Hence, in the present passage, Liu explained that re-establishing the harmony of heaven and earth depends on rectifying human natures, hearts, and bodies. In speaking of "rectification" (*zheng* 正) of the heart, or "making the heart true," he is following the language of *The Great Learning*.

6. This issuing appearance is the Mandate of Heaven, as in Diagram 1.5: "The issuing appearance that becomes the Mandate is the issuing appearance of the Real Ruler."

7. This passage may be inspired by *The Great Learning* (cf. *Chinese Gleams*, pp. 10, 85) and/or by this passage from *The Doctrine of the Mean* (22):

Only [those who have] the utmost sincerity (*cheng*) under heaven can fully realize their nature. Able to fully realize their nature, they can give full realization to the nature of the human. Able to give full realization to the nature of the human, they can give full realization to the natures of things. Able to give full realization to the natures of things, they can assist the transforming and nurturing of heaven and earth. Able to assist the transforming and nurturing of heaven and earth, they can form a triad with heaven and earth.

In the Islamic context, parallel discussions can be found under the rubric of Adam's role as God's vicegerent or the cosmic function of the perfect human being. For example, Jāmī wrote:

The Real discloses Himself to the heart of the perfect human being, who is His vicegerent. The reflection of the lights of His self-disclosures is effused from his heart into the cosmos, which subsists through the arrival of this effusion. As long as this perfect one subsists in the cosmos, he seeks from the Real the aid of the self-disclosures of His Essence. . . . So, the cosmos is preserved by this seeking of aid and by the effusion of self-disclosures as long as the perfect human being is within it.   (*Naqd*, p. 9)

8. This is a frequent theme in Islamic theology; the position is epitomized in the Koranic verse, "God creates you and what you do" (37:96). Ibn al-'Arabī expended much effort explaining why the prescriptive command, which "compels people to be free" as he liked to put it, is itself a corollary of the engendering command, making possible certain modalities of exis-

tence that could otherwise not be actualized (such as punishment in hell and reward in paradise). For some of his explanations, see *Sufi Path*, chap. 17.

9. As Ibn al-'Arabī and others explain, Real Existence, *al-wujūd al-ḥaqq*, is *muṭlaq* (nondelimited, unconditioned, absolute) and consequently omnipresent, "shared in common" by all things. Thus the things are called *al-mawjūdāt*, "the existents," a word derived from *wujūd* that points precisely to the fact that everything shares *wujūd* in common. It is this commonly shared existence that is often called "expanded" or "deployed" (*munbasiṭ*), that is, spread out among all things as the Breath of the All-merciful, in which every existent thing is an articulated divine word.

People are "rooted in the Root Suchness embedded within each" because each individual partakes of his or her own delimited, confined, and constricted share of Nondelimited Being. Each is a fixed entity that has been given existence by the divine command "Be!" People seek for the Root Suchness shared in common inasmuch as they strive to achieve the perfection of the human state through reunion with the Nature of Continuity. This perfection is achieved by the all-comprehensive engendered being (*al-kawn al-jāmiʿ*), who has actualized the form of Nondelimited Existence; Ibn al-'Arabī called this being's perfection the Muhammadan Station and the Station of No Station.

10. People in their finiteness can never know God in his infinity. In Ibn al-'Arabī's axiom, "None knows God but God." By the same line of reasoning, nothing loves God but God, and nothing seeks God but God. The individual *qua* individual does not strive for God; rather, it is the presence of God within him that does the seeking and the finding. The theme is common in Sufism, and we will meet it again under Diagram 4.8. Liu could have been familiar with it from Jāmī's commentary on the first chapter of *Lamaʿāt* (*Rays*, pp. 39–43; cf. *Flashes*, p. 73); or from the twenty-first Gleam, which ends with this quatrain:

> O You toward whom no one journeys but You,
>     neither mosque nor monastery is empty of You!
> I saw all the seekers and everything sought—
>     all are You, with no one else in the midst.  (*Chinese Gleams*, p. 174)

11. In Sufism, this discussion commonly goes on in terms of "annihilation" and "subsistence," a pair of terms derived from the Koranic verse, "All that dwells on the earth is undergoing annihilation, and there subsists the face of your Lord, Possessor of Majesty and Generous Giving" (55:26). 'Irāqī discussed it in several places, including this:

If God's majesty charges into the World of Spirits from inside the veil of meaning, it will take the lover away from himself such that neither name nor trace will remain. The lover will not find the joy of witnessing, nor will he taste the flavor of existence. This is the *annihilation* of "him who was not" and the *subsistence* of "Him who ever was."   (*Rays*, p. 73; *Flashes*, p. 88)

## 4.6
### 聖功實踐圖

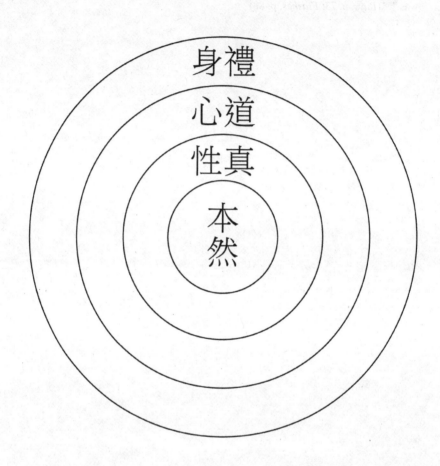

# 4.6
## Diagram of the True Practice
## of Sage Endeavor

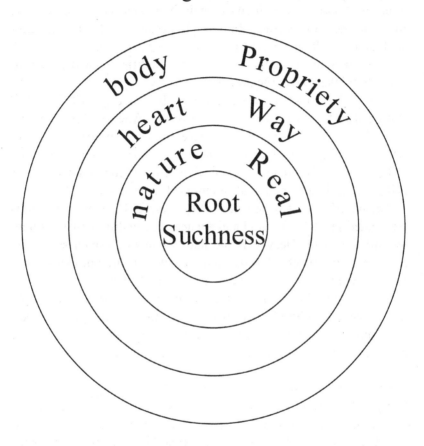

Heaven and earth, up and down, humans and things, outward and inward—all are the ongoing flow of the Root Suchness. Only the sages have the power of true practice with which to hasten toward this realm. The sages take the Nature of Continuity as their own nature. The Nature of Continuity is undifferentiated sameness with the Root Suchness of the Real Ruler. Only because of this undifferentiated sameness do they have the power of true practice.

Someone said: Since they already have undifferentiated sameness, why should they have true practice?[1]

I said: True practice means that they flow and go with the Real Ruler's Root Suchness. They encompass everywhere and reach everyplace. Only after they reach everyplace do they fully realize the substance and function of undifferentiated sameness. Only after they fully realize the substance and function of undifferentiated sameness is it possible to talk about undifferentiated sameness.

The undifferentiated sameness of the Former Heaven is the undifferentiated sameness of void and silence. The undifferentiated sameness of the Latter Heaven is the undifferentiated sameness of true practice. "True practice" and "void and silence" are not two realms. Where there is true practice, there are void and silence.[2]

The sage knows that the multitudes are not capable, and he deeply hopes that the multitudes will become capable. In the midst of their incapability, he directs them and exhibits to them the [three] paths of true practice: The first is called "Propriety," the second "the Way," and the third "the Real."[3]

Propriety is the rules of behavior for daily interaction; this is the true practice of the body. The Way is the tendency to resist things and to circle back to the Real; this is the true practice of the heart. The Real is deep unification with the Root Suchness, which becomes the reality-moment of Propriety and the Way; this is the true practice of nature.[4]

The true practice of nature is the true practice of the Root Suchness. It is not that nature does not have these three at root, or that they are artificially established to be exhibited to the people. Because of the ongoing flow of the Root Suchness in humans and for the sake of the regulated principles inherent in humans, the sage arranges and differentiates the sequence so as to direct and exhibit it.

Those in whose bodies the Root Suchness flows and goes have the heavenly precedence and the heavenly order that are called "Propriety." Fully realizing Propriety is the true practice of the Root Suchness that flows and goes in the body.

Those in whose hearts the Root Suchness flows and goes have the genuine knowledge and genuine power that are called "the Way."[5] Fully realizing the Way is the true practice of the Root Suchness that flows and goes in the heart.

Those in whose natures the Root Suchness flows and goes have the Complete Substance and Great Function that is called "the Real." Returning to the Real is the true practice of the Root Suchness that flows and goes in nature. Therefore I said, "Where there is true practice, there is void and silence." These are not the void and silence of the alien learning.[6]

## Notes

1. This is an important issue in Islamic texts. If we say that the Shariah and the Tariqah exist in order to make it possible for people to reach the Haqiqah, then, once the Haqiqah is reached, the Shariah and the Tariqah have served their purpose and can be discarded. This is the "antinomian" position for which many Sufis have been taken to task, both by jurists and by fellow Sufis. Ibn al-'Arabī frequently argued against it, explaining, among other things, that everyone must follow the path of the Prophet, who continued to practice the Shariah and the Tariqah until the end of his life, even though—or rather, precisely because—he was the perfect embodiment of the Haqiqah (see *Sufi Path*, chap. 11; Chittick, *Imaginal Worlds*, chap. 3).

Picking up on one of Ibn al-'Arabī's many arguments, 'Irāqī wrote that someone who arrives at God may imagine that the path has come to an end, but in fact, the "Journey in God"—as opposed to the "Journey to God"—is endless. Jāmī quoted 'Irāqī's text (in boldface type below) and explained it as follows:

**Those who have quenched their thirst,** that is, who have reached the first levels of arrival, which is the end of the Journey to God, and who have drunk their fill from the spring of union, **imagine that, having arrived, they have attained the desired goal. They rest content with, "Unto Him you shall be returned"** [Koran 2:28]. **Beware, beware! The way stations on the road of arrival,** which are the levels of the Journey in God, **will never be cut off for all eternity,** for the divine tasks and attributes, which are followed by the self-disclosures, have no end. **There is no returning,** after completion of the Journey to God, **to the place of emergence,** where the reality of the servant was configured from Him. **How could the wayfaring,** which is, first, the Journey to God and second, the Journey in God, **be cut off? Where would the road come to an end?** For, even if the Journey to God reaches an end and the servant returns thereby to the [divine] name from which he was configured, he does not stop there. Rather, he enters into the abyss of arrival and dives in it forever, finding at every instant a new pearl. . . . **If the place of arrival were the same as the place of emergence,** and, after returning to the name from which he emerged he came to a stop, **what profit would there have been in coming?** (*Rays*, pp. 117–18; *Flashes*, p. 107).

2. The association of sagehood with emptiness, silence, and stillness is prominent in Daoism, although it is also found in the *Analects* (e.g., 8.5). Certainly the point being made here recalls Zhuangzi:

The sage is still not because he takes stillness to be good and therefore is still. The ten thousand things are insufficient to distract his heart—that is the reason he is still. . . . In stillness the sage's heart is the mirror of heaven and earth, the glass of the ten thousand things. Emptiness, stillness, limpidity, silence, inaction—these are the level of heaven and earth, the substance of the Way and its Virtue.   (13:1–2; Watson, p. 142)

3. As noted in the introduction, these three stages are commonplace in Chinese Islam and correspond to the well-known triad Shariah, Tariqah, and Haqiqah. Both *Goal* and *Path* mention this triad in their prologues, and *Goal* immediately provides a lengthy explanation (*Goal*, pp. 210/41–42, 213–16/45–49; *Path*, pp. 3/28, 162/180).

4. In other words, Propriety (the Shariah) brings one's body and activities into harmony with the Self-so, the Way (the Tariqah) turns one's heart and consciousness away from the lower tendencies of the ego, and the Real (the Haqiqah) is the realization of the nature of continuity (the Muhammadan Spirit), which then spontaneously manifests itself in the body's observation of propriety and the heart's following the Way. At this stage, individual endeavor has been reintegrated into the Self-so, and the engendering and prescriptive commands coincide.

5. There is an allusion here to Mencius 7.A.15: "The power possessed by people without having learned it is genuine power, and the knowledge possessed without thinking is genuine knowledge." Zhu Xi explained that here

the word genuine (*liang* 良) denotes the goodness of the Root Suchness (Legge). In this passage Legge renders *liang* as "intuitive," and Lau translates it as "true."

6. That is, Buddhism and, to some degree, Daoism. Cf. Wang Daiyu's critique of these notions in his *Great Learning* (*Chinese Gleams*, pp. 108–10).

## 4.7

## 聖賢智愚圖

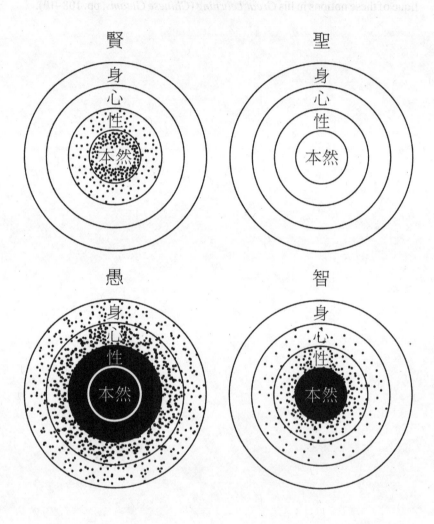

# 4.7
## Diagram of Sage, Worthy, Wise, and Ignorant

worthy         sage

ignorant       wise

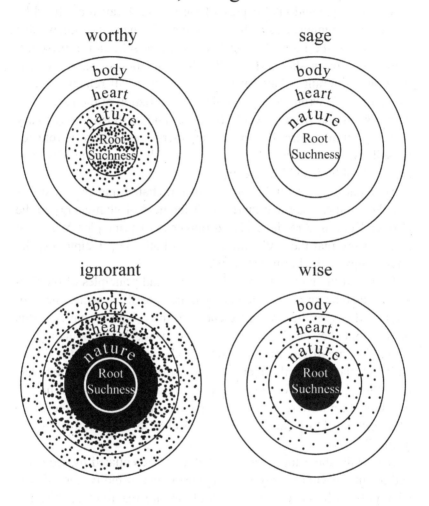

The differentiation of sage, worthy, wise, and ignorant[1] is a differentiation by the principle and vital-energy of the Former Heaven, and also a differentiation by the knowledge and action of the Latter Heaven.[2]

The principle and vital-energy of the Former Heaven are fixed by heaven, and humans cannot have any share in them. The knowledge and action of the Latter Heaven are reliant on self, and in these humans can have a share. Hence the differentiation of sage, worthy, wise, and ignorant is half fixed by heaven and half reliant on self.[3] Therefore, it is wrong to say that the differentiation of the four levels emerges entirely from heavenly firmness, and it is also wrong to say that it is not made firm by heaven but emerges entirely from reliance on self.[4] When human affairs are united with heavenly affairs, then the levels of high and low are divided.

Someone said: If vital-energy is differentiated into pure and turbid, then you can say that there are differences of vital-energy in the Former Heaven. Are there also differences of principle? Why is it that you say that the differentiation is in both the principle and the vital-energy of the Former Heaven?[5]

I said: At the moment when the natures and principles of the Former Heaven begin to be differentiated, they are of the same, one, root origin. After they become differentiated, the principles have no this or that, but they do have sequence. Sequence is the boundary by which they are differentiated. If we talk about them before the differentiation, then originally there was no sequence. But once there has been the Chief Manifestation [1.5], and once the natures and principles have been differentiated and separated in the midst of the Chief Manifestation [1.6], how can it be possible for there not to be sequence?

If we talk about the principles that are differentiated by sequence and about the vital-energy that has purity and turbidity, then this is what is fixed by heaven. Heavenly affairs are fixed before this, and human affairs are differentiated after this. This is the reason why sage, worthy, wise, and ignorant become differentiated in the end and why their levels do not transgress each other.

Human affairs are knowledge and action.[6] Although knowledge and action belong to human affairs in the Latter Heaven, what brings forth differences in depth and shallowness, ease and exertion, is all due to the pure and turbid vital-energy that is endowed by the Former Heaven.

In the midst of the pure is the utmost pure. This is the vital-energy endowed on the sages; this vital-energy excels in the purity of wind. That which cannot obtain the utmost purity is the vital-energy endowed upon the worthies; this vital energy excels in the purity of water. That which dwells next to this purity is the vital-energy endowed on the wise; this vital-energy excels in fire.[7]

The number of the pure is one or two out of ten, and the number of the turbid is eight or nine out of ten. This is the vital-energy endowed upon the ignorant; this vital-energy excels in soil. "Ignorant" means the multitudes. These sorts of people are not the most stubborn or unapproachable.

The sages are rooted in the utmost purity of vital-energy, and this becomes their knowledge and action. Their true action and real knowledge are an undifferentiated sameness with the Root Suchness in one body.

Both worthies and wise are rooted in the vital-energy with which they are endowed, and this becomes their knowledge and action. The worthies hope to be sages, and the wise hope to be worthies. In each case their knowledge and action are equal to their root capacity, and there they stop. The worthies are able to put the regulated principles of nature into practice, but they are not able to obtain undifferentiated sameness with the Root Suchness. The wise are able to put the regulated principles of the heart into practice, but their nature and allotment are not yet fully realized.

The ignorant are rooted in the vital-energy of little purity and much turbidity, and this becomes their knowledge and action. Their knowledge is merely customs, and their actions merely old regulations. Although they are able to put the regulated principles of the body into practice, their heart and nature are not yet clarified. Moreover, by no means are they able to discern the reasons why the regulated principles of the body emerge. This is the reason why the ignorant become ignorant in the end.

Someone said: In each of the sages, worthies, wise, and ignorant, knowledge and action are caused by the vital-energy endowed by the

Former Heaven. That is why there are ease and exertion, shallowness and depth. This means that all human affairs are bound by heavenly affairs. When there is only heavenly firmness and no self-reliance whatsoever, how can you say that half is made firm by heaven and half is reliant on self?

I said: In the midst of the heavenly firmness, there is self-reliance, but this self-reliance exists in subtle concealment. In the midst of self-reliance there is self-reliance, but this self-reliance exists in the function of the excelling heart.

Why did I say that there is self-reliance in the midst of heavenly firmness? Because there are principle and vital-energy in heavenly firmness. The principle is heaven, the vital-energy is self. Self is where vital-energy is. Having self is the taproot of self-reliance.

Why is there self-reliance in the midst of self-reliance? Because all the affairs arise from the function of the excelling heart, and all come to be from the function of the excelling heart. In each case [the excelling heart] causes the endowed vital-energy to become knowledge and action; so there is heavenly firmness in the midst of self-reliance. Everything ends up at the excelling heart, through which there are knowledge and action; so there is self-reliance in the midst of self-reliance.

When the heart excels in something, the endowed vital-energy is not able to limit its domain. Even if the endowed vital-energy is finally able to limit its domain, the heart never wants its domain to be limited. This is why there is no realm in which the function of the excelling heart comes to a halt. The excelling heart belongs neither to the principle of the Former Heaven nor to the vital-energy of the Former Heaven. Is it not possible to say that it belongs to the self-reliance of the Latter Heaven?

In the extreme case, the most stubborn and most ignorant consider opposing the principle as enjoyable and approaching the principle as not enjoyable. Their knowledge and action are extreme and outside [the norms of] mankind. This, too, is the function of the excelling heart. So, without doubt, their activities are reliant on self.

Thus is it said that the differentiation of sage, worthy, wise, and ignorant is half fixed by heaven and half reliant on self.

## Notes

1. The issue of the differentiation of human beings into types is much discussed by Neo-Confucians. Chen Chun explained the general position:

Regarding the different kinds of people, their endowment from Heaven on High is the same, but what happens to man differs in purity or impurity, greater or lesser amount. The sage, for example, has received the clearest vital-energy and is therefore born with knowledge from the start. . . . From the sage down, each one has his own degree. . . . A worthy has received much clear vital-energy and little impure vital-energy. There is a small amount of dreg in its purity. . . . Those below the great worthy may be half pure and half impure, or more impure than pure, and are thickly darkened. . . . There are those whose endowment is clear and bright and can discern moral principles but do not practice earnestly and fail to be a vehicle of truth. . . . There are also those who like to reason but strongly hold on to their own views and set up a school of their own opinions. In this case, while the endowed vital-energy is pure, it has been struck and disturbed by some perverse force. (*Terms*, pp. 40–42)

In differentiating people into four types, Liu was inspired by Part IV of *Path*, where Rāzī addressed the issue of the return (*ma'ād*) of the souls of both the felicitous and the wretched, that is, the saved and the damned. At the outset he reiterated the standard teaching that the Return amounts to going back to the Origin, as demanded by the Circle of Existence. But, everyone does not go back to the same "place" (e.g., some end up in paradise, some in hell), and this has everything to do with the fact that "at the beginning of their created nature (*fiṭra*), the spirits had four ranks" (*Path*, p. 345/ 335). The first rank is that of the spirits of the prophets and the elect among the saints, who stand in the station of having no "intermediary" (*wāsiṭa*) between themselves and God. This corresponds to Liu's "Nature of Continuity." The second rank belongs to the spirits of the common saints and the elect believers. The third is that of the common believers and the elect among the disobedient. The fourth is the spirits of the common disobedient, the hypocrites, and the unbelievers (*Path*, pp. 345/335–36). In the four chapters of this part of *Path*, Rāzī explained how the four ranks of spirits (determined in the Former Heaven) then become manifest through human activity and practice as four sorts of soul (in the Latter Heaven).

The designations of the four sorts of soul on the ascending arc of the Latter Heaven derive from the Koran and were much discussed in Sufi texts, although usually not as elaborately as in *Path*. These are the soul that commands to evil (*nafs-i ammāra*), the blaming soul (*nafs-i lawwāma*), the inspired soul (*nafs-i mulhama*), and the tranquil soul (*nafs-i muṭma'inna*). Rāzī pointed out that there are three subranks in the second through the fourth sorts of soul, corresponding in each case to the Companions of the Right, the Companions of the Left, and the Foremost (terminology deriving from Koran 56:10).

Nūr al-Ḥaqq, in his commentary on Root Classic 4:48–51, explained that the sages (the prophets, *anbiyā'*) have reached union with the Real, but the other three classes are touched by darkness (*ẓulma*) and thereby become veiled from the Real. The worthies (the sincere, *mukhliṣ*) may become deluded (misguided, *ḍāll*), for when they see charismatic acts (*karāmāt*, i.e., miracles) appearing from themselves, they may be confused about their own relation with God's power. The wise (the ulama) may become heretics (innovators, *mubtadi'*), for they may give legal pronouncements based on their own opinions. The ignorant (*jāhil*) may become hypocrites (*munāfiq*) or unbelievers (*kāfir*) by denying religious obligations or articles of belief (*Sharḥ*, pp. 126–27/92).

2. Notice that Liu is saying that differentiation occurs both as a result of the Former Heaven's Mandate (the engendering command) and as a result of practice, or the realization of the Mandate in the Latter Heaven (observance of the prescriptive command). The passage of *Path* cited in note 1 to this section makes the differentiation of spirit pertain to the Former Heaven, which is to say that it is already fixed in the created nature (*fiṭra*) of the spirits. But the whole thrust of Rāzī's four chapters on the Return is that people earn their places in the next world by their activities and practices in this world. Right at the beginning of the section, he distinguished the two sorts of Return: the "voluntary" (*bi-ikhtiyār*), which determines the rank achieved in the next world by the felicitous, and the "compulsory" (*bi-iḍṭirār*), which belongs to the wretched, those who do not attempt to follow the Way.

3. This is the typical position of Islamic theology, the middle point between predestination and free will. Predestination follows upon the absolute authority of God, the sole giver of existence, who measures out everything in the universe in a wise measure (*qadar*) in keeping with the engendering command. Free will follows upon God's creation of man in his own form, bestowing upon him a certain freedom of choice—which no sane person denies—and then addressing him with the messages of the prophets and the teachings of the sages (the prescriptive command). These delineate the Way that must be followed in order to achieve harmony with heaven and earth and felicity in the next stage of the cosmic flow.

4. This is a standard rejection of the two extremes of absolute compulsion and unlimited free choice.

5. The questioner is objecting because the general Neo-Confucian position is that principle pertains to the formless realm (the Former Heaven) and vital-energy to the realm of forms (the Latter Heaven). These two passages from Zhu Xi illustrate how he dealt with the issue:

Man's nature and mandate exist before form, and vital-energy exists after form. What exists before form is the one principle harmonious and undifferentiated, and is invariably good. What exists after form, however, is confused and mixed, and good and evil are thereby differentiated. (*Source Book*, p. 597)

Considering the fact that all things come from one source, we see that their principle is the same but their vital-energy different. Looking at their various substances, we see that their vital-energy is similar but their principle utterly different. The difference in vital-energy is due to its purity or impurity, whereas the difference in principle is due to its completeness or partiality. (Ibid., p. 637)

6. In Islamic sources, the corresponding terminology is *'ilm* and *'amal*, and the two are considered precisely the constituents of human affairs. The Prophet said, "Knowledge without action is a tree without fruit." Real knowledge is understanding the way things are, and that demands recognition of the ultimate realities. Proper action is to act rightly and appropriately on the basis of correct knowledge. Without knowledge, even right action is faulty. Thus the Prophet is also reported to have said, "An ardent worshiper without understanding is like a donkey in a mill" (Hujwīrī, *Kashf al-maḥjūb*, p. 17).

7. Liu explained this under Diagram 3.10.

# 4.8
# 障礙層次圖

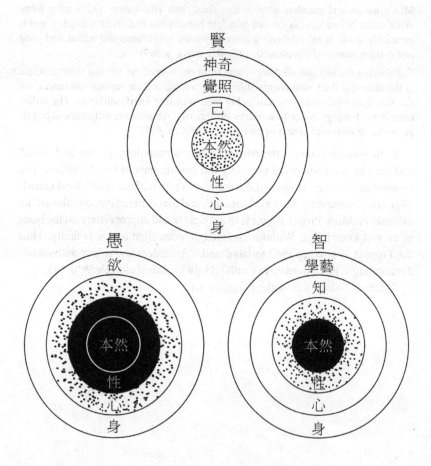

# 4.8
# Diagram of the Order of the Layers of
# Veils and Obstacles

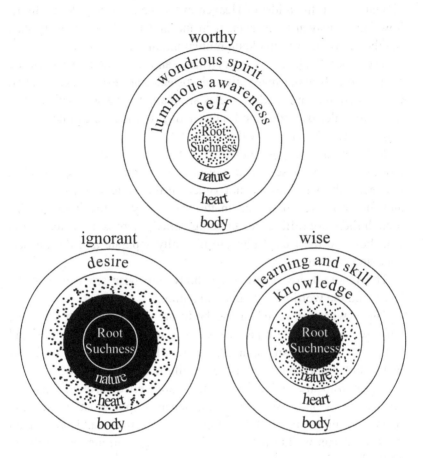

Heaven is Heaven because of humans,[1] and humans are human because of Heaven.[2]

There are veils and obstacles without any cause.[3] The I's and the Real Ruler are mutually separate and never pervade one another.[4] Humans are in the midst of Heaven every day, but they do not know how close Heaven is. Heaven is in the midst of humans every day, but they have no way to obtain mutual union.

The Root Suchness is everywhere, and veils and obstacles are everywhere. It is not that veils and obstacles are everywhere; rather, everywhere the veils and obstacles are made by the self. This is why the Real Ruler pervades the I's every day, but the I's can never pervade the Real Ruler on any day.[5]

Not only are the ignorant veiled, but also the wise cannot avoid it. Not only are the wise veiled, but also the worthies cannot avoid it. However, the worthies are not veiled in the same way as the wise, and the wise are not veiled in the same way as the ignorant. Although there are differences in being veiled, there is no difference in that they and the Real Ruler are mutually separate and do not pervade one another.

The ignorant are veiled in the body, the wise are veiled in the heart, and the worthies are veiled in nature.[6]

Those who are veiled in the body are veiled through what the body seeks. What the body seeks exists in sound, color, smell, and taste. Sound, color, smell, and taste are all veils. How can we know that sound, color, smell, and taste are all the Root Suchness?

Those who are veiled in the heart are veiled through what the heart depends upon. What the heart depends upon exists in hearing, seeing, learning, and skill. Hearing, seeing, learning, and skill are all veils. How can we know that hearing, seeing, learning, and skill are all the Root Suchness?

Those who are veiled in nature are veiled through nature's not reaching transformation. Nature is the Root Suchness of the Lord, and it is the name and allotment of having the I. Before nature is entered undifferentiatedly, the name and allotment of the I are still preserved. There is always the wondrous spirit, but the wondrous spirit exists in the I, not in the Lord. There is always luminous awareness, but luminous awareness exists in the I, not in the Lord. This means that both the wondrous spirit and the luminous awareness are veils. How can we know that, when endeavor and strength reach here, the wondrous spirit and luminous awareness of the Root Suchness are still the veils and obstacles of the Root Suchness?

Thus it was said that everywhere is the Root Suchness, and everywhere veils and obstacles come to be. So, for the sage, veils and obstacles are everywhere, and the Root Suchness is everywhere.

Nature is the self-manifestation of the Root Suchness; if the nature of the Root Suchness circles back to the Root Suchness, how can there be veils? The heart is that through which the Root Suchness flows and goes and becomes perfected; if the heart through which the Root Suchness flows and goes and circles back to the Root Suchness, how can there be veils? The body is where the Root Suchness correctly begins as the original being so as to flow and go and be perfected; if the body of the Root Suchness properly and fully realizes the intention of the ongoing flow of the Root Suchness, how can there be veils?

This is why the ears, eyes, mouth, and nose of the Root Suchness, existing day by day in the midst of sound, color, smell, and taste, begin to obtain the full realization of the function of ears, eyes, mouth, and nose.[7] They are not veils.

This is why the attentiveness, clarity, wisdom, and knowledge of the Root Suchness, expounding day by day the affairs of hearing, seeing, learning, and skill, begin to obtain the full realization of the endeavor of attentiveness, clarity, wisdom, and knowledge. They are not veils.

This is why the Complete Substance and Great Function of the Root Suchness, manifesting day by day the powers of the wondrous spirit and luminous awareness, begin to obtain the full realization of the subtlety of the Complete Substance and Great Function. They are not veils.

The sage is the person who governs the veils and obstacles of the worthies, the wise, and the ignorant, and circles back to the Root Suchness. He also transforms the veils and obstacles of the worthies, the wise, and the ignorant. Yet he does not preserve any trace of circling back to the Root Suchness.[8]

## Notes

1. In Ibn al-'Arabī's terms, this is to say that the Lord (*rabb*), by the very fact of being Lord, has "servants" (*'abd*), who are the ones "lorded over" (*marbūb*). So also the God (*al-ilāh*), by the fact of being the God, has divine thralls, literally, those "godded over" (*ma'lūh*). See *Sufi Path*, chap. 4. As Wang Daiyu put it, in answering someone who asked why God in his transcendence would bother to create the universe:

If there were no heaven and earth, humans, and spirits, how could the Lord be the Lord of the ten thousand things? According to your statement, it is not necessary for the greatly honored to manifest himself. This would mean that it is possible for him to be a king without ministers and multitudes. Were there none of these people, who would make him a king?   (*Chinese Gleams*, p. 45)

2. Ibn al-'Arabī made this point by saying that the defining characteristic of human beings is not "rational speech," as the philosophers would have it, but rather the Divine Form (*al-ṣūrat al-ilāhiyya*) in which they were created (*Futūḥāt*, 3: 154; *Sufi Path*, p. 276). Wing-tsit Chan says that the notion of the unity of Heaven and human beings, already present in some of the earliest extant Chinese sources, "was to dominate the course of Chinese history" (*Source Book*, p. 10). As Cheng Hao put it, "When the Way and principle are followed, Heaven and man will be one and can no longer be separable" (ibid., p. 532); or again, "Heaven and man are basically not two. There is no need to talk of combining them" (ibid., p. 536).

3. That the cosmos is nothing but the veils of the Real is a common discussion in Sufism, again brought to the fore by Ibn al-'Arabī. The notion has strong roots in the hadith literature, as when the Prophet says of God, "His veil is light." This and other sayings, combined with various Koranic allusions and the depiction of God as "the light of the heavens and the earth" (24:35), quickly led to the notion that heaven and earth and everything in between are veils. Another version of the hadith of God's veils, not grounded in the earliest sources but much more frequently cited, says that God has seventy, or seventy thousand, "veils of light and darkness." The veils have no "cause" because they belong to the very reality of the cosmic flow; so they are simply the Self-so. On veils in general, see Chittick, *Sufism*, chap. 10; for Ibn al-'Arabī, see *Self-Disclosure*, chaps. 3–4.

4. This is a constant theme of Islamic theology. It is commonly called the "incomparability" (*tanzīh*), or transcendence, of God, as contrasted with his similarity, or immanence (*tashbīh*). Ibn al-'Arabī has numerous passages asserting both perspectives, whether separately or together (e.g., *Sufi Path*,

pp. 68–76). His declaration "He / not He" combines the two standpoints. In a typical passage, he wrote concerning God's separation:

There is no interrelationship or correlation between the Real and creation—on the contrary, He is "Independent of the worlds" [Koran 3:97], and this belongs to no existent essence save the Essence of the Real—so no engendered thing is tied to the Essence, no eye perceives It, no limit encompasses It, and no demonstration gives knowledge of It. (*Futūḥāt*, 2: 226; *Sufi Path*, p. 64)

5. This statement is reminiscent of Ibn al-'Arabī's typical rumination on the Koranic verse, "He is with you wherever you are" (57:4). For example:

He did not say, "And you are with Him," since the manner in which He accompanies us is unknown. He knows how He accompanies us, but we do not know how He accompanies us. So witness is affirmed for Him in relation to us, but it is negated from us in relation to Him. (*Futūḥāt*, 2: 582; *Sufi Path*, p. 364)

6. In his commentary on Root Classic 4:60–64, which this diagram illustrates, Nūr al-Ḥaqq continued the discussion of the previous lines by summarizing the three stages of obscuration in terms of light and darkness. He called Root Suchness "the Reality" (*al-ḥaqīqa*) and nature "the soul" (*al-nafs*). In the case of the sincere (the worthy), their realities are veiled from the light of the Real by the darkness of egoity (*anā'iyya*). When they perform charismatic acts, they become proud and ascribe the acts to their own power. As for the ulama (the wise), both their realities and their souls are veiled by the darkness of passing thoughts (*khawāṭir*) in their hearts. Their learning keeps them distracted from the Real; so their sciences become their veils. As for the ignorant, the darkness of appetites in the body veils their hearts, souls, and realities; thus the Koran (3:14) says, "Made attractive to people is the love of their appetites—women, children, heaped up mounds of gold and silver" (*Sharḥ*, pp. 127–31/93–95).

7. Here the most obvious parallel with early Islamic sources is the famous divine saying, narrated by the Prophet (and found in the standard hadith collections), in which God says that his servant keeps on approaching him through good works until God loves him. Then, when God loves him, God becomes his hearing through which he hears, his eyesight through which he sees, his hand through which he grasps, and his foot through which he walks. In his chapter on the purification of the heart, Rāzī cited this saying twice. For example,

In this station, the heart reaches the reality of being a heart and returns to its original soundness and limpidness. . . . Here the commander is neither the heart nor the spirit, lest some of the soul's attributes conform and some not conform. Rather, the commanding Sultan of "Faces are humbled unto the Living, the Self-Standing" [Koran 20:11] has emptied the court of the heart from the jostling of "others" and made it into His own specific throne, for "My earth and My heaven embrace Me not, but the heart of My believing servant does embrace Me." After this, the Real's command prevails over all the organs and attributes. . . . No organ or attribute is able to act freely by its own nature (*ṭab'*), only by the command and indication of the Real. For, "I am his hearing, his eyesight, his tongue and his hand, and through Me he hears, through Me he sees, through Me he speaks, and through Me he grasps." (*Path*, pp. 208–9/218–19)

On the basis of the full text of this hadith, which mentions "obligatory acts" (*farā'iḍ*) and "supererogatory acts" (*nawāfil*), Ibn al-'Arabī and his followers discussed two complementary sorts of nearness (*qurb*) to God (see *Sufi Path*, pp. 325–31). Jāmī explained the difference between the two in his introduction to *Rays* (pp. 15–16) and referred to it again in his commentaries on the sixth and ninth flashes (cf. *Flashes*, pp. 138, 142–43).

8. The distinction between sage and worthy was much discussed by Chinese thinkers. What Liu says here agrees with a point made by the Daoist master Wang Bi (d. 249), who explained why Confucius was a sage, but Laozi and Zhuangzi were only worthies: "The Sage [i.e., Confucius], being identified with non-being, realized that it could not be made the subject of instruction and so felt bound to deal with being (*yu* [*you*]). Lao and Chuang, however, not yet having completely escaped from the sphere of being, constantly spoke of that in which they were themselves deficient" (Fung Yu-lan, *History of Chinese Philosophy*, 2: 170).

Ibn al-'Arabī made a similar point when he described the station of the "Muhammadans," meaning those saints and prophets who achieve the full realization of all the qualities embodied in Muḥammad, the Utmost Sage. The lowest-ranking saints are the ascetics and are distinguished by pious works. The second rank is occupied by the Sufis, who display their spiritual accomplishments to the people in order to attract them to God.

The third group . . . do not distinguish themselves from the faithful who perform God's obligations by any extra state whereby they might be known. They walk in the markets, they speak to the people, and none of God's creatures sees any of them distinguishing himself from the common people by a single thing; they add nothing to the obligatory works or the Sunna customary among the common folk. They are alone with God, firmly rooted, not wavering from their servanthood for the blink of an eye. (*Futūḥāt*, 3: 35; *Sufi Path*, p. 374)

This way of looking at human perfection helps explain why the general Muslim understanding of Jesus—God's messenger, spirit, and word, according to the Koran (4:171)—is that his spiritual reality predominated over his mortal, human reality, and hence he failed to realize the full range of perfections present in the divine form that is human nature, a range actualized by Muḥammad. Nonetheless, Ibn al-'Arabī could still remark that "Jesus is a Muhammadan" (*Futūḥāt*, 3: 507; *Sufi Path*, p. 377), meaning that he achieved the same human/divine fullness as Muḥammad.

## 4.9
## 疑信累德圖

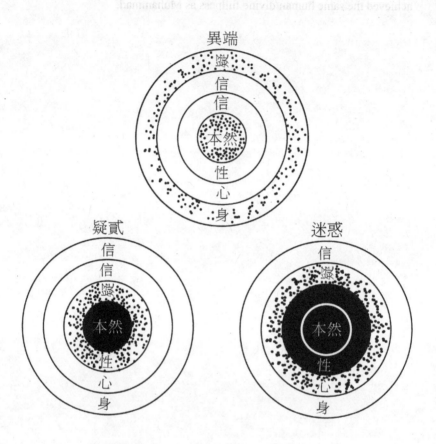

# 4.9
## Diagram of the Burdens of Virtue in Doubt and Faithfulness

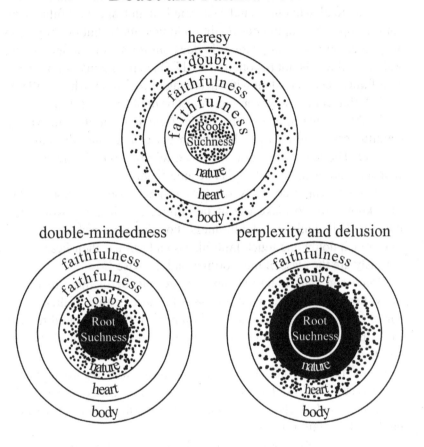

Erlifu said, "Even if your eyes are full of things, doubt will not arise. Even if heaven and earth are all rolled up, faithfulness will not arise."[1]

Perhaps the meaning of these words is that when the Real is united with the Real without sound and smell, doubt and faithfulness no longer apply. Not only does doubt no longer apply, but doubt has no way to come into being. Not only does faithfulness no longer apply, but faithfulness is not begotten in itself. Once the germs of doubt and faithfulness become silent without arising or perishing, where will virtue be? Below this, however, there must be doubt and faithfulness.[2]

Doubt is departure; to depart from right is to be near to wrong. Faithfulness is firmness; to be firm in purity is to stay distant from mixture. The involvement of doubt and faithfulness with heaven and humans, nature and mandate, is not superficial.

Ignorant people do not know how to make use of doubt, nor do they know how to make use of faithfulness; so it is not worth discussing their doubt and faithfulness. For the most part, those who have much doubt and much faithfulness and can use their hearts dangerously are the class of the worthies and the wise.[3]

Doubt and faithfulness do not emerge outside of three realms—body, heart, and nature. Faithfulness is beautiful virtue. If their faithfulness is right, then of course faithfulness in the body, faithfulness in the heart, and faithfulness in nature will all be beautiful. It is useless to discuss this.

Doubt is dangerous. The disease of those who regard doubt as doubt is still shallow. The disease of those who regard doubt as faithfulness is much deeper; most kinds of the worthies and the wise regard doubt as faithfulness.

It is still possible for the doubt of those who regard doubt as doubt to return and come home to faithfulness. As for the doubt of those who regard doubt as faithfulness, the longer it lasts, the deeper it becomes. Finally, there will be no day of returning by oneself.

Doubts are distinct, however, in shallowness and depth. The doubt of those whose doubt stops in the body is shallow. The doubt of those whose doubt enters the heart is deep. The doubt of those whose doubt arises in their nature becomes disease, and they cannot be rescued.

What is it that is called "doubt in the body"? It is that someone betrays the regulated principles of the body at the moments of the daily interactions; he establishes something new and novel that has not been experienced or seen.[4] This is the meaning of doubt in the body. Doubt in the body is a burden of virtue, but one can still wait for return.

What is it that is called "doubt in the heart"? It is that at the moment of darkly and vaguely searching for the Real, someone betrays the regulated principles of the heart and joyfully hastens toward the deviated paths and byways. "He is like a traveler on a path who turns the carriage south to seek for north."[5] This is the meaning of doubt in the heart.

Doubt in the heart is a heavier burden, but, if there is a day of ruthless self-examination, there can still be return from doubt. If there is return from doubt and coming home to faithfulness, then it will still be possible to use the heart. Then the disease will not reach the point beyond rescue. Steps will still remain waiting for his return.

What is it that is called "doubt in nature"? On the day when together body and heart arrive—precisely the time when the regulated principles of the root nature issue forth and appear, when spiritual penetration reaches everywhere and the luminous awareness goes everyplace—this is precisely the moment one should let go of clinging to the cliff by coming home to the Real, and nothing is more dangerous than this ground. Yet, a doubt may arise here and someone may say, "Is this my power or is this the power of the Lord? Does my power match that of the Lord? Am I the Lord?"

If someone comes to the ground of utmost danger and of no turning around and still has irresolute and unsettled suspicions like this, how can the Real Ruler forgive such great rebellion appearing before Him? Even if he wishes to return by himself, there will be no steps remaining by which to retire from this ground, nor will time wait for him. This is why rescue is impossible when doubt arises in nature. The deeper the endeavor, the more dangerous the realm. The nearer to the Lord, the more impossible it is to turn doubt around.

These are the mistakes of the worthies and the wise who misuse their attentiveness and clarity. Thus the words of Erlifu can truly be said to be a mirror of returning to the Truth and coming home to the Real.

## Notes

1. Erlifu is perhaps a transliteration of *'ārif,* "gnostic." Sufi texts often quote sayings from an anonymous "gnostic," meaning saint or sage. Erlifu's saying refers to a discussion that typically goes on in Sufi texts in terms of the contrast between "faith" (*īmān*) and "unbelief" (*kufr*), a major topic in theology. He is saying that those who reach the goal of the Path transcend the distinction between these two. The well-known Sufi teacher 'Ayn al-Quḍāt Hamadānī (d. 1131) explains this transcendence like this:

A great man said, "Faith and unbelief are two stations beyond the Throne, two veils between God and His servant." This is because a true human being must be neither unbeliever nor Muslim. The one who is still with unbelief and faith is behind these two veils. (*Tamhīdāt*, pp. 122–23).

Maḥmūd Shabistarī, one of the many Sufi poets who speaks of transcending this duality, referred to it in these two verses in terms of the unity of the two in their divine source, the Haqiqah. He was explaining the perfection achieved by the Perfect Human Being:

He makes the Shariah his shirt,
   he makes the Tariqah his coat,
But, know that the station of his essence is the Haqiqah,
   so he combines faith and unbelief. (*Gulshan*, vss. 349–50)

For a study of various sides to this issue in the Sufi tradition, see Lewisohn, *Beyond Faith and Infidelity.*

2. Faithfulness (*xin*), as noted, is one of the five constant virtues, often contrasted with doubt (*yi* 疑). Chen Chun (*Terms*, p. 86) said that some interpret it to mean "being beyond doubt," but he preferred Cheng Hao's understanding, that it means "making things real" and "following things without any deviation."

The relevant lines from the Root Classic begin with the sentence, "Being faithful to the principle and doubting affairs / is to become a heretic" (4:65–66). Nūr al-Ḥaqq translated and explained these lines like this (the bold script represents the text of *Subtleties*):

**Some acknowledge the Real**, that is, God and His messenger, in their hearts, **but** their beliefs **deviate in some of the affairs of the religion** from the path of the Sunnis; **they are among the innovators**, that is, those who oppose the Prophet and the Rightly Guided Caliphs in some beliefs. (*Sharḥ*, pp. 131–32/95–96)

In other words, Nūr al-Ḥaqq took faithfulness to mean adherence to right beliefs as expressed in the Koran and the Sunnah, and "doubt" to mean deviation from that adherence. This seems to be in line with Cheng Hao: "There is only one principle in the world. . . . And to be faithful is to be faithful to this principle" (*Source Book*, p. 534).

3. The dangers of the path to God are commonly discussed in Sufi texts. Rāzī, for example, compared the servanthood of seekers to a tree that becomes more luxuriant as they progress in the Shariah and the Tariqah. When the blossoms of good deeds sprout up, however, many cold winds will threaten them, for, as a purported hadith has it, "The sincere are in great danger" (*Path*, pp. 362–64/351–53).

4. In other words, this sort of doubt pertains to the level of Propriety (the Shariah). Specifically, it entails modifying the law without following the traditional procedures. In Arabic, *bid‘a* or "innovation" can carry precisely this meaning. See Nūr al-Ḥaqq's explanations quoted under 4.7.

5. A Chinese proverb.

# 4.10
# 順逆分支圖

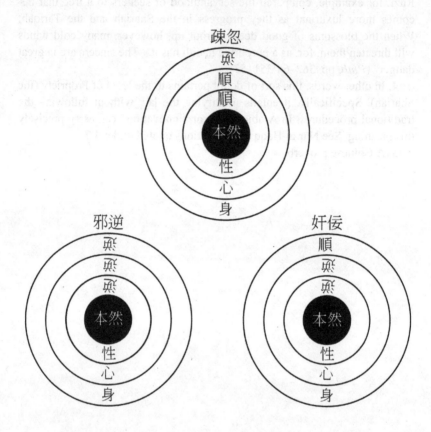

# 4.10
# Diagram of the Differentiated Branches
# of Obedience and Rebellion

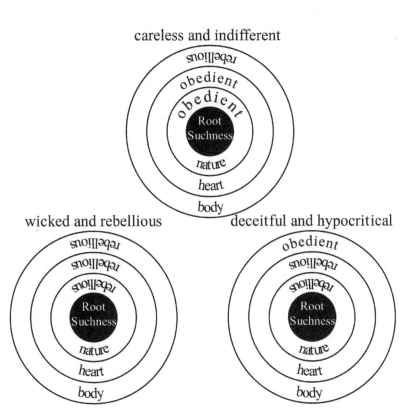

Relying on the principle of heaven and not going along with the privateness of human desire is called "obedience." Having merely human desire and not uniting with the truth of the heavenly principle is called "rebellion."[1]

The two extremes of obedience and rebellion are certainly the one great, general gate of the differentiated branches and distinct groups of all good and evil, public and private, false and true, loyal and deceitful.

When there is obedience and rebellion, human affairs are not equal, and without obedience and rebellion, the creative transformation would not be subtle. The mechanism and circumstances of the creative transformation are lodged in the midst of obedience and rebellion.[2]

The body and heart of humans come to be when the four agents are collected together. When the natures of the four agents oppose one another and infringe upon one another, there is more rebellion and less obedience.[3] The mechanisms and bindings of obedience and rebellion are already lurking in the midst when the four agents are collected together. When diverse affairs and activities issue forth as obedience and rebellion, the wonder of the creative transformation becomes manifest. Without obedience, rebellion would not be shown, and without rebellion, obedience would not be displayed.

By enumerating obedience and rebellion together, we can differentiate some into acts of obedience and some into acts of rebellion. When obedience and rebellion become manifest, the border between the heavenly principle and human desire becomes even more obvious, without anything shaded. When the border between the heavenly principle and human desire becomes manifest, the original subtlety of the Real Ruler's Root Suchness becomes more splendid, and all is displayed to the ears and eyes. The Real Ruler becomes manifest through the manifestation of obedience and rebellion. This is the subtlety of the mechanism and circumstances of the creative transformation.

Only the sages neither obey nor rebel, not because they have no obedience and rebellion, but because their obedience is of course obedience, and even their rebellion is obedience. The sages are those who cannot be bound by the four agents.

Those beneath them, however, have no power; so some are begotten to be obedient, and some are begotten to be rebellious. Some seem not to be obedient but in reality are obedient. Some seem not to be rebellious but in reality are rebellious. Those who rebel first and obey later have something over those who obey first and rebel later.[4] Those who seem not to obey but are really obedient are as far apart from those who seem not to be rebellious but really rebel as heaven is from earth.[5]

There is the same one obedience, yet there are hundreds of thousands of different gates to this obedience; thus, in the midst of obedience, it is impossible not to argue about this and that. There is the one rank of rebellion, yet there are hundreds of thousands of different groups in this rebellion; thus, in the midst of rebellion, there are still differences between fine and coarse. In this multiplicity and complexity, each regards himself as right.

How do we know that the obedient are few and the rebellious many? How do we know that those who are really obedient want to borrow the name of the rebellious so as to conceal their obedience, not wanting to display the name "obedient"? How do we know that those who are really rebellious skillfully borrow the name "obedient" so as to conceal their rebellion, not wanting to be manifest as dwelling with the title "rebellious"?

Those who are obedient once but rebellious forever afterward skillfully borrow the name "obedient" so as to conceal their rebellion. Finally, however, their rebellion cannot be concealed. Why? Because it is impossible to deceive the Real Ruler.

Those who are rebellious once but obedient forever afterward simply borrow the name "rebellion" to conceal their obedience. Finally, however, their obedience cannot perish. Why? Because the Real Ruler would never be in darkness and be ungrateful to the people.

If this is the case, then it is not only that the original subtlety of the Real Ruler's Root Suchness becomes manifest relying only on human obedience and rebellion but also that the luminous awareness of the Real Ruler's Root Suchness is increasingly shown forth relying only on human obedience and rebellion. Thus it was said, "The Real Ruler becomes manifest through the manifestation of obedience and rebellion." However, if we are able to manifest the Real Ruler through rebellion, how much more so can we manifest Him through obedience! This is the place of human judgment and a path of dignity and honor that people can bring upon themselves.

### Notes

1. Obedience (*shun* 順) is the virtue that children should have toward their parents, and rebellion (*ni* 逆) the lack of it. The *Doctrine of the Mean* (20) discusses obedience in the context of explaining the five relationships: "There is a way to be trusted by one's friends: If one is not obedient to his parents, he will not be trusted by his friends. There is a way to obey one's parents: If one examines himself and finds himself to be insincere, he will not be obedient to his parents" (*Source Book*, p. 107). Heaven is one's ultimate parent; so, as Mencius puts it, "Those who obey Heaven are preserved; those who rebel against Heaven perish" (4.A.7). Nūr al-Ḥaqq took the two terms as translations of "obedience" (*ṭā'a*) and "disobedience" (*ma'ṣiya*), a basic Koranic pair. Obedience is to observe the divine commandments—to follow propriety—and disobedience is to go against them. Disobedience is a generic Koranic term for "sin"; Adam's sin was precisely that he disobeyed (Koran 20:121).

2. How obedience and rebellion shape the creative transformation is explained in what follows, but it is worth noting that Ibn al-'Arabī frequently discussed the manner in which human shortcomings are demanded by the "Self-so," as Liu would put it, that is, by the very reality of the way things are. Typically, he grounded this discussion in the diversity of the divine names, which call for diverse creatures. In reference to the issue of disobedience and rebellion, for example, he liked to quote this saying of the Prophet: "By Him in whose hand my soul is, if you had not sinned, God would have removed you and brought a people who do sin, then ask God's pardon and are forgiven." In other words, without sin, God would have no one to forgive, but God is by definition the Forgiver (*al-ghafūr*); so his eternal attribute of forgiveness demands the existence of sin in the world of time.

Humans are not mere puppets, however, but co-creators of the cosmos—the cosmos being defined as "everything other than God," a term that includes all prenatal and posthumous realms, that is, the full expanse of what the Indian traditions call samsara. Over the long term, human freedom and its attendant responsibility—that is, the fact that people answer for both virtue and vice—provide the very *raison d'être* of diverse realms of being, such as paradise and hell. See Chittick, *Imaginal Worlds*, chap. 7.

3. As noted under Diagram 1.12, the four humors—each of which has the qualities of one element—mix together to form the blend (*mizāj*), or constitution, of a thing. According to Ibn al-'Arabī, when the Koran says about God's creation of Adam, "He proportioned him and balanced him" (82:7), it is referring to God's shaping and molding of Adam's clay "with His own two hands" (38:75). By doing so, God gave him "a constitution that receives every form" (*Futūḥāt*, 4: 19; *Self-Disclosure*, p. 106). Then God blew "of His own spirit" (32:9)—that is, the "Ascribed Spirit"—into the clay. Each person, however, has a uniquely proportioned body; so each has a different receptivity toward the Spirit, and this results in differences of aptitude, intelligence, and virtue.

Hence the soul becomes manifest between the divine inblowing and the proportioned body; this is why the constitution displays traces in the souls and why souls come to be ranked according to excellence. For, in respect of the divine inblowing, there is no ranking in excellence. Ranking in excellence occurs only in the receptacles. (*Futūḥāt*, 2: 568; *Self-Disclosure*, p. 271)

4. According to general Islamic teachings, sinners who repent (*tawba*) of their wrongdoing will be forgiven, but not those who are obedient for a time but end up in wrongdoing.

5. Muslim texts generally consider hypocrisy (*nifāq*), which is to profess Islam outwardly but not to accept it in the heart, as the worst shortcoming of the soul. It is the opposite of sincerity (*ikhlāṣ*), the foremost of virtues, which is to act on the basis of *tawḥīd*, that is, for the sake of God alone. The Koran and Hadith place the hypocrites in the deepest pit of hell. Here Liu was pointing both to the ugliness of hypocrisy and to the praiseworthiness of not making a show of one's religiosity. Judging from some of the discussion in the rest of this section, especially the clause, "those who are really obedient want to borrow the name of the rebellious so as to conceal their obedience," Liu may have had in mind the Sufi notion of "blame" (*malāma*). Briefly, the "blameworthy" are those who follow Islamic teachings with sincerity but act in socially unacceptable ways to avoid the admiration of people. Ibn al-'Arabī took the concept to such a degree that he looked upon the "blameworthy" (*malāmiyya*) as the highest rank of human beings, calling them also the "Muhammadans," because they stand in the station of the prophet Muḥammad himself (*Sufi Path*, pp. 372ff).

# 4.11
## 修進功程圖

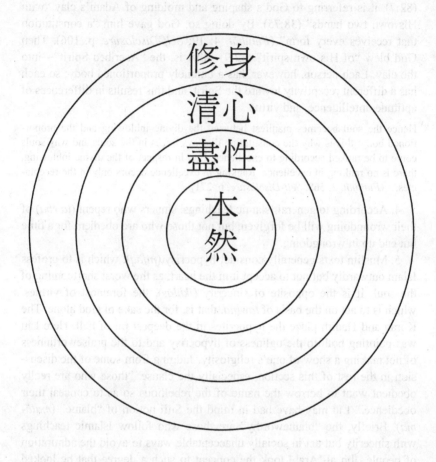

修身

清心

盡性

本然

# 4.11
## Diagram of the Procedure and Endeavor of Cultivation and Progress

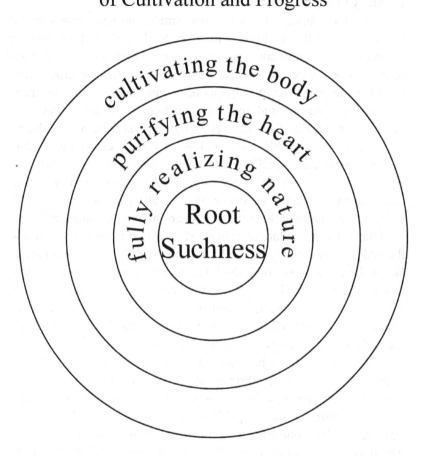

If humans had been begotten without appetite and desire, they could not comprehend the subtlety of sound, color, smell, and taste. If they did not have the endeavor of cultivation,[1] they could not circle back gradually to the Real that is the Root Suchness.

As for the subtlety of sound, color, smell, and taste, how can this be anything but the Real that is the Root Suchness?[2] Before reaching the endeavor of cultivation, however, body, heart, nature, and mandate may be burdened by any sound, color, smell, or taste. After reaching the endeavor of cultivation, sound, color, smell, and taste will be everywhere, and the Root Suchness will be everywhere. What is not separate from ears, eyes, mouth, and nose will be everywhere, and the invisible and inaudible will be everywhere. Seeing, hearing, tasting, and smelling will be everywhere, and the movement and stillness of the Root Suchness will be everywhere.[3] How, then, could one say that the endeavor of cultivation is involved superficially and insignificantly with body, heart, nature, and mandate?

What is the procedure of endeavor? It is said to be first rectifying the body, second purifying the heart, and third fully realizing nature. When the body is rectified, the body becomes the mirror of the true face of the Root Suchness. When the heart is purified, the heart becomes the light that reflects and is illuminated by the light of the World of Principles. When nature is fully realized, nature becomes the principle of the unity of Heaven and human.

How is the body to be rectified? The five affairs of the Sage's teaching are these: remembrance, by which one knows the place of coming home; propriety, by which one practices on the path of coming home; setting aside, by which one releases oneself from loves; fasting, by which one cuts oneself off from things; and assembly, by which one goes home to the Real.[4] In the midst of effort, all the meanings of pointers are embedded. Relying on the outside realm, they point to the inside meanings.

Among the five affairs, the pointers are profound and long-lasting only in the midst of propriety. In rising, standing, kneeling, and sitting, one sees in stillness the nature of the Root Suchness of the things and the I. One searches out and seeks the pointers of each affair, and, in relying on the pointers, the endeavor becomes continuous and thorough. Thereby the body can be rectified.[5]

How, then, is the heart to be made pure? Purification of the outside realm is to keep it without disturbance. More important is purification of inner virtue, which is to keep it without shade. The heart has seven layers, within which lodge the seven virtues. It also has five senses, each of which has a subtle function.

What does it mean to say that the heart has five senses? The heart has a subtle eye with which it can see the colors of the formless. The heart has a subtle ear with which it can hear the words of the voiceless. The heart has a subtle nose with which it can smell the fragrance of the subtle world. The heart has a subtle mouth with which it can taste the flavor of pleasing the Lord. The heart has a subtle discernment with which it can comprehend the principles of the fine and the coarse. Fully realizing the function of the five senses, it goes back to the seven virtues without deficiency and lack. Then the heart can be pure.[6]

How, then, is nature to be fully realized? By the heart's full realization of its ability to know, and, more important, by the form's full realization of its ability to practice. When the heart regards reflected luminosity as knowledge, then the principle leaves out no principle. When the form regards obedient response as practice, then the form comes home to the formless. When the Complete Substance is known and, furthermore, when the Great Function is known, then the nature of the I will be clear and the nature of the ten thousand things will not be outside it. When one practices what should be and one also practices why it should be so, one will expose and fully realize the subtlety. Then there will be no separation between the Majestic [Heaven] and this [nature].

Form and color are nature. Those who do not know take form and color as form and color. Those who know see that form and color are all heavenly nature.[7] Before the practice of form and color, there is no talk of nature. When there is the ability to practice form and color, there is still no talk of nature. When form is no different from nature, and nature is no different from form, then nature can be fully realized.

Reaching the pure heart from the rectified body and reaching fully realized nature from the pure heart are the cultivation and progress of ordinary people. This is from the outside to the inside. This is gradual cultivation.

When nature is fully realized, the heart is pure in itself, and when the heart is pure, the body is rectified in itself. This is the cultivation and progress of the sage. It is from the inside to the outside. This cultivation has no waiting. The cultivation and progress of the sage, however, is not something that one dares to wish for.[8]

### Notes

1. Cultivation (*xiu* 修) is the process of nurturing and refining oneself, and especially one's activities, by observing Propriety. It is what one needs to do in order to follow Confucius' instructions concerning perfect virtue: "To subdue one's self and return to propriety is perfect virtue" (*Analects* 12:1). The *Great Learning* associates it with the body, and Zhu Xi made it the fifth of the eight steps that lead to perfection: "Those who wished to cultivate their bodies would first make their hearts true." Legge translated this, "Wishing to cultivate their persons, they first rectified their hearts." The word suggests as its Arabic equivalent *tazkiyat al-nafs*, "the cultivation of the soul," a phrase derived from Koran 91:6–10 and commonly discussed as the means of achieving perfection (as in *Path*, chap. 3.6).

2. "Subtlety" (*miao*), as we have seen (under Diagram 1.3), is the invisible root of a thing, its spiritual principle. Liu was saying, in Islamic terms, that sensory phenomena can be nothing but the signs and traces of the divine names.

3. In other words, after realization, phenomena cease beings veils and become instead faces—"Wherever you turn, there is the face of God" (Koran 2:115). Ibn al-'Arabī frequently discussed the transformed vision that is achieved through cultivation. As for the situation as it is in itself, he described it this way:

"God is Subtle to His servants" [Koran 42:19]. Part of God's subtlety (*lutf*) is that it is He who comes to them in everything in which they are, but the servants' eyes fall only upon the occasions that they witness, so they attribute what they are in to these occasions. Thus the Real becomes manifest by being veiled, so He is the Manifest/the Veiled. He is the Nonmanifest because of the veil, not because of you, and He is the Manifest because of both you and the veil. So glory be to Him who veils Himself in His manifestation and becomes manifest in His veil! No eye witnesses anything other than Him, and no veils are lifted from Him.    (*Futūḥāt*, 3: 547; *Self-Disclosure*, p. 129)

4. That is, the five pillars of Islam, or the five bodily activities required of every Muslim: bearing witness to God's unity and Muḥammad's prophecy

(Shahadah), performing the ritual prayer (*ṣalāt*), paying the alms-tax (*zakāt*), fasting during the month of Ramadan, and making the pilgrimage (hajj) to Mecca. Liu listed the pillars here in terms of their deeper significance, not their external appearance. Elsewhere, as we have seen, he equated *li*, "propriety" or "ritual," with the Shariah, but here he identified it with the daily prayers, which are the most characteristic ritual practice of Islam, one that the Prophet called the "centerpole" of the religion. As noted in the first chapter of the Introduction, Liu provided a detailed explanation of the five pillars in four of the twenty chapters of *Tianfang dianli*, describing them in the manner of books on jurisprudence, but with greater concision. In Chapter 5 of that book, "A General Explanation of the Five Endeavors," he described how the pillars are the basis for cultivating the Way and achieving union with Heaven. In explaining the Shahadah, he called it, as here, "remembrance" (*nian* 念). Chapter 6 deals with *ṣalāt*, which he again called *li*, and Chapter 7 with both fasting and *zakāt*, which he called "tax" (*ke* 課) rather than "setting aside" (*she* 舍). Chapter 8 addresses assembly, that is, the hajj.

5. The fundamental importance that Liu gave to the *ṣalāt*, the ritual prayer, is typical of the whole tradition, beginning with the Koran and the Hadith. The Sufis are no exception, although they tend to stress *dhikr*, the remembrance of God—the ritual repetition of God's name—because it can be performed constantly, and because the essence of the *ṣalāt* is remembering God. As God says in the Koran, "Perform the *ṣalāt* to remember Me" (20:14). On the utter centrality of the ritual prayer for Ibn al-ʿArabī, see Chodkiewicz, *Ocean Without Shore*, chap. 5.

6. This paragraph is based on the following passage in Rāzī, found in the chapter "Explaining How to Make the Heart Limpid According to the Code of the Tariqah":

The soundness of the frame lies in the health of its senses, for it can perceive the whole of the Visible World with those five senses. In the same way, the heart has five senses. When they are healthy, it can perceive with them all of the Sovereigntarial and spiritual beings of the Unseen World.

Thus the heart has an eye through which it sees witnessings in the Unseen Realm. It has an ear through which it listens to the speech of the inhabitants of the Unseen and the speech of the Real. It has a nose through which it smells scents of the Unseen. It has a mouth through which it finds the taste of love, the sweetness of faith, and the flavor of gnosis.

Just as the frame's sense of touch is in all the organs so that all may benefit from touchable things, so also the heart has the intellect, so that the entirety of the heart may take benefit from all the intelligibles through the intellect. . . . This is exactly what God says in the Koran: When the senses of someone's heart are healthy, he has achieved deliverance and high degrees: "Those who come to God with a healthy heart" [26:89].   (*Path*, pp. 192–93/205–6)

7. This discussion can be taken as a commentary on Mencius 7.A.38: "Form and color are the heavenly nature. Only after someone becomes a sage can he put the form into practice." Legge's freer translation helps clarify the sense of the passage, but loses its more general significance: "The bodily organs with their functions belong to our Heaven-conferred nature. But a man must be a sage before he can satisfy the design of his bodily organization." Lau translates: "Our body and complexion are given to us by Heaven. Only a sage can give his body complete fulfillment."

8. Here Liu provides an Islamic answer to the Zen debate over whether enlightenment is to be achieved suddenly or gradually: only the prophets reach sudden enlightenment. As an example of a parallel Zen text, one can cite the *Platform Scripture*, which is attributed to the Sixth Patriarch, who died in the early eighth century:

Good and learned friends, in method there is no distinction between sudden enlightenment and gradual enlightenment. Among men, however, some are intelligent and others are stupid. Those who are deluded understand gradually, while the enlightened achieve understanding suddenly. But when they know their own hearts, then they see their own nature, and there is no difference in enlightenment. (*Source Book*, p. 434)

4.12

全體歸眞圖

## 4.12
## Diagram of the Coming Home to the
## Real of the Complete Substance

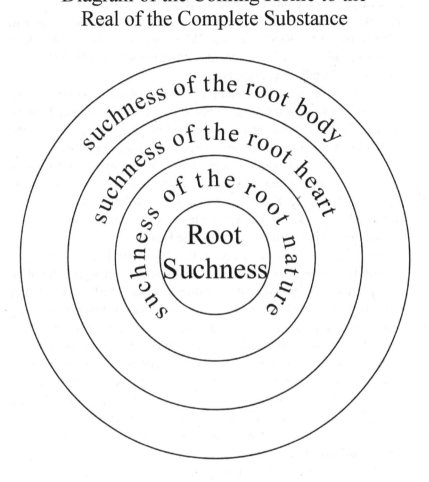

The Real cannot easily be talked about in terms of coming home.[1] If one seeks to come home before the period of cultivation, one will have no path of coming home to the Real. If one seeks to come home after the period of cultivation but without transformation, one will come home to the Real with self. When one has had no path, there cannot be talk of coming home, and when the self is still there, there also cannot be talk of coming home.

If you talk about coming home on the day of knowing the coming home, then knowing the coming home is not coming home. To have the act of coming home and to have the knowledge of coming home are two; you cannot talk of coming home when there are two.

If you talk about coming home while not knowing that there is coming home on the day of your own coming home, then not knowing is like knowing. Knowing that you do not know is also knowledge.[2] When you know, you cannot talk about coming home.

How then will you come home to the Real?

I say: Seeking to come home on the day of not knowing that you are coming home is to make use of cultivation. Through cultivation one sharpens and polishes the vital-energy and stuff[3] of the Latter Heaven. If you seek to come home while on the brink of coming home, then you should wave away and cast aside cultivation. For, if you cultivate but do not know how to wave it away and cast it aside, all cultivation will become an obstacle in coming home to the Real. Moreover, if you know how to wave it away and cast it aside, but you are not able to wave it away and cast it aside thoroughly, then all the waving away and casting aside will become an obstacle in coming home to the Real. Hence, the more you seek to come home, the less you are able to come home.

What is the way to wave it away and cast it aside?

I say: First you forget the anxious desires to come home, you forget the cultivation, and you also forget the Real.[4] Forgetting is the mechanism of coming home. So, in which ground should you forget? The place of forgetting is in seeing, hearing, speaking, and acting. In the ground of seeing, hearing, speaking, and acting, you may betray the Real, you may remember the Real, and you may forget the Real.

For example, if in seeing, you must seek for what the Real makes suitable to see, then certainly your seeing is not the Real. If in hearing, you must seek for what the Real makes suitable to hear, then certainly your hearing is not the Real. The heart that seeks the suitable is an obstacle to seeing and hearing. If there are obstacles, how can you talk of coming home?

If in speaking and acting, you must seek everything that is suitable for the Real, then certainly the speech and acts are not the Real. The heart that seeks the suitable is an obstacle to speaking and acting. If there are obstacles, how can you talk of coming home? Therefore, the more you seek to come home, the less you are able to come home.

How, then, do you forget? You forget the principle by which you see, and at the same time you forget the I that is seeing. You forget the principle by which you hear, and at the same time you forget the I that is hearing. You forget the principle by which you speak and act, and at the same time you forget the I that is speaking and acting.

If you know that you have forgotten, you cannot say that there is forgetting. You must forget the reason you have forgotten, and, more important, you must forget that you have forgotten the reason you have forgotten. This then would be real forgetting.

The one who really forgets is without the I and without others. When you are without the I and without others, the trace of coming home fades away. Only when the trace of coming home has faded away is it possible to come home to the subtle realm of the Real. Cultivating by way of not cultivating, progressing by way of not progressing, obtaining by way of not obtaining—only then can one come home without coming home. This is the meaning of the Complete Substance's coming home to the Real.[5]

## Notes

1. In translating Root Classic 4:86, "the Complete Substance comes home to the Real," Nūr al-Ḥaqq took "complete substance" as an adverb, "entirely" (*bi'l-kulliyya*), and explained that it means "with their bodies, their hearts, and their souls" (*Sharḥ*, p. 136/99). In other words, the return to

the Complete Substance and Great Function embraces all three levels of the human substance—body, heart, and nature.

2. There is a reference here to *Analects* 2.17: "Knowledge means . . . to know what you know and to know what you do not know." Daoists were especially fond of pointing to the wisdom of not-knowing, as in Zhuangzi: "Understanding that rests in what it does not understand is the finest" (Watson, p. 44), or (in another translation of the same passage), "He who knows to stop at what he does not know is perfect" (*Source Book*, p. 187). Neo-Confucians discussed the sage as the one who achieves the perfection of not knowing. Zhang Zai wrote: "When there is not knowing, then there is [true] knowing; if there is no 'not knowing,' there is no [true] knowing" (Kasoff, *The Thought of Chang Tsai*, p. 108). Or again:

Being "without knowledge" lies in there being nothing you do not know. If you say you have knowledge, then there are things you do not know. Only because [Confucius] was "without knowledge" was he able to "fully present both sides." This is what the *Change* [the *Yijing*] calls "quiescent and unmoving; when stimulated, then it penetrates." (Ibid.)

Sufis frequently discussed the theme of achieving the perfection of knowledge by not knowing, although its *locus classicus* is a saying by the Prophet's companion Abū Bakr, which Ibn al-'Arabī cited in the following:

The most knowledgeable of the knowers is he who knows that he knows what he knows and that he does not know what he does not know. . . . Abū Bakr said, "Incapacity to attain perception is itself perception." In other words, he perceived that there is something that he is incapable of perceiving. So this is knowledge / not knowledge. (*Futūḥāt*, 2: 619; *Sufi Path*, pp. 155–56)

3. As noted under Diagram 3.6, "the nature of vital-energy and stuff" is a Neo-Confucian term used to differentiate the individual nature from the nature shared in common. The process of cultivation aims at bringing this individual nature into harmony with the nature of heaven and earth.

4. The terminology here goes back at least to Zhuangzi, especially 5.8: "If virtue is preeminent, the form will be forgotten. When people do not forget what can be forgotten, but forget what cannot be forgotten—that may be called sincere forgetting" (cf. Watson, p. 75). Liu may also have in mind the Sufi concept of annihilation (*fanā'*), especially "the annihilation of annihilation" (*fanā' al-fanā'*), which Jāmī discussed in *Gleams* (*Chinese Gleams*, pp. 148–51).

5. Ibn al-'Arabī often discussed the paradoxes of practice. For example,

Since you have no escape from returning to Him, you should know that you are at Him from the first step, which is the first breath. So do not weary yourself by seeking ascent to Him, for that is nothing but your emerging from your desire such that you no longer witness it. For "He is with you wherever you are" [Koran 57:4], so your eyes will fall on none but Him. However, it remains for you to recognize Him. Were you to distinguish and recognize Him, you would not seek to ascend to Him, for you would not have lost Him.    (*Futūḥāt*, 4: 424; *Self-Disclosure*, p. 21)

# Volume 5

## Summary

Volume 5 is a supplemental explanation that summarizes those meanings of the macrocosm and the microcosm whose details have not yet been fully realized. The meaning is doubly fine and deep, but it does not go beyond the One Real. In the midst of the supplemental explanation is lodged the intention of sweeping away and obliterating. To supplement is to beautify, and to sweep away is to supplement. The finer the supplement, the more fully realized the sweeping; the quicker the sweeping, the more marvelous the supplement.

The principle is in a realm as if of neither being nor nonbeing, the text is between the explainable and the unexplainable, and the reader measures his strength and realizes his heart to the fullest. The explainable is to be explained by explanation, and the unexplainable is to be explained by not explaining. This is the good way of explanation in this book. If we were to explain the explainable with the unexplainable and explain the unexplainable with the explainable, then not only would the book be unexplainable, but also the reader would not be able to understand.[1]

## Notes

1. The summary sets the tone for the volume, especially the discussion under the last five diagrams. The basic theme is the coincidence of opposites, or the mysteries of union with the Real. Ibn al-'Arabī adopted a similar tone when he said that the furthest degree of perfection, which he sometimes called "the station of no station" (*maqām lā maqām*), is none other than bewilderment or perplexity (*ḥayra*).

Arrival at bewilderment in the Real is itself arrival at God. Bewilderment is the most magnificent thing that belongs to the folk of self-disclosure, because the forms are diverse for them in the One Entity. The limits are diverse because of the diversity of the forms, but limit does not apply to the Entity. The Entity is not witnessed, just as It is not known. Those who stop with the limits that follow upon the forms are bewildered, but those who know that there is an Entity that fluctuates through forms in the eyes of the viewers but not in Itself know that there is an Unknown Essence that is not known and not witnessed. (*Futūḥāt*, 4: 43; *Self-Disclosure*, p. 84)

## 5.1
### 眞一三品圖

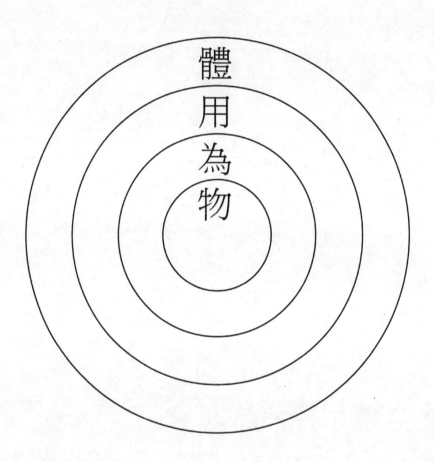

## 5.1
## Diagram of the Three Levels
## of the Real One

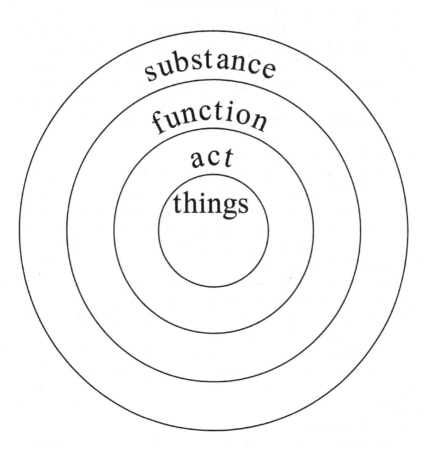

In the midst of the deep and dark that cannot be seen is the Real One, the Lord Ruler of the ten thousand beings. To be silent without attachment is called "substance"; to be luminously aware without leaving anything out is called "function"; to enumerate and differentiate without fail is called "act."[1]

Three levels are thus designated.[2] Function arises from substance, and act arises from function. This is the order that advances from inside to outside. Act is not separable from function, nor is function separable from substance. These are different names, yet they are the same reality in their essence. Hence, all the ten thousand beings of the unequal things are the manifestation and display of the different names of the same reality.

Nonetheless, there have never been three levels.[3] "Real" means not false. "One" designates not two. To be Real and to have substance, to be Real and to have function, to be Real and to have act—all of these are false. If they are false, how is there the Real? To be One and to have substance, to be One and to have function, to be One and to have act—this is not only to be two, it is also to be three. If they are three, how is there One?

Hence, in the midst of the Real One, there is no going or coming, no delusion or awakening, no movement or stillness, no rising or perishing. How can there be substance? How can there be function? How can there be act?

But, without substance, from whence does function arise? Without function, from whence is act begotten? Without act, from whence do the ten thousand beings of the unequal things become manifest? Thus we know that the Real One must have substance, it must have function, and it must have act. How could we know that this is not so?

The Real One has never been without substance, but It has never had substance. The Real One has never been without function, but It has never had function. The Real One has never been without act, but It has never had act. This is the root realm of the Real One.

There has never been substance without its being the substance of the Real One. There has never been function without its being the function of the Real One. There has never been act without its being the act of the Real One. This is the manifestation and display of the Real One.

The realm of manifestation and display is not the True Being of the root realm. The manifestation and display of the three levels is still not the True Being of the Real One's root realm. Much less can the ten thousand things that the three levels manifest and display be the True Being of the root realm.

Although the ten thousand beings of the unequal things are not the True Being of the Real One's root realm, the ten thousand manifested and displayed things have never been without the manifestation and display of the Real One's Root Suchness.

The sage said, "Hidden it is named 'Real'; manifest it is named 'thing.' "[4] This means that there is nothing that is not the Real. When it becomes manifest as a formless thing, the formless thing is the Real. When it becomes manifest as a thing with form, the thing with form is the Real. When it becomes manifest as the time of the ongoing flow, the time is the Real. When it becomes manifest as a fixed place, the place is the Real. Since there is no place that is not manifest, there is no place that is not the Real. This is what makes the Real One the Real One.

## Notes

1. This paragraph summarizes Diagrams 1.2–1.4. It may be based on Gleam 35 (*Chinese Gleams*, pp. 206–7), in which Jāmī described the reality of the Real Being as Essence, attributes, and acts. As Ibn al-'Arabī wrote, the "Divine Presence" (*al-ḥaḍrat al-ilāhiyya*, i.e., the sphere of reality that pertains strictly to God) is "the Essence, the attributes, and the acts" (*Futūḥāt*, 4: 196, 407). As explained by Nūr al-Ḥaqq under Diagram 1.4, all three terms designate the same Real Being, but from different standpoints. The Essence is the very reality of God in himself as known only to himself; this is the God of negative theology, from whom qualities can only be negated. The attributes (also called the names) are the qualities and characteristics of this supreme Reality the moment we think of it as "God," that is, as the Creator of the universe, or as the Living, Knowing, Desiring, and Powerful Being who gives rise to reality as we know it. The "acts" are the diverse modalities of creative activity, or the creatures themselves envisaged in their relationship to the Root Being.

2. The discussion of the three levels of the Real One under Diagrams 5.1–5.3 subdivides each level into three further levels in a manner that

parallels Wang Daiyu (*Chinese Gleams*, pp. 84–100). Liu, however, did not seem to be indebted to the details of Wang's discussion, and this whole section is one of the more original parts of the book.

If we look only at this diagram and its explanation, it seems that the three levels of oneness are no different from those described in Diagrams 1.2–1.4. The text of the Root Classic, however, alerts us to the fact that Liu was looking at the levels while making a clear differentiation between Origin and Return, rather than, as in 1.2–1.4, speaking only of the Origin. Liu said several things in the Root Classic that he did not repeat here in Volume 5, and these deserve some explanation. Chapter 5 of the Root Classic begins:

> Only the One is not a number,
>> but all numbers are the One.
>> At the beginning, the True Being
>> governs the One and governs the numbers.
>> Oneness is its substance,
>> and the numbers are its functions.   (5:1–6)

The discussion of these two sorts of oneness, supra-numerical and numerical, is common among Ibn al-'Arabī's followers, who often referred to them as Exclusive Unity (*aḥadiyya*) and Inclusive Unity (*wāḥidiyya*). Ibn al-'Arabī himself sometimes called them "the unity of the One" (*aḥadiyyat al-aḥad*) and "the unity of manyness" (*aḥadiyyat al-kathra*; *Sufi Path*, pp. 25, 260, 337–38; cf. *Rays*, pp. 98–99; and *Flashes*, pp. 99, 148). The One is the Real Existence, and to speak of its unity is precisely to talk about *waḥdat al-wujūd*, "the Oneness of Existence." But that same One, inasmuch as it is conscious and aware, is omniscient, and in this respect we can speak of "the manyness of [the divine] knowledge" (*kathrat al-'ilm*). The many objects of knowledge are the infinite fixed entities. Hence, "Oneness is the substance" of the Real Existence, and the numbers—manyness, the infinite entities—are its functions. When functions are differentiated from acts, then the activity of God is to give existence to the entities, which have no being of their own at the stage of divine knowledge, for there is no being but the Real Being. The Root Classic continues:

> The undifferentiated suchness of Substance and function
>> is named "the Real One."
>> The Substance's giving rise to the functions
>> is named "the Numerical One."
>> The functions' returning and coming home to the Substance
>> is named "the Embodied One."   (5:7–12)

Real One and Numerical One have parallels in Exclusive Unity and Inclusive Unity, but Liu's explanation is closer to what is said about the Most Holy Effusion (*fayḍ-i aqdas*) and the Holy Effusion (*fayḍ-i muqaddas*), which Jāmī discussed in Gleam 36 (*Chinese Gleams*, pp. 206–9). The Most Holy Effusion is the Real's self-consciousness, which is luminous awareness of everything demanded by its own infinity, namely, the cosmos and all that it contains for all eternity. The Holy Effusion is then the appearance of the cosmos, which is nothing but the manifestation of the Real Being's infinite possibilities.

It is more difficult to suggest parallel terminology for the Embodied One, which is the return of the many to the One. We are not aware that there is any Arabic word that expresses this idea quite so explicitly. Certainly, when Ibn al-'Arabī analyzed the nature of the Perfect Human Being, the whole discussion circles around the annihilation (*fanā'*) of apparent multiplicity and the subsistence (*baqā'*) of true unity. Nothing is left at the end of the journey but the Real in his self-disclosure. There cannot be two, only the One. This is why Ibn al-'Arabī and his followers disliked the term employed by some Sufis, *ittiḥād*, "unification"—it implies that two have become one. In fact, the One remains in its oneness as it ever was, and illusory multiplicity disappears.

Nūr al-Ḥaqq was aware that the Arabic and Persian sources offer no synonym for Liu's "Embodied One." In his translation of the Root Classic, he used the standard "Exclusive Unity" and "Inclusive Unity" for the first two levels, but for the third, he coined the term *muttaḥidiyya*, "unifiedness." *Muttaḥid*, meaning unified or united, is an adjective derived from *ittiḥād*, "unification," and the suffix *iyya* turns it into an abstract noun. Faced with the passage, "The three ones are not three:/They are one with three meanings" (5:13–14), Nūr translated and commented (boldface marks quotations from *Subtleties*):

**The three ones**, that is, Exclusive Unity, Inclusive Unity, and Unifiedness, **are not three** independent realities; **rather,** they are **a single reality**, that is, the reality of the Real Existence, **that has three meanings**, that is, levels: the level of nonmanifestation, which is called "Exclusive Unity"; the level of manifestation, which is called "Inclusive Unity"; and the level of nonmanifestation after manifestation, which is called "Unifiedness." In reality these three are the reality of the Real Existence. As for manifestation and nonmanifestation, firstness and lastness, these are Its relations and respects. The Prophet said, "Glory be to Him who subtilized Himself and called it 'Real,' and glory be to Him who densified Himself and called it 'creation'!"

This is like an ocean without shore or limit. From it vapor rises into the air, becomes amassed, and is called "clouds." The clouds turn into drops and are called "rain." The rain gathers together and is called "flood." The floods gather together and are called "rivers." When the rivers return to the ocean, this is the original ocean, so there is nothing but the ocean from which "levels" appeared. (*Sharḥ*, pp. 141–42/102)

Liu's next three lines clarify the differing functions of the Three Ones: "The Real One gives rise to transformation, / the Numerical One perfects transformation, / the Embodied One transforms transformation" (5:15–17). Nūr understood transformation to mean "creation" (*takhlīq*). If he were to say, however, in the third of these lines, "creates creation," that would be the meaning of the first line; so he understands it to mean "annihilates" in the sense that the term has generally been understood in the Sufi tradition. He was careful to note that the "annihilation" of things takes place through "witnessing" (*shuhūd*), that is, seeing things as they truly are. He translated and commented on the passage:

**Exclusive Unity originates creation**, which is to say that when He desires to create the existent things, He discloses His Essence to His Essence in knowledge, thus actualizing the fixed entities in His knowledge. The level of **Inclusive Unity actualizes** creation, since He first makes manifest the First Engendered Being with the command "Be!," and then [He makes manifest] the rest of the beings in the Sovereignty and the Kingdom. **And** the level of **Unifiedness annihilates it**, that is, annihilates creation within Exclusive Unity through the eye of witnessing. (*Sharḥ*, pp. 142/102–3)

3. From here to the end of this section, Liu engaged in a *coincidentia oppositorum* argument typical of the school of Ibn al-'Arabī, although he carried it out in Chinese terms. The basic question is how the Real Being can be one and simultaneously named by many names and attributes—precisely the issue addressed in Nūr al-Ḥaqq's analogy of water and the various forms it takes. The discussion has been a constant one in Islamic theology, especially in its Sufi and philosophical forms. Even the Ash'arite theologians, forced to address the fact that the Divine Reality cannot fit into the either-or categories of Aristotelian logic, had to come up with contradictory formulas such as "The attributes are neither He nor other than He."

4. This may be Jāmī, in particular his statement, "The cosmos is the manifest of the Real, and the Real is the nonmanifest of the cosmos" (*Chinese Gleams*, p. 184). The discussion of all things as the manifestation of the Real could easily be based on Gleam 27 (ibid., pp. 194–95).

## 5.2
數一三品圖

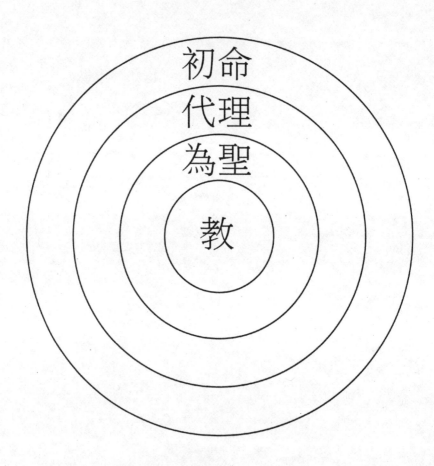

## 5.2
## Diagram of the Three Levels
## of the Numerical One

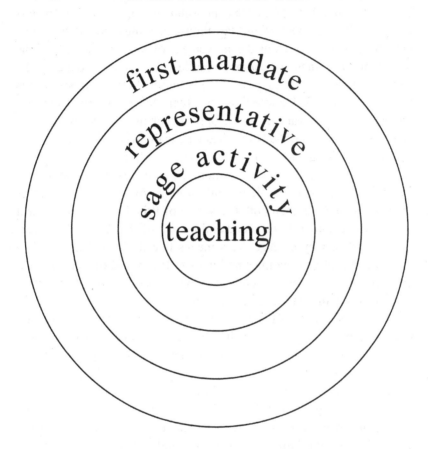

first mandate

representative

sage activity

teaching

The oneness of the Real One means its uniqueness. It means that the Unique One has no mate, the Honored Unique One has no mate, the Great Unique One has no mate, the Real Unique One has no mate.

The oneness of the Numerical One is that from which numbers begin.[1] The numbers of the ten thousand principles arise from this One, and the numbers of the ten thousand things extend from this One. Its being arises from the movement of the one thought of the Real One,[2] and then it becomes manifest. It is the opposite of the Real; so the Real One is real, and the Numerical One is illusory.[3] It is the opposite of the Honored; so the Real One is lord, and the Numerical One is servant. It is the opposite of the Great; so the Real One is the ocean, and the Numerical One is the waves.[4]

These are designated as One, yet they are different. If we compare them, no one would be so presumptuous as to make the Numerical One match the Real One. If we talk in terms of the root measure of the Numerical One, then both the World of Principles and the World of Images become differentiated and branch off from this Numerical One, and then they emerge. This means that the Real One that follows the World of Principles and goes to the World of Images must also follow this to emerge. Only then will it become manifest and be displayed according to its own intention.

The root measure of the Numerical One is also like this. The origin of its beginning and end, its root and branches, also has three levels. These are called "the First Mandate," "the representative," and "sage activity."[5]

The First Mandate is the chief manifestation of the Real One, and it is the earliest beginning of the act of the Mandate. The representative comes into being from this First Mandate and, on behalf of the Real One, exposes the affairs of transforming and nurturing. Sage activity also has the meaning of representative, but, through having the body of color,[6] living in the world, governing the people by the people, and representing the Real One, it broadly proclaims the utmost Way.

These are called "the three levels." These three levels do not come into being as three levels by the Numerical One's own act of lordly sustaining. The Numerical One becomes manifest and comes into being from the movement of the one thought of the Real One. Then the

Numerical One moves because of the movement of this one thought. It moves such that it cannot not move, and it moves as the Real One desires it to move without itself ever knowing why it moves. Thus the movement of the representative comes into being from the First Mandate. It represents such that it cannot not represent, not that the Numerical One itself has sovereignty. The movement of sage activity comes into being from the representative. The sage is such that he cannot not be a sage, not that the Numerical One itself has sovereignty.

Although the subsequent movement truly arrives incessantly, if we ask the Numerical One how there can be this movement that cannot cease for a moment, the Numerical One does not know. The reason that the Numerical One cannot know is again that it is the Real One's self-activity of manifestation and display.

The reason that the Real One's self-activity of manifestation and display must be entrusted to the Numerical One is that the Real One is not tainted with the illusory or mixed with numbers. Not to be tainted with the illusory is to be the Ultimate Real; not to be mixed with numbers is to be the Utmost One. That which is the Utmost Real and the Utmost One, in which illusion and number have no share, is the root realm of the Real One. The Real One has no illusion or number, yet it is between hidden and manifest according to its own intention. This is why the Real One is subtly the Real One, and the Numerical One is also subtly the Real One.

## Notes

1. The contrast between the Real One and the Numerical One may be based on Gleams 17 and 19 (*Chinese Gleams*, pp. 160–63, 168–69); or on *Rays*, pp. 98–99; or *Flashes*, p. 99.

2. In Buddhism, there is a good deal of discussion of one thought (*yinian* 一念), or one instant of thought, in relation to the achievement of detachment and freedom. As the *Platform Scripture* puts it, "If one single instant of thought is attached to anything, then every thought will be attached. That is bondage" (*Source Book*, p. 434). Here the text means the unitary knowledge of God, the self-awareness of the Hidden Treasure. "Movement" (*dong*) most likely translates *tajallī*, "self-disclosure." In Gleam 16 Jāmī

said that "the First Self-disclosure" is that the Essence "discloses Itself by Itself to Itself." Liu rendered this as "the Root Substance . . . saw by Itself within Itself" (*Chinese Gleams*, pp. 158–59). Jāmī went on to say that after the First Self-disclosure, there is a Second Self-disclosure, then a Third, and so on; Liu translated these as First, Second, and Third Movement.

3. This is a relative illusoriness, deriving from the application of *tawḥīd*: "There is no god but God," so "There is none real but the Real." In other words, nothing is truly one and truly real but the Real One.

4. Ocean and waves are standard imagery in Sufi poetry. Jāmī offered an example in *Gleams*, one of the few instances in which Liu translated the poetry into Chinese (*Chinese Gleams*, pp. 194–95).

5. In Wang Daiyu's discussion of the three levels of the Numerical One, only the second has the same name (*Chinese Gleams*, pp. 93–95). As seen in Diagram 1.5, the First Mandate is the engendering command "Be!," also called the Breath of the All-merciful, because within it is articulated every divine word, that is, every created thing. As the one word that gives rise to all words, the engendering command comprehends every possibility in its unity, and the "beings" are simply its differentiations, although it remains forever one, just like our own breath when we speak. As noted, Nasafī's favorite term for this mandate is Ascribed Spirit (Liu's "Nature of Continuity").

"Representative" may be a translation of *khalīfa*, "vicegerent." According to the Koran (2:30), God created Adam to be his vicegerent in the earth. For Ibn al-ʿArabī and others, vicegerency is the supreme human function, achieved only by prophets and perfect human beings. Rāzī wrote of this rank after having mentioned God's unique favors bestowed only on Adam, such as kneading his clay with his own two hands and blowing into him of his own spirit (i.e., the Ascribed Spirit). The goal of human life should be to actualize the potentialities of the Spirit within:

The perfection of the level of the [human] spirit lies in its becoming adorned with the attributes of Lordship so that it may be worthy for the vicegerency of that Presence. (*Path*, p. 211/221)

The reality of the vicegerency lies in this: God discloses Himself to [man] through His Essence and all Lordly attributes so that all the attributes may come to exist within him. (*Path*, p. 328/322)

In his version of the diagram, Nūr al-Ḥaqq called the Numerical One "Inclusive Unity" and he named the three levels "Command" (*amr*), "Sanctity" (*walāya*), and "Prophecy" (*nubuwwa*). At the center, in place of "teaching," he has *al-islām*. Although this word, in a narrow sense, means the religion that nowadays goes by the name, in a broader, Koranic sense, it designates the attribute of submission and surrender to God characteristic of all prophets and their sincere followers; thus the Koran (e.g., 2:132) can talk about Abraham and other pre-Islamic figures as "Muslims."

Nūr's explanation is largely based on a section of Nasafī called "On the True Knowledge of Sanctity and Prophethood," and this may indeed be one of Liu's sources. Nasafī wanted to show that the Command/Mandate is the Muhammadan Spirit, and as such it is receptive to God on one side and active toward the world on the other; he called its receptivity *walāya*, or "sanctity," and its activity "prophethood."

The word *walāya* is derived from *walī*, an important Koranic term that means "friend," "someone given nearness," and "someone given authority." God has "friends" to whom the Koran promises paradise, and God himself is the "friend" of the believers. One of the heated topics of discussion among theologians and Sufis was the relationship between prophets and friends. In Western scholarship, *walī* is usually translated as "saint," although most scholars are well aware that this English/Christian term can be misleading. Ibn al-'Arabī pointed out that friendship with God extends into the afterlife, whereas being God's prophet or messenger pertains only to this life, since there is no need for prophets in the next realm. For this and other reasons, he considered sanctity as the highest human station, even higher than prophethood or messengerhood. Nonetheless, prophets are first and foremost friends of God, and their prophetic functions are added to their sanctity and show that their ranking in the hierarchy of human beings is beyond that of ordinary saints. Every messenger is a prophet, but not every prophet is a messenger; likewise, every prophet is a saint, but not every saint is a prophet. Hence the normative hierarchy—messenger, then prophet, then saint—is preserved. Liu translated the term *walī* as "worthy" and understood it precisely in this normative sense—those whose virtuous traits place them above the believers and below the prophets (as, for example, in Diagram 1.6).

In explaining the relationship between prophethood and sanctity, Nasafī wrote:

The First Substance [i.e., the Ascribed Spirit] does two things: First, it receives effusion from God, and second, it conveys effusion to God's creatures. If it is said that Muḥammad does two things—that he takes from God and conveys to the creatures—this is correct, since the First Substance is the same as the spirit of Muḥammad. . . . The name of the side of the First Substance that takes from God is "sanctity," and the name of the side of the First Substance that conveys to God's creatures is "prophethood." Hence, sanctity is the inner side of prophethood, and prophethood is the outer side of sanctity; both are attributes of Muḥammad.    (*Goal*, pp. 245/82–83; cf. *Sharḥ*, pp. 143–45/104–5)

6. The body of color (*seshen* 色身) is the phenomenal body, the fleshly body.

5.3

體一三品圖

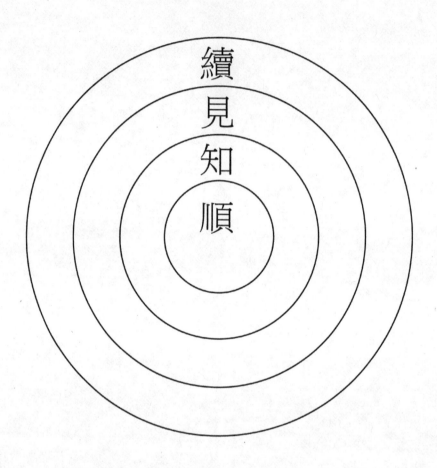

## 5.3
## Diagram of the Three Levels
## of the Embodied One

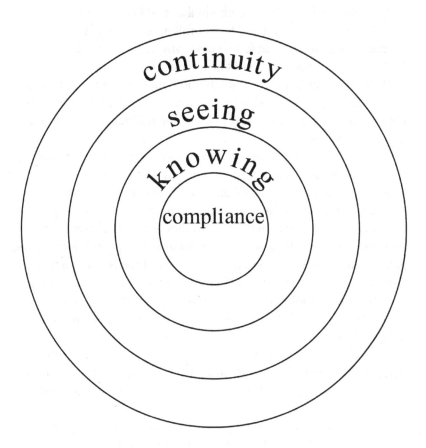

When humans are begotten, there are three bodies—the bodily body,[1] the heart body, and the nature body. In embodying the Real One with the body, there are also three, and that is embodiment with these three bodies.

With the bodily body we embody the Real One; our endeavor is to comply and follow.[2] To comply and follow is to know what ought to be done without being able to know why it is so. At this level we know the name, but we do not know the reality.

With the heart body we embody the Real One; our endeavor is to understand. To understand is to see why it is so but not to be able to obtain why it is so. At this level we see the differentiation, but we do not see the union.

With the nature body we embody the Real One; our endeavor is to be without interval. To be without interval is to be rooted in why it is so and to be undifferentiated from why it is so; this is the utmost.

These three levels have been the comprehensive meaning of the cultivation of the Real from ancient times until now.[3] Sometimes the sequence of these three levels is contained in the endeavor of one person, and sometimes the sequence of the three is differentiated to make three sorts of people. In the midst of the three levels, those who embody through knowing are shallow, those who embody through seeing are deep, and those who embody through nature are too deep to be fathomed.[4]

To embody the One through nature, however, is to embody it while having the I.[5] If it is embodied while having the I, the I still has coming and going. If it has coming and going, traces are still preserved.

If the One embodies the I, there will be no coming and going. But, if the One embodies the I and the I still knows that the act of the One has embodied the I, then the traces have not yet been transformed; if the I does not know that, then the traces have disappeared.

Even if the I does not know that the One has embodied the I, the I cannot be certain that the One itself does not know. If the One knows, then there is still knowledge; so there is not yet transformation. Only when the I does not know that there is the One who has embodied the I, and the One also does not know that there is an I that can be embodied, is there transformation.

## Notes

1. In the expression "bodily body," *shenti* 身體, *shen* designates the physical body that is contrasted with the heart, and *ti* designates the body that is also embodiment and substance. One might also translate it as "bodily substance," in which case, the other two terms would be "heart substance" and "nature substance."

2. What Liu is saying here is that each of the three levels of the human substance needs to be transformed appropriately. The body can achieve transformation by following the Shariah (Propriety), the heart by conforming to the Tariqah (the Way), and nature by realizing the Haqiqah (the Real). Those who perform only the practices know what is to be done but not why they should do it; they follow the rules of propriety without understanding the theological, metaphysical, and moral roots. Those who understand in the heart grasp the rationale behind what is to be done and achieve a vision of the way things actually are, but they have not yet achieved unmediated vision, integration of the soul, and realization. Those who achieve perfection rejoin the Nature of Continuity and return to the Real itself. It is the last group who follow the Prophet's footsteps on the *mi'rāj*, the ascent to God.

3. This view of things accords easily with the Koran's depiction of the universality of *tawḥīd* and prophecy and the understanding that "religion" deals with the three basic levels of Shariah, Tariqah, and Haqiqah; or *islām*, *īmān*, and *iḥsān*; or transformation of body, heart, and nature.

4. This paragraph is a clear reference to another tripartite scheme, one that Nūr al-Ḥaqq incorporated into his version of the diagram. From this standpoint, the discussion circles around three sorts of "certainty" (*yaqīn*) mentioned in the Koran: "knowledge" (*'ilm*) of certainty, "eye" (*'ayn*) of certainty, and "truth/reality/real" (*ḥaqq*) of certainty. Jāmī explained them like this:

When someone closes his eyes and has knowledge of the existence of fire by way of the evidence of heat, this is "knowledge of certainty." When he opens his eyes and sees the fire face to face, this is "the eye of certainty." When he falls into the fire and becomes nothing, and when the attributes of the fire—like burning and giving illumination—become manifest from him, this is "the truth of certainty." . . .

The possessor of the knowledge of certainty seeks for the object of his knowledge (*ma'lūm*) to become the object of his witnessing (*mashhūd*); so he has no serenity or ease in his knowledge. The possessor of the eye of certainty seeks for annihilation in what he witnesses, disappearance of his own entification, and knowledge and vision of himself as the same as what he witnesses; so he has no serenity in his witnessing. When his entification disappears, however, and when the object of his witnessing sits in place of him, then he has realized the truth of certainty. He has achieved serenity, and no level remains in knowledge for which to seek.   (*Rays*, pp. 138, 140, commentary on *Flashes*, pp. 119–20)

In Root Classic 5:22–24, Liu wrote that obeying the Real results first in knowledge, then in seeing, and then in not being cut off. Nūr al-Ḥaqq said that obedience (*ṭā'a*) begins in knowledge, then reaches witnessing, and finally results in not being cut off (*inqiṭā'*), a stage that he equated with "union" or "joining" (*wiṣāl*) with God, a standard Sufi expression. He explained as follows:

One begins these acts of obedience by knowledge, that is, first, by knowing God and the rulings (*aḥkām*) of the Shariah, while these are linked with worthy acts (*al-a'māl al-ṣāliḥa*). This is called "the knowledge of certainty," and it belongs to the folk of the Shariah.

Second, there is disciplining the soul by denying it its own caprice (*hawā*) and burdening it with the observances handed down from the Prophet and received from the chain (*silsila*) of the pure (*aṣfiyā'* [the Sufi teachers]), namely, the rules for purifying and cultivating the soul, making the heart limpid, and adorning the spirit; finally, one may reach witnessing, that is, witnessing of the Real. This is called "the eye of certainty," and it belongs to the folk of the Tariqah.

The furthest end of these acts of obedience is never to be cut off from the Real. This is called "the truth of certainty," and it belongs to the folk of the Haqiqah.

Thus, the level of Unifiedness also has three levels: the knowledge of certainty; the eye of certainty, which is witnessing; and the truth of certainty, which is union. (*Sharḥ*, pp. 146–47/106)

Liu noted that Root Classic 5:18–24 is derived from *Path*, but we have not been able to find any passage there that makes these points in such condensed fashion. Certainly, this is the general theme of the book, whose very title includes the phrase, "from the Origin to the Return." Several passages could be taken as the inspiration for this diagram, such as the following (note the lapse into paradoxical language typical of texts that speak of the ultimate perfection):

These are the benefits that accrue from the attachment of the spirit to the body: it recognizes the pure Essence of the Real through unity, and it discerns all the attributes of the Divinity—the knowable as seeable, the seeable as reachable, the reachable as tasteable, the tasteable as be-able, the be-able as not be-able, and the not be-able as be-able. . . . Had the spirit not achieved these perceptions through its attachment to the frame and had it not gained tools, instruments, means, and preparedness pertaining to the Unseen and the Visible, it would never have been able to reach this station in asserting the unity (*tawḥīd*) of and knowing the Essence and attributes of [God, who is] the Knower of the Unseen and the Visible. (*Path*, pp. 124–25/147)

5. From here to the end of this section, Liu meditated on the mysteries of annihilation in the One; this may be a further explanation of "forgetting the forgetting," mentioned under Diagram 4.12. Ibn al-'Arabī and his followers addressed these issues in a variety of ways. The basic principle is that the absolute oneness of God allows for no multiplicity whatsoever; in order for true realization of the Real to occur, the traces of cosmic existence must disappear. In this sort of context, Ibn al-'Arabī often mentioned the formula "None knows God but God." To the extent human knowledge is tainted by body, soul, or spirit, it cannot be true knowledge of unity. Nearness is achieved when the servant's attributes disappear and God becomes "the hearing with which he sees," and so on (cf. *Sufi Path*, pp. 325ff). Among Liu's sources, *Rays* deals with the mysteries of annihilation and subsistence in the most detail, given that 'Irāqī's *Flashes* is concerned mainly with the achievement of union with God through love.

**5.4**

三一通義圖

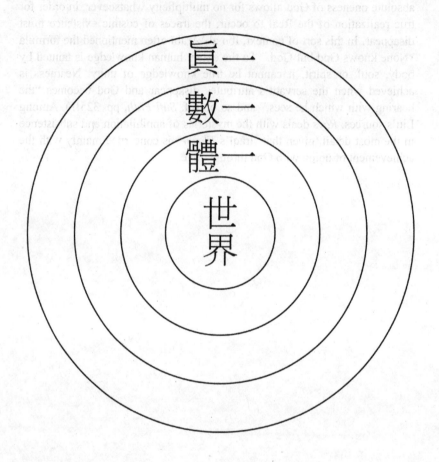

## 5.4
## Diagram of the Meaning of the
## Pervading of the Three Ones

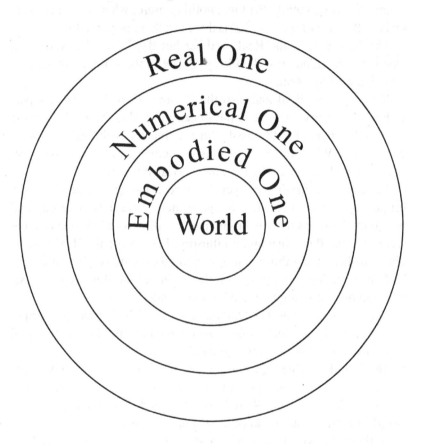

"Pervading" means that they are three while being one.[1]

When this pervades that, it is called "pervading"; there must be that if this is to pervade it. When that pervades this, it is called "pervading"; there must be this if that is to pervade it. If we suppose that there is only the One, merely the One, nothing more, what could pervade? Only in the case of the One that is three can there be pervading.[2]

The Real One is the Real, nothing but the Real. The Numerical One is the Real, but also the illusory.[3] The Embodied One is the illusory, but also the Real.

If there is the Real and also the illusory, then the Real has pervaded the illusory. If there is the illusory and also the Real, then the illusory has pervaded the Real. But the illusory is the manifestation of the Real. When the Real of illusory being has pervaded the Real of the Root Being, then the Real has pervaded the Real.

Time has the bright day, yet, because it has the black night, the bright day can be discerned. Suppose there were only pure day and no night. How could the bright day be discerned? Suppose there were only the Pure Real and no illusory. How could the Real One be distinguished? As a thing, moreover, the Real One is silent suchness without direction and place. The Real without the illusory is one silent suchness, nothing more. What then could it pervade?

Thus we know that it is One but also three. It is three and cannot not be three. That which is three and cannot not be three is the Real One's own act of hiding and manifesting.

The world is where the three Ones lodge as a whole and where pervading can be manifest. Outside the world there is a world, and that is the world of the Real Principle. Inside the world there is a world, and that is the world of the Human Ultimate.

Without the world of heaven and earth, the world of the Human Ultimate would have no assistance. Without the world of the Human Ultimate, the world of the Real Principle would have no position. Without the world of the Real Principle, the world of the Human Ultimate and the world of heaven and earth would have no way of becoming manifest by themselves. Thus the being of the world is a being that cannot not be. The being that cannot not be is the Real One's own act of hiding and manifesting.[4]

When the Real One manifests itself as the Numerical One, the Numerical One is the Real One's pervading. It is not that there is a distinct Numerical One outside the Real One. When the Numerical One manifests itself as the Embodied One, the Embodied One is the Numerical One's pervading. It is not that there is a distinct Embodied One outside the Numerical One.

The Three Ones become manifest in the world, and the world is what is pervaded by the Three Ones. Because of the pervading of the Three, there is a world. Because of the world, it is possible for the pervading of the Three to become manifest. The whole is the Real One's own act of hiding and manifesting.

The Real One's own act of hiding and manifesting is what the Real One arouses with the movement of the one thought. If the movement of the one thought were to be eliminated, we do not know whether there would still be the possibility of the pervading of the Three Ones.

## Notes

1. The basic issue here is why the many must be present in the One "before" there can be a universe, and why the many can be nothing but the manifestation of the One. The key term is *tong* 通, "pervading," often translated as "penetration," although in Buddhist contexts it takes on the meaning of being free and unrestricted. Given that the Real Being is one, all apparent or "illusory" being must be a manifestation of the One Being, and all things must somehow be present within the One.

2. Ibn al-'Arabī has a parallel discussion in which he explained the role of triplicity (*tathlīth*) both in God and in creation (see Murata, *Tao*, pp. 151–53); Jāmī amplified on his discussions in some of his books (e.g., *Naqd*, pp. 194–97). For example, Ibn al-'Arabī wrote:

Obviously, nothing comes to be from one. The first of the numbers is two, and nothing whatsoever comes to be from two unless there is a third thing that couples the two, ties one of them to the other, and brings them together. At this point what is engendered from them will be engendered, according to the situation of the two, whether they be two divine names, or two supraformal or sensory things—whatever they may be.   (*Futūḥāt*, 3: 126)

3. In the Muslim philosophical and theological perspectives, the contrast between what Liu is calling "real" (*zhen*) and "illusory" (*huan*) typically proceeds in language such as "Necessity" (*wujūb*) and "possibility" or

"contingency" (*imkān*), and "eternal" (*qadīm*) and "newly arrived" (*muḥ-dath*). Generally, these schools are averse to speaking of appearances as "illusion." In contrast, Ibn al-'Arabī and his followers were happy to pair "Real" (*ḥaqq*) with "imagination" (*khayāl*). The latter term also means "image" (as in a mirror image), and it can have the same sort of negative connotations as "illusion," especially in phrases like *wahm wa khayāl*, which in Persian is a likely candidate to translate "illusion." Nonetheless, the negative connotations of "illusion" in English are too strong to suggest what Ibn al-'Arabī had in mind, given that in his view, imagination/image is simply the self-disclosure of the Real. It plays the role of "illusion" only if we fail to see it for what it is. (The parallels with the Advaitan concept of Maya are obvious.)

In Ibn al-'Arabī's way of looking at things, *khayāl* (and so also its near synonym *barzakh*, or "isthmus") is the perfect word to express the ambiguity of everything in the cosmos. All things simultaneously manifest and hide the Real. The Koran tells us: "Everywhere you turn, there is the face of God" (2:115), but each face of God is also his veil (*Self-Disclosure*, chaps. 3–4). Everything is He/not He, at once Real and not Real, Being and nonbeing; or, as Liu put it here, "the Real One's own act of hiding and manifesting." The cosmos as a whole, defined as "everything other than God," is imagination, even "God's dream." Nonetheless, as Jāmī wrote, "Yes, the world is all imagination, but/within it Reality discloses Itself eternally" (*Chinese Gleams*, p. 188). In a quatrain, he put it this way:

> Let me tell you without concealment a story of the Friend:
> All is from Him and, if you look closely, all is He.
> His beauty is unveiled in every atom of being,
> your veil is your many-layered imagination.    (*Rays*, p. 65)

Nasafī had much to say along the same lines. In explaining the views of the "Folk of Oneness," he wrote:

Existence is of two sorts: true (*ḥaqīqī*) and imaginal (*khayālī*). True Existence is the existence of God, and imaginal existence is the existence of the cosmos and everything within it. . . . The cosmos and everything within it are all mirages and appearances, and in reality the existent things have no existence. But, because of the characteristic of True Existence, which is God's existence, they appear to exist, just like existent things that appear in dreams or in water but in reality have no existence. . . . God's Essence is Being that appears as nothingness, and the cosmos is nothingness that appears as being.    (*Goal*, pp. 252–53/91–92)

4. When Muslim philosophers and Sufis say, as Liu did, "the being of the world is a being that cannot not be," they do not mean that it exists on

its own. Avicenna and others often made the point by saying that God's Being is the Necessary Existence (*al-wājib al-wujūd*), which is to say that it cannot not be. The world's being is then "necessary through the Other" (*al-wājib bi'l-ghayr*), which is to say that God makes it necessary by bringing it into existence, not that it is necessary in itself.

## 5.5
## 自然生化圖

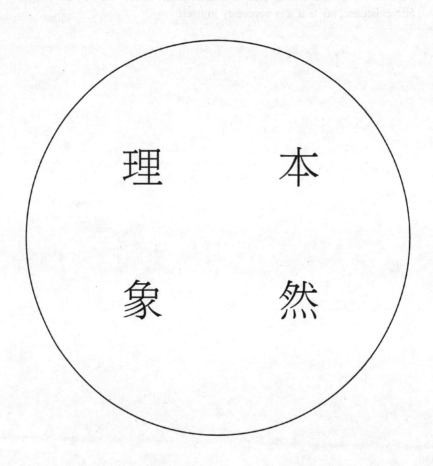

## 5.5
## Diagram of Begetting and Transforming
## by the Self-so

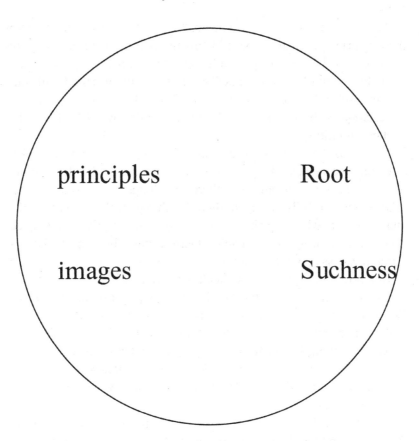

In begetting and transformation, created things do not go beyond the two sides—what cannot be seen, which is principle; and what can be seen, which is image.[1] These two are begotten without begetting and transformed without transformation. Both are rooted as such in the Self-so.[2]

To be as such in the Self-so means that in the midst of the Self-so there is principle, and in the midst of the Self-so there is image. In the midst of the Self-so, principle and image enter into each other. Although principle has no expectation of becoming paired with image, by itself it has the mechanism of pairing. Although image has no expectation of becoming united with principle, by itself it has the subtlety of uniting.

If there is the slightest arrangement and deployment in the midst, it is because created things employ heart in the midst. Employing heart in the midst means that there are things fully arranged and other things not fully arranged; there are things deployed with spirits and others in which spirits are not fully realized. Even if created things are skillful and capable, there cannot but be deviations through excess and deficiency.[3]

But, how can anything be as such in the Self-so?

Answer: Principles in the World of Principles and images in the World of Images are begotten and come into being, but in reality nothing is begotten. They are transformed and come into being, but in reality nothing is transformed. The Root Suchness has being by itself, now hidden, now manifest. Before manifestation, there is neither increase nor decrease. After manifestation, there is neither voidness nor fullness.

The diverse and different kinds of principle in the World of the Principles, and the diverse and different kinds of image in the World of the Images, were like this at root and will be like this forever. They were like this at root; so they were begotten without begetting and transformed without transformation. They will be like this forever; so they will be begotten without begetting and transformed without transformation.

The being of the World of the Principles does not come to be before the World of the Images, and the being of the World of the Images does not come to be after the World of the Principles. Principles and images have being in the Root Being, where there is no differentiation of before and after.

To have before and after is still to have the trace of begetting and transformation, and this cannot be considered the Self-so. Only in manifestation are there before and after. When the Self-so is hidden, its hiddenness is not far away from manifestation, and when the Self-so is manifest, its manifestation is not separate from hiddenness. Hidden yet manifest, manifest yet hidden—all are the Root Suchness's self-activity of real and illusory. This is not begetting and transformation.

The Root Suchness does not belong to begetting and transformation. If we say that both principle and image come into being because of begetting and transformation, this would be to say that there are two: principle and image, and the Root Suchness. This indeed would be far from being the Self-so.

## Notes

1. In other words, the ongoing flow of the creative transformation has but two realms, "unseen" (*ghayb*) and "visible" (*shahāda*), or the spiritual realm known as the Sovereignty (the World of Principles) and the corporeal realm known as the Kingdom (the World of Images).

2. One can translate the discussion under this Diagram into the language of Islamic philosophy by saying that the Self-so is the Necessary Being, which cannot not be and which cannot not be just as it is. Then the cosmos, with its two basic realms, is "the necessary through the Other," which is to say that it is as it is not of itself, but because of the Self-so. Ibn al-'Arabī and his followers stressed that what is "necessary" is nothing but Being itself, and that Being can only be one. This is what Jāmī and other late followers of his school meant when they spoke of "the Oneness of Existence" (*waḥdat al-wujūd*). In Persian poetry, the idea is commonly expressed by the refrain, "All are He" (*hama ūst*). Jāmī wrote:

In terms of its reality and being, each thing is either entified Being; or it is the entification that has occurred for Being, and the entification is the entified thing's attribute. . . .

Neighbor, companion, fellow voyager—all are He.
In beggar's rags, in king's satin—all are He.
In the banquet of dispersion and the private hall of gathering,
all are He, by God—by God, all are He! (*Chinese Gleams*, p. 176)

In a passage of *Rays* that Liu may have had in mind here, Jāmī explained the ascription of being to the existent things in terms of the appearance of an image (the thing) in a mirror (Being). The visible event appears to be an actual occurrence in the mirror, but the rational mind knows that this is not the case. So also, the ascription of being to the thing means simply that the cause of the thing's appearance is being; the thing itself is not being. As Jāmī has already explained, the thing itself is an entity fixed in God's knowledge, and it never leaves its state of "nonexistence" (*'adam*), that is, its essential lack of self-being. Any appearance of the thing is in fact the self-disclosure of the Real Being.

In reality, the mirror adds nothing to the appearance of the form other than appearance. When the form vanishes, only its appearance vanishes. There is no doubt that the altering and changing of relationships bring about no alteration or imperfection in the mirror.    (*Rays*, p. 9)

In explaining lines 5:27–30 of the Root Classic, Nūr al-Ḥaqq wrote (boldface marks quotations from *Subtleties*):

**Creation emerges** from the Real **by the requirement of the Unitary Essence**, that is, by the actual situation, without any exertion of effort (*takalluf*), exactly like what is required by the natures of things, such as the ascent of fire, the fall of water, and the appearance of shadows from light. **And, at the end, its return**, that is, the return of the created thing to the Real by means of the eye of witnessing, **is** also **by the requirement** of the Unitary Essence. **Whatever is not required** by this, such as the effort exerted by the servants in their acts of obedience, **is not from** the Presence of **the Unitary Essence**. This is because exerting effort comes from incapacity and deficiency, and these are not permissible for God.    (*Sharḥ*, pp. 148–49/107–8)

3. Liu may well have had in mind the Koranic verse, "I seek refuge in the Lord of the Dawn from the evil of what He has created" (113:1–2). A hadith clarifies the implication: "All good is in Thy hands, and evil does not go back to Thee." Evil goes back to the created realm itself, which is by definition other than the perfection of the Real, hence a realm of deficiency and excess. Jāmī discussed good and evil in these terms (*Chinese Gleams*, pp. 200–201), and Rāzī went to great lengths in *Path* to explain how the defects of mankind—indicated in the verse of the Trust with the words, "surely [man] is a great wrongdoer, ungrateful" (33:72)—are precisely what allows for the appearance of love and aspiration; these alone drive the quest for perfection, which is the quest for God (see the comments under Diagram 3.10).

## 5.6
### 名相相依圖

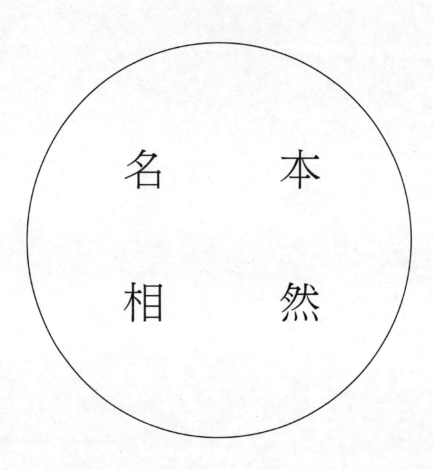

## 5.6
## Diagram of the Mutual Dependence
## of Names and Guises

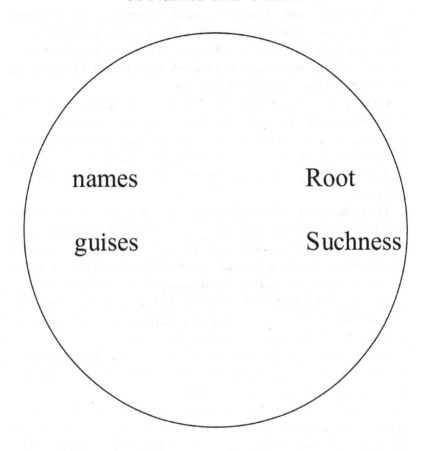

When two things adhere to each other, this is called "dependence." We never see anything that makes itself dependent upon itself. If there is only one thing, we can say only that it stands alone, not that it is mutually dependent.

"Dependence" here does not mean the mutual dependence of one thing on another. Rather, it means that the name of self and the guise of self are mutually dependent; the guise of self and the substance of self are mutually dependent; and the substance of self and the name and guise of self are mutually dependent.[1]

Guise is the manifestation of substance. The kind of substance will determine the kind of guise. Guise depends on substance, but guise and substance are not two things. The name is the designation of the guise. The kind of guise will determine the kind of name. The name depends upon the guise, but the name and guise are not two things.

The name is not different from the guise, and the guise is not different from substance. They are one, simply that. However, as a thing, name is voidness, and as a thing, guise is illusion. Voidness and illusion do not seem to be close to the Real. But, if there were no names, the guises would not be designated, and if there were no guises, the Real would not be manifest. In reality, voidness and illusion are the self-act of the Real One's alteration and transformation and the self-act of designating and naming.

What can be different is one in substance, although its guises are not the same. Not to be the same, however, is not enough to be different. Each of the guises that is not the same is the Complete Substance of the Real One's one-and-the-sameness. The Real One's guise is without measure and number; so the Complete Substance of the Real One's one-and-the-sameness is also without measure and number.

Is the Complete Substance numerous? When one guise arises, the Complete Substance of the Real One's one-and-the-sameness appears. When one guise perishes, how can the Complete Substance of the Real One's one-and-the-sameness perish? It is never numerous and never perishes.[2] There is only this one Complete Substance. When it appears in this, this is the Complete Substance of the Real

One's one-and-the-sameness. When it appears in that, that is the Complete Substance of the Real One's one-and-the-sameness.

One appearance, two appearances, no appearance—none of this detracts from the one-and-the-sameness of the Complete Substance of the Real One. A hundred appearances, a thousand appearances, innumerable appearances—none of this adds to the one-and-the-sameness of the Complete Substance of the Real One.

The guise is the appearance. The appearance is hidden yet manifest. The guise is the real. The guise depends on the substance in the midst of having no place on which to depend, and we are forced to give it the name "dependent." The name is what expresses the reality of the guise.

Each guise surely has the meaning of one guise and the function suitable for one guise. When guise becomes manifest, the Complete Substance appears. The guise cannot itself express in detail either the necessary meaning of this one guise nor the suitable function of this guise.

When the name arises, all the necessary meanings and suitable functions are fully realized together in the name. Those who do not know the meaning of the guise or its function can obtain the meaning and know the function by going into detail concerning the name. Therefore, the name of this one guise is the register of this one guise, and the name of that one guise is the register of that one guise. The register expresses the reality of the root guise; so the name is the guise of the guise. When the name is established, the guise is shown. When the guise is shown, the Complete Substance of the Real One is manifest and further manifest.

If there were a name and no guise, what kind of name would that be? If there were a guise and no name, what kind of guise would that be? Name and guise are two, yet one and not dependent. Name depends on guise in the midst of having no place on which to depend, and we are forced to give it the name "dependent."

In the guise, the Complete Substance of the Real is seen, and in the name, the differentiated number of the guise is seen. The Complete Substance and the differentiated number are not two. There is nothing outside the Real One.

## Notes

1. The gist of Liu's discussion is that the guises of things are self-disclosures of the Real, and the names of the things are specified and designated because of the guises. Nūr al-Ḥaqq translated "names and guises" (*mingxiang*) as "names and forms" (*asmā' wa ṣuwar*). He explained that forms are the appearance of things, and names are designations that we give to the appearances. His explication of the meaning of Root Classic 5:31–36 runs as follows (boldface marks quotations from *Subtleties*):

Here, a question comes up: it seems that he is saying that the Unitary Essence becomes manifest in the Inclusive Unity, and the latter becomes manifest in the Unifiedness; so there is change from state to state. Change, however, is one of the marks of new arrival (*ḥudūth*), and this cannot be correctly ascribed to the Real [whose attribute is eternity, *qidam*].

He answers with his words, **As for It**, that is, the Unitary Essence in Itself, **It is not clothed** by anything of the created beings. **It is clothed only by** the **names** of Its tasks (*shu'ūn*) **and** the **forms** of Its tasks. What is meant by these [names and forms] is the forms of the existent things and their names, for they are the manifestations of the diverse divine tasks, since each manifestation has a form, and every form has a name, such as "heaven and earth." So, the created beings are the tasks and names of the Real, but they have no existence in reality.

The names of the tasks and the external forms have no realization (*taḥaqquq*) in anything. Their only realization is a realization in the recognition and belief of the mind (*dhihn*). And this recognition does not continue; rather, it changes with the changing of the forms and their names. This is because a thing is a thing only through its form; its names are marks that follow the form. This is like the forms and names of seeds. When they are planted in the earth, their forms change, and their name is "crops." When they are harvested, their forms change, and their name is "rice." When they are cooked, their forms change, and their name is "food." When the later forms—like crops and what follows—become manifest, the earlier forms—like seeds—are annihilated.    (*Sharḥ*, pp. 149–51/108–9)

2. In Root Classic 5:37–40, Liu focused on the dissolution and disappearance of all names and guises while insisting that their "principles" remain. If "principles" here mean the spiritual roots of things as in Diagram 1.6, then the names and guises would be the World of Images. Nūr al-Ḥaqq, however, translated "principle" here as "reality" (*ḥaqīqa*) and interpreted it to mean the fixed entity; thus the principles would be the things as known eternally in the divine knowledge. This would be more in keeping with the position of Ibn al-'Arabī and Jāmī. Ibn al-'Arabī held that these fixed realities of the things are their "faces"; it is they that are meant in one of the readings of the Koranic verse, "Each thing is perishing except its face"

(28:88), that is, except the thing's face, which is none other than the face of God turned toward the thing in God's own self-awareness (*Self-Disclosure*, chap. 3).

Liu cited *Rays* as the source of lines 37–40. Perhaps he had in view the following explanation of the traces left by the fixed entities in manifest Being:

The trace of the fixed entities in the Real Existence is that both It and Its attributes become entified and delimited. Existence in Itself is nondelimited and has no entification or delimitation, and so also are Its names and attributes. When It becomes colored by the properties and states of one of the fixed entities, It becomes entified and delimited because of that coloring. Through Its entification and delimitation, Its names and attributes also become entified and delimited. This is because the names and attributes become manifest in keeping with the preparedness of the entities. There is no doubt that the preparedness of each entity requires some kind of entification and delimitation, whether of the Essence or of the names and attributes.   (*Rays*, p. 13)

## 5.7

## 萬物全美圖

## 5.7
## Diagram of the Complete Beauty of the Ten Thousand Things

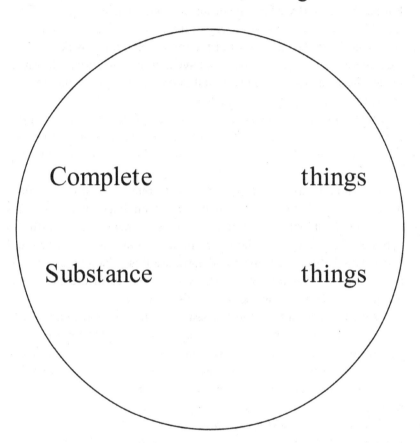

Things fill what is between heaven and earth, and heaven and earth are also things. The Real One transforms everything; so there is nothing whatsoever that is not completely beautiful.[1] If we look at substance from inside, there is nothing that does not have the principle of the Former Heaven. If we look at substance from outside, there is nothing that does not have the vital-energy of the Latter Heaven. If we look at substance from the standpoint of the mutual union of inside and outside, there is nothing that does not have a proper function. All principle is complete principle and all vital-energy is complete vital-energy; so the function is by itself complete function.

Things are great and small, but in the place of their complete beauty, they are neither great nor small. Things are fine and coarse, but in the place of their complete beauty, they are neither fine nor coarse.

Heaven and earth are things of utmost greatness and utmost fineness. If you freely take up a thing of utmost smallness and coarseness and compare it with the complete beauty of heaven and earth, its complete beauty will not be differentiated from that of heaven and earth. This is because heaven and earth are this principle, and the tiniest speck is also this principle. Heaven and earth are this vital-energy, and the tiniest speck is also this vital-energy.[2]

Heaven and earth have the necessary function of heaven and earth, and the tiniest speck has the necessary function of the tiniest speck. The necessary function of heaven and earth, however, functions in heaven and earth; so its function is universal. The necessary function of the tiniest speck functions in the tiniest speck; so its function is minute.

If we take the tiniest speck in the ultimate allotted measure of its function and allow it to extend and broaden, its function will be comparable to that of heaven and earth. There is already a heaven and earth, however; so there is no need for another heaven and earth. There is already the necessary function of a heaven and earth; so there is no need for another necessary function of heaven and earth. Each tiny speck is settled and at ease in its allotment; it simply realizes fully the function of a tiny speck.

When we talk of complete beauty, heaven and earth are this complete beauty, and the ten thousand things are also this complete beauty.

Someone said: Among the things between heaven and earth, nothing is completely beautiful. Heaven itself does not fill the west and the north, nor does earth fill the east and the south. If heaven and earth cannot be completely beautiful, how much more so for the rest!

I replied: Incompleteness is precisely where completeness is perfected.[3] Anything that crosses beyond complete beauty would not be complete beauty. In the midst of unmixed yang, one yin is concealed, so the measure of unmixed yang is not yet complete. Were there no concealment of this one yin, from whence would yin be begotten on the day when yang is fully realized? This means that yang's incompleteness is precisely where its completeness is perfected. In the midst of unmixed yin, one yang is concealed, so the measure of unmixed yin is not yet complete. Were there no concealment of this one yang, from whence would yang come back on the day when yin is fully realized? This means that yin's incompleteness is precisely where its completeness is perfected.

The Complete Substance of the sage is the Non-Ultimate and the utmost purity.[4] In the midst of this purity, there will surely be one speck. This means that the measure of unmixed purity is not yet complete. But, were this one speck not concealed, where would be lodged the mechanism of the ceaseless begetting and begetting of the human way? This means that purity's incompleteness is precisely where its completeness is perfected.

The principle of yin and yang is like this, and the principle of the sage is like this. Why do you have doubts about heaven, earth, and the ten thousand things?

Someone said: If each one of the ten thousand things has the substance of completeness, how can there be incomplete functions? When the function is complete, benefit is seen in the place of function. But when the function is incomplete, harm is seen in the place of function.

I replied: The ten thousand things are what issue forth and appear from the Root Suchness. There is no incompleteness in the Root Suchness; so how can there be incompleteness in its responding function?[5] It is only that, in the midst of the creative transformation, there is the subtlety of time and location. When the time is suitable and the allotted location is there, how can there be incompleteness? When the time is not suitable, the allotted location changes; so completeness is used in the ground of incompleteness. This is an error of those who use the ten thousand things, not an error of the functions of the ten thousand things.[6]

Looked at more broadly, the world is one world of complete beauty. Time is one time of complete beauty. When what is suitable in the south dwells in the north, however, and when what is suitable in the north dwells in the south, then you have an awareness that the world is incomplete. When you wear the fur of the winter in summer, and when you wear the light clothing of summer in winter, then you have an awareness that time is incomplete. When the function is not complete or beautiful, it is only that it has not been used suitably. How can you blame time and the world?

## Notes

1. This could be a translation of the Koranic verse, "He made beautiful everything that He created" (32:7), and it can be seen as a corollary of the principle enunciated in the prophetic saying "God is beautiful, and He loves beauty." Ibn al-'Arabī put the argument in a nutshell:

Know that the divine beauty through which God is named "Beautiful" and by which He described Himself in His messenger's words, "He loves beauty," is in all things. There is nothing but beauty, for God created the cosmos only in His form, and He is beautiful. Hence all the cosmos is beautiful. (*Futūḥāt*, 2: 542; *Self-Disclosure*, p. 27)

In *Flashes* 'Irāqī wrote: "Whatever you see is the mirror of His beauty; so everything is beautiful. He loves everything," for, as Jāmī commented: "It is His beauty that has appeared in the mirror of the things" (*Rays*, p. 69; *Flashes*, p. 86).

2. In Islamic terms, this theme is frequently discussed with Koran 2:115 in view: "Wherever you turn, there is the face of God." In brief, God discloses himself in each thing through his all-pervading existence and his names and attributes. On the Confucian side, one can find explicit statements of the unity of principle and vital-energy on one hand and the omnipresence of the Supreme Principle on the other. For example, Zhu Xi wrote:

Principle has never been separated from vital-energy. . . . Principle is not a separate entity. It exists right in vital-energy. (*Source Book*, p. 634)

The Great Ultimate is simply the principle of the highest good. Each and every person has in him the Great Ultimate and each and every thing has in it the Great Ultimate. (*Source Book*, p. 640)

3. This could almost be a translation of Ibn al-'Arabī: "Part of the perfection of existence is the existence of imperfection within it" (*Futūḥāt*, 2: 307; *Sufi Path*, p. 296). Rāzī made the point in terms of the Koranic verse about the Trust offered to the heavens, the earth, and the mountains; all of them refused, "And the human being carried it—surely he is very ignorant, a great wrongdoer" (33:72). Rāzī argued that it is precisely these two attributes of ignorance and wrongdoing that provide human beings with "the two wings" with which to fly to God, for they are nothing other than caprice and wrath transformed into love and zeal, as explained under Diagram 3.10 (*Path*, p. 185/199).

4. This is the only instance in the text where Liu employed the expression Non-Ultimate (*wuji*). As noted under Diagram 4.4, Wang Daiyu called the Non-Ultimate the seed and the Human Ultimate the fruit. This could be what Liu had in mind, i.e., that the sage is the Muhammadan Reality, the Logos in God, the seed from which the entire cosmos is born.

5. This passage may have been inspired by Jāmī's discussion of the privative nature of evil in Gleam 31 (*Chinese Gleams*, p. 200). Nūr al-Ḥaqq translated and explained the relevant lines of the Root Classic (5:45–50) this way (boldface marks quotations from *Subtleties*):

**Which thing is not** the manifestation of **the Existence of the Real**, that is, Its self-disclosure through the tasks of Its knowledge in the external realm? . . . **Which task** among the tasks of heaven, earth, and the things **is not the task of the Real?** In respect of what is manifest, their tasks seem to be their own tasks, but in reality all are the tasks of the Real. **So**, given that this is the situation, **each thing** within the limits of itself in relation to the Real **is pure**, or unmixed, **and perfect**, or not deficient.

Nonetheless, each thing's perfection is in the measure of its own state, for each thing has a perfection that is not appropriate for anything else. The perfection of earth is not like the perfection of heaven, the perfection of the moon is not like the perfection of earth, the perfection of the saints is not like the perfection of the prophets, and the perfection of a bow is not like the perfection of an arrow, for the perfection of the one is in its straightness and that of the other in its curve.

**Who would say** about something "whose creation He made beautiful" [Koran 32:7] that it is **deficient**, or imperfect, **and contaminated**, or impure? **Because** the reality of **each speck of dust and each grain**, although these are the smallest of things, is one of the tasks of the Real, so each is perfect and pure. . . .

So, there is nothing that is not perfect and pure in the eyes of witnessing and in regard to the thing's reality, even if some things are not beautiful in the eyes of those who are veiled and in regard to the things' forms.   (*Sharḥ*, pp. 154–55/111–12)

6. Again, this can be an allusion to the principle implied in the Koranic verse, "I seek refuge in the Lord of the Dawn from the evil of what He has created" (113:1–2).

## 5.8
## 小中見大圖

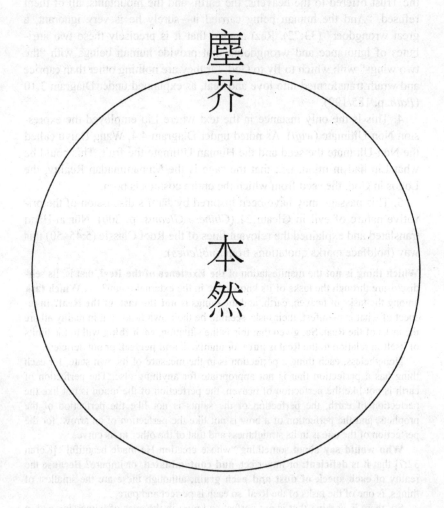

塵
芥

本
然

## 5.8
## Diagram of Seeing the Great in the
## Midst of the Small

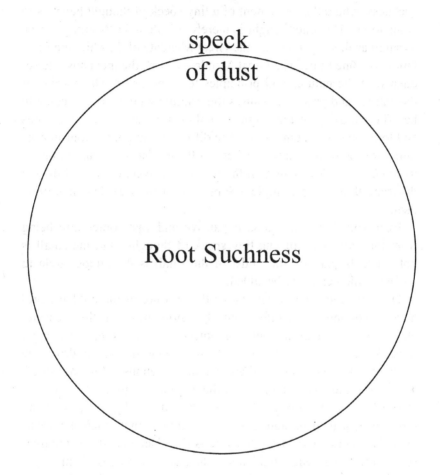

speck
of dust

Root Suchness

The smallness of things under heaven reaches a mustard seed or a tiny speck, which is the ultimate, utmost smallness. But we should not look at them as small.[1]

Let us try to look at the Real One in the state of signless, silent suchness, where the movement of a tiny speck of thought happens to come to be. This one thought is merely one thought. Nothing can be as small as this, yet it causes the Great Mandate of the chief manifestation to come to be. The Great Mandate causes the inexhaustible sequence of the natures and principles to come to be. The surplus of the natures and principles causes the original vital-energy to come to be. The exposing of the original vital-energy causes the two wings and four images to come to be. The differentiation of the four images into pure and turbid causes heaven, earth, and the ten thousand things to come to be. Once again, in the midst of heaven, earth, and the ten thousand things, the Complete Substance of the Real One manifests itself.

Even something that is so expansive and vast comes into being from the movement of one tiny speck of thought. But, the small is not small, because in the midst of the small is the utmost great to which nothing can ever be added.

Ouzaier[2] said, "The Real One is the treasure of the hidden storehouse. Nothing is manifest but this storehouse of the treasure. Heaven and earth are the one storehouse of the treasure, and a single thing is the one storehouse of the treasure. One speck, one drop, one blade of grass, one grain—all are the one storehouse of the treasure." This also is the meaning of seeing the great in the midst of the small.

But I have not yet spoken extensively and broadly. If I extend and broaden this, then thought and deliberation cannot reach the greatness. The storehouse of the treasure is the place that stores the treasures of the Real One's hidden storehouse. A storehouse is merely a storehouse, nothing else. It is nothing but the place that stores the substance that is the silent suchness, without direction and place, nothing else.[3]

Although it is great, we still have not seen the utmost greatness. Why? We talked about the storehouse, but we have not yet talked about issuing forth. When it issues forth, the Complete Substance of the Real One, which is stored in a tiny mustard seed, exposes again the Great Function of its Complete Substance. This is like the earlier exposing and it brings forth at present the ageless heaven and earth. When there are heaven and earth, there are the ten thousand things that are ceaselessly begotten and begotten.

Each of the ten thousand things embraces the Real One, which is without border and boundary.[4] One thing is the one Real, and the ten thousand things are ten thousand Reals. Countless and innumerable things are countless and innumerable Reals. All emerge from the midst of a tiny mustard seed. Is the tiny mustard seed small? Its greatness is beyond thought and deliberation. There is no place that is not small, and there is no place where the great is not seen in the midst of the small. It is a pity that the seeing of none but a few people arrives here. Oumoer[5] said, "I have never seen anything without seeing the Complete Substance of the Real One." This is a case of someone who can see.

## Notes

1. The texts of Diagrams 5.8 and 5.9 discuss the relativity of things, an essential part of complementary thinking generally. Zhuangzi in particular liked to highlight the seeming paradoxes that arise as soon as we look on things in these terms, e.g.: "There is nothing in the world bigger than the tip of an autumn hair, and Mount T'ai is tiny. No one has lived longer than a dead child, and P'eng-tsu died young" (Watson, p. 43).

In Islamic texts, the notion that the Real Being can be seen in every speck of dust follows on the reality of Being's Oneness. "Wherever you turn, there is the face of God" (Koran 2:115), that is, the very Essence and Reality of the Real One, which is Being. Wherever Being discloses itself, it is accompanied by all its perfections, which are the divine names and attributes. Jāmī made this point and then quoted a verse from the midst of a similar discussion by Shabistarī in the *Gulshan-i rāz*:

The Reality of Being, along with all the tasks, attributes, relations, and respects that are the realities of all the existents, pervades the reality of each existent. This is why it has been said, "Everything is in everything." The author of the *Gulshan-i rāz* says,

Split the heart of a single drop—
out will come a hundred pure oceans.   (*Chinese Gleams*, p. 196)

In his translation of the relevant verses of the Root Classic (5:51–54), Nūr al-Ḥaqq added to the text "the one who is annihilated" (*al-fānī*) in order to make explicit who it is that sees the great inside the small (boldface marks quotations from *Subtleties*):

**In every breath that leaves and enters** the mouth of **the one who is annihilated** in God **is unveiled to him** everything **that there is from the first of the** creation of the **cosmos to its last,** namely the affairs of the times that cannot be counted or calculated; no one knows their length but God. For, when the Perfect Man, annihilated in God, reaches the station of "With Me there is no morning or evening," it is possible for him to embrace fully in every one of his breaths everything that there is from the first of this world to its annihilation, as will be explained.

In the same way, when this annihilated one reaches the station of "I have never looked upon anything without seeing God within it," then **he may see** with the eye of "through Me he sees" the manifestation of the tasks of **the larger inside** something **small,** like a speck of dust or a mustard seed; **and even see the heavens,** the earth, and the things, with all their greatness in size, **embraced by,** or manifest in the locus of manifestation of, **a grain.** For, there may become manifest from their reality, in respect of the fact that they are the tasks of the Real, the forms of the heavens, the earth, and the things.   (*Sharh*, pp. 155–56/112)

2. This is a transliteration of 'Uzayr (the Arabic form of the name Ezra). No doubt Liu meant Nasafī, whose first name is 'Azīz. In the Arabic script (which is not vocalized), the difference in spelling is a single dot; missing a dot, z becomes r, so 'Azīz becomes 'Uzayr. The passage from Nasafī that Liu had in mind is:

"God has the storehouses of the heavens and the earth" [Koran 63:7]. The storehouses are heavenly, and no matter how much is spent from these storehouses, they never become less: Every intellect is a storehouse, every sphere is a storehouse, every star is a storehouse. As for the storehouses of the earth, soil is a storehouse, water is a storehouse, air is a storehouse, and fire is a storehouse. Every seed is a storehouse, every tree is a storehouse, and every animal is a storehouse.

I have handed you the thread. Think how many storehouses there are in the heaven, and how many storehouses there are in the land! He says, "Naught is there, but its storehouses are with Us, and We send it not down but in a known measure" [Koran 15:21].   (*Goal*, p. 244/81)

3. Here Liu may have had in mind the already quoted divine saying "I was a Hidden Treasure."

4. Concerning the presence of the Divine Essence in all things, a presence that is indicated by the Koranic verse, "He is with you wherever you are" (57:4), Nasafī wrote:

God is not far from some, and close to others. God is with everything. All of the existent things are equal in nearness to Him. The highest of the high and the lowest of the low are the same in nearness to Him. Talk of "nearness" and "distance" is in relation to our knowledge and ignorance, which is to say that whoever is more knowledgeable is closer. Otherwise, God is with every speck among the existent things through His Essence; He encompasses it and is aware of it. (*Goal*, p. 235/71)

5. This is 'Umar, the second caliph, to whom a similar saying is sometimes attributed. Liu cited both *Rays* and *Path* for this section. The quotation is found in both, although in slightly different forms and completely different contexts. In the first passage, 'Irāqī described what happens when God says "Be!" to the "lovers," that is, the fixed entities, or the creatures in God's knowledge before their creation.

The morning of manifestation breathed, the breeze of solicitude blew, the sea of generosity began to move. The clouds of effusion rained so much of the rain of "He sprinkled them with His light" on the earth of preparedness that "the earth shone with the light of its Lord" [Koran 39:69]. The lover was satiated with the water of life. He got up from the sleep of nonexistence and put on the cloak of existence. He placed the hat of witnessing on his head, bound the belt of yearning around his waist, and set forth with the foot of sincerity on the path of seeking. . . . The first time he opened his eyes, his gaze fell on the beauty of the Beloved. He said, "I have never seen anything without seeing God before it." (*Rays*, pp. 47–48; *Flashes*, p. 76)

Rāzī cited the saying while explaining the characteristics of the illumined perception that is achieved by following the Way:

He perceives the three hundred sixty thousand worlds of the Kingdom and the Sovereignty with these outward and inward organs of perception. . . . Each speck of these worlds manifests one of the Lordly attributes and has within itself one of the Real's signs; it throws off the veil from its face and displays to his vision the beauty of the Real's sign. . . . Here he can recognize the pure Essence of the Real in Its unity, and he can contemplate the attributes of the Divinity with the eye of certainty. It is this station about which that great man said, "I have never looked upon anything without seeing God within it." (*Path*, p. 118/139)

5.9

大中見小圖

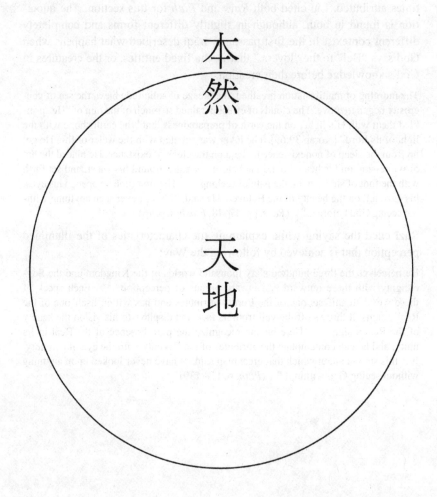

## 5.9
## Diagram of Seeing the Small in the Midst of the Great

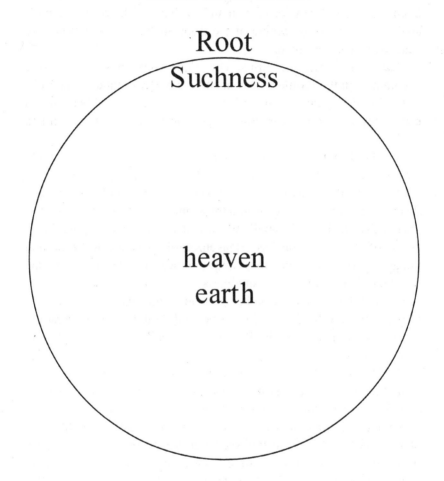

Root
Suchness

heaven
earth

Of all things, nothing is greater than heaven and earth.[1] If we see them as great, however, they are great, and if we see them as small, they are small. It is all in regard to how we see.

As long as seeing has not yet gone back to the seeing of the Root Suchness, we will not see heaven and earth as small. When seeing is able to go back to the seeing of the Root Suchness, we will not see heaven and earth as great.

Heaven and earth are forms. The formed heaven and earth were begotten from the formless heaven and earth. If we stand in the midst of the formless heaven and earth and look at the formed heaven and earth, they will be no more than a speck in the midst of heaven and earth.

We should not see anything as small, however. Not only should we not see heaven and earth as small, but also we should not see the ten thousand things as small. Why? Heaven, earth, and the ten thousand things are not fixed in greatness and smallness. When that is greater than this, this is small. When that is smaller than this, this is aware of its own greatness. Heaven, earth, and the ten thousand things are not fixed in greatness and smallness, because the Real One is not fixed in greatness and smallness.

It is not that the Real One has greatness and smallness. If we talk of greatness, the Real One is great beyond thought and deliberation. If we talk of smallness, the Real One is small beyond thought and deliberation.

Yezide[2] said, "Aershi has come and gone in a corner of my heart many times, yet I am still unaware of it." This is what Yezide thought about seeing the small in the midst of the great.

Among the things under heaven, the utmost smallness is like that of a grain of sand or a mustard seed, yet these certainly have insides. If they have insides, it is possible to enter into their midst and break them. The smallness of the Real One is such that it has no inside. If it has no inside, how can anything enter into its midst and break it? It is of the utmost smallness, but how is it possible for the Real One actually to be small?

When we say that nothing breaks it, we mean that the substance of the Real One is the utmost voidness and the utmost silence. There is no way to obtain a differentiated border so as to enter into it. When people see this, they have the strongest desire to display its greatness outwardly, but they cannot fully realize its greatness. Thus they return to smallness and fully realize it.[3]

To talk about smallness is precisely to talk about greatness. To talk about greatness is to know that heaven, earth, and the ten thousand things have places from which they come. All of them come from the midst of the great. To talk about smallness is to know that the One that begets heaven, earth, and the ten thousand things is without taint. How can It be seen as without taint? Without inside, It has no way whatsoever to be tainted.

## Notes

1. Almost a quotation from the Koran: "Certainly the creation of the heavens and the earth is greater than the creation of humans" (40:57); or from Shao Yong: "Among large things, there are none larger than heaven and earth" (Birdwhistell, *Transition*, p. 102). Nūr al-Ḥaqq said that Diagram 5.8 "explains the greatness of the Perfect Man in respect of the fact that he never looks upon anything without seeing the Real within it," whereas this Diagram deals with the Perfect Man's vision. In explaining the relevant lines from the Root Classic (5:55–56), he wrote (boldface marks quotations from *Subtleties*):

He also **may see**, with the eye of witnessing, **in the majesty of the Real the things' smallness, and even view the heavens,** the earth, and the things **beyond a speck,** that is, smaller than it. For, when he is annihilated from the forms of the things, he sees only their realities, which are their forms in the Real's knowledge. In the eye of his witnessing, these realities relative to the Real's majesty are like a speck of dust or even smaller. That is why [Abū] Yazīd said, "Were the Throne and everything around it a hundred thousand times in my heart, I would not feel it."

This is the explanation of the greatness of the Real, such that the things relative to His greatness are like a speck of dust.

Know also that, in respect of their forms, some bodies are larger than others. But, in respect of their realities, they do not have a designated smallness or a distinct largeness. So, when the viewer looks upon something with the eye of form, he will see only its form; then he will have seen the small as small and the large as large. But, when he looks upon it with the eye of witnessing, he will have seen its reality; then he will see the larger in the smaller, just as he sees the Real in a speck. And, it may be the opposite, as when he sees things in the Real such that he sees them smaller than a speck in relation to Him.   (*Sharḥ*, pp. 157–58/113–14)

2. Liu probably took this saying (quoted in Arabic by Nūr al-Ḥaqq in the passage just cited) from *Flashes*, where 'Irāqī gave it in Persian translation, having taken it from the Arabic text provided by Ibn al-'Arabī in the *Fuṣūṣ* (*Rays*, p. 122; *Flashes*, p. 110).

3. Liu here provided still another way of formulating a major theme of both Islamic and Chinese spirituality: the realization of completion and wholeness depends upon an initial realization of nothingness. Subsistence (*baqā'*) is preceded by annihilation (*fanā'*). The fullness of human possibility is reached by way of emptiness. The mirror of the heart must be polished and emptied of forms before it can reflect the Truth. One must be God's servant (*'abd*) before one can be his vicegerent (*khalīfa*). In order to be wealthy and independent (*ghanī*), one must be utterly poor (*faqīr*). And so on.

## 5.10
## 一息終古圖

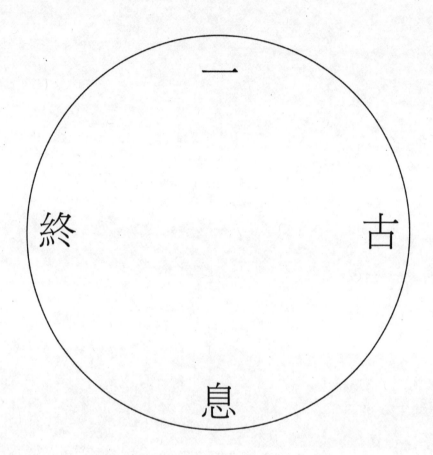

## 5.10
## Diagram of the One Breath
## as the Final Antiquity

One exhalation and one inhalation are called a "breath." One breath is the shortest of times.[1] In one breath the affairs and tasks of the final antiquity are complete.[2] The life of humans does not easily reach this one breath. When someone reaches this one breath, heaven and earth follow him and are rolled up.[3]

In the midst of the one breath, he sees past, present, and future. In the midst of the one breath, he sees the principles existing in the past world of principles, the images existing in the present world of images, and the principles and images existing in the future of both worlds.

In the midst of the one breath, he sees what has gone, although in reality nothing ever goes; he sees what is present, although in reality nothing ever exists; and he sees what is future, although in reality nothing ever comes.

In the midst of the one breath, he sees that nothing has gone, although in reality there is nothing that has not gone; he sees that nothing is present, although in reality there is nothing that does not exist; he sees that nothing is future, although in reality there is nothing that will not come.

In the midst of the one breath, he sees that nothing has gone, and simultaneously the seeing transforms itself to enter into the midst of the nothing that has gone. He sees that nothing is present, and simultaneously the seeing transforms itself to enter into the midst of the nothing that is present. He sees that nothing is future, and simultaneously the seeing transforms itself to enter into the midst of the nothing that is future.

In the midst of the one breath, it is like this, and in the midst of the one breath, it is also like that. It is not that there should be another breath outside the one breath. All this is fully realized in the one breath.

In the midst of the one breath, there is emergence and entrance. In the midst of the one breath, spirit emerges and spirit enters. In the midst of the one breath, nothing emerges and nothing enters.

In the midst of the one breath, entrance follows the Former Heaven, and emergence follows the Latter Heaven. In the midst of the one breath, entrance follows the Latter Heaven, and emergence follows the Former Heaven.

In the midst of the one breath, entrance follows the measureless and numberless, and emergence follows the One. In the midst of the one breath, entrance follows the One, and emergence follows the measureless and the numberless.

In the midst of the one breath, entrance follows what has neither color nor subtlety, and emergence follows what has color and subtlety. In the midst of the one breath, entrance follows what has color and subtlety, and emergence follows what has neither color nor subtlety.

In the midst of the one breath, entrance follows the place of entrance, and emergence follows the place of no emergence. In the midst of the one breath, entrance follows the place of no entrance, and emergence follows the place of emergence.

In the midst of the one breath, entrance follows what has no beginning and end, and emergence follows what has beginning and end. In the midst of the one breath, entrance follows what has beginning and end, and emergence follows what has no beginning and end.

In the midst of the one breath, entrance follows what has no purity or filth, and emergence follows what has purity and filth. In the midst of the one breath, entrance follows what has purity and filth, and emergence follows what has no purity or filth.

In the midst of the one breath, entrance follows what has a gate, and emergence follows what has no gate. In the midst of the one breath, entrance follows what has no gate, and emergence follows what has a gate.

It is not that there is another breath outside the one breath. All this is fully realized in the one breath. In the one breath, the affairs and tasks of the final antiquity are complete.

This one breath is not the one breath of the I; it is shared by the I and the Lord.

When the I shares with the Lord, sometimes, in the midst of the one breath, only the I is seen, and the Lord is not seen.

When the Lord shares with the I, sometimes, in the midst of the one breath, only the Lord is seen, and the I is not seen.

In the midst of the one breath, sometimes the Lord is not seen, and the I also is not seen.

The subtlety of the final antiquity is fully gathered together and contained in the midst of the one breath. Such is the ultimate subtlety of the one breath. The ascent on high of our sage was merely an affair of the one breath. He was provided with the seeing and discernment of all that have principles, images, and affairs from the beginning of the rise of transformation until the full realization of the coming home and going back. This is clear proof of the one breath as the final antiquity.

Once when Erli[4] was on horseback, he was provided with the transmission of a complete account of learning from the beginning to the end of heaven and earth. This comes close to the flourishing of the one breath that ascends on high. This also is clear proof of the one breath as the final antiquity.

## Notes

1. *Xi* 息 (breath) here is apparently a literal translation of Arabic *nafas* (breath), which also means moment or instant. Ibn al-'Arabī's doctrine of the renewal of creation "at each instant" (discussed in the notes under Diagram 2.12) means literally "at each breath." Ibn al-'Arabī also spoke of the "world of the breaths" as the realm in which visionary realities come to be unveiled on the path to God (*Sufi Path*, p. 402*n*18). The one breath in which the gnostic's vision opens up to the Real is nothing other than the Breath of the All-merciful, the Ascribed Spirit through which God taught Adam "all the names."

2. "Final antiquity" translates *zhonggu* 終古. *Zhong* means "end," "finality," "death"; *gu* means "ancient," "old," "antiquity." Mathews says that the two together mean "throughout antiquity, for a long time past," and under Diagram 3.7 we translated the expression as "from oldest antiquity." Here, however, Liu was apparently not using it in the usual sense. Rather, he was stressing the coincidence of opposites that occurs when the seeker reaches what Ibn al-'Arabī called "bewilderment." This is why Nūr, in the instance where it occurs in the Root Classic (5:52), translated it "from the first to the last of the cosmos." In short, "final antiquity" designates the final moment of the unfolding of the cosmos, when it returns to its beginning, i.e., the point where the Arc of Ascent rejoins the Arc of Descent, or where the Latter Heaven reunites with the Former Heaven.

This is perhaps the most obscure section of the book. Certainly the overall thrust is clear: Liu wanted to describe the coincidence of opposites witnessed by the realized sage when he lives in the eternal present, the moment without duration, which lasts forever. Everything comes together, the same yet distinct. Each is He / not He, and the viewer is "bewildered"—to use Ibn al-'Arabī's expression—by the fact that the middle is not excluded, and the present moment is both/and, or neither/nor. We are not aware of an Islamic precedent, however, for the yin/yang-style play on exhalation/inhalation, emergence/entrance, and the implied and sometimes explicit correlation with the two arcs, the Former Heaven and the Latter Heaven.

This section may be a commentary on one or both of the following passages from *Flashes*, in which 'Irāqī discussed time as a phenomenon arising from the existence of human awareness situated between the beginningless (*azal*) and the endless (*abad*), that is, God as the First who has no first and the Last who has no last. If individual awareness can be erased through annihilation, only the eternal present will remain.

The depth of this ocean is called "the beginningless" and its shore "the endless." . . . The isthmus (*barzakh*) is your you-ness. The ocean is one, but it appears to you as two because of your imaginary you-ness. If you give yourself over to the ocean's water, the isthmus that is your you-ness will disappear, and the ocean of the beginningless will mix with the ocean of the endless. The First will come forth in the color of the Last, and the Last in the color of the First. . . . Then, when you open your eyes, all will be you, but you will not be there.   (*Rays*, pp. 51–52; *Flashes*, p. 78)

When [God's lover] throws off the robes of form and dives into the ocean of Unity, he is not aware of chastisement or bliss, he knows nothing of expectation or dread, he recognizes neither fear nor hope. For fear and hope depend on past and future, and he is drowned in a sea that has neither past nor future—all is now upon now. (*Rays*, p. 82; *Flashes*, p. 91)

Nūr al-Ḥaqq's explanation of the relevant passage from the Root Classic (5:57–60) makes one think of Plato's cave, although it is doubtful that he had that specifically in mind, given that it was not a well-known image even in Islamic philosophical texts (boldface marks quotations from *Subtleties*):

**When time undergoes expansion for** this annihilated one in the station of "there is no time with God, nor any location," then **in each breath** of his, the affairs of the **first and** the **last** will all become present to him and witnessed by him, such that nothing will be hidden from him in this breath. It was to this station that the Prophet alluded with his words "I have a moment with God when neither proximate angel nor sent-out prophet embraces me." This is because his knowledge here is God's unseen knowledge, and he sees through His presence. So, nothing is hidden from him in this breath, just as nothing is hidden from God. That is why all the affairs of this world, from the first of it to the last, are present in his every breath.

The likeness of this is a man in a well. He does not see heaven except in the measure of the width of the well's mouth. When he leaves the well all at once, he sees all of heaven in one glance. So, the person who is veiled is like a man in a well. He sees only what is present with himself. The Perfect Man, annihilated in God, is like the man who has come out of the well all at once. So, he sees in a glance from the first of this world to its annihilation, and nothing is hidden from him, for his vision has become vision in God's presence.

This, then, is the explanation of the Perfect Man inasmuch as the affairs of first and last are present with him and witnessed by him in every presence. (*Sharḥ*, pp. 159–61/114–15)

3. Perhaps a reference to Koran 21:104: "On the day when We shall roll up heaven as a scroll for writings is rolled." The verse refers to the Last Day, but such verses are often interpreted in terms of the "greatest resurrection," which is, as one thirteenth-century author put it, "The state of arrival achieved by the gnostic, that hour when in his eyes the two engendered worlds are erased and obliterated in the light of unity, and nothing remains but the Living, the Self-subsistent" (Chittick, *Faith and Practice*, p. 102).

4. This is ʿAlī, the cousin and son-in-law of Muḥammad, who is often considered the repository of the Prophet's wisdom. Thus the Prophet said, "I am the city of knowledge, and ʿAlī is its gate." The quotation here seems to refer to ʿAlī's well-known saying, "O people! Ask of me before you lose me, for I have the knowledge of the earlier and the later folk."

5.11
終古一息圖

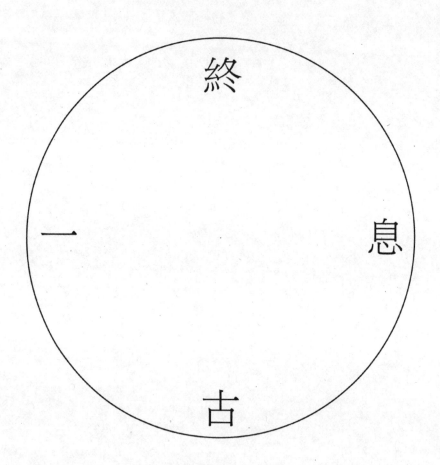

# 5.11
## Diagram of the Final Antiquity
## as the One Breath

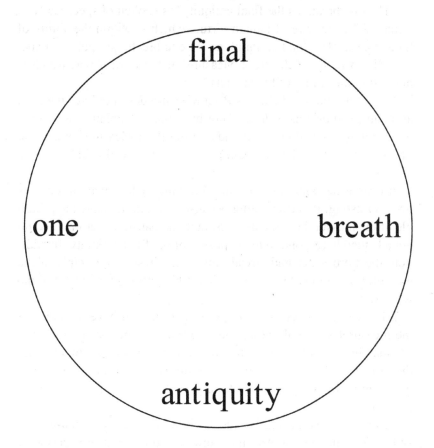

"Antiquity" means the beginning. "Final" means the time of the beginning of antiquity. The completion of this one affair of the creative
transformation is called "the final antiquity."[1] It is not possible to
measure this time by the turning of the years.[2]

"The one breath as the final antiquity" is spoken of specifically in
terms of the measure of human virtue, which is within the ability of
human acts. "The final antiquity as the one breath" is spoken of specifically in terms of the Root Measure[3] of the Lord Ruler, which is
not within the ability of human acts.[4]

Originally[5] the Lord Ruler's Root Measure does not have the final
antiquity, and originally it does not have the one breath, for there is
no morning or evening in the midst of the Root Measure.[6] We speak
of what are called "the final antiquity" and "the one breath" in terms
of time.[7]

It cannot be said, however, that the time of the final antiquity is
not everlasting. It is everlasting because, if it did not have the principle of the measureless, numberless, and inexhaustible period, it could
not adequately respond to the exposing of the final antiquity. In addition, the Lord Ruler had already made manifest the principle of the
measureless, numberless, and inexhaustible period in the midst of the
Root Measure.[8]

Likewise, it is everlasting because, if it did not have the color of
the measureless, numberless, and inexhaustible period, it could not
adequately respond to the portrayal of the final antiquity. In addition,
the Lord Ruler had already made manifest the color of the measureless, numberless, and inexhaustible period in the midst of the Root
Measure.

So also it is everlasting because, if it did not have the vital-energy
and stuff of the measureless, numberless, and inexhaustible period, it
could not adequately respond to the continuity of the final antiquity.
In addition, the Lord Ruler had already made manifest the vital-
energy and stuff of the measureless, numberless, and inexhaustible
period in the midst of the Root Measure.

If it is like this, how can we not say that what becomes manifest is
numerous? To say that it is numerous is enough to see the wealth of
the final antiquity, but it is not enough to see the wonder of the final
antiquity. The great wonder is that the wealth of the final antiquity

cannot be measured; an even greater wonder is that its wealth cannot be fathomed.

With one world of the Mandate, it enters all the worlds of the Mandate, and with all the worlds of the Mandate, it enters one world of the Mandate. But this does not ruin the final antiquity of its guise.

With one world of vital-energy, it enters all the worlds of vital-energy, and with all the worlds of vital-energy, it enters one world of vital-energy, but this does not ruin the final antiquity of its guise.

With one storehouse of the treasure, it enters all the storehouses of the treasure, and with all the storehouses of the treasure, it enters one storehouse of the treasure, but this does not ruin the final antiquity of its guise.

With one root suchness, it enters all the root suchnesses, and with all the root suchnesses, it enters one root suchness, but this does not ruin the final antiquity of its guise.

With one manifest suchness, it enters all manifest suchnesses, and with all manifest suchnesses, it enters one manifest suchness, but this does not ruin the final antiquity of its guise.

With one time, it enters all times, and with all times, it enters one time, but this does not ruin the final antiquity of its guise.

With one heaven and earth, it enters all heavens and earths, and with all heavens and earths, it enters one heaven and earth, but this does not ruin the final antiquity of its guise.

How can we not say that the final antiquity is wealthy? How can we not say that it is wealthy and wondrous? Finality is the unfathomable principle, and again finality is the unfathomable number. Finality is the unfathomable form, and again finality is the unfathomable subtlety. How can we not say that the time of the final antiquity is wealthy and everlasting?

In the midst of the Root Measure of the Lord Ruler, however, there is but one breath. A former worthy said, "The duration of heaven and earth is the time of a half day," because it is said that the World of the Principles makes up one half of a day, and the World of the Images makes up the other half of the day.

Another former worthy said, "The Lord Ruler creates and transforms the worlds of both the principles and the images as one exhalation and one inhalation."[9]

Perhaps the two worthies who said this had undifferentiated suchness in the presence of the Real One, not knowing the difference between day and night.

If we speak, however, of the ultimate extension of the Root Measure of the Real One, the explanation of the one breath is still superfluous. In the midst of the Root Measure of the Real One, there is originally nothing that can be called "the final antiquity." How, then, can there be the one breath?

## Notes

1. Again, Liu was saying that the final point on the circle of creation is identical with the initial point. One should not imagine, however, that once the seeker reaches the top, he then continues back around the circle to experience once again the stages of creation in the Former Heaven. That this is not the case is made clear in the mythic model of the stages of the Latter Heaven, that is, the Prophet's climb to God on the "ladder" (*mi'rāj*). According to those accounts, once he had encountered God, he came back to his community by way of the same steps by which he had climbed. Once the seeker reaches the endpoint, which is none other than the beginning point, creation is complete; there is no retrogression, but rather an ongoing, never-ending journey in God (cf. the discussion of the Two Arcs in the notes under Diagram 4.3 and of the two journeys under Diagram 4.6).

2. Nūr al-Ḥaqq explained the meaning of Root Classic 5:59–60 and this diagram in these terms (boldface marks quotations from *Subtleties*):

**When the moments** of the duration of this world **are folded up**, then, with the eye of his witnessing [the one who has been annihilated] sees that **the first and the last** of time, all of it, despite its length, **are like one breath** of his own in relation to the majesty of the Real, for surely the duration of this world, although we see it as long, in relation to the beginningless and endless length that pertain to the Real, is like a breath, or even shorter than that.

This, then, is the explanation of the Real's majesty in respect of the fact that, in relation to the Real, all time, from the first of this world to its annihilation, despite its tremendous length, is like one breath. (*Sharḥ*, pp. 161–62/115–16)

3. Root Measure (*benliang* 本量) is mentioned under Diagram 5.2 as pertaining to the Numerical One (Inclusive Unity). It is the realm of the divine knowledge, within which all things are differentiated as fixed entities and from which the World of Principles and the World of Images come into manifestation. As the corresponding Arabic term for *liang*, Liu may have had in

mind *qadar*, "measure" or "measuring out," a Koranic term that theologians put at the center of debates over free will and predestination. The saying of Ouzaier (Nasafī) to which Liu referred under Diagram 5.8 quotes a key Koranic verse using the term: "Naught is there, but its storehouses are with Us, and We send it down only in a known measure" (15:21), which is to say that everything's measure is known to God, but not to us.

4. In other words, Diagram 5.10 addresses the achievement of the Nature of Continuity by the worthy, when all is seen as present in the vision of Oneness. In contrast, Diagram 5.11 addresses the primal unity of all things in the Breath of the All-merciful.

Islamic texts often talk of two standpoints in the meeting of the divine and human. One of the most common ways of doing so is in terms of two sorts of nearness (*qurb*), to which reference is made in the notes to Diagram 4.8. Jāmī explained the difference like this:

The result of the nearness of supererogatory acts is that the faculties, organs, and limbs of the traveler come to be identical to the Real, which is to say that the side of Realness dominates over the side of creatureliness, and the side of creatureliness is dominated and subjugated. . . . The wayfaring servant acts and perceives, and the Real is his tool. Reference to this is found in the hadith "I am his hearing with which he hears, his eyesight with which he sees." . . .

The result of the nearness of obligatory acts is the annihilation of the wayfarer's essence and the absorption of the side of creatureliness in the side of Realness. . . . In this nearness, the Real acts and perceives, and the wayfarer, with his own faculties, organs, and limbs, is like the tool. Reference to this is found [in the hadith] "God speaks on the tongue of His Prophet," or "His servant." (*Rays*, pp. 15–16)

Ibn al-'Arabī discussed the two-sidedness of realization in many ways, not only in terms of the two sorts of nearness. Take this passage, which has a number of parallels with what Liu has been discussing:

It was said to the Prophet, "Have you seen your Lord?" He replied, "He is a light. How should I see Him?" This is because engendered existence is darkness, and light is the Evident Real. Light and darkness never come together, just as night and day never come together. On the contrary, each of them conceals its companion and makes itself manifest. He who sees the day does not see the night, and he who sees the night does not see the day. The actual situation is manifest and nonmanifest, since He is the Manifest and the Nonmanifest. So there is a Real and a creation. If you witness creation, you will not see the Real, and if you witness the Real, you will not see creation. So you will never see both creation and the Real. On the contrary, you will witness the former within the latter, or the latter within the former—a witnessing by way of knowledge—since one of them will be a wrapper and the other enwrapped. (*Futūḥāt*, 2: 496; *Sufi Path*, p. 225)

5. Notice that here "originally" (*yuan* 原) means at the level of the Real Substance, or *in divinis*, or *sub specie aeternitatis*. It does not mean at the temporal beginning of creation.

6. The Arabic saying (perhaps a hadith) of which this sentence may be a translation was cited by Nūr al-Ḥaqq under Diagram 5.8.

7. Time is literally "light and shade" (*guangyin* 光陰), that is, the turning of the days. Here, however, it clearly refers to the realm of change (*yi* 易), that is, the realm in which yang and yin (literally, "sun and shade") exercise their effects. Nūr al-Ḥaqq translated the one occurrence of this expression in the Root Classic (5:57) as *zamān*, which means time in the sense of the passing of the days and the turning of the spheres. A better translation would be *ḥudūth*, which means "new arrival," or "occurring," or "coming to be," and which is used as the opposite of *qidam*, "eternity," that is, that which is outside time and beyond any sort of change and becoming.

8. This and the next two paragraphs explain that "the time of the final antiquity," or the eternal present realized by those who have rejoined the Origin, embraces the World of Principles (the Former Heaven), the World of Images or "color" (which makes the Former Heaven manifest), and the world of the ascending arc, where vital-energy rises up in the stages of the Latter Heaven. In each case, Liu reminded us that heaven, earth, and the ten thousand things are prefigured in the Root Measure (the Numerical One, Inclusive Unity); all things are fixed entities, known eternally by God.

9. This may be a reference to Ibn al-ʿArabī's doctrine of the Breath of the All-merciful.

## 5.12
## 眞一還眞圖

## 5.12
## Diagram of the Real One Circling
## Back to the Real

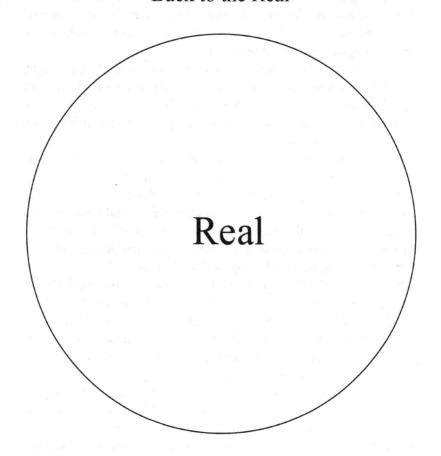

Before the movement of the one thought, the Real One is Nondesignation and Silent Suchness, and the Real One's name does not stand
by itself.[1] How is it possible for the Real to circle back?[2]

"Circling back" means to return to the beginning. Humans surely
have something dissimilar to the beginning so that they may later return to the beginning. How can the Real One have something dissimilar to what It has in the beginning?

I say: On Its own the Real One has the movement of one thought,
and all that is comes into being because of this one thought. The one
thought is the place where the Real issues forth and falsehood arises.
Falsehood cannot last long without corruption; it cannot be absent
long without coming home.[3]

Heaven and earth, humans and things, arise from numbers that are
self-so and principles that cannot but be so. When the numbers are
exhausted and the principles reach the ultimate, then heaven and
earth, humans and things, always renounce and discard form and stuff
and come home to the Real One. How is it that only the Real One
does not reject and separate itself from feeling and desire, and yet it
thinks of circling back and going back to the Real?

Someone said: The one-thought movement of the Real One is
nothing but the movement of one thought. It seems not to taint the
Complete Substance. What is the use of its circling back? Moreover,
the one thought is extremely minute. When it arises, it becomes the
illusory, and when it is transformed, it becomes the Real. How is it
possible for the Real to circle back?

I replied: Although the movement of one thought is not enough to
burden the Complete Substance, the Complete Substance always
knows the movement of this one thought. When the Complete Substance "knows," then the Complete Substance "moves."[4] How then
can it be said that this does not taint the Complete Substance?

As for what was said, "When it arises, it becomes the illusory, and
when it is transformed, it becomes the Real," it is permissible to talk
about this in terms of those who cultivate the Real, but it is not permissible to talk about it in terms of the Root Substance of the Real
One. When the thinking and acting of those who cultivate are transformed to enter into the Real One and are fully realized, impurity

will be entrusted to the Real One and will comply with the Self-so.[5] That's all.

Those who cultivate can comply with the Real One, but with whom will the Real One comply? When the illusory enters the Real, illusion becomes firmly the Real, and when the Real mixes with the illusory, the Real also becomes the illusory.

But the Real One never congeals and stagnates like this. How can It circle back?

It is also said that It circles back without having a place to which It circles back, that's all.

Those who move and appear in the principle comply with the principle, that's all. They need not ask whether this principle has another place where it is preserved or issues forth.

Those who move and appear in vital-energy comply with its full realization, that's all. They need not ask whether vital-energy has another place where it gathers inside and opens to the outside.

Those who move and appear in images and numbers comply with disappearance, that's all. They need not ask whether these images and numbers have another place where they arise and perish.

If we desire to gather together those of principle, vital-energy, and images and numbers and return them all to the Real, the Real One will never congeal or stagnate.

The one thought that already moves fuses with its place of movement, and its trace is nowhere preserved. The one thought that does not yet move is at ease in its nonmovement, and its mechanism nowhere issues forth. At this moment there is only silence without effect, only muteness and signlessness. Real and illusory are not differentiated; substance and function are not distinguished. If you want to discriminate, there is no way to discriminate, and if you want to designate, there is no way to designate. It is still the one realm of the earliest beginning, nothing else. What, then, is circling back?

## Notes

1. Naming depends upon manifestation and duality; names result from the existence of both namer and named. "The name that can be named is not the final name" (Laozi 1). Or, in Liu's terms, the name depends on the guise, and the guise on the substance (Diagram 5.6).

2. Nūr al-Ḥaqq began his explanation of the final passage in the Root Classic by employing Ibn al-'Arabī's distinction between Lord (*rabb*) and vassal (*marbūb*, the one "lorded over"), or God (*ilāh*) and divine thrall (*ma'lūh*, the one "godded over"). The moment we have a universe, we have the relationships of Lord and vassal, Creator and creature, Knower and known, and so on. The Divine Reality demands the world, and the world demands the Divine Reality. Only in the Essence per se, the level of Non-designation (Diagram 1.1), is all duality transcended; otherwise, to speak of "God" is to speak of "what is other than God," that is, the cosmos. (This is a yin/yang relationship not in terms of earth and heaven but in terms of heaven, earth, and the ten thousand things on one hand and the Supreme Principle on the other; see Murata, *Tao*, pp. 57ff.) Once nothing remains in human consciousness but the Real Being, as it ever was and ever will be, then and only then is Unifiedness established. (Boldface marks quotations from *Subtleties*.)

When he is annihilated in God; **when the three ones go back to the Essence**, that is, Unifiedness goes back to Inclusive Unity, and Inclusive Unity goes back to Exclusive Unity; and when **the heavens and man fade away**. Here what is meant by the heavens is every corporeal thing, and what is meant by man is every spiritual thing. The meaning is that none of the corporeal or spiritual forms veils him; so he never looks upon anything without seeing the Real within it. Nothing remains in the eye of his witnessing except God alone.

**Now the things**, whether corporeal or spiritual, all of them, **and the I**—myself, my descriptions, my traces, all of this—**withdraw to the Real. Or rather**, the level of **Exclusive Unity**, which is the Essence, attributes, and acts of the Real, thereby including the level of Divinity, also withdraws **to Nondelimited Existence**. For Divinity is only so in relation to the divine thrall. When the divine thrall has been negated, everything ascribed to it is also negated. So, nothing remains in the eye of his witnessing save the Nondelimited Existence, disengaged from relations and aspects.

When the one annihilated in God arrives at this level, **no form of anything** whatsoever **veils him**. In sum, the forms of the things do not cease to exist in actual fact, but rather they do not veil him from the Real. When he looks upon them, he sees nothing within them but the Real. **And no human appetite**, such as women, children, possessions, status, and so on, **holds him back** from the Real. For the root of appetite is following caprice, and when his caprice has been removed, the root of his appetite has been cut off. So how could it obstruct him? He does nothing except for the sake of God, so he loves for God and hates for God, he gives for God and holds back for God.

Since [Liu] wanted to explain the withdrawal of Exclusive Unity to the Nondelimited, he says, **When all things,** whether the heavens, the earth, or other things, **manifest their subtle meanings,** that is, the characteristics deposited within them by God, then **he,** the annihilated one, **witnesses the Real** within them, for their characteristics are among Its attributes, so within them he witnesses the Real beyond the veils of their forms. For the Real is manifest through the veils but hidden without them, in contrast to created beings.

So, **in the** moment of the **beginning, the Real discloses Itself** to Itself in Its knowledge **through** a universal task that brings together all **the** divine and created **realities** and tasks, **and now,** that is, at the moment of the end, the Real discloses Itself to him who reaches It in his witnessing, **through their forms,** that is, the forms of the realities. For the external forms are the traces of the realities.

**When he witnesses** the tasks of **the Real in the forms,** that is, in the heavens, the earth, and the things, **the seed and the fruit are complete.** Here by "seed" he means the realities of the things, and by "fruit" their forms. Just as the fruit is the same as the seed, so also the forms are the same as the realities. Neither of the two comes to be except through the self-disclosure of the Real. (*Sharḥ,* pp. 161–64/ 116–19)

3. If light appears, there must also be darkness. If the real/truth (*ḥaqq*) reveals itself, there must also be the unreal/false (*bāṭil*). The creative transformation, in other words, demands both up and down, bright and dark, yang and yin. If falsehood cannot last without corruption, this is because the Real alone is truly real, and all else by definition partakes of unrealness and therefore perishes. Koranic verses that Liu may have had in mind include "Everything is perishing but His face" (28:88) and "The Real (*ḥaqq*) has come and falsehood (*bāṭil*) has vanished; surely falsehood is ever bound to vanish" (17:81).

4. This can be a reference to a basic principle of Ibn al-'Arabī's teachings, that is, that the knower always follows the known, and, more specifically, that God as knower responds to the cosmos as known. God knows the cosmos and all that it contains as a concomitant of his knowledge of himself, and the creative flow is simply the "movement" whereby he gives existence to what he knows. The objects of his knowledge are the infinite fixed entities, and his giving existence to them is his one word, "Be!" Thereby things become articulated in the One Breath, which is to say that thereby the Most Holy Effusion gives rise to the Holy Effusion.

5. Ibn al-'Arabī often spoke of the transformation of evil into good as taking place during the return to God after death, because of the divine ac-

tivity mentioned in Koran 25:70, "God will change their ugly deeds into beautiful deeds." He also pointed out that some seekers come to see this here and now:

It will be unveiled to him that the one who acted was God, no one else. So the acts were God's, and His acts are all perfect in goodness, without any imperfection or ugliness. . . . Some people see this in this world. They are the ones who say that all God's acts are good, that there is no one who acts except God, and that the servant has no act other than the performance that is attributed to him.   (*Futūḥāt*, 3: 403; *Sufi Path*, p. 208)

# *Epilogue*

# Tu Weiming

Confucianism emerged as a local culture in the sixth century BCE in Qufu on the Shandong peninsula. It took the followers of Confucius several centuries to develop it into the mainstream of Chinese culture. We may refer to the period from the sixth century BCE to the third century CE as the first epoch of Confucian humanism. During the second epoch, which began in the tenth century and lasted into the mid-nineteenth century, Confucianism spread to Vietnam, Korea, and Japan, evolving from an enduring intellectual tradition of Chinese culture into an East Asian way of life. By then, the Chinese mind had been deeply influenced by Indian spirituality through Buddhism, which dominated the Chinese religious landscape for half a millennium. Meanwhile, Daoism re-emerged not only as a philosophy but also as a major religion. In the eighteenth century, at the height of the second epoch, Confucianism, Buddhism, and Daoism were often referred to as the Three Teachings. Some innovative scholars, such as Lin Zhaoen 林兆恩, attempted to amalgamate them into one coherent religion honoring Confucius, Buddha, and Laozi in the same temple. Such eclecticism never attracted much support from the sophisticated literati, but it reflected a particular mentality of the time: seeking unity in diversity. For political, social, and

cultural reasons, it is not far-fetched to characterize the Middle Kingdom as Confucian China. Yet religious diversity is a defining characteristic of "Confucian" China.

The famous Jesuit Matteo Ricci fully recognized this phenomenon
and adjusted his missionary strategy accordingly. He prepared himself
for more than a decade in the periphery of Macau and gradually
worked his way to Nanjing, then the center of power and influence. It
is widely claimed that his success in converting leading Confucian intellectuals to Catholicism and earning the sympathy of many scholar-
officials at court was the result of his accommodating theology and
practice. In other words, his conscientious effort to make his faith
compatible with the Confucian way was the reason behind his success.
His celebrated treatise, *The Real Meaning of the Lord on High* (*Tian-
zhu shiyi* 天主實義), has often been cited to substantiate this claim.
For a while, it was the scholarly consensus that Ricci was a Confucian
Christian or an outward Confucian and an inward Christian.

Recent scholarship has demonstrated that Ricci's ambition was not
accommodating but hegemonic.[1] His letters in Latin to the Vatican
clearly indicate that he deliberately undermined the Confucian discourse prevalent at the time in order to create a new ethos in which Catholicism could readily be accepted by committed Confucians without
arousing suspicion. His tactic seemed deceptively simple. By evoking
pre-Confucian sacred ideas, such as Heaven and the Lord on High, he
merely urged Confucians to return to the roots of Confucian teaching.
He convincingly showed that Confucius himself was very much a
product of and a contributor to this legacy. An implication of this
clever move was to reorient the Confucian literati to a source of inspiration that had been forgotten and lost. Instead of directly challenging
them, he claimed that what they had inherited for decades, if not centuries, was a radical departure from the original Confucian teaching, a
teaching that they must endeavor to remember and rediscover.

In the intellectual context of the seventeenth century, what Ricci
attempted to do was to raise fundamental questions about the authenticity and legitimacy of the second epoch of Confucianism, as shaped
by Zhou Dunyi 周敦頤, Zhang Zai 張衡, Cheng Hao 程顥, Cheng
Yi 程頤, Zhu Xi 朱熹, Lu Xiangshan 陸象山, and Wang Yangming
王陽明. Specifically, he seemed to argue that the conceptual frame-

work they had taken pains to formulate was based on a serious misunderstanding of the "real meaning" of Confucius, not to mention deeply influenced by Daoism and Buddhism. In his interpretation, seminal ideas such as *taiji* 太極 (the Great Ultimate), *li* 理 (principle), *qi* 氣 (vital-energy), *xing* 性 (nature), *xin* 心 (heart), and *tianli* 天理 (Heavenly Principle) lost their potency. The effort of the Song-Ming masters to transmit the Learning of the Way was condemned as erroneous and misleading.

This serves as a background for introducing the Islamic thinkers responsible for the Han Kitab, notably Wang Daiyu 王岱與, Ma Zhu 馬注, Liu Zhi 劉智, and Ma Dexin 馬德新. Since they are virtually unknown in the mainstream of Chinese studies, a few preliminary remarks are in order. For the sake of brevity, I will not refer to the two Mas. Also, to avoid repeating some of the pertinent points covered in Sachiko Murata's informative and insightful Introduction, I would like to begin with a personal reminiscence. With the gracious collaboration of Seyyed Hossein Nasr, I organized an Islamic-Confucian dialogue at the Harvard Inn in Cambridge in 1994. Only half a dozen or so scholars from either side attended the meeting. One of the participants, Osman Bakar, proposed at the end of the meeting that the University of Malaya sponsor a second dialogue in Kuala Lumpur the following year. Originally conceived as a small gathering, the conference grew over the subsequent months to several hundred participants and more than a thousand attendees. The main reason was the sponsorship and active participation of Deputy Prime Minister Anwar Ibrahim.

At this 1995 conference, Lee Cheuk Ying 李焯然, a historian from Singapore National University, presented a paper on Wang Daiyu. I was fascinated by his reference to *Qingzhen daxue* 清眞大學 (*The Great Learning of the Pure and Real*, or simply *The Islamic Great Learning*). It was an illuminating experience for me to encounter in Wang's text a compelling vision. When I probed further, I was intrigued by my deepening impression that the text was both intimately familiar and strangely incomprehensible. My joint venture with Murata to make sense of Wang Daiyu's project is one of the most fruitful scholarly collaborations I have ever undertaken.

For the next decade, at the initiative of Hua Tao 華濤 at Nanjing University, the Harvard-Yenching Institute sponsored three major conferences on Islamic-Confucian dialogue in China, in Nanjing, Ningxia, and Kunming. They opened my eyes to a world of ideas and practice with inexhaustible potential for exploration by scholars in the humanities and social sciences. As my horizon of Islamic culture expanded, I realized that those whom the Islamic scholars took for granted as the four shapers of the life of the mind in the Chinese Muslim communities were creative thinkers and exemplary teachers.

My first reading of Liu Zhi's *Tianfang xingli* 天方性理 (especially the elaborate diagrams) evoked in me an electrifying feeling that what was unfolding in front of my eyes might be one of the most comprehensive articulations of the meaning of life in Chinese intellectual history. As I delved into the text with Murata and William Chittick, an accomplished scholar in Islamic philosophy, I was convinced that Liu Zhi's accomplishment is rare in Chinese philosophy and unique in Ming-Qing thought. A comparative observation may be helpful here. *Renpu* 人譜 (The human profile) by Liu Zongzhou 劉宗周 (1578–1645) is a brilliant analysis of the human condition. Despite its brevity, it offers a penetrating inquiry into the process whereby a seriously flawed concrete and living human being, here and now, can transcend overwhelming odds through self-cultivation to become a true, real, and authentic person taking an active part in forming one body with Heaven, Earth, and the myriad things. *Renpu*'s core text, even with all the appended stories illustrating the key points, is relatively short, but it presents a holistic interpretation of learning to be human that is richly textured and highly inspiring. I have taught this text in graduate seminar three times at Berkeley and four times at Harvard. Although several English versions of *Renpu* have been made, none of them has been published. What Liu Zhi accomplished can be compared to what *Renpu* could have been if a few of the nuanced details that Liu Zongzhou intended to cover had been fleshed out or conveyed in a "thick description."

To the casual observer, the comparison is inadequate. *Renpu* is one of the most succinct philosophical essays in Ming Confucian thought, whereas *Tianfang xingli*, composed of thousands of complex phrases with seventy diagrams, is arguably the longest philosophical treatise in Chinese thought. In Liu Zongzhou's will, he instructed his only son to burn all his writings except the *Renpu*. Liu was one of the most respected scholar-officials at the end of the Ming dynasty. He was a teacher of Huang Zongxi 黃宗羲, and his biography and writings feature prominently in Huang's intellectual history of famous Ming Confucians. His martyrdom is recorded in the dynastic history. Furthermore, he is celebrated by modern scholars, notably Mou Zongsan 牟宗三, as a profound thinker, indeed the last philosophical giant of the second epoch of Confucian development. In contrast, Liu Zhi is virtually unknown in sinological circles. There is no evidence that he wielded much influence during his lifetime outside the intellectual circle of the Chinese Muslim community. His voluminous works were written for Confucians as well as Muslims. He cherished the hope that what he did would not only influence his fellow Muslim thinkers but also have an impact on the Chinese intellectual world at large.

Liu Zhi's autobiographical sketch gives us a clue. Reared in a scholarly family, he was well educated by both Confucian scholars and "scripture hall" (*jingtang* 經堂) masters. His putative encounter with Ma Zhu, a towering figure in Islamic studies, seems to have been an isolated occasion. His main teacher, Yuan Ruqi 袁汝琦, exerted great influence on him by exposing him to a wide range of intellectual pursuits. In addition to Arabic and Persian texts essential for his spiritual self-identity, he acquired enormous information and knowledge in Chinese studies. In his own words, he had read books in the categories of the classics, history, fiction, astronomy, music, mathematics, Buddhism, and Daoism. His erudition could have oriented him toward the path of a prolific literatus rather than an original and profound thinker, but his methodical approach to Confucian learning compelled him to hold on to the Six Classics as the standard of judgment in his life of the mind.

Thanks to his father's conscientious guidance, Liu Zhi was educated in a most sophisticated and cosmopolitan Muslim community. His father belonged to a Muslim intelligentsia who took advantage of broad learning and linguistic facility and dedicated themselves to the transmission and promulgation of Islam. Their purpose was twofold: to preserve the best "scripture hall" educational tradition for their faith community and to transform a "local knowledge" into wisdom meaningful to all interested people "under Heaven" (*tianxia* 天下).

The critical self-consciousness with which they shaped a sinophone Islamic discourse was unprecedented. Liu Zhi, in putting his father's dying wish into practice, determined to learn to be a transmitter and a promulgator. In the spirit of Confucius and Yan Hui 顏回, "fondness of learning" (*haoxue* 好學) motivated him. In a seal carved by him only two characters, *yuanxue* 願學 (willing to learn), accompany his name. He circumspectly entered the Confucian world of ideas. Mencius may have been his source of inspiration, although so far there is little documentary proof to substantiate this claim. Yet the philosophy he later developed is in perfect accord with the School of Heart and Mind (*xinxue* 心學), which is rooted in Mencian thought. He also studied Xunzi 荀子, Han Yu 韓愈, the Cheng brothers, Zhu Xi, and Lu Xiangshan. The intellectual ethos nurtured him to become an accomplished Han Kitab writer seasoned in both the Confucian and the Islamic worlds of thought. His aspiration, true to his father's expectation, was to articulate an authentic Islamic theology in Confucian terms. He cherished the hope that his works would be acknowledged and appreciated by Confucian scholar-officials as well as Muslim theorists and practitioners. Unsurprisingly he fulfilled the duty of a filial son beyond the requirements of the *Analects*: "Without changing the will of the father for three years."[2]

Underlying Liu Zhi's purpose of acquainting Confucian literati with Islam by interpreting Islam in Confucian terms was the coexistence of two spiritual universes symbolizing two complementary forms of cosmopolitanism. On one hand, he intended to present the local wisdom of the Muslim community to the cosmopolitan world of Confucian learning. At the same time, he wanted to familiarize the Confucian intellectual world with the learning of the "Heavenly Realm" so that Chinese scholar-officials could appreciate the true manifestation of the Ultimate Reality by the Utmost Sage. The point of departure for his lifelong work was a mutually edifying dialogical relationship between the self-understanding of the Chinese Muslim educated elite and the communal critical consciousness of the Confucian literati. His great aspiration was to think through and commit to writing a holistic and integrated vision of learning to be human inspired by Confucian as well as Islamic modes of thinking.

Liu Zhi dedicated his life to this intellectual and spiritual quest at the expense of his family affairs. He used all his financial resources to purchase books and travel to libraries to enhance his learning as preparation for his great work. In the journey of the mind, he noted that he spent eight years studying Confucianism, six years reading Arabic and Persian texts, three years investigating Buddhism, and one year exploring Daoism. He traveled to Shandong, specifically to Qufu to pay tribute to Confucius, and Henan, Hunan, Hubei, Shanxi, and Gansu to research archives. During his time as a peripatetic scholar, he discovered a Persian text on the life of Muhammad. Later it became the basis for his extensive study of the life of the Prophet, whom he respectfully regarded as the "utmost sage" (*zhisheng* 至聖).

Liu's devotion to thinking and writing is rare in the Confucian world. Even among Buddhists and Daoists, it is unusual. For example, Dong Zhongshu, the great Han cosmologist, spent three years reading the classics without looking at the garden in front of his house. This anecdote has been repeatedly cited as exemplifying seriousness in intellectual pursuit. Cheng Yi's predilection for the ideal life, half a day quiet-sitting and half a day reading, remained wishful thinking. The common saying of studying for ten years in front of a freezing window refers to the strenuous rote learning needed for the examinations in order to enter officialdom. Moral or spiritual self-cultivation was subsidiary to this rigorous discipline in classical studies.

Confucians, including those who have gained stature as prominent thinkers, are what we may refer to as "public intellectuals." They are politically concerned and socially engaged. Virtually all Confucians in the second epoch, especially in the Song and Ming dynasties, were scholar-officials. They were immersed in court politics and the governance of local communities. They were not meditative thinkers like the Greek philosophers, spiritual leaders like the Hindu gurus, or monk-scholars like many Christian priests during the medieval period. Of course, the matter is complex. Their philosophical reflections, spiritual practices, and scholarly pursuits involving exegeses, commentaries, essays, and recorded conversations exerted a profound influence on defining the core values and shaping the climate of opinions throughout China. Their earthly activities were different from submission to the status quo. Their quest for the meaning of life has an enduring historical significance beyond wealth and power. Although they were not philosophers, gurus, or monks, their impact on society was not restricted to the economic and political spheres. They exercised "soft power" and accumulated "cultural capital" not unlike otherworldly spiritualists.

However, as followers of Confucius and Mencius, they were committed to the improvement of the human condition here and now: "I cannot herd with birds and beasts; how can I not associate myself with my fellow human beings?"[3] Such a commitment compelled them to take an active part in politics. Political activities were vitally important in their lives.

Their self-realization entailed "regulation of the family, governance of the state, and bringing peace to all under Heaven." No matter how much they were alienated from and prosecuted by corrupt officials at court, they served the dynasty as loyal servants, upright officials, righteous critics, or courageous dissidents. They never considered leaving politics altogether. Even when they were wrongly punished for crimes that they had never committed and banished to remote areas for the wrong reasons, their concern for the well-being of the state remained strong. Strictly speaking, the primary preoccupation of these scholar-officials was political engagement rather than scholarly pursuit or philosophical reflection. This is evident from a superficial glance at their collected works. As a rule, official documents feature prominently in the entire corpus of their literary works, perhaps next only to poetry, which was often composed for social gatherings with other scholar-officials.

By contrast, Liu Zhi deliberately and determinedly chose to commit to scholarship and philosophy at fifteen. Confucius in his pithy autobiography recalls that "at fifteen, I set my heart upon learning."[4] But Confucius traveled for decades to rectify politics through moral persuasion. Only after he had been utterly disappointed at his abortive attempts to moralize politics did he reluctantly return home to work on the classics in his late sixties. Liu, in contrast, began a lifelong career as a philosopher, guru, and scholar at a much younger age. He learned to do philosophy, to guide students, and to write down what he had mastered through his extensive archival research and close reading of books in Chinese and Persian. Liu's style of life resembles that of professional academicians at leading universities today. To be sure, under Manchu rule, many Qing philologists also engaged in pure scholarship throughout their adult lives, but they defined their intellectual endeavor in terms of empiricism and realism. With the exception of a few outstanding philologists, notably Dai Zhen 戴震, none were interested in doing philosophy. Like Song and Ming Confucians, especially Wang Yangming's followers in the seventeenth century, they practiced what they taught to spread the Way among ordinary people. They would have condemned Liu Zhi's philosophizing as an exercise in "empty talk."

In the history of Confucian thought, Liu Zhi is exceptional, if not unique. In what sense can he be characterized as a Confucian? The intellectual self-definition of the aforementioned four giants of Chinese Islamic thinking is pertinent. The term Huiru 回儒 can be straightforwardly rendered as "Muslim Confucian," but generically it seems also to mean "Muslim scholar," "Muslim literatus," or "Muslim intellectual." I would contend that "Muslim Confucian" is most appropriate because these men self-consciously envisioned their conversation partners as Confucian scholar-officials. Liu Zhi did study Buddhism and Daoism. He also used Buddhist and Daoist terminology to articulate his ideas. Yet, I readily accept Professor Murata's characterization of Liu Zhi's "Sage Learning" as "Islamic Thought in Confucian Terms." I am critically aware of the difficulty of substantiating this claim. Chittick and Murata have successfully identified three Sufi thinkers as major Islamic sources for Liu. Detailed study of the Confucian sources that he tapped to build his philosophical system is a more challenging task.

In my opinion, in order to understand Liu, it is neither necessary nor desirable to undertake such a study, even if it were doable. My assumption is that Liu's proficiency in Confucian language enabled him to construct an original Islamic theology purely in classical Chinese. This is, so far as I know, a significant event in Islamic theology. It has often been assumed that Arabic and the languages that employed the Arabic script—Persian, Turkish, and Urdu—were the languages for expounding original Islamic thinking before the nineteenth century. If classical Chinese could also facilitate such a subtle and sophisticated task in the seventeenth and eighteenth centuries, it means that Islam is more than a regional phenomenon in philosophy. It also means that classical Chinese can extend its scholarly community beyond the so-called Confucian cultural area. Thus, what Matteo Ricci and his fellow Jesuits accomplished was not exceptional.

It is well documented that the Chinese Islamic thinkers were aware of the Catholic missionary activities. Indeed, Ricci and Wang Daiyu were contemporaries, and both were present in Nanjing at the same time. They could have met and engaged in an interfaith dialogue. The Islamic thinkers may have benefited from the presence of Catholic theologians. Liu Zhi reported that he had read 137 Western books. These were probably works translated by the Jesuits, but the Jesuits do not seem to have noticed the Muslims just around the corner.

A further observation is in order. Liu Zhi's relationship to Neo-Confucian thought was intimate. It was natural for him to philosophize with its terminology. It is appropriate to characterize his approach as presenting Islam in Neo-Confucian terms. Although such a characterization is correct, it may give the misleading impression of being instrumental. For instance, it may suggest that he deliberately employed Neo-Confucian terms as a tool to expound the Islamic Truth. In a way, this is exactly what he did. We have ample evidence to show that he conscientiously expressed his commitment to Truth and Reality as a Muslim thinker by availing himself of obvious Confucian ideas. I would contend that the underlying reason for him to adopt that "strategy" may have been much more complex. An inquiry on the historical moment may help us to figure out the reason behind his mode of thinking.

I would suggest that in a deeper sense Liu Zhi had no choice but to use Confucian ideas. His philosophy is so much an integral part of the manner in which he did philosophy that it is a clear case of "style as thought." In other words, the Confucian terms that he ingeniously and imaginatively used to articulate his Islamic faith essentially define the distinctive content of his philosophy. Liu Zhi does not seem to have been motivated by a wish to seek for amalgamation or eclecticism between his faith and the Neo-Confucian Way. Nor did he, like Lin Zhaoen, search for synthesis. To a certain extent he was in favor of accommodation, but in sharp contrast with Ricci's project, there is no indication that he made an attempt to undermine the transmission of the Way initiated by Zhou Dunyi, continued by Zhang Zai, Cheng Yi, and Cheng Hao, culminating in Zhu Xi, and further developed by Wang Yangming. In fact, Liu Zhi made it explicit that his mission was to demonstrate the compatibility, convergence, and unity of his faith and "the Way of Confucius and Mencius" (Kong-Meng *zhi dao* 孔孟之道). He took it for granted that the genealogy represented by the Song-Ming masters was his own Way. He did philosophy in the language of *li* (principle), *qi* (vital-energy), *ti* 體 (substance), *yong* 用 (function), *xin* (heart and mind), and *xing* (nature). To him it was not even a "rejected possibility" that Neo-Confucians were not faithful transmitters of the teaching of Confucius and Mencius.

To be sure, as a faithful Muslim and an Islamic thinker, his ultimate concern was fundamentally different from the Neo-Confucians' commitment to this-worldliness. The Neo-Confucian way of learning to be human, informed by the political culture of the time, is apparently at odds with Liu Zhi's perception of what a human being ought to be. He must have been critically aware of the tensions, conflicts, and contradictions between these two life-orientations. His internal dialogue should have oriented him to the incompatibility, divergence, and disunity between Islam and Confucianism as well. Did he simply ignore the obvious? Did he agonize over the impossibility of reconciliation? Or, was he so insensitive to the actual situation that he failed to recognize that his project was unrealizable?

We may find a tentative answer in the context of Liu Zhi's three major works. I propose that we take the work translated here, in strategy as well as in logic, as the first book. It was followed by the carefully structured monumental study on ritual. The third work is the story of the Prophet. In fact, he succinctly defined his three works, using only one word for each of the first two: *Principle* (*li* 理) is to expound the Way (*dao* 道) and *Ritual* (*li* 禮) to describe the teaching (*jiao* 教). The third he described with two words: *Utmost Sage* (*zhisheng*) epitomizes the origin of the source of "the Teaching and the Way." He believed that the three books are indivisible and should be conceived as three integrated and fundamental components of a holistic vision. He made it explicit that "they are three yet actually one whole" (*saneryizhe* 三而一者) and stated that his purpose in composing the trilogy was to "show all under Heaven the evidence of the Way in its entirety."

In the book on the Way, translated here, his self-assigned task was to define Truth and Reality in a comprehensive and integrated manner. Inspired by both the Neo-Confucian mode of thinking and Islamic philosophy, he intended to show that his intellectual and spiritual quest led him to conclude that both Confucian and Islamic wisdom point in the same direction and arrive at the same conclusion. His conviction enabled him to conduct one of the most original and systematic inquiries into the "anthropocosmic" vision of the unity between Heaven and Humanity. It seems that he intentionally rejected the strategy of justifying the truth of Islamic faith or the validity of the Neo-Confucian worldview in two different languages. He opted for one consistent interpretive process to articulate his philosophy.

Undeniably, given the intellectual ethos of the time, Liu Zhi was prompted by a strong desire to make "parochial" Islam acceptable to the "cosmopolitan" Confucian world. I hasten to point out that it is not Islamic universalism, as the exemplification of Truth and Reality, that is parochial, but rather, in terms of the prevailing Confucian culture in Liu's time, the Islamic teaching in the Chinese Muslim community was parochial. It seems natural for him to employ the presumably Buddhist method of expedient means (*upaya*) to convey his message. Textual evidence suggests that, in his considered opinion, the Classic (*jing* 經) symbolizing the Islamic Way is a specific manifestation of Muslim culture, whereas principle belongs to all under Heaven. Since the Islamic Way greatly resembles "the intention (*zhi* 志) of Confucius and Mencius," in order to make the voice of Islam audible to all people under Heaven, the major challenge was for him to demonstrate conclusively that Islamic learning is also "impartial learning" (*gongxue* 公學), publicly accountable and answerable to the vitally important issues confronting the human condition.

This may have been the underlying justification for the fact that revelation and devotional spirituality, undoubtedly central tenets of Islam, are veiled, whereas self-realization predicated on the mutuality between Heaven and humanity in the spirit of the "unity of Heaven and humanity" (*tianrenheyi* 天人合一) is accentuated. "Immanent transcendence," rather than radical transcendence, is highlighted. It should be noted that Liu's Islam and Ricci's Catholicism were fundamentally different in this regard. The idea of the "wholly other," a form of absolute otherness, impelled Ricci to reject the philosophy of Principle embraced by all Neo-Confucian masters. Whereas Neo-Confucians took "immanent transcendence" for granted as part of the authentic transmission of the Way of Confucius and Mencius, Ricci, in his hegemonic stratagem, was adamant to subvert it. He presupposed that the philosophy of principle is totally incompatible with the Christian idea of God and the doctrine of revelation. Liu, on the other hand, constructed his theology on the basis of the philosophy of principle and considered it a continuous source of inspiration for his philosophizing.

An illustration of this is found in Liu's characterization of the Prophet as the "utmost sage" in his chronological biography of Muhammad, which is an interpretive translation of a Persian text. The idea of the sage is central to Confucian learning. The practice of "learning for the sake of the self" is also conceived as "learning of the body and heart-mind," "learning of nature and mandate," "learning of the profound person," and "learning to become a sage." In this connection, sagehood is the most authentic, real, and true manifestation of humanity. The biography contains quite a few apparently Confucian features. In his depiction of how the Prophet conducted his life in this world, he offers thirty-five brief narratives.

They are (1) demeanor, (2) virtue, (3) learning, (4) bathing, (5) worship, (6) keeping the Lord in mind, (7) reciting the Classic, (8) fasting, (9) alms, (10) pilgrimage, (11) speech, (12) moving and resting, going and coming, (13) father and mother, (14) progeny, (15) marriage, (16) husband and wife, (17) older and younger brothers, (18) slaves and servants, (19) interacting with people, (20) dealing with things and affairs, (21) banquets, (22) treating disciples, (23) making friends, (24) harmonizing neighbors, (25) arts and career, (26) pleading, (27) travel, (28) negotiation, (29) healing, (30) divination, (31) interpreting dreams, (32) dwelling, (33) clothes, (34) eating and drinking, and (35) visiting the sick.

Confucian motifs and themes are pervasive and conspicuous in several of these narratives. I will mention a few as illustrations:

learning (no. 3) contains several emblematic Confucian ideas, such as "the myriad things are established in sincerity" (*cheng* 誠), "making your heart-mind constant and your will rectified," and "enlightening the Way must be the purpose of the transmission of learning." Marriage (no. 15) is the beginning of the human way. It is the source of transformation and the root of establishing oneself and completing the family and the country. The section on brothers (no. 17) states that if we can sympathetically understand the heart of our parents and apply it to the way we treat our brothers, the family will always be harmonious. The part on interacting with people (no. 19) observes that in teaching there is no discrimination with regard to status and wealth. Similarly humaneness and compassion regard age and position as one body without differentiation. Liu's comments on the arts and one's career (no. 25) refer to the four occupations: scholar, farmer, worker, and merchant. The reason that scholar is ranked first is because he can serve as the teacher of kings. Finally, the section on dwellings (32) recommends that in choosing one's residence, quality of neighborhood takes precedence over the value of the house.

The other monumental treatise of the trilogy, *The Rules and Proprieties of Islam* (*Tianfang dianli*), deals with a subject central to the Confucian tradition. Some Confucian scholars, notably those in the anglophone sinological community, obviously under the influence of Xunzi and the twentieth-century American philosopher Herbert Fingarette, advocate that propriety or the rites, especially in the *Analects*, define the Confucian Way better than the idea of humanity (*ren*). Interpreters of Confucian learning in Cultural China, following the Neo-Confucian legacy, either of the Cheng-Zhu 程朱 School (School of Principle) or the Lu-Wang 陸王 School (School of Heart and Mind), insist that humanity precedes propriety, but they never deny the importance of propriety in determining Confucian ethics, politics, society, and philosophy. James Frankel has made an admirable and thorough explanation of *Rules and Proprieties* in his doctoral dissertation, "Liu Zhi's Journey Through Ritual Law to Allah's Chinese Name: Conceptual Antecedents and Theological Obstacles to the Islamic-Confucian Harmonization of the *Tianfang Dianli*." There is no need to make extensive comments. Suffice it to offer a few examples. A glance at the table of contents is instructive. Among the twenty chapters, the tenth to thirteenth address the five basic human relationships: husband-wife, father-son, ruler-minister, brothers, and friends. Frequent reference to Confucian practices is unmistakable, especially in the comments on the rites of marriage, mourning, and burial. Without doubt, the announced purpose of the text is to defend, preserve, maintain, continue, and develop Islamic rites as practiced by the Muslims in their practical living. However, the culturally specific purpose was to contextualize Islamic rites in a language accessible to non-Muslims so that educated non-Muslim Chinese could readily see its reasonableness and meaningfulness.

Liu was much more than a philosopher and theologian. He was also a teacher, educator, commentator, investigator, explorer, and interpreter. He was charged with seemingly inexhaustible energy and resources to make Islam an integral part of Chinese philosophy. His *Displaying the Concealment of the Real Realm* (*Zhenjing zhaowei* 眞境昭微) is an incisive and penetrating meditation on the mystery of the Islamic "real realm," but he also composed several texts for children and novices as well as for the educated elite. The *Islamic Three-Character Classic* (*Tianfang sanzijing* 天方三字經), or *The Meaning of the Islamic Three-Character for Children* (*Tianfang sanzi youyi* 天方三字幼義), merits special attention here.

Modeling his work on the *Three-Character Classic* (*Sanzijing*), the ubiquitous Confucian morality book for children, Liu Zhi composed this thoughtfully constructed and elegantly presented three-character rhyming prose for beginning students of Islam. Unlike the Confucian version, which begins with the Mencian conviction that "in the origin human nature is good," the Islamic text begins with a cosmological discourse on the Real Lord's creative transformation of the universe. However, following the emergence of the human as the intelligent and spiritual being, the process of learning to be human is conceived purely in Confucian terms. Moral education takes reflection on the things at hand as its point of departure. Filial piety, serving one's parents and teacher, recognizing the proper order of the young and old, differentiating the hierarchy of the honored, knowing humanity and deference, practicing propriety and ritual behavior, respecting words and deeds, and being aware of wrongdoing constitute elementary education. After these values are internalized, the practice of the

Way commences. Only after the discussion of the Way's embodiment, involving the efforts of "vigilant solitariness" (*shendu* 慎獨) and "sincerity of the will" (*chengyi* 誠意), are specific Muslim practices offered.

It is certainly inadequate to depict Liu Zhi as an Islamic apologist or propagandist. Undeniably, he was motivated by a fervent interest in promulgating the Islamic Way. He did not compose his magnificent work as a value-neutral analysis. Nor did he regard himself as a disinterested scholar. He seems to have had a strong passion for his intellectual pursuit with an obvious agenda. This brings us to an intriguing methodological issue. Liu Zhi's mode of apprehending Truth and Reality was not through propositional knowledge but through experiential understanding. My idea of "embodied knowing" (*tizhi* 體知) is pertinent here.

Liu was firmly convinced that his quest for Truth and Reality is an intrinsic value independent of any instrumental or strategic missionary considerations. His *Nature and Principle* is intended to show that his faith in Islam must transcend any distorted or partial representation. Rather, it is based on a worldview that offers an adequate understanding of what Truth and Reality is. Ontological insight rather than empirical investigation is the proper method for grasping this. Deduction as well as induction is required. Thinking so conceived is more than cognition. It involves not only the brain and mind but also the heart and body. It is inexorably a transformative act. From a positivistic point of view, the danger of subjectivism and solipsism looms large. This approach seems incompatible with disinterested objective inquiry. Yet personal knowledge is not derived from private opinion, conjecture, or speculation. It is the outcome of multifaceted intellectual reflection, rigorous spiritual exercise, persistent meditation, and profound rumination. As a form of experiential understanding, it is neither private nor subjective. Indeed, it is diametrically opposed to subjectivism and solipsism, but not at all in conflict with objectivity, disinterestedness, and impartiality.

Liu's attempt to grasp Truth and Reality in its all-encompassing fullness was predicated on his commitment to ritual practice, erudition in literate culture, familiarity with history, and extensive learning. This kind of "embodied knowing" entails logic, research, and meditation. It can deepen self-understanding and foster an open and resourceful subjectivity that enables one to transcend egoism, parochialism, ethnocentrism, and anthropocentrism, let alone subjectivism and solipsism. Mencius' idea of "getting it by oneself" (*zide* 自得) is relevant here:

A profound person steeps himself in the Way because he wishes to find it in himself. When he finds it in himself, he will be at ease in it; when he is at ease in it, he can draw deeply upon it; when he can draw deeply upon it, he finds its source wherever he turns. That is why a profound person wishes to find the Way in himself.[5]

Liu's "getting it oneself" implied that his philosophical inquiry was motivated by purpose and that he did it with an agenda. On the surface, he seems to have violated two basic requirements of any unbiased scientific investigation—disinterestedness and value-free neutrality. However, if we examine Liu's modus operandi in conducting his scholarship, we realize that he moved from word to word, sentence to sentence, chapter to chapter, and diagram to diagram with a seriousness and sophistication not unlike the high Qing masters of Evidential Learning, notably Dai Zhen. In fact, he was so conscientious in his detailed and nuanced scholarly work that he trained himself in philology, phonology, textual analysis, and several other relevant disciplines. This is displayed in his *Explaining the Meaning of Islamic Letters* (*Tianfang zimu jieyi* 天方字母解義). In this supposedly educational manual, he explained each letter thoroughly. Furthermore, he described each stroke with illustrations. Beyond doubt Liu was seasoned in evidential methodology, which in the twentieth century was acclaimed by Hu Shi 胡適 as a significant demonstration of proto-scientific spirit in imperial China.

Nevertheless, his learned competence was not the result of empirical studies; nor was it the consequence of observing natural phenomena. Rather, it was a manifestation of the "investigation of things" (*gewu* 格物) in the *Great Learning*, especially the kind construed by Zhu Xi. To both, the "investigation of things" is a prerequisite for the ultimate intellectual and spiritual understanding of all humanly constructed forms of rationality. Although Liu Zhi was thoroughly familiar with this kind of study, his inspiration came from the wisdom of Confucian masters and Sufi thinkers. It was not a matter of rigid adherence to dogma without rigorous examination. He was well prepared to defend every word he put down on paper. He did not merely describe what he had learned from the Neo-Confucian masters and Sufi thinkers. He was able to expound Truth and Realty from within because he had totally internalized their terms, languages, and modes of thinking. Indeed, he presented his integrated work through them and with them. His systematic construction was the result of digging as well as building. By digging, I mean that he tapped internal spiritual resources and utilized information and knowledge acquired by empirical observation. Instead of merely building an intellectual edifice, he drew from many sources.

At first glance, I had the impression that Liu Zhi had opted for a simple and clear presentation. The text seemed to be lucid with the aid of his elegantly designed diagrams. After I studied the text intensely and seriously for a while, however, I became aware of the complexity of his grand system. Beneath the clarity and simplicity, complex sentences and words with multiple meanings are everywhere. Even the diagrams with only one character are pregnant with a meaning that overflows the character's apparent denotation. There are many undercurrents beneath the surface tranquility. Having devoted numerous afternoons to a close reading for six years with Murata and Chittick, I learned that there is a fruitful ambiguity in many seemingly unproblematic phrases. I was convinced what I had been reading closely is an informed, rich, and exceeding creative book. It is a major contribution to Neo-Confucian thought from a comparative philosophical perspective. I also suspect that it is one of the most significant Islamic masterpieces in the golden age of the Chinese Muslim cultural renaissance. I have no doubt that it will become an important reference for Islamic scholarship in Arabic and Persian. I will offer a personal account of this magnum opus.

Liu Zhi's frequent reference to paradoxes, such as apparent/ hidden, manifest/obscure, obvious/subtle, ordinary/unusual, and simple/complex and his fascination with "complementary bipolarities," such as yin/yang, substance/function, former/latter, principle/ vital-energy, principle/image, body/heart, ascend/descend, coming/ returning, nature/principle may mislead us into believing that the "either-or" mode of analysis is his basic methodology. To be sure, he used dichotomies as an expedient means to drive home his main theses, but he built his complex system with a subtle reasoning and brilliant interpretation in sharp contrast with any simpleminded dichotomous thinking. The tangible structure he constructed is buttressed by many layers of substrata invisible to those who read about rather than read from the labor of his "heart and blood" (*xinxue* 心血). Of course, he philosophized with his brain and mind, but his thorough immersion in the sacred task implies that he did not think with his head alone but with his entire person. This kind of knowing is more profound and embracing than mental activities stimulated by cerebral and cognitive functions. It reflects an experiential understanding, a dynamic process, and an ever-deepening subjectivity. Knowledge so acquired has transformative power.

This reminds me of an anecdote about the alleged progenitor of the twentieth-century New Confucian movement, Xiong Shili 熊十力. He criticized Feng Youlan 馮友蘭 (Fung Yu-lan) straightforwardly and bluntly to his face when the famous historian of philosophy labeled "innate knowledge" or "primordial awareness" (*liangzhi* 良知) an assumption, a hypothesis. Xiong insisted that it should be understood as a manifestation, an experienced reality. We may question this seemingly dogmatic approach. Either analytical or linguistic philosophers would condemn it as poetic and meaningless. Actually what Xiong advocated is philosophy as a way of life. Life is a puzzle that cannot be resolved by detached analysis without the personal participation of the analyzer.

The explication of this kind of philosophical text entails practice. Without practice or, more appropriately, spiritual exercise, it is difficult if not impossible to hear the authorial voice. To read closely such a text one must read from it rather than about it. It presupposes a mental attitude. This may have prompted Tang Junyi 唐君毅, a second-generation intellectual giant of the New Confucian movement, to assert that "respect" is required for understanding one's own tradition. Doing philosophy so understood is not fundamentally different from religious acts such as worship, prayer, and participation in sacred rites. Practice, as a form of spiritual exercise, is not necessarily social praxis in the Marxist sense, but as a transformative act it inevitably, sometimes inadvertently, makes a difference in the behavior, attitude, and belief of the practitioner. Indeed, our world-view, social interaction, and personal knowledge are profoundly affected by this ostensibly cerebral function. It is inconceivable that after we have closely read a book, not to mention a classic, we are not transformed by that experience. Much more so, if we commit ourselves to putting in writing what we have pondered for years.

The demand for personal engagement needs clarification. As I have mentioned, "personal" is radically different from "private." Private suggests a closed space protected by law or convention. Personal is sharable and publicly accountable. I will most likely conceal my private opinions, but I feel impelled to share and defend my strongly felt ideas or experiences. In my personal reading of Liu Zhi's masterwork, I am awed by his ability to offer richly textured and nuanced interpretation of all his theses. He combines an all-inclusive framework with detailed explication. The compelling way he integrates humanity with Heaven is rare in the entire history of Chinese thought. He apparently does so by argumentation and persuasion, but in a deep sense he is guided by a "firm and hard" faith in Truth and Reality. He takes it for granted that there is an Islamic-Confucian simultaneity and synchronicity. He was totally convinced that Confucius, Mencius, Neo-Confucian masters, and the Sufi thinkers were fellow seekers of Truth and Reality. This conviction was the beginning rather than the conclusion of his intellectual enterprise. In other words, it was not a considered opinion derived from a focused investigation, but the presupposition as a point of departure for his philosophizing. The convergence and unity of Islamic and Confucian paths were so evident to him that his fidelity to both of them was the foundation of his theory and practice.

It would be misleading to assume that Liu Zhi's interpretive stance indicates his failure to notice the difference between Confucianism and Islam. He seems naïvely to have accepted the claim that Truth and Reality is so transparent that either Confucius and Mencius' Way or the Muslim path, if pursued intelligently and rigorously, will necessarily lead to convergence. He seems also to believe that it matters very little whether the path is Confucian or Islamic; if it is pursued to the ultimate end, the result will be identical. His inclusivity may be wrongly perceived as inadvertently giving in to abstract universalism without proper attention to the multiplicity of lived concreteness. On the contrary, although he preferred to under-score commonality, he was not at all blind to difference.

Unlike Matteo Ricci, he was neither accommodating nor subvert-ing. Ricci regarded the Neo-Confucian project, either the Cheng-Zhu or the Lu-Wang version, as an obstacle to his missionary work. He was an outsider and refused to engage his contemporary Confucians in an edifying conversation. To him they were subjects of conver-sion. Ricci chose to depict the evolution of the Confucian tradition from the first to the second epoch as a misrepresentation of the teaching of Confucius and Mencius. His well-calculated strategy was to condemn the transmitters of the Confucian Way. He believed that they suffered from forgetting what the authentic Confucian message was. Actually he implicitly asserted that the only way to recover the lost message was to hark back to the pre-Confucian era when the idea of a personal God (Shangdi) was still vibrant.

This deliberate choice to alienate himself from the Neo-Confucian ethos reminds us of the work of the Japanese Confucian Ogyu Sorai. In his critique of Zhu Xi, Sorai advocated a similar idea. He urged his contemporary Confucians to return to the pre-Confucian age when the Lord-on-High and Heaven took on the form of a personal-ized, transcendent reality fundamentally different from the ideas of Principle and Nature in Neo-Confucian thought. Like Ricci, Sorai considered the critique of Zhu Xi's onto-cosmological vision as a point of departure for articulating his authentic interpretation of the sage intention.

By contrast, Liu Zhi openly acknowledged his indebtedness to the Confucian masters of the second epoch. He cherished the hope that his endeavor would be recognized as an integral part of Confucian self-understanding. He was an insider and felt at home in the Confu-cian intellectual environment. He would not and could not abandon his Confucian roots. His philosophical reflection was based on them and his philosophical growth was sustained by them. Neo-Confucian thought was an inseparable part of his mentality.

As already mentioned, Liu Zhi did not use Confucian terms in-strumentally as tools. They were the manifestations and constitutive parts of his philosophical reflection. They were the reason behind the complexity and richness of his brilliant construction. These terms helped him to think through the vital issues he encountered in his interpretive task. They not only shaped his style of thinking but also defined the contour of his thought. Therefore, Confucian terms that appear in Liu Zhi's musing on nature and principle are pregnant with far-reaching implications for those committed to the Confucian tradition. Even a single word is full of meaning. Each of the generic terms that designate all-encompassing concepts such as Being (*you* 有), Real (*zhen* 眞), Substance (*ti*), and Human (*ren*) seems to provide an inexhaustible supply of food for thought. The four terms cited above appear in the four diagrams symbolized by only one character. None of them is simplistic. All are essential to Liu Zhi's project.

Professor Murata has already narrated Liu Zhi's story with an emphasis on the Muslim side from a comparative civilizational perspective. She convincingly shows that he was an authentic Islamic thinker thoroughly loyal to the teachings of the Prophet and that he was a seasoned Sufi philosopher methodically accurate in presenting the main streams of Islamic thought. I would like to make a few observations from the Confucian side and offer my idiosyncratic interpretation of his historical significance and contemporary relevance in Chinese thought and religion.

Liu Zhi divided his *Explication of the Root Classic* into five volumes. Each of them is guided by a coherent vision. He begins with the root text, symbolized by ten diagrams; this is followed by an inquiry into cosmic transformation, followed by a portrayal of nature, a description of human growth, an elucidation of the process of self-realization, and an exposition of the ultimate return to the Real. Each theme is illustrated by twelve diagrams. The ten diagrams of the root text give a panoramic view of the whole project. Ostensibly, his self-assigned task is to present a treatise on Islamic theology in a language understandable to the Confucian intellectual community, thought-provoking to those familiar with the Chinese Muslim world of ideas, and inspiring to those committed to the development of Han Kitab. It is evident that he spent a great deal of time and energy on establishing a platform for Islamic-Confucian dialogue with the purpose of promoting recognition, acceptance, and respect for the Muslim way of life among Confucian scholar-officials. His essay on explaining the Huihui is a testament to this kind of effort. It is also evident that he considered it an important part of his mission to help his fellow Chinese Muslim teachers and scholars understand directly and intimately the primary sources of Islam. His work on explaining the meaning of Islamic letters with a focused investigation on the Arabic alphabet is a testimony to this mission.

I will follow the rhetoric of the diagrams and offer brief comments on each of the five volumes:

1. Onto-cosmological inquiry on creation
2. Portrayal of heaven and earth
3. Thick description of the advent of the human
4. Elucidation of self-realization
5. Exposition of the ultimate return

Arguably, like the overwhelming majority of his contemporary Confucian scholars, Liu followed the Mencian line, although Xunzi remained a significant reference. Specifically, his worldview is in perfect accord with the onto-cosmological vision of the *Book of Change* and the *Doctrine of the Mean*. Among the Neo-Confucian thinkers, Zhou Dunyi readily comes to mind. Zhou's explanation of the Diagram of the Great Ultimate serves as an illuminating reference. Liu Zhi's decision to name his first diagram the "nondesignation of the very beginning" (0.1, 1.1) is particularly relevant here. The long debate on the relationship between the Great Ultimate and the Ultimate of Nonbeing in Confucian cosmology is focused on the issue of being and nothingness. Since Zhou appropriated the diagram from the Daoist tradition, in Confucian sensibility the original design of placing nonbeing beyond the Great Ultimate must be rejected or reinterpreted. Otherwise the beginning would be designated as nothingness, which is inconceivable from the Confucian perspective. The solution is to regard nonbeing as the indescribability of the Great Ultimate. It does not have an ontological status. It functions only as an indication of the "nondesignation" of the Great Ultimate. Wing-tsit Chan's effort to render the first part of the Diagram as "the Ultimate of Nonbeing and also the Great Ultimate" is an ingenious effort to fuse the two in a new vision. Similarly Liu Zhi, given his commitment to Islam and Confucianism, could not have used the single character *wu* 無 to designate the beginning. The choice of "non-designation" (*wucheng* 無稱) was measured and wise.

The diagram of "nonattachment to the real substance" (1.2) appears to be Daoist or Buddhist. The idea of "nonattachment" (*wuzhuo* 無着) may give that impression, but it is merely a qualifier. The key word is "substance." It is substantially different from the Daoist "nothingness" (*wu* 無) or the Buddhist "emptiness" (*kong* 空). The function that is directly deduced from substance is the great function in which knowledge and power are not differentiated (1.3). This undivided nature precedes the act in which substance and function begin to divide (1.4). The act inevitably gives rise to conscious functions such as looking, hearing, granting, depriving, begetting, and transforming, necessarily occasioned by the separation of knowledge and power. Analogously the "flow of the real principle" entails the perfect unity between principle and nature (1.5). In the spirit of the opening line of the *Doctrine of the Mean*, "what is endowed by Heaven is nature," Heaven is the ultimate source of nature and the *raison d'être* of the wisdom that is inherent in human nature. Yet when nature and principle begin to divide, the ontological realm transforms itself into the cosmological and existential realms (1.6). In the world of principles, human nature evolves from the natures of stone, metal, grass, trees, birds, and beasts. This reminds us of a similar statement in Xunzi: "Fire and water possess vital-energy but are without life. Grass and trees have life but no consciousness and feeling. Birds and beasts have consciousness and feeling but no sense of rightness. The human possesses vital-energy, life, consciousness, and feeling, and, in addition, a sense of rightness."

According to the thesis of the "continuity of being," the emergence of the human does not imply radical separation. Rather, the human is interconnected with the myriad things. Even the "vast sediment" is no exception. It is not far-fetched to point out that there is consanguinity between the human and all other modalities in the universe. I suppose that this is the underlying reason that human beings can form one body with Heaven, Earth, and the myriad things.

However, the principle of differentiation is implicit in the idea of continuity, consanguinity, and oneness. Each of the emerging properties such as life, consciousness, and rightness has its distinctiveness, which is not reducible to the genetic conditions underlying its emergence. Life, which has evolved from vital-energy, must be comprehended at a higher level and in a more complex structure. By analogy, consciousness, which has evolved from vital-energy and life, can no longer be comprehended in terms of them alone. The advent of the human signifies the presence of a new reality. Although humanity is rooted in vital-energy, life, and consciousness, it cannot be reduced to any one of them or all of the three combined. Thus, the uniqueness of the human must be sought from both its sources and its ability to go beyond its rootedness.

The same principle is applicable to Liu Zhi's differentiation of the human into levels of attainment, presumably through self-cultivation. From commoners to the utmost sage, the range of perfection, in an ascending order, encompasses good, pure and upright, wise, great worthies, average sages, ambassador sages, and great sages. This strikes a chord with the Mencian perception of the stages of human perfection:

The desirable is called good (*shan* 善).

To have it in oneself is called true (*xin* 信).

To have it sufficiently and fully is called beautiful (*mei* 美).

The sufficiency and fullness that shines forth brilliantly is called great (*da* 大).

The greatness that transforms is called sage (sheng 聖).

The sagehood that is beyond comprehension is called spiritual (*shen* 神).[6]

Good, true, beautiful, great, sage, and spiritual constitute the entire scope of realizing authentic humanity. The true emerges from the good, but it cannot be understood in terms of the good. By inference, sagehood, as the culminating point of the human quest for excellence, entails goodness, truth, beauty, and greatness. At the same time, it rises beyond greatness. In the Confucian personality ideal, it is difficult to imagine that there is a category, namely the spiritual, above the attainment of the sage. I believe that "spiritual" here is used to describe the transforming power of the sage as ineffable, indeed mysterious.

Ambassador sage is not a familiar category in the Confucian tradition, but it seems to convey a sense of respect and reverence. The idea of different degrees of sage manifestation is not at all alien to Confucian thinking. Mencius' characterization of types of sages, the hierarchy specifying different levels of attainment, is evident in Liu Zhi's diagram. Mencius made it abundantly clear that he followed the Confucian Way, but he put Confucius in a comparative context to illustrate his preference. Bo Yi 伯夷 was a pure sage, Yi Yin 伊尹 was a responsible sage, and Liu Xia Hui 柳下惠 was a harmonizing sage, whereas Confucius was a timely sage.[7] It seems that Mencius wanted to demonstrate that "timeliness" (*shi* 時) was more congenial to his personal choice, but certainly not superior to purity, responsibility, and harmony. It is plausible that he envisioned timeliness as a more encompassing category that can incorporate the other three into its rich, flexible, balanced, and suitable quality. In contrast with this parallel approach, Liu Zhi's hierarchical structure emphasizes that the "utmost sage" is way above the others. Obviously his standards of excellence were dictated by a revelatory transcendence significantly different from the Confucian predilection for immanence. Even in this regard the difference is not pronounced. After all, the Mandate of Heaven expresses itself in ideas such as "human nature is ordained by Heaven." The transcendent dimension is also essential to Confucian humanism.

The diagram of the "display of vital-energy and the hiddenness of principle" (1.7) offers a highly suggestive reading of the subtle relationship between principle and vital-energy. In Chinese Confucian thought, the intra-philosophical debate in the Song-Ming period (the Second Epoch) was between the School of Principle and the School of Heart and Mind, whereas in the Choson dynasty, under the influence of Yi Toegye 李退溪 and Yi Yulgok 李栗谷, it was between the School of Principle and the School of Vital-Energy. It seems unlikely that Liu Zhi was aware of the Korean intellectual scene, but his evocation of "original vital-energy" in his onto-cosmological deliberation is in accord more with the Korean than with the Chinese style of reasoning. The idea of principle hidden in the manifested vital-energy was familiar to Zhu Xi, and the positive appraisal of vital-energy as the origin of creativity is embraced by both the School of

Principle and the School of Heart and Mind. Some contemporary scholars in the People's Republic of China characterize Zhang Zai as the progenitor of materialism. This is a misreading and wrong. There is no equivalence in pre-twentieth-century Chinese philosophy of the so-called controversy between Materialism and Idealism. It is a recent phenomenon unprecedented in the entire history of Chinese thought resulting from the imposition of the Western dichotomy on the Chinese mode of thinking. A central thesis in the Neo-Confucian tradition was the "oneness of principle and the multiplicity of its manifestations" (*liyifenshu* 理一分殊). For instance, Feng Youlan admitted that it is difficult to identify unequivocally an indigenous Song-Ming school of vital-energy.

The three diagrams of yin-yang—the division of the beginning, the end of the division, and alteration and transformation (1.8)—narrate the critical phases by which the "original vital-energy" engenders fire, air, soil, and water. The Four Images appear to be a subset of the Five Elements, without metal. It will take a while to explain how the "beginning of the forms" through "the ascending pure and the descending turbid" evolved into the "differentiated forms of above and below" (1.9). It is relatively easy to show the logic of the generative power of earth in producing the ten thousand things through the evolution of metal, wood, and life and that this evolutionary productivity is oriented toward Heaven (1.11). The previous diagram, "the firm position of Heaven and Earth," is a precondition for the appearance of the human (1.10). The designation of the human as "the level of completeness of the great perfection" (1.12) strikes a sympathetic resonance with the elegant depiction in Zhou Dunyi's Explanatory Essay: "It is the human alone who receives the highest excellence of the five elements. Therefore, the human is the most spiritual (*ling* 靈). Its physical form comes into being. Its spirituality arouses wisdom."[8]

The discussion of substance and function, the flow of the principle, the interplay between principle and vital-energy, the division of yin and yang, the positioning of heaven and earth, and the emergence of the myriad things are all motifs in Confucian onto-cosmology. It is interesting to learn that in Liu Zhi's ontology and cosmology the culminating point, "diagram of the level of the completeness of the great perfection," is symbolized by the single word "human." My characterization of the Confucian "faith" in anthropocosmic terms can very well be perceived as Liu Zhi's chosen style in formulating his thought.

In Murata's introduction and the detailed footnotes she and Chittick prepared, they convincingly explain the Islamic sources that Liu Zhi tapped to formulate his interpretive stance. It is not surprising that in their judgment he was faithful to the expository comments of the three Sufi masters. They also identified specific texts to substantiate their claim. On the Confucian side, Zhou Dunyi's diagram and the "Former Heaven" and "Latter Heaven" in the numerology of Shao Yong 邵雍 were plausible inspirations for him, but it seems impossible to pin down his Confucian sources. In my judgment, though, there is no need to identify his indebtedness to specific Confucian masters. His communal critical self-consciousness enabled him to philosophize from within. The Confucian legacy, like the air he breathed, was the atmosphere in which he found his personal identity. Arguably, his Sufi knowledge was purposefully acquired through rigorous study, even though as a devoted Muslim he had been brought up in the Islamic doctrine, ritual, and practice.

In Liu Zhi's "portrayal of heaven and earth" (Volume 2), his description of sagehood, human nature, astronomy, and geography clearly uses Islamic terminology, but the framework of the design of heaven and the pattern of earth would have been understandable to Confucians of his time. The dichotomies of "form and vessel" and "principle and image" are familiar Neo-Confucian terms originating in the *Book of Change*. The static picture and the dynamic process of the "nine heavens," the position of the "four agents" (without the metal in the "five agents"), the alternation of the four seasons, the division of the earth, and the differentiated boundaries of heaven are not distinctly Confucian categories, but the evocation of the idea of "one thread" (*yiguan* 一貫) in the "diagram of the overspreading of the one" is revealing.

The term "one thread," which refers in the *Analects* to Confucius' ability to tie all his virtues into a coherent wholeness, is employed here to show the dynamic union of the former and the latter heavens. The expression "one thread" does not mean there is oneness beyond the two heavens. The idea of "overspreading" (*yangyi* 洋溢) suggests that the union is dynamic, robust, and overflowing. These Confucian elements are constitutive parts of Liu Zhi's frame of mind. They were an integral part of the way he expressed his faith. To reiterate the point repeated above, he did not appropriate Confucian terms to help him express his Islamic faith. To him Islam and Confucianism share the same faith in human flourishing. As a Chinese Muslim, he arduously struggled to make sure that Islam would be properly appreciated by Confucian scholar-officials. He presupposed that Islam can significantly enrich Confucian discourse and empower Confucians to attain the highest good in their quest for moral excellence. This suggests an ongoing internal dialogue signifying mutual reference and mutual learning.

The first two diagrams in Volume 2 can serve as an illustration. The "Diagram of the Levels of the Natures of Former Heaven" (2.1) is reminiscent of the "Diagram of the Beginning of the Differentiation of the Natures and the Principles" in Volume 1 (1.6). Diagram 2.2, perhaps the most elaborate among all seventy diagrams, is apparently anthropomorphic. It connects all the evolutionary stages even before the appearance of the human with moral qualities: obstinacy and dullness for stone, fixity and firmness for metal, issuing and nurturing for grass and trees, and knowledge and awareness for birds and beasts. The nine levels of humanity are also clearly differentiated. How humans handle knowledge and power determines where they stand in the hierarchy of moral attainment: selfish use of knowledge and power (common people), following and practicing (good people), firmly guarding (pure and upright), embodied recognition (wise people), hoping for and looking toward (great worthies), manifesting and elevating (average sage), obedient response (ambassador sage), freely using (great sage), and undifferentiated sameness (utmost sage). Whether or not Confucians would use the same expressions, they could without difficulty appreciate the reasonableness of the total picture.

Liu Zhi's "thick description of the advent of the human" is both intriguing and unsurprising (Volume 3). The elaboration of the growth of the human body in the fetus is rare in Confucian literature. It may have been derived from medical knowledge of his time. However, the concern for pregnancy, not to mention the prominence given to "fetus education" (*taijiao* 胎教), recalls that Confucians of his age would appreciate his concentration on the evolution of the human body before birth. The Confucian attentiveness to self-cultivation from youth to old age is an experiential and logical extension of this process of becoming fully human. Liu Zhi displayed loving care of the body in his narrative of human growth. I suppose that he would have been delighted had he known that in recent times Confucian moral teaching has been classified as care ethics.

The manifestation of the function of nature, heart/mind, and body and the ascendance from body and heart/mind to spirit/life are root metaphors in Confucian humanism, perceptively explicated in Murata's introduction as "spiritual anthropology." A salient feature of this comprehensive and integrated humanism is the rich texture of the body. The body is definitely not "the prison house of the soul." Its inward and outer apertures are the physical, mental, and spiritual openings for the five internal organs—heart, lungs, spleen, kidney, and liver. They can communicate with the outside world through brain, eyes, ears, mouth, nose, the four limbs, and other constitutive members of the body.

Liu Zhi's developmental psychology is embedded in religious ethics. The three natures, namely the nature of vital-energy, root nature, and the nature of continuity (3.10–3.12), offer a whole range of values for human flourishing in the spiritual as well as the emotional sense. The nature of vital-energy embodies a variety of virtuous qualities including knowledge, love, hate, bravery, boldness, laughter, speech, and awareness. It is endowed with authentic possibilities and realizable potentialities already present "at the beginning of emergence and departure from the mother's belly." The root nature expresses itself in the determining will, clear awakening, luminous intelligence, and the inner urge in search of wisdom. In the nature of continuity, "the complete substance and the great function" of body and heart/mind are manifested and revealed.

The root nature (*benxing* 本性) is a principal concern of Neo-Confucian thinkers. As inheritors of the Mencian line, they were particularly interested in exploring the inner resources for self-cultivation. They believed that cardinal virtues, such as humanity, rightness, propriety, and wisdom, all have their germs in the human heart/mind. Since the heart/mind is a defining characteristic of being human, human nature is intrinsically good and godlike. Thus Mencius avows that if we can fully realize our heart/mind, we will know our nature, and, through knowing our nature, we will know Heaven. Liu Zhi declares in his discussion of the nature of vital-energy that "humans are the spiritual of the ten thousand things." In the diagram of the root nature, he explicitly states: "Within the root nature are embedded all the ten thousand principles and all the ten thousand affairs without leaving aside anything, and it is equipped with all the ten thousand things." As Murata and Chittick observe in their note, this is a direct quote from *Mencius*: "All the ten thousand things are there in me." Actually, similar ideas appear in the *Book of Change*, the *Doctrine of the Mean*, and the works of Neo-Confucian thinkers, notably Cheng Hao, Lu Xiangshan, and Wang Yangming.

The nature of continuity (*jixing* 繼性) is unfamiliar to Confucians. The term is virtually unknown in Neo-Confucian literature. Without the background of the monotheistic God, it is difficult to understand the significance of this nature as what Murata and Chittick assert, the "Muhammadan spirit, the First Intellect, and the Ascribed Spirit." Yet Liu Zhi describes "the original nature of the Real Ruler's chief Manifestation" as shared in common by heaven/earth and humans/things. This can be readily apprehended by those familiar with and committed to Cheng Hao's and Wang Yangming's idea of "forming one body with heaven, earth and the myriad things" and in Zhang Zai's insistence that "nature is not something individual." By implication, it is intimately connected with the world in the most inclusive sense. The way that Zhang Zai in his *Western Inscription* envisions the human is pertinent here: "Heaven is my father and earth is my mother, and even such a small creature as I finds an intimate place in their midst. Therefore that which fills the universe I regard as my body and that which directs the universe I consider as my nature. All people are my brothers and sisters, and all things are my companions."

The fusion of the immanent and the transcendent evokes a form of religiosity that can very well be characterized as "immanent transcendence." Liu Zhi's allusive way of approaching his "devotional spirituality" by unifying the macrocosm with the microcosm strikes a sympathetic resonance with the Confucian onto-cosmology elegantly presented in the *Book of Change*, the *Doctrine of the Mean*, and *Mencius*. It seems Liu Zhi self-consciously offered a theology that underscores continuation rather than annihilation. The positive assessment of the human as a spiritual being is sharply contrasted with self-denial: "He sees and experiences the nothingness of his own separative self and participates with full awareness in the Real's self-disclosure" (notes on 3.12). This makes Liu Zhi a Confucian Muslim par excellence.

This line of thinking naturally leads to the "Diagram of the Meeting and Uniting of Heart and Nature" (4.1). The focus on self-realization is predicated on the malleability, improvability, and perfectibility of human nature through personal, ethical, and spiritual cultivation. The ultimate concern of Confucius' and Mencius' way is realizing the authentic humanity. In the *Analects*, learning is perceived as "for the sake of the self." It is the way transmitted by the ancient sages and worthies. Character-building rather than social utility is the priority of self-realization, which requires a conscientious effort to animate the past in order to revitalize the present. This perception entails rigorous practice, not as a subjectivist endeavor but as a publicly accountable transformative act, putting forward the spirit of continuity. Continuity so conceived, in the understanding of Lu Xiangshan, is embodied by ancient and present-day sages in east, west, south, and north. Core ideas such as "real heart" (*zhenxin* 真心), "first heart" (*chuxin* 初心), and "root suchness" (*benran* 本然) are Neo-Confucian elucidations of Mencius' instruction that "learning consists of nothing but the quest for the lost heart."[9] Daoist or Buddhist influence is evident, but the center of attention and the context are different.

Liu Zhi explained human flaws in terms of inertia, limitation, and self-deception rather than evil as a positive force. This explanation is commensurate with Liu Zongzhou's explication of human mistakes (*guo* 過) in the *Renpu*. Admittedly Liu Zongzhou's account is much more elaborate and nuanced, but Liu Zhi's six diagrams illustrating heresy, double-mindedness, perplexity, indifference, rebellion, and hypocrisy (4.9–10) are a thoughtful exhibition of the veils and obstacles on the way to authentic existence as a faithful Muslim. His contention that attaining "root suchness" requires "cultivation of body, purification of heart, and realization of nature" could have been articulated by Liu Zongzhou as well (4.11).

The fifth volume, "exposition of the ultimate return," gives the strong impression that, in the concluding chapter of Liu Zhi's magnum opus, he decides to make a firm assertion of his self-definition as a Muslim thinker. In the introductory summary, he labels the volume as a supplement to his highly complex and yet lucid presentation of the Islamic principle and nature from a palpably Confucian perspective. Whether by design or by default, these are the least Confucian of all his diagrams. Even in his noticeable reference to indigenous sources, Daoist or Buddhist rather than Confucian material is used. Specifically, in the discussion of the mutual implications of microcosm and macrocosm, he draws heavily from the insights of Zhuangzi 莊子 (5.8–5.9), and in his observation that one breath is eternal antiquity and that eternal antiquity is one breath, the inspiration seems to come from Tiantai 天台 Buddhism (5.10–5.11).

Nevertheless, as strong undercurrents, Confucian ideas are ubiquitous. The distinction between substance and function and the idea of the oneness of principle and the multiplicity of its manifestations are observable exemplifications. Mutuality between Heaven and the Human in the notion of the "human ultimate" (*renji* 人極) is worth noting:

Without the world of heaven and earth, the world of the Human Ultimate would have no assistance. Without the world of the Human Ultimate, the world of the Real Principle would have no position. Without the world of the Real Principle, the world of the Human Ultimate and the world of heaven and earth would have no way of becoming manifest by themselves. Thus the being of the world is a being that cannot not be. The being that cannot not be is the Real One's own act of hiding and manifesting.   (5.4)

With the exception of reference to the Real One toward the end, Real Principle (*zhenli* 眞理) is almost indistinguishable from the Heavenly Principle (*tianli*) advocated by Cheng Hao. In the case of the evident reference to God (the Real One)—"The being that cannot not be is the Real One's own act of hiding and manifesting"—this is understandable in the spirit of *cheng* (sincerity, authenticity, truth, and reality) in the *Doctrine of the Mean.*

Having briefly discussed each of the themes of the five volumes and the sixty diagrams, I will reflect on the themes of the root text and the ten diagrams accompanying it:

0.1 Nondesignation of the very beginning

0.2 The transformation of principles in the Former Heaven

0.3 Transformation of forms in the Latter Heaven

0.4 Alteration and transformation of forms in the womb

0.5 Manifestation and display of the nature of the spiritual

0.6 Macrocosm's following in the circle of creation and transformation

0.7 Microcosm's original beginning and final return

0.8 Differentiated levels of Heaven and humans

0.9 Heaven and humans united as one

0.10 Undifferentiated transformation of Heaven and humans

The text begins with the "nondesignation of the very beginning" and ends with the "undifferentiated transformation of Heaven and humans." In between, four parallel structures are employed to outline the essential steps for self-realization. In 0.2 the sequence of the Former Heaven explicates the transformation of the principle, and in 0.3 the sequence of the Latter Heaven explicates the transformation of the forms. Together they offer the onto-cosmological interplay between principle and vital-energy. Whereas principle is above form, vital-energy is within form. They depict the emergence of the human in naturalistic terms.

Diagram 0.4 is an analysis of the physical development of the body focusing on the growth of vital organs from the seed (presumably the fertilized egg). The emergence of the heart-and-mind signifies a human quality that fundamentally transforms the body and gives meaning to human existence. Unambiguously what Liu Zhi presents here is a philosophy of life. Diagram 0.5 illuminates the manner in which all cosmic qualities are involved in the manifestation and display of spiritual nature, beginning with hardness and firmness, the quality of stones and inanimate things. This is followed by the nature of growth, which pertains to plants, the nature of awareness, which pertains to animals, the nature of vital-energy, which belongs to humans generally, and the spiritual nature, which pertains to human maturity. The culmination of this process is the consolidation of the "nature of continuity," in which the great function and complete substance reside.

Diagram 0.6 depicts the creation and transformation of the macrocosm (the great world). Humans evolve from the vast sediment of original vital-energy. The division of yin and yang, the crystallization of the four elements (air, fire, water, and soil), the participation of heaven and earth, and the additional supplement of wood and metal give rise to the living kinds. We may add that the living kinds are differentiated into plants and animals. Humans are animals to be sure, but they are unique in their ability to realize "principle and nature" (*lixing* 理性) through rooting in the original substance, exercising authentic function, performing socially proper acts, and waiting with steadfastness for the Mandate of Heaven. Diagram 0.7 denotes the original beginning and final return of the microcosm (the small world). This refers to the internal transformation of the human. The ultimate realization is the attainment of the "nature of continuity." This nature is distinctly Islamic. Nonetheless, emergence of the root nature from bodily apertures (the physical nature), body and mind/heart, four roots, pure and turbid, and seed is readily understandable from the Confucian perspective. Actually, I would maintain if the Confucian masters had been exposed to this way of thinking, they would have regarded it as reasonable and persuasive.

Diagrams 0.8 and 0.9 are not at all alien to Confucian morality and spirituality. They lead to the "undifferentiated transformation of Heaven and human," the most authentic, true, and real manifestation of humanity (0.10). Admittedly, technical terms such as "embodied one," "numerical one," and "real one" are perplexing to Confucian moral and religious reasoning, but the implicit anthropocosmic vision is Confucian to the core.

To substantiate this claim, I would offer a focused investigation of Liu Zhi's *Displaying the Concealment of the Real Realm*, putatively a translation of 'Abd al-Raḥmān Jāmī's seminal work, *Lawā'iḥ*. This was published some years after *Nature and Principle in Islam*. Murata and Chittick conclusively demonstrate that, notwithstanding Liu Zhi's intention to truthfully represent Jāmī's Sufi reading of the tenets of Islam, his interpretive translation is an articulation of his own philosophical orientation. Murata asserts in her *Chinese Gleams of Sufi Light* that *Displaying* "appears as a Neo-Confucian treatise that stresses the transcendence and uniqueness of the Principle on the one hand, and the manner in which the Principle brings about the ten thousand things through various levels of differentiation on the other."[10] I would suggest that the underlying thesis in the "translation" is to provide an ontological basis for self-cultivation. Liu followed Jāmī in dividing the text into two complementary sections: the endeavor to search for and cultivate the Way (the first twelve chapters) and the illumination of the meaning of the concealment and visibility of the Real Principle (the remaining twenty-four chapters). This interplay between the microcosm and the macrocosm reminds me of the opening statement of *Zhongyong* 中庸 (*On the Practice of the Mean*). It seems that, in this connection, Andrew Plaks's interpretive translation is pertinent:

By the term 'nature' we speak of that which is imparted by the ordinance of Heaven; by 'the Way' we mean that path that is in conformance with the intrinsic nature of man and things; and by 'moral instruction' we refer to the process of cultivating man's proper place in the world.

What we take to be 'the Way' does not admit of the slightest degree of separation therefrom, even for an instant. For that which does admit of such separation is thereby disqualified from being the true Way.

Given this understanding, the man of noble character exercises utmost restraint and vigilance towards that which is inaccessible to his own vision, and he regards with fear and trembling that which is beyond the reach of his own hearing.

For, ultimately, nothing is more visible than what appears to be hidden, and nothing is more manifest than matters of imperceptible subtlety. For this reason, the man of noble character pays great heed to the core of his individuality.[11]

Surely Liu Zhi's repeated reference to the "Real Being," which as Murata points out, "is not employed in the Chinese classics" and his "constant mention of the term 'Real' is perhaps the major indication of the book's Islamic provenance." Nevertheless, his vision of "Real Being," "One Principle," or "Divine Essence" is resonant with *Zhongyong*'s discourse on *cheng* (Sincerity, Authenticity, Truth, or Reality).

I would like to conclude with four observations:

1. Liu Zhi's accomplishment is widely acknowledged by Chinese Muslim theorists and practitioners as one of the most sophisticated, systematic, original, and creative articulations of Islamic philosophy in the golden age of Islam in China. He will be recognized as a profound resource for Chinese Islamic intellectual self-definition.

2. *Nature and Principle in Islam* is a major contribution to Confucian thought in the late Ming and early Qing dynasties as well as to Muslim-Han dialogue. It will broaden the philosophical horizons of Confucian thinkers and compel Chinese intellectual historians to re-examine their underlying assumptions about the Three Teachings.

3. It has enriched and enlarged the Confucian discourse comparable to and in several areas more significantly than the great work of the Jesuits, notably the endeavor of Matteo Ricci.

4. It will undoubtedly stimulate new research and interpretation in the comparative study of religion and philosophy as well as in Chinese and Islamic studies.

# Reference Matter

# Chronology of Cited Sources
# and Authors

## Confucianism and Taoism[1]

*Yijing* 易經 (*I Ching*, The Book of Change). 2nd–1st millennium BCE. A foundational classic of Chinese thought, much quoted and discussed by both Confucians and Daoists. The basic text, consisting of eight trigrams (sets of three broken and/or unbroken lines), is ancient, traditionally dated to Fu Xi in the third millennium BCE. The eight trigrams were developed into sixty-four hexagrams sometime later. The "Ten Wings" or commentaries, including *Shuogua* and *Dazhuan*, are attributed to Confucius.

Confucius (Kong Fuzi 孔夫子). 551–479 BCE. The greatest sage of the Confucian tradition. His teachings are summarized in the *Analects*, one of the Four Books canonized by Zhu Xi.

Laozi 老子 (Lao Tzu). 571–480 BCE. Author of the *Daodejing* (*Tao Te Ching*), the oldest and most famous text of Daoism.

*Great Learning* (*Daxue* 大學). 5th century BCE. Chapter 42 from the *Classic of Rites*. Traditionally attributed to Confucius, it was canonized by Zhu Xi as one of the Four Books.

*Doctrine of the Mean* (*Zhongyong* 中庸). 5th century BCE. One of the Four Books. Attributed to the grandson of Confucius, it was incorporated into the *Classic of Rites* as Chapter 31.

Mencius (Mengzi 孟子). 372–289 BCE. The most respected authority in the Confucian tradition after Confucius. Zhu Xi canonized his collected sayings, called by his name, as one of the Four Books.

Zhuangzi 莊子 (Chuang Tzu). 360–280 BCE. Author of the second great classic of Daoism, known by his name.

Wang Bi 王弼. 226–49 CE. A Daoist scholar, famous for his commentary on the *Yijing*.

Shao Yong 邵雍. 1011–77. A Confucian author with Daoist leanings.

Zhou Dunyi 周敦頤. 1017–73. Important Neo-Confucian scholar.

Zhang Zai 張載. 1020–77. Ditto.

Cheng Hao 程顥. 1032–85. Ditto.

Cheng Yi 程頤. 1033–1107. Ditto. Cheng Hao's brother.

Zhu Xi 朱熹. 1130–1200. Typically considered the greatest of the Neo-Confucians.

Lu Xiangshan 陸象山. 1139–92. Another great Neo-Confucian thinker, although he disagreed with Zhu Xi on many points.

Chen Chun 陳淳. 1159–1223. Student of Zhu Xi and author of *Neo-Confucian Terms Explained* (*Beixi zi yi* 北溪字義).

Wang Yangming 王陽明. 1472–1529. A major Neo-Confucian thinker.

## Islam

Koran (al-Qur'ān). 620–32 CE. The scripture of Islam, traditionally understood as the Word of God revealed to the prophet Muḥammad (570–632 CE) over a twenty-three-year period.

Hadith (*ḥadīth*). The body of sayings attributed to Muḥammad himself and distinguished from God's Word, the Koran; also, one such saying. The Hadith literature was gradually codified during the eighth and ninth centuries into a number of more or less canonical collections. Muslim scholars have often debated the authenticity of individual sayings.

Abū Bakr. 573–634. A close companion of Muḥammad and his first successor (caliph) as political leader of the nascent Muslim community.

'Umar. ca. 584–644. Another close companion of Muḥammad, and his second successor.

'Alī. 599–661. Muḥammad's cousin and son-in-law, his fourth successor, and the first Imam of the Shi'ite branch of Islam (as contrasted with Sunnism).

Ja'far al-Ṣādiq. 702–65. A great authority in transmitted learning, a master of the intellectual sciences, and the sixth Imam of the Shi'ites.

Abū Yazīd (Bāyazīd) of Bastam. 804–74. One of the greatest of the early Sufis, to whom numerous aphorisms are ascribed.

Junayd of Baghdad. 830–910. A great Sufi teacher.

Ash'arite theology. 10th century onward. The most prominent of several schools of Kalam (dogmatic theology), founded by Abu'l-Ḥasan al-Ash'arī (874–936).

Avicenna (Ibn Sīnā). ca. 980–1037. Author of many books and treatises, he is generally considered the greatest of the Muslim philosophers, at least of the Peripatetic (Aristotelian) school. He was also an outstanding physician and wrote numerous books on medicine.

Ghazālī, Abū Ḥāmid al-. 1058–1111. One of Islam's foremost scholars, he was the author of important books in jurisprudence, Kalam, philosophy, and Sufism. He wrote mainly in Arabic, but also in Persian.

Hamadānī, 'Ayn al-Quḍāt. 1098–1131. Author of Persian and Arabic works on Sufism with a focus on love.

Suhrawardī al-Maqtūl, Shihāb al-Dīn Yaḥyā. 1155–91. Founder of the Illuminationist school of philosophy and author of important books in both Arabic and Persian.

Rāzī, Fakhr al-Dīn. 1149–1209. Author of numerous works in Kalam and philosophy; especially famous for his *Great Commentary* on the Koran.

Kubrā, Najm al-Dīn. 1145–1221. Eponymous founder of the Kubrawī Sufi Order; known as "the saint-carver" because of his many prominent disciples.

Ibn al-'Arabī. 1165–1240. Called the "Greatest Master" (al-Shaykh al-Akbar) by the Sufis, he wrote a massive corpus of extremely high-level Arabic writings that have shaped the formulation of the intellectual tradition down to the present.

Ḥammūya, Sa'd al-Dīn. 1190–1252. A disciple of Kubrā, he himself became a great shaykh and wrote many books in Arabic and Persian. His influence seems to have reached later generations mainly through the writings of his disciple Nasafī.

Rāzī, Najm al-Dīn. 1177–1256. Also a disciple of Kubrā, he was a great Sufi teacher and author of *Path*, probably the single most influential Islamic text to be translated into Chinese, and Liu's most important source in *Tianfang xingli*.

Rūmī, Jalāl al-Dīn. 1207–73. Not only was he one of the greatest poets of the Persian language, but he was also a prominent spiritual teacher whose 25,000-couplet *Mathnawī* has inspired seekers of God down to modern times.

Qūnawī, Ṣadr al-Dīn. 1207–74. Ibn al-'Arabī's stepson and most influential disciple, he wrote several highly focused philosophical presentations of the Path of Realization.

'Irāqī, Fakhr al-Dīn. ca. 1213–89. An important Persian Sufi poet, he studied Ibn al-'Arabī's *Fuṣūṣ al-ḥikam* with Qūnawī and was inspired to write *Flashes*, a Persian prose classic on divine love. Jāmī's *Rays* is the most influential of several commentaries on the book.

Jandī Mu'ayyid al-Dīn. d. 1291. A student of Qūnawī, he authored the earliest detailed commentary on Ibn al-'Arabī's *Fuṣūṣ al-ḥikam*.

Farghānī, Sa'īd al-Dīn. d. ca. 1295. Another student of Qūnawī, he wrote a highly influential Persian commentary on the 600-verse *Poem of the Way* of Ibn al-Fāriḍ (d. 1235), the greatest Sufi poet of the Arabic language, on the basis of Qūnawī's lectures. He then composed an expanded Arabic version.

Nasafī, 'Azīz. d. ca. 1295. A disciple of Ḥammūya, he produced several clear and simple Persian books important in the spread of theoretical Sufism; his *Goal* was the second important Sufi text to be translated into Chinese.

Bayḍāwī, Qāḍī Nāṣir al-Dīn 'Abdallāh. d. ca. 1300. He was chief judge of Shiraz and author of many Arabic books in the Islamic sciences, the most famous of which is his Koran commentary.

Kāshānī, 'Abd al-Razzāq. d. 1335. A student of Jandī, he is the author of theoretical works in both Arabic and Persian and is most famous for his commentary on Ibn al-'Arabī's *Fuṣūṣ al-ḥikam*.

Shabistarī, Maḥmūd. d. ca. 1340. A Sufi teacher, famous for his 1,000-verse Persian summary of theoretical Sufism, *Gulshan-i raz* (The rose garden of the mystery).

Qayṣarī, Sharaf al-Dīn. d. 1350. A student of Kāshānī and author of many Arabic works, like his teacher he wrote a highly regarded commentary on the *Fuṣūṣ al-ḥikam*.

Āmulī, Sayyid Ḥaydar. d. after 1385. A Shi'ite theologian, his commentary on the *Fuṣūṣ al-ḥikam* is probably the longest ever written, although only its introduction has been published.

Jāmī, 'Abd al-Raḥmān. 1414–92. Prolific Persian poet, he also wrote many scholarly books in Arabic and Persian on a variety of topics, not least theoretical Sufism.

Mullā Ṣadrā. ca. 1571–1641. Considered in Iran the greatest of the Muslim philosophers, he wrote numerous books, mainly in Arabic, and is the founder of the school of Transcendent Wisdom (*al-ḥikmat al-muta'āliya*).

Wang Daiyu 王岱輿. 1584–1660.[2] With the publication of his *Zhengjiao zhenquan* 正教眞詮 (The real commentary on the true teaching) in 1642, he became the founding author of the Han Kitab.

Ma Zhu 馬注. 1640–1711. Another major author of the Han Kitab.

Liu Zhi 劉智. 1670–1730. Author of the Tianfang Trilogy.

Ma Dexin 馬德新 (Ma Fuchu. 馬復初). 1794–1894. Prolific author of works on theoretical Sufism.

Ma Lianyuan. 馬聯元 (Nūr al-Ḥaqq). 1841–1904. Author of *Subtleties* and *Explanation of the Subtleties*, as well as several books in Chinese.

# Notes

N.B. This section contains the notes to the Preface, Chapters 1–5 of the Introduction, the Epilogue, and the Chronology. The notes to the Translation follow each section of that work. For complete bibliographic information on works cited here in short form, see the Bibliography, pp. 637–44. See pp. xvii–xviii in the front matter for the abbrevations used here.

## Preface

1. Needham provides a review of the scholarship on the issue and devotes a long section to it in the chapter, "Fundamental Ideas of Chinese Science" (*Science and Civilisation in China*, 2: 279–345). John B. Henderson's study, *The Development and Decline of Chinese Cosmology*, provides a sweeping view of what he calls "correlative thought" in Chinese history, mainly in relation to "scientific" ideas.

2. Schwartz, *The World of Thought in Ancient China*, p. 350.

3. See, e.g., *Confucian Thought* and *Centrality and Commonality*.

4. Jonathan N. Lipman provides a good overview of the earlier figures of this school in *Familiar Strangers*, pp. 72–85.

5. "Liu Zhi's Journey Through Ritual Law to Allah's Chinese Name: Conceptual Antecedents and Theological Obstacles to the Confucian-Islamic Harmonization of the *Tianfang Dianli*," Columbia University, 2005.

6. In 1999, Jin Yijiu, a well-established scholar of Chinese Islam, published *Zhongguo yisilan tanmi: Liu Zhi yanjiu* (Exploration of Chinese

Islam: a study of Liu Zhi), which surveys the role of Sufism in China while focusing on Liu's writings, especially his *Tianfang xingli*; he provides a good summary of Liu's main themes and modes of thinking. In 2004, Jin's student Sha Zongping published his Ph.D. dissertation under the title *Zhongguo de Tianfangxue: Liu Zhi zhexue yanjiu* (The Islamic learning of China: a study of Liu Zhi's philosophy). The first chapter reviews the development of Islam in China and compares Liu's use of key terms with that of Wang Daiyu, the second analyzes the meaning of the term "Real One" in Liu's writings, and the third suggests some of his Neo-Confucian sources. On the Islamic side, the author shows some knowledge of the early Muslim philosophers, finding parallels between Liu and al-Fārābī. Also, beginning in 2002, a translation of parts of *Tianfang xingli* with study and commentary has been appearing in Japanese. In the introduction to the first of these, *Yakuchū Tenpō seiri* (Translation of and commentary on *Tianfang xingli*), Minoru Satō and Toshiharu Nigo explain that a team of ten Japanese specialists, some in Chinese thought and some in Islam, met together for three years and jointly translated the first of Liu's five explanatory volumes. In 2005 and 2006, some of the team published a translation and study of vol. 4, and half of vol. 2. In 2008 Satō published *Ryū Chi no shizengaku*, a study of Liu Zhi's "natural learning," much of which is dedicated to explaining the manner in which Liu harmonizes the four- and five-element theories. He also has chapters on the treatment of the brain and its faculties, the levels of sagehood, the various editions of Liu's trilogy, and he provides a new edition of the Chinese text.

## *Chapter 1*

1. Benite (*Dao*, pp. 159–60) traces the use of the expression "Han Kitab" to *Tianfang zhengxue* 天方正學 (The true learning of Islam), published by Lan Zixi 藍子義 in 1852. The word "Huiru" is found as early as 1681, in one of several prefaces written by Muslim scholars to an important book by Ma Zhu 馬注, who is discussed shortly (ibid., p. 143).

2. Ibid., p. 119.

3. Ibid., p. 37.

4. Ibid., pp. 39–43. Tazaka (*Chūgoku*, pp. 1358–59) and Bai Shouyi (*Minzu*, pp. 401–4) call him by his style name Hu Puzhao.

5. Benite, *Dao*, p. 131.

6. Ibid., p. 138.

7. Ibid., pp. 144–45.

8. For the Chinese text of this passage with translation, see ibid., p. 146.

9. Frankel ("Liu Zhi's Journey," p. 88) is also convinced that Liu used European books.

10. Benite, *Dao*, pp. 150, 156.

11. Frankel, "Liu Zhi's Journey," chap. 6.

12. Ibid., p. 235. Contrary to what Frankel suggests, this is not a uniquely Chinese adaptation, because the Koran insists that God sent numerous prophets to all peoples, beginning with the first prophet, Adam himself. The Koran presents itself as the restoration of the purest form of the previous revelations, in particular the monotheism of Abraham, the father of the three Semitic religions.

13. Liu Zhi, *Tianfang dianli*, p. 9.

14. See Benite, *Dao*, pp. 151–52; and *Chinese Gleams*, p. 34.

15. On Ding (fl. 1650–95), see Benite, *Dao*, pp. 173, 188–91.

16. Frankel, "Liu Zhi's Journey," p. 163.

17. For an analysis of the whole Islamic tradition along these lines, using another well-known triad—*islām*, *īmān*, and *iḥsān*—see Murata and Chittick, *The Vision of Islam*.

18. In his translation of *Tianfang zhisheng*, Mason (*The Arabian Prophet*, p. 91) clarifies that Tianfang is a name of the Kaaba and is used by Muslims to refer to Arabia. He quotes Liu as saying that Tianfang is the kingdom of Mecca and, elsewhere, that it corresponds with "Asia," apparently meaning the Muslim empire at its height: "Of all the dependent countries of 'T'ien Fang,' the central one was Arabia, and on the east was Fars (Persia) and Hindustan, on the west Syria and Misr (Egypt), on the south Yemen and Abyssinia and on the north Roman Territory and Irak, in all ten countries."

19. In some of the later editions of the text, the name of the book is also given in Arabic script. For a list of all the books, see Leslie and Wassel, "Arabic and Persian Sources Used by Liu Chih."

20. For an English translation of the text by Hamid Algar, see Rāzī, *The Path of God's Bondsmen*.

21. This book was translated into Chinese in 1679, shortly after *Path*, by one of the most prominent of the early Huiru, She Yunshan 舍蘊善 (*Chinese Gleams*, pp. 32–33; Leslie et al., *Islam*, p. 74, no. 14). The book's importance was recognized early in the West, and it was translated into English by E. H. Palmer in 1867. A better translation was made by Lloyd Ridgeon in *Persian Metaphysics and Mysticism*.

22. Jāmī, *Nafaḥāt*, p. 431.

23. E.g., Landolt, "Le paradoxe de la 'face de Dieu.' "

24. Western scholars have generally followed Muslim scholars in considering the idea controversial; those sympathetic with its critics have often

labeled it "pantheism." But this is a massive oversimplification of one of the most sophisticated and subtle thinkers of Islamic history, as more recent scholarship has tended to acknowledge. Moreover, the expression *waḥdat al-wujūd* itself is not found in Ibn al-'Arabī's writings and, when ascribed to him—whether by sympathizers or critics—it is typically understood in an idiosyncratic way. For a history of the usage of the term, see Chittick, "Rūmī and *Waḥdat al-wujūd*." For a sample of the controversies surrounding Ibn al-'Arabī's teachings, see Knysh, *Ibn 'Arabi in the Later Islamic Tradition*.

25. And continuing on with Mu'ayyid al-Dīn Jandī (d. 1291), 'Abd al-Razzāq Kāshānī (d. 1330), and Dāwūd Qayṣarī (d. 1350), the most important commentators on Ibn al-'Arabī's most famous work, the *Fuṣūṣ al-ḥikam*. Jāmī did this both in his biographies of the saints, *Nafaḥāt al-uns*, and in his thorough review of Ibn al-'Arabī's teachings, *Naqd al-nuṣūṣ*, from which we have occasion to quote in our annotations.

26. For a translation of the text and discussion of its role in the school of Ibn al-'Arabī, see *Flashes*.

27. The thirty-two diagrams Ma uses are 0.6, 1.1–1.6, 1.8, 1.9b, 1.10, 1.11, 2.6, 2.8–2.11, 3.1–3.5, 4.3, 4.7, 5.1–5.3, 5.5, 5.8–5.12. For his own diagrams, see pp. 18/14, 25/19, 34/27, 36/29, 37/29, 67/50 (from the *Futūḥāt*), 69/53 (ibid.), 98/73.

28. The name can be translated as "The Servant of the Wise, the hajji [the person who has gone on the pilgrimage to Mecca], the Sayyid [descendent of the Prophet], Muḥammad, the Light of the Real, the son of the Sayyid, Luqmān, of China." The "Wise" is a divine name mentioned many times in the Koran, and "wisdom" is the standard Arabic translation of "philosophy" when *falsafa*, the transliteration of the Greek word, is not used. So, the Wise is God inasmuch as he is the source of wisdom and philosophy. A second reference is found in the personal name of Ma's father, Luqmān, the name of a legendary figure after whom Surah 31 of the Koran is named. The Koran accords him the same respect that it gives to the prophets, but it calls him a *ḥakīm*, a wise man or sage. This is one of several Koranic passages that Muslim philosophers cited in support of their own pursuit of wisdom, and it could not have been missed by Chinese Muslims, who were much concerned to acknowledge the universality of wisdom and sagehood. A third reference can be seen in the author's personal name, Muḥammad Nūr al-Ḥaqq. It was and is common for Muslim men to be named "Muḥammad" with the addition of another name, to distinguish this individual from all other Muḥammads. In this case, "the Light of the Real" is a suggestive name, given the prominence of light in Sufism and philosophy. Take, for example, a purported saying of the Prophet, cited by Nasafī

toward the beginning of *Goal*: "Intelligence (*'aql*) is a light in the heart, by which the Real is discerned from the unreal," or "by which the truth is discerned from falsehood."

29. The text is full of marginal notes, and, to make sure that the reader does not imagine that they were added by someone else, Nūr al-Ḥaqq signed each of them.

30. On these, see Lipman, *Familiar Strangers*. Since some of the secondary literature suggests that these names refer to clearly demarcated groups, Lipman's many caveats are well worth reading. As he remarks in his final paragraph, "The narrative told in this [250-page] book cannot be simplified accurately."

31. Jaschok and Shui, in *The History of Women's Mosques in Chinese Islam*, are aware of the importance of what they call "ancient Persian," even if what they mean is none other than what is technically known as "modern Persian," the same language that has been spoken over the past millennium in Iran, Afghanistan, and Tajikistan. The two authors do not seem to grasp that Persian had at least the same status as Arabic among members of the Han Kitab into the nineteenth century. They write,

A history of neglect of women's concerns has also produced the phenomenon of an educational curriculum . . . which has not changed in language (ancient Persian) or content (seventeenth century morality fused with Islamic doctrine) since first compiled and copied in the First Cultural Movement of late Ming / early Qing China [i.e., the period of Wang Daiyu and Liu Zhi]. . . . Literate, more often than not semi-literate, only in ancient Persian, the lack of Arabic and Chinese literacy compounds [the female leaders'] difficulty to retain respect for their leadership. (pp. 21–22)

32. See Ma Lianyuan, *Tianfang xingli benjing zhushi*; the translator was Ruan Bin. The publication of this book in Chinese (in Yunnan) compounds what Lipman (*Familiar Strangers*, p. 226) calls the "extraordinary irony" inherent in the fact that "Muslim scholars in Yunnan, teaching among Muslims who read Arabic and Persian but not Chinese, have translated some of the *Han kitab* texts into Arabic for instruction in the *madrasa*." Lipman reports this on the basis of correspondence with an informant. It may be that what is at issue is the teaching of Nūr al-Ḥaqq's commentary rather than an ongoing process, and this would help explain the need for a Chinese translation of the Arabic text.

## Chapter 2

1. For the importance of realization in Ibn al-'Arabī's conceptual universe, see *Sufi Path* and especially *Self-Disclosure*.

2. A typical Koranic verse cited to justify this position is 4:59: "O you who have faith! Obey God, and obey the Messenger and those in authority among you."

3. Mullā Ṣadrā, *The Elixir of the Gnostics*, p. 79.

4. *Futūḥāt*, 3: 120. For the passage with more context, see *Sufi Path*, pp. 238–39. See also *Self-Disclosure*, pp. 216–19, where Ibn al-'Arabī discussed the sort of knowledge achieved by those who possess the kernels.

5. *Goal*, p. 238/74.

6. See Heath, *Allegory and Philosophy*.

7. Ḥammūya, *al-Miṣbāḥ*, introduction, p. 33. Ḥammūya purposefully transposed "prophets" and "saints" to play on the usual version of this saying, which is found in Ibn al-'Arabī and others: "The ends of the saints are the beginnings of the prophets" (Ibn al-'Arabī, *Futūḥāt*, 2: 51; *Sufi Path*, p. 222). In other words, the perfections of the prophets begin where those of the saints leave off; the fact that a person is a prophet presupposes his being a saint.

8. This is not to say that this world—or any other world—is beginningless and endless. Only God has that attribute. But God is always "Creator," and unlike the worlds that he creates, he is not conditioned by time.

9. *Futūḥāt*, 3: 363; cited in Chittick, *Imaginal Worlds*, p. 34. For other passages from Ibn al-'Arabī, see "macrocosm" in the indexes of *Sufi Path* and *Self-Disclosure*; and for the discussion in a broader context, see Murata, *Tao*, especially chap. 1.

10. We make no attempt in this study to distinguish between existence and being in English. We translate *wujūd* in quoted passages as "existence," and *you* 有 as "being," but in the Introduction and notes we use "being" and "existence" more or less interchangeably; we capitalize the words when they are clearly used as divine names. In passages translated from Persian, "being" is *hastī*, a synonym for *wujūd*. We use "engendered being" for Arabic *kawn*, a word that refers to created being, not the uncreated *wujūd* that is God.

11. For representative schemes, see Chittick, "The Five Divine Presences"; also *Flashes*, pp. 6–17 (with diagrams).

12. Jāmī, *Naqd*, p. 55 (quoting from Qūnawī).

13. Ibid., pp. 60–61. Jāmī covers some of the same ground in Gleam 17 (*Chinese Gleams*, pp. 160–61).

## Chapter 3

1. Benite (*Dao*, pp. 147–48) also translates it as "Reason and Principle of Islam." Frankel ("Liu Zhi's Journey," p. 137) translates *xingli* as "metaphysics."

2. *Source Book*, p. 14.

3. The eight steps were codified by Zhu Xi, the most influential of the Neo-Confucian thinkers, in his commentary on *The Great Learning*. See *Source Book*, p. 84; *Chinese Gleams*, p. 69.

4. This is the fourth of fifteen definitions in *Webster's Third New International Dictionary* (1968); nothing like it is found in the twenty definitions provided by *Webster's Encyclopedic Unabridged Dictionary* (2001).

5. *Concepts*, pp. 27–42, 367–83.

6. *Source Book*, p. 640.

7. Ibid., p. 641.

8. Ibid.

9. Chan, *Zhu Xi*, p. 186; see also *Source Book*, pp. 630–31.

10. Ching, *Religious Thought*, p. 96.

11. *Terms*, pp. 46–47.

12. The recognition of the spiritual dimension of "nature" was, of course, not limited to theologians; it infused the medieval worldview and was only gradually lost with the Renaissance and the industrial revolution. Feminist scholars in particular have been concerned to map out the way in which views of nature changed with the rise of a mechanistic understanding of the universe. See, e.g., Merchant, *The Death of Nature*.

13. The quote is from Marcel Granet, *La pensée chinoise* (Paris: Albin Michel, 1934), p. 478; cited by Roger T. Ames in "Confucian Harmony (*he*) as *Creatio in Situ*." Ames struggles valiantly to show that in Chinese thought there is nothing "outside" the cosmos. The Islamic metaphysics from which Liu drew would see no contradiction between what Ames calls *creatio in situ* and a Creator God (again, Ibn al-'Arabī provided sophisticated explanations of how this apparent contradiction is the only correct way to understand things; see, for example, *Sufi Path*, part 3).

14. Needham, *Science and Civilisation in China*, 2: 475.

15. For some of al-Ghazālī's explanations, see Murata, *Tao*, pp. 257–60.

16. On the heart in Chinese thought, see *Concepts*, pp. 391–409; *Terms*, pp. 56–61.

17. 'Alī ibn Abī Ṭālib, *Nahj al-balāgha*, sermon no. 222 (p. 342).

18. *Zhuangzi* 7.8. Both Watson (p. 97) and Chan (*Source Book*, p. 207) translate *xin* here as "mind," and Utmost Human as "perfect man." Buddhists also compare the heart to a mirror, as in the Platform Scripture: "The heart is the tree of perfect wisdom. / The body is the stand of a bright mirror. / The bright mirror is originally clear and pure. / Where has it been defiled by any dust?" (*Source Book*, p. 432).

19. On the heart in Islamic thought, see Murata, *Tao*, chap. 10.

20. *Goal*, pp. 269–70/110–11.

21. *Path*, p. 52/78.

22. In *Subtleties*, Nūr usually translated *li* as *ḥaqīqa*, "reality." This is completely appropriate in Sufism and philosophy, where *ḥaqīqa* typically means the intelligible essence of the thing; or its "form" in the Aristotelian, hylomorphic sense of the term; or its "quiddity" (*māhiyya*) as contrasted with its existence (*wujūd*).

23. In the Islamic philosophical tradition, a parallel discussion goes on in terms of Aristotelian hylomorphism: form (*ṣūra*) becomes manifest by means of hyle (*hayūlā*), also called matter (*mādda*).

24. See *Concepts*, pp. 127–39; *Terms*, pp. 37–46.

25. Schwartz, "The Ethical and the Meta-Ethical," p. 59.

26. Graham, *Studies in Chinese Philosophy*, p. 20. The dilemma can be seen clearly in the chapters on *ming* in *Concepts* or *Terms*; see also the chapter on *ming* in Chan, *Zhu Xi*, pp. 212–21.

27. *Analects* 2.4.

28. Graham, *Studies in Chinese Philosophy*, p. 54.

29. *Shuogua* 1.1; Wilhelm, *I Ching*, p. 262.

30. The word *takwīnī* is an adjectival form from the noun *takwīn*, which is derived from the same root as *kun*. Literally, *takwīn* means "to say 'Be' to something," or "to make something come to be." For the contrast between the two sorts of command in Ibn al-ʿArabī's teachings, see *Sufi Path*, pp. 291ff.

31. For a good review of the meanings of *tian* in Chinese thought, see Ching, *Religious Thought*, pp. 54–60.

32. Rūmī, *Mathnawī*, Book 3, verse 4404. For detailed quotes from the Koran and Muslim authors on the complementarity of heaven and earth, see Murata, *Tao*, especially chap. 4.

33. Anne Birdwhistell (*Transition*, p. 86) explains that the Fu Xi chart was said to be earlier, hence former, and thus she translates "the Former Chart of Heaven." She adds that scholars have translated *xiantian* in various ways—"former heaven, prior heaven, pre-creation, *a priori*, what antedates Heaven, Prior to Heaven, and the former sky or celestial [plan]. The source of much of the disagreement appears to arise from our ignorance of the development of the uses of this term and the great number of different meanings that it has" (ibid., pp. 84–85).

34. Wilhelm (*I Ching*, pp. 266, 269) calls these "the sequence of earlier heaven, or primal arrangement" and "the sequence of later heaven, or inner-world arrangement."

35. *Source Book*, p. 482.

36. Birdwhistell, *Transition*, p. 66.

37. Ibid., p. 85.

38. See *Concepts*, pp. 240–57.

39. Ching, *Religious Thought*, p. 12.

40. In Chinese philosophy, *ti* and *yong* can be context dependent, much like yin and yang: What is *ti* from one point of view can be *yong* from a different standpoint (Cua, *Encyclopedia*, pp. 720–21). Muslim cosmologists also see the parallel Arabic terms as context dependent (Murata, *Tao*, pp. 130–33, 161–68).

41. According to Matsumoto, "An Analysis of the 'Whole Substance and Vast Operations' (*quanti dayong*) in Ma Fuchu's Philosophy."

42. Ibn al-'Arabi, *Futūḥāt*, 2: 124. For more on the all-comprehensiveness of the human form, see *Sufi Path*, pp. 274–78; and Murata, *Tao*, pp. 33–37, 95–101.

43. For the text, see Legge, *Chinese Classics*, 1: 365–66.

44. *Source Book*, p. 585.

45. Ching, *Religious Thought*, p. 12.

46. *Source Book*, p. 580; Benite, *Dao*, pp. 166–67.

47. Benite, *Dao*, pp. 184–85.

48. Cheng, "*Ti*: Body or Embodiment," in Cua, *Encyclopedia*, p. 717.

49. Ibid., p. 718.

50. *Source Book*, p. 791.

51. Cheng, in Cua, *Encyclopedia*, p. 718.

52. Tu, *Confucian Thought*, pp. 180–81. Cf. *Source Book*, p. 17.

53. *Source Book*, p. 524.

54. Ibid., p. 523.

55. Ibid., p. 497.

56. Chan, *Instructions*, pp. xxxix, 272.

57. *Dazhuan* 5.1–2; Wilhelm, *I Ching*, pp. 297–98.

## Chapter 4

1. We have already noted that cosmological diagrams are not uncommon in Islamic sources. They are also well known in the Chinese tradition; Zhou Dunyi's *Diagram of the Great Ultimate* is a famous example. For it and several more, see Yi T'oegye's *Ten Diagrams on Sage Learning*, translated by Michael Kalton in *To Become a Sage*. On the Islamic side, the most elaborate metaphysical and cosmological diagrams that we have seen are the twenty-eight provided by Sayyid Ḥaydar Āmulī (d. after 1385) in his *Kitāb Naṣṣ al-nuṣūṣ*, a commentary on Ibn al-'Arabī's *Fuṣūṣ al-ḥikam*.

2. On the importance of memorization in the Han Kitab—an importance that was matched in centers of learning throughout the Islamic world—see Benite, *Dao*, pp. 88–97.

3. Nūr, *Sharḥ*, pp. 2–3/1–2.

## Chapter 5

1. In Liu's list of sources, he rarely mentioned authors. Rather, he gave a brief title, usually consisting of the title's first word in transliteration, and then a Chinese translation of the full title (in the Root Classic itself, he mentions only the translated name). In the 1863 edition of *Tianfang xingli* we consulted, the brief title in the list of sources is also given in Arabic script. According to Leslie and Wassel in their article on Liu's sources, there were many earlier editions of the book, but this was the first to have the Arabic, as also was the 1862 edition of *Tianfang dianli*.

## Epilogue

1. See Zhang Qiong, "Cultural Accommodation or Intellectual Colonization?: A Reinterpretation of the Jesuit Approach to Confucianism During the Late Sixteenth and Early Seventeenth Centuries" (Ph.D. diss., Harvard University, 1996).

2. *Analects* 1.11.

3. *Analects* 18.6.

4. *Analects* 2.4.

5. *Mencius* 4.B.14.

6. *Mencius* 7.B.25.

7. *Mencius* 5.B.5.

8. *Source Book*, p. 463.

9. *Mencius* 6.A.11.

10. *Chinese Gleams*, p. 121.

11. Andrew Plaks, trans., *Ta Hsüeh and Chung Yung (The Highest Order of Cultivation and On the Practice of the Mean)* (London: Penguin Books, 2003), p. 25.

## Chronology

1. We follow *Concepts*, pp. 487–89; some of the dates, especially the earlier ones, are disputed.

2. The dates of the Chinese Muslim scholars are approximate at best; we follow Leslie, Yang, and Youssef, *Islam*, pp. 165ff, 295.

# Bibliography

## Han Kitab

Hei Mingfeng 黑鳴風. (*Tianfang*) *xingli benjing zhushi* (天方)性理本經註釋. Canton, 1875.

Lan Zixi 藍子羲. *Tianfang zhengxue* 天方正學. Beijing, 1923.

Liu Zhi 劉智. "Huihui shuo" 回回説. In idem, *Tianfang zhisheng shilu* (q.v.), chapter 20.

———. *Tianfang dianli* 天方典禮. 1740. Shanghai, 1923, 1924.

———. *Tianfang sanzijing* 天方三字經. 1858. English trans. F. J. M. Cotter and L. Reichelt, "The Three Character Classic for Moslems." *Chinese Recorder* 48 (1917): 645–52; also in *Moslem World* 8 (1918).

———. *Tianfang xingli* 天方性理. Shanghai, 1863; Beijing, 1922; Shanghai, 1928; also in Satō, *Ryū Chi no shizengaku*, pp. 279–362. Modern Chinese (*baihua* 白活) translation by Ma Baoguang 馬宝光 and Li Sansheng 李三胜, Zhongzhou: Guji chubanshe, n.d. For Japanese translations of vol. 1, half of vol. 2, and vol. 4, *see* Aoki et al.

———. *Tianfang zhisheng shilu* 天方至聖實錄. 1872. For the English translation, *see under* Mason; Japanese translation, *under* Tanaka.

———. *Tianfang zimu jieyi* 天方字母解義. 1879.

———. *Zhenjing zhaowei* 眞境昭微. Beijing, 1925. English trans. Murata, *Chinese Gleams*, pp. 129–209.

Ma Lianyuan 馬聯元 (Muḥammad Nūr al-Ḥaqq ibn al-Sayyid Luqmān). *Sharḥ al-laṭā'if*. Kanpur: 1320/1902; 2d ed., Kanpur: Maḥmūd al-Maṭābi',

1343/1924–25. Chinese trans. Ruan Bin 阮斌, *Tianfang xingli benjing zhushi* 天方性理本經注釋. Kunming: Jingxueyuan, 1983.

———. *Xingli weiyen* 性理微言. *Laṭā'if.* Yunnan, 1898.

Wang Daiyu 王岱輿. *Qingzhen daxue* 清眞大學. Beijing, 1921. English trans. Murata, *Chinese Gleams*, pp. 81–112. Japanese trans. Kadono Tatsudō 角野達堂, *Kaikyō-ken* 回教圈 2 pts., 5, no. 4 (1941): 31–43; 5, no. 5 (1941): 12–24.

———. *Zhengjiao zhenquan* 正教眞詮. 1642, 1657, 1873. Beijing, 1921.

———. *Zhengjiao zhenquan* 正教眞詮, *Qingzhen daxue* 清眞大學, *Xizhen zhengda* 希眞正答. Ed. Yu Zhengui. Yinchuan: Ningxia renmin chubanshe, 1987.

## Other Sources

'Alī ibn Abī Ṭālib. *Nahj al-balāgha.* Ed. Ṣubḥī Ṣāliḥ. Beirut, 1967.

Ames, Roger T. "Confucian Harmony (*he*) as *Creatio in Situ*." In *The Harmony and Prosperity of Civilizations: Selected Papers from the Beijing Forum* (2004). Beijing: Peking University Press, 2005, pp. 301–21.

Āmulī, Sayyid Ḥaydar. *Kitāb Naṣṣ al-nuṣūṣ fī sharḥ fuṣūṣ al-ḥikam.* Ed. Henry Corbin and O. Yahia. Tehran: Bibliothèque Iranienne, 1975.

Aoki Takashi 青木隆, Satō Minoru 佐藤実, and Nigo Toshiharu 仁子寿晴. "Yakuchū *Tenpō seiri* kanshi" 訳注天方性理 卷四. *Chūgoku islanshisō kenkyū* 中国伊斯蘭思想研究 1 (2005): 16–214.

Aoki Takashi 青木隆, Satō Minoru 佐藤実, Nakanishi Tatsuya 中西竜也, and Nigo Toshiharu 仁子寿晴. "Yakuchū *Tenpō seiri* kanni sono ichi" 訳注天方性理 卷二その一. *Chūgoku islanshisō kenkyū* 中国伊斯蘭思想研究 2 (2006): 62–201.

Avicenna, *see* Ibn Sīnā.

Bai Shouyi 白壽彝. *Huizu renwuzhi* 回族人物志. Yinchuan: Ningxia renmin chubanshe, 1992.

———. *Minzu zongjiao lunji* 民俗宗教論集. Beijing: Beijing shifan daxue chubanshe, 1992.

———. *Zhongguo Yisilanjiao shi cungao* 中國伊斯蘭史存稿. 1948. Reprinted—Yinchuan: Ningxia renmin chubanshe, 1983 (1982?).

Bayḍāwī, al-Qāḍī al-. *Tafsīr al-Qur'ān* (*Anwār al-tanzīl wa asrār al-ta'wīl*). N.p.: al-Maṭba'at al-'Uthmāniyya, 1329/1921.

Benite, Zvi Ben-Dor. *The Dao of Muhammad: A Cultural History of Muslims in Late Imperial China.* Cambridge: Harvard University Asia Center, 2005.

Bernard, Henri. *Matteo Ricci's Scientific Contribution to China.* Beijing, 1935. Reprinted—Westport, CT: Hyperion Press, 1973.

Birdwhistell, Anne D. *Transition to Neo-Confucianism: Shao Yung on Knowledge and Symbols of Reality*. Stanford: Stanford University Press, 1989.

Burckhardt, Titus. *Mystical Astrology According to Ibn 'Arabi*. Gloucestershire: Beshara Publications, 1977.

Chan, Wing-tsit. *Instructions for Practical Living and Other Neo-Confucian Writings by Wang Yang-Ming*. New York: Columbia University Press, 1963.

———. *A Source Book in Chinese Philosophy*. Princeton: Princeton University Press, 1963.

———. *Zhu Xi: New Studies*. Honolulu: University of Hawaii Press, 1989.

Ch'en Ch'un (Chen Chun). *Neo-Confucian Terms Explained*. Trans. Wing-tsit Chan. New York: Columbia University Press, 1986.

Chen, Hui-Hung. "The Human Body as a Universe: Understanding Heaven by Visualization and Sensibility in Jesuit Cartography in China." *Catholic Historical Review* 93, no. 3 (2007): 517–52.

Ching, Julia. *The Religious Thought of Chu Hsi*. Oxford: Oxford University Press, 2000.

———. *To Acquire Wisdom: The Way of Wang Yang-ming*. New York: Columbia University Press, 1976.

Chittick, William C. *Faith and Practice of Islam: Three Thirteenth Century Sufi Texts*. Albany: State University of New York Press, 1992.

———. "The Five Divine Presences: From al-Qūnawī to al-Qayṣarī." *Muslim World* 72 (1982): 107–28.

———. *Imaginal Worlds: Ibn al-'Arabī and the Problem of Religious Diversity*. Albany: State University of New York Press, 1994.

———. "Rūmī and *Wahdat al-wujūd*." In *Poetry and Mysticism in Islam: The Heritage of Rūmī*, ed. A. Banani, R. Hovannisian, and G. Sabagh. Cambridge: Cambridge University Press, 1994, pp. 70–111.

———. *The Self-Disclosure of God: Principles of Ibn al-'Arabī's Cosmology*. Albany: State University of New York Press, 1998.

———. *The Sufi Path of Knowledge: Ibn al-'Arabī's Metaphysics of Imagination*. Albany: State University of New York Press, 1989.

———. "Waḥdat al-Shuhūd." In *Encyclopaedia of Islam*, 10: 37–39.

Chodkiewicz, Michel. *An Ocean Without Shore: Ibn Arabi, the Book, and the Law*. Albany: State University of New York Press, 1993.

Cua, Antonio S., ed. *Encyclopedia of Chinese Philosophy*. London: Routledge, 2002.

*Daodejing, see* Laozi.

*Dazhuan*, The Great Commentary on the *Yijing*, *see* Wilhelm, *The I Ching*.

*Doctrine of the Mean, see* Legge; also Chan, *Source Book*, pp. 95–114.

*Encyclopedia of Islam.* Leiden, 1960–2005.

Farghānī. Sa'īd al-Dīn. *Mashāriq al-darārī.* Ed. S. J. Āshtiyānī. Tehran: Anjuman-i Islāmī-i Ḥikmat wa Falsafa, 1358/1979.

————. *Muntaha'l-madārik.* Cairo: Maktab al-Ṣanā'i', 1293/1876.

Fletcher, Joseph F. *Studies on Chinese and Islamic Inner Asia.* Aldershot: Valiorum, 1995.

Forbes, A. D. W. "Liu Chih." In *Encyclopaedia of Islam,* 5: 770–71.

Ford, J. F. "Some Chinese Muslims of the Seventeenth and Eighteenth Centuries." *Asian Affairs* 61 (1974): 144–56.

Frankel, James D. "Liu Zhi's Journey Through Ritual Law to Allah's Chinese Name: Conceptual Antecedents and Theological Obstacles to the Confucian-Islamic Harmonization of the *Tianfang Dianli.*" Ph.D. diss., Columbia University, 2005.

Fu Tongxian 傅統先. *Zhongguo huijiao shi* 中國回教史. Japanese trans. Itō Ken 伊東憲, *Shina kaikyōshi* 支那回教史. Tokyo: Okakura shobō, 1942.

Fung Yu-lan. *A History of Chinese Philosophy.* 2 vols. Princeton: Princeton University Press, 1952, 1953.

Ghazālī, Abū Ḥāmid al-. *Mishkāt al-anwār: The Niche of Lights.* Text and trans. David Buchman. Provo: Brigham Young University Press, 1998.

Graham, A. C. *Studies in Chinese Philosophy and Philosophical Literature.* Albany: State University of New York Press, 1990.

Hamadānī, 'Ayn al-Quḍāt. *Tamhīdāt.* Ed. 'A. 'Usayrān. Tehran: Dānishgāh, 1341/1962.

Ḥammūya, Sa'd al-Dīn. *al-Miṣbāḥ fi'l-taṣawwuf.* Ed. N. Māyil Hirawī. Tehran: Mawlā, 1362/1983.

Heath, Peter. *Allegory and Philosophy in Avicenna (Ibn Sînâ), with a Translation of the Book of the Prophet Muḥammad's Ascent to Heaven.* Philadelphia: University of Pennsylvania Press, 1992.

Henderson, John B. *The Development and Decline of Chinese Cosmology.* New York: Columbia University Press, 1984.

Hujwīrī, 'Alī ibn 'Uthmān. *Kashf al-maḥjūb.* Ed. Maḥmūd 'Ābidī. Tehran: Surūsh, 1383/2004.

*I Ching, see* Wilhelm.

Ibn al-'Arabī. *Fuṣūṣ al-ḥikam.* Ed. A. 'Afīfī. Beirut: Dār al-Kutub al-'Arabī, 1946.

————. *al-Futūḥāt al-makkiyya.* Cairo, 1911. Reprinted—Beirut: Dār Ṣādir, n.d.

Ibn Sīnā. *al-Najāt*. Ed. M. Ṣabrī al-Kurdī. 2d ed. Cairo: Maṭbaʿat al-Saʿāda, 1938.

Ījī, ʿAḍud al-Dīn al-. *al-Mawāqif fī ʿilm al-kalām*. Beirut: ʿĀlam al-Kutub, n.d.; also, with the commentary of al-Jurjānī, 8 vols., Cairo: Maṭbaʿat al-Saʿāda, 1325/1907.

ʿIrāqī, Fakhr al-Dīn. *Lamaʿāt*. Ed. J. Nurbaksh. Tehran: Khānaqāh-i Niʿmatullāhī, 1353/1974. Trans. William C. Chittick and Peter Lamborn Wilson, *Fakhruddin ʿIraqi: Divine Flashes*. New York: Paulist Press, 1982.

Jāmī, ʿAbd al-Raḥmān. *Ashiʿʿat al-lamaʿāt*. Ed. Ḥ. Rabbānī. Tehran: Kitābkhāna-yi ʿIlmiyya-yi Ḥāmidī, 1352/1973.

———. *Lawāʾiḥ*. Persian text ed. Yann Richard. Paris: Les Deux Océans, 1982. Trans. W. C. Chittick, in Murata, *Chinese Gleams*, pp. 128–210.

———. *Nafaḥāt al-uns min ḥaḍarāt al-quds*. Ed. Maḥmūd ʿĀbidī. Tehran: Intishārāt-i Iṭṭilāʿāt, 1370/1991.

———. *Naqd al-nuṣūṣ fī sharḥ naqsh al-fuṣūṣ*. Ed. W. C. Chittick. Tehran: Imperial Iranian Academy of Philosophy, 1977.

Jaschok, Maria, and Shui Jingjun. *The History of Women's Mosques in Chinese Islam: A Mosque of Their Own*. Surrey: Curzon Press, 2000.

Jin Yijiu 金宜久. *Zhongguo Yisilan tanmi* 中國伊斯蘭探秘. Beijing: Dongfang chubanshe, 1999.

Kalton, Michael. *To Become a Sage*. New York: Columbia University Press, 1988.

Kasoff, Ira E. *The Thought of Chang Tsai* (1020–1077). Cambridge: Cambridge University Press, 1984.

Knysh, Alexander D. *Ibn ʿArabi in the Later Islamic Tradition: The Making of a Polemical Image in Medieval Islam*. Albany: State University of New York Press, 1999.

Kuwata Rokurō 桑田六郎. "Minmatsu Shinsho no kaiju" 明末清初の回儒. In *Shiratori hakushi kanreki kinen tōyōshi ronsō* 白鳥博士還暦記念東洋史論叢. Tokyo: Iwanami Shoten, 1925, pp. 377–86.

———. "Ryū Chi no saikyō shomoku ni tsuite" 劉智の採經書目に就いて. In *Ichimura hakushi koki kinen tōyōshi ronsō* 市村博士古稀記念東洋史論叢. Tokyo: Fuzanbō, 1933, pp. 335–53.

Landolt, Hermann. "Le paradoxe de la 'face de dieu': ʿAzīz-e Nasafī et le 'monisme ésoterique' de l'islam." *Studia Iranica* 25 (1996): 163–92.

Laozi (Lao Tzu). *Daode jing* (*Tao te ching*). In Legge, *The Texts of Taoism*. Many other English translations are available, including several on-line.

Lau, D. C. *Mencius*. London: Penguin Books, 1970.

Legge, James. *The Chinese Classics*. Vol. 1: *Confucius: Confucian Ana-lects, The Great Learning, & The Doctrine of the Mean*. Vol. 2: *The Works of Mencius*. Oxford: Clarendon Press, 1893–94.

———. *The Texts of Taoism*. Sacred Books of the East. Oxford: Oxford University Press, 1891.

Leslie, Donald D. *Islamic Literature in Chinese*. Canberra: Canberra College of Advanced Education, 1981.

Leslie, Donald D., and Muhammad Wassel. "Arabic and Persian Sources Used by Liu Chih." *Central Asiatic Journal* 26 (1982): 78–104.

Leslie, Donald D., Yang Daye, and Ahmed Youssef. *Islam in Traditional China: A Bibliographical Guide*. Sankt Augustin: Institut Monumenta Serica, 2006.

Lewisohn, Leonard. *Beyond Faith and Infidelity*. Surrey: Curzon Press, 1995.

Lipman, Jonathan N. *Familiar Strangers: A History of Muslims in North-west China*. Seattle: University of Washington Press, 1997.

Mason, Isaac. *The Arabian Prophet: A Life of Mohammed from Chinese and Arabic Sources, a Chinese-Moslem Work by Liu Chia-lien*. Shanghai: Commercial Press, 1921.

Mathews, R. H. *A Chinese-English Dictionary*. Shanghai, 1931. Reprinted— Cambridge: Harvard University Press, 1943.

Matsumoto, Akiro. "An Analysis of the 'Whole Substance and Vast Opera-tions' (*quanti dayong*) in Ma Fuchu's Philosophy." Proceedings of the *Nanjing University–Harvard-Yenching Forum for Dialogue Between Chinese and Islamic Civilizations: The Global Significance of Local Knowledge*, June 16–18, 2006, Yunnan University, Kunming, China, pp. 163–73.

Mencius, *see under* Lau and Legge.

Merchant, Carolyn. *The Death of Nature: Women, Ecology, and the Scien-tific Revolution*. San Francisco: Harper & Row, 1980.

Mullā Ṣadrā. *al-Asfār al-arba'a*. Ed. M. Ḥ. Ṭabāṭabā'ī. Qum, 1378/1959.

———. *The Elixir of the Gnostics*. Text and trans. W. C. Chittick. Provo: Brigham Young University Press, 2003.

Murata, Sachiko. *Chinese Gleams of Sufi Light: Wang Tai-yü's "Great Learning of the Pure and Real" and Liu Chih's "Displaying the Con-cealment of the Real Realm."* Albany: State University of New York Press, 2000.

———. *The Tao of Islam: A Sourcebook on Gender Relationships in Is-lamic Thought*. Albany: State University of New York Press, 1992.

Murata, Sachiko, and William C. Chittick. *The Vision of Islam*. New York: Paragon, 1994.

Nasafī, ʿAzīz. *Bayān al-tanzīl*. Ed. S. ʿA. Mīrbāqirī. Tehran: Anjuman-i Āthār wa Mafākhir-i Farhangī, 1379/2000.

———. *Kashf al-ḥaqāʾiq*. Ed. A. Mahdawī-yi Dāmghānī. Tehran: Bungāh-i Tarjama wa Nashr-i Kitāb, 1344/1965.

———. *Kitāb al-insān al-kāmil*. Ed. M. Molé. Tehran: Département d'Iranologie de l'Institut Franco-Iranien, 1962.

———. *Maqṣad-i aqṣā*. Appended to Jāmī, *Ashiʿʿat al-lamaʿāt*, pp. 210–85. English trans. Ridgeon, *Persian Metaphysics*, pp. 41–128.

Nasr, Seyyed Hossein, ed. *Islamic Spirituality: Manifestations*. New York: Crossroad, 1991.

Needham, Joseph. *Science and Civilisation in China*. Cambridge: Cambridge University Press, 1954–2004.

Nūr al-Ḥaqq. *Sharḥ al-laṭāʾif*. Kanpur: 1320/1902; 2d ed., Kanpur: Maḥmūd al-Maṭābiʿ, 1343 (1924–25). *See also under* Ma Lianyuan.

Nūrbaksh, Jawād. *Bāyazīd-i Basṭāmī*. N.p.: Chāpkhāna 110, 1373/1994.

Qūnawī, Ṣadr ʿal-Dīn. *al-Nuṣūṣ*. Ed. S. J. Āshtiyānī. Tehran: Markaz-i Nashr-i Dānishgāhī, 1362/1983.

Rāzī, Najm al-Dīn. *Mirṣād al-ʿibād min al-mabdaʾ ilaʾl-maʿād*. Ed. M. A. Riyāḥī. Tehran: Bungāh-i Tarjama wa Nashr-i Kitāb, 1352/1973. English trans. Hamid Algar, *The Path of God's Bondsmen from Origin to Return*. Delmar, NY: Caravan Books, 1982.

Ricci, Matteo 利瑪竇. *Kunyu wanguo quantu* 坤輿萬國全圖. In *Li Madou Zhongwen zhuyi ji* 利瑪竇中文著譯集. Shanghai: Fudan daxue chubanshe, 2002.

Ricci, Matteo, and Zhu Weizheng 朱維錚. *Qiankun tiyi* 乾坤體義. In *Li Madou Zhongwen zhuyi ji* 利瑪竇中文著譯集. Shanghai: Fudan daxue chubanshe, 2002.

Ridgeon, Lloyd. *ʿAzīz Nasafī*. Richmond, Surrey: Curzon, 1998.

———. *Persian Metaphysics and Mysticism: Selected Treatises of ʿAzīz Nasafī*. Richmond, Surrey: Curzon, 2002.

Rūmī, Jalāl al-Dīn. *The Mathnawī*. 8 vols. Ed. R. A. Nicholson. London: Luzac, 1925–40.

Satō Minoru 佐藤実. *Ryū Chi no shizengaku: Chūgoku islanshisō kenkyū josetsu* 劉智の自然学: 中国イスラーム思想研究序説. Tokyo: Kyūko shoin, 2008.

Satō Minoru 佐藤実 and Nigo Toshiharu 仁子寿晴, eds. *Yakuchū Tenpō seiri* 訳注天方性理卷一. Tokyo: Tōkyō daigaku bunka kenkyūjo, 2002.

Schwartz, Benjamin I. "The Ethical and the Meta-Ethical." In *Confucian Spirituality*, ed. Tu Weiming and Mary Evelyn Tucker. New York: Crossroad, 2003, 1: 56–61.

———. *The World of Thought in Ancient China*. Cambridge: Harvard University Press, 1985.

Sha Zongping 沙宗平. *Zhongguo de Tianfangxue: Liu Zhi zhexue yanjiu* 中國的天方學: 劉智哲學研究. Beijing: Beijing daxue chubanshe, 2004.

Shabistarī, Maḥmūd. *Gulshan-i rāz*. In Lāhījī, *Sharḥ-i Gulshan-i rāz*, ed. M. Barzgar Khāliqī and 'I. Karbāsī. Tehran: Zuwwār, 1381/2002.

*Shuogua*, "Discussion of the Trigrams," *see* Wilhelm, *I Ching*.

Suhrawardī al-Maqtūl, Shihāb al-Dīn Yaḥyā. *Majmū'-yi āthār-i fārsī*. Ed. S. H. Nasr. Tehran: Imperial Iranian Academy of Philosophy, 1977.

Tanaka Ippei 田中逸平. *Tenpō shisei jitsuroku* 天方至聖實錄. Tokyo: Dainihon Kaikyō kyōkai, 1941.

Tazaka Kōdō 田坂興道. *Chūgoku ni okeru Kaikyō no denrai to sono gutsū* 中国における回教の傳來とその弘通. Tokyo: Tōyō bunko, 1964.

Tu, Weiming. *Centrality and Commonality: An Essay on Confucian Religiousness*. Albany: State University of New York Press, 1989.

———. *Confucian Thought: Selfhood as Creative Transformation*. Albany: State University of New York Press, 1985.

———. *Neo-Confucian Thought in Action: Wang Yang-ming's Youth (1472–1509)*. Berkeley: University of California Press, 1976.

Watson, Burton. *The Complete Works of Chuang Tzu*. New York: Columbia University Press, 1968.

Wilhelm, Richard. *The I Ching or Book of Changes*. London: Routledge & Kegan Paul, 1968.

Wolfson, H. A. "The Internal Senses in Latin, Arabic, and Hebrew Philosophic Texts." *Harvard Theological Review* 28 (1935): 69–133.

Yampolsky, Philip. "The Origin of the Twenty-Eight Lunar Mansions." *Osiris* 9 (1950): 62–83.

Yang Huaizhong 楊懷中 and Yu Zhengui 余振貴. *Yisilan yu Zhongguo wenhua* 伊斯蘭與中國文華. Yinchuan: Ningxia renmin chubanshe, 1995.

*Yijing*, *see* Wilhelm, *I Ching*.

Yu Zhengui 余振貴 and Yang Huaizhong 楊懷中. *Zhongguo Yisilan wenxian zhuyi tiyao* 中國伊斯蘭文獻著譯提要. Yinchuan: Ningxia renmin chubanshe, 1993.

Zhang Dainian. *Key Concepts in Chinese Philosophy*. Trans. and ed. Edmund Ryden. New Haven: Yale University Press, 2002.

Zhuangzi (Chuang Tzu), *see* Watson.

# Index

compound (*murakkab*), 107, 155,
244, 260, 285, 391. *See also under* simple
comprehensive awareness (*zongjue*
總覺), *see under* awareness
configuration (*nashw*), 127, 320,
368, 383, 389
Confucianism (and Islam), 6–8, 16,
18–19, 24, 49–53, 60–64, 67,
72–78, 591–92, 599–602;
epochs of, 581–85; Song-Ming,
583, 587, 589, 591, 606; cosmopolitanism of, 586, 592; and
politics, 587–88
Confucius, 94, 218, 468, 600; *Analects*, 6, 9, 62, 84, 189, 260, 412,
433, 445, 452, 486, 494, 586,
588, 594, 608, 612
Constancy, Possessors of
(*ulu'l-'azm*), 113, 224, 277
constitution (*mizāj*), 155, 259–60,
325, 374, 481
contingent (*mumkin*), *see under* necessity
continuity (*ji* 繼), *see under* nature
contraction (*qabḍ*), 105, 320, 332
cosmology, 11, 14, 25, 35–36, 60,
72, 77–78, 284, 595; onto-, 601,
603, 606–7, 612, 614
cosmos (*'ālam*), 30, 480, 526; map
of, 31–39, 65; levels of, 32–34,
36–37. *See also* world
creation (*zao* 造, *khalq, takhlīq*),
33–34, 52–53, 58, 63–64, 68,
106–10, 114, 123, 137, 147,
202, 216–18, 238, 288, 378–79,
467, 503, 505–6, 530, 538, 550–
51, 571; reason for, 36, 44–45,
72, 131, 260–63, 271, 337, 347,
431, 532; ceaseless renewal of,

34, 278, 293, 300, 336–37,
444, 543, 562. *See also* circle;
cosmos; *and under* command;
transformation
cultivation (*xiu* 修, *tazkiya*), 130,
140, 262, 330, 403, 482–87,
492–94, 577; of the soul/self,
66, 86, 396, 486, 520, 584,
587–89, 605, 610–13, 616; of
the Real, 518, 576

*da* 大, 605
Dai Zhen 戴震, 589, 597
*dā'irat al-wujūd*, 82
*ḍāll*, 460
Dao 道, 8, 51, 79, 591
*Daodejing, see* Laozi
Daoism, 24, 94, 186, 199, 444,
452, 581, 583, 589, 603–4,
613
*darādī*, 227
darkness (*an* 暗, *ẓulma*), 136–39,
289, 367, 460. *See also under*
light
*de* 得 (obtaining), 426
*de* 德 (virtue), 271, 426
decision (*duan* 斷), 166–67,
386–88, 390
deliberation (*lü* 慮), 166–67,
259, 386–88, 390
demons (*gui* 鬼), 262. *See also*
jinn; Satan
dense (*kathīf*), 354. *See also under* subtle
dependence (*yi* 依), 118, 298,
464; mutual, 534–37
deployment (*inbisāṭ*), of existence, 202, 216, 300, 446
descent (*jiang* 降, *nuzūl*). *See
under* ascent